Development or Deterioration?

Development or Deterioration?

WORK IN RURAL ASIA

edited by
Bruce Koppel, John Hawkins, William James

LYNNE
RIENNER
PUBLISHERS

BOULDER
LONDON

Published in the United States of America in 1994 by
Lynne Rienner Publishers, Inc.
1800 30th Street, Boulder, Colorado 80301

and in the United Kingdom by
Lynne Rienner Publishers, Inc.
3 Henrietta Street, Covent Garden, London WC2E 8LU

Library of Congress Cataloging-in-Publication Data
Development or deterioration? : work in rural Asia / edited by Bruce
    Koppel, John Hawkins, William James.
    Includes bibliographical references and index.
    ISBN 1-55587-471-1
    1. Rural industries—Asia—Employees—Case studies. 2. Labor—
Asia—Case studies. 3. Asia—Economic conditions—1945– —Case
studies. I. Koppel, Bruce. II. Hawkins, John N. III. James,
William E.
HD8653.5.D48 1994
331.12'5'095—dc20   93-40819
                                                                          CIP

British Cataloguing in Publication Data
A Cataloguing in Publication record for this book
is available from the British Library.

Printed and bound in the United States of America

    The paper used in this publication meets the requirements
 ∞ of the American National Standard for Permanence of
    Paper for Printed Library Materials Z39.48-1984.

To the memory of Edna Angeles–Reyes

Contents

Tables

Figures

1

Rural Transformation and the Future of Work in Rural Asia

Bruce Koppel and John Hawkins

What is the future of work in rural Asia? Two broad trajectories appear available. The first—often associated with the agrarian transformation and postwar industrialization experiences of Japan, Korea, and Taiwan—can be called a developmental trajectory. It is characterized by a relatively egalitarian distribution of land and a low incidence of rural households without access to land but dependent on production agriculture for their livelihoods. Rising agricultural incomes and productivity generate savings, investment in education, and increased demand for nonfarm goods. Meanwhile, farm household labor is increasingly freed for productive participation in nonfarm work for supplemental income. Wages for nonfarm income gradually match and then grow higher than agricultural wages—in part because of diversification within the nonfarm sector and expanding possibilities for occupational mobility across the nonfarm sector into the urban sector.

A second trajectory—often associated with the juxtaposition of high agrarian population growth and densities, stagnant agricultural productivity growth, skewed distribution of access to land, and significant numbers of landless rural households nevertheless dependent on agriculture (described especially in South Asia)—can be called a deterioration trajectory. It is marked by an increasing incidence of nonfarm employment and income, reflecting the increasing difficulties agrarian households face in maintaining their basic welfare. Wages for nonfarm income tend to be low, and occupational diversification within the nonfarm sector tends to be confined to unskilled positions. Residential mobility to the urban sector is usually associated with a comparable unskilled occupational role.

Both off-farm and nonfarm employment are on the rise throughout rural Asia (Shand, 1986). But what is the significance of this diversification, in theoretical and policy terms? In terms of income, productivity, mobility, and welfare, under what conditions is this diversification broadly indicative of a developmental trajectory? And under what conditions does it indicate a deterioration trajectory?

1

We return, therefore, to the initial question, What is the future of work in rural Asia? A World Bank report summarized the rural employment prospects in Bangladesh in the mid-1980s.

> The absorption of one million new entrants to the labor force per annum in the context of increasing landlessness and the existing structure of the economy is a formidable job. In addition . . . open unemployment in Bangladesh is low because people often engage in part-time or short du-ration work in order to survive, but underemployment is high. . . . Un-fortunately there are no easy or quick solutions for creating productive employment of this magnitude. This is particularly because the majority of the poor have no assets, and very few of the skills necessary for engag-ing in productive activity. . . . However, if immediate and direct action is not taken, the situation can only grow worse (World Bank, 1984: 15).

Although the magnitude of the problem varies throughout Asia, the se-riousness conveyed by the report's conclusions are not confined to Bangladesh. G. Edgren and N. Muqtada (1987: 7) begin an overview of Asia's rural employment situation with a somber introduction:

> Against the backdrop of existing levels of unemployment, underemploy-ment, poverty, economic inequality and landlessness in several countries of the Asia-Pacific region, the need to generate rural employment on a substantial scale can hardly be exaggerated. While the development plans in all of the region's countries are concerned with improving the condi-tions of the rural poor, most of the programs have failed to effectively ad-dress the target population.

Recognition of the scope of rural poverty in Asia is certainly not new. However, the economic dynamism of the region in the 1980s (especially in Southeast and East Asia) diverted the attention of many governments, de-velopment assistance donors, and mainstream analysts away from both the persistence of large-scale rural poverty in South and Southeast Asia and the significant and systematic rural stagnation in parts of East Asia (e.g., the graying of the farm population in Japan and Korea and the lack of suc-cessor farmers).

Until relatively recently, the problems of rural poverty—when they were noticed—were viewed principally as agrarian issues. They were be-lieved to be related to problems of low land productivity and even lower labor productivity, uncertain access to adequate productive resources (land, water, and technology), unstable agricultural incomes, and insuffi-cient government investment in and support for the human resource devel-opment that could foster a better understanding and application of new production technologies and information.

In the 1950s and 1960s, the principal solutions to these problems were generally thought to be labor-intensive rural public works aimed at providing employment for large numbers of landless laborers and seasonally unemployed agricultural workers. Land reform was advocated, in some cases, as a solution to widespread rural unemployment, but this course appeared politically infeasible, especially in reformist settings. Agricultural performance was a concern, but there was widespread skepticism and even pessimism about the prospects for improving agricultural productivity among "peasant" producers. In the 1970s and 1980s, this skepticism was essentially reversed as a result of several measures focused on improving agricultural organization and performance. These measures were optimistically thought to be corrections for what were seen as fundamentally agrarian problems.

Most notable among these measures was what was called the "green revolution"—the application of science and technology to basic cereal grain production in developing Asia (and later applied to other areas). This green revolution was supposed to address the issue of persistent low agricultural productivity. It would do this through breeding programs, particularly at the International Rice Research Institute in the Philippines, that generated cereal grain seeds that were inherently more productive and, at the same time, more responsive to complementary inputs, notably water and fertilizer. The availability of this technology helped, in turn, to rationalize massive investment (generally via loans and grants from foreign aid agencies) in agricultural infrastructure—especially irrigation and farm-to-market roads and a variety of subsidization programs designed to encourage increased fertilizer use (particularly in areas deemed most suitable for grain production). All this was supposed to reduce excessive variability in crop yields and improve physical access to markets. To some, analyses of successful economic development experiences in Japan, Korea, and Taiwan suggested that growth in agricultural productivity and incomes could significantly improve levels of savings and investment by rural households and thus help to finance industrialization.

However, this view of an industrialization process pushed along by agricultural development was overshadowed by another interpretation in the mid-1970s. In the new interpretation, there was a growing emphasis on export-led industrialization, which again implicitly equated agriculture with traditional (as opposed to modern) economic development.[1] In effect, the cause of rural poverty was not believed to be low agricultural productivity per se, nor even the political economy of agricultural organization (a point made strongly by Latin American and South Asian analysts); more precisely, it was the persistence of peasant agriculture.

What was needed was not improved productivity in peasant agriculture—a necessary but insufficient condition for improving rural welfare—but rather a supplementation of the fundamental mode of production in peasant households. Interests in strategies of formal, nonformal, and informal education (especially in China and India)—including community development and resource management and participatory development—suggested that there was a strong potential for raising labor productivity through local resource mobilization and economic diversification. Strategies to promote rural industrialization and rural enterprise development were seen as avenues for absorbing "excess" rural labor, channeling rural investment and entrepreneurship to more productive purposes, and facilitating agricultural-nonagricultural linkages within rural areas through a variety of programs in job training and small enterprise development (Koppel, 1989). Particularly in the 1980s, advocates of economic policy reform for places such as Bangladesh, Indonesia, and the Philippines argued that excessive government intervention in agricultural factor markets had, in fact, distorted those markets (e.g., through credit and fertilizer subsidies) and ultimately strengthened disincentives to investment and savings by agricultural households.

To the degree that employment, rather than income, was recognized in these different measures as a crucial and distinct dimension of the rural poverty question, it was still visualized principally in relation to agricultural and agrarian processes. This focus was captured in the growing interest in "off-farm" employment, that is, employment by members of farm households in activities off their own farms. The major apparent exception to embedding rural employment issues in agrarian processes was a large body of literature on rural-to-urban migration. But in fact, most of this literature was not an exception. The causes of migration were generally tied to underemployment in agriculture. And much of the migration literature argued implicitly that the alternative to participation in agrarian labor markets in rural areas was participation in nonagricultural labor markets in urban areas. Consequently, rural and agrarian were viewed as equivalent.

More recently, however, the literature on rural poverty in Asia has started to move beyond the earlier and narrower focus on agrarian income alone (e.g., Edgren and Muqtada, 1987; Khan and Lee, 1985; UNDP, 1990 and 1991; World Bank, 1991). An exploration of the fuller complexities of rural labor processes in Asia has begun. The critical question, however, is this: In what context should this exploration be framed? Several answers have been proposed, four of which stand out.

One answer is to maintain the agrarian focus and therefore continue to see rural labor processes as offshoots of fundamentally agrarian processes. The extensive literature on labor seasonality and off-farm rural employment exemplifies this. Much of this literature views seasonality in agricultural labor demand as the major driving force behind the variability in demand for labor in agricultural labor markets; it also defines off-farm employment as equivalent to other-farm employment. The seasonality of labor demand is seen principally as an outcome of population growth and, secondarily, of the way in which agricultural production is organized in terms of cropping intensity. This answer appears relevant in purely agrarian settings, but is arguably problematic in other contexts.

Another answer is to see the rural economy as dominated by but not limited to agrarian processes. This leads to the recognition that (1) there is a distinction between off-farm (i.e., off "own" farm but on "other" farm) and nonfarm work *within* rural areas, and (2) there are possibilities of distinct although linked labor markets for these different forms of employment. As illustrated in particular by analyses of the economic development experience in Taiwan and Korea during the 1960s, as well as growing research in the 1980s on the roles of women in rural development, this view invites an exploration of agriculture-nonagriculture linkages as both an intrarural and a rural-urban question. In practice, the research has concentrated heavily on the rural household as a unit of analysis—a concentration based on assumptions about the unity and stability of rural households and the equivalence of the residential household and the family. These assumptions may not always be viable (Wilk, 1989).

A third answer is to reject the underlying primacy of the urban-rural dichotomy altogether and argue that labor processes in rural areas are increasingly articulating with (and hence, often indistinguishable from) broader labor processes that function on national and even transnational scales. The factors driving this articulation include: the internationalization of capital and commodity markets (McMichael, 1992); the development of transnational commodity systems with associated political economies of control and divisions of labor; and, particularly in Asia, the emergence of new and especially intense forms of rural-urban interaction—characterized by patterns of mixed land use and employment—that may represent a distinct "third" settlement trajectory (McGee, 1987; Ginsburg, Koppel, and McGee, 1991). From this perspective, a crucial issue is to determine the significance of specific patterns of articulation and incorporation for the characteristics of local (in this case, rural) labor processes. An insistence on the reality of macro-micro linkages is not always matched, however, by compelling evidence of how these linkages evolve or how they actually influence and are influenced by local resource allocation processes.

A fourth answer, which really crosses the first three, is to see rural labor processes in terms of relationships between the state and the economy. There are two major variants to this answer. One focuses on an assessment of the impacts of macroeconomic policy regimes (and possibly sectoral policies as well) on sectoral performance (e.g., through estimates of bias and effective protection). A second variant examines relationships among the state, class formation and the division of labor, and trajectories of economic development. Both variants explore the ways in which the activities and interests of the state influence and are influenced by the political organization of rural economies. Here, too, however, analyses of linkages have focused on assessments of largely presumed outcomes rather than processes that have been discovered and evaluated. This leaves open the issue of potential variabilities among structures, processes, and outcomes.

Each of these four alternatives constitutes an arena for important theoretical, policy, and empirical debates. But which of these perspectives is the most appropriate for understanding the significance of and context for changes in rural labor processes in Asia? And when and where is that perspective applicable? The purpose of this book is to gain a better understanding of these questions, both conceptually and empirically. To do this, the focus is on the emergence and significance of nonfarm nonagricultural employment within rural Asia. The studies that follow were cooperatively designed by all the authors to offer perspectives that are diverse—drawing from the traditions of anthropology, economics, geography, regional development, political science, and sociology—but that also converge in placing the emergence of nonfarm rural work in contexts that are broader than a strictly agrarian one.[2] To do this, the studies identify the characteristics of employment differentiation processes in selected parts of rural Asia, giving special emphasis to the growing importance of nonagricultural work in rural areas. The authors indicate how these characteristics are related to wider processes of structural transformation in terms of (1) relationships between the state, the rural economy, and class development; (2) broader patterns of economic integration and technological change; (3) the gender implications and economic and technological change; and (4) local processes of demographic, economic, and political change. This is not to suggest that the authors believe that a more traditional, agrarian-focused explanation will never suffice but rather that for the areas they considered, restriction to an agrarian context would be inadequate.

The studies are presented in a progression of contexts. The first are essentially extensions of processes of agrarian differentiation in Malaysia, the Rajasthan area of India, and Bangladesh. Next are contexts influenced by the emergence of significant non-agrarian-based economic interests—especially in the service sector—within rural areas of the Philippines, Thailand, and Indonesia. The final study explores contexts in which urban and industrial forces are playing especially important roles in driving processes of rural transformation in southern China.

The purpose of this opening chapter is to introduce several of the major issues that are considered in the studies that follow. But clearly, there are no easily transferable conceptual frameworks or policy generalizations that can be comfortably applied across all cases. This is because the diversity of what is unfolding in rural Asia exceeds what has been previously conceptualized and because the significance of this diversity cannot be adequately assessed solely through morphological (or structural) comparisons of the contrasting labor processes in rural areas.

More specifically, in this chapter, we will review Asia's rural employment situation, giving special attention to issues of nonfarm rural employment. We will also draw attention to significant limitations in understanding the changing characteristics of work in rural Asia, derived from problems within existing theoretical debates about rural and agrarian change. We will propose a perspective that views transition in work as a social, economic, and political process closely correlated both with local processes involving the changing social significance of the family, community, and rural enterprises and with wider processes involving the changing relationships between the state and the economic organization of rural areas. And finally, we will identify a number of research topics, emphasizing the importance of one integrating issue—understanding the processes associated with the evolution, maintenance, and consequences of a commitment by rural individuals and households to identities that define nonagricultural rural work as something other than a temporary attribute.

Asia's Rural Employment Situation

By 1983, agriculture accounted for more than half of the gross domestic product (GDP) in only two Asian countries, Bhutan and Nepal. Throughout the region, the relative contribution of agriculture to GDP is declining (Figure 1.1), while the relative contributions of manufacturing and service

Figure 1.1 The Declining Role of Agriculture in Asia, 1960–1988

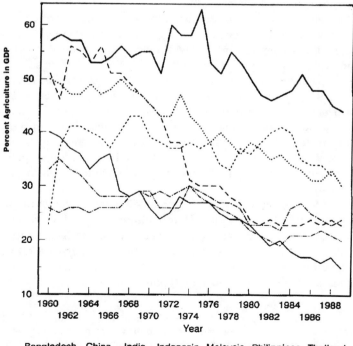

Bangladesh   China   India   Indonesia   Malaysia   Philippines   Thailand

activities are increasing (Table 1.1). However, across South and Southeast Asia, conventional national demographic and employment statistics show that the agriculture sector's share of the total labor force continues to substantially exceed one-half of the GDP (Table 1.2). What these statistics directly reflect is the fact that even though the structures of Asia's economies are differentiating in directions that give increasing prominence to manufacturing and services, the majority of Asia's people still live in areas classified as "rural"—an attribution routinely assumed to be equivalent to the dominance of agricultural economic activities and agrarian social organization.

Labor force participation, however, is a notoriously problematic concept in developing economies generally and especially in agrarian settings. In any case, it is not the same as productive employment. Despite significant increases in land productivity, the average annual growth of agricultural output per worker in Asia's agriculture continued below 2 percent in the 1980s, not nearly enough to provide productive employment in agriculture for an expanding rural labor force nor to generate the surpluses needed for meaningful levels of savings and investment—hence, hardly enough to significantly reduce continuing problems of rural poverty and inequality (Khan and Lee, 1985). In fact, as can be seen in Table 1.3, growth rates in Asian agriculture showed a tendency to stagnate and even decline throughout the later 1980s.

Although variations reflect differences in weather, policies, environmental degradation, and technological infrastructure, there is rising concern that growth rates are slowing to levels below those needed to maintain the welfare of the contemporary agricultural population and, in some cases, to avoid jeopardizing food security for those in vulnerable income, age, and gender groups in both urban and rural areas. Certainly, the levels of agricultural productivity growth are not adequate to support appreciable increases in levels of productive employment absorption in agriculture. Rural labor forces throughout the region are growing at annual rates in the 3 to 6 percent range (ESCAP, 1989: 10), well beyond aggregate growth rates for agriculture and real growth rates of value-added in agriculture (Table 1.4).

Awareness of these issues has generated greater interest in productive employment in rural areas outside agriculture (Fong, 1988; Shand, 1986). However, several problems have emerged that make it difficult to document the existing scope and rate of growth of nonagricultural rural employment. For example, in an early overview of the issues, Dennis Anderson and Mark Leiserson (1980: 228) point out:

> Measurement of rural nonfarm employment is . . . made difficult by the continually changing patterns of employment over the agricultural cycle. Estimates of labor force by economic activity generally provide a

classification of workers at a single point in time according to their principal sector of employment or occupation. They are, therefore, likely to underestimate the extent of nonfarm work in rural areas, which is commonly a secondary source of income on a part-time or seasonal basis.

Most of what is known on this topic, particularly in South and Southeast Asia, comes from income and expenditure surveys. These surveys reveal that large proportions of farm household income (estimates of 30 to 40 percent are common) are being attributed to off-farm sources. However, the surveys tend to concentrate on households that are primarily engaged in agricultural activities. If other households, such as those of landless families and residents in market towns and villages, were appropriately sampled, estimated proportions of total rural household income derived from nonfarm sources would likely be even higher. For example, the "agricultural" category in national employment and occupational statistics is very "lumpy." This lumpiness is typically the product of a sampling scheme that oversamples agricultural areas, further assumes that all households within these areas are principally agricultural,[3] and finally takes the self-identification of the residential household head (frequently predefined as a male) as the principal occupation of all adults in the household. This obscures considerable work diversification both within and between rural households. For instance, there are increasing numbers of part-time farmers as well as landless households that are marginal and periodic participants in agricultural labor markets. Indeed, many of the households described in national statistics as "agricultural" are not agricultural at all but are involved in other sectors (Deolalikar, 1987; Islam, 1986; Mangahas, 1987; Quisumbing and Cruz, 1986).

As another example, a World Bank report (1986: XVII) on employment conditions in Indonesia notes:

> The number of manhours spent in the major agricultural labor market— rice—is only a small part of the total labor time supplied to the market even by landless households. Typically the proportion of total time utilized on agricultural wage labor is 30–40% for landless workers. The rest of the labor time is devoted to a variety of activities in trade, services, handicrafts, and sometimes to nonagricultural wage labor outside the villages.

Another World Bank report (1984: 7–8) makes a complementary point about Bangladesh that has wide applicability throughout rural Asia:

> Rural poverty and rural wages are significantly linked: Because of the high incidence of landlessness almost half the rural population depend on work off their own land. Agricultural labor is generally employed for 185 days per worker year, including 115 days in crop production and 70 days in other allied activities. Accordingly they need either high wages for

Table 1.1 Structure of GDP in Developing and Developed Countries of the Asia Pacific, 1960–1989 (percentage of GDP in current market prices)

	1960[a]				1970				1980				1989[b]			
	Agri-culture	Manu-facturing	Indus-try[c]	Services	Agri-culture	Manu-facturing	Indus-try[c]	Services	Agri-culture	Manu-facturing	Indus-try[c]	Services	Agri-culture	Manu-facturing	Indus-try[c]	Services
Developing countries																
NIEs																
Hong Kong[d]	3	22	12	63	2	29	7	62	1	23	8	68	0	21	7	72
Korea	37	14	6	43	26	21	8	45	15	30	12	44	10	31	13	46
Singapore	4	12	6	79	2	20	10	67	1	30	9	60	0	30	7	63
Taiwan	29	22	8	42	15	29	8	48	8	36	10	47	5	36	8	58
ASEAN-4																
Indonesia	51	9	6	33	45	10	8	36	24	13	29	34	23	18	19	39
Malaysia	33	8	10	49	29	12	13	46	22	21	17	40	21	19	16	44
Philippines	26	20	8	46	28	23	7	43	23	24	12	40	24	25	8	43
Thailand	40	13	6	41	26	16	9	49	23	21	10	46	15	25	12	47

South Asia																
Bangladesh	57	5	2	36	55	6	3	37	50	10	5	35	44	7	7	41
Burma	33	8	4	55	38	10	4	48	47	10	3	41	48	10	3	39
India[d]	50	14	6	30	45	15	7	33	38	18	8	36	30	18	10	41
Nepal[d]	65	3	8	23	67	4	8	21	62	4	8	26	58	5	8	28
Pakistan	46	12	4	38	37	16	6	41	30	16	9	46	27	17	8	49
Sri Lanka[d]	32	15	5	48	28	17	7	48	28	18	12	43	26	15	12	47
China	23	na	48	29	39	3	10	18	36	36	13	15	32[f]	34[e,f]	14[f]	20[f]
Developed countries																
Japan	13	34	11	43	6	36	11	47	4	29	13	54	3[f]	30[f]	11[f]	56[f]
United States	4	28	10	58	3	25	9	63	3	22	12	64	2[f]	17[f]	12[f]	69[f]

Sources: Republic of China, Directorate-General of Budget, Accounting, and Statistics, *Statistical Yearbook of the Republic of China* (Taipei: Directorate-General of Budget, Accounting, and Statistics), various issues; World Bank, 1991; East-West Center, Program on International Economics and Politics, Asia-Pacific Data-base, computer tapes, 1988.

ASEAN = Association of Southeast Asian Nations.

na = not available.

NIEs = newly industrialized economies.

[a] 1965 for Nepal.

[b] 1986 for Burma and 1984 for Malaysia.

[c] Includes mining, utilities, and construction.

[d] Percentage of GDP in current factor cost.

[e] World Bank estimates.

[f] GDP and its components are shown at purchase values.

Table 1.2 Structure of the Labor Force in the Countries of the Asia Pacific, 1960–1989 (in percentages)

	1960[a]				1970[b]				1980[c]				1989[d]			
	Agri-culture	Manu-facturing	Indus-try[e]	Services	Agri-culture	Manu-facturing	Indus-try[e]	Services	Agri-culture	Manu-facturing	Indus-try[e]	Services	Agri-culture	Manu-facturing	Indus-try[e]	Services
Developing countries																
NIEs																
Hong Kong	5	38	7	50	4	46	6	44	1	42	8	48	1	30	9	60
Korea	53	11	4	33	50	14	6	31	34	22	7	37	20	28	7	45
Singapore	na	na	na	na	3	20	7	70	1	29	6	63	0	29	7	63
Taiwan[f]	50	15	5	30	37	21	7	35	20	33	10	38	13	34	8	45
ASEAN-4																
Indonesia	68	5	2	25	64	6	2	27	55	9	4	32	55	9	4	32
Malaysia	na	na	na	na	na	na	na	na	37	16	8	39	31	16	7	47
Philippines	60	10	3	27	51	11	4	33	52	11	5	33	45	11	5	39
Thailand	82	3	1	14	78	4	2	16	71	8	2	19	64	9	3	24

South Asia															
Bangladesh	86	4	1	9	77	5	0	18	77	5	0	18	57	10	2	31
Burma	na	na	na	na	69	7	2	22	67	1	2	30	65	9	2	24
India	73	9	2	16	72	9	2	16	63	10	2	25	na	na	na	na
Nepal	94	2	0	4	94	1	0	4	91	0	0	8	na	na	na	na
Pakistan	na	na	na	na	58	14	4	24	53	15	6	27	51	13	7	29
Sri Lanka	49	9	3	39	41	8	3	49	50	17	10	23	46	22	4	28
Developed countries															
Japan	24	24	8	43	19	26	8	47	10	25	11	54	8	24	10	58
United States	6	27	8	59	4	26	8	62	4	22	9	66	3	18	8	70

Sources: International Labour Office, *Yearbook of International Labour Statistics* (Geneva: ILO), various issues; Republic of China, Council for Economic Planning and Development, *Taiwan Statistical Data Book 1989* and *Taiwan Statistical Data Book 1991* (Taipei, Taiwan: Republic of China).

na = not available.

[a] 1961 for Indonesia, Bangladesh, India, and Nepal; 1963 for Sri Lanka; 1965 for Japan; and 1966 for Hong Kong and Korea.
[b] 1971 for Hong Kong, Indonesia, India, Nepal, Pakistan, and Sri Lanka; 1973 for Burma; and 1974 for Bangladesh.
[c] 1981 for Bangladesh, India, and Nepal.
[d] 1984 for Bangladesh; 1985 for Indonesia; 1986 for Sri Lanka, Thailand, and India; and 1987 for Malaysia and Burma.
[e] Includes mining, utilities, and construction.
[f] Structure of employment.

Table 1.3 Agricultural Production (per capita) Annual Growth Rates in the Asia Pacific, 1971–1990 (in percentages)

	1971–1980	1981–1985	1986–1990	1981–1990
ASEAN-4	2.18	2.27	1.72	2.44
Indonesia	2.60	3.45	2.06	3.17
Malaysia	2.60	3.45	2.06	3.17
Philippines	2.53	-3.59	−0.25	−1.59
Thailand	1.80	2.19	0.55	0.17
Indochina				
Burma	0.18	4.34	−6.63	−1.24
Cambodia	−5.07	10.61	1.73	5.22
Laos	2.27	4.00	1.51	1.88
Vietnam	1.33	1.51	2.60	2.35
South Asia				
Bangladesh	0.0	0.13	0.12	−0.03
Bhutan	0.69	−0.20	−3.39	−1.73
India	−0.16	1.55	6.38	3.20
Nepal	−1.04	−0.15	2.89	0.49
Pakistan	0.52	0.27	0.16	0.61
Sri Lanka	0.77	0.05	−2.37	−1.39
China	1.23	4.98	2.67	3.43

Sources: United Nations Food and Agricultural Organization, *FAO Production Yearbook* (Rome: FAO), various years.

agricultural work to carry them through the lean period, or they need additional non-farm jobs. [However] there are no reliable data explaining the extent of non-farm employment opportunities.

Even when there is evidence of growth in the aggregate of rural household income coming from off-farm and nonfarm sources, there are inadequate and inconsistent data on the actual earnings available from specific off-farm and nonfarm employment opportunities in rural Asia. In particular, there is not enough data, in many instances, to document wage rates and terms of employment in the nonfarm rural sector. What data there are, however, suggest a troubling trend: Throughout South and Southeast Asia, rural wage rates outside the agriculture sector are not always higher than real agricultural wages. More troubling yet is evidence, in some places, of declining real agricultural wage rates. The resulting picture, however sketchy, shows employment and income differentiation occurring in a context of stagnant and even declining productivity.

For example, Islam (1986: 165) concludes from the data presented in Table 1.5 that "low returns to non-farm activities are not only a feature of wage-employment; non-farm family enterprises are also characterized by low productivity and hence low returns." However, to repeat, evidence on

Table 1.4   Real Growth of Value-added in Agriculture in the Asia Pacific,
1961–1989 (average annual growth, in percentages)

	1961–1969[a]	1970–1979[b]	1980–1989[c]
NIEs			
Korea	5.6	3.3	1.7
Singapore	4.8	2.3	−4.8
Taiwan	4.2	2.3	0.6
ASEAN-4			
Indonesia	2.6	4.4	3.7
Malaysia	na	5.2	3.9
Philippines	4.5	4.6	2.5
Thailand	4.8	4.2	4.3
South Asia			
Bangladesh	3.0	1.6	1.9
Burma	4.9	4.1	5.6
India	2.3	1.3	4.4
Nepal	−2.3	1.1	4.2
Pakistan	4.6	2.7	5.1
Sri Lanka	3.4	2.6	3.8
China	8.8	3.6	5.5

Sources: Republic of China, Directorate-General of Budget, Accounting, and Statistics, *Statistical Yearbook of the Republic of China* (Taipei: Directorate-General of Budget, Accounting, and Statistics), various issues; World Bank, 1991; East-West Center, Program on International Economics and Politics, Asia-Pacific Data-base, computer tapes, 1988. na = not available.
[a] 1962–1969 for Taiwan and 1966–1969 for Nepal.
[b] 1971–1979 for Malaysia.
[c] 1980–1986 for Burma, 1980–1989 for the United States, and 1980–1988 for Japan.

this point is very sketchy. One estimate for the Philippines concludes that from 1975 to 1983, the ratio of agricultural to nonagricultural incomes per worker (in current prices) declined from 46 percent to 34 percent (World Bank, 1985). But this estimate is based on pooled urban and rural household data. Because other data show that the rural-to-urban income ratio during the same period declined from 75 percent to 48 percent (Mangahas, 1987), the implication is that the bank's analysis overestimated nonagricultural wage incomes in rural areas. Interpretation is further complicated by evidence in the Philippines (and throughout Asia) of declining real wage rates in agriculture (Table 1.6). Finally, rural income statistics often do not distinguish between wage, self-employment, family enterprise, and remittance income sources. This is an especially crucial point for understanding the developmental significance of rural income diversification, given evidence from several countries about the importance of remittances from relatives in urban areas and foreign countries and growing evidence that female and child labor may be dominant in rural self-employment

Table 1.5 Selected Data on Nonfarm Employment in Rural Asia

Country and Village	Nonfarm Employment[a] as a Percentage of Total Employment	Percentage Share of Income from Nonfarm Self-Employment	Wage Employment in Nonfarm Activities as Percentage of Total Employment
Bangladesh			
Village near Dhaka	59.2	25.6	56.8
Village near Chittagong	64.6	22.5	65.2
India			
Cluster of villages in West Bengal	40.7	na	30.1
Pakistan			
Village "A" in Faisalabad	51.4	23.8	53.8
Village "B" in Faisalabad	45.1	15.0	66.7
Village in Jhelum	88.8	28.9	67.3
Sri Lanka			
Village in Kandy	44.3	8.4	81.0
Village in Kurunegala	46.2	10.5	77.2
Thailand			
Village in Suphan Buri	39.8	22.0	44.7
Village in Kalasin	59.6	36.0	40.6
Village in Chiang Mai	81.8	46.6	43.0

Source: Data from Islam, 1986: 153–174.
na = not available.
[a] Person-days per year spent on nonfarm activities.

activities (Hart, 1986a; Heyzer, 1986; Rosenberg and Rosenberg, 1980; Wolf, 1986). This last point is addressed by Shelley Feldman, Gillian Hart, and Miriam Sharma in their studies in this volume.

In fact, as limited as the Philippine data are, they are better than those from many other parts of Asia. Throughout Asia, there is a lack of fundamental and reliable time-series data on levels and trends in earnings from off-farm and nonfarm rural activities. What information there is, however, reveals numerous issues about the structural changes characterizing rural Asia. For example, characteristics of the linkages among wages, employment, and output appear to vary at regional and even village levels throughout the area. How wide is this variation, and what are the primary underlying socioeconomic conditions accounting for it?

Similarly, there is important evidence of renewed interlinkages among land, capital, and labor markets through a variety of institutional arrangements that "tie" labor recruitment and compensation (Hart, 1986b; Hayami and Kikuchi, 1982; Hayami, Mariano, and Rambo, 1987; Kikuchi and

Table 1.6   Real Wage Rates in Agriculture in Asia Pacific Countries, 1960–1981 (indices: 1970 = 100)

	1960	1965	1975	1981	Average Annual Growth Rate 1970–1981 (%)
East Asia					
Japan	43.1	76.7	140.0	142.0	3.4
Republic of Korea	61.5	71.5	136.0	135.0	9.3
Southeast Asia					
Indonesia	90.2[a]	77.0[b]	93.7	97.4	0.2
Malaysia[a]		101.4	92.0	121.2	1.5
Philippines	133.0	127.0	97.8	82.0	−2.2
South Asia					
Bangladesh	104.4	112.8	75.3	69.7	−2.6
Burma	82.4	116.2	45.8	45.3	−7.2
India					
Maharastra	86.3	80.4	69.2	76.1	−2.6
Kerala	89.3	91.1	92.9	104.5[c]	0.9[d]
West Bengal	117.6	104.7	88.2	127.1[c]	1.2[d]
Pakistan		79.8	126.6	190.7	5.3
Sri Lanka[a]	101.8	812.4	126.7	168.5	1.8

Source: Data from ESCAP, 1986: Table I-27.
 [a] plantation workers.
 [b] 1966.
 [c] 1979/1980 (crop year).
 [d] 1966–1980.

Hayami, 1980). These arrangements appear to be most likely in places where combinations of social relations of production and growing landlessness operate in a Boserup-type dynamic to depress rural wages and increase supervision costs. One result is the evolution of permanent labor arrangements in a situation in which there is a significant surplus of labor. Why is this refeudalization pattern occurring in some cases, while in other cases, relationships between agricultural and nonagricultural labor markets appear to be relatively independent?

Harry Oshima (1983 and 1984) and others (e.g., Ho, 1986) have pointed to the seasonality of demand for agricultural labor, especially in Asia's tropical monsoon climates, as a principle *cause* of the variability of rural labor markets in Asia. They suggest seasonality has a primary influence on the evolution and performance of rural labor markets for both agricultural and nonagricultural activities and, in fact, that it is the major reason why South and Southeast Asia might not replicate the rural non-farm employment experiences of Japan, Korea, and Taiwan.

However, this conclusion, even as a hypothesis, does not appear persuasive. The dynamics and particularly the variability of the influence of seasonality on the differentiation of rural labor markets in Asia, though extensively described, remain fundamentally unexplained. Seasonal labor demand has been seen as an endogenous product of agricultural intensification patterns, but it also (and often simultaneously) has been seen as exogenous to a variety of agrarian institutions. These institutions, in turn, are frequently viewed as induced responses to the seasonality of labor demand (e.g., Binswanger and Ruttan with Uri Ben-Zion, 1978; Oshima, 1983 and 1984; Otsuka, Chuma, and Hayami, 1992; Roumasset, 1979). But it is at least as plausible to suggest that seasonality is not exogenous to the organization of agrarian relations (and through that to rural labor markets) but rather that seasonality is an endogenous product of the interaction between agrarian organization in general and rural labor processes in particular. Although seasonality undoubtedly is a factor in the variation of labor supply and wages, it may be more important to understand why, across seasons, poorer households might be more vulnerable to low-wage nonagricultural employment than better-off households (Wolf, 1986). Similarly, how do markets for factors of agricultural production (land and capital) influence the evolution and performance of linkages between agricultural and nonagricultural rural labor markets? For instance, how are changes in the organization and performance of rural credit markets associated with household savings and welfare behavior, migration patterns, and the creation of rural enterprise (Bardhan, 1980; Floro, 1987a)? Under what conditions are rural households actually subsidizing the participation of their members in the nonagricultural labor force, and what are the impacts of these costs on the household's overall welfare position?

Summarizing this section, existing research on the changing significance of work in rural Asia has maintained a fundamentally agrarian focus: problems of seasonality in agricultural labor demand, "surplus" labor created by population growth in relation to land productivity, labor absorption within agriculture in relation to levels of technology and land use intensity, and off-farm employment supplementing an essentially agricultural income base. The results have prompted interest in a variety of processes that could reduce the pressures of "excess" rural labor—most notably during the last decade, international labor migration to the Middle East—and about the possibilities of "smoothing" seasonal agricultural labor demand through agricultural intensification (e.g., triple-cropping), the well-established use of rural public works programs, and the periodic advocacy of rural industrialization as ways to absorb underemployed and unemployed rural labor. Conceptually, the main consequence has been to view nonfarm and off-farm labor activities as derivatives (and even residuals) of processes of agrarian differentiation.

Fundamental gaps remain. Does agrarian differentiation alone determine labor market differentiation in rural Asia? Although recognition of the importance of increasing employment, labor productivity, and income in rural Asia is high, the context in which these problems are defined and the means generally advocated to address the problems may be too narrow. What is needed is more explicit attention to the broader structural changes characterizing rural Asia and their relationships to rural work.

The Development Studies Debate
on the Transformation of Rural Asia

The broader dimensions of Asia's rural transformation include the relationships of socioeconomic change in rural areas with processes of urbanization, industrialization, expanded international trade in rural natural resources, and technological change in agriculture (Jones, 1984; Koppel, 1988; Lo and Salih, 1978; Lo, Salih, and Douglass, 1981; Pakkasem, 1979; Rondinelli, 1986; Rondinelli and Ruddle, 1978). The consequences of these processes are evident in the changing social organization of agriculture; the growing significance of secondary and tertiary urban centers for rural socioeconomic life; the increasing importance for national economic development of international trade in rural natural and human resources; the rising importance of nonrural and nonagricultural economic power in and for rural economic life; and the burgeoning complexities, capacities, and ambitions of contemporary national bureaucracies, communication, and political systems.

These examples reflect three significant longer-term characteristics of rural transformation in Asia. First, the transformation process is uneven in terms of which individuals, groups, institutions, and social, economic and political relationships are affected—and when and how they will be affected. It is not clear at all—from historical experiences in East Asia or contemporary experiences in South and Southeast Asia—that the transformation process can proceed without significant social costs nor that these costs will be distributed in a manner consistent with broad-based development. To this point, Asia's rural transformation has involved two processes that have not always worked in tandem: (1) an *evolution* of the structure, composition, and functions of traditional rural socioeconomic and political institutions, and (2) an *imposition* of relationships, structures, and processes that can significantly modify and ultimately displace existing patterns of rural resource management, economic development, social mobility, and political determination.

One example is the discussion around Michael Lipton's (1977) "urban bias" hypothesis. Is the political economy of the urban bias a reflection of nonrural forces, or can it be indicative of both the hegemony of nonrural forces and the processes of differentiation and subordination *within* rural political economies (Koppel, 1986)? An illustration is given by the types of changes under way in rural credit systems. Writing about her research in the Philippines, Sagrario Floro (1987b) concludes:

The uneven spread of agricultural development and commercialization allows for the coexistence of diverse groups of lenders. Their different economic considerations lead to a sorting phenomenon whereby trader-lenders prefer to lend to rich households while farmer-lenders prefer to lend to poor households. This lender-sorting behavior has resulted in market fragmentation.

Asia's rural transformation is also characterized by the coexistence (but not necessarily the correlation) of numerous transformations. Consequently, equating rural transformation with only one process—which is done when it is described purely as a nonmarket-to-market, agriculture-to-industry, or rural-to-urban transition—discounts many other processes that are also occurring. These include political assimilation and mobilization; social differentiation and integration; and cultural-religious innovation, revitalization, and suppression. These omissions are crucial because they deflect attention away from the richness of the heterogeneous transformation patterns that appear to be present (see, e.g., Alexander, Boomgaard, and White, 1991; Harriss and Moore, 1984).

Furthermore, there is evidence that in some circumstances, Asia's rural transformation may well represent the emergence of a new form of socioeconomic organization, neither urban nor rural as conventionally defined but rather the product of increasingly intense interaction between urban and rural socioeconomic activities. Within these zones of more intense economic interaction (e.g., the Jakarta-Bandung-Bogor triangle in Java, Central Luzon in the Philippines, or Guangdong Province in China), one already sees an increase in nonagricultural activities (trading, transportation, services, and industry), high population mobility, and intense mixtures of land use with agriculture, cottage enterprises, industrial establishments, and a wide variety of trade and service activities, all coexisting side by side (McGee, 1987). If there is a "new" socioeconomic form emerging, then what variabilities (for instance, in rate, structure, and impacts) is this form displaying and why?

The distinctiveness of the concepts "rural"—usually thought of as interchangeable with agrarian—and "urban"—usually thought of as interchangeable with industry and services—is becoming less reliable as a way of understanding economic development in Asia (Koppel, 1986 and 1991). The concepts "rural" and "urban" do continue to be meaningful in some instances as descriptors of land use systems. However, these terms are becoming less meaningful in many parts of Asia in distinguishing different patterns of socioeconomic development. Socioeconomic change is not as neatly arranged along rural-urban lines (spatially or functionally) as previously thought. The impacts of transportation, communication, and energy infrastructure development; the rise and spread of the service economy; significant rates of mixed agricultural, industrial, and service land uses; the increasing incidence of household participation in both agrarian and nonagrarian labor and capital markets; and new processes of interlinkage and segmentation between labor and capital markets in rural areas are just a few illustrations of the blurring distinction between socioeconomic activities in many rural and urban Asian areas. Yet interpreting these blurring distinctions has proven to be a problem.

Existing theoretical strategies for describing and explaining rural transformation processes have focused on the roles and impacts of the market, technology and technological change, the state, population growth and human resource development, and cultural change and assimilation. Broadly speaking, there is a neo-Marxist-liberal economic axis along which specific perspectives on these transformation instruments are configured within contemporary development studies (primarily covering anthropology, sociology, economics, and political science). However, as is increasingly being acknowledged, the debate generated by these configurations appears to be near (if not actually at) an impasse (Booth, 1985; Burawoy, 1984; Hart, 1986a; Laclau, 1977; Otero, 1987; Perkins, 1983; Rosen, 1985). This is especially apparent if one wants to understand how broad transformation processes influence work and labor in rural areas.

The problem for development studies on Asia is not that there are too many ways of conceiving the nature of the change processes. Rather, it is that there is a tension weaving through all the major conceptions—a tension that is sometimes characterized as existing between different scales (macro-micro) but that really centers on an argument over the imperatives of structure and culture, the domains of discipline and area, and the possibilities of universalism and particularism. Caught between the demands of the imperatives, domains, and possibilities, development studies—born of the search to construct a composite bridge—has wandered, instead, into a cul-de-sac. In that cul-de-sac, at least four problems can be identified in the existing theoretical debates on transformation processes characterizing and affecting rural Asia. These problems cross the ideological boundaries of the debate.

Metaphors

Theory is typically built through images and metaphors. The challenge is to ensure that the metaphors are robust enough to encompass a significant range of social and historical experience while maintaining a heuristic role as a vehicle for a theory's central insights. As empirical research on rural Asia has proceeded, attempting to employ the preferred metaphors of development theory, real doubts have arisen about the robustness and heuristic values of many key metaphors. For example, rural (actually agrarian and, even more accurately, peasant) differentiation categories often appear strained and artificial when compared to the variety of patterns and contexts they purport to reference and interpret. Increasingly, research is diverted from efforts to understand those patterns and contexts by the prior need to generate and maintain confidence that the metaphors being used are actually "appropriate."

Rural households throughout Asia typically appear to be involved in several economies, each of which traditionally has been described in dichotomous terms—rural/urban, formal/informal, agrarian/nonfarm, and so forth. Intrahousehold division of labor—for example, by gender, age, birth order, or affinity—appears to vary significantly even within communities. Markets display wide variety in forms of segmentation based on economic, ethnic, religious, political, spatial, and commodity forces. And a maze of "quasi" and hyphenated categories arise from neo-Marxists, liberal economists, and strongly functionalist forms of anthropology and sociology— a shared recognition of content that does not lie within the boundaries of existing metaphors and metaphors with boundaries that are not synchronous with observed relationships.

Faced with such anomalies, it is natural to focus strongly on methodological issues and ask, in effect, if the data are reliable? The pursuit of this question has led to both greater sophistication of methodology and increasing recognition that the methodological problems are a Trojan horse for a variety of basic assumptions about what data are, how they can be known, and who owns the data (Contreras, 1991; Crocker, 1989). Faced by these conundrums, it is appropriate to ask: At what point should there be a more active assessment of the existing array of metaphors? For example, at what point is it counterproductive to argue that exchange relationships can be seen as functioning "as if" there were a free market (thereby permitting the application of the tools of market analysis), when it might be just as reasonable (although considerably more inconvenient for those who want to use those tools) to argue that the relationships are better comprehended using another metaphor for exchange relationships—one that provides more illumination?

That much might appear intuitive to many, but consider other metaphors that are just as casually used. Take, for instance, "household." The household is a metaphor for a minimal and stable social unit within which labor allocation, child socialization, gender relations, resource management, and other processes occur. Indeed, it is common to speak of household reproduction as a key element of rural class development and as a central feature of resource allocation and capital accumulation in market system development. Yet it is rare to ask if the household is, in practice, what theory claims it to be. As the studies in this volume by Feldman, Hart, and Sharma attest, this metaphor, too, needs to be challenged. It must be challenged to avoid tautological traps in hypotheses about reproduction and to avoid confusing the residential household for the basic family unit. It should also be challenged to consider that processes of social differentiation in parts of rural Asia do not necessarily build from or yield a social formation that meaningfully corresponds to the conventional household metaphor or to the roles that households are presumed to have in agrarian social processes. In fact, whether from the left (in terms of perspectives on the household in the context of semiproletarianization) or from the right (in terms of the expansion of market principles of exchange and resource allocation), there is a disturbing common tendency. Having identified the context and the guiding dynamics, household characteristics and behaviors are primarily deduced. Variation in these characteristics and behaviors is lost to the imperative of the metaphor.[4]

Many theories of agrarian change, on both the left and the right, are proving to be quite limited in their capacity to illuminate diversification in rural areas in relation to the dynamics of structural change in rural economies. These limitations derive, in part, from a problem many of these theories share—an exclusive preoccupation with what is only one dimension of rural differentiation. This is the persistence of small-scale forms of agricultural production operated primarily with family labor, the retention of land, and production fundamentally for home consumption. Against this background, the peasant household is idealized as a solidary unit of production. Where employment and income differentiation occur, as in the movement of some agrarian household members into nonagricultural wage labor, they are seen simply as elements of commoditization and proletarianization processes and the expansion of capitalist markets. The assumption is that the solidary character of the household is undermined by these *exogenous* forces.

These approaches will sometimes be appropriate. The problem is that an uncritical acceptance of the underlying metaphors dulls sensitivity to inappropriate applications of such understandings. This problem arises because the predominant metaphors principally focus attention on what are fundamentally morphological attributes—forms of the employment relationship—when, in fact, more attention is needed to the technical and sociopolitical content of the relationships. A morphological concentration assumes that the content of the relationship *is* the form (the Marxist position that wage labor *is* proletarianization) or that the form of the employment relationship is determined by and hence reflects the content (the liberal economic position on material determinants of agrarian institutions). In fact, the dynamics of diversification cannot be easily deduced simply from quantitative indicators of changes in income patterns, land distribution, cropping patterns, and so on. These often indicate diversification, but by themselves, they are insufficient evidence of the specific processes that yielded the diversification (and the indicators). That this problem of tautology has been ignored testifies to the power of the metaphors to substitute as explanations of diversification. What is needed are metaphors that support more direct understandings of the processes by which resources and labor are mobilized and deployed and of the ways in which these processes are shaped by and then act upon larger structures of economic and political power.

It is important to emphasize that the problem of metaphors, in our attempts to understand rural change in Asia, is not semantic but rather epistemological: How do metaphors explicitly organize and orient learning, and how do they implicitly select and value what can be learned? Assuming that metaphors from some source will always be employed, it is important to find some perspective—both intellectual and political—from which to continually question whether these metaphors are adequate for identifying and organizing information. This leads to the question of what is being lost by any strategy to selectively recognize and value information—in this case, about employment diversification in rural areas. Here, there is an irony in the development studies cul-de-sac. Instead of building an intellectual composite that can encompass diverse empirical content, development studies may actually be driving a wedge. If too much information is ignored, lost, or distorted, there is a powerful tendency for theory and research to disarticulate: Theory tends to retreat into disciplinary debates about categories, and research retreats into idiosyncratic area and village studies. Thus, an "old" problem remains: Theory and research about rural Asia must be better articulated. An important starting point may be a reassessment of the metaphors themselves.

Discontinuity

There is a strong tendency to conceive of the impacts and characteristics of social processes as being composed of a few significant discontinuities—from family to wage labor, from peasant to market production, from human to mechanized labor, from rural to urban sociocultural organization, and so on. The processes and historical characteristics of socioeconomic (primarily agrarian and peasant) differentiation and cultural adaptation and the cumulative characteristics of population growth in relation to land are frequently recognized. However, theoretical understanding is not adequately oriented to social *process* as much as it is to describing the social *location* of what is *presumed* to be a process in terms of a theory's map of stages and categories. The results, which often amount to reductionist arguments about the causative roles of class or the market, can oversimplify and possibly misrepresent patterns of social change and the significance of these patterns at particular points in time or in specific portions of a social system.[5]

A primary example of the association between conceptions of process that are discontinuous and explanatory arguments that are reductionist is the utilization of wage labor as an indicator of rural proletarianization. Although wage labor could certainly be assigned this significance in specific circumstances, the assignment is problematic as a general proposition for all circumstances. First, by assuming that all wage labor is fundamentally comparable because of the wage relationship, it sidesteps the evaluation of the significance in different wage labor shares in total income, different wage labor sources, and other nonwage characteristics of employment relations for overall peasant household income, welfare, and class position. Second, even if one assumes that participation in wage labor alone is evidence of participation in rural class formation processes, this still does not establish the coherence, inclusiveness, or unidirectionality of those class formation processes. A related example has been the excessive reliance of classical Marxists, neoclassical economists focusing on material determinants (e.g., Binswanger and Rosenzweig, 1984 and 1986), and functionalist anthropologists (e.g., Harriss, 1981) on analyses of modes of production to explain rural political and organizational behavior. This strategy depends on maintaining sharp distinctions between peasants and wage laborers—distinctions that it is additionally assumed extend to and are reflected by differentiated social and political interests. As James Scott (1985) and Reynaldo Ileto (1983) have argued, this additional assumption of instrumental interest formation may be far too simplistic conceptually and empirically, and, in turn, it may make the scope of the presumed differentiation between peasants and rural wage laborers problematic.

More generally, analysis has been weak on issues of articulation—between processes at different scales (local, national, international) and between processes at the same scale (e.g., the differentiation of rural labor and capital markets). For example, issues of relationships between the state and class development processes are often reduced to propositions about degrees of hegemony (or autonomy) that are, in fact, rarely demonstrated. It is appropriate, therefore, that interest is turning away from an insistence on the pervasiveness of hegemonic processes in state development to an understanding of discontinuities in relations between state development and local processes of social, economic, and political differentiation.

Variability

Heterogeneity of context has proven to be a major stumbling block in conceptualizing the significance of rural labor market differentiation. Rural Asia is far more variable than the central insights of most development theory would admit. Specific transformation processes display wide variation across rural Asia, a point that, in principle, can be accommodated. The problem is that the fundamental contexts in which these patterns function also display substantial variation—a fact that much theory has not readily confronted. This is a crucial omission because these contexts may represent considerably more than neutral or passive settings in which specific global transformation patterns appear and grow. As each of the studies in this volume suggests, specific national and local rural contexts can

have very significant roles in defining the meaning and system of relationships in which the transformation patterns preferred by theory actually
function. In other words, there may be a difference between the contextual
definition of pattern (and the consequent meaning that pattern has) and a
theory's interpretation of pattern (and the possible meanings it can recognize). However, can theory that is not sufficiently interactive with the field
know this?

For example, one can speak about the emergence of surplus production, the appearance of intermediation arrangements that tie local capital
markets to regional or urban markets, or capital and labor substitution
events associated with land consolidation. But are these always best understood as indicators of "the" commercialization process? For instance,
one can cite the substitution of tractors for human labor in agriculture, but
is this incontrovertible evidence in all cases of "the" mechanization
process? Commercialization and mechanization processes certainly would
have different meanings in the resettlement areas of Malaysia, the middle
hills of Nepal, or the Bicol region of the Philippines. In each case, the specific context presents numerous nontrivial historical, cultural, socioeconomic, and political characteristics that together give particular socioeconomic or technological events local meaning; they do this chiefly by
defining the primary systemic relations of which these events are part.
There is a troubling tendency in contemporary development theory to acknowledge historical specificity and cultural influence but to nevertheless
insist on global meaning. As research struggles with the association between the particular and the universal, an understanding of variation and
heterogeneity is frequently sacrificed to a theory's need for self-preserva-
tion—a need that is exhibited by insistence on the priority of universalis-
tic imperatives. Both neo-Marxists and liberal economists have been seriously inclined to practice this ritual.

Agency

Perhaps the most troublesome problem in the development studies debate
about rural Asia is how broad transformation processes are believed to relate to human action. Indeed, agency has become a highly contentious
issue in social theory generally, with writers such as Anthony Giddens,
Jürgen Habermas, and Paul Ricoeur differing sharply with the postmod-
ernists. What this issue reflects is a broader and long-standing dilemma
within the social sciences—namely, how to consider the relationships between macrolevel and microlevel processes and structures. As noted earlier, reductionist arguments based most notably on class, mode of production, the market, and the state have portrayed rural sociopolitical action as
simplistic in form and unidirectional in significance. The research in this
volume, however, demonstrates that such arguments are highly selective

about what sorts of action they recognize. Both the complexity and variability in the sources, scale, form, and consequences of rural sociopolitical action are considerably greater than much development theory typically accepts.

One example comes from the strong arguments for policy reform, economic liberalization, and "getting the prices right" as environmental prerequisites for the emergence of market-determined outcomes in resource allocation. This macro-micro relationship is expected because of the "distortions" that existing macrolevel policies introduce to microlevel incentives. However, in practice, it often is not clear how this particular type of macroeconomic environmental change leads to alterations in specific resource allocation decisions. For example, what are the relationships among macroeconomic policies, intermediate institutions that set boundaries on the organization of labor processes (principally centralization of wage setting, regulation of union activity, and income protection arrangements), and labor processes and choices at the local level? If responses (in terms of the direction and incidence of predicted resource allocation decisions) are not those expected, the usual conclusion is that liberalization and reform have not proceeded far enough.

Yet the issue of how the liberal economic market actually emerges is not examined directly, in part because of the premise that because the market is a natural phenomenon, it is the nonemergence and nonprimacy of market forces that are the legitimate objects of study. What is missing, consequently, are analyses that examine the articulation between changing policy and state environments and changing local systems of exchange and allocation. Of special importance is the possibility that agency is not restricted to the unidirectional macro-micro relationship but that agency operates and is also institutionalized in micro-macro relationships (e.g., the political economy of economic policy), micro-micro relationships (e.g., market segmentation and factor market linkages), and macro-macro relationships (e.g., between macroeconomic and sectoral policies) (Klitgaard, 1991; Koppel, 1990b, 1992, and 1993).

> It has become a commonplace, in the macroeconomic literature on industrialized countries, to regard differences in labour market institutions as critical determinants of macroeconomic performance. Yet, the far greater variety of institutional arrangements in the Third World has almost entirely been neglected as an explanator of the equally divergent macroeconomic performance (Banuri and Amadeo, 1991: 171).

Although it is not appropriate to expect any theory to link broad historical and social forces to the actions of specific individuals, it is troubling that the linkage between important macroprocesses and patterns of individual and collective action remains so mechanical. Choice in terms of individual action is frequently trivialized in the sense that a priori choice does not exist (except through some form of false consciousness or as an exercise of irrationality). Elaborate patterns of organization, leadership, affiliation, interest formation and expression, and commitment are subsumed by increasingly abstract categories of social position (such as class or "rurality") and motivation (such as economic utility or cultural tradition).

Toward a More Relevant Research Agenda on Rural Work

Although agrarian-based employment remains a primary source of income for most households in rural Asia, there is a growing awareness that for a variety of reasons and under a variety of circumstances, increasing proportions of the income generated by rural households is coming from off-farm and nonfarm sources. This has drawn some attention from both academics and policymakers, but the phenomenon is not well documented, nor are the diverse dynamics of the processes involved well understood. For example, under what conditions are we witnessing a *transformation* of work and labor relations that bodes well for rural development, and under what conditions are we witnessing a *reproduction* of immiserating employment characteristics that does not bode well?

Certainly, it is clear that the challenge of productive employment in rural Asia during the 1990s will be substantial. Failure to adequately meet this challenge holds the potential for dramatically increasing the number of rural people who are marginalized in terms of productive skills and, consequently, productive income. In an earlier time, the principal strategies for meeting this challenge were the exploitation of new lands, agricultural intensification, and urban-based industrialization. Today, however, the opportunities for increased productive labor absorption through further agricultural extensification or intensification appear limited—at least in comparison to what was achieved for cereal grains in the 1960s and 1970s. In most parts of Asia, all cultivable lands (and increasingly, lands that should not be farmed) are already being cultivated. At the same time, productive labor absorption in Asia's primary cities has not been strong—especially outside Japan, Korea, Taiwan, Hong Kong, and Singapore—and there is little reason to believe this pattern will change soon.

Numerous innovations in policy that go beyond agriculture, rural industrialization, and urban enterprises may well be required, and new directions in development studies that move past traditional sectoral metaphors may need to be embraced. However, we must understand several issues considerably better than we currently do if these conceptual and policy innovations are to emerge and new directions are to be recognized.

Key to addressing these issues is the resolution of two fundamental conceptual problems.

1. First, it is essential to improve our understanding of relationships between diverse local processes of socioeconomic and political change in rural Asia and the growth and exercise of state power and influence there (Hart, 1986b; Herring, 1984; Huber, 1990). How are these micro- and macroprocesses interrelated, and what are the consequences for employment diversification and class differentiation in rural areas?

2. Second, it is essential to improve our understanding of the theoretical significance of nonfarm employment in rural areas. Should such employment be understood primarily in relation to processes of agrarian differentiation, which has been the predominant perspective? Should it be viewed in relation to processes of urbanization, which is really another way of reaffirming the agrarian metaphor as the paramount perspective on rural socioeconomic processes (Koppel, 1986 and 1991)? Or are distinctive theoretical connections needed—connections, for example, that would not limit nonfarm employment in rural areas to a residual outcome of agrarian processes (implicit in the term *nonfarm*)? For instance, what is the theoretical significance of different forms of nonagricultural labor specialization in rural areas? What is the theoretical importance of participation by rural household members in nonagricultural labor for an understanding of the rural household's developmental significance?

Clearly, there are deep pitfalls in seeing rural employment problems too narrowly and too rigidly. For this reason, a broad concept of "work" is advocated as a preferable starting point for understanding contemporary employment issues in rural Asia.

"Work relates to social transactions as well as to material production and it generates specific identities for those involved in particular forms of it, and the control of these often implies control over the values ascribed to them" (Long, 1984: 16). This starting point directs attention to the social context of rural work and the rural work experience, specifically by inviting a focus on the learning, commitment, identity, and power relations that develop within rural workplaces. That focus, in turn, draws attention to the close connections between work, worker, and the primary social arenas where labor relations and work experience occur and from which they draw their social, cultural, and political substance: family, community, and rural enterprise. Tamara Hareven (1982: XI) states the perspective for relationships between work and family, and similar perspectives could be stated for work in relation to community and enterprise: "Family behavior can be better understood in relation to the workplace, on which its survival and success depend; similarly workers' behavior must be seen as founded on familial traditions and expectations, which, along with external forces, shape the patterns of labor response."

Such connections are crucial because Asia's broader patterns of economic development are transforming these same primary social institutions. Within this intricate context, one can ask: Under what conditions are rural families becoming, in effect, more productive, and under what conditions are they slipping further into a more vulnerable welfare position? Figure 1.2 illustrates this perspective by schematically presenting the way in which rural households can combine various economic activities to sustain themselves. An important point highlighted in this figure is that it is not enough to speak about employment in terms of time allocation alone—which has frequently been all that the statistical systems describing the composition of rural employment in Asia could hope to do. Similarly, the incidence of employment in terms of household members as well as different classes of rural households is important to document, but it also is not enough.

Research is needed that extends understandings of relationships between rural transformation and changing characteristics of work in rural areas to a focus on one crucial behavioral issue: how commitment to nonagricultural work roles in rural areas is acquired, lost, maintained, amplified, or transmitted. An understanding of commitment and the terms under which it functions is crucial because it frames the choices and investments people can be expected to make as they move through their work experiences. This, in turn, is important for understanding the significance of work as a social relationship and of how public investments in employment creation, education, and other strategies can actually succeed. Underlying factors that account for variations in commitment processes must be examined, with special emphasis on the roles of broader changes in village and regional economic, social, and natural resource systems. The following sets of questions illustrate the types of issues that such research would address.

1. What kinds of employment are available (for example, between wage, self-employment, and family enterprises or between different sectors), and how are these characterized in terms of wages and productivity? How, in particular, are the kinds of available employment influenced by levels and forms of agricultural development (in terms of land and labor productivity, enterprise scale, market orientation, diversification, and so forth), by characteristics of regional development, and by the policy environment?

2. What drives demand for nonagricultural employment by different types of rural households? How do these factors relate to household characteristics, including size and composition; wealth and assets; ethnicity; gender differentiation of labor and household reproduction

Figure 1.2 The Social Context of Rural Work

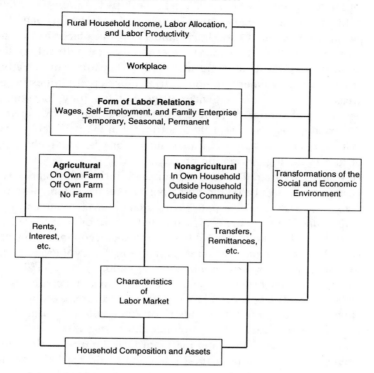

responsibilities; physical accessibility; sources, levels, and variability of income; food security, education, employment, and migration experience; and nonfood consumption patterns?

3. How, where, and when do individuals acquire the skills needed to obtain and hold nonagricultural rural work? How are these processes related to the types of work and workplaces available?

4. What are the terms of employment for nonagricultural rural work (including recruitment, tenure, wages, and working conditions), and how do these terms relate to social and political relationships beyond the organization of labor processes directly? How are they related, for example, to family structure, class, power, and conflict issues within rural communities?

5. What are the characteristics (in terms of employment conditions, productivity, wages, power relations, and competitiveness) of local agricultural and nonagricultural labor markets (and their interlinkages)? If labor markets are segmented, what are the sources, characteristics, and impacts of this segmentation? If segmentation is age

or gender specific, what are the relationships to family and household structure? If segmentation is related to the socioeconomic or political positions of rural households, how does labor market performance relate to the wider socioeconomic and political relations in which the households are involved? What forms of selectivity are exhibited by emerging nonagrarian labor opportunities in rural areas—in terms of skills, gender, wage, age, ethnicity, location, education, and similar variables? How do these patterns compare to the existing distribution of these attributes in the rural labor force? What are the implications of mismatches for who are likely to gain or lose in the transformation process?

6.   How are patterns and rates of urbanization influencing land use, investment, savings behavior, and labor market development in rural areas? How are specific patterns of change in the composition of employment in rural areas affecting the socioeconomic viability of smaller rural communities? What are the socioeconomic impacts of small towns in rural areas on rural labor market evolution and performance, patterns of economic diversification, and so on? How do changes in transport, communication, education, and credit systems influence rural labor, rural labor markets, and rural workplaces?

7.   How are those rural households most vulnerable to welfare crises and potentially least able to mobilize the resources needed for migration—landless, poor, and marginal farm families—affected by emerging nonagricultural rural labor and credit markets and linkages among these markets and agrarian labor, land, and capital markets? Under what conditions is nonfarm employment in rural areas a fundamentally positive factor in the survival of the poorest rural groups? And under what conditions do the levels of real wage rates for nonagricultural rural work relative to agricultural work exacerbate existing rural income distribution problems?

8.   What is the most appropriate unit of analysis for assessing these questions? Specifically, is the residential household the appropriate unit, or does this need to be supplemented or replaced by other units of analysis, such as age cohorts, gender groups, classes, subcommunity- or communitywide groups?

Examples of Research Themes

Several important areas of current research can serve as bridges from the more established focus on the economics of agrarian employment relations to a focus on understanding the changing social significance of rural work in light of the broader transformation of rural Asia. Four examples will be discussed here.

The Changing Status of Rural Natural Resources

Changes in the management and utilization of rural natural resources are a key factor in (re)defining both rural work and rural workplaces. Rural natural resources, especially those directly involved in agriculture, are the objects of processes of agrarian organization and differentiation. Beyond the resources usually associated with agriculture, principally land and water, a wider range of natural resources in rural areas—including non-agricultural land, forest materials, and minerals—provide additional directions for resource-based economic development. They also attract nonrural economic and political interests and can influence the broader claims to rural power based on the political economy of agriculture. Thus, the status of rural natural resources can have significant consequences for the transformation of both workplaces and work in rural areas.

However, given the importance of agricultural resources for the definition and evolution of rural social structure, the most crucial question related to rural resources involves the future of agriculture. In most of Asia, agriculture—directly and indirectly—will continue to provide a significant employment base and exercise a significant influence on the evolution of nonagricultural rural economic opportunities. The future of work in rural Asia, therefore, is closely tied to the future of agriculture.

Since the early 1960s, overall production of major food grains in Asia has increased dramatically. For example, rice productivity in South Asia rose from 1,500 kilograms per hectare in 1965 to over 2,500 in 1985 (one hectare equals 2.54 acres). In Southeast Asia, average yields increased from close to 1,600 kilograms per hectare in 1965 to almost 3,000 in 1985. However, despite the success of agricultural production in Asia as an aggregate, there are many warning signals to suggest that the foundation underlying this success is not impregnable. In parts of South and Southeast Asia, per capita food production has grown only marginally during the last three decades, and in some places that have experienced productivity growth associated with the green revolution, grain yields seem to be leveling (Table 1.3). At the least, the success in aggregate land productivity masks considerable variability in agricultural labor productivity, and there is little indication that significant numbers of new entrants to the agricultural labor force can be productively absorbed. Yet this is only one of the factors that will determine the future of agriculture in Asia. Additional issues are emerging.

Agriculture's future is increasingly being mediated by processes external to agriculture (Koppel and Zurick, 1988). Some, most notably the expansion of agriculture's relationships to broader product and factor markets, have been under way for some time already. Contemporary indicators of these processes include: the dramatic increase over the last twenty-five years in the importance of purchased inputs (e.g., fertilizer, pesticides, and gasoline) "imported" into producing areas and incorporated into production systems, the increasing share of production that is marketed outside producing areas (even when food needs in producing areas have not been met), the increasing proportion of farm household income derived from off-farm sources, and the rising share of disposable farm household income that goes to nonfood purchases. Moreover, additional manifestations of these processes are on the horizon.

A technology transformation is in progress. Science and technology are holding out the enticing prospect of substantially increased and more stable production—but in the framework of production systems that may be very different from those common today. Biotechnology already shows a significant potential not simply to modify (or in some cases, enhance) the existing technological bases of agricultural production, food processing, and animal husbandry but also to be very compatible with a restructuring of the economic, institutional, and political foundations of Asia's agriculture. For example, what will hybridization of basic food crop seeds mean for Asia's small farmers, when the vast majority of them do not now buy seed and are not likely to be able to do so in the future without weakening their income positions? Other trajectories for biotechnology development in agriculture will link specific purchased seed varieties to proprietary chemicals. Will income inequalities within agrarian Asia be exacerbated, with the better-endowed farmers, input suppliers, and millers capturing most of the benefits of technological developments like hybridization? Obviously, the broad changes associated with biotechnology have fundamental implications for the roles of public agricultural research and extension and for the types and consequences of privatization that may occur in Asian agriculture (Koppel, 1985).

Other technology transformations influencing the future of agriculture in Asia include the growing availability of processed foods for Asian consumers, the introduction of new preservation technologies that permit longer-term storage and marketing of perishable foods, and transportation technologies that will affect the marketing areas for various agricultural products. These are all signs that postproduction dimensions of Asia's food and agriculture systems are becoming more important. Such changes may have very significant implications for the organization and performance of rural factor markets, and they will increasingly test the boundaries of what falls within the category of "agricultural employment."

The Changing Characteristics of Rural Social Organization

Rural work draws significant meaning from the social context in which it functions. Important dimensions of the social context can change and can be changed by transitions in rural work. As a social phenomenon, work in rural areas is intimately related to rural social organization, principally as the context from which the social meanings of work are obtained and expressed. The status of rural communities and organizational behavior shape workplace size, management, and performance. They influence relationships between labor specialization and resources and affect associations between occupational mobility and worker skills. They also offer both the standards and the social arrangements for interpreting and enforcing the criteria that workers use to evaluate their work and workplaces. The distribution of rural socioeconomic status, the processes of rural class formation (Desai, 1982; Eder, 1982; Hane, 1982; Oommen, 1984; Scott, 1985; Tharamangalam, 1981), and the changing division of labor within rural households (Bernstein, 1983; Cho and Koo, 1983; Dixon, 1982; Heyzer, 1986; Jeffrey, 1982; Sharma, 1985; Strange, 1981) have already attracted considerable attention as social correlates of changing rural labor relations. But other pertinent dimensions of changing social organization throughout contemporary rural Asia that can influence the social significance of rural work have not been adequately assessed.

One important example is the relationship between rural work and the social organization of rural resource management (Ahmed, 1984; Castillo, 1977; Cernea, 1985; Chan, Madesen, and Unger, 1984; Ledesma, 1982; Popkin, 1979; Scott, 1976; Stranch, 1981). Local organizational resources—those that exist and can be mobilized on approximately a community scale—are receiving considerable attention from the development assistance community. From the *Zanjera* of the Philippines to Nepal's *Moeya* to Bali's *Subak*, indigenous irrigation associations—primary examples of locally organized resource management—have been "discovered" (Bagadion and Korten, 1986). The growing awareness that direct administration of rural natural resources by large public bureaucracies can be profoundly problematic (Hurst, 1990; Kummer, 1991) is leading to a substantial rethinking of rural development strategy. And several strategies are currently being advocated to enhance the growth and participation of local organizational resources in the management and governance of local natural resources in rural areas, most notably biomass and water.

In the context of Asia's rural transformation and its implications for rural work, at least two important issues arise. The first is the question of who governs. During the 1950s and 1960s, community development in South and parts of Southeast Asia "gave" rural communities a chance to provide certain amenities for themselves, but in most cases, there was no intent to empower rural communities (individually or as a group) in altering (favorably) fundamental characteristics of their relationships with the state. Community organization strategies have attracted considerable new interest in recent years, but these strategies do not represent significant departures from basic relationships between the state and the rural periphery. This will likely have important implications for the forms and directions of social learning that go on within these organizations.

This leads to a second issue: What is the status of local organizational resources as rural resources? This issue really involves the question of what is governed. "Old" rural organizational resources (such as the social organization of labor reciprocity, the household as a foundation of the division of labor, and culturally or ethnically based property management regimes) may be replaced by "new" ones (such as tenant or farm worker unions, local chapters of national political groupings, or the privatization of natural resource management). Complex relationships between old and new organizational resources and other rural resources can result—sometimes inviting new forms of conflict, and at other times reinforcing existing patterns of stratification (Bhaduri, 1982; Castillo, 1983). This, too, will have a significant impact on the evolution of work as a social relationship.

Outcomes of State Development and Intervention

In recent decades, the institutions that make up the public support system for rural (principally agricultural) development have been among the most visible and readily recognized features of Asia's rural development experience. These institutions include the support systems for agricultural production, processing, transport, storage, marketing, credit, and education, as well as a range of agricultural and economic policy management systems. Together, these institutions have served as mechanisms for moving goods and services both to and from rural areas and for influencing the allocation of land, labor, and capital within rural resource systems. Given the roles the institutions have acquired in allocating and regulating the flows of goods and services within rural economies and between rural and national economies, it has become clearer that processes affecting the allocation of administrative resources can significantly influence the management and distribution of rural resources.

For example, the acceleration of state intervention to control rural commodity systems, purportedly to stabilize domestic prices and production in the face of volatile international markets, appears to be a pervasive phenomenon throughout Asia, from Japan to Burma. It is precisely against this background that what are now commonly called "parastatal" organizations have arisen. These are quasi-state corporations that have been given government powers to regulate, allocate, and tax but that are not routinely accountable to "normal" government staffing, financial management, and reporting conventions. Parastatals have acquired important roles as exclusive agents of the state for commodity trading in many countries of the region. Such state participation in rural economic development can have significant implications for the organization and performance of affected rural commodity markets and can be closely associated with the emergence (and state endorsement) of monopsony power in rural resource marketing systems. These kinds of changes also can have profound consequences for the characteristics of rural labor relations, working conditions, and wage levels. The coconut and sugar industries in the Philippines became primary examples of this during the 1970s (Clarete and Roumasset, 1982 and 1983; David, 1982; De Dios, 1984; Hawes, 1987).

Currently, there is strong interest in policy reform and other strategies to reduce the level of government participation in rural commodity markets. But here, too, there are potentially significant implications for rural labor because though policy reforms may alter the surface relationships between government bureaucrats and the economy, they may also veil an even closer relationship between specific and class interests (Harriss, 1984; Koppel, 1990a). For instance, adjustment problems associated with such reforms—most notably the closing of urban factories, price inflation, and declining real wages (Koppel, 1992)—can lead to an increase in urban-to-rural labor migration. Beyond these adjustment problems, however, lies the fundamental question of what policy reform actually is. Policy reform can be a strategy for reducing government's role in rural commodity markets—the presumed relationship. But this leaves open the issue of what kind of rural markets are being restored. Here, it is necessary to consider that policy reform can also be a strategy for enhancing the state's role in rural commodity markets by depoliticizing important dimensions of the transformation process (Clarete, 1985; Dell, 1983). For example, minimum wage standards may be relaxed based on the argument that there is no public interest in how private economic power is acquired or exercised, while at the same time, union activity is suppressed based on the argument that it is "antimarket." Yet, in fact, there may be a significant public interest in improving the efficiency of rural factor markets, threatened not only by inappropriate government intervention but also by the private economic power exercised by rural elites. Clearly, rural labor markets must be understood in the context of relationships between the state and the rural economy.

Transitions in Rural Economic Organization: The Roles of Services

Services are not a new element in rural economic organization. The growth of rural services—including activities in petty transport and communications, as well as a variety of personal, trading, and marketing enterprises—traditionally has been associated with the expansion of rural marketing and exchange relationships and the extension of urban economic and political interests to rural areas. However, the estimated size of the service economy in many parts of Asia, under economic conditions as diverse as those in Korea and in Bangladesh, suggests more may be happening in rural areas than urbanization, market expansion, or agricultural diversification. Statistics disaggregated by area on service economies in

Asia are not available, but aggregate evidence on the growth of small towns and estimated labor participation rates in agriculture, cottage enterprises, and rural small industries clearly shows that the share of services in rural GDP formation already exceeds agriculture in most countries. Nonetheless, the characteristics of employment relations in the rural service sector are not well understood. One example involves the evolution of labor skills and relations. How do people working in the service sector in rural areas acquire their work? How do they learn the skills required by the work? What are the characteristics of working conditions, especially tenure and compensation? What forms of stratification and segmentation do service sector labor markets exhibit? How do such markets in rural areas articulate with labor markets normally associated with urban areas, as well as with other factor markets? These and related gaps in understanding are important because there is a widespread assumption, based primarily on interpretations of the East Asian experience, that rural services can serve as an economic base for productive employment and income expansion in rural areas. Yet, it is not clear when and under what conditions this is a reasonable expectation.

Conclusion

In the seven studies that follow, complex issues associated with the emergence and significance of nonfarm labor in rural areas of Asia are illustrated and evaluated. The studies are not designed to be—nor could they be—conclusive. The variabilities across Asia and the conceptual conundrums that surround any analysis of nonfarm employment combine to make assessments preliminary and exploratory. However, at this stage, precisely what is needed is more grounded evidence of what is actually happening.

The reader will also confront a variety of disciplinary perspectives. This is unusual, and according to conventional wisdom, it endangers the possibilities for comparative inference. We see the problem differently. The absence of adequate pluralism in perspectives on nonfarm employment has created a core piece of conventional wisdom—that nonfarm employment processes derive from processes of agrarian differentiation. This essential and pervasive assumption has not only guided analysis of nonfarm employment issues, it has also encouraged a preeminent comparative inference to the development experiences of Japan, Korea, and Taiwan, where the appearance of nonfarm employment is correlated with the growth of agricultural productivity, on one side, and the growth of the industrial economy, on the other.

We believe there is enough evidence to suggest that both the assumption and the inference should be challenged. The more appropriate position is not to assume that nonfarm employment is a derivative of agrarian differentiation processes but rather to treat that assumption as a hypothesis. Similarly, the appropriate inference for comparative purposes is not necessarily to East Asia or even to a model based on East Asia; rather, again, such an assumption should be treated more carefully as a hypothesis.

There is another reason why this volume features studies based on different disciplines. The emergence of nonfarm labor in rural Asia is a significant example of the transformation processes affecting rural areas throughout the region. And there is no reason to assume that any specific discipline or conceptual tradition has a preferential position in defining and interpreting these processes. Consequently, this volume encompasses a variety of disciplinary and methodological styles. In the concluding chapter, we will offer our own interpretation of some of the principal issues addressed by the studies, but readers—coming from diverse conceptual and methodological orientations—should likewise consider the variety of perspectives as an invitation to reassess contemporary wisdom and to consider directions for new understandings.

Notes

1. Although there was increased investment in agricultural development in the 1960s, it would not be completely accurate to conclude that governments were giving agrarian development priority. Throughout the region—from China to the Philippines to India—priorities were clearly centered on industrialization. Governments extracted considerably more out of agriculture than they put into it.

2. In addition to the authors, Gelia Castillo of the University of the Philippines at Los Baños, Harry Oshima, visiting Rockefeller professor at the University of the Philippines in Manila, and Graham Johnson of the University of British Columbia also participated in research planning meetings in 1989 and 1990.

3. In some cases, this is a direct product of conceptual predefinition. In other cases, it is more directly the result of focusing on areas serviced by agricultural extension agents and other agricultural support programs.

4. This issue is not restricted, of course, to analyses of rural Asia or rural areas anywhere. The persistence of the household metaphor in advanced industrial societies is also a topic of current concern. See Coontz, 1992; Gordon, 1988; May, 1988; Skolnick 1991.

5. Discontinuity has become a central issue in contemporary social theory, principally through the influence of Michel Foucault's work.

References

Ahmed, Imtiaz. 1984. "Political Economy of Communalism in Contemporary India," *Economic and Political Weekly*, Vol. 19 (June 2), pp. 903–906.

Alexander, Paul, Peter Boomgaard, and Ben White, eds. 1991. *In the Shadow of Agriculture: Non-farm Activities in the Javanese Economy, Past and Present* (Amsterdam: Rural Tropical Institute).

Anderson, Dennis, and Mark W. Leiserson. 1980. "Rural Nonfarm Employment in Developing Countries," *Economic Development and Cultural Change*, Vol. 28, pp. 227–248.

Bagadion, Benjamin U., and Frances F. Korten. 1986. "Developing Irrigators' Organizations: A Learning Process Approach," in Michael Cernea, ed., *Putting People First: Sociological Variables in Rural Development* (New York: Oxford University Press), pp. 52–90.

Balisacan, A. 1992. "Rural Poverty in the Philippines: Incidence, Determinants, and Policies," *Asian Development Review*, Vol. 10, pp. 125–163.

Banuri, Tariq, and Edward Amadeo. 1991. "Worlds Within the Third World: Labour Market Institutions in Asia and Latin America," in Tariq Banuri, ed., *Economic Liberalization: No Panacea* (Oxford: Clarendon Press), pp. 171–220.

Bardhan, P.K. 1980. "Interlocking Factor Markets and Agrarian Development: A Review of Issues," *Oxford Economic Papers*, Vol. 32, pp. 82–98.

Bautista, R.M. 1986. *Domestic Price Distortions and Agricultural Incomes in Developing Countries* (Washington, D.C.: International Food Policy Research Institute).

Bernstein, Gail Lee. 1983. *Haruko's World: A Japanese Farm Woman and Her Community* (Stanford, Calif.: Stanford University Press).

Bhaduri, Arnit. 1982. "Agricultural Cooperatives and Peasant Participation in the Socialist Republic of Viet Nam," in Arnit Bhaduri and Md. Anisur Rahman, eds., *Studies in Rural Participation* (New Delhi: Oxford and IBH Publishing), pp. 34–57.

Binswanger, Hans, and Mark Rosenzweig. 1984. "Contractual Arrangements, Employment and Wages in Rural Labor Markets: A Critical Review," in Hans Binswanger and Mark Rosenzweig, eds., *Contractual Arrangements, Employment and Wages in Rural Labor Markets in Asia* (New Haven, Conn.: Yale University Press), pp. 1–40.

———. 1986. "Behavioral and Material Determinants of Production Relations in Agriculture," *Journal of Development Studies*, Vol. 22 (April), pp. 503–539.

Binswanger, Hans, Vernon W. Ruttan, with Uri Ben-Zion. 1978. *Induced Innovation: Technology, Institutions and Development* (Baltimore, Md.: Johns Hopkins University Press).

Booth, David. 1985. "Marxism and Development Sociology: Interpreting the Impasse," *World Development*, Vol. 13, pp. 761–787.

Bourdieu, Pierre. 1977. *Outline of a Theory of Practice* (Cambridge: Cambridge University Press).

Bradford, Colin I., Jr. 1986. "East Asian 'Models': Myths and Lessons," in John P. Lewis and Valeriana Kallab, eds., *Development Strategies Reconsidered* (Washington, D.C.: Overseas Development Council), pp. 115–128.

Burawoy, Michael. 1984. "The Contours of Production Politics," in Charles Bergquist, ed., *Labor in the Capitalist World Economy* (Beverly Hills, Calif.: Sage Publications), pp. 23–48.

Castillo, Gelia. 1977. *Beyond Manila: Philippine Rural Problems in Perspective* (College, Laguna: University of the Philippines at Los Baños).

———. 1983. *How Participatory Is Participatory Development? A Review of the Philippine Experience* (Manila: Philippine Institute for Development Studies).

Cernea, Michael, ed. 1985. *Putting People First: Sociological Variables in Rural Development* (New York: Oxford University Press).

Chan, Anita, Richard Madesen, and Jonathan Unger. 1984. *Chen Village: The Recent History of a Peasant Community in Mao's China* (Berkeley: University of California Press).

Cho, Uhn, and Hagen Koo. 1983. "Economic Development and Women's Work in a Newly Industrializing Country: The Case of Korea," *Development and Change*, Vol. 14, pp. 515–531.

Clarete, Ramon. 1985. *Debt Crisis, Trade Liberalization, and Agricultural Policy Reform: The Philippines* (Honolulu: East-West Center Resource Systems Institute).

Clarete, Ramon, and James Roumasset. 1982. *Economic Policy and the Philippine Coconut Industry*, Working Paper WP-82-6 (Honolulu: East-West Center Resource Systems Institute).

———. 1983. *An Analysis of the Economic Policies Affecting the Philippine Coconut Industry* (Manila: Philippine Institute for Development Studies).

Contreras, Antonio P. 1991. "Power and Discourse: Development from the World System to the Philippine Uplands" (Ph.D. dissertation, University of Hawaii).

Coontz, Stephanie. 1992. *The Way We Never Were: American Families and the Nostalgia Trap* (New York: Basic Books).

Crocker, Joanna. 1989. "Proprietorship of Knowledge: The Politics of Social Science Research in the Third World" (Ph. D. dissertation, University of Hawaii).

David, Cristina C. 1982. *An Analysis of Agricultural Policies in the Philippines* (College, Laguna: University of the Philippines at Los Baños, Department of Economics).

De Dios, Emmanuel, ed. 1984. *An Analysis of the Philippine Economic Crisis* (Quezon City: University of the Philippines, School of Economics).

Delfs, Roben. 1987. "Lesson from Sunan," *Far Eastern Economic Review*, Vol. 137 (June 4), pp. 78–80.

Dell, Sidney. 1983. "Stabilization: The Political Economy of Overkill," in John Williamson, ed., *IMF Conditionality* (Washington, D.C.: Institute for International Economics), pp. 17–45.

Deolalikar, A. 1987. "Rural Employment Creation in India and Nepal," in Asian Development Bank, *Rural Employment Creation in Asia and the Pacific* (Manila: Asian Development Bank), pp. 91–134.

Desai, Meghnad, ed. 1984. *Agrarian Power and Agricultural Productivity in South Asia* (New Delhi: Oxford University Press).

Dixon, Ruth B. 1982. "Mobilizing Women for Rural Employment in South Asia: Issues of Caste, Class and Patronage," *Economic Development and Cultural Change*, Vol. 30, pp. 373–390.

Eder, James. 1982. *Who Shall Succeed? Agricultural Development and Social Inequality in a Philippine Frontier* (New York: Cambridge University Press).

Edgren, G., and N. Muqtada. 1987. "Rural Employment Creation in Asia and the Pacific: An Overview," in *Rural Employment Creation in Asia and the Pacific* (Manila: Asian Development Bank), pp. 7–12.

ESCAP (United Nations Economic and Social Commission for Asia and the Pacific). 1986. *Economic and Social Survey of Asia and the Pacific 1985* (Bangkok: ESCAP).

———. 1989. *Economic and Social Survey of Asia and the Pacific 1988* (Bangkok: ESCAP).

Floro, Sagrario L. 1987a. "Credit Relations and Market Interlinkage in Philippine Agriculture" (Ph.D. dissertation, Stanford University).

———. 1987b. "Technical Change and the Structure of the Informal Credit Market," paper presented to the First Workshop on the Differential Impact of Modern Rice Varieties on Favorable and Unfavorable Production Environments, Los Baños, Laguna, Philippines, International Rice Research Institute, March 23–25.

Fong, Pang Eng, ed. 1988. *Labor Market Developments and Structural Change* (Singapore: Singapore University Press).

Fujita, N., and W.E. James. 1990. "Export-Oriented Growth of Output and Employment in Taiwan and Korea, 1973/74–1983/84," *Weltwirschaftliches Archives*, Vol. 126 (Winter), pp. 737–753.

Giddens, Anthony. 1981. *A Contemporary Critique of Historical Materialism* (Berkeley: University of California Press).

Ginsburg, Norton, Bruce Koppel, and Terry McGee, eds. 1991. *The Extended Metropolis in Asia* (Honolulu: University of Hawaii Press).

Glassburner, B. 1985. "Macroeconomics and the Agricultural Sector," *Bulletin of Indonesian Economic Studies*, Vol. 21 (August), pp. 51–73.

Gordon, Linda. 1988. *Heroes of Their Own Lives: The Politics and History of Family Violence* (New York: Viking).

Hane, Mikaso. 1982. *Peasants, Rebels and Outcasts: The Underside of Modern Japan* (New York: Pantheon).

Hareven, Tamara K. 1982. *Family Time and Industrial Time* (New York: Cambridge University Press).

Harriss, Barbara. 1984. "Agrarian Change and the Merchant State in Tamil Nadu," in P. Bayliss-Smith and Sudhir Wanmali, eds., *Understanding Green Revolutions: Agrarian Change and Development Planning in South Asia* (Cambridge: Cambridge University Press), pp. 53–83.

Harriss, J., and M. Moore, eds. 1984. *Development and the Rural-Urban Divide* (London: Frank Cass).

Harriss, Marvin. 1981. *Cultural Materialism: The Struggle for a Science of Culture* (New York: Random House).

Hart, Gillian. 1986a. "Interlocking Transactions: Obstacles, Precursors or Instruments of Agrarian Capitalism," *Journal of Development Economics*, Vol. 23, pp. 177–203.

————. 1986b. *Power, Labor and Livelihood* (Berkeley: University of California Press).

Hawes, Gary. 1987. *The Philippine State and the Marcos Regime: The Politics of Export* (Ithaca, N.Y.: Cornell University Press).

Hawkins, John, and Bruce Koppel. 1991. "Special Economic Zones and Education in China: Bold Reform or Timid Experiment?" in Irving Epstein, ed., *Chinese Education: Problems, Policies, and Prospects* (New York: Garland Publishing), pp. 172–195.

Hayami, Yujiro. 1964. "Demand for Fertilizer in the Course of Japanese Agricultural Development," *Journal of Farm Economics*, Vol. 46 (November), pp. 776–779.

————. 1987. "Innovations in the Fertilizer Industry and Agricultural Development: The Japanese Experience," *Journal of Farm Economics*, Vol. 49 (May), pp. 403–412.

Hayami, Yujiro, and Masao Kikuchi. 1982. *Asian Village Economy at the Crossroads* (Tokyo: University of Tokyo Press).

Hayami, Yujiro, and Vernon W. Ruttan. 1970. "Factor Prices and Technical Change in Agricultural Development: The United States and Japan, 1880–1960," *The Journal of Political Economy*, Vol. 78 (September–October), pp. 1115–1141.

————. 1985. *Agricultural Development: An International Perspective*, 2d ed. (Baltimore, Md.: Johns Hopkins University Press).

Hayami, Yujiro, Esther B. Mariano, and Luisa M. Rambo. 1987. *Kasugpong in Central Luzon: "Indianization" of the Philippine Rice Bowl?* Department of

Agricultural Economics Paper No. 87–22 (Los Baños, Laguna, Philippines: International Rice Research Institute).

Herring, Ronald J. 1984. "Economic Consequences of Local Power Configurations in Rural South Asia," in Meghnad Desai, Susanne Hoeber Rudolph, and Ashok Rudra, eds., *Agrarian Power and Agricultural Productivity in South Asia* (Berkeley: University of California Press), pp. 198–249.

Heyzer, Noeleen. 1986. *Working Women in South-East Asia: Development, Subordination and Emancipation* (Philadelphia, Pa.: Open University Press).

Ho, Samuel P.S. 1979. "Decentralized Industrialization and Rural Development: Evidence from Taiwan," *Economic Development and Cultural Change*, Vol. 32 (October), pp. 77–96.

———. 1986. *The Asian Experience in Rural Nonagricultural Development and Its Relevance for China* (Washington, D.C.: World Bank).

Hsieh, Sen-Chung, and Teng-Hui Lee. 1966. *Agricultural Development and Its Contribution to Economic Growth in Taiwan* (Taipei: Chinese-American Joint Commission on Rural Reconstruction).

Huber, Joan. 1990. "Macro-Micro Links in Gender Stratification," *American Sociological Review*, Vol. 55 (February), pp. 1–10.

Hurst, Philip. 1990. *Rainforest Politics: Ecological Destruction in Southeast Asia* (London: Zed Press).

Ileto, Reynaldo. 1983. *Pasyon and Revolution* (Manila: Ateneo University Press).

Islam, Rizwanul. 1986. "Non-Farm Employment in Rural Asia: Issues and Evidence," in R.T. Shand, ed., *Off-Farm Employment in the Development of Rural Asia*, Vol. 1 (Canberra: Australian National University National Centre for Development Studies), pp. 153–174.

Ito, T. 1992. *The Japanese Economy* (Cambridge, Mass.: MIT Press).

James, William E., S. Naya, and G.M. Meier. 1989. *Asian Development: Economic Successes and Policy Lessons* (Madison: University of Wisconsin Press).

Jeffrey, Patricia. 1982. *Frogs in a Well: Indian Women in Purdah* (London: Zed Press).

Johnston, B., and P. Kilby. 1975. *Agriculture and Structural Transformation* (London: Oxford University Press).

Johnston, B., and J. Mellor. 1961. "The Role of Agriculture in Economic Development," *American Economic Review*, Vol. 51 (September), pp. 566–593.

Jones, Gavin. 1984. "Links Between Urbanization and Sectoral Shifts in Employment in Java," *Bulletin of Indonesian Economic Studies*, Vol. 20, pp. 120–157.

Khan, Azizur Rahman, and Eddy Lee, eds. 1985. *Poverty in Rural Asia* (Bangkok: International Labor Organization).

Kikuchi, Masao K., and Yujiro Hayami. 1980. "Inducements to Institutional Innovation in an Agrarian Community," *Economic Development and Cultural Change*, Vol. 29 (October), pp. 21–36.

Klitgaard, Robert. 1991. *Adjusting to Reality: "State Versus Market" in Economic Development* (San Francisco, Calif.: International Center for Economic Growth).

Koppel, Bruce. 1985. "Themes on Genes: Comments on Biotechnology, Agricultural Research and Rural Sociology," *The Rural Sociologist*, Vol. 5 (March), pp. 79–88.

———. 1986. "Janus in Metropolis: An Essay on the Political Economy of Urban Resources," *The Developing Economies*, Vol. 24, pp. 3–25.

———. 1988. "The Future of Official Development Assistance to Rural Asia," *The Developing Economies*, Vol. 26 (June), pp. 103–124.

————, ed. 1989. *Rural Transformation: Issues for Policy, Planning and Project Development* (Tokyo: Asian Productivity Organization).

————. 1990a. "Mercantile Transformations: Understanding the State, Global Debt, and Philippine Agriculture," *Development and Change*, Vol. 21 (October), pp. 579–619.

————, ed. 1990b. *Structural Adjustment and Policy Reform: Impacts on Small and Medium Enterprises in Asian Economies* (Tokyo: Asian Productivity Organization).

————. 1991. "The Rural-Urban Dichotomy Re-examined: Beyond the Ersatz Debate?" in Norton Ginsburg, Bruce Koppel, and Terry McGee, eds., *The Extended Metropolis: Settlement Transition in Asia* (Honolulu: University of Hawaii Press), pp. 47–70.

————. 1992. "Between Ballot and *Balut*: Emerging Issues in Philippine Labor Markets and Industrial Labor Relations," in Chung H. Lee and Park Fun Koo, eds., *Emerging Labor Issues in Developing Asia* (Seoul: Korea Development Institute), pp. 98–143.

————. 1993. "The Politics of Economic Reform: Insights from Indonesia, the Philippines and Thailand," in David Timberman, ed. *The Politics of Economic Reform in Southeast Asia* (Manila: Asian Institute of Management), pp. 117–147.

Koppel, Bruce, and David Zurick. 1988. "Rural Transformation and the Future of Agricultural Development Policy in Asia," *Agricultural Administration and Extension*, Vol. 28, pp. 283–301.

Kummer, David M. 1991. *Deforestation in the Postwar Philippines* (Chicago: University of Chicago Press).

Kuo, S. 1981. *The Taiwan Success Story* (Boulder, Colo.: Westview Press).

Laclau, Ernesto. 1977. *Ideology and Politics in Marxist Theory* (London: New Left Books).

Lau, L.J., ed. 1986. *Models of Development* (San Francisco, Calif.: Institute for Contemporary Studies Press).

Ledesma, Antonio J. 1982. *Landless Workers and Rice Farmers: Peasant Subclasses Under Agrarian Reform in Two Philippine Villages* (Los Baños, Laguna, Philippines: International Rice Research Institute).

Lee, Teng-Hui. 1971. *Intersectoral Capital Flows in the Economic Development of Taiwan* (Ithaca, N.Y.: Cornell University Press).

Lipton, Michael. 1977. *Why Poor People Stay Poor: Urban Bias in Third World Development* (London: Temple Smith).

Lo, Fu-Chen, and Kamal Salih. 1978. *Growth Pole Strategy and Regional Development Policy: Asian Experience and Alternative Approaches* (New York: Oxford University Press).

Lo, Fu-Chen, Kamal Salih, and Mike Douglass. 1981. "Rural Urban Transformation in Asia," in Fu-Chen Lo, ed., *Rural-Urban Relations and Regional Development* (Singapore: Maruzen Asia), pp. 7–43.

Long, Norman, ed. 1984. *Rural Societies: Perspectives on Non-Wage Labour* (London: Tavistock Publications).

Mangahas, Mahar. 1987. "Rural Employment Creation in the Philippines and Thailand," in Asian Development Bank, *Rural Employment Creation in Asia and the Pacific* (Manila: Asian Development Bank), pp. 135–192.

May, Elaine Tyler. 1988. *Homeward Bound: American Families in the Cold War* (New York: Basic Books).

McGee, T.G. 1987. *Urbanisasi or Kotadesasi? The Emergence of New Regions of Economic Interaction in Asia*, Working Paper 87–08 (Honolulu: East-West Center Environment and Policy Institute).

McMichael, Philip D. 1992. "Tensions Between National and International Control of the World Food Order: Contours of a New Food Regime," *Sociological Perspectives*, Vol. 35, pp. 343–365.

Mellor, J. 1976. *The New Economics of Growth: A Strategy for India and the Third World* (Ithaca, N.Y.: Cornell University Press).

Myers, R.H. 1991. "The Economic Development of the Republic of China, " in L.J. Lau, ed., *Models of Development* (San Francisco, Calif.: Institute for Contemporary Studies Press), pp. 13–64.

Myint, H. 1975. "Agriculture and Economic Development in the Open Economy," in L. Reynolds, ed., *Agriculture in Development Theory* (New Haven, Conn.: Yale University Press).

Ohkawa, Kazashi. 1980. *Dualistic Development and Phases: Possible Relevance of the Japanese Experience to Contemporary Less Developed Countries* (Luxemburg, Austria: International Institute for Applied Systems Analysis).

Ohkawa, Kazashi, and Bruce F. Johnston. 1969. "The Transferability of the Japanese Pattern of Modernizing Traditional Agriculture," in E. Thorbecke, ed., *The Role of Agriculture in Economic Development* (New York: National Bureau for Economic Research, Columbia University Press), pp. 277–300.

Ohkawa, K., and H. Rosovsky. 1973. *Japanese Economic Growth: Trend Acceleration in the Twentieth Century* (Stanford, Calif.: Stanford University Press).

Ohkawa, Kazashi, Bruce F. Johnston, and Hiromitsu Kaneda, eds. 1969. *Agriculture and Economic Growth: Japan's Experience* (Tokyo: University of Tokyo Press).

Oommen, T.K. 1984. *Social Transformation in Rural India: Mobilization and State Intervention* (New Delhi: Vikas Publishing House).

Oshima, Harry T. 1983. *The Transition to an Industrial Economy in Monsoon Asia*, Asian Development Bank Staff Paper No. 20 (Manila: Asian Development Bank).

———. 1984. *The Significance of Off-Farm Employment and Incomes in Post-War East Asian Growth*, Asian Development Bank Staff Paper No. 21 (Manila: Asian Development Bank).

Otero, Gerardo. 1987. "Proletarianization in Rural Mexico: Class, State and Culture," paper prepared for presentation at the Rural Sociological Society meetings, Madison, Wis., March.

Otsuka, Keijiro, Hiroyuki Chuma, and Yujiro Hayami. 1992. "Land and Labor Contracts in Agrarian Economies: Theories and Facts," *Journal of Economic Literature*, Vol. 30, pp. 1965–2017.

Pakkasem, Phisit, ed. 1979. *Rural-Urban Relations in the Bangkok Metropolitan Dominance Subregion* (Nagoya, Japan: United Nations Centre for Regional Development).

Perkins, Dwight H. 1983. "Research on the Economy of the People's Republic of China: A Survey of the Field," *Journal of Asian Studies*, Vol. 42, pp. 345–372.

Popkin, Samuel. 1979. *The Rational Peasant* (Berkeley: University of California Press).

Power, J.H., and G. Sicat. 1971. *The Philippines: Industrialization and Trade Policies* (New York: Oxford University Press).

Quisumbing, Agnes R., and Concepcion J. Cruz. 1986. *Rural Poverty and Poverty Programs in the Philippines*, Center for Policy and Development Studies Working Paper No. 86–01 (College, Laguna: University of the Philippines at Los Baños).

Ranis, G., J. Fei, and S. Kuo. 1979. *Growth with Equality: The Case of Taiwan* (New York: Oxford University Press).

Rondinelli, Dennis A. 1986. "The Urban Transition and Agricultural Development: Implications for International Assistance Policy," *Development and Change*, Vol. 17, pp. 231–263.

Rondinelli, Dennis A., and Kenneth Ruddle. 1978. *Urbanization and Rural Development: A Spatial Policy for Equitable Growth* (New York: Praeger).

Rosen, George. 1985. *Western Economists and Eastern Societies* (Baltimore, Md.: Johns Hopkins University Press).

Rosenberg, Jean G., and David A. Rosenberg. 1980. *Landless Peasants and Rural Poverty in Indonesia and the Philippines* (Ithaca, N.Y.: Cornell University Rural Development Committee Special Series on Landlessness and Near-Landlessness).

Roumasset, James. 1979. "Sharecropping, Production Externalities and the Theory of Contracts," *American Journal of Agricultural Economics,* Vol. 61 (November), pp. 640–647.

Scott, James. 1976. *The Moral Economy of the Peasant* (New Haven, Conn.: Yale University Press).

———. 1985. *Weapons of the Weak: Everyday Forms of Peasant Resistance* (New Haven, Conn.: Yale University Press).

Shand, R.T., ed. 1986. *Off-Farm Employment in the Development of Rural Asia,* Vols. 1 and 2 (Canberra: Australian National University National Centre for Development Studies).

Sharma, Miriam. 1985. "Caste, Class and Gender: Production and Reproduction in North India," *Journal of Peasant Studies,* Vol. 12, pp. 57–88.

Skolnick, Arlene. 1991. *Embattled Paradise: The American Family in an Age of Uncertainty* (New York: Basic Books).

Stranch, Judith. 1981. *Chinese Village Politics in the Malaysian State* (Cambridge, Mass.: Harvard University Press).

Strange, Heather. 1981. *Rural Malay Women in Tradition and Transition* (New York: Praeger).

Tharamangalam, Joseph. 1981. *Agrarian Class Conflict: The Political Mobilization of Agricultural Labourers in Kuttanad* (Vancouver: University of British Columbia Press).

UNDP (United Nations Development Program). 1990. *Human Development Report 1990* (New York: Oxford University Press).

———. 1991. *Human Development Report 1991* (New York: Oxford University Press).

Vogel, E. 1991. *The Four Little Dragons: The Spread of Industrialization in East Asia* (Cambridge, Mass.: Harvard University Press).

Vyas, V.S., and W.E. James. 1988. "Agricultural Development in Asia: Performance, Issues, and Policy Options," in S. Ichimura, ed., *Challenge of Asian Developing Countries* (Tokyo: Asian Productivity Organization), pp. 133–168.

Wilk, Richard R., ed. 1989. *The Household Economy: Reconsidering the Domestic Mode of Production* (Boulder, Colo.: Westview Press).

Willis, Paul. 1977. *Learning to Labour* (Hampshire, England: Gower Publishing).

Wolf, Diane. 1986. "Factory Daughters, Their Families, and Rural Industrialization in Central Java" (Ph.D. dissertation, Cornell University).

World Bank. 1984. *Bangladesh: Employment Opportunities for the Rural Poor* (Washington, D.C.: World Bank).

———. 1985. *The Philippines: Recent Trends in Poverty, Employment and Wages,* Report 5456-PH (Washington, D.C.: World Bank).

———. 1986. *Indonesia: Wages and Employment* (Washington, D.C.: World Bank).

———. 1991. *World Development Report 1991* (New York: Oxford University Press).

2

The Dynamics of Diversification in an Asian Rice Region

Gillian Hart

Longitudinal studies in different parts of South and Southeast Asia are pointing to the proliferation of nonagricultural income sources among what are ostensibly agricultural households (Alexander, Boomgard, and White, 1991; Harriss, 1991; Hart, Turton, and White, 1989). A sizable proportion of households are becoming occupationally more diverse and spatially more dispersed while still retaining links to agricultural land. Consequently, small-scale holdings often exhibit remarkable tenacity, and concentration of landholdings has been far more gradual than many observers anticipated in the early years of the green revolution.

Theories of agrarian change are typically quite limited in their capacity to relate diversification to the dynamics of structural change and class formation. These limitations derive, in part, from a preoccupation with production relations in agriculture. Analysis of diversification has also been thwarted by notions of the household as an undifferentiated unit of production and consumption.[1]

Efforts to address diversification fall into two main categories. First are the models derived from East Asian experience that portray diversification in rather idyllic terms and that typically invoke some form of technological determinism. F. Bray (1983 and 1986), for example, argues that managerial diseconomies of scale in wet-rice agriculture place a brake on land concentration and perpetuate small-scale household production. Agricultural and nonagricultural household enterprises combine in ways that contribute both to intrarural equality and to "palliating to some extent the growing economic gap between rural and urban areas" (Bray 1983: 25). A related set of theories dealing with diversification at the regional rather than the household level posit that agricultural growth stimulates the expansion of nonagricultural activities in a manner that is mutually reinforcing and that it contributes to intrarural equality (Ranis and Stewart, 1987). Taiwan is often taken as the ideal-type case.

A second body of theory views diversification as an essentially immiserating process. These theories come in different forms, but most boil down to the functionalist assertion that "semiproletarianization" is

47

conjured up by the workings of capitalism and/or the state to ensure both cheap labor and cheap food.[2]

The most obvious problem with these efforts to construct monocausal theories is their failure to explain the wide variety of diversification patterns within and across regions. For example, even in predominantly wet-rice regions, it is becoming clear that diversification can assume forms that diverge markedly from the idealized East Asian pattern. Recent research in the main rice regions of Java shows how diversification can reflect and intensify differentiation (White and Wiradi, 1989). Larger landowners diversify in order to accumulate, whereas for many landless and near-landless people, diversification is part of a struggle for survival. Broadly similar patterns have been observed in the main rice regions of Bangladesh (Huq, 1984).

In this chapter, I will illustrate yet another pattern based on longitudinal evidence from a community in Muda, the main rice region of Malaysia.[3] This evidence spans a ten-year period (1977–1987), during which rice production in Muda became heavily mechanized. Along with mechanization, there was a rapid proliferation of nonagricultural income sources, especially among men belonging to very small landholding households. Within this category of extremely small landholders, one can discern two very different processes of diversification operating simultaneously: First is a dynamic, familiar among poor households in many other parts of the world, by which married women take over agriculture while men move into nonagricultural jobs. The second trajectory of diversification signifies the emergence of an aggressive new class of brokers since the late 1970s, along with the decline of agricultural patronage. Though apparently divergent, these paths of diversification are, in fact, closely linked.

Neither theory of diversification outlined earlier can explain patterns like these. In fact, the Muda evidence dramatizes the limitations of theories that explain diversification in terms of either the technological imperatives of wet-rice production or the needs of capitalism. My purpose in this chapter is to offer an alternative framework that allows us to understand diversification both as a reflection of larger economic and political processes and as a source of pressure and change in the larger system. In particular, I will argue that social institutions and the exercise of power at different levels of society are crucial to understanding the varied forms and trajectories of diversification, as well as their connections and common elements. Rather than a monocausal and/or universal theory, we need to clarify within a comparative and historical framework (1) how different groups and classes use, manipulate, and contest the rules, rights, and obligations governing access to and control over resources and labor, and (2) how larger configurations of political and economic forces set the conditions of these struggles and are, in turn, affected by them.

Reconceptualization of "the household" is particularly critical. We must set aside the notion of a bounded unit of production and consumption that acts according to some kind of unified logic and think instead in terms of multiple sets of implicit and explicit "contracts" or arrangements that are subject to ongoing renegotiation and contestation (Hart, 1992a and 1992b; Moore, 1992). Diversification of "household" income sources is the outward manifestation of shifts in the structure and exercise of power between women and men and between elders and juniors, in relation both to one another and to wider structures of political and economic power. Explicit specification of these macroeconomic and political configurations is crucial to the analysis of diversification and class formation.

To illustrate this approach, I will start by outlining key features of the macroeconomic and political context that have set the conditions of local-level struggles over resources and labor. I will then describe changing patterns of regional- and household-level diversification in Muda. How to explain these patterns becomes the central focus as I argue that they can only be understood in terms of shifts in the structure and exercise of power at different levels of society. Finally, I will try to show how a detailed understanding of diversification in a particular setting can illuminate larger processes of structural change and class formation.

The Macroeconomic and Political Context

Race-Class Conflict and the Structure of the Macroeconomy

Until the late 1970s, Malaysia had a classic export enclave economy, characterized by limited industrialization and heavy dependence on exports of plantation crops and tin. The Malaysian economy was strikingly undiversified, even in relation to economies with far lower levels of per capita gross national product (GNP) (Saith, 1986). In contrast to most newly independent nations, the postcolonial state in Malaysia was strongly laissez-faire in orientation (Jomo, 1986).

Both the role of the state and the structure of the economy changed dramatically with the launching of the New Economic Policy (NEP) in 1971. The NEP has reshaped and intensified the class-race divisions in Malaysian society that developed during the colonial period. British colonial strategy in Malaysia operated through the elaboration of an ideology of racial difference (Hirschman, 1986; Lim, 1984). In return for extracting resources on plantations and mines with cheap indentured labor from India and China, the British tried to maintain the prestige and social status of the Malay sultans and territorial chiefs, a key element in this effort was the preservation (if not creation) of a "traditional" Malay rice peasantry (Roff,

1967). Racially defined class divisions were clearly demarcated by the close of the colonial era in 1957, and the stage was set for the race-class conflicts that surfaced in the late 1960s—conflicts that the NEP was ostensibly designed to tackle.

With its stated aims of eradicating poverty and restructuring the economy in favor of Malays, the NEP generated a markedly more interventionist role for the state, which was facilitated by growing revenues from oil and other commodity exports. Rapid economic growth during the 1970s was accompanied by important shifts in the structure of the economy. In addition to a proliferation of public enterprises, foreign-owned export industries, many of them located in free trade zones and employing a predominantly young and female Malay work force, dominated the pattern of industrialization during the 1970s. This industrialization strategy produced little in the way of male employment, which was largely contingent on a rapidly expanding bureaucracy. By the early 1980s, the proportion of the Malaysian work force in bureaucratic employment was one of the highest in the non-Socialist world. Construction, another important source of employment for Malay men, was also heavily contingent on government contracts.

The redistributive phase of the NEP ended quite abruptly in the mid-1980s. Falling commodity prices and rising debt precipitated a major shift to supply-side structural adjustment policies, privatization, and deregulation. Following a severe slump in 1985–1986, there was an acceleration of economic growth, although unemployment levels remained quite high. In addition, recent research suggests that a "labor flexibilization" process has been gaining strength, involving a move away from employment security and a shift of employment risk from companies to workers (Standing, 1989).

These shifts in macroeconomic policy and structure are crucial in understanding the patterns of diversification taking shape in the Muda region. As I will show later, certain groups continue to enjoy NEP privileges while others have become increasingly vulnerable to macroeconomic instability and the withdrawal of many protective measures. The political struggles to which I now turn have played a major role in determining gainers and losers.

The Political Imperatives of the State's Agrarian Strategy

The disproportionate political influence of the predominantly Malay rice-producing regions in the north of the country is one of the most important elements in the state's agrarian strategy. Rice accounts for only about 2 percent of GDP and is the principal source of livelihood for roughly 8 percent of Malaysia's population. However, the chief threat to the coalition in control of the state comes from the northern rice-producing regions in the form of the fundamentalist Islamic party, Partai Islam (PAS). PAS represents an orthodox Islamic and populist ideology that challenges the interests of those who control the ruling party, the United Malay National Organization (UMNO), which joined with several Chinese and Indian parties to form the National Front government.

In a continuing effort to undermine (or at least contain) PAS, the state has pumped huge subsidies into these regions, so that it is now considerably more expensive to produce rice domestically than it would be to import it.[4] The official justification for rice subsidies invokes the need for national self-sufficiency, as well as the alleviation of the poverty of rice producers. In practice, these and other subsidies are directed toward ensuring the conditions of accumulation in the national economy by securing the rural political base (Doshi, 1988).

The mechanisms by which state resources are channeled into rural regions are particularly critical for understanding the conditions of access to resources and opportunities. First, through massive infrastructural investments, the state has come to assume an extremely important role in defining the conditions of rice production. The largest of these is the Muda Irrigation Scheme, a M$270-million system of canal irrigation (M$ = Malaysian dollars) installed in the late 1960s and administered by the Muda Agricultural Development Authority (MADA). MADA exercises firm control over water distribution, access to inputs, crop timing, maintenance of the irrigation system, and so forth. The state has also taken over most of the purchasing and milling of rice. In short, state control over the conditions of production and distribution is extremely rigid, and the disbursal of agricultural price and input subsidies is organized in such a way that most cultivators do have access to them.

The allocation of other categories of state resources in rural regions is far more discretionary and is typically channeled through strategically placed groups. Under the aegis of NEP efforts to create an indigenous Malay bourgeoisie, large farmers who—at least until recently—formed the main base of UMNO support in the countryside captured a disproportionate share of these resources (Scott, 1985; Shamsul, 1986). Yet, as I will discuss later, there was a period in the mid-1970s when prominent PAS members also received a sizable share of state-dispensed resources.

The deep factional divisions represented by PAS and UMNO cut vertically across class lines (Mansor, 1978). Dominant UMNO groups, the chief recipients of state resources, are expected to bring at least a significant proportion of the poor along politically (Scott, 1985). At the same time, the PAS elite try to strengthen and consolidate their position by mobilizing the support of their poorer neighbors.

During the 1970s, the ties between rich and poor were defined mainly by agricultural production relations. J. Scott (1985) has shown how, with the intensification of agricultural production following the installation of the Muda Irrigation Scheme, larger landowners revitalized and elaborated older forms of agrarian patronage to cope with burgeoning labor requirements. He argues that the patronage strategies through which large landowners tried to ensure an adequate, hardworking, and deferential work force also helped to create a loyal political following. Although this analysis needs to be qualified to take into account gender differences in labor and political relations (Hart, 1991), there is no doubt that agricultural production relations were of preeminent importance in defining relations between rich and poor. These conditions changed dramatically in the late 1970s with the rapid spread of mechanization and other forms of labor-saving technology in rice production. Today, in essence, the rich no longer need the agricultural labor of the poor.[5]

This transformation of production relations in agriculture coincided with intense political conflict at the national level. Acting in conjunction with one another, during a period of increasing unstability in the macro-economy, these conflicts created the conditions at the local level for a fundamental restructuring of patronage relations and systems of access to resources. In the following pages, I will show how these shifts in larger political and economic conditions are essential in explaining the emerging patterns of diversification in the Muda region and interpreting their significance.

Diversification in the Muda Region

Agricultural Growth and Diversification of the Regional Economy

The experience of the Muda region contradicts the expectations of those who claim that agricultural growth stimulates expansion in nonagricultural sectors of the regional economy. Following the construction of the Muda Scheme in 1970, there was, indeed, an initial spurt of nonagricultural growth. Since then, both economic growth and structural change in Kedah state, which encompasses most of the Muda region, have lagged behind the Malaysian economy as a whole despite massive increases in government spending. In fact, government services account for a large proportion of the increase in nonagricultural employment (Wong and Anwar, 1987). The disappointing performance of the regional economy reflects several forces by which capital is channeled out of the region (Hart, 1989 and 1993).

Both survey data and village studies point to the stabilization of relatively small-scale owner-operators in the first phase of agricultural growth.[6] In 1975, researchers at Universiti Sains Malaysia conducted a complete enumeration of cultivators in the Muda Scheme and compared

Table 2.1   Size Distribution of Operated Paddy Farms, Muda Irrigation Scheme

Farm Size Class (hectare)	Percentage of Total Number of Farms		Percentage of Total Area	
	1955	1975/76	1955	1975/76
0.01 – 0.57	13.6	20.7	2.2	4.2
0.58 – 1.15	18.8	25.9	7.9	12.8
1.16 – 1.72	20.3	19.5	14.0	16.7
1.73 – 2.30	15.0	11.1	14.5	13.4
2.31 – 2.87	14.4	8.3	18.4	13.0
2.88 and above	17.9	14.5	43.0	39.9
Total	100.0	100.0	100.0	100.0
Total number of farms	46,547	61,164		
Total area (hectare)			99,950	99,002

Source: Gibbons et al., 1981.

Table 2.2   Tenurial Patterns in the Muda Scheme, 1955 and 1975

	1955		1975	
	Percentage of Households	Percentage of Area	Percentage of Households	Percentage of Area
Owner-operators	37.6	30.9	56.1	45.3
Tenants	42.1	40.0	24.5	22.7
Owner-tenants	20.3	29.1	19.4	32.0

Source: Gibbons et al., 1981: Table 78.

the results with a 1955 survey (Tables 2.1 and 2.2). Along with a sharp decline in pure tenancy, these data suggest there has been a large increase in
the proportion of owner-operators in the very small size group. The proportion of those in the largest size group fell, although less rapidly than the
amount of land they cultivated. Several in-depth studies note that increasing income and productivity rendered small-scale producers better able to
resist indebtedness and dispossession (Wong, 1983; Scott, 1985). There
are also indications of a decline in the proportion of income derived from
nonagricultural sources by rural households (FAO/IBRD, 1974; Jegatheesan, 1977).

The process that some have termed the *repeasantization* of the Muda
economy did not follow in an automatic way from the technological characteristics of wet-rice production. Among the critical factors have been
huge state subsidies of rice production, combined with uniform access to
state-subsidized resources. These, in turn, reflect the political imperatives
discussed earlier, together with the growing role of state agencies in controlling the conditions of production.

Sharp increases in agricultural wages were likewise important in boosting the incomes of small producers who also worked as wage laborers. From an index base of 100 in 1970, R. Goldman and L. Squire (1982: 758) estimate that nominal planting wages increased to 245, and harvesting wages grew to 201 by 1976. The price index (excluding rice) rose to only 140 over the same period.

The 1970s were a period of intensifying struggles over the mobilization and control of labor, although mechanisms of labor recruitment and control were sharply differentiated along gender lines (Hart, 1991 and 1992b). As a rule, men were hired and paid as individuals. In contrast, poorer women were increasingly organizing themselves into labor gangs that confronted and challenged the interests of larger landowners.

The initial phase of agricultural growth in Muda was heavily labor intensive. Since the late 1970s, however, there has been a massive substitution of capital for labor. MADA and larger landowners used labor-saving technology as a means to exercise greater control over the labor process. Combine harvesters, which displaced female labor in harvesting and male labor in threshing, began to be widely used in the latter part of the 1970s, and by the early 1980s, virtually the entire Muda region was being harvested by combines. Today, even the smallest cultivators purchase combine services with the cash coupon component of the rice subsidy, which is now simply passed on to machine owners. Most of these owners are Chinese syndicates that operate at the supravillage level, although some wealthy Malays have been entering the combine business (Md. Ikmal, 1989). The market for machine services is organized by Malay brokers, who have emerged as extremely powerful actors on the rural scene.

Labor displacement has been massive despite the creation of some new jobs for men. The only labor-intensive task in rice production that persists to some extent is transplanting, although this, too, has been the target of efforts to reduce labor requirements—in this case, by replacing transplanting with broadcast sowing. The proportion of land that was broadcast rose from 20 percent in 1982 to 65 percent in the first season of 1986, although it has since fallen to 50 percent. Broadcast sowing and combine harvesters together reduce average labor requirements by about 80 percent (MADA, 1987: 127). Apart from transplanting, the work involved in rice cultivation is now very limited and is mainly managerial in nature.

Mechanization has effectively eliminated the managerial diseconomies that Bray (1983 and 1986) and others regard as the key determinant of small-scale units of production in wet-rice agriculture. This, together with the heavy input and price subsidies that increased in the late 1970s, would suggest there are tendencies toward land concentration. As Md. Ikmal (1989) has shown, there is, indeed, a small but significant category of extremely large landowners who operate at the supravillage level and who expanded their scale of operations when labor-displacing technology became available.

There are no data for the Muda region as a whole on how the distribution of landholdings changed in the postmechanization period. However, the panel data from a Muda village that I will now discuss show that land concentration does not necessarily imply the disappearance of small-scale units of production.

Shifts in Landholding and Income Patterns: Sungai Gajah, 1977–1987

I based my study in a village that I shall call Sungai Gajah to take advantage of earlier studies done there in 1976–1977 (Mohd. Shadli, 1978) and again in 1979–1980 (Wong, 1983). Through the generosity of Mohd. Shadli, I was able to draw on raw data from his study to trace what had happened to each person over the ten-year period in which mechanization had taken hold, as well as movements into and out of the village. In addition to data on shifts in demographic, occupational, and landholding patterns, I collected qualitative evidence on changes in intra- and inter-household relations, as well as changing connections in the larger political-economic system.

The population of the village increased from 616 in 1977 to 646 in 1987 (Tables 2.3 and 2.4) or to only 629 if one excludes the 18 young people studying outside the village in 1987. These figures understate the degree of population mobility because they omit those who left the village and returned within the ten-year period—most notably, poorer men engaged in labor circulation. Together, out-migration (162 people) and in-migration (107 people) were more important sources of turnover than births (123) and deaths (37). Of the 107 people who moved into the village, 71 were couples in their twenties and thirties, along with young children. As I will show later, the large majority of men in the group held nonagricultural jobs and comprised the core of the new middle class. Overall, about 35 percent of the people living in the village in 1977 had been replaced by others in 1987.

The number of residential units rose from 132 to 144, and there was a slight decline in average size (4.7 to 4.5). Survey data on landholdings typically equate "the household" with the residential unit, and this is the definition that I have used in presenting the Sungai Gajah data on changing patterns of landholding (Table 2.5). In fact, however, this definition can be quite misleading, especially in interpreting the increase in landlessness. For example, an increasing number of elderly people lived alone but were provided for by married children living in an adjacent house. Part of the increase in landlessness reflects this type of arrangement. There were also several cases of ostensibly landless young couples who were working their

Table 2.3 Sungai Gajah: Age-Sex Structure of Village Population, 1977–1987

Age Group	1977						1987					
	Female (no./%)		Male (no./%)		Total (no./%)		Female (no./%)		Male (no./%)		Total (no./%)	
1–5	39	(12.4)	29	(9.6)	68	(11.0)	39	(11.6)	38	(12.2)	77	(11.9)
6–10	44	(14.0)	53	(17.6)	97	(15.7)	36	(10.7)	36	(11.6)	72	(11.1)
11–15	46	(14.6)	41	(14.0)	88	(14.3)	36	(10.8)	29	(9.3)	65	(10.1)
16–20	37	(11.7)	37	(12.3)	74	(12.0)	42	(12.5)	44	(14.1)	86	(13.3)
21–30	46	(14.6)	34	(11.3)	80	(13.0)	50	(14.9)	39	(12.5)	89	(13.8)
31–40	43	(13.7)	38	(12.3)	80	(13.0)	48	(14.3)	33	(10.6)	81	(12.5)
41–50	31	(9.8)	23	(7.6)	54	(8.8)	39	(11.6)	39	(12.5)	78	(12.1)
51–60	18	(5.7)	32	(10.6)	50	(8.1)	26	(7.8)	22	(7.1)	48	(7.4)
61+	11	(3.5)	14	(4.7)	25	(4.0)	19	(5.7)	31	(10.0)	50	(7.8)
	315	(100)	301	(100)	616	(100)	335	(100)	311	(100)	646	(100)

Table 2.4 Age-Sex Structure of People Who Moved in or out of Sungai Gajah, 1977–1987

Age Group	Age Structure in 1977 of People Who Moved out of the Village Between 1977 and 1987			Age Structure in 1987 of People Who Moved into the Village Between 1977 and 1987		
	Female (no.)	Male (no.)	Total (no.)	Female (no.)	Male (no.)	Total (no.)
1–5	6	7	13	1	7	8
6–10	10	8	18	8	10	18
11–15	25	16	41	7	7	14
16–20	22	26	48	5	2	7
21–30	12	10	22	12	8	20
31–40	5	6	11	12	12	24
41–50	4	1	5	4	5	9
51–60	2	1	3	2	3	5
61+	1	0	1	2	0	2
	87	75	162	53	54	107

parents' land. As I will discuss, mechanization has enhanced elderly parents' capacity to delay handing over their land to children.

As mentioned earlier, the data from Sungai Gajah on land distribution in 1977 and 1987 illustrate a very important point—namely, that land concentration does not necessarily imply the disappearance of small-scale units. Concentration of landholdings is an inference that could be drawn from the 13 percent decline in the total amount of land operated by village residents. Although it was not possible to trace every land transaction over the decade, there were several cases like that of a landowner from outside the village who withdrew a 10–hectare plot of land previously cultivated

Table 2.5   Sungai Gajah: Distribution of Rice Land Ownership and Operation, 1977–1987

Farm Size Group (relong[a])	1977				1987			
	Households		Land		Households		Land	
	(no.)	(%)	(area)	(%)	(no.)	(%)	(area)	(%)
Ownership								
0	39	29.8	—	—	49	34.0	—	—
.1 – 3.99	47	35.9	96.0	21.2	57	39.6	105.50	25.6
4 – 9.99	31	23.7	188.5	41.6	26	18.1	163.50	39.7
10+	14	10.6	168.75	37.2	12	8.3	143.00	34.7
	131	100.0	453.25	100.0	144	100.0	412.00	100.0
Operation (including noncultivators)								
0	11	8.4	—	—	31	21.5	—	—
.1 – 3.99	54	41.2	114.75	17.2	54	37.5	106.25	18.4
4 – 9.99	45	34.4	274.00	41.2	42	29.2	248.50	43.2
10+	21	16.0	276.75	41.6	17	11.8	221.50	38.4
	131	100.0	665.50	100.0	144	100.0	576.25	100.0
Operation (excluding noncultivators)								
.1 – 3.99	54	45.0	114.75	17.2	54	47.8	106.25	18.4
4 – 9.99	45	37.5	274.00	41.2	42	37.1	248.50	43.2
10+	21	17.5	276.75	41.6	17	15.1	221.50	38.4
	120	100.0	665.50	100.0	113	100.0	576.25	100.0

[a] 1 relong = 0.28 hectare.

by village tenants and hired a manager from another village to supervise cultivation.

Despite a significant tightening of the rental market, the distribution of cultivated holdings among village households remained extraordinarily stable (Tables 2.5 and 2.6). Average farm size fell by about 8 percent as the total amount of land cultivated by villagers declined more rapidly than the number of cultivating households. A slight downward shift in the distributional structure can be discerned, in the sense that the proportion of households and land in the smallest farm size group increased in relation to the others. These changes are small, however, and what is perhaps more surprising is how little land distribution within the village community seems to have changed in a period when the organization of production was radically restructured. Indeed, the number of households operating what MADA designates as "subviable holdings"—less than 4 relong (1.15 hectares)—remained the same.

The tenacity of these tiny holdings in the face of mechanization was accompanied by major shifts in occupational patterns. Between 1977 and 1987, the number of people receiving some form of nonagricultural

Table 2.6   Sungai Gajah: Tenurial Arrangements for Rice Land, 1977–1987

	1977			1987		
	Total Number	Total Area[a]	Average Farm Size	Total Number	Total Area[a]	Average Farm Size
Owner-operators	29 (24.2%)	129.00 (19.4%)	4.45	26 (23.0%)	114.25 (19.8%)	4.39
Owner-tenants	32 (26.7%)	271.50 (40.8%)	8.48	35 (31.0%)	252.25 (43.8%)	7.20
Tenants	29 (24.1%)	118.50 (17.8%)	4.08	28 (24.8%)	93.00 (16.1%)	3.32
Operating landlords	30 (25.0%)	146.50 (22.5%)	4.88	24 (21.2%)	116.75 (20.3%)	4.86
Totals	120 (100%)	665.50 (100%)	5.55[b]	113 (100%)	576.25 (100%)	5.10[b]
Nonoperating landlords	1	.50[c]		10	38.75[b]	

[a] Area operated (in relong).
[b] Weighted average for all farms.
[c] Area owned and rented out (in relong).

Table 2.7   Sungai Gajah: Nonagricultural Occupational Patterns, 1977–1987

	1977			1987		
	Women	Men	Total	Women	Men	Total
Primary nonagricultural occupation						
Self-employment	2	4	6	10	15	25
Wage employment	0	2	2	3	12	15
Government employment	0	1	1	2	9	11
	2	7	9	15	36	51
Secondary nonagricultural occupation						
Self-employment	2	20	22	10	22	32
Wage employment	0	9	9	1	13	14
Government employment	0	0	0	0	0	0
	2	29	31	11	35	46

income increased sharply (Table 2.7), particularly among married men.[7] The proportion of married men primarily engaged in nonagricultural activities rose from 5 percent (i.e., six men) in 1977 to just under 30 percent (thirty-six men) in 1987. Of this latter group, 75 percent belonged to households that cultivated some land—more than 80 percent of which had holdings of less than 1 hectare. Excluding households composed of elderly individuals and couples, 60 percent of landless and small landholding households contained men primarily engaged in nonagriculture, and an additional 25 percent of men with small landholdings were actively seeking nonagricultural jobs.

Men with primary nonagricultural occupations fall into two quite different groups:

1. Fifteen men were employed in low-wage jobs—mainly lorry driving, construction, quarry work, and rice-mill labor—that paid between M$10 and M$12 per day. As discussed more fully later, poor men's relationships with influential brokers were key determinants of access to nonagricultural jobs. In the early 1980s, many of these men had gone to work as construction laborers in Kuala Lumpur and Singapore in three- to six-month stints. By 1987, however, such jobs had dried up, and many of the low-wage jobs in the region were sporadic and insecure. Construction workers, for example, would report to work every day but would not always be employed. These and other poor men who were often openly unemployed frequently pieced together a variety of odd jobs.

2. The other twenty-one men primarily involved in nonagricultural occupations earned incomes at least triple those of the low-wage groups and, in some cases, considerably higher. These more lucrative pursuits included work in trade and transport enterprises requiring capital and contacts, in highly prized government jobs, and in brokering and contracting services. With the exception of a few medium landowners, the landholding patterns of this group are identical to those of the low-wage group.

In fact, quantitative indicators of income and landholdings provide only a very partial picture of the profound differences between the two groups. These differences are more clearly evident in the division of labor, the organization of "the household," and the nature of the conjugal tie.

In households where men held (or were seeking) low-wage nonagricultural jobs, a high proportion of women were engaged in agricultural work, both on their own tiny farms and as wage laborers. Further, "the household" was not the salient unit of production for the poor. Instead, poor women organized themselves into labor gangs or "share groups" (Hart, 1991 and 1992b). These women retained a high degree of control over their own earnings, facilitated in part by transfers of cash, food, and other resources among members of such groups. At the time of my study, a number of poor men had few income-earning options, and the dominant role of women in ensuring household reproduction was quite palpable. In some cases, it was also a source of considerable tension between husbands and wives.

The conjugal tie in poor households also became more spatially elastic in the early 1980s when a number of poor men moved temporarily to urban areas in search of construction work. Jobs of this type had dried up in 1987, but poor men would undoubtedly resume labor circulation if such jobs were to become available again. Generally speaking, "the household" became a more sectorally and spatially divided set of arrangements for the poor.

Men engaged in more lucrative nonagricultural occupations were enmeshed in an entirely different set of "intrahousehold" arrangements. They were married to women who typically described themselves as "housewives" and who, with two exceptions, did not engage in income-earning activities. These men did not perform manual agricultural labor, but they assumed full responsibility for managing their agricultural enterprises. Such men were quick to note their capacity to provide for their wives, in contrast to poor men who often had to live off women's earnings. Women frequently used such claims to invoke men's responsibility to provide for them and their children (Hart, 1991). For this group of people, the household has become a more tightly bounded unit that exemplifies a decisive break with an older agrarian existence and the emulation of a modern bourgeois family that, until quite recently, was a largely urban phenomenon.

In short, the apparent tenacity of very small holdings in the face of mechanization masks two quite different processes of diversification. As I will now show, these patterns present a number of puzzles, particularly when viewed in terms of standard theories.

Divergent Paths of Diversification

On the face of it, diversification in poor households conforms to a classic pattern observed in many other parts of the world—namely, the "feminization" of agriculture, together with men's shifting into nonagricultural occupations and circular migration.

One common interpretation of these patterns is that women's subsistence production in agriculture subsidizes the reproduction of the nonagricultural work force and thereby provides a subsidy to capital. In fact, this interpretation is far too simplistic. It is, indeed, true that poor women's labor is critical to the retention of land and that this has provided a buffer for men (and younger women) who have become increasingly vulnerable to rising instability in the national economy: In fact, the role of land in providing a modicum of security in the face of fluctuating economic conditions was a point that people constantly stressed. In the Malaysian case, however, the subsidy function of women's labor is highly questionable for the state itself provides generous subsidies to rice producers in the form of free fertilizer and price supports to which even the smallest producers have access.

There is another very important way in which diversification among the poor diverges from the semiproletarianization model, which tends to portray women as peasants and men as emerging proletarians. In Muda, the forms of poor women's labor organization seem far more conducive than men's to something approximating a working-class consciousness (Hart, 1991). In the premechanization period, poor men were bound to the rich through diffuse relations of patronage, based on agricultural production relations. But the employment of poor men in nonagricultural jobs has entailed their becoming enmeshed in new relations of dependency. To understand these relations and their significance, one must explain why other men were able to diversify successfully.

This second pattern of diversification also presents a series of puzzles. In the first place, education provides only a very partial explanation of access to more highly paid jobs. Most of the men with government jobs had an average of nine years of schooling, but they represent less than half of the men with lucrative nonagricultural occupations. In terms of age and education, the remaining men are indistinguishable from those in the low-wage group.

In fact, one can distinguish two fairly clear subgroups among men with lucrative occupations:

1. The better-educated men with government jobs, many of whom had been in the army in 1977, had returned to the village in the early 1980s after retiring from the army and moving into these much-sought-after jobs. This career trajectory is apparently a fairly common one in the region. However, a number of other men who were in the army in 1977 did not return to the village and have been far less successful in finding jobs in other parts of the country.
2. A second subgroup was living in the village in 1977. Some members had part-time nonagricultural occupations, but for the most part, they were medium landholders primarily engaged in agriculture at that time. Mainly through selling or leasing out their land, they had acquired cars or trucks that they used in trading, taxi, and trucking services, all of which were contingent on obtaining licenses and contracts.

Not all medium landholders in 1977 diversified, however. A group of men (roughly comparable in terms of age and education to those just described) remained primarily involved in agriculture between 1977 and 1987. Some expanded their landholdings through inheritance, leasing, or both, but the majority did not cultivate significantly larger holdings in 1987 than they had in 1977. In terms of the division of labor and the organization of the household, this group retained a distinctly "middle-peasant" character; the men who were engaged in more thorough and intensive cultivation than those with nonagricultural occupations, as well as most women, were involved in transplanting their own land through exchange labor arrangements. Failure to diversify was not deliberate—indeed, these men often complained about the limited options for nonagricultural diversification.

The critical question, then, is why certain men managed to diversify successfully. There are two key elements here. First, all these men are tied to large landowners through actual or fictive kinship, and within these kinship relations, there have been major shifts in the intergenerational distribution of power over the past decade. Second, the conditions of access to resources and opportunities have been shaped in critical ways by larger political struggles. Together, these forces have led to the emergence of a new category of rural inhabitants who are engaged in brokering resources of the state and/or those of urban capitalists.

Multiple Layers of Struggle:
The Emergence of a New Class of Brokers

The massive reorganization of production that accompanied mechanization brought about major shifts in the intergenerational balance of power within the propertied class. Until fairly recently, mobilizing and controlling the labor of adult children—particularly sons—was an acute problem confronting wealthier parents. Kinship tenancies and other forms of intergenerational transfers of land were the main mechanisms by which parents sought to control their children's labor (Wong, 1983). As parents aged, they tended to hand over the operation of land—although not necessarily ownership—to their children.

Labor-displacing technologies have made it considerably easier for larger landowners to retain control over land as they grow older. One indication of this is the fact that very few of those in the largest landholding category (i.e., those operating more than 10 relong or 3 hectares) experienced downward mobility in terms of landholdings between 1977 and 1987, despite considerable mobility in the smaller landholding categories. Sixty-five percent of the largest landholders in 1987 had belonged to the same landholding category in 1977, and another 18 percent had operated only slightly less than 10 relong in 1977. This stability is reflected in a pronounced upward shift in the age structure of larger landholders.

The decline in the area cultivated by large landowners was primarily a reflection of changes in the land rental market that made long-term cash leasing—mainly to outsiders—an extremely attractive proposition. The spread of combine harvesters also encouraged long-term leasing arrangements known as *pajak* that entail up-front cash payment for the entire amount of the rent. In Sungai Gajah and other villages (e.g., Barnard,

1981; Scott, 1985), *pajak* arrangements increased sharply in the period immediately following the spread of combine harvesters. Moreover, those who rented out most of their land on *pajak* in 1987 included some quite wealthy elderly people. Such arrangements represented a sharp break with earlier practices of renting land to children and other close relatives.

Both of these shifts have meant that children of large landowners have less access to their parents' land than was the case ten years earlier. Thus, the typically diminutive pieces of land cultivated by middle-class men are indicative of the capacity of wealthy parents to delay land transfers.

Although kinship ties were not a particularly fruitful source of access to land in the 1970s, they did enable certain strategically well placed men to take advantage of new opportunities that arose in that period. I will now examine the genesis of these opportunities and the conditions of access to them.

Political Struggles and the Capture of New Opportunities

The restructuring of accumulation and employment brought about by the rapid spread of combine harvesters in the late 1970s coincided with the eruption of intense political struggles. In the state of Kedah, these struggles were accompanied by a massive escalation in levels of state resources and shifts in the conditions of access to them. The emergence of a new class of brokers in Sungai Gajah—and possibly also in many other parts of the Muda region—is partly a product of the larger conflicts that erupted in this period.

As mentioned earlier, heavy rice subsidies and government spending on rural development were part of an effort by the ruling party (UMNO) to contain the challenge posed by the fundamentalist Islamic party (PAS). There was, however, a temporary rapprochement at the national level from 1973 to 1977, during which PAS joined UMNO in the National Front coalition. This was the initial phase of implementation of the New Economic Policy when large amounts of money were flowing into rural regions, and the state apparatus at different levels was being restructured to enhance the power of politicians in relations to bureaucrats. As Shamsul A.B. (1986) and others have shown, the *wakil rakyat* (representatives in the state and federal assemblies) came to wield enormous influence in the disposition of government funds during this period.

Although dominant UMNO members have always been favored recipients of government resources, the PAS-UMNO rapprochement meant that at least some members of the PAS elite in the countryside got in on the ground floor and managed to establish or enhance their bases of accumulation. For example, during the 1970s, the most influential *wakil rakyat* in the district where Sungai Gajah is located was a member of PAS. A wealthy businessman in the local town and also the owner of large tracts of land, he was actively engaged in furthering accumulation and using at least some of his wealth to secure a political following. At the time of the 1977 survey in Sungai Gajah, at least eight or nine households were renting land from him on highly favorable terms. And according to several informants, a number of other PAS supporters in the village received jobs, credit, and so on from this supravillage patron.

During the early and mid-1970s, village-level PAS patrons were also elaborating their power bases. Hassan T., the most influential PAS member in Sungai Gajah, is actually the tenant of a very large landowner based in the city of Alor Setar who acquired the land in the 1930s. In 1976, Hassan brought Ismail M., the present combine broker, into the village as his adopted son (*anak angkat*), followed in 1977 by Syed A., a building contractor. Through his connections with wealthy syndicates outside the village and with an organized crime network that extends throughout the region, Ismail established himself as a particularly powerful figure.

Since the late 1970s, the options available to PAS supporters in Sungai Gajah and elsewhere in the Muda region have been sharply curtailed, and dominant UMNO groups are in a far stronger position. This shift in the pattern of access to opportunities and resources along party lines can be traced to the expulsion of PAS from the National Front coalition prior to the 1978 general election. Although UMNO won the election, the margin in Kedah was very narrow, and the ruling party moved quickly to consolidate its position. Immediately following the election, all PAS members were dismissed from every village committee in the state of Kedah. As Scott (1985: 274) noted, "This step not only set the stage for the denial of government benefits to all PAS members, but also indicated that, henceforth, the opposition would have no legitimate role in community politics."

There were also large increases in government spending in Kedah. For example, in the plan period following the 1978 election, rural development spending in Kedah rose by 168 percent, compared with 16 percent in Peninsular Malaysia as a whole (Gibbons, 1985: 42). (One might note here that Kedah is Prime Minister Mahathir Mohammad's home state.) This massive increase in government spending goes a long way toward explaining shifts in the regional economy. As noted earlier, government services account for a large proportion of the increase in nonagricultural income and employment in the regional economy. At the village level, increases in government spending in the early 1980s were manifested not only in rising rice subsidies but also in infrastructural projects, such as electrification, piped water, and village roads. This was also the period in which discretionary grants to dominant UMNO groups at the village level were quite common, including those documented by Scott (1985) in the village of Sedaka.

In Sungai Gajah, as in Sedaka and many other communities, village society was torn apart by the exclusion of PAS from the *Jawatan Kuasa*

Kemajuan Kampong, or village security and development committee (commonly known as the JKKK), which oversees the disposition of most of these funds. Diana Wong (1983: 313), who conducted research in Sungai Gajah shortly after what is now known as the *pecah* ("split"), reports that there were only two UMNO members on the JKKK at the time of the expulsion of PAS men. Since then, the JKKK has been composed entirely of UMNO supporters, appointed by district-level officials in consultation with "village leaders." In practice, almost all the JKKK members are the sons and sons-in-law of prominent village families with large landholdings. At the time of my own study in 1987, 80 percent of the members of the JKKK were precisely those men engaged in lucrative nonagricultural activities. They include Ismail M., the combine broker and criminal originally brought into Sungai Gajah by an influential PAS supporter now widely identified with UMNO.

For those with the appropriate connections, the restructuring of village government and increases in government spending at all levels of the local and regional economy in the early 1980s meant the proliferation of opportunities, and out of this process, a new class of brokers is beginning to emerge. Several of the men who have risen to prominence on the village committee had left the village in the early 1970s but moved back with their wives and children in the late 1970s and early 1980s to take advantage of government jobs in the region and obtain access to resources and influence through the village committee. Village committee members also include all but one of the men engaged in trade and transport. These are men who appeared to experience downward mobility in landholdings between 1977 and 1987, but who, in practice, were in a far more influential position by 1987. For the most part, it is membership in prominent families with UMNO credentials that has enabled these men to grasp and use new opportunities. Conversely, those men of comparable age and education who failed to diversify were all members of PAS.

Although access to government resources is more or less blocked to PAS supporters, there are some PAS men in Sungai Gajah—particularly those who are close associates of Hassan T., the main PAS patron mentioned earlier—who still have links to important outside accumulators, most notably a combine- and tractor-owning syndicate in the local town. Like their UMNO counterparts, these men have access to outside resources through kinship-cum-political ties: Virtually all them are relatives or fictive kin of Hassan. By the same token, options are far more limited for PAS men who do not have close connections with Hassan and hence with outside capitalists.

By exploring the connections by which particular people in Sungai Gajah gained—or failed to gain—access to opportunities through kinship-cum-political ties, we can see how the new middle class in Sungai Gajah is the product of (1) massive increases in government spending that accompanied intensified power struggles at the national and regional levels, (2) changes in terms of those who control the allocation of government spending and patronage at the regional and village levels, and (3) a shift in the locus of accumulation occasioned by the spread of combine harvesters and by the concentrated patterns of ownership and control of capital. Those who grasped and those who missed new opportunities were positioned to do so by the contingencies of local history, but the conditions were set by forces extending far beyond the boundaries of the village. What is most important to understand, however, is how these larger political-economic structures are now being subject to a new set of pressures from below.

From Patronage to Brokerage

The emergence of this new category of rural inhabitants signifies a shift from older forms of agriculturally based patronage to new forms of brokerage. By 1987, brokers had taken over from large landowners (often their fathers or fathers-in-law) the task of managing the poor—or at least a segment of them—by providing poor men with access to nonagricultural income. The mechanisms by which brokers used their influence and access to resources to ensure a loyal political following were both direct (contracts for projects that employed poor men) and indirect (via influence with large contractors, state agencies, machine syndicates, etc.). In other words, the apparently separate paths of diversification were actually closely linked.

This system of brokering outside resources differs significantly from older forms of patronage based on agricultural production relations. In the first place, these systems of brokerage operate between rich and poor men, and they exclude women. This exclusion is, I suggest, one of the elements in poor women's capacity to construct and sustain class-based forms of labor organization, in contrast to poor men who sought the "protection" of a broker (Hart, 1991).

However, brokers are not interested in accommodating all those who seek their protection. As Scott (1985) has pointed out, political operatives who rely on outside resources are likely to pursue what he terms a "minimum winning coalition." Agricultural patrons, on the other hand, were concerned with ensuring an adequate and reliable labor force. Accordingly, brokers tend to have a far more limited reach. As I have mentioned earlier, a sizable proportion of poor men failed to secure regular nonagricultural employment in the region at the time of my fieldwork in 1987 and depended on odd jobs. They were also becoming quite resentful. Far from providing a subsidy to capital, the existence of a poor, marginalized semiproletariat that falls outside the purview of state clientilism poses a potential political threat to larger structures of accumulation.

From the viewpoint of the state of the accumulating classes, ensuring a base of political support in the countryside was becoming an increasingly expensive and problematic endeavor by 1987. These problems were intensified by fiscal constraints that became quite severe in the mid-1980s with the collapse in prices of export commodities. In addition to being less reliable in their capacity to bring the poor along politically, the new brokers were both willing and able to put enormous pressures on the state. Simultaneously, the World Bank and other international agencies were urging the Malaysian government to lift rice subsidies. In fact, the state was under great pressure not only to continue the agricultural support system but also to accelerate nonagricultural subsidies to rural regions like Muda. Because of the mechanisms that channel capital out of the region (Hart 1989 and 1993), these subsidies did very little to stimulate productive reinvestment and employment within the region. The intensifying tensions in regions like Muda contributed to the Malaysian political crisis, which had become quite serious by 1987.

Since the late 1980s, the Malaysian economy has grown very rapidly, driven in large part by foreign investment from Taiwan and Japan. Economic growth has alleviated the political-economic crisis that was so evident at the time of my field research. It is very likely, however, that the dynamics of diversification within and from regions like Muda will continue to play an important role in the larger political economy.

My inquiry into institutional dynamics suggests two possibilities. First, men and younger women from poor households have undoubtedly migrated to the booming industrial regions of the country. It is very likely, however, that there will be a concerted attempt to retain access to small landholdings and that older women will serve as the main anchors in poor rural regions. In the absence of a comprehensive system of pensions, unemployment, and health insurance, one can anticipate that land will increasingly come to play the role of ensuring social security and that efforts to consolidate land for more "rational" agricultural uses will be met with considerable resistance.

It is also likely that the rural brokers who were making their presence felt in the middle to late 1980s have consolidated their position and continue to demand state largesse. Indeed, it is precisely these forms of rentier accumulation that help to explain why Malaysian growth is so heavily dependent on foreign investment.

Conclusion

For all its particularities, the Muda case helps to move us beyond the debate over whether diversification of income sources signifies either immiseration or equalization along East Asian lines. In the first place, the retention of tiny holdings and the increase in nonagricultural incomes in Muda between 1977 and 1987 were, in fact, the reflection of multiple processes operating simultaneously—namely, the emergence of an aggressive new class of brokers of state resources, along with what is often termed semiproletarianization. To characterize this latter process as the outcome of efforts to ensure cheap labor and cheap food is, however, to misunderstand some of its most important features in the Malaysian context.

The more general point is that diversification can assume multiple forms that cannot be understood in narrowly economic terms. In this chapter, I have tried to show how understanding the dynamics of diversification requires explicit attention to politics and the exercise of power at different levels of society—between genders and generations, among agrarian classes, and in the larger configuration of economic and political power of which they are a part.

Notes

1. This approach is characteristic of both neoclassical farm household models (e.g., Barnum and Squire, 1979; Singh, Squire, and Strauss, 1986) and the "forms of production" literature (e.g., Friedmann, 1980; Kahn, 1982; see also Scott, 1985).

2. See Deere (1986) for a review and critique of this literature.

3. This research was supported by a fellowship from the Rockefeller Foundation's program on "Changing Gender Roles" and was carried out in affiliation with the Centre for Policy Research at Universiti Sains Malaysia. Panel data on demographic and socioeconomic changes between 1977 and 1987 are summarized in Hart (1988).

4. Tan (1987) estimated that in 1985, it cost Malaysia almost M$5 to US$1 to produce rice locally, compared to an import cost of M$2.3 to US$1. The policy instruments for the rice subsidy include a guaranteed minimum price, a price subsidy, and a fertilizer subsidy. The total cost of direct assistance to the rice sector was M$491.6 million in 1986, representing 94 percent of domestic production valued at import prices.

5. Mechanization in rubber and oil palm has been far less successful than in rice production, and plantations are heavily dependent on cheap, illegal immigrant workers, many of whom come from Indonesia.

6. MADA estimates that 5 relong (1.4 hectares) of owner-operated, double-cropped land is the minimum necessary for an average-sized family to earn an adequate income from agriculture alone and to accumulate a modest surplus (Yamashita et al., 1981). Holdings below 4 relong (1.1 hectares) are considered "subviable."

7. Most of the women who were engaged in nonagricultural activities in 1987 were poor, elderly women who had been displaced from agricultural labor and who were working in petty trade.

References

Afifuddin, H.O. 1974. "Some Implications of Farm Mechanization in the Muda Irrigation Scheme," in M. Barnett and H. Southworth, eds., *Experience in Farm*

Mechanization in Southeast Asia (New York: Agricultural Development Council).

Alexander, P., P. Boomgard, and B. White, eds. 1991. *In the Shadow of Agriculture: Non-Farm Activities in the Javanese Economy, Past and Present* (Amsterdam: Royal Tropical Institute).

Barnard, R. 1981. "Recent Developments in Agricultural Employment in a Kedah Rice-Growing Village," The Developing Economies, Vol. 19, No. 2, pp. 207–228.

Barnum, H., and L. Squire. 1979. "An Econometric Application of the Theory of the Farm Household," *Journal of Development Economics,* Vol. 6, pp. 79–102.

Bell, C., P. Hazell, and R. Slade. 1982. *Project Evaluation in Regional Perspective* (Baltimore, Md.: Johns Hopkins University Press).

Bray, F. 1983. "Patterns of Evolution in Rice Growing Societies," *Journal of Peasant Studies,* Vol. 11, pp. 431–443.

———. 1986. *The Rice Economies: Technology and Development in Asian Societies* (Oxford: Oxford University Press).

Deere, C. D. 1987. "The Peasantry in Political Economy: Trends of the 1980s," Occasional Papers Series No. 19. Program in Latin American Studies, University of Massachusetts, Amherst.

Doshi, T. 1988. "Peasants, the State, and Policy Constraints: The Political Economy of Rural Development in Peninsular Malaysia," *Journal of Peasant Studies,* Vol. 15, pp. 473–499.

FAO/IBRD (Food and Agriculture Organization/IBRD Cooperative Program). 1974. *The Muda Study,* 2 vols. (Bangkok: FAO).

Friedmann, H. 1980. "Household Production and the National Economy: Concepts for the Analysis of Agrarian Formations," *Journal of Peasant Studies,* Vol. 7, No. 2, pp. 159–184.

Gibbons, D., 1985. "Rural Development and the Political Process in Peninsular Malaysia Since Merdeka: An Overview," paper presented to the Consumer Association of Penang's seminar on "Problems and Prospects of Rural Malaysia."

Gibbons, D., et al. 1981. *Hak Milik Tanah di Kawasan Perairan Muda* (Universiti Sains Malaysia, Penang: Center for Policy Research).

Goldman, R., and L. Squire. 1982. "Technical Change, Labor Use, and Income Distribution in the Muda Irrigation Project," *Economic Development and Cultural Change,* Vol. 30, No. 1, pp. 753–755.

Harriss, J. 1991. "The Green Revolution in North Arcot: Economic Trends, Household Mobility, and the Politics of an 'Awkward Class,'" in P. Hazell and C. Ramaswany, eds., *Green Revolution Reconsidered: The Impact of High Yielding Varieties in North India* (Baltimore, Md.: Johns Hopkins University Press).

Hart, G. 1988. "Adjusting to Mechanization: Indicators of Change in Malay Rice Growing Community," Harvard Institute for International Development.

———. 1989. "The Growth Linkages Controversy: Lessons from the Muda Case," *Journal of Development Studies,* Vol. 25, pp. 571–575.

———. 1990. "Does Agricultural Growth Stimulate Rural Industrialization?" manuscript in author's possession.

———. 1991. "Engendering Everyday Resistance: Gender, Patronage, and Production Politics in Rural Malaysia," *Journal of Peasant Studies,* Vol. 19, No. 1, pp. 93–121.

———. 1992a. "Imagined Unities: Constructions of a Household in Economic Theory," in S. Ortiz and S. Lees, eds., *Understanding Economic Process* (Lanham, Md.: University Press of America).

———. 1992b. "Household Production Reconsidered: Gender, Labor, Conflict, and Technological Change in Malaysia's Muda Region," *World Development,* Vol. 20, No. 6, pp. 809–823.

———. 1993. *Regional Growth Linkages in the Era of Liberalization: A Critique of the New Agrarian Optimism,* World Employment Working Paper No. 37 (Geneva: International Labor Office).

Hart, G., Andrew Turton, and Benjamin White, eds. 1989. *Agrarian Transformations: Local Processes and the State in Southeast Asia* (Berkeley: University of California Press).

Hirschman, C. 1986. "The Making of Race in Colonial Malaysia," *Sociological Forum,* Vol. 1, pp. 45–73.

Horii, K. 1972. "The Land Tenure System of Malay Padi Farmers," *The Developing Economies,* Vol. 5, pp. 45–73.

Huq, S. 1984. "Patterns and Distribution of Rural Employment Opportunities: A Comparative Study of Two Bangladeshi Villages" (Ph.D. dissertation, Boston University).

Jegatheesan, S. 1977. "The Green Revolution and the Muda Irrigation Scheme," research paper for the Muda Agricultural Development Authority, Alor Setar, Malaysia.

Jomo K.S. 1986. *A Question of Class: Capital, the State, and Uneven Development in Malaysia* (Singapore: Oxford University Press).

Kahn, J. 1982. "From Peasant to Petty Commodity Production in Southeast Asia," *Bulletin of Concerned Asian Scholars,* Vol. 14, pp. 3–15.

Lim T.G. 1984. "British Colonial Administration and the 'Ethnic Division of Labour' in Malaysia," *Kajian Malaysia,* Vol. 2, No. 2, pp. 28–66.

MADA (Muda Agricultural Development Authority). 1987. *Matlamat dan Pencapaian* (Alor Setar, Malaysia: MADA Pejabat Pengurus Besar).

Mansor Haji Othman. 1978. "Hak Milik Tanah Padi dan Politik di Kedah" (master's thesis, School of Comparative Social Science, Universiti Sains Malaysia).

Md. Ikmal Said. 1989. "Large Farmer Strategies in an Undiversified Economy," in G. Hart, Andrew Turton, and Benjamin White, eds., Agrarian Transformations: *Local Processes and the State in Southeast Asia* (Berkeley: University of California Press).

Mohd. Shadli Abdullah. 1978. "The Relationship of the Kinship System to Land Tenure" (master's thesis, Universiti Sains Malaysia).

Moore, H. 1992. "Households and Gender Relations: The Modelling of the Economy," in S. Ortiz and S. Lees, eds., *Understanding Economic Process* (Lanham, Md.: University Press of America).

Ranis, G., and F. Stewart. 1987. "Rural Linkages in the Philippines and Taiwan," in Francis Stewart, ed., *Macro Policies for Appropriate Technology in Developing Countries* (Boulder, Colo.: Westview Press).

Roff, W. 1967. *The Origins of Malay Nationalism* (Ithaca, N.Y.: Cornell University Press).

Saith, W. 1986. "Location, Linkage and Leakage: Malaysian Rural Industrialization Strategy in National and International Perspective," *National Spatial Plan Study* (Government of Malaysia/UNDP).

Scott, J. 1985. *Weapons of the Weak: Everyday Forms of Peasant Resistance* (New Haven, Conn.: Yale University Press).

Shamsul A.B. 1986. *From British to Bumiputera Rule: Local Politics and Rural Development in Malaysia* (Singapore: Institute of Southeast Asian Studies).

Singh, I., L. Squire, and J. Strauss. 1986. *Agricultural Household Models* (Baltimore, Md.: Johns Hopkins University Press).

Standing, G. 1989. *The Growth of External Labour Flexibility in a Nascent NIC: Malaysian Labour Flexibility Survey,* World Employment Working Paper (Geneva: International Labor Office).

Tan Siew Hoy. 1987. *Malaysia's Rice Policy: A Critical Analysis* (Kuala Lumpur: Institute for Strategic Studies).

White, B., and G. Wiradi. 1989. "Agrarian and Nonagrarian Bases of Inequality in Nine Javanese Villages," in G. Hart, Andrew Turton, and Benjamin White, eds., *Agrarian Transformations: Local Processes and the State in Southeast Asia* (Berkeley: University of California Press), pp. 266–302.

Wilson, T.B. 1958. *The Economics of Padi Production in North Malaya,* Bulletin No. 103 (Kuala Lumpur: Ministry of Agriculture).

Wong, D. 1983. "The Social Organization of Peasant Production: A Village in Kedah" (Ph.D. dissertation, University of Bieleveld).

Wong Poh Kam, and Anwar Ali. 1987. "Economic Base Survey," unpublished report (Majlis Pebandaran Kota Setar).

Yamashita, M., et al. 1981. *MADA-TARC Cooperative Study* (Alor Setar: Muda Agricultural Development Authority).

3

Profiting from the Poor: Income Generation Schemes and Women in Rural India

Miriam Sharma, with Urmila Vanjani

The challenge of providing productive rural employment throughout Asia in the 1990s and beyond is critical. Not only does it affect the dramatically rising number of people who are being marginalized in terms of productive skills and hence income, it also affects political outcomes in terms of how the state will control the increasing number of the poor. On the one hand, a structurally narrowed labor market in the urban-industrial sector, unable to absorb a growing work force, makes it advisable to prevent peasant production from disintegrating. On the other hand, statistics reveal just how limited the possibilities are for household reproduction solely through farming activities. With meaningful agricultural land reform an apparent mirage in most of South and Southeast Asia, the possibility or hope that rural employment will act as a pacification mechanism to divert the potential explosiveness of a pauperized rural subproletariat has taken on critical proportions. At this juncture, the very survival of the absolutely impoverished and the needs of the state coincide with a form of capital accumulation from the rural sector that, in fact, represents "profiting from the poor."

The World Bank's "basic needs" policy, first enunciated in 1973 as part of its war against absolute poverty (World Bank, 1972),[1] has followed the strategy of "investment in the poor" (Bennholdt-Thomsen, 1988: 51). However, two decades of developmental efforts had failed to reduce the pressures of growing unemployment and underemployment, inadequate food supplies, and increasing absolute poverty. Faith in the trickle-down theory waned as rapid economic growth failed to automatically reach the poor or reduce poverty. Trickle-down was replaced by the view that "in the long run they [upper-income groups] may even benefit from the 'trickle-up' effects of greater productivity and purchasing power of the poor" (Bennholdt-Thomsen, 1988: 53). The strategy of investing in the poor to benefit the rich of developing countries has led to a reevaluation of the function of peasants. No longer viewed as the remnant of a precapitalist mode of production that would disappear with incorporation into a

73

capitalist economy, the peasantry now exists in a form that has been shaped and perpetuated by capitalist development.

During the continuing economic crisis of the 1970s and 1980s, occurring despite increased "green revolution" productivity, attention turned to those who bore the brunt of responsibility for maintaining the survival and reproduction of the household—women. In India, the commercialization of agriculture has meant the displacement of men while women are still retained in large numbers in the rural labor force (and the converse—the decline of women in modern sectors—is equally true). It is men's work, not women's, that is being mechanized as the labor-intensive areas of agriculture increasingly become, a female preserve.[2] Women are not being left out of the modernization process, as developmentalists have feared. Rather, the problem is that they are integrated in a manner that "generates and intensifies inequalities, making use of existing gender hierarchies to place women in subordinate positions at each level of interaction between class and gender" (Beneria and Sen, 1981: 288). Women are participating in the processes of production and accumulation from a traditionally weak position (Beneria and Sen, 1982).

It is our contention that in the headlong rush to provide programs and income generation schemes for women—by both international development agencies and the state—too little attention has been given to fundamental inconsistencies between what these projects assume are the existing roles of women, what those roles actually are, and what roles the projects require. Although much of the rhetoric is addressed to increasing the incomes of the poor through the generation of self-reliant productive employment, actual policies proceed from the premise that the female contribution to meeting basic needs is through household and subsistence production. A strategy for women has evolved "within the framework of their traditional responsibilities," while at the same time, the contradictory vision of promoting their economic independence and rise in status was propounded.[3] It has been left to a host of scholars and others to give voice to the realities. And the general consensus of critical views, as Lourdes Beneria and Gita Sen (1982: 158) note, has been that "women are instrumental to programs of population control, increased food production, and the provision of other basic needs. There is little concern, at the official level, with the subordination of women or with the impact of class processes on this subordination."

Income generation programs created for rural women, such as those in India, often have been designed and implemented in ways that reinforce the preexisting status of women, including especially their limited mobility and traditional responsibilities in the domestic sphere. Various forms of putting-out contract work and animal husbandry programs have assumed increasing importance as quick panaceas to deep-rooted problems of poverty, subordination, and ill health.[4] The result has been a "welfare" bias in policies that confers the necessary gender specificity to programs targeting the rural sector but does nothing about changing the structures underlying entrenched patterns of differentiation (Leon, 1987: 93). Such policies for the poor have, in turn, proven extremely profitable in terms of capital accumulation.

The following theoretical section provides a framework to explore the meaning and impact of rural work programs on class differentiation and gender relations and links them to the general processes of capital formation among the peasantry. It is within this context that "profiting from the poor" becomes a reality. We then present a case study of a village in northwestern India and a discussion of the implications of introducing an income-generating dairy scheme for poor women. Finally, we will offer some conclusions regarding programs of rural income generation for women.

Production and Reproduction in Capital Accumulation from the Poor

The ways in which a specific woman is incorporated into rural work programs are mediated by the particular nexus of production and reproduction relations located within her domestic unit—the household. Nancy Folbre (1986: 27ff) has pointed "to the recognition of certain complementaries between patriarchal and capitalist mechanisms of control over labor. They may often coincide." The analysis of intrahousehold inequalities within the context of class positionality provides an understanding not only of the links between such systems at the micro and macro levels but also of the linkages between different levels of capital accumulation and extraction.

The bulk of all peasant women's economic activities relates to agricultural production and to rural household reproduction.[5] The latter category includes not only biological reproduction, child care, and nurturing functions but also all the domestic chores that maintain and reproduce the household on a daily basis. Poor rural women bear the heaviest reproductive load for they lack even the basic social infrastructure (water, fuel, fodder) and their domestic technology is the most rudimentary. In addition, these poor women have the primary responsibility for providing income critical to the survival of the household unit. All peasant women participate in some tasks of agricultural production, harvesting, and postharvesting. Poor women also must labor for others. Female responsibility for household reproduction is a major source of inequality because the working day of a woman is longer than that of a man (Deere and Leon, 1987: 4).

A focus on reproduction foregrounds the relationships of dominance and subordination within the patriarchal household and the way that women's roles and locations in the development process are conditioned by their roles in the reproductive sphere (Beneria and Sen, 1982: 167). It directs attention to women's economic contributions, to the material basis of their oppression, and to the implications of these patterns for policy and action. Equally important is attention to class in understanding the work women do. Characteristics of choices and participation in rural wage labor markets differ significantly according to a household's access to the means of production.

Because of the dual nature of their tasks in production and reproduction, women are incorporated into wage labor under unfavorable conditions. First, because they are still tied to the production of subsistence and use values, they are not completely proletarianized. Further, the complex intermesh of class and gender disadvantages combine to ensure that poor women have the least access to all social resources. As Hilary Standing (1985) has elaborated in the case of urban Bengal, unequal access to family resources—for example, education and movable property (where they exist)—reinforces a woman's material dependence on male kin, whatever their situation in the labor market. This is also reflected in the unequal capacities of men and women to compete in the labor market for scarce or better-paid jobs. When status and dependency ideologies enmesh with objective inequalities to reproduce disadvantage and when employment opportunities coincide with women's traditional work and lack of mobility, then employers "see women as a cheap and relatively compliant source of labor" (Standing, 1985: 225).

Veronika Bennholdt-Thomsen's provocative piece makes the strongest case for why investment in the poor is a profitable venture and investment in poor women perhaps the most profitable of all. The goal is to increase the productivity of "self-employed producers" by providing productive (i.e., wage) employment in rural areas that supplements the workers' possession of the means of production (land or skills).[6] This form of production is "particularly exploitable for the accumulation process" (Bennholdt-Thomsen, 1988: 54) since subsistence production subsidizes low wages, and there is no incentive to raise them to cover the costs of reproduction. Through the self-exploitation built into the "independence" of these workers, agricultural and other goods are produced cheaply. This also helps to keep the wage packets of industrial workers low, and it fuels greater capital accumulation in that sector as well.[7]

The argument so far has postulated that modern capital accumulation proceeds where the costs of reproducing the labor force are lowest. In predominantly agrarian societies, this may be best achieved when it is linked to continued subsistence production. Current levels of industrialization can absorb only a small fraction of the rural poor. And the vast majority of them are not fully proletarianized (i.e., to the point where their wages cover reproduction costs) but continue to eke out a marginal existence from subsistence production amidst a falling standard of living. When subsistence production is linked to the reproductive responsibilities of women, labor becomes the most profitable of all. A close look at the implications of an attempt to introduce a dairy development scheme for women in rural India provides a vivid illustration.

Class and Gender in Village Shankpur

For seven months during 1986–1987, we lived in a village called Shankpur in northern India.[8] Villagers will tell you that the arid hill country of eastern Rajasthan surrounding their homes is a *bukkha mullak*—a region of hunger. It is hunger that forces many of the poorest of the poor to migrate annually to the more fertile Punjab, where they work as seasonal laborers, harvesting cotton or rice. Sometimes, especially for those called Bhangis (untouchable, low-caste sweepers), the move becomes permanent as they find employment cleaning the streets in the small towns dotting the Punjab. The village itself is located midway between the district headquarters in Alwar and the nearby *tehsil* (block development headquarters) town. Further on, the road links up with the national highway running between Jaipur and Delhi, some ninety miles away, and midway between the capital and the village is the large industrial area of Rewari in Haryana. Surprisingly, few villagers have found more than occasional employment there.

The village represents a fascinating mix of ethnic groups, castes, and religions. Forty-four percent of the 1,800 inhabitants are Punjabi Jats, members of a caste that had migrated to the area at the time of Partition in 1947. Originally coming from the fertile land of the five rivers in Multan (now part of Pakistan), Jats are known as sturdy peasants who live across northern India from Punjab to Uttar Pradesh. They are the agriculturists who have created the green revolution in Punjab. The next largest group in the village is composed of the Scheduled Castes, making up 25 percent of the population. These include Chamars (traditionally leatherworkers) and Bhangis (sweepers and scavengers), the latter representing only 5 percent. The Ahirs, traditional cowherders and agriculturists, comprise 14 percent of the village population today. Like a small segment of the Punjabi Jats, they all live together in a separate hamlet (*dhani*) near their fields. They own a proportionately larger amount of land than any other caste. Muslims represent 10 percent of Shankpur. These include Meos (some of whom live in their own *dhani*)[9] and Fakirs. The three remaining castes in the village are Kumhars (potters—6 percent), Banias (merchants—1 percent), and Nais (barbers—2 households out of a total of 252).

Shankpur represents a fairly egalitarian village in terms of status, landownership, and wealth: The great disparities visible in other villages and parts of India are not readily apparent here. The reasons for this seem to be twofold. On the one hand, the traditional pattern of land concentration in place before 1947—where the "dominant" caste and premier landholders were the Meos (many being extremely large landlords)—was broken by their migration to Pakistan and the reallocation of this land in small plots to Punjabi refugees. Landownership also became a reality for a number of Chamar families. On the other hand, the rather limited success of the green revolution, due to the scarcity of water, has retarded the acquisition and alienation of land (the transfer of title) that has become a hallmark of areas of highly capitalized agriculture (Tables 3.1 and 3.2).

This is not to say that traditional markers of caste status are not present. All acknowledge the Punjabi Jats to be dominant—if not in terms of wealth determined by landownership, then in terms of education, salaried positions outside the village, power and leadership within the village, and general sophistication and advancement. The coming of the Punjabis some forty years ago affected all aspects of local life. One of the most important effects, which has relevance for the dairy schemes being promoted today, was the constriction of the numbers of milch animals and the amount of grazing land available.

Traditionally, the Ahirs and other castes kept a lot of cattle. Because most of the village land was considered *banjar* (wasteland suitable only for grazing), it could support large numbers of animals. Irrigated plots were confined to the small areas around the wells, and agriculture was not pursued by many because of the scarcity of water. Grazing land and the cattle previously supported by it soon disappeared, however, with the allotment of land to the Punjabi refugees and the extension of irrigation facilities. Government promotion of buffaloes, which yielded more milk, combined with the introduction of large-scale milk sales, further depleted the village cattle stock. Yet even today, Rajasthan has the largest number of milch animals, especially cows. During the droughts from 1984 through 1987, it was not unusual to see the main highways clogged with herds of cattle—hundreds at a time—migrating to the Punjab and Haryana in search of grazing land after crops there are harvested.

Although the majority of villagers are engaged primarily in agricultural pursuits, what is most striking today is the wide range of activities pursued by different male individuals within a household as well as by the single individual in order to ensure survival of the domestic unit. Hardly any men (and definitely no women) received a "living wage" or "family wage" to cover all the reproduction costs or provide social security for illness and old age. The gap between income and expenditure was widest among the landless and marginal holders, and it led to a state of permanent indebtedness (see also Mies 1986: 95, 98, 108). Most households combined wage employment with agriculture for their subsistence.

A distinction must be made, however, between the sorts of pursuits that individual household members engage in and the class status of the

Table 3.1 Land Ownership by Caste in Shankpur, India

Caste	Caste as Percentage of Population	Ownership by Size of Holdings (percent)				
		Landless	.5–6.99 bighas[a]	7–13.99 bighas	14–21.99 bighas	22+ bighas
Bhangi	5	84	16	0	0	0
Chamar	20	21	55	20	4	0
Kumhar	6	1	42	27	10	20
Meo	10	0	7	36	50	7
Ahir	14	0	4	33	30	33
Jat	43	8	15	36	33	8
Bania/Nai	2	68	0	32	0	0

[a]1 bigha = 0.64 acre; 4 bighas = 1 hectare.

Table 3.2 Landlessness by Caste in Shankpur, India

Caste	Caste as Percentage of Population	Percentage of Caste Landless	Total Number of Households	Total Number of People[a]	Percentage of Total Population
Bhangi	5	84	12	72	4
Chamar	20	21	13	75	4
Kumhar	6	1	1	1	.05
Meo	10	0	0	0	0
Ahir	14	0	0	0	0
Jat	43	8	11	60	3
Bania/Nai	2	68	4	23	1.2
Total	100	13	41	231	13

[a] Village population = 1,800.

domestic unit. The occasional driving job that a landless Chamar may find is not of the same order as the driving done as an occupation by a relatively large landholding Ahir or Punjabi. Secondly, the range and numbers of those engaged in pursuits other than agriculture are closely associated with the class and educational background of household units.[10] Kumhars, Ahirs, and Meos, all primarily landowners, are still preeminently agriculturalists. Those Meos classified as laborers belong to related households of land-poor villagers. To some extent, it is below the dignity of a Meo or an Ahir to find such employment, and only dire necessity would prompt them to do so.

But it is a comparison of the various occupations of the Punjabi Jats and Untouchable Chamars that is most interesting (Table 3.3). The single largest category of employment for Chamar males is "laborer," which includes both agricultural and construction work. Beyond this, the scope

Table 3.3   Male Occupations by Caste in Shankpur, India

	Bhangi	Chamar	Bania	Kumhar	Meo	Ahir	Jat	Total
Basketmaker	6							6
Laborer	4	25			5		9	43
Carpenter/mason	1	22		2			4	29
Blacksmith							3	3
Shepherd	3							3
Military serviceman	3				3	2	7	15
Policeman		1					1	2
Tonga driver		1						1
Government worker		5				1	4	10
Electrician		2						2
Driver		1			4	3	9	17
Shopkeeper		3	2				7	12
Television repairman		1						1
Mechanic						2	5	7
Factory worker		6					17	23
Sweets maker (halwai)		3						3
Tailor		3			1		5	9
Leatherworker		1						1
Barber		2						2
Potter				5				5
Pot seller				3				3
Agriculturist[a]	2	35		16	21	34	94	202
Teacher			1		3		7	11
Engineer						1		1
Hotel worker					1			1
Guard						1		1
Forest department worker							6	6
Flour mill worker							4	4
Dairy worker							3	3
Waterworks employee							1	1
Photographer							1	1
Printer							1	1
Medical assistant							1	1
"Doctor"							4	4
Village council (panchayat) secretary						1	1	
Postman							2	2
Vegetable seller							1	1
Cold storage worker							1	1
Camel cart driver							1	1
Rickshaw driver							1	1
Chef							2	2
Singer							1	1
Totals	19	111	3	26	38	44	203	444

[a] Agriculture is often combined with other occupations, especially when the holding is small.

and quantity of jobs are quite narrow: policeman, cart driver, truck driver, factory worker, tailor, shopkeeper, electrician, sweet maker, government employee, or television repairman. None of these jobs requires extensive education, and in our study population, there was only one college graduate, employed in a bank. Even the electrician's knowledge may be obtained without formal education: A son, for example, may apprentice himself to his father and learn while working beside him. In cases where apprenticeship is not possible, there are courses available in the city to learn the requisite skills in electronics, tailoring, and other fields. These are usually of several months' duration. In contrast, the numbers and range of workers among the Punjabis who obtained a cash income to supplement subsistence needs was impressively larger and more diverse.

And what of women's work and employment? One of the most striking things about a village in Rajasthan is the intensity and duration of women's work. On a walk down the main street of Shankpur, at perhaps any time of the year except when mustard and wheat are being harvested in April and May, an observer will find a number of men playing cards in small groups. By contrast, at any time of the year (excluding the two summer months), few women will be seen between 8:00 A.M. and 4:00 P.M.; it is definitely difficult to meet a woman or a teenage girl from a nuclear family. Moreover, girls are disproportionately kept from attending school, and it is not uncommon to see little ones of just six or eight assuming all the household and nurturing tasks while their mothers work in the fields.

Women go to the fields twice a day to cut and collect the huge headloads of fodder that they carry home, where the animals (buffaloes or cows) are kept tethered in the courtyard or nearby. Twice a day, they will feed and milk the animals, also cleaning the shed or area where they are tied and collecting the dung to make into fuel cakes. During the three winter months, they will make almost daily six-hour-long trips to the hills near the village to collect firewood, the main source of fuel. They will be at the wells bathing and washing their children, animals, and clothes. Twice a day, they will need to balance ceramic pots on their heads and carry water from the well to the home for drinking, cooking, and cleaning. If they are poor Meo, Punjabi, or Chamar women, they also will be working in someone's fields, earning 6 to 7 rupees a day.[11] If they own land, they will be laboring in their fields during sowing, reaping, and irrigating times. Most postharvest activities are also performed by women.

In Rajasthan, women do all the work that men do, except ploughing,[12] and men do none of what is considered women's work. And so, it is not surprising that elderly Punjabi women all uniformly bemoaned the fate that had brought them to the *bukkha mullak* of Rajasthan. In their pre-Partition home in western Punjab, women did little work outside the home other than harvesting the cotton crop. But just as their families could not have survived those early years in Shankpur if women did not do all types of work, a family cannot survive today without the work of its women. Despite this, wage labor is the only area in which women have become visible in formal statistics.

Most Bhangi women (except for two new brides and the wives of those in the military) are sweepers who clean the homes and collect the dung from animal areas of village homes (Table 3.4). Practically all Chamar women work in the village (and occasionally in others nearby) as seasonal laborers in onion production and at harvest times. When famine-relief work became available in the district, these women (as well as men) also cut stones out of the hillside near the village for use in widening the road. This was done in the hottest months, from April onward.[13] Joining them as laborers were the poorest of the Punjabi, Meo, and Kumhar women. Some of the Bania, merchant caste, women worked at their shops or at pushcarts in the village, as did two Punjabi women. One Bhangi woman continued her traditional work as a midwife (*dai*). Only three women were employed outside the village—all were Punjabis. One was a teacher in a nearby village, a second was a trained midwife and village health worker who traveled daily to work in another village eleven miles away, and the third taught girls how to use a knitting machine in a small town, also eleven miles away. There widows took the responsibility for agricultural production as no grown son was available to take over these responsibilities.

Table 3.4 Women's Work for Others by Caste and Class in Shankpur, India (number of women)

	Bhangi	Chamar	Bania	Kumhar	Meo	Ahir	Jat
Sweeper	11						
Laborer		a		2	4	1	10–20
Agriculturist[b]		2					1
Shopkeeper			3				
Midwife	1[c]						1
Nurse							1
Knitting instructor							1
Teacher							2
Totals	12	2	3	2	4	1	16–26

Note: These are rough estimates from an initial census questionnaire.

a Practically all Chamar women work as seasonal agricultural laborers for others.

b These women are widows with no grown sons to take care of the farming activities.

c This woman had recently stopped working as a traditional midwife (dai).

A comparison of the work done by men and women in the village reveals that the women were a much more homogeneous occupational group. The range of employment outside their homes and their village was greatly restricted (see also Mies, 1986: 95). Yet it is clear that when these productive activities—of both paid and unpaid labor—were added to reproductive responsibilities, the double-day became more than a matter of rhetoric. It had implications for women's inability to engage in full-time, paid production, as well as for their need to accept positions in the labor market (Beneria and Sen, 1982: 167). There were also poor women who worked a triple- or even a quadruple-day: They carried out reproductive and domestic tasks within the household, worked on their own land and/or that of others, and cared for animals. In addition to the inequalities and subordination that poor women suffered by virtue of belonging to the lower class, they were also impacted by the inequalities engendered by the patriarchal family.

The distribution of resources within the household appears to be inversely related to the amount of work performed. Furthermore, the distribution of nutrition, health, education, movable property, and access to income operates against women. Overwork and the lack of adequate nutrition are the two main causes for most of the women's ailments, and multiple pregnancies take a terrible toll on those already in such a weakened and overworked state. Although, for example, the universal practice of a woman eating last—after husband and children—may be regarded as a cultural value displaying respect, in fact it means she eats the least: There are not always leftovers. Men, not women, eat meat, and boys receive preferential treatment in the dispensing of clarified butter (*ghee*), milk, and other important nutrients.

The incidence of good health in Shankpur, as elsewhere in India (see Zurbrigg, 1984), has a definite class and gender bias. And the poorest women are not only the most overworked and already weakened by multiple pregnancies, they also have the poorest diets. Most commonly, there is a morning "meal" of dry *roti* (bread without *ghee*) and perhaps some *dal* (lentils), preceded by a cup of tea. The evening meal basically consists of *roti* or rice, more *dal,* or a seasonal vegetable. Hunger between meals is quenched by consuming leftover *roti*. In addition to their low-caloric diet, these women also have the least access to medical care. There are three "doctors" who have medical stores in the village, where they sit and dispense their pills and injections. Such medical care is not cheap—a few pills can cost 2 to 5 rupees and an injection 5 to 10. With a female laborer earning just 6 rupees for a full day's, work, it is understandable that they wait for a long time before going to the doctor. What often occurs is that their illnesses progress until it is beyond the capacity of the village doctors to treat them, and the women must be taken to a government hospital in a nearby bazaar-village, an hour's walk away.

This was the situation of life, work, and general well-being (or lack thereof) in the village of Shankpur when representatives of the Rajasthan state dairy at Alwar came to discuss a joint project to provide loans to poor women for the purchase of buffalo and encourage them to establish their own dairy cooperative.[14]

A Revolution of a Different Color?

Parading under the guise of an income-generating scheme for small and marginal farmers as well as agricultural laborers that will also provide an improved nutritional standard, Operation Flood is the government of India's massive program for developing the dairy industry. A white revolution was to follow upon—indeed, build upon—the green revolution that had transformed productivity in basic food grains. Operation Flood has gone through several incarnations, but critical assessments do not attribute much success either to its design or its performance in achieving the stated goals: boosting dairy production (as distinguished from procurement), improving the lives of the peasants (especially the rural poor and landless), and providing reasonably priced milk for urban consumers (George, 1985: 9, 275–300; see also Alvares, 1985: 99-112).

Shanti George (1985: 4) highlights the issues involved in (re)building India's dairy sector "toward large scale, high speed, discontinuous change." The original motivation for Operation Flood grew out of the need for the European Economic Community (EEC), the world's largest producer of skimmed milk powder and butter oil, to dispose of huge surpluses in the late 1960s. Today, India's continuing dependence upon foreign aid from the EEC in the form of surplus dairy commodities is a key issue. Indeed, the entire Indian dairy network has become dependent upon these supplies, which vary according to external market conditions. This importation of dairy products has a considerable impact on India's balance of payments, and it has undercut domestic production, which cannot compete with the lower prices of the imports (George, 1985: 241; Doornbos et al., 1990: 51ff).

This was corroborated in an address by V. Kurien, chair of the National Dairy Development Board and "father" of Operation Flood, at the twenty-third dairy industry conference. He warned that "stiff prices and poor quality of [domestic] milk has eaten into the milk market" and threatens its expansion. As a result, dairies are faced with unsold supplies, and cooperatives are declaring milk holidays. Simultaneously, cooperatives are producing expensive by-products strictly for upscale and foreign markets, while "milk has begun to disappear from rural India" (*India Abroad*, 1990). Inappropriate, capital-intensive imported technology has also raised the cost of indigenous milk. The Tetrapak, a Swedish container designed to extend the shelf life of milk to six months, is the most expensive form of retaining milk fluid and will hardly be within the means of those who cannot afford a refrigerator (George, 1985: 189). Thus, it may be fairly concluded that this foreign aid has transformed milk processing but achieved little in the way of a revolution in milk production.[15]

An evaluation of Operation Flood by A.H. and Geeta Somjee (1989) described the project in very favorable terms.[16] However, an extensive and more careful study to explore the interface of dairy aid and development is offered in a book on the Indo-Dutch Programme on Alternatives in Development (Doornbos et al., 1990), which looked closely at Operation Flood as an "alternative in development." It documented how "India had in effect become dependent on cheap imports or foreign aid" (Doornbos et al., 1990: 293) to adequately cover the full costs of the milk processing and marketing system. To date, the central government has resisted subsidizing this sector on a permanent basis out of domestic resources or passing the costs on to consumers (many of whom are already priced out of the market!). Meanwhile, several states (especially Gujarat and Maharastha) have declared milk holidays during the flush season when the surplus milk cannot be marketed. Doornbos et al. (1990: 293ff) also note the depressing impact of cheap imports on domestic production.

And what of the production process itself and the impact of the dairy scheme on solving the problems of poor producers? As Shanti George (1985: 130) notes:

> The white revolution that Operation Flood promises must therefore be viewed in the perspective of both the green revolution which it follows and the red revolution that it attempts to fend off. It is feared that growth in production without simultaneous egalitarian distribution of the returns therefrom will aggravate structural strains until deprivation and its consequent tensions reach a point of no return. The green revolution brought both augmented production and increased disparity: the white revolution promises the former without the latter, and further, claims to narrow the gap between rich and poor that the green revolution was responsible for widening.

Shifting milk production to a commercial basis with high-value inputs of fodder, feed, and medical costs for the milch animals does not benefit the poor. Nor is it the most advisable path to follow if malnutrition and ill health are to be truly addressed. The *Times of India* (1985) highlighted the distortions created by excessive emphasis on dairy development in the famed Kaira district, where the dairy program gained its fame "while basic causes of poverty remained untackled." Despite such distressing news, the pattern of cooperatives has spread through the dairy departments of all states, along with its policy of capital-intensive inputs based on Western technology.

When government planners discovered that women had been left out of the development process, they also came to realize that female labor is the mainstay of the dairy sector (e.g., Chen et al., 1986: VII, 1). And yet, even if the nutritional status of the family undergoes a change for the better, that of the women and female children may scarcely be affected. Therefore, the neglect of women's role in livestock maintenance and dairy production not only strengthened the pattern of unequal access to resources between men and women but also had an adverse affect on production itself (Chen et al., 1986: 13–14). Women "activists" and the Ford Foundation attempted to remedy this inequity in 1980 by initiating measures to facilitate ownership of animals by women and to set up dairy cooperatives for them. Their major concern was to draw the millions of women already engaged in dairying into the mainstream of dairy development and to increase their income and knowledge about the modernizing industry (Chen et al., 1986: foreword). Such programs utilized the preexisting institutional infrastructure of the cooperative pattern in conjunction with the government Integrated Rural Development Program (IRDP). IRDP is basically a bank-loan-cum-subsidy scheme that is part of a number of antipoverty programs instituted to stem the considerable unrest in rural areas due to increasing inequalities of the green revolution.[17] Together, IRDP and Operation Flood attempted to "create an alternative asset base for land-poor households" as well as for women (Chen et al. 1986: 20).

Even studies sympathetic to the basic premises of Operation Flood still draw attention to basic flaws in the system. Marty Chen et al. (1986: 41, 50–53, 78–80) note that the workload increase for women falls disproportionately on the poor, that obtaining adequate fodder is difficult, and that participation of poor Scheduled Caste females is also problematic. Devaki Jain takes a close look at the famous "milk producers of Kaira." She confirms that the burden of animal care falls most heavily on the landless women and that the "infrastructure for making the investment [of a buffalo or cow] viable is not accessible except to those with large resources" (Jain, 1980: 108). She also notes that women felt no real change had occurred with household participation in the dairy cooperatives, except perhaps in terms of food consumption and health. Finally, she questions whether income enhancement can really be achieved for mid- and low-level peasant households and whether the development pattern promotes self-reliance and participation in decisionmaking (Jain 1980: 107, 109). Although dairying is popular among those planning employment for rural women (Jain, 1980: 107–110), the question of the hidden costs for women rarely arises.

Although a milk cooperative has been in existence in Shankpur for the past fifteen years, its performance is less than admirable. Perhaps as many as forty villagers (most all male) sell their milk to the cooperative in the peak winter season; as few as eight or nine do so in the dry summer months. Rough estimates of the milk collected from the villagers vary from only 8 kilos daily in the summer to 90 kilos daily during the winter months. Most villagers still prefer to sell to the *dudhwallah* (the traditional milk procurer), who comes by bicycle. He may pay a little less, but the payment is on time (and often advanced), and the dudhwallah comes to their door. As George perceptively notes (1985: 214), for "women having their hands and their time full with housework, child care, buffalo-tending, and agriculture labor," the convenience of not having to go to the cooperative and wait to deposit a small amount of milk is immeasurable.

The Shankpur dairy cooperative was also fraught with mismanagement and misuse of funds. The previous secretary was an acknowledged thief who stole cooperative monies. Women also accused the incumbent secretary of many irregularities, such as not measuring the butterfat content correctly, not entering the correct amount of milk in the account books, retaining the 50 grams of milk taken to test the fat from each member, taking the money that accrues as daily profit to the cooperative, and never paying the members a bonus.

Why, then, should a women's cooperative be established when a cooperative already exists in the village? Why give loans specifically to women? During a government-sponsored "dairy camp" held in the village, a number of answers to these questions emerged. But many more are still needed.

Eighteen women chosen on the basis of poverty, according to the criteria of the government Integrated Rural Development Program, attended a twelve-day training session from noon to 4:00 P.M. every day and received 6 rupees for their time. Each woman whose income level was verified in a subsequent investigation was then eligible to receive a loan-cum-subsidy of 2,500 rupees for the purchase of a buffalo in her own name. Such loans represent just one of a number of development schemes coming out of the IRDP. In this particular case, it merged with the Rajasthan government's Operation Flood program that was to displace the traditional village milk procurers with a women's cooperative, selling milk directly to the Alwar dairy.

There are a number of problems inherent in this program as an income-generating and status-enhancing mechanism. The officials who came to "teach" the women revealed their own ignorance about the extent of women's knowledge and workload, local poverty, the fodder crisis, and the prevalence of liquor consumption in the village—all factors that impacted the economic viability of supporting this scheme and even of maintaining the buffalo among land- and cash-poor households. A number of policy statements relating to the intent of Operation Flood and the establishment of women's cooperatives were also proclaimed during dairy camp. It became clear that the chief aim of the cooperative movement is to increase milk procurement for the urban centers and to keep the cities free of animals. According to officials, extending credit to men for the purchase of milch animals has often proved unsuccessful: They misuse the money (for consumption), do not pay it back, and do not reliably deliver milk to the cooperatives. But women, they declared, are "more honest and will repay their loans." Further, the officials proclaimed, women would also benefit because their ownership of an income-producing asset would enhance their status and independence.

Ironically, however, more comes to mean even less when the consumption of milk products is explored, for with the sale of fluid milk, vital nutrients are no longer available to the producing household or the poor. Previously, home production of *ghee* provided a large part of the population's lactic nutrition in the form of the by-product buttermilk (*lassi*), which was generously distributed to the poor. But those who now sell their milk relinquish these nutrients because cooperatives deal in fluid milk, not *ghee*. Consequently, critical assessments of the dairy development program conclude that "animal husbandry for direct human consumption (either as meat or milk) does not appear to be the most efficient way of producing food energy" (Doornbos et al., 1987: 162). There is, then, a contradiction between the traditional dairy system, geared toward subsistence and provision of important nutrients, and a modern one, geared toward production for sale. Further, a true concern for the diet of the poor—one of Operation Flood's objectives and certainly the chief aim of all income-generating schemes—would focus on their need for cereals and pulses. Yet increasing urban demand for milk and milk products leads to the diversion of agricultural resources from basic food crops to fodder crops.

Transforming dairying in this way also ignores the fact that those who produce may not be able to buy and that those who buy may not necessarily be those in need. More than ever, milk is rapidly being transformed into a luxury food, and in the priorities for the distribution of luxuries, poor women are at the bottom of the list. What, then, are the benefits of selling milk? Where does the money that is earned get spent? It is certainly not spent on the women who worked so hard to produce it. Instead, it may go into general, everyday needs for the family—food, clothing, and so forth. It may contribute to educating a son, and, most important, it may aid in providing for their children's necessary marriage expenses.

Problems beyond those associated with nutrition and income disposition remain. Obtaining adequate fodder often is a major feat for women. Communal grazing lands in the village have long since disappeared, and the forests and land along the main road are off-limits. Since the construction of a paved road into the village, even that grassy area has also disappeared. Increasing mechanization of agriculture is accentuating this situation since harvesting by hand is required to provide crop residues. Land-poor women in Shankpur totally depend on foraging, the "kindness" of their employers, and pilferage.[18] Occasionally, they have to scrape up the money to purchase fodder. One of the saddest scenes is of children, usually little girls, going along the dry field channels with pieces of discarded *saris* slung around their shoulders, bending over to pull up blades of grass, one by one.

Unfortunately, the imported strategies and "minikits" for dairy production do not provide land, and without this commodity, the strategies and kits are not of much benefit. Even marginal farmers can ill afford to divert any part of their present holdings from the already insufficient production of food, and any attempt to cultivate green fodder on unirrigated land in Shankpur, where staple crops have dried up, is futile. The dairy camp women would certainly have agreed with the view that current development schemes, preoccupied with constructing splendid dairies to process and distribute the expected flood of milk without giving sufficient thought to the animal feed required, are building "dairies in the air" (George, 1985: 77). Yet the women were still willing to participate in such schemes.

A poor woman with a buffalo needs to add approximately 3.5 to 4.5 hours of labor daily to accommodate work related to milk production. One of her first tasks upon waking is to clean the animal shed or area, collect the dung, and feed, water, and milk the animal. These activities take about 1.5 hours. Later in the morning, she will go to the fields for the first of two trips to collect fodder, and she will often be one of two people required to cut the fodder. Both of these activities take another 2 hours. Then the buffalo must be bathed and watered at the village well in the late afternoon, its evening feed must be prepared, and it must be milked. This is another hour's work. Studies show that belonging to a dairy cooperative requires even greater inputs of time and labor from women in landless households, in addition to their ongoing household work and grueling but low-paid agricultural labor. One wonders where these poor women will find the time and energy to manage this additional strain, unaccompanied as it will be by any nutritional improvement (George, 1985: 257).

Projecting into the future, it is expected that the struggle and drudgery of fuel collection by the poorest women will increase for crop residues—utilized by the owners for dry fodder—will no longer be as freely available for domestic fuel. This erosion of the agricultural laborers' traditional right to these residues and fodder collection from the patron's land exemplifies the wider currents of the backlash effect from the extension of dairying (George, 1985: 152). Nor were dairy camp officials calculating labor costs into the overall equation when they spoke about the profitability of taking a buffalo loan for milk production. The scheme could only make sense if it is assumed that labor costs are nil. In reality, then, the average net income to the women, combined with all the costs and risks involved, will (hopefully) be just enough to repay the bank loan. Further, the risks involved in becoming "entrepreneurs" may well be too great for these women. In addition to natural "dry" periods, there is always the possibility that the animal will become sick or die, and fodder may be impossible to obtain. Finally, one wonders what would happen if the Alwar dairy should stop buying milk when it oversteps its capacity in the flush season.

Conclusion

While a study of a single village puts flesh and blood on more generalized analyses, several broad conclusions do emerge from this examination of milk production as an income-generating scheme for poor women. These relate to the perpetuation of nutritional apartheid, effects on food crop production, creation of more work rather than more jobs, and replication of the class and gender inequalities inherent in the green revolution. And a fundamental question remains: Why do the women seek to participate in a project that they realize is fraught with more work and risks for them?

Nutritional apartheid refers to the differential benefits of increased milk production in terms of consumption. It appears that neither the rural areas in general nor women in rural areas specifically gain from the dairy scheme. Urban areas are provided with wholesome milk in stable supply and "reasonable" (but for whom?) prices. Yet the overriding needs of 50 percent of the population below government-defined poverty levels are to increase food energy and to maintain a well-balanced diet. These goals are obtainable more cheaply by augmenting the supply of cereals and other grains. The converse side of nutritional apartheid refers to gender differentiation in food access: Women are the last to benefit from any increase in family consumption. Ultimately, improvement in their health and nutritional status will require a reshaping of the family power structure and associated gender roles.

Because Operation Flood and the women's dairy cooperatives will not make any drastic change in the milk production process, concentrating instead on the circulation and marketing of the commodity, these programs cannot claim to create jobs in the production of milk they merely collect (George, 1985: 78).[19] A close look at female participation in dairying in Shankpur discloses that what the proposed scheme really creates is more work, not more jobs, and an increased burden of stress for poor women. Added to all their other worries will be that of caring for the buffaloes and repaying their loans. (After all, women's greater concern and integrity about loan repayment was foremost in the minds of the dairy officials who claimed that "women are more honest than men.")

Should their cooperative become a reality, the women will also face further stress from men's opposition to their active participation (see also Chen et al., 1986: 88ff). Hints of such reactions occurred during the dairy camp itself. Several men in the village commented to the women about acting in an unbecoming manner by attending the camp or about "getting 'big heads.'" Others looked askance—especially in the first few days— when the women all marched boldly down the main street, chatting excitedly. The women felt proud to be in the training camp; for most, it was the only sort of schooling they had ever had. Nevertheless, it is not unreasonable for the women to anticipate tremendous opposition should they really try to organize and run a cooperative and attempt thereby to achieve a measure of independence from their husbands. The women understand the unrealistic promises and premises inherent in the scheme that the officials chose to ignore.

This brings up the final point—the replication of green revolution class and gender inequalities. A main aim of the spread of women's cooperatives in Operation Flood is to provide employment, income, and increased status for rural women. Claiming to deliver large-scale voluntary income redistribution without conflict or confrontation and, by implication, restructuring society, Operation Flood was designed to avoid the inequalities of the green revolution. However, poor women face serious problems in Shankpur, including the fact that they cannot compete on an equal basis with more affluent households. The inputs required for modern dairying present a built-in scale bias for the larger farmer, and the white revolution unavoidably imitates its green predecessor in the use of high-cost, high-risk productive technology.

Congruent with this class bias is one based on gender. Women have been and continue to be integrated into dairy development along lines that reinforce the current division of labor and status hierarchy within their society. Females will continue to do what they have always done in the labor-intensive care of animals. It is a gender-based "internal colonialism," in which the functioning and capital accumulation of the modern dairy system, represented by the male-controlled processing and marketing centers in the city, depend upon the cheap, labor-intensive work of females in the rural sector. Even in the dairy camp, the officials revealed a patronizing and paternalistic attitude to the producers, and the women's main concerns were never addressed. The officials operated under the assumption that low productivity was due to lack of education and training rather than a paucity of land and other inputs.

Along with the class and gender biases discussed here, Operation Flood also perpetuates the idea that basic shortages and poverty can be eliminated by loan-cum-subsidy programs operating within a system of extreme inequalities. In this regard, milk cooperatives appear doomed to the same fate as the sugar cooperatives (Matson, 1983). It is difficult to avoid concluding, as the critics of dairy development policies in India do, that success will remain elusive without a restructuring of society in terms of radical land reforms, the transformation of gender roles, and a mass mobilization on behalf of ecological concerns.

The broader ramifications of similar income-generating schemes are echoed in many other critical studies, especially those on Latin America (see Mies, 1986: 120ff, and Bennholdt-Thomsen, 1988: 57–58). These stem from the fact that such development programs do not focus on women as peasants or as wage workers but as propertyless, petty commodity producers. Because women have neither capital nor an adequate wage, their production must be based on credit, which becomes an instrument to control their labor and their product. The market economy penetrates rural areas through the credit system and engages households in the process of capital accumulation. The generation of monetary income comes from linking this production to the market economy. Maria Mies details the connection between development schemes based on bank credit and the pauperization process of small or marginal peasant and agricultural laborers. She finds that through the credit system and such nonviable schemes as the dairy program, poor women enter into a "new bondage system which ties them to banks instead of to the money-lenders, all in the name of development" (Mies 1986:126).

This permits what Veronika Bennholdt-Thomsen identifies as the "formal subsumption of labor." Control arises from granting credits to small producers. Mediated through credit, a capitalist obtains control over producers, and that means he or she has a direct hold over their surplus labor. The giver controls by specifying what the loan will be used for because otherwise, there is always the danger that the credit will go toward meeting subsistence needs and not the expected surplus product.[20] For example, lenders prefer to give buffalo loans to the women of Shankpur for they may be relied on to use the monies for that purpose. Bennholdt-Thomsen also outlines the contradictions inherent in the formulation of a credit strategy that regards the "consumption fund" of the poor only marginally, if at all. Since profit is secured for the development programs through repayment guarantees, the major concern is to ensure mechanisms for extracting the produce. "As the minimum subsistence level has been identified as the basic problem, presumably the strategy would be aimed at raising that level. But in reality the concern is not to increase the peasants' consumption but to increase the marketable output!" (Bennholdt-Thomsen, 1988: 57–58).

Maria Mies further expands on this. Commodity production defined as an "additional income-generating activity" obscures the exploitation of the women and men engaged in the schemes. The exploitation is even higher than in the case of wage labor.

> The net result was over-exploitation and exhaustion, and hardly any additional money or material benefit on the side of the actual producers, mainly the women. On the other hand, the state marketing monopoly . . . and the banks made profits. Women's work in these schemes was at low costs for those who control the marketing of their products (Mies, 1986: 58).

Such an arrangement is extremely profitable because capital does not need to assume the full reproduction cost of the labor force (see also Spindel, 1987).[21] But for the women involved, activities linked to the home are characterized by low investment and low productivity level, and they are not very profitable.

On close inspection, income-generating projects, by providing women with access to cash, do not appear to contribute to greater female autonomy (Deere and Leon, 1987: 8). As Hilary Standing noted, urban Bengali women control at least some of their income in a narrow sense. But the social matrix within which decisions are made overwhelmingly mitigates against personal accumulation or personal expenditure on the part of women—activities fully sanctioned for men. She questions, "Are women who put money into a personal bank account to save for their daughters' dowries acting in a meaningful sense as autonomous agents?" (Standing, 1985: 234). To what extent do poor rural women "control" their income when all of it is immediately used to meet the family's basic subsistence needs?

The main limitations of such income-generating policies geared to providing work for rural women stem from begging the issues of agrarian reform and patriarchal subordination. The preference is to define the problems of persistent poverty through a focus on the consequences of poverty—for example, the inabilities of rural poor to provide for their basic needs—rather than on the causes—such as lack of access to land. As the dairy scheme illustrates, a program based on such preferences will not be sufficient to even partially reverse some of the associated macro phenomena, such as deterioration in the agricultural sector and the peasant economy (Leon, 1987: 93). Similarly, as long as agricultural policies continue to focus on women as instruments in productive activities, they will not support them but will make them even more vulnerable economically and socially (Arizipe and Botey, 1987: 91).

Why, then, do women continue to seize upon such ill-advised programs? Why did all of the women participating in the dairy camp at Shankpur uniformly say that it was a good scheme? It is not a matter of being overpowered by the arguments and persuasion of the officials. Nor is it simply a matter of having internalized compliance and consensus in a system that disadvantages them. Rather, it is a question of the extent to which strategies are meaningfully available to the women within the context of the structure of their class and gender relations. In her study of gender transformation among women coir workers in Sri Lanka, Carla Risseeuw (1988: 205) points out "how crucial to the workings of power relations is the fact that they can be misrecognized at the time of operation, and thus seem to owe nothing to the 'logic of exploitation'." It is this logic of exploitation embedded in a particular structural process of social relations that has been critical in influencing the village women's acquiescence to the buffalo scheme being offered. Within Shankpur, it is the confluence of the women's class position and gender roles as described earlier that has determined this.

Female coir workers as workers in Sri Lanka have been able to participate, albeit seldom as primary agents, in the increasing legitimacy of an alternative discourse on class—one that questions the existing hegemonic view. However, a comparable "counterpoint" on gender that has found acceptance and legitimacy both for the individual women as well as the village as a whole has not been forthcoming. This has consequences for possible strategies of resistance (Risseeuw, 1988: 255ff). "Women are both aware and unaware [i.e., conscious of their exploitation], but above all, there is no perspective of an alternative. Male and female behavior is imbued with notions of 'being natural'; one is accustomed to being a man or a woman almost before being human" (Risseeuw, 1988: 287). Such a view permits us to better understand how, despite all the problems and increased workload, these desperately poor women welcome any possible source of income, "no matter how skewed and uneven the division of labor between men and women may be" (Mies, 1986: 82). Under such conditions, "profiting from the poor" will be around for a long time.

Notes

1. For critiques of this policy, see, for example, Feder (1976), Payer (1980 and 1982), Bennholdt-Thomsen (1988).

2. Deere and Leon (1987, introduction) find that women are not being marginalized or displaced in the agricultural wage labor force with the development of capitalism in Latin America. They are increasingly employed as seasonal wage workers in laborious tasks of export agriculture. Islam (1985: 5) cites a major study that found about 42 percent of all rural workers in Bangladesh are engaged primarily in nonfarm activities; among female workers, some 59 percent are engaged in rural industries (of which 49 percent are in family industries).

3. For example, Maria Mies analyzes the Programme on Rural Women in Andhra Pradesh (India) of the International Labour Organisation's World Employment Program. Its goal is to "contribute to an improvement in the social and economic conditions and status of rural women" by promoting "group social and economic activities on a self-reliant and participatory basis (Mies, 1986: v). Mies particularly studies the impact of milk credit schemes on poor women. Beneria and Sen also noted the key aspects of the ILO's initial statement of 1976: "One is to enable them to contribute more effectively to the satisfaction of their families' basic needs, within the framework of their traditional responsibilities. The other, which is a fundamental need for women themselves, is to ease their work burden while furthering their economic independence and their more equitable integration into the community, beyond the narrow circle of the family" (quoted in Beneria and Sen, 1982: 169).

4. See Mies (1985) on the lace-making export industry and Rao and Hussain (1987) on the garment export industry.

5. This is true even if the family is engaged in craft production.

6. The wage form, as Bennholdt-Thomsen (1988: 61) notes, is clearly not the only—and certainly not the most important—means of extracting profit.

7. Lester Brown, of the Overseas Development Council, stated the main reason for helping the poor: "Idle manpower constitutes a valuable but wasted resource. . . . That this will simultaneously help to meet food needs (keeping food

prices lower for everyone) . . . is a further incentive for pursuing such a strategy" (quoted in Bennholdt-Thomsen 1988: 53).

8. The names of the village and villagers have been changed to respect their privacy. The research for this fieldwork was supported monetarily by a Smithsonian Foreign Currency Senior Fellowship during 1986–1987 and by the friendship of a host of others.

9. Alwar is in the area traditionally known as "Mewat"—land of the Meos. Before the holocaust of the Partition of the subcontinent, the Meos were the largest and dominant group in the village and the region. The majority left for Pakistan.

10. Although, of course, caste is still coterminous with class to a large extent, this is increasingly not the case.

11. In 1987, when we began our fieldwork, there were 14 rupees to the dollar.

12. There were, however, two cases where women did plough in the past: one involved a woman whose husband was in prison, and the other involved a widow and her daughter.

13. One day, we tried to follow the daily routine of one of our Chamar friends. We went with her to the mountain by 7:00 A.M. As the sun beat down and with no shade in sight, the women made a small area for us to sit by placing two sacks over a bit of scrub nearby. When they stopped to rest or to eat, we all crowded in that small space. Some women just used their large head shawls (*ordni*) as protection against the scorching heat (it must have been about 104 degrees). We left at noon, and one of us suffered from heatstroke.

14. A more detailed analysis of this is presented in Sharma and Vanjani (1989), and the following summary draws upon that article. Maria Mies's analysis (1986: 120ff) of the implications of a comparable scheme on a single family in a Telengana village in Andhra Pradesh (India) corroborates our own findings.

15. See also Alvares (1985) on "imperialism through food aid" and "economics and politics for food aid" and Parthasarathy (1991) for the impact on landless labor.

16. The Somjees study was deeply problematic. In their study of milk cooperatives in western India, they saw the role of individual dairy officials as critical in making a difference for poor, low-caste communities. They concluded that the poor "now need a *human* agency . . . to help them retrace their position back to a full humanhood . . . for such a socially diminished people, the mere provisions of five-year plans and policies are not enough" (Somjee and Somjee, 1989: 136, their emphasis). They further stated, "The poor in the rural communities always needed a human intermediary, at least initially, to help them benefit from any development opportunity" (Somjee and Somjee, 1989: 143). Elsewhere, low-caste poor are characterized as "a heap of human wreckage whose will and capacity to be able to get out of their economic adversity, and social indignity, is reduced to different degrees of ineffectiveness" (Somjee and Somjee, 1989: 145–146). For the Somjees, the solution to poverty lies in enlightened individuals showing the shining path of development of this "human wreckage."

17. IRDP is concerned with increasing the productivity and life chances of "weaker sections" and is implemented primarily through credit loans. The Seventh Five-Year Plan advocated an integration of the main antipoverty program (IRDP) and Operation Flood. Critical assessments of the effectiveness of IRDP in generating income for the rural poor are found in Dreze (1990) and in Gopal and Ramulu (1989).

18. See also Chen et al. (1986: 29, 80) for estimates of expenses incurred in obtaining fodder.

19. However, transforming the traditional dairy system will also have an adverse effect on staple crop production. Inputs and land will be diverted to produce

fodder. Poor women will be denied access to their patrons' green fodder and crop residues for their own animals and fuel use.

20. In market subsumption, small producers own the means of production and have free access to the market. It is the "blind mechanism" of circulation that subordinates for they cannot influence the prices they get for their products. Forced to sell under extremely disadvantageous conditions, the small producers must minimize the cost of physical reproduction of labor power, resulting in self-exploitation (Bennholdt-Thomsen 1988: 54–55).

21. This may also explain why it is "economic" for the very poor to have more children—i.e., more laborers—to ensure household survival.

References

Alvares, Claude, ed. 1985. *Another Revolution Fails: An Investigation into How and Why India's Operation Flood Project, Touted as the World's Largest Dairy Development Programme, Funded by EEC, Went Off the Rails* (New Delhi: Ajanta Publishers).

Arizipe, Lourdes, and Carlota Botey. 1987. "Mexican Agricultural Development Policy and Its Impact on Rural Women," in Carmen D. Deere and Magdalena Leon, eds., *Rural Women and State Policy: Feminist Perspectives on Latin American Agricultural Development* (Boulder, Colo., and London: Westview Press), pp. 67–83.

Beneria, Lourdes, and Gita Sen. 1981. "Accumulation, Reproduction, and Women's Role in Economic Development: Boserup Revisited," *Signs,* Vol. 7, No. 2, pp. 279–298.

————. 1982. "Class and Gender Inequalities and Women's Role in Economic Development—Theoretical and Practical Implications," *Feminist Studies,* Vol. 8 No. 1, pp. 157–174.

Bennholdt-Thomsen, Veronika. 1988. "'Investment in the Poor': An Analysis of World Bank Policy," in Maria Mies, ed., *Women: the Last Colony* (New Delhi: Kali Press for Women), pp. 51–63.

Boserup, Ester. 1970. *Women in Agricultural Development* (New York: St. Martin's Press).

Chen, Marty, Manoshi Mitra, Geeta Athreya, Anita Dholakia, Preeta Law, and Aruna Rao. 1986. *Indian Women: A Study of Their Role in the Dairy Movement* (New Delhi: Shakti Books, Vikas Publishing House Pvt.).

Deere, Carmen D., and Magdalena Leon, eds. 1987. *Rural Women and State Policy: Feminist Perspectives on Latin American Agricultural Development* (Boulder, Colo., and London: Westview Press).

Doornbos, Martin, Frank van Dorsten, Manoshi Mitra, and Piet Ternal. 1987. "Assessing Dairy Development: Towards a Research Approach to India's Operation Flood," *Netherlands Review of Development Studies,* Vol. 1, pp. 149-164.

————. 1990. *Dairy Aid and Development: India's Operation Flood* (New Delhi/Newbury Park/London: Sage Publications).

Dreze, Jean. 1990. "Poverty in India and the IRDP Delusion," in *Economic and Political Weekly* (Bombay), Vol. 25, No. 39, pp. A95–A104.

Feder, Ernest. 1976. "The New World Bank Programme for the Self-Liquidation of the Third World Peasantry," *Journal of Peasant Studies,* Vol. 3, No. 3, pp. 343–354.

Folbre, Nancy. 1986. "Cleaning House, New Perspectives on Households in Economic Development," *Journal of Development Economics,* Vol. 22, pp. 5–40.

George, Shanti. 1985. *Operation Flood: An Appraisal of Current Indian Dairy Policy* (Delhi: Oxford University Press).

Gopal, G. Hara, and C.H. Bala Ramulu. 1989. "Poverty Alleviation Programmes, IRDP in an Andhra Pradesh District," *Economic and Political Weekly* (Bombay), Vol. 24, No. 35–36, pp. 2025–2034.

Hossain, Hameeda. 1987. "Capitalist Penetration into Handicrafts Manufacture: A Historical Review of Women's Work for the Market in Bangladesh," in Andrea M. Singh and Anita Kelles-Vitanen, eds., *Invisible Hands* (New Delhi: Sage Publications), pp. 165–174.

India Abroad, January 26, 1990.

Islam, Shamima. 1985. *Invisible Labour Force: Women in Poverty in Bangladesh* (Dhaka, Bangladesh: Center for Women and Development, BRAC Printers).

Jain, Devaki. 1980. "Milk Producers of Kaira," in Devaki Jain, ed., *Women's Quest for Power: Five Indian Case Studies* (Ghaziabad, India: Vikas Publishing House Pvt.), pp. 77–120.

Leon, Magdalena. 1987. "Colombian Agricultural Policies and the Debate on Policies Toward Rural Women," in Carmen D. Deere and Magdalena Leon, eds., *Rural Women and State Policy: Feminist Perspectives on Latin American Agricultural Development* (Boulder, Colo., and London: Westview Press), pp. 84–104.

Matson, Jim. 1983. "Class Struggles in Cooperative Development: The Subordination of Labor in the Cooperative Sugar Industry of Maharasthra, India," *Bulletin of Concerned Asian Scholars,* Vol. 15, No. 3, pp. 18–29.

Mies, Maria. 1985. *Lacemakers of Narsapur* (London: Zed Press).

———. 1986. *Indian Women in Subsistence and Agricultural Labour* (Geneva: International Labour Office).

Mones, Delkis, and Lydia Grant. 1987. "Agricultural Development, the Economic Crisis and Rural Women in the Dominican Republic," in Carmen D. Deere and Magdalena Leon, eds., *Rural Women and State Policy: Feminist Perspectives on Latin American Agricultural Development* (Boulder, Colo., and London: Westview Press), pp. 35–50.

Parthasarathy, G. 1991. "White Revolution, Dairy Co-operatives and Weaker Sections," *Economic and Political Weekly* (Bombay), Vol. 26, No. 52, pp. A177–A183.

Payer, Cheryl. 1980. "The World Bank and the Small Farmer," *Monthly Review,* Vol. 15 (November), pp. 30–45.

———. 1982. *The World Bank* (New York: Monthly Review Press).

Rao, Rukmini, and Sahba Hussain. 1987. "Invisible Hands: Women in Home-based Production in the Garment Export Industry in Delhi," in Andrea M. Singh and Anita Kelles-Vitanen, eds., *Invisible Hands* (New Delhi: Sage Publications), pp. 51–67.

Risseeuw, Carla. 1988. *The Fish Don't Talk About the Water: Gender Transformation, Power and Resistance Among Women in Sri Lanka* (Leiden/New York/Kobenhaven/Koln: E.J. Brill).

Sharma, Miriam, and Urmila Vanjani. 1989. "Women's Work Is Never Done: Dairy 'Development' and Health in the Lives of Rural Women in Rajasthan," *Economic and Political Weekly* (Bombay), Vol. 24, No. 17, pp. WS 38–44.

Somjee, A.H., and Geeta Somjee. 1989. *Reaching Out to the Poor: The Unfinished Revolution* (London: Macmillan Press).

Spindel, Cheywa R. 1987. "The Social Invisibility of Women's Work in Brazilian Agriculture," in Carmen D. Deere and Magdalena Leon, eds., *Rural Women and State Policy: Feminist Perspectives on Latin American Agricultural Development* (Boulder, Colo., and London: Westview Press), pp. 51–66.

Standing, Hilary. 1985. "Resources, Wages, and Power: The Impact of Women's Employment on the Urban Bengali Household," in Haleh Afshar, ed., *Women, Work, and Ideology in the Third World* (London and New York: Tavistock Publications).

Times of India, June 12, 1985.

World Bank. 1972. *Agricultural Sector Working Paper* (Washington, D.C.: World Bank).

Zurbrigg, Sheila. 1984. *Rakku's Story: Structures of Ill-Health and the Source of Change* (Madras: Sidma Offset Press Pvt.).

4

Class Relations
and Labor Market Differentiation
in Rural Bangladesh

Shelley Feldman

Recent development policies as well as scholarship on Third World labor markets have focused on the growing segment of the rural population engaged in off-farm and nonfarm employment. These policies and studies generally assume that nonfarm and off-farm employment growth has been a response to the changing organization of agricultural production and the increasing numbers of farm households forced to meet part of their subsistence needs from wage labor. Although the recent decline in the number of rural households able to provide for their subsistence solely through agricultural production has likely increased the demand for off-farm and nonfarm rural employment, it is also true that the rural economy has always embraced a diversified set of income-earning opportunities. This employment diversity has included artisans and petty commodity producers, traders, service workers, and a range of professionals such as doctors and medical practitioners, lawyers, and clerks.

What is the nature of the relationship between the commercialization of agricultural production and the expansion of the nonfarm rural sector? How has this relationship been theorized, and what kind of empirical research has shaped analyses of the linkage between agricultural and industrial production and employment? How have contemporary development policies shaped both the nature of this relationship and the future configuration of the rural labor market? What are the conditions of the present historical conjuncture that make an answer to these questions important?

This chapter will examine the changing complexity of the rural labor market in Bangladesh. My point of departure is a view of the rural economy that includes both farm and nonfarm employment opportunities and various arenas of production, types of employment, and social relations of production.[1] To avoid semantic confusion, I use the terms *nonfarm rural production* and *nonfarm employment* as historicized concepts that reflect the autonomy of rural petty commodity production. By autonomy, I mean that changes in the pattern of nonfarm production engage with but are not solely determined by changes in agrarian relations. This definition is important because it defines changes in nonfarm production and employment as the outcome of various processes of diversification stemming from changing state policies and patterns of migration and industrial transformation as well as from changes in agricultural production. This means that the demand for nonfarm and off-farm employment is not simply a reaction to shifts in the organization of agricultural production. It also means that the dynamics of the nonfarm labor market generate conditions distinct from those in agricultural production per se. These conditions increase the demand for labor so that the relationship between changes in agricultural production and the expansion of nonfarm rural employment cannot be viewed simply as a direct and causal one.

Three subthemes are embedded in the discussion that follows. These themes characterize analyses of the transformation of work and labor relations as this process shapes rural employment opportunities and restructures both the labor market and the household division of labor. The first theme draws attention to the transformation of women's work, which moves from invisible to visible forms of labor deployment as women move from work in the household to more generalized participation in the labor market. The invisibility of women's work refers to the location of forms of female labor deployment, once focused primarily within the household, to the often overlooked participation of women in household and cottage industry production, and to women's contribution to agricultural production. In the Bangladesh context, rural women's labor has been limited to primarily *bari*-based (courtyard) activities, and their participation in agricultural production has been tied specifically to grain processing rather than field production.

The transformation of women's participation in agricultural production and their increasingly diversified participation in nonfarm activities helps to identify the ways which government development policies build upon assumptions regarding labor availability within the household. The emphasis on women is especially relevant in Bangladesh, where the proportion of females in the labor market has been systematically miscalculated by estimates that exclude or underrepresent the labor of women engaged as household workers, petty commodity producers, and casual and daily laborers in farm and nonfarm work (ESCAP, 1981; Dixon, 1982; NORAD, 1984).

In addition to the critical assessment of the ways in which women's labor has been underestimated in studies of labor market dynamics, there are analyses of household resource diversification that also ignore the ways in which various household members engage in remunerative activity. The second theme examines the analyses of household resource and income diversification that often assume that only male farmers, rather than farm household members, seek alternative or additional sources of income to secure the conditions for family reproduction. An appreciation of the range of household members engaged in remunerative activity draws attention to the interface between farm, off-farm, and nonfarm work in shaping labor supply and demand. A more complex understanding of household income and resource diversification also draws attention to the increasing demand for wage employment that is likely to come from women and other household members who have previously worked as "free" household laborers.

A third theme embedded in analyses of the nonfarm rural employment sector is the salience of government-sponsored rural infrastructural development programs in shaping opportunities for work. Infrastructural development involves primarily temporary, short-term construction work for poor men and women. For a small minority, longer-term employment is available in the maintenance of irrigation facilities, fish tanks, and roads (Chen and Ghaznavi, 1977; Marum, 1982; CARE, 1983). These rural works initiatives were originally relief efforts to provide work and food for those without other productive assets. More recently, they have evolved into more permanent forms of nonfarm employment, and they are indicative of the changing relationship between state-sponsored employment generation efforts and the rural labor market.

In this chapter, employment as delimited by participation in the formal sector is treated as a subset of the broader category called "work." Formal sector employment includes all work that is defined and accounted for in census and manpower surveys. Subsistence production, informal work, and informal labor exchanges are another subset of work. This latter arena of labor deployment is more difficult to gauge because national surveys have yet to devise techniques and concepts capable of capturing its range and complexity.[2] However, I will draw on a rich set of micro studies that suggest patterns of work masked by census surveys (Islam, 1987; Hossain, 1987; Feldman, 1982 and 1984).

Theoretical Background

Studies of the rural economy and rural labor markets in South Asia traditionally have examined only the agricultural sector and have explored the expansion of agricultural wage labor and sharecropping relations as exemplars of rural transformation and employment generation. The green revolution and the effects of differential access to land and to new biological and mechanical technologies were one focus of these studies. A second focus was the challenge the diffusion of new resources posed to existing agricultural labor relations. It was presumed that the capitalization of agricultural production would reshape rural labor supply and demand by creating a group of large-scale surplus producers, on the one hand, and a cadre of agricultural laborers, on the other (Byres, 1981; Hirashima and Muqtada, 1986).

Within the context of agrarian transformation, two broad perspectives predominate. One suggests that large-scale commercial producers and agricultural wage laborers have complementary interests: The generation of new production relations stimulates increases in productive capacity by enabling land consolidation and the adoption of capital-intensive techniques. Increases in production, in turn, support a rural labor force whose wages are assumed to expand and sustain the demand for agricultural commodities and consumer goods and also improve the returns to labor of those dispossessed of landed property.

The second perspective argues that agrarian differentiation generates contradictory and conflictual class interests between agricultural producers and wage laborers. The benefits to be generated by the consolidation of landholdings accrue to large, capitalized farmers, while the costs of landlessness are borne by agricultural wage laborers for whom the loss of productive resources and exploitative wage relations result in increasing impoverishment and immiseration, lack of political control, and an inability to generate conditions for capital accumulation.

In the literature on these perspectives, passing reference is made to the expected growth in those rural industries that foster the expansion and diffusion of green revolution practices (Zaman, 1987; Wood, 1978 and 1981; Rahman and Islam, 1987). Within these agro-focused perspectives, small-scale rural industrial development has been examined as an arena for employment generation in concert with the need to provide work for those dispossessed of land and as new production practices require the production of mechanical and biological inputs. The need for new production inputs generates the conditions for developing a market and trade network and thus shapes the development of production, trade, and service occupations in the countryside. To the extent that attention focused on employment in the nonfarm sector, the relationship between agricultural work and rural employment was examined in the context of supplemental employment among subsistence producers and as a relation characterizing new patterns of household income diversification (Hirashima and Muqtada, 1986). In other words, nonfarm rural employment generation has remained an untheorized aspect of rural transformation and has been of only secondary empirical interest in studies of the rural economy. The linkage between agricultural and nonfarm production has been viewed as a determinant one: As agricultural differentiation increased, so did the demand for nonfarm employment among a growing number of landless laborers.

The determinant role of the agrarian economy in patterning nonfarm employment opportunities is theoretically grounded both in theories of modernization and in the debate between Vladimir Lenin and Aleksandr Vasilevich Chayanov. Modernization theory and the neoclassical perspective shape much of the research on the benefits to be gained from increased agricultural productivity brought about by the adoption of green revolution practices and by the new social relations that are emerging as new patterns of production and accumulation are formed.

A less well-known debate on the rural economy among Western social scientists is that between Lenin and Chayanov on the changing structure of rural class relations. Lenin (1974) argued that in the long-term, capitalizing the agricultural sector would polarize producers into a class of capitalist farmers and a class of landless laborers. Processes of polarization represent the reorganization of production from subsistence to commercial production, expressed in terms of new land and labor relations as well as new patterns of consumption and exchange. But despite Lenin's careful analysis of peasant differentiation, social policy concerns, as they shaped nonfarm employment, were neither adequately theorized nor empirically examined. Nor was the salience of state policy initiatives in defining the nature of the agrarian transformation and new rural class relations well integrated within his careful analysis of the capitalization of agriculture. Rather, changing productive forces and the nature of the process of capitalist penetration generated particular forces that created the conditions for rural class formation. In other words, Lenin's view was limited because he ignored the importance of state policy in shaping processes of rural class formation.

An opposing interpretation of the view that processes of capitalist development in agriculture would transform agricultural production as it would industrial production was advanced by the Russian populists (Chayanov, 1986). They held that the logic and rationale of peasant economies differ from those of the capitalist firm because the former are premised on the notion of meeting consumption needs and the latter assume an interest in profit and expansion. The Chayanovian view recognizes the noncorporate character of the household as a production unit, but it asserts that demographic factors internal to the structure of the household shape the production opportunities and rationale that each household employs. For Chayanov, household characteristics mold rural class formation.

However, though this view is grounded in the demographic characteristics of households, Chayanov does not conceive of a differentiated household that may exhibit both consensus and conflict among its members. Interests may be differentiated by class, gender, age, and ethnicity, factors that shape both short- and long-term goals among household members. Despite the shortcomings of a household model premised on shared interests, the Chayanovian position has gained increased currency in light of a growing interest in the household division of labor, the domestic life cycle, and studies of household labor allocation, especially among feminist scholars.[3]

The elaboration of the Lenin-Chayanov debate has defined much of the contemporary theoretical and empirical insight regarding the rural economy. In that economy, an agricultural one, changes in the processes of agricultural production and the relations of agricultural producers illuminate processes of rural class formation, differentiation and proletarianization: Changes in agricultural relations and a growing dependence on off-farm employment and income garnered primarily from other agricultural opportunities generate the conditions for rural class formation and shape patterns of agrarian differentiation.[4]

It should be emphasized, however, that agricultural wage labor has never been the sole arena of off-farm employment, nor has the agricultural labor market ever been expected to provide sufficient opportunities for the growing demand placed on it by changing agrarian relations. Even during the early years of the green revolution (1961–1971) when the agricultural sector held center stage, it was recognized that increased opportunities for off-farm work would be generated by the demand for new inputs such as irrigation facilities and machinery, as well as by the trade and marketing networks necessary to support an increasingly capitalized agricultural sector. During this period, government policies incorporated the need to generate and subsidize infrastructural development for the creation of small factories, agro-based industries, machine repair shops, and market and input distribution services.

In the 1980s, the view of agriculture as the mainspring of rural transformation and employment differentiation shifted to a conception of the rural economy that incorporated rural industrialization and employment differentiation as autonomous arenas of social reproduction.[5] Thus, rural nonfarm employment was reconceptualized from a residual category of agricultural employment to a sector molded by distinctive social practices and characterized by different patterns of class formation than those that typically structure agrarian differentiation (Feldman, 1990b). Epitomizing this distinction between a determinant and an autonomous rural nonfarm sector are studies of rural credit, artisanal production, and home-based commodity production (Friedmann, 1980; Amin, 1981; Kahn, 1982; Roseberry, 1983; Smith, 1984; Hossain, 1985; McCarthy, 1989; Feldman, 1990b). These studies, along with Gillian Hart's chapter in this volume, recognize various forms of commodity production and the ways in which nonfarm labor relations and conditions of reproduction differ from those that characterize agricultural production.[6]

Complementing these studies of rural differentiation is the growing interest in household survival strategies, household income and resource diversification, and evaluations of the contribution women make to family and household reproduction. These studies are distinguished by their concern with rural class relations as distinct from agrarian social relations and are often informed by feminist analysis (McCarthy, Sabbah, and Aktar,

1979; Amin, 1981; Ahmed, 1987; Feldman, 1989a, 1989b, 1990a, and 1990b). They represent a commitment to documenting the complex labor relations that determine subsistence production and highlight women's contribution to agricultural production, petty commodity production, and informal sector activity.

Feminist scholarship has also enriched, if not transformed, theoretical analyses of subsistence production, the rural household, and rural work.[7] A focus on the household and the labor relations that mold both remunerative and maintenance activities within the household has enriched our understanding of rural nonfarm relations because it has emphasized the diverse labor activities and relations that are necessary for social reproduction. Such analyses have also differentiated between the integration of farm and nonfarm labor allocation among petty commodity producers, workers in cottage and small-scale industries, and trade and service workers—all areas of work not generally represented in labor force statistics. In this context, processes of rural differentiation are more broadly defined than when they are delimited by the capitalization of agriculture.

The Structure of the Bangladesh Rural Economy

During the early years of Bangladesh independence, agricultural commodities constituted the bulk of that country's exports. In 1973/74, for example, income earned from agricultural goods, including jute, fish, and processed food originating from agriculture, represented approximately 95 percent of total exports. Agriculture also accounted for about 80 percent of total employment. At the same time, however, agriculture was undercapitalized: The sector received only 10 to 15 percent of total public development expenditure (excluding water and flood control expenditures), 10 percent of institutionalized bank credit, and 7 to 9 percent of total private investment (de Vylder, 1982: 29; Feldman and McCarthy, 1984; Feldman, 1990b).

After 1974, jute and leather exports stagnated, and there were only modest increases in tea exports. This was the result of falling world prices and the ban on jute exports to Cuba promoted by the United States. These exports continued to stagnate between 1975 and 1985 but began to increase during the first three years of the Third Five-Year Plan (1985–1990). Nontraditional exports also increased during this period at the unexpected rate of 11.5 percent, against a target of 4.6 percent, and traditional exports increased at the rate of 4.5 percent (Government of the People's Republic of Bangladesh, 1985).

As the export profile for agricultural commodities has changed, agricultural underemployment and unemployment have grown. A declining proportion of agriculturalists continue as small-scale owner-cultivators, and many households have become functionally landless. By 1978, the total number of landless households was estimated at approximately 29 percent of the rural population; including functionally landless households that owned less than 1 acre, the percent of landless households increased to almost 80 percent. All these households are likely to require off-farm employment, but it should be noted that this percentage of nonfarm employment demand is a conservative one because it excludes (1) members of households owning between 1 and 2.5 acres who are also likely to seek off-farm work to subsidize reproduction costs, and (2) the small proportion of households with more than 2.5 acres who supplement agricultural incomes with seasonal agricultural wage labor (UNDP, 1988: 11–13). Thus, there is a growing demand for off-farm employment among households needing to subsidize subsistence and family reproduction and to diversify investments and earnings. Unfortunately, however, it is not anticipated that this growing supply will be met by a sufficient increase in demand for agricultural labor.

At present, off-farm employment primarily involves the production of food grains, which alone account for nearly two-thirds of wage labor requirements in agriculture. Crop processing is the second largest source of agricultural employment after crop production, providing an estimated 460 million days of work. Eighty percent of this employment is in rice processing, which is the major source of employment and income for landless women.[8] In addition, there is the work generated by noncrop agriculture: livestock, fisheries, and forestry (Feldman, 1982 and 1987).

Since the mid-1970s, development projects and programs have supported expanding credit and training facilities to increase both crop and agro-industrial production as well as the nonfarm service sector (Feldman, Akhter, and Banu, 1980; Grameen Bank, 1980–1985; Huq, 1981; Jahangir et al., 1983). The nonfarm sector includes the myriad of trade, transport, and other service workers; manufacturing employees; government workers; professionals; and petty commodity producers. Although there are no reliable data showing recent employment trends in the nonfarm sector, it is clear that rural wage employment opportunities are limited and that the rural work force will likely come to depend on self-employment. Those classified as self-employed tend to be ignored in official statistics and can best be conceptualized as part of the informal sector. Data available on cottage industries also ignore home-based producers, and thus no national survey data are available on employment in this sector. Data on small-scale industries, on the other hand, provide a regionally dispersed view of this segment of nonfarm workers but, as will be indicated later, they also have not been disaggregated by occupational group, gender, wages, and hours worked. In general, however, the 1983/84 Labor Force Survey indicates that nonagricultural employment accounts for 41.1 percent of total employment. Although the overall employment in the agricultural sector has remained unchanged during the past two decades, the nonagricultural sector has shifted dramatically, and the growth in rural employment has been absorbed primarily by the nonfarm sector.

Changing National Policy Initiatives

The state responses to processes of rural and agrarian differentiation and the expanding demands placed on the rural labor market have changed over time. First in concert with the concentration of agricultural production and later in response to it, national policies addressed the demand for rural employment through an expansion of medium-sized enterprises, with support to rural elite interests. As early as 1957, the East Pakistan (now Bangladesh) Small and Cottage Industries Corporation (BSCIC) supported the establishment of rural industrial estates. These estates were envisioned as mechanisms to promote investment in local industry development, to generate rural employment opportunities for those displaced from agriculture, and to provide consumer goods for local markets. In other words, they were envisioned as infrastructural resources to expand traditional enterprises (such as jute processing, glass making, and handloom and textile manufacture) and to support agro-based industrial growth and the production of consumer goods, including cooking and eating utensils, farm implements, batteries, chemicals, pharmaceuticals, food, clothing, and shoes.

It has taken, on average, 14.5 years for the industrial estates to be brought to completion. This has been done through a 20, 40, or 60 percent nominal subsidy for building costs. Estates have 3 to 81 enterprises, with an average (excluding the largest one located in the capital city) of 19 industries per estate. Investments on the estates represent capital- rather than labor-intensive enterprises with high loan default rates (Chowdhury, 1987).

The employment generated by estate enterprises has not been as high as anticipated. Figures for 1981 reveal that employment and type of enterprise vary significantly by region. Among the 403 enterprises for which information is available, aggregate average employment is 21.6 jobs per enterprise, with a total employment of 8,697. Excluding Dhaka, which accounts for 52 percent of the total estimated employment, enterprises employ from 6 to 54 people, with an average employee base of 13. Jute, glass-making, and textile firms are the largest enterprises, account for the largest proportion of employment generated, and tend to be located in the more urban industrial estates of Dhaka, Chittagong, and Rajshahi. The largest proportion of enterprises are food-processing businesses, which account for 33 percent of all firms, followed by engineering and textile-manufacturing firms, which account for 20 percent and 17 percent of all firms, respectively (NORAD, 1984; Chowdhury, 1987).

The failure of the industrial estates to become established centers of production and generators of employment is one indication of the collapse of an industrialization and employment effort premised on medium- and large-scale, public sector and highly subsidized private sector industrial growth. During the 1970s and 1980s, therefore, national policy initiatives attempted to stimulate the expansion of the small and cottage industries sector. Major donor agencies supported credit extension and infrastructural development through the Ministry of Industries, and they institutionalized credit institutions to stimulate increased domestic resource mobilization among rural entrepreneurs. Rural programs previously limited to agricultural initiatives were expanded to include a broad array of rural activities, such as parastatals to develop handicraft production and agroprocessing for rural markets.[9] During this period as well, there was a growing interest in the denationalization of public sector enterprises and the development of export-processing enclaves under the government's New Industrialization Policy (NIP).

The later 1980s witnessed a proliferation of semiautonomous and nongovernmental organizations (NGOs) providing credit and training opportunities for nonfarm production activities to village and provincial town entrepreneurs. These were expected to increase employment by generating demand for hired labor (Feldman and McCarthy, 1984; Grameen Bank, 1980–1985; Hossain, 1987).[10] Support for NGO and semiautonomous initiatives parallels the national policy shift toward forms of private production and small-scale credit schemes. Such support also parallels donor interest in removing agricultural subsidies, privatizing large- and medium-sized industrial production, and promoting small-scale and cottage enterprises through specialized credit and training programs to develop rural entrepreneurship. The focus on private sector development and the restructuring of the organization of production represents a shift of emphasis from public sector employment toward export-led growth and urban manufacturing employment and the creation of a cadre of rural self-employed entrepreneurs.

The Donor Community and Global Restructuring

Changes in the international division of labor have helped to shape recent interest in new forms of employment in Bangladesh. Global economic restructuring, for example, has enhanced employment opportunities for labor-intensive production among small- and medium-sized firms through subcontracting initiatives and the specialized production of local crafts. Support for an export-led growth strategy and the development of export-processing enclaves is premised on the assumption that Bangladesh has a comparative advantage because of low labor costs, relatively weak labor organizations, and donor financing to develop a basic infrastructure.

Donor financing, technical assistance, and the ability to buy policy reform, in other words, have shaped the current investment environment, policy and planning strategy, policy discourse, and employment patterns.

At the Paris Aid Consortium for Bangladesh in 1982, for example, discussion focused on the nature and magnitude of the rural employment problem, including the limited capacity of the crop sector to absorb the growing number of rural unemployed, the rising salience of self-employment, and the crucial role of the NGOs in generating home-based and cottage industry production (World Bank, 1983; Ahmed et al., 1990; Chowdhury, 1987). This discussion emphasized the importance of rural employment for poverty alleviation,[11] and it drew attention to the salience of the rural nonfarm sector in generating new work opportunities. It also acknowledged the range of activities that comprised nonfarm rural production that could be expanded to create new employment opportunities.

The initiatives addressed at this meeting focused on private sector growth and employment generation. This is indicated by the World Bank technical assistance in preparing the New Industrial Policy in 1982 and by the growth in national budget allocations for private sector development between the First and Third Five-Year plans, a shift from 11 percent to 35 percent of plan allocations (Government of the People's Republic of Bangladesh, 1985). It is also indicated by increased expenditures on rural infrastructure development, tax and tariff reform, and improved terms and expanded access to rural credit.

This chapter focuses on the rural nonfarm sector, but it is important to note that expanded employment opportunities for educated women in the export-processing sector have created new patterns of household and individual migration for rural women. Despite the major growth of these firms, however, total employment still remains at approximately 200,000 (Feldman, 1990b). Although only a small segment of the rural population has been employed in export manufacturing, such employment has reconfigured the rates of female participation in the labor force and provided opportunities for women whose family status had previously kept them off the labor market. Because of a commitment to the proscriptions of *purdah* ("a veil or screen," which refers to the seclusion of women from public observation), unmarried, educated women were generally limited in the employment they could undertake. But with expanded opportunities in "modern sector" work, these women have used their access to the labor market as a mechanism for upward mobility in the creation of marriage contracts (Feldman, 1993). Women who secure employment tend to have good social networks both in the rural areas and in the cities. The point to emphasize here regarding rural nonfarm employment is that urban employment generation has shaped the kind of employment desired by rural residents.[12]

In terms of the national economy, the strategy to expand rural off-farm employment opportunities and support small-scale entrepreneurs and self-

employment schemes redirects state policy from an employment generation strategy to one that encourages private investment and private initiative among a cadre of self-employed. This fosters forms of economic
independence that hold individuals responsible for their own social reproduction and promote the interests of larger entrepreneurs in the expansion
of export production. In this context, social welfare initiatives can be reduced, and increased attention can be paid to the creation of an ideology
premised on individualism and self-reliance. This policy shift makes a relatively poor segment of the rural population more self-reliant and mitigates their demands on the public sector for services.

The strategy to promote individualized production, however, is contradictory in its effects. On one hand, the shift highlights a development
thrust that holds people responsible for their own survival and thus limits
the state's responsibility to support social welfare initiatives to meet the
subsistence needs of the poor. On the other hand, providing access to training and credit opportunities to potential rural entrepreneurs increases their
dependence on government-financed public services, despite the fact that
such services are provided on a fee-for-service basis. The best example of
these services is the credit programs linking households to forms of dependence and obligation different from that characteristic of money-lend-
ing arrangements.[13] The new relations that are generated between state services and a growing cadre of the rural nonfarm population can also be said
to represent the strategy to capitalize what has traditionally been part of
the informal sector.

The Growth in Rural Labor Demand

Income Diversification Among Agricultural Producers

Following the theoretical debates previously outlined, it is reasonable to
assume that development assistance to increase agricultural productivity
has changed the structure of agriculture from a predominance of small-
scale owner-cultivators to large-scale commercial producers. This reorganization of agricultural production has driven inefficient owner-cultivators
from agriculture and generated a rural labor force to maintain commercial
agriculture and the subsidiary industries created to foster commercialized
production. Those whose lands have been appropriated, sold, or mortgaged
now provide labor for large-scale producers unable to sustain production
with family labor alone. Others seek employment in the industries generated by rural development efforts, including those that result from the need
for new agricultural technologies.

A recent study of the effects of the green revolution on the demand
for hired agricultural labor reveals that only 44 percent of the total labor

required for agricultural production is hired. The distribution of labor use by farm size is presented in Table 4.1. The table reveals that the majority of field production from all landholding classes is carried out by family labor. Although the proportion of hired labor to family labor increases with farm size, even large landowners only engage hired labor for 58 percent of their labor requirements, and those with less than 2 acres engage hired labor for only 33 percent of the work (Ahmed, 1987). As expected, the agricultural sector has been unable to absorb those seeking off-farm and nonfarm wage employment.

Table 4.1   The Pattern of Labor Use in Bangladesh by Size of Farms, 1982

Size Group (acres)	Labor Days per Household			Labor Days per Acre of Cropped Land			Percentage Use of Hired Labor
	Family	Hired	Total	Family	Hired	Total	
Small owner (up to 2.0)	68.7	33.7	102.4	37.6	18.5	56.1	32.9
Medium owner (2.01 to 5.0)	114.0	82.3	196.3	29.5	21.3	50.8	41.9
Large owner (5.01+)	159.4	218.3	377.7	20.3	27.8	48.1	57.8
All farm households	96.6	76.2	172.8	28.7	22.6	51.3	44.1

Source: Abstracted from Ahmed (1987: 109).

Unfortunately, the use of hired labor has not been disaggregated by task. However, other data suggest that hired labor is employed for ploughing, weeding, and harvesting among medium and large owner-cultivators; among households owning less than 2 acres and without draft animals, the labor of those renting draft animals may be employed for ploughing operations. Also, though the demand for employment in harvesting was once limited to male laborers, more recent evidence suggests that women are increasingly visible in fieldwork (McCarthy, n.d.). The increased participation of women as field labor is one marked response to increasing levels of poverty; it is also a response to the migration of male household heads in search of seasonal or full-time employment. This increased substitution of male and female labor is eroding the gender division of labor assumed to characterize Bangladeshi *purdah* (Feldman and McCarthy, 1983).

On the other hand, increasing numbers of farmers who had previously employed female laborers to husk paddy are instead having their rice processed at commercial mills: The proportion of paddy husked commercially increased from 17 percent in 1967 to close to 30 percent by 1981. As a result of this mechanization, employment opportunities for landless women are being destroyed at an estimated rate of 3.6 million to 5.1 million work-days each year (Harriss, 1977; McCarthy, 1980 and 1981; World Bank, 1983). The contradictory processes of labor substitution and marginalization characterize the changing patterns of participation by females in the rural labor force.

In refining analyses of changes in labor demand, the type of demand created and the gendered distribution of labor use are important themes to emphasize. For example, the type of labor employed by different groups of owner-cultivators determines the employment opportunities available to rural households. With each distinctive type of labor, moreover, different patterns of employment will shape a household's income diversification strategy. For instance, daily laborers are likely to be the most vulnerable of labor force participants for they must seek and secure work on a daily basis. The work that is available to them is often seasonal, with wages changing according to both the demand for labor and its supply. Thus, daily laborers must depend on other household members to contribute to the purchase of food and other subsistence items.

Given the insecurity of employment and the low wage rates usually associated with casual work, households that depend on daily agricultural wage labor opportunities are among the most likely to require that more than one household member seek employment and contribute to family income. In these households, women and children often contribute to household resources through nonwage or in-kind exchanges as well as wage employment.[14] These households are also among those most likely to participate in dry season construction and road maintenance work through Food for Work programs (CARE, 1983). Between 1982 and 1986, these programs increased their labor demand by 38 million days. A second rural works program (Vulnerable Group Development), targeted at poor women, increased the demand for female labor by nearly 55 million days at Tk12 per day (Tk = taka)—the equivalent of US$.40 per day (World Bank, 1986).

Many of the rural underemployed come from households that have been able to maintain agricultural production but at below-subsistence levels. And current estimates reveal that the number of below-subsistence farm households continues to increase. In 1983, approximately 70 percent of all farm households owned less than 2.5 acres, an increase of almost 20 percent since 1960. Moreover, average farm size is estimated to have decreased from 3.5 acres in 1960 to 2.3 acres by 1983/84 (Ahmed, 1987). In seeking to diversify their incomes, individuals from these households have increased the demand for seasonal or casual employment in agriculture and in agro-based cottage and small-scale enterprises. Sadly, the needs, interests, and costs of the green revolution for this segment of the rural population have never received the attention given to those of the landless, and thus, this segment remains an unrecognized proportion of the rural economy demanding expanded opportunities for work.

One reason for the limited attention given to analyses of the relationship of land-poor households to the labor market is the assumption that such demands are likely to be transitional and that the land-poor will eventually share the characteristics of landless households. This undifferentiated view of households with landed property masks the complexity of agrarian relations and the differentiated needs and interests that shape rural labor market dynamics. A few studies have examined households that are dependent on both agriculture and off-farm and nonfarm employment to meet subsistence needs. Recent studies conceptualize this integration of various forms of work in the context of household survival strategies. These studies begin with a disaggregation of agricultural households and examine the range of nonfarm activities in which they are engaged. Mahabub Hossain (1987), for example, drawing on data from the Bangladesh Institute of Development Studies, the census, and the Land Occupancy Survey, examines three farm size groups and compares the percentage of workers in different occupations and cottage industries. These data indicate that in all landowning household classes, a proportion is engaged in both off-farm and nonfarm occupations. This information is summarized in Table 4.2.

What is clear from the figures is the heterogeneity of the household occupation and employment structure. Although agricultural wage labor accounts for the largest proportion of employment in those households owning less than 2 acres, trade and business accounts for a proportion of the income earned in all landowning categories. The salience of service work for all household categories is also interesting to note.

A disaggregation of workers by landownership and gender, presented in Table 4.3, indicates a range of differences by industry type. Industries involved in the processing of fiber (grain straw, bamboo, coir) are dominated by female laborers, the great majority of whom represent households that own less than half an acre of land. Gur making (gur is a palm syrup), on the other hand, is a male occupation in households with large landholdings (Hossain, 1987: 27). Not surprisingly, a significant proportion of all workers come from households with less than one-half acre, highlighting the demand likely to come from this expanding segment of the rural population.

It is also interesting to point out that women who work within the household compound come from households that tend to own less than one-half acre of land. This type of employment has traditionally been excluded from labor force statistics; it is thus not surprising that the rate of female participation in the labor force was estimated at only 4 percent in 1974. The Rural Industries Survey carried out in 1980, however, indicates that about 33 percent of rural industry workers are female, and the 1983/84 Labor Force Survey indicates that commodity and personal services and manufacturing account for 28.2 percent and 24.6 percent, respectively, of

Table 4.2 Occupational Structure for Landless and Small Landowning Groups in Bangladesh, 1980 and 1982

	Percentage of Total Workers Engaged in the Occupation					
	RISP Survey 1980			BGP Survey 1982		
	0 to 0.5 Acres	0.51 to 2.0 Acres	Over 2.0 Acres	0 to 0.4 Acres	0.41 to 2.0 Acres	Over 2.0 Acres
Cultivation	22.8	76.5	88.8	22.9	68.8	75.7
Agricultural wage labor	39.4	11.6	1.0	35.6	11.1	—
Cottage industry	24.5	16.2	10.2	23.3	9.5	2.4
Trade and business	19.2	18.2	21.3	20.9	15.3	9.3
Transport service	2.6	1.9	0.7	4.5	2.8	0
Other services	8.3	6.0	7.8	8.8	12.9	20.1
Miscellaneous occupations	10.9	11.6	3.2	13.7	7.6	1.9
All occupations[a]	127.7	142.0	133.0	129.7	128.0	109.1
Number of workers in the sample	1165.0	595.0	295.0	2663.0	1507.0	821.0

Source: Data from Hossain (1987: 26).
GBP = Grameen Bank Project.
RISP = Rural Industries Study Project.
  [a] The column totals exceed 100 because some of the workers are engaged in more than one occupation.

Table 4.3 Distribution of Nonfarm Workers in Bangladesh by Land Ownership and Sex, 1980

Industry	Percentage of Workers from Different Landholding Households			
	>0.50 Acres	0.51 to 2.0 Acres	Over ≥2.0 Acres	Percentage of Female Workers
Dairy products	72.3	22.2	5.5	9.8
Oil pressing	74.3	18.6	7.1	42.5
Rice husking	87.5	11.7	0.8	56.0
Gur making	7.1	63.4	27.6	0
Carpentry	82.2	15.9	1.9	4.4
Mat making	64.1	34.7	1.1	62.8
Bamboo products	5.4	20.3	4.4	49.0
Coir products	87.6	12.4	0	64.3
Net making	89.7	9.0	1.3	63.3
Handloom weaving	73.0	16.9	6.6	37.6
Blacksmithing	65.0	25.0	10.0	2.4
Pottery	83.1	13.0	3.9	47.0
All industries	79.4	20.6	9.7	32.3
Bangladesh	42.4	24.2	33.4	9.8

Source: Hossain (1987: 27), Table 2.4.

the employed population over the age of five (Hossain, 1987: 27; BBS, 1984: 33). Additionally, the Bangladesh Manpower Survey of 1980 indicates that 31.8 percent of rural women between the ages of fifteen and sixty-four are engaged in the production and transport sector (BBS, 1982: 36).

M. Muqtada and M.M. Alam (1987), in their study of hired labor, note that although off-farm employment opportunities differ among landholding groups, nonagricultural household income represents a growing proportion of income for all household types. In four distinct village types,[15] nonagricultural income represented more than 43 percent of the income of all households in the villages studied. In the village with a low level of agricultural growth, where one might expect a limited demand for agricultural labor, the landless earned 36 percent of their income from nonagricultural activities. Not surprisingly, only in the village near the industrial center did the landless earn 65 percent of their income from these nonagricultural sources (Muqtada and Alam, 1987: 62).

As indicated in many of the projections on labor absorption in crop production, only a limited proportion of the expected labor demand is likely to secure off-farm employment. World Bank (1983) figures reveal that the demand for agricultural employment far exceeds the expected growth in the labor absorptive capacity of crop production. It is anticipated, for example, that only 29 percent of the increased labor demand will be employed in crop production.

These results assume a continued expansion in food grain production of 3.7 percent per annum and the maintenance of minor crop production at 1985 levels. This assumption is premised on the use of both more extensive and more intensive productive practices: The area used for growing high-yielding varieties (HYVs) is expected to have expanded from 5.4 million acres in 1981 to 11 million acres in 1988, and cropping intensity should have increased from 138 to 155. This should increase the demand for labor by 13 percent over the 1978 level; at the same time, the labor force is expected to have increased by nearly 24 percent (World Bank, 1983: 32–33). Thus, crop production is expected to have absorbed, on average, approximately 22 percent of the expected growth in the labor force during the 1978–1988 decade.[16] These figures represent an increasing labor absorptive capacity during November to December and May to August but not during the major slack periods, especially mid-September to mid-October when attention shifts to the nonfarm sector to meet employment needs (World Bank, 1983: 34).

The Rural Nonfarm Sector

The discussion thus far has been limited to changes among landowning households and their shifting demands for agricultural wage labor. This ignores the increasing complexity of the nonfarm rural sector and the changing proportion of households represented among different segments of the rural population. To be recalled at this juncture, therefore, are the employment demands of a diversified rural population that includes non-agricultural wage workers, traditional artisans, small and petty business entrepreneurs, professionals and government servants, and those engaged in the transportation of goods and services. In other words, the discussion must include those in the rural population who have been landless for generations and who are not dependent on agricultural production or agricultural skills for their livelihood. Tables 4.4 and 4.5 indicate the changing pattern of rural household types and projects the proportion of households in different farm and nonfarm categories through the year 2006.

One problem with the figures presented in Tables 4.4 and 4.5 is the inconsistent definitions of employment used by the census during the 1960–1983 period. This has caused what appear to be unexpected negative changes in the various categories of nonagricultural households. The major proportion of the change noted reflects the decline of farm households and the definition of all farm households with less than 0.5 acres as rural, nonagricultural, landless labor households (Ahmed, 1987). This redefinition accounts for the magnitude of change indicated for the 1977–1983 period. Changes during this period can also be explained as a consequence of the independence war and the 1974 famine, which generated a slow erosion of household security and resulted in distress sales of land (Feldman and McCarthy, 1983; Ahmed, 1987). Also increasing during this period were the number of households seeking urban employment and migrating to Dhaka, Chittagong, and a number of peripheral cities.

As noted earlier, in the shift to promote the private sector, rural industrialization and rural employment generation have become central concerns of both domestic policy and donor assistance. For example, recent national policy, with support from multilateral and bilateral agencies through the BSCIC, has sustained an effort to expand the participation of traditional artisans and nonfarm petty commodity producers in entrepreneurial activity. The BSCIC also provides credit and technical support to small- and cottage-industry entrepreneurs, with small-scale entrepreneurs sometimes using resources made available through support to the industrial estates.

As on the estates generally, BSCIC activities include the production of consumer goods, processed food items, and other agro-industrial products; they also encompass handicraft production, petty trade, and service enterprises, including repair and maintenance work. The types of enterprises supported indicate an effort to improve the linkages between agricultural and industrial production.

Embedded within this approach to rural employment generation is an employment strategy paralleling the generalized patterns of production

Table 4.4   Changing Shares of Various Subgroups in the Total Population and
Households of Bangladesh, 1960–2006 (in percent)

Share of Population by Type of Household	1960	1977	1983	2006[a]
Total urban	5.1	7.2	15.5	19.1
Total rural	94.9	92.8	84.5	80.9
Agricultural	76.7	53.0	80.7	72.3
Nonagricultural	21.3	47.0	19.3	27.7
Landless labor	92.8	89.2	89.2	91.8
Other nonagriculture	7.2	10.8	10.8	8.2

Source: Adapted from Ahmed (1987: 93, Table 2, and 106, Table 9).
[a] Assumes growth in urban population of 3.7 percent per annum.

Table 4.5   Annual Growth Rates of Various Types of Households During the
Intercensal Years in Bangladesh, 1960–2006 (percent change)

Period by Type of Household	1960–1977	1977–1983	1960–1983	1983–2006[a]
Total households	2.8	2.7	2.8	2.8
Total urban	4.9	15.4	7.6	3.7
Total rural	2.7	1.2	2.3	2.6
Agricultural	0.3	8.1	2.4	2.1
Nonagricultural	7.3	–13.7	1.8	4.2
Landless labor	7.1	–13.7	1.7	4.3
Other nonagriculture	10.6	–15.1	3.6	3.0

Source: Adapted from Ahmed (1987: 92, Table 1 and 106, Table 9).
[a] Assumes growth in urban population of 3.7 percent per annum.

fragmentation and global economic restructuring. For instance, the spatial redistribution of commodity production among regions within countries and the generalized fragmentation of the labor process have enhanced opportunities for small-scale, cottage-based, and home-based enterprises. Small, labor-intensive enterprises build upon the organization of production that is characteristic of the Bangladesh domestic economy of tailors, weavers, potters, metal and brass workers, goldsmiths and blacksmiths, and mat and basket weavers.

Subsidizing BSCIC industries has tended to favor small-scale rather than cottage-based producers, especially if they are located on the industrial estates. In the long run, the subsidies may serve as a disincentive for cottage-based entrepreneurs who cannot compete with the small-scale producers; the latter pay lower interest rates on credit, which provides them with a better return to capital than is found in the cottage-industry sector. This advantage is already visible in the growth rates of 16.6, 13.1, and 11 percent, respectively, in rice, oil, and saw milling between 1962 and 1978 (Hossain, 1987).

Unfortunately, the employment generated by small-scale and cottage-based entrepreneurs has been insignificant. The labor power that has been mobilized is provided by those who may be variously defined in the category of nonfarm self-employed, rather than those recently forced out of agriculture. Although expanding opportunities for self-employment may not automatically generate wage employment, it has alleviated the demand for work among a growing number of semiskilled and skilled artisans. Moreover, although cottage-industry production is generally more labor intensive, the small size of the cottage enterprises and their dependence on family labor limit their overall demand for wage labor.[17] This information is indicated in Table 4.6, which represents one of the largest BSCIC credit schemes to small and cottage entrepreneurs. Norwegian Development Assistance, Ministry of Development Cooperation (NORAD) credit has been distributed to 305,410 enterprises, with 79 percent of the supported enterprises dispersed throughout the rural district towns (NORAD, 1984: 14). The average number of workers per enterprise in the scheme ranges from 1.6 to 3.4. Differences reflect both the proportion of family labor to hired labor and the type of enterprise financed. Two broad patterns are noteworthy: In districts such as Dhaka, Chittagong, and Rajshahi, where a competitive medium- and large-scale industrial sector operates, workers seek wage income and secure employment in large- or medium-sized enterprises, as well as in the small-scale and cottage-industries sector. This reflects a growing and increasingly complex labor force where hired labor in small and cottage enterprises supported by NORAD credit range between 22 percent and 32 percent. In districts where families are less dependent on wage income and where self-employment in small-scale and cottage industries predominates the nonagricultural rural economy, hired labor represents a relatively small proportion of those securing income in these enterprises.

The use of hired labor, rather than family labor, represents a distinct form of production. Hired laborers are likely to work in centralized production sites, usually engaging some form of mechanized technology with a greater likelihood of fixed capital investment. These enterprises are more often classified as small-scale rather than cottage units of production. Wages are paid on a daily, weekly, or longer-term contract basis and are more likely than cottage enterprises to fall under the laws governing minimum wages.

Cottage enterprises, on the other hand, draw heavily on family labor, although they may hire labor on an irregular basis or to carry out a single task in the overall production cycle. Generally operating within the home, the domestic group jointly provides labor, may possess a part of the means of production, and often disposes of at least part of the product of its labor (Friedmann, 1980). The production site, in other words, is organized around the household gender division of labor, and the patterns and relations of inequality that characterize "factorylike" production have little

Table 4.6 Employment Generated by NORAD Credit to the Bangladesh Small and Cottage Industries Corporation, 1983–1984

District	Number of Industries	Number of Persons Employed			Percent Hired per Firm	Average Number of Workers per Industry
		Hired	Family	Total		
Dhaka	40,360	42,592	88,824	131,416	32	3.3
Mymensingh	17,344	3,702	43,075	46,777	8	2.7
Tangail	5,746	2,487	11,839	14,326	17	2.5
Jamalpur	8,867	1,324	12,945	14,269	9	1.6
Faridpur	17,480	5,090	43,587	48,677	10	2.8
Chittagong	22,444	15,921	56,986	72,907	22	3.2
Noakhali	9,461	3,518	21,634	25,152	14	2.7
Comilla	18,800	7,577	44,104	51,681	15	2.8
Sylhet	18,554	11,438	43,789	55,527	21	3.0
Chittagong Hill Tracks	1,755	1,443	2,893	4,336	33	2.5
Khulna	19,066	8,775	47,046	55,821	16	2.9
Barisal	18,522	7,782	45,543	53,325	15	2.9
Patuakhali	6,933	2,176	18,898	21,074	10	3.0
Jessore	18,683	5,620	52,787	48,407	10	2.6
Kushtia	9,451	3,970	19,803	23,773	17	2.5
Pabna	10,735	2	28,842	36,810	0	3.4
Bogra	9,807	4,652	25,540	30,192	15	3.1
Rajshahi	17,502	16,621	38,185	54,806	30	3.1
Rangpur	22,129	8,694	53,022	61,716	14	2.8
Dinajpur	14,771	3,958	34,832	38,790	10	2.6
Total	305,410[a]	157,342	734,174	899,782	16	

Source: Data from NORAD (1984: 14).
[a] Total excludes salt producers.

place in the household context. Hossain (1987) suggests that in home-based, cottage industries, women comprise a significant percent of the work force. These industries are also among the least likely to hire labor, and they come to depend on the hidden contribution of women and children (Kobayashi, 1989; Feldman, 1989b and 1990a). What often plays a critical role in cottage-industry production are new relations of gender exploitation that may emerge with the intensification of productive responsibility within the home.

In areas where there has been a tradition of small-scale entrepreneurship, it is not surprising that a larger proportion of labor is hired and that production is organized on a slightly larger scale than is typically the case in the cottage sector. Despite such differences, opportunities for employment generation in both these enterprise types is quite low. In the cottage-industry sector, however, the deployment of family labor may reduce the effective labor demand among people working in these enterprises. Thus, traditional craftspeople and artisans may now put fewer demands on the agricultural and unskilled rural labor market to subsidize their small production units. The increased deployment of female household members may also pressure women to expand the number of hours they work to include labor in subsistence and petty commodity production, while continuing to meet household responsibilities. In almost all comparisons of gender differences in hours worked, women are engaged for longer hours than men in a combination of paid and unpaid labor.

As intimated earlier, policy initiatives that focus on the rural household as an arena of production tend to assume rather than help to theorize and examine the intrahousehold division of labor. By assuming and thereby maintaining the household as an undifferentiated set of social relations, proscriptions for expanding household production have underestimated the degree to which the household is a contested terrain where the differential interests of its members are subject to continuous negotiation (Folbre, 1986; Hart, Chapter 2 in this volume; Bruce and Dwyer, 1988). Such proscriptions and the new resources that may accompany income diversification and resource-generating schemes have also assumed that family labor, especially women's labor, is underutilized and thus would be available to meet the labor requirement of home-based production.

An assumption of consensual household relations ignores the contradictory consequences of changes in household resource control. Such an assumption, for example, underestimates the extent to which new relations of inequality and exploitation may emerge in the process of expanding household resources and employment opportunities. Alternatively, given that resources may be provided directly to women, the increased access that these women have to credit, training, and technical inputs may augment their opportunities for negotiation. Also likely to be enhanced is their degree of authority regarding the division of labor, control of income, and domestic responsibilities and expenditures.

Although this chapter has emphasized the theoretical and policy logic in the construction of off-farm and nonfarm employment, three themes that generally frame analyses of rural employment should also be noted. These themes include the changing pattern of employment in the formal sector and its characteristic occupational structure; analyses of poverty as the stimulus for an investigation of underemployment, unemployment, and differential wage rates; and a review of informal sector opportunities. These themes have not been privileged in this discussion because formal sector wage employment accounts for only a marginal proportion of rural employment. Moreover, the formal sector is unlikely to be an arena for expanding employment opportunities, given a policy focus on denationalization and a general critique of public sector employment as well as the inability of the state to mobilize domestic resources and interest for industrial development. However, a few comments on each of these themes are in order.

Tables 4.7 and 4.8 summarize the occupational distribution of the civilian labor force and indicate the growth rates within occupations for

Table 4.7   Employed Bangladesh Population 10 Years of Age and Older and
Annual Growth Rates by Occupation Group, 1961 to 1983/84

Occupational Group	Employed Population (000)			Average Annual Growth Rates (%)	
	1961	1974	1983/84	1961–1974	1974–1983/84
Professional, technical	205	405	994	5.4	9.4
Administrative, managerial	36	34	164	–0.5	17.0
Clerical	184	229	505	1.7	8.2
Sales	574	1,018	3,102	4.5	11.8
Service	325	423	2,695	2.0	20.3
Agriculture, forestry, and fisheries	14,239	16,855	16,323	1.3	–0.3
Production, transport	1,194	2,444	3,587	5.7	3.9
Total employment	16,828	21,408	27,972	1.9	2.7

Source: Abstracted from BBS (1984: 30).

the periods 1961 to 1974 and 1974 to 1983/84. The fastest-growing occupations during the second period were service work, which grew by 20.3
percent, administrative and managerial work, which grew at an annual rate
of 17 percent, and sales, which averaged an 11.8 percent annual increase.
What is most significant in Table 4.8 is the decline in the percentage of
male agricultural workers, from 86 percent to almost 72 percent of those
employed in the rural areas during this same period.

It should be emphasized that in both these tables, female employment
has been variously defined in different census periods. This makes accurate accounting and comparison of female employment across time impossible. Moreover, because of the invisibility of women's participation in
subsistence agriculture and home-based production, female participation
rates are generally underestimated in all periods. In 1974, it was estimated
that less than 5 percent of all women were employed (ESCAP, 1981). Present estimates indicate that the proportion of women in the labor force will
increase from 11 percent in 1980 to 23 percent by the year 2000 (World
Bank, 1983)—an increase that only accounts for women employed in the
public and private sectors. However, what is interesting is the distribution
of females within the occupational hierarchy. Among women, for example,
48.6 percent are employed in services and 24 percent in production and
transport; only 10.6 percent of all women employed are engaged in agriculture.

In the discussion of poverty alleviation, employment generation has
played a major role because it has been assumed that underemployment
rather than the lack of resource control is the primary determinant of
poverty (Government of the People's Republic of Bangladesh, 1988). In

Table 4.8 Employed Bangladesh Population 10 Years of Age and Older by Broad Occupation Group and Sex, 1974, 1980, and 1983/84

Occupational Group	National (percent distribution)			Urban			Rural		
	1974	1980	1984[a]	1974	1980	1984	1974	1980	1984
Male									
Professional and technical	1.9	2.2	3.3	4.3	9.8	7.8	1.6	1.7	2.6
Administrative and managerial	0.2	0.3	0.6	1.2	1.6	2.9	0.1	0.1	0.3
Clerical	1.1	1.8	1.1	5.9	8.8	4.9	0.6	1.0	1.3
Sales	4.8	5.5	11.4	20.9	21.1	23.9	3.1	3.8	9.5
Service	2.0	3.7	6.2	7.5	15.2	22.7	0.9	2.5	3.6
Agricultural	78.7	74.0	63.0	14.7	10.8	19.8	86.1	80.1	71.7
Production and transport	11.4	12.5	11.8	45.5	32.6	20.8	7.6	10.4	10.4
Not reported	—	—	1.8	—	—	7.3	—	—	1.0
Female									
Professional and technical	2.6	2.4	5.4	11.8	4.5	4.3	1.4	2.1	5.6
Administrative and managerial	—	—	1.8	0.4	—	0.5	—	—	—
Clerical	0.3	1.5	1.3	1.6	7.7	1.7	0.1	0.5	1.2
Sales	1.3	4.2	5.5	3.0	5.8	5.7	1.1	2.9	5.5
Service	10.5	19.6	52.7	58.3	74.4	72.0	4.3	11.6	48.6
Agriculture	72.6	47.7	8.9	7.7	4.5	1.2	81.1	54.7	10.6
Production and transport	12.6	24.6	21.2	17.3	3.2	7.7	12.0	28.2	24.0
Not reported	—	—	4.9	6.7	—	—	—	—	4.6

Source: BBS (1984: 31).
— indicates less than 0.05 percent.
a 1984 = 1983/84 fiscal year and includes data for persons 5 to 9 years of age, accounting for about 2 percent of total employment.

most discussions of poverty, attention is drawn to the role of work programs to create short-term employment for the poor. The limited capacity
of the state to support these initiatives in the long term has been a stimulus for expanding the cottage-industries sector and promoting urban informal employment (World Bank, 1986). In the rural sector, the promotion of
cottage industries and home-based enterprises is equivalent to expanding
urban informal sector opportunities, but such efforts have contradictory effects because they create ties to forms of credit and training that require a
reconceptualization of informal sector activity.

The Household as a Unit of Analysis

Although the data presented in the preceding discussion suggest a rapid
transformation of rural production relations, they may underestimate the
actual demand for rural employment because the figures are likely to be
based on the primary income of male household heads rather than on the
multiple employment activities of all household members. However,
households often diversify their resource bases by expanding the number
of jobs a single member undertakes or by increasing the number of household members securing work to meet subsistence needs. This latter point
recognizes that nonagricultural households also place increasing demands
on the labor market.[18]

Various strategies are used by households to expand income-earning
capacity or to increase participation in the labor market. These strategies
include: (1) increasing the number of days working in or the returns from
agricultural production through crop diversification and/or the intensification or extensification of production, (2) generating cottage or home-based
productive activity, (3) seeking agricultural employment, (4) seeking employment in small and cottage enterprises, government service, or trade,
(5) securing work in government rural works programs (a strategy the poor
might pursue), (6) migrating for seasonal agricultural and nonfarm work,
or (7) permanent migration to urban centers.

Household strategies constitute a fertile and important area for analyses involving ethnographic and microlevel forms of inquiry. To understand
the ways in which households identify possible resources, opportunities,
risks, and costs, we must first understand the processes used by household
members (and members of the extended family and village community) to
choose an appropriate household strategy. Household survival and employment strategies, in other words, are not outcomes to be measured
using cross-sectional survey data; rather, they are processes that depend on
a complex set of relationships among intrahousehold, interhousehold, and
community relations, resources, and risks. These strategies also depend on
the institutional environment and the demographic and life-cycle profile of
the household that shape the household opportunity structure. To date,

most studies of household survival strategies actually posit, a priori, a strategy based on a household's behavior over time. Such research is unable to shed light on the structural factors, antecedent conditions, and mechanisms faced by and negotiated by households as they choose or reject various opportunities before them.

At the present juncture, we are limited to extrapolating information from Tables 4.4 and 4.5 in order to understand broad categories of households and the ways these various household groupings are likely to increase their demand for employment. Changes in the shares of various household and employment categories anticipated through the year 2006 suggest that the urban population will account for almost 20 percent of all household types, with nonagricultural rural households expected to increase from 19.3 percent in 1983 to 27.7 percent of all rural households by 2006. Among the highest growth categories are nonagricultural rural and landless households, anticipated to grow at annual rates of 4.2 percent and 4.3 percent, respectively. Given low rural wage rates, it could be hypothesized that there either will be an increasing number of households surviving at below-subsistence levels or that an increasing proportion of household members will be required to seek wage employment to meet household resource requirements. This latter strategy undoubtedly expands the demand for rural nonfarm wage employment.

For those unable to secure employment or increase self-employment opportunities, there is likely to be a rise in instability. This is being expressed in the *gharaoing* (the encircling, taunting, and restraining) of government officials for increased rural resources or for the more equitable distribution of existing resources. Rural instability is also expressed in the riots that have accompanied the distribution of food or clothing to the poor. These expressions have created a pressure on the state to generate or create conditions for expanding rural employment opportunities or for increasing credit and training schemes to support self-employment initiatives.

Conclusion

The demand for employment in rural Bangladesh can be characterized as a response to the capitalization of agriculture, the lack of a domestic market for consumer goods, a stagnating rural and urban industrial sector, and the restructuring of the organization of production. The capitalization of agricultural production has generated greater land consolidation and a decline in the number of subsistence agriculturalists and landowning households. This has increased the number of functionally landless households and created a cadre of rural unemployed forced either to seek off-farm or nonfarm rural employment or to migrate to urban cities and towns in search of wage employment. The number of those able to secure urban and town employment has been relatively small, given that industrial growth has expanded more slowly than the demand for work from rural landless household members.

Average farm size has also declined, which has generated a demand for both part-time and full-time off-farm employment to supplement agricultural incomes. Those seeking supplemental household income include male household heads looking for work during the slack seasons (especially between mid-September and mid-October) and those looking for casual and daily employment throughout the growing season.

Female household members, particularly those from landless rural households, are often forced to secure either in-kind or wage employment because of the low wages of male casual laborers. The declining family wage has meant that each household member is increasingly forced to secure his or her own reproductive costs. The introduction of commercial rice mills has reduced the demand for women's agricultural labor in rice processing and has thus forced them to seek nonfarm employment. Securing work as a household laborer without also engaging in rice-processing work has significantly reduced wage rates for household laborers, thereby forcing more and more women onto the nonfarm rural labor market.

In very poor households, children are also likely to seek part-time or full-time work. Thus, it is not surprising that the age structure of the labor force is skewed toward the very young. In general, the labor force is expected to grow more than 3 percent annually, with one-third of the labor force being below the age of twenty-five by the year 2000 (World Bank, 1983). Census data for 1974 indicate that economic participation rates for those between the ages of ten and fourteen was already 35.1 percent for males and 3.0 percent for females (BBS, 1982).

The demand for nonfarm employment is also likely to increase among households engaged in home-based cottage industries. This is especially likely among very small producing units where the scale of production is insufficient to employ all the household members and meet the costs of household reproduction. To satisfy this growing demand for nonfarm employment, state policy and resource allocations have shifted from an emphasis on the agricultural sector to the promotion of rural industries. Support for rural industries comes from the donor community that has financed the development of the 1982 New Industrial Policy and efforts to liberalize the economy and promote private sector initiatives, including the expansion of credit and training opportunities to stimulate rural entrepreneurial activity. Though there has been a burgeoning of credit and skills-development projects that have expanded the number of households engaged in cottage production, the scale of these enterprises has generated only limited rural employment opportunities. Instead, such initiatives have reduced the demand for rural wage employment among the growing number of petty commodity producers.

Three brief substantive conclusions are important. One highlights the need to incorporate a theory of the rural economy into analyses of nonfarm work. This would enable us to include (but not limit) labor market differentiation in agrarian change, and it would invite more textured analyses of changing labor relations in commodity production. A definition of the rural economy that includes nonfarm relations of production would also help to focus on the determinants of nonfarm labor demand in facilitating or constraining forms of agricultural production and agrarian production relations.

The second substantive conclusion focuses attention on the farm and/or household and rural household as a differentiated arena of contestation and negotiation. The different interests that shape intrahousehold relations include those of ethnicity, age, gender, and class. These differentiated interests also mold interhousehold relations and labor market strategies. In Bangladesh, the ideology of Bengali *purdah,* which has changed its articulation of the rules and behavioral proscription that define social interaction between men and women, has played a special role in legitimation patterns of female exclusion.

The concluding issue concerns the policy initiatives taken by the Bangladesh government and shaped by processes of global restructuring and by international aid and assistance. As is conventionally believed, policy initiatives respond to changing relations of production and exchange, as well as to changing patterns of migration, household formation, and resource mobilization. What I have suggested in this chapter is that policies also *shape* these patterns of social organization and guide social practices in particular ways. The increased need for nonfarm employment among a growing number of households, in other words, is one response to agrarian policy and policies that mold rural petty commodity production and require that individuals take responsibility for their own social reproduction. This suggests that we will see the evolution of new village and community relations, new relations between urban and rural employment, and new relations of nonfarm rural work.

Notes

1. Although the emphasis in the chapter is on the rural sector, there are important points of intersection between rural and urban employment markets and the increasing salience of household migration strategies that link and integrate labor market opportunities within the household. These relations will be suggested as relevant.

2. For an elaboration on the range of activities to be included under the concept of work, see Pahl (1980).

3. As noted later, though the household as a unit of production and consumption has drawn the attention of recent scholars, definitions of relations within the household remain an arena of debate and theoretical innovation.

4. Concurrent with analyses of agricultural employment differentiation, there are studies of urban employment that have focused on policies and incentives promoting large-scale industrial expansion. Not surprisingly, a dual economy perspective has shaped much of these analyses for the issues they examine were considered distinct from those used in exploring agricultural expansion and rural employment.

5. See Edholm, Harris, and Young (1977: 105–106) for an analysis of social reproduction that includes human and biological reproduction, the reproduction of the labor force, and the "reproduction of the conditions of social production in their totality." This conception moves away from both determinist theories of reproduction and those that tend toward structural teleology.

6. For an argument exploring the specific conditions that differentiate agricultural production from other forms of production, see Mann and Dickinson (1978), Mooney (1982 and 1987), and Davis (1980).

7. The wealth of microstudies now available on women's work in agriculture has occasioned renewed interest in the complexity of work relations within households. However, though these studies acknowledge women's invisible contribution to social reproduction and provide a growing body of descriptive detail on women's participation in agricultural production, they have been less successful in challenging the theoretical limitations of analyses of rural differentiation and the growing concern with the articulation of agricultural and nonfarm tasks among rural producers.

8. With the increase in mechanical rice milling, estimated at 40 percent of total output, between 3.5 and 5 million employment days per year have been lost, affecting approximately 2 million women who are now forced to seek employment elsewhere.

9. See, for example, the Bangladesh Rural Development Board (BRDB, previously the IRDP) objectives that provide credit, training, and technical support for both farm and nonfarm productive activities.

10. The Grameen Bank Project (GBP) is an internationally known small credit scheme for landless men and poor rural women to initiate agricultural and cottage-based industrial production. Project support comes from international agencies, such as the International Fund for Agricultural Development (IFAD), NORAD, and the Ford Foundation. The BSCIC is a semiautonomous government agency with credit schemes supported by the U.S. Agency for International Development (USAID), NORAD, and other members of the donor community.

11. Research on the nonfarm sector has often grown out of the need to diversify income earning among those dispossessed of landed property. Although forms of income diversification may be stimulated by the need to replace agricultural production with nonfarm work, processes to alleviate poverty, diversify income, or devise income-earning strategies are not synonymous because each may generate a different pattern of labor market participation and restructure the economy in diverse ways. Moreover, nonfarm employment has an independent historical trajectory that should not be equated with the ways in which nonfarm employment interfaces with changes in agricultural production.

12. One problem with expanding employment in export-processing zones is the difficulty such arrangements pose for workers who are generally not protected by minimum wage rate standards and minimum conditions of health and safety. In a majority of export-processing firms, for example, bathroom facilities were either limited in number or in disrepair, the production floor was overcrowded, and machinery was not operated with safety devices in place for fear that productivity levels would decline (Feldman, 1984). Moreover, employment in subcontracting firms

in the zone or in informal sector operations generally makes it difficult for workers to organize to protect their interests and articulate their demands because labor unions are illegal and workers have no organizational mechanism with which they can engage with management. Workers also remain vulnerable to the vagaries of the market for quick turnover and short-term demand characterize production in those subcontracting firms tied to garment and electronics manufacture in the export-processing zone.

13. Moneylending is also contradictory in its effects, but the point remains that it is not implicated as a relation of independence.

14. Rice-processing workers and daily household laborers are often paid in kind and receive wage equivalents of rice paddy or meals (McCarthy, 1980). The labor of children is discussed by Cain (1977), but his findings likely underestimate the work of young girls.

15. These four village types include one village with low agricultural growth, one village with high agricultural growth, one village near an industrial center, and one village far from an industrial center (Muqtada and Alam, 1987).

16. Wennergren (1983) suggests that fisheries and rural works are likely to expand their proportion of the work force more rapidly than crop production, livestock-rearing, and forestry sectors.

17. The growth in the demand for work represents those recently forced out of agriculture, those whose holdings are insufficient to realize reproduction and who attempt to supplement subsistence production with wage labor, and those who desire to diversify income-earning opportunities as a hedge against declining wages and agricultural prices.

18. Though not the focus of this study, rural wage rates in agriculture and the small-scale and cottage-industries sector remain low and often require that individuals meet their own reproductive costs (Feldman, 1989a). In this context, the family wage is completely undermined.

References

Ahmed, Muzaffar, Philip English, Shelley Feldman, Mosharaff Hossain, Eirik Jansen, Florence E. McCarthy, Koen de Wilde, and Roger Young. 1990. *Rural Poverty in Bangladesh.* Dhaka, Bangladesh: University Press Limited.

Ahmed, Raisuddin. 1987. "A Structural Perspective of Farm and Nonfarm Households in Bangladesh," *The Bangladesh Journal of Development Studies*, Vol. 15, No. 2, pp. 87–112.

Amin, A.T.M.N. 1981. "Marginalisation vs. Dynamism: A Study of the Informal Sector in Dhaka City," *The Bangladesh Journal of Development Studies*, Vol. 9, No. 4, pp. 77–112.

BBS (Bangladesh Bureau of Statistics). 1982. *Manpower Situation in Contemporary Bangladesh: Findings of the Bangladesh Manpower Survey of 1980* (Dhaka, Bangladesh: Ministry of Planning).

———. 1984. *Preliminary Report on Labour Force Survey, 1983–1984* (Dhaka, Bangladesh: Ministry of Planning).

Bruce, Judith, and Daisy Dwyer. 1988. "Introduction," in Daisy Dwyer and Judith Bruce, eds., *A Home Divided: Women and Income in the Third World,* Stanford, Calif.: Stanford University Press, pp. 1–19.

Byres, T.J. 1981. "The New Technology, Class Formation and Class Action in the Indian Countryside," *Journal of Peasant Studies*, Vol. 8, No. 4, pp. 405–454.

Cain, Mead. 1977. "The Economic Activities of Children in a Village in Bangladesh." *Population and Development Review*, Vol. 3, No. 3, pp. 201–228.

CARE. 1983. *Attitudinal Study of the Preventive Maintenance Program Pilot Schemes* (Dhaka, Bangladesh: Dhanmondi).

Chayanov, A.V. 1986. *The Theory of Peasant Economy.* Madison: University of Wisconsin Press.

Chen, M., and R. Ghaznavi. 1977. *Women in Food-for-Work: The Bangladesh Experience* (mimeographed) (Dhaka: Bangladesh Rural Advancement Committee).

Chowdhury, Nuimuddin. 1987. *BSCIC's Industrial Estate Programme: An Assessment,* Research Report No. 59 (Dhaka: Bangladesh Institute of Development Studies).

Davis, John E. 1980. "Capitalist Agricultural Development and the Exploitation of the Propertied Laborer," in Frederick H. Buttel and Howard Newby, eds., *The Rural Sociology of the Advanced Societies: Critical Perspectives* (Montclair, N.J.: Osmun), pp. 133–153.

de Vylder, Stefan. 1982. *Agriculture in Chains: Bangladesh—A Case Study in Contradictions and Constraints* (London: Zed Press).

Dixon, Ruth B. 1982. "Women in Agriculture: Counting the Labor Force in Developing Countries," *Population and Development Review*, Vol. 8, No. 3, pp. 539–566.

Edholm, Felicity, Olivia Harris, and Kate Young. 1977. "Conceptualising Women," *Critique of Anthropology*, Vol. 3, No. 9/10, pp. 101–130.

ESCAP (Economic and Social Commission for Asia and the Pacific). 1981. *Population of Bangladesh*, Country Monograph Series No. 8 (New York: United Nations).

Feldman, Shelley. 1982. "The Role of Women in the Bay of Bengal Fishing Project in Bangladesh," FAO, Bay of Bengal Project, manuscript.

———. 1984. Fulbright Islamic Civilization Research Program field notes, Grant No. 83-006-IC (10-4-83).

———. 1987. "Household Crafts and Rural Industries in the Sundarbadans: Extrapolations from Existing Bangladesh Data," paper presented to the Sundarbans Workshop, sponsored by the Smithsonian Institution and Joint Committee on South Asia of the Social Science Research Council and the American Council of Learned Societies, Washington, D.C., November 20–21.

———. 1989a. "Engendered Development: Entrepreneurship or New Forms of Domestic Exploitation for Bangladeshi Women," paper presented to the International Colloquium on Gender and Class, University of Antwerp, Belgium, September.

———. 1989b. "The Transformation of the Domestic Economy: New Household Labor Relations in Bangladesh," paper presented to the Association of Women in Development Conference, "The Global Empowerment of Women," Washington, D.C., November 17.

———. 1990a. "Formalizing the Informal Sector: New Forms of Domestic Exploitation of Bangladeshi Women," paper presented to the 42nd annual meeting of the Association for Asian Studies, April.

———. 1990b. "Rural Industrialization: The Shaping of 'Class' Relations in Rural Bangladesh," in Rhonda Levine, Scott McNall, and Rick Fantasia, eds., *Bringing Class Back In: Contemporary and Historical Perspectives* (Boulder, Colo.: Westview Press), pp. 119–138.

———. 1992. "Crisis, Islam and Gender in Bangladesh: The Social Construction of a Female Labor Force," in Lourdes Beneria and Shelley Feldman, eds., *Unequal Burden: Economic Crises, Persistent Poverty, and Women's Work* (Boulder, Colo.: Westview Press), pp. 105–130.

130   Shelley Feldman

————. 1993. "Contradictions of Gender Inequality: Urban Class Formation in Contemporary Bangladesh," in Alice W. Clark, ed., *Explorations of South Asian Systems*. New Delhi: Oxford University Press.

Feldman, Shelley, and Florence E. McCarthy. 1983. "Disaster Response in Bangladesh," *International Journal of Mass Emergencies and Disasters,* Vol. 1, No. 1, pp. 105–124.

————. 1984. *Rural Women and Development in Bangladesh* (Oslo: NORAD).

Feldman, Shelley, Farida Akhter, and Fazila Banu. 1980. *The Research and Evaluation Study of the IRDP Pilot Project on Population Planning and Rural Women's Cooperatives* (Dhaka, Bangladesh: Ministry of Local Government and Rural Development).

Folbre, Nancy. 1986. "Hearts and Spades: Paradigms of Household Economics," *World Development,* Vol. 14, No. 2, pp. 245–255.

Friedmann, Harriet. 1980. "Household Production and the National Economy: Concepts for the Analysis of Agrarian Formations," *Journal of Peasant Studies,* Vol. 7, No. 2, pp. 158–184.

Government of the People's Republic of Bangladesh. 1985. *The Third Five-Year Plan (1985–1990)* (Dhaka, Bangladesh: Planning Commission).

————. 1988. *Memorandum for the Bangladesh AID Group 1988–89* (Dhaka, Bangladesh: Ministry of Planning, Planning Commission and External Resources Division).

Grameen Bank. 1980–1985. *Annual Reports* (Dhaka, Bangladesh: Grameen Bank).

Harriss, Barbara. 1977. "Paddy Milling: Problems in Policy and the Choice of Technology," in B.H. Farmer, ed., *Green Revolution* (London: Macmillan), pp. 276–300.

Hirashima, S., and M. Muqtada. 1986. "Hired Labour and Rural Labour Market in Bangladesh," in S. Hirashima and M. Muqtada, eds., *Hired Labour and Rural Labour Markets in Asia* (New Delhi: ILO), pp. 1–19.

Hossain, Hameeda, Roushan Jahan, and Salma Sobhan. 1987. "Industrialisation and Women Workers in Bangladesh: From Home-Based Work to the Factories," in Noeleen Heyzer, ed., *Daughters in Industry: Work Skills and Consciousness of Women Workers in Asia* (Kuala Lumpur: Asian and Pacific Development Center), pp. 107–135.

Hossain, Mahabub. 1985. *Credit for the Rural Poor: The Grameen Bank in Bangladesh* (Dhaka: Bangladesh Institute of Development Studies).

————. 1987. "Employment Generation Through Cottage Industries—Potentials and Constraints: The case of Bangladesh," in Rizwanul Islam, ed., *Rural Industrialisation and Employment in Asia* (New Delhi: ILO, Asian Employment Programme), pp. 19–57.

Huq, Shireen. 1981. *A Report on Grameen Bank Prokalpa,* Draft report (Dhaka: Bangladesh Institute of Development Studies).

Islam, Rizwanul. 1987. *Rural Industrialization and Employment in Asia* (New Delhi: International Labour Organization, Asian Employment Programme).

Jahangir, B.K. et al. 1983. *An Evaluation of Grameen Bank—A Case Study of Narandia Union* (mimeographed) (Dhaka, Bangladesh: Center for Social Studies).

Kahn, Joel S. 1982. "From Peasants to Petty Commodity Production in Southeast Asia," *Bulletin of Concerned Asian Scholars,* Vol. 14, No. 1, pp. 3–15.

Kobayashi, Emiko. 1989. "Rural Entrepreneurship and Small-Scale and Cottage Industries in Bangladesh" (master's thesis, Cornell University, Department of Rural Sociology).

Lenin, Vladimir. 1974. *The Development of Capitalism in Russia* (Moscow: Progress Publishers).

Mann, Susan A., and James M. Dickinson. 1978. "Obstacles to the Development of a Capitalist Agriculture," *Journal of Peasant Studies,* Vol. 5, No. 4, pp. 466–481.

Marum, M.E. 1982. *Women at Work in Bangladesh* (Dhaka, Bangladesh: USAID).

McCarthy, Florence E. N.d. "Female Household Workers in Four Districts in Bangladesh" (mimeographed).

————. 1980. *Patterns of Employment and Income Earning Among Female Household Labour* (Dhaka, Bangladesh: Ministry of Agriculture).

————. 1981. *Patterns of Involvement and Participation of Rural Women in Post Harvest Processing Operations* (Dhaka, Bangladesh: Ministry of Agriculture).

————. 1989. "Formalizing the Unorganized Sector: Issues in the Capitalization of Petty Commodity Production," paper presented to the South Asian Studies Annual Meeting, Madison, Wis., November.

————.1991. "Purdah," in Helen Tierney, ed., *Women's Studies Encyclopedia,* Vol. 3, *History, Philosophy, and Religion* (New York: Greenwood Press).

McCarthy, Florence E., Saleh Sabbah, and Roushan Aktar. 1979. *Rural Women Workers in Bangladesh: A Working Paper* (Dhaka, Bangladesh: Women's Section, Planning and Development Division, Ministry of Agriculture and Forests).

Mooney, Patrick H. 1982. "Labor Time, Production Time and Capitalist Development in Agriculture: A Reconsideration of the Mann-Dickinson Thesis," *Sociologia Ruralis,* Vol. 22, No. 3/4, pp. 279–292.

————. 1987. "Toward a Class Analysis of Midwestern Agriculture," *Rural Sociology,* Vol. 48, No. 4, pp. 563–584.

Muqtada M., and M. M. Alam. 1987. "Hired Labour and Rural Labour Markets in Bangladesh," in S. Hirashima and M. Muqtada, eds., *Hired Labour and Rural Labour Markets in Asia* (New Delhi: ILO), pp. 20–73.

NORAD. 1984. *Field Study Concerning Norwegian Financial Assistance to Small and Cottage Industries in Bangladesh* (Dhaka, Bangladesh: NORAD).

Pahl, R.E. 1980. "Employment, Work and the Domestic Division of Labor," *International Journal of Urban and Regional Research,* Vol. 4, No. 1, pp. 1-20.

Rahman, Atiq, and Rizwanul Islam. 1987. "An Empirical Account of Hired Labour Market in Rural Bangladesh," *The Bangladesh Journal of Development Studies,* Vol. 15, No. 1, pp. 129–142.

Roseberry, William. 1983. "From Peasant Studies to Proletarianization Studies," *Studies in Comparative International Development,* Vol. 18, No. 1/2, pp. 69–89.

Smith, Carol A. 1984. "Labor and International Capital in the Making of a Peripheral Social Formation: Economic Transformations in Guatemala, 1850–1980," in C. Bergquist, ed., *Labor in the Capitalist World-Economy* (Beverly Hills, Calif.: Sage Publications), pp. 135–156.

UNDP (United Nations Development Program). 1988. *Bangladesh Agriculture: Performance, Resources, Policies and Institutions* (Dhaka: Bangladesh Agriculture Sector Review).

Wennergren, E. Boyd. 1983. *An Assessment of the Agricultural Sector of Bangladesh* (Dhaka, Bangladesh: USAID).

Wood, Geof. 1978. "Class Differentiation and Power in Bandokgram: The Minifundist Case," in Ameerul Huq, ed., *Exploitation and the Rural Poor* (Comilla, Bangladesh: BARD), pp. 60–96.

————. 1981. "Rural Class Formation in Bangladesh, 1940–1980," *Bulletin of Concerned Asian Scholars,* Vol. 13, No. 4, pp. 2–17.

World Bank. 1983. *Bangladesh Selected Issues in Rural Employment,* World Bank Report No. 4292–BD (Washington, D.C.: World Bank).

————. 1986. "Rural Employment and the Urban Informal Sector," in *Bangladesh: Recent Economic Developments and Medium Term Prospects,* World Bank Report No. 6049 (Washington, D.C.: World Bank).

Zaman, H.Q. 1987. "Agrarian Structure, Rural Development and Class Formation in Bangladesh," in Chowdhury E. Haque, ed., *Bangladesh Politics, Economy and Society* (Winnipeg: University of Manitoba, Bangladesh Studies Assemblage), pp. 117–139.

5

Nonfarm Work in the Philippine Rural Economy: An Omen of Change or a Change of Omens?

Edna Angeles-Reyes

All the rural economies under analysis in this book have nontrivial incidences of growing nonfarm rural employment. The question is: What does this growth of nonfarm rural employment signify beyond the obvious fact of labor market differentiation? The question arises because of the diversities in the characteristics of agrarian organization, the levels of agricultural performance, the distribution of rural poverty, and the political economy of industrialization. Consequently, the answer to this question cannot be pursued in isolation from perspectives on the trajectory of the wider rural and national economies. In the case of the Philippines—with its history of sluggish industrialization, stagnant agricultural productivity growth, high population growth, and extensive and persistent rural poverty—a troubling question arises. Is a growth in nonfarm rural employment an omen of basic changes within the rural economy, or does it represent the appearance of a new omen for long-standing problems of low productivity?

In this chapter, I will trace the growth of nonfarm activities in the rural Philippines and examine the sources and consequences of this growth. In particular, I will describe the composition of nonfarm economic activities in the rural sector, how this has changed over time, and how this change has been influenced by the various policies and programs implemented by the government, both directly and indirectly.

The chapter is organized into two major sections. The first proceeds from the assumption that the evolution of the rural nonfarm sector must be understood in the context of structural change in the rural sector in general and the agricultural sector in particular. The second section discusses growth of the rural nonfarm sector with special attention to the kinds of nonfarm work available in terms of industry, occupation, sex, income, and linkages with agriculture. Data come primarily from the Census of Agriculture and the Integrated Survey of Households, each of which are conducted regularly by the National Statistics Office. Additional data come

from a series of intensive village and household surveys conducted by Yujiro Hayami and the International Rice Research Institute in Los Baños,
Laguna (Hayami, 1987; Hayami, Mariano, and Bambo, 1989).

The Rural Economy in the Philippines

The Philippine economy remains predominantly rural. Almost 60 percent
of the population still lives in rural areas. Agriculture continues to employ
half of the labor force; it contributes more than a quarter of gross domestic production and earns about two-fifths of export revenues (APST,
1986). No fundamental structural transformation has taken place in the
economy since the late 1960s. The proportion of the population classified
as living in rural areas has remained high despite significant rural-urban
migration flows: From 68.2 percent in 1970, the share of population living
in rural areas went down to 62.7 percent in 1980. Estimates of the National
Economic and Development Authority (NEDA) placed this share at 57
percent by 1992. Although the direction of change is consistent with expected forms of economic transformation in which the role of agriculture
declines relative to the roles of manufacturing and services, the rates of
change are considerably lower and the direction of change considerably
less consistent than what has been seen elsewhere in Southeast Asia
(Montes, 1991: 101–110).

The structure of production in the Philippine economy has changed little since the mid-1960s. Agriculture accounted for about a third of gross
domestic production in the 1960s. By 1980, agriculture's share had declined to about a quarter of GDP. However, the relative importance of
agriculture then *increased* during the mid-1980s to more than 28 percent
of GDP. This was matched by a significant decline of 11.5 percent in industry's relative share of GDP during the period 1980–1987. The decline
was associated with the collapse of the Philippine economy associated
with the accumulation of and subsequent default (in 1983) on a large external debt and the worsening of a domestic political crisis around the final
stages of the Ferdinand Marcos administration.

In terms of employment, the picture shows little change since 1960.
Industrial employment continues to hover between 9 and 11 percent of
total employment. Agriculture's share of total employment is the highest,
estimated to be 46.1 percent in 1988. This represents a decline from 1960
levels of more than 60 percent. However, because of problems in measuring income and occupational identification and given high levels of unemployment and underemployment, especially in rural areas, it is likely that
the proportion of the population dependent on agriculture as a principal
source of food and income exceeds the proportion of those estimated to be
in the labor force. Labor force participation is measured in the Philippines,

as it is in more advanced economies, by surveys to determine whether someone is employed or looking for employment at the time of the survey. But looking for employment in the sense of actively seeking work has little meaning in poor countries because in many cases, there is no employment to be had. It does not follow, however, that those who are not "actively looking" have voluntarily removed themselves from the labor force. Labor force participation is consequently underestimated, and the employment rate is actually overestimated (Tidalgo and Esguerra, 1984).

Nevertheless, there is strong evidence of significant change in the structure of employment in two areas. The employment sector that has grown the fastest has been the service sector: from 23 percent of employment in 1960 to a 38 percent share in 1988. This is problematic in developmental terms, however, because employment stability and wage levels in the service sector are both generally low. Although employment in manufacturing is typically regular salaried employment, employment in most service industries (as well as transport and construction) operates principally on the *pakyao* system, in which hiring and payment are conducted on a daily basis. What has also happened, especially since the early 1980s, is that new nonagricultural employment has gone more to females than males while lost employment affects males more than females. This reflects the growth and feminization of the service sector, the growth of female wage employment in industry, and the weaknesses of the Philippine labor movement outside of industrial activities (Koppel, 1992).

Numerous analyses have documented how both macroeconomic and sector-specific economic policies have suppressed the country's comparative advantage in agriculture by deepening an incentive structure that penalized the agricultural sector (David, 1983; de Dios, 1984; Clarete, 1985; Clarete and Roumasset, 1983; APST, 1986). In fact, the penalties imposed, if considered as implicit taxes, have been estimated to amount to more than 20 percent of the agricultural value added throughout the 1970s and 1980s. This has been a significant drain on the sector's resources, even when those resources were not in surplus. For example, biases in the government's industrialization strategies consistently favored capital-intensive, Manila-based industries and discouraged increased labor absorption in the industrial sector and decentralized industrial location. This placed an additional burden on the agricultural sector to absorb surplus labor in rural areas.

What is remarkable is that despite these problems, the agricultural sector, on the whole, has been a more efficient earner and saver of foreign exchange than the industrial sector (APST, 1986). However, this is only in comparison to a stagnant, protected, sometimes declining, and generally very inefficient industrial sector. In fact, many parts of the Philippine agricultural sector have maintained a predominantly subsistence character. In 1960, about two-thirds of all farms were planted to food crops. By 1980, this had not changed significantly.

What is most problematic about the Philippine agricultural sector is its continuing low productivity. For example, despite the presence of the International Rice Research Institute in the Philippines and extensive investment in irrigation, roads, and other agricultural and land infrastructure, Philippine rice, corn, and sugar yields have consistently remained among the lowest in Asia.[1] Moreover, since the early 1980s, agricultural productivity growth, already historically low, turned stagnant; for some crops, it was even negative. Exacerbating the income and employment effects of this lack of productivity growth is the fact that there is a long-term trend of a small-farm rural economy becoming an even smaller-farm rural economy. Average farm size has continuously declined, falling, for example, from 3.59 hectares in 1960 to 2.83 hectares in 1980. Similarly, the number of farms of less than 3 hectares increased by 58.8 percent over a three-decade period (Table 5.1). In the 1960s, 62.4 percent of the 2.17 million farms were less than 3 hectares. This figure declined slightly to 61.1 percent in 1971 but increased significantly again in 1980 to about 69 percent. This trend varies by crop (Castillo, 1979): In 1971, for example, 80 percent of tobacco farmers, 69 percent of rice farmers, 65 percent of corn farmers, and 79 percent of pineapple growers were operating farms of less than 3 hectares. However, only about 44 percent of the sugarcane and coconut farmers belonged to this category.

Although all these figures indicate the predominance of small farmers and the problem of low productivity, they do not present the entire picture. Indeed, the problems of low productivity, poverty, and rural unemployment are often seen as symptoms of a deeper issue: the social and political structure of Philippine agriculture. The total farm area operated remains largely in the hands of large farm owners (i.e., those with farms of 5 hectares or more). For instance, although only about 15 percent of the farms in 1971 were 5 hectares or larger, more than 50 percent of the total farm area was operated by farmers with 5 hectares or more. These farmers were primarily engaged in the production of pineapple, sugarcane, and banana.

Seventy percent of the pineapple farms are less than 3 hectares, but about 93 percent of the pineapple farmland is being operated on farms of 50 hectares or more. For sugarcane farms, about 44 percent are less than 3 hectares, but 66 percent of the sugar land is on 50-hectare or larger farms. About 82 percent of banana farms are smaller than 5 hectares, but 47 percent of the total banana-producing area is on farms of 10 hectares and more. This dualism is present even for basic food crops. For example, 90 percent of rice farms are smaller than 5 hectares, but 35 percent of all rice grown is cultivated on farms of 5 hectares or more. Eighty-seven percent of the corn farms are smaller than 5 hectares, but 42 percent of all corn lands are on farms of 5 hectares or more.

In 1960, the proportion of farms fully or partly owned was about 60 percent of the total farms reported; about 40 percent were tenanted under various arrangements (Table 5.2). The proportion of farms fully or partly owned increased to 69.3 percent in 1971 and 74.4 percent in 1980.[2] According to census data, the share of tenanted farms declined to 26.5 percent in 1971 and to 25.5 percent in 1980.

The case of rice and corn is of interest because these were the only crops covered by the land reform program of the Marcos government. Tenanted farms amounted to 36.8 percent of all rice farms and 30.4 percent of all corn farms in 1971. However, in terms of all farms, rice tenancy farms in 1971 constituted only 15.1 percent; corn tenancy farms represented just 6.8 percent of all farms. In other words, as of 1971, only 21.9 percent of all rice and corn farms, representing 13.2 percent of the farm area planted to rice and corn, were even subject to land reform. Gelia Castillo (1979: 41), on the basis of these figures and some additional information, has succinctly expressed reservations about the extent to which the land reform program could really change the patterns of landownership in the country.

> Considering that almost half of the tenanted rice and corn landholdings that are operated by 57% of the tenants are owned by landlords who have only 7 hectares or less and, therefore, are not likely to be included in land transfer to the tenants, the total effective hectarage for redistribution may be only about one-half of the tenanted rice and corn area, which roughly means less than 10% of total farm area. Land transfer, although regarded as a major instrument for achieving greater income equality, is not likely to drastically shake up the prevailing patterns of landownership because about three quarters of the farm area is operated by full or part-owners whose holdings are not part of the redistribution plan. Furthermore, their farms are larger than the tenanted farms. These data underscore the reality that the present land reform program cannot be expected to bring about equality or solve poverty in a major way.

This expectation was borne out (Koppel, 1987).

The farm size distribution and tenancy situation for agriculture is reflected in the overall income situation in the rural areas. In 1971, about 59 percent of all families in the country were classified as low-income, families—earning 3,000 pesos or less per month. Of those, 82 percent were living in the rural sector, with 69 percent of them engaged in agriculture (Castillo, 1979). Moreover, the urban-rural income gap, already substantial in the 1960s, widened in the 1980s. In 1971, for example, urban incomes were more than twice as high as rural incomes. A World Bank (1985) study estimated the number of families living in poverty in 1975 to be about 61 percent, some three-quarters of whom were in the rural areas. A 1984 report by the National Economic and Development Authority (NEDA) indicated that the number of poor families in rural areas increased from 2.5 million in 1971 to 2.8 million in 1980–1983. The NEDA study revealed that the urban-rural disparity widened as (1) underemployment in rural areas grew, (2) profit margins accruing to farmers went down, and

Table 5.1 Number and Distribution of Farms in the Philippines by Size, 1960, 1971, and 1980

	1960		1971		1980	
	No.	%	No.	%	No.	%
All farms	2,166,216	100.00	2,354,469	100.00	3,420,323	100.00
Under 1.00 ha.	249,773	11.53	319,363	13.56	775,791	22.68
1.00 to under 2.99 ha.	1,100,974	50.82	1,117,581	47.47	1,578,044	46.14
3.00 to under 4.99 ha.	404,882	18.69	558,347	23.71	588,151	17.20
5.00 to under 9.99 ha.	289,730	13.37	243,847	10.36	360,006	10.53
10.00 ha. and over	120,857	5.58	115,331	4.90	118,331	3.46

Sources: Republic of the Philippines, National Census and Statistics Office. *Census of Agriculture* (Manila: NCSO), various years.

Table 5.2 Number and Distribution of Farms in the Philippines by Tenure, 1960, 1971, and 1980

	1960		1971		1980	
	No.	%	No.	%	No.	%
All farms	2,166,216	100.00	2,354,469	100.00	3,420,323	100.00
Owned	967,725	44.67	1,364,990	57.97	1,993,293	58.28
Partly owned	310,944	14.35	268,665	11.41	367,304	10.74
Tenanted/leased	864,538	39.91	624,821	26.54	871,536	25.48
Other farms	23,009	1.06	95,993	4.08	188,190	5.50

Sources: Republic of the Philippines, National Census and Statistics Office. *Census of Agriculture* (Manila: NCSO), various years.

(3) labor productivity in agriculture continuously declined. Reyes, Milan, and Sanchez (1989) show that labor productivity in agriculture fell at an average rate of 0.53 percent from 1980 to 1985—a drastic decline from an average growth rate of 4.92 percent in 1975–1980. In 1985–1987, the level of productivity improved slightly at an annual growth rate averaging 0.78 percent.

Using the "bottom 30 percent" definition and the per capita income cutoff of 1,269 pesos, based on the Family Income and Expenditure Surveys (FIES) in 1985, around 3.1 million families were identified in the bottom 30 percent of the income distribution. Of these families, 72.8 percent were in the agricultural sector (NEDA, 1989). Among those who are considered to be particularly poor in the rural areas, the largest groups are the families of corn and coconut farmers, subsistence fishermen, and landless laborers (DAR, 1989). It is relatively easy to get actual figures for the first group of farmers, but the size of the last two groups is more difficult to estimate for no direct measure is possible given available census and survey data. There are numerous studies of these groups, especially the landless laborers (see studies cited in Castillo, 1979), but they do not provide a basis for reliable national estimates. However, if the census figures on wage and salaried workers in agriculture are at all indicative, then the extent of landlessness amounted to 1.2 million in 1980 but rose to 2 million by 1986 (Koppel, 1992: 127). The severity of poverty among landless farm laborers has been cited in various studies for different areas in the country. For instance, USAID (1981) demonstrated that for the Bicol region, the incidence of poverty was highest among farm laborers and among farmers cultivating crops other than rice, corn, and coconut (Table 5.3).

Trends in Labor Absorption in the Rural Sector

The total labor force in the rural sector has been increasing by about 4.1 percent annually (Table 5.4), which is approximately 40 percent greater than the expansion rate of the rural population between 1975 and 1988. The labor force participation rate has been increasing, too. As of 1988, the rural labor force participation rate was 67.7 percent. However, two points should be noted here. First, growth in reported labor participation (0.7 percent annually) has been significantly *lower* than growth in the rural labor force. Second, as discussed earlier, the reported participation and employment rates are very sensitive to the definition of participation and employment and the timing of measurement surveys.

In terms of occupational distribution, agriculture is predominant, although its share declined about 12 percent over a period of twenty-three years (Table 5.5). From about 74 percent of total rural employment in 1965, this share dropped to 64 percent by 1988. The shift has primarily

Table 5.3 Incidence of Poverty in Selected Agricultural Occupations and
         Subsectors in Bicol, 1981

Selected Agricultural Occupation and Subsectors	Percentage of Poor
Farmer owner	59.5
Farmer part-owner	57.8
Farmer tenant	66.1
Farmer (not specified) and tuber gatherers	73.9
Farm laborer	80.0
Fishermen	55.6
Subsector	
Rice and corn farming	60.8
Coconut farming	70.3
Other crops	76.6
Fishing	55.6

Source: USAID (1981: p. 6).

Table 5.4 Rural Labor Force Participation Rate and Employment Status in
         Bicol, 1975–1988 (number of persons in the labor force in thousands)

	Labor Force Participation Rate (%)	Total Labor Force	Employed		Unemployed		Underemployed	
			No.	%	No.	%	No.	%
1976	61.7	10,045	9,690	96.5	355	3.5	2,650	27.35
1977	59.6	10,049	9,739	96.9	310	3.1	1,801	18.49
1978	65.1	11,390	11,020	96.8	370	3.2	2,158	20.06
1980	62.2	12,056	11,614	96.3	442	3.7	2,691	23.17
1981	64.4	12,847	12,339	96.0	508	4.0	3,182	25.79
1982	62.0	12,751	12,211	95.8	540	4.2	3,201	26.21
1983	67.3	14,243	13,709	96.3	534	3.7	4,085	33.45
1984	66.9	13,202	12,738	96.5	464	3.5	4,714	36.96
1985	66.0	13,426	12,841	95.6	585	4.4	3,218	25.06
1986	66.3	14,030	13,480	96.1	549	3.9	3,986	32.36
1987	68.2	14,316	13,339	93.2	978	6.8	3,661	27.35
1988	67.7	16,631	13,766	94.1	865	5.9	3,593	26.10

Source: NEDA (1989: pp. 11-1–11-2).
Note: Data on years 1975–1986 were based on the past third quarter reference period, data
on 1987 were based on the past week reference period.

been to services, wholesale and retail trade, and transportation, storage,
and communications. The majority of workers in rural areas are own-
account workers, mostly in agriculture (Table 5.6). What is noteworthy,

Table 5.5 Rural Employment by Industry in the Philippines, 1965–1988 (in thousands)

Major Industry Group	1965 No.	1965 %	1975 No.	1975 %	1980 No.	1980 %	1985 No.	1985 %	1988 No.	1988 %
Agricultural, fishery, and forestry	5,545	73.7	7,053	74.3	7,885	67.9	8,546	66.6	8,885	64.5
Mining and quarrying	20	0.3	27	0.3	80	0.7	100	0.8	121	0.9
Manufacturing	653	8.7	711	7.5	925	8	931	7.1	1,026	7.4
Electricity, gas, and water	0		.9	0.1	27	0.2	28	0.2	31	0.2
Construction	162	2.2	200	2.1	313	2.7	322	2.5	399	2.9
Wholesale and retail trade	522	6.9	614	6.5	839	7.2	1,112	8.1	1,326	9.6
Transportation, storage, and communications	144	1.9	241	2.5	336	2.9	407	3.2	430	3.1
Financing, insurance, real estate, and business services	0		0		87	0.7	86	0.7	87	0.6
Commercial, social, and personal services	468	6.2	620	6.5	1,118	9.6	1,309	10.2	1,459	10.6
Industry, not adequately defined			16	0.2	4	0.03	0			
Total	7,527		9,491		11,614		12,841		13,766	

Source: Republic of the Philippines, National Statistics Office, computer tapes.

Table 5.6 Rural Employment by Class of Worker in the Philippines, 1965–1988 (in thousands)

Class of Workers	1965 No.	1965 %	1975 No.	1975 %	1980 No.	1980 %	1985 No.	1985 %	1988 No.	1988 %
Wage and salary workers	1,774	23.6	2,548	26.8	3,498	30.1	4,315	33.6	4,903	35.6
Own-account workers	3,509	46.6	4,210	44.4	5,161	44.5	5,845	45.5	6,013	43.7
Unpaid family workers	2,237	29.7	2,720	28.7	2,954	25.4	2,681	20.9	2,850	20.7
Total	7,527		9,491		11,614		12,841		13,766	

Source: Republic of the Philippines, National Statistics Office, computer tapes.

however, is the continuous increase in the shares of own-account and un-paid family workers and the decreasing shares of wage and salary work-ers in total rural income. The share of own-account and unpaid family workers increased from about 24 percent in 1965 to 36 percent in 1988, an increase of roughly 51 percent in a span of more than twenty years.

Major Policy and Institutional Changes

There is a long history of government policies aimed at redressing poverty and improving productivity and overall welfare in the Philippine rural sec-tor. Agrarian reform has been viewed as perhaps the most potent policy for addressing the roots of persistent poverty in the Philippines. The nation's experience with land reform dates back to the start of the twentieth cen-tury, when the United States purchased church lands for redistribution to tenant farmers. The program was a failure as a reform of agrarian structure associated with overcoming poverty, low productivity, and social stratifi-cation, but it was successful in building a rural elite loyal to the United States. Most of the redistributed lands eventually went to large corpora-tions and wealthy families (Thiesenhusen, 1990). Succeeding programs under different administrations were primarily a reaction to peasant unrest and insurgency activities and were focused more on regulating tenancy con-tracts than on restructuring the distribution of land ownership. These pro-grams had little effect on the conditions and prospects of Filipino peasants.

For example, legislation enacted during the Ramon Magsaysay era (1953–1955) was heavily diluted by the landholding members of Congress who provided for a large landlord retention limit. Lands planted to export crops were excluded, and the program also suffered from a lack of ade-quate funding for administration. Similarly, the Operation Land Transfer program of the Diosdado Macapagal administration in the mid-1960s ben-efited relatively few peasants, continued the exclusion of lands planted to export crops, and was plagued by the same problems of inadequate politi-cal and financial support that paralyzed previous programs. In addition, the Macapagal land reform, like the earlier Magsaysay land reform, relied on resettlement on public lands (particularly in Mindanao) as a way to relieve pressures in areas of Central Luzon in particular. Often, the amount of land provided was inadequate (James, 1983). Moreover, by the early 1960s, most public land that was available had been settled (Crisotomo-David and Barker, 1972).

Presidential Decree (PD) 27 was issued in 1973, early in the Marcos martial law period, making land reform the flagship program of the New Society. The law covered all farms planted to rice and corn throughout the country. It also lowered the ceiling for landholdings to 7 hectares. The law stipulated that share tenants who were renting land from a holding of 7 hectares or more could purchase land they tilled up to a maximum of

3 hectares for irrigated land and 5 hectares for nonirrigated land, subject to the landlord's retention rights; share tenants on holdings of less than 7 hectares would become leaseholders. The lease rent was fixed at 25 percent of the average normal harvest for three years before 1972, net of seed and other costs. Landlords were to be compensated following a complex and continually controversial formula. Under this program, tenants were issued Certificates of Land Transfer (CLTs) at the time of land transfer and an Emancipation Patent (EP) when payments were completed. The issuance of an EP required membership in an agrarian reform cooperative called a *Samahang Nayon*. It is estimated that about one-third (190,000) of the potential beneficiaries received EPs covering 265,000 hectares. This translates to an average of only 1.4 hectares of farm land per beneficiary.

The program had serious defects. One was the lack of support services to the new landholders. This became more serious as the government's overall ability to provide support services declined due to domestic budget problems and the farmers' growing credit indebtedness to the system, rising input prices, and declining rice prices. As a result, some farmers had to sell out. Others covertly sublet their lands to a new set of tenants, often rural landless and marginal peasants.

A second major defect was that the reform in one sense bypassed and in another sense exacerbated the problem of rural landlessness and unemployment. It bypassed the problem by focusing only on tenants, and it exacerbated the problem by recognizing only primary tenancy and ignoring complex patterns of subtenancy. The effect was to convert significant numbers of marginal peasants (estimated at 50,000 households) into landless workers (Ledesma, 1982). Other problems included the tendency to distribute poor-quality lands; the slow rates at which CLTs and EPs were distributed; the exemption of all nontenanted lands, which prompted landlords to ease out tenants; the fact that coverage was restricted to only corn and rice lands; the continuing exemption of plantation crops and exportables; and finally, the high land-payment defaults among beneficiaries, which ran as high as 90 percent.

The impacts of agrarian reform on farm incomes and productivity of beneficiaries have been studied extensively, and the consensus is that though farm incomes and/or productivity did improve, these improvements were not directly due to tenurial change per se. The change in tenure status experienced by beneficiaries gave them collateral that they could use to increase their access to and utilization of production inputs. At the same time, however, this relationship forced some beneficiaries to sell out because of the indebtedness they accumulated.

When the Corazon Aquino government took over, land reform was again made the centerpiece of the state's rural development program. Supposedly more comprehensive in coverage, the program encompassed about 10.3 million hectares and, if fully implemented, would have affected about

3.9 million households. However, implementation of the program did not move far beyond the areas originally targeted in the Marcos land reform. Neither the political will nor the needed financial resources were available (e.g., Koppel, 1987; Koppel et al., 1988) to extend comprehensive land reform to agricultural lands beyond the rice and corn properties already designated by the Marcos program.

Consequently, the rural economy of the Philippines has remained strongly agrarian—with increasing numbers of small farms, low productivity, and some degree of technological and scale dualism between food crop and export crop production. The predominance of agrarian characteristics is not limited to prevailing modes of production and foundations for rural income and employment, although those would be important enough. The rural economy is predominantly agrarian in a political sense as well because local politics and power structures continue to be significantly built on control over agricultural resources and the concentration and exercise of agrarian power. As already noted, the rural economy has also historically been the target of a macroeconomic policy regime and a broader political economy that is oriented in favor of an (unsuccessful) import-substitution industrialization strategy, along with managed domestic competition, and against fundamental alterations in the economy's structural characteristics. These biases have been unfavorable for agriculture but not necessarily for agrarian power. This is because traditional agrarian power in the Philippines has two faces. One face looks toward the rural economy and is clearly agrarian. The other face, however, looks toward a range of urban and industrial activities (such as manufacturing, insurance, and real estate).

Growth of the Rural Nonfarm Sector

Some Conceptual Issues

Economic theorizing within neoclassical economics on the growth of the nonfarm sector was pioneered by Stephen Hymer and Stephen Resnick (1969) with the introduction of the so-called Z-goods sector. The major proposition of the H-R paradigm was that in a two-sector agrarian economy, nonagricultural activities (Z-activities) will decline as the economy grows. The critical assumption is that Z-activities producing Z-goods are basically small household or village activities that are primarily geared for home consumption and that these goods are of inferior quality compared with imported goods produced in the urban/metropolitan areas, the supply of which tends to increase as the economy expands.

Attempts to further study the displacement phenomenon espoused in the H-R model resulted in various propositions. For instance, utilizing a small, open, two-sector model composed of an agricultural sector and the

Z-goods sector, R. Bautista (1971) pointed out that inferiority of the Z-goods is not sufficient to bring about decline in the sector. Further, Raul Fabella (1985: 499) showed that "in a rural economy model with a food sector, a more dynamic manufacturing sector and a Z-goods sector, it is specialization in commodities where the rural economy has some comparative advantage rather than inferiority that dictates the rise of the more dynamic manufacturing sector and augurs the demise of the Z-goods sector."

The experience of the East Asian countries provided an exception to the conclusions of the H-R model. Oshima (1984), for instance, has shown that off-farm incomes in Japan, Korea, and Taiwan have experienced substantial increases in both levels and shares as these countries moved through various stages of development. Oshima (1987) offers a model involving different stages of growth that aptly captures the growth experiences of the Asian countries with emphasis on the role of the nonagricultural activities and incomes. The focus of his discussion is the argument that, basically, it is the low farm incomes in monsoon settings that have held back Asia historically and that the transition from agriculture to industry is not possible without a substantial and sustained rise in these incomes. Farm family incomes must rise not only with an increase in yields per hectare but with multiple-cropping and diversification and with nonagricultural activities. His framework basically involves a three-stage agro-industrial transition and, ultimately, movement to a service-oriented economy.

In the first stage of the agro-industrial transition, nonagricultural activities are largely traditional, and the supply of labor is largely seasonal. The volume of nonagricultural activities is large in employment terms but small in value because of low productivity and earnings, which are lower than those in agriculture on a per day basis. These nonagricultural opportunities would be in transport, construction, and services. In the middle stage of the first transition, there is a rise in semimodern industries and further improvement in infrastructure facilities; with a rise in farm incomes, demands for nonagricultural goods expands—demands that are then easily supplied by the growing import-substituting industries in cities. The semimodern industrial activities are higher valued and use more capital-intensive technologies; hence, they are larger than the traditional handicraft production in homes. This is particularly true with the labor-intensive factories in urban centers to which farm workers begin to commute to work for periods longer than a season. In effect, the commitment to nonfarm work is enhanced with better roads and transportation facilities. In the later stage of the first transition, off-farm work in manufacturing takes the lead over construction and services. Handicraft industries continue to decline, but this decline is matched by an expansion of factory industries. The labor-intensive industries may start to produce goods for export. There is also an expansion of crop diversification, and the commercialization of agriculture reduces subsistence farming.

A second transition is primarily marked by a major acceleration in nonagricultural incomes. Labor scarcities emerge as full employment is attained. Meanwhile, migration to big cities in response to higher wages slows down. As the cities expand, smaller firms start to move toward areas heavily populated by farm workers. With the expansion of education toward these areas, firms are able to get more workers, who can be paid lower wages than in the big cities. Thus, the proliferation of smaller enterprises in rural areas results in increased nonagricultural income for rural workers.

The third stage of the transition is the final move toward a service society. In this stage, modern services dominate the economy. Trade declines and is replaced by personal services as the dominant activity in the services sector. Higher-valued services in education, health, recreation, and culture increase significantly.

These various developmental stages summarize what happened especially in Japan, Taiwan, and Korea. Gustav Ranis (1990) attempted to develop variants of the H-R model to describe the experiences of the Philippines and Taiwan. They came up with both colonial and postcolonial archetypes, each one having both favorable and unfavorable cases. In doing this, they pointed to several major departures from the H-R model.

1. In the H-R model, the Z-goods sector is considered to be broadly homogeneous and carried out in individual households or at the village level. In fact, Z-goods are not really homogeneous. Nonagricultural activities range from very small-scale household and village production to small modern factories using modern technology and producing higher-quality products. Hence, the Z-sector is divided into one sector covering traditional household and village production and another sector covering the nontraditional modern rural industries.

2. The existence of a U-sector (a modern industrial sector located predominantly in urban areas) results in a U-displacement—the U-sector displaces the Z-goods. This is more dominant than the displacement of Z-goods by imports.

3. The agricultural sector should be divided into two subsectors—the agricultural cash crop export sector and the domestically oriented food-producing agricultural sector. The former is usually capital intensive, and it operates in large units with hired wage workers. The latter is based on small owner-operated holdings and is labor intensive. Domestically oriented agriculture has growth potential as land- and labor-augmenting technologies are applied to modern seed varieties. This means it can release land and labor for other uses. Increasing farm incomes also give rise to stronger linkages between domestic agriculture and rural nonagriculture.

4. The H-R assumption of improving terms of trade or improving opportunities for export agriculture does not seem to hold true in the
postcolonial era. The terms of trade of most less-developed countries (LDCs) have either remained constant or deteriorated.

The application of the model puts the Philippines under the unfavorable colonial category, which basically resembles the H-R case. In the
postcolonial era, the Philippines exhibits both favorable and unfavorable
characteristics.

Trends in Rural Nonfarm Work

Various estimates of the size of the nonfarm sector in the country use rural
nonfarm employment or income as indicators. For example, Fabella (1985)
and Oshima (1987) estimate the share of off-farm income of farm households in the Philippines to be over 30 percent. Using a less liberal definition of farm households, distinguishing specifically between farmers and
part-time farmers, F. Medalla (n.d.) suggests that the average share of
strictly off-farm rural incomes could be lower than 10 percent.

The share of nonfarm employment relative to total employment in the
rural sector has been increasing but at a relatively slow pace (Table 5.7).
The proportion of workers engaged in nonagricultural activities was close
to 36 percent in 1988, an increase of about 35 percent over a period of
twenty-three years. This contrasts with Taiwan, where the share of labor
force in nonagricultural activities increased from 29 percent in 1956 to 67
percent in 1980—an increase of 131 percent in a span of some twenty-four
years (Ranis and Stewart, 1990).

Table 5.7   Distribution of Rural Employment in the Philippines in Agricultural
and Nonagricultural Activities, 1965–1988 (percent)

	Agricultural	Nonagricultural
1965	73.7	26.3
1975	74.3	25.7
1980	67.9	32.1
1985	66.6	33.4
1988	64.5	35.5

Source: Republic of the Philippines, National Census and Statistics Office. *National Sample
Survey of Households, Labor Force Surveys* (Manila: NCSO-NSSH), various years.

Looking more closely at the occupational distribution of rural workers
doing nonagricultural work, the share of manufacturing declined while there
was a significant increase in the shares of services and trade (Table 5.8).

The increasing participation of females in the rural labor market is also evident. The proportion of females in the rural labor force has increased from about 30 percent in 1965 to 34 percent in 1988.

Previous studies have claimed that much of the nonagricultural employment in rural areas is temporary work due to the seasonal nature of work in agriculture. This implies that during peak agricultural seasons, there should be less employment in nonagricultural activities. Fabella (1985) demonstrated some seasonal variation in the share of the labor force in nonagricultural activities. Slight variations were evident in the share of nonagricultural activities for males, with the peak season share being lower than that of the slack season. This trend was also evident among females and wage and salary workers, whose shares tended to fall somewhat during the peak month. However, on the whole, his general observation was that "while there appears to be some competition for labor across seasons, the nonagricultural activities seem to hold their own pretty well" (Fabella, 1985: 503). The explanation offered was the possibility that some components of nonagricultural activities are largely complementary to rather than competing with agriculture. Further, the existence of surplus labor allows for less competition for labor between the two sectors.

Table 5.9 similarly suggests that among wage and salary workers, the nonagriculture share was increasing until 1980 and ranged from 60 percent to 69 percent. Even among own-account workers, the nonagricultural share rose to nearly 28 percent by 1988. Because the proportion of females among wage and salary workers has also been increasing, it is likely that the participation of females who are wage and salary workers in nonagricultural work has also been increasing.

In terms of off-farm income, the share of nonagricultural sources has also been increasing. From about 49 percent in 1971, this share went up to 53 percent in 1985, and further to 57 percent in 1988 (Tables 5.10, 5.11, and 5.12). The bulk of this income originated from wages and salaries, with about half as much coming from entrepreneurial sources.

On the demand side, there is little information available to indicate the size of the rural nonfarm sector. However, a survey of establishments in regions outside metro Manila conducted jointly by NEDA and the University of the Philippines Institute for Small Scale Industries does provide some useful information. The survey sample included establishments that were primarily rural-based. Micro-, cottage-, and small-sized establishments were included.[3]

Data from the survey reveal that 52 percent of all enterprises were manufacturing concerns, with trading and services comprising 27 and 21 percent, respectively. In terms of actual sizes measured by employment size, most of the manufacturing establishments employed less than 10 workers, with about 61 percent of them employing only 1 to 3 workers. The same was true for trading and service activities, where establishments

Table 5.8 Distribution of Rural Employment in the Philippines by Industry and Sex, 1965–1988 (percentage)

Major Industry Group	1965			1975			1980			1985			1988		
	Total	Male	Female	Total	Male	Female	Total	Male	Female	Total	Male	Female	Total	Male	Female
Agriculture, fishery, and forestry	73.7	78.2	21.8	74.3	79.6	20.4	67.3	75.7	24.3	66.6	73.8	26.2	64.5	73.6	26.1
Mining and quarrying	0.3	100.0		0.3	96.3	0.6	0.7	82.5	13.8	0.8	42.0	7.0	0.9	89.2	10.7
Manufacturing	8.7	32.9	67.1	7.5	41.9	58.1	8.0	46.5	53.4	7.2	43.9	56.1	7.4	47.0	53.0
Electricity, gas, and water	0			0.1	100.0	0	0.2	92.6	7.4	0.2	78.6	21.4	0.2	80.6	19.4
Construction	2.2	97.5	2.5	2.1	99.0	1.0	2.7	98.7	1.0	2.5	98.4	1.2	2.9	99.5	0.5
Wholesale and retail trade	6.9	34.1	65.9	6.5	33.6	66.4	7.2	28.1	71.9	8.6	27.2	72.8	9.6	28.7	71.3
Transportation, storage, and communications	1.9	96.5	2.5	2.5	97.9	2.1	2.9	98.5	1.5	3.2	97.5	2.5	3.1	97.9	2.1
Financing, insurance, real estate, and business services	0			0			0.7	74.7	25.3	0.7	70.9	29.1	0.6	70.1	24.9
Commercial, social, and personal services	6.2	45.7	54.3	6.5	43.9	55.8	9.6	44.9	55.1	10.2	39.6	60.4	10.6	44.3	55.7
Industry, not adequately defined or reported	0			0											
Total	100.0	70.1	29.9	100.0	72.3a	27.7	100.0	68.3	31.7	100.0	65.6	34.4	100.0	66.1	33.9

Source: Republic of the Philippines, National Statistics Office, computer tapes.
a Of this total, 0.2 percent is from "Industry, not adequately defined."

Table 5.9   Distribution of Rural Employment in the Philippines by Agricultural
and Nonagricultural Activities and Class of Worker, 1965–1988
(percentage)

	Wage and Salary Workers	Own-account Workers	Unpaid Family Workers
Agricultural			
1965	40.36	77.54	94.23
1975	42.03	81.02	94.41
1980	31.05	79.52	91.23
1985	39.17	74.92	92.39
1988	40.28	72.33	89.86
Nonagricultural			
1965	59.64	22.46	5.77
1975	57.97	18.98	5.59
1980	68.95	20.48	8.77
1985	60.83	25.08	7.01
1988	59.72	27.67	10.14

Sources: Republic of the Philippines, National Census and Statistics Office. *National Sample Survey of Households, Labor Force Surveys* (Manila: NCSO-NSSH), various years.

Table 5.10   Distribution of Rural Families and Income in the Philippines by
Source of Income, 1971 (percentage)

Main Source of Income	Families	Income
Wages and salaries	33.1	35.1
Agricultural	14.0	10.6
Nonagricultural	19.0	24.5
Entrepreneurial activities	61.7	48.9
Trading	4.3	5.5
Manufacturing	2.7	2.8
Transport	1.3	2.0
Other enterprises	0.5	0.6
Practice of profession or trade	0.4	0.7
Farming (livestock and poultry)	47.3	31.8
Fishing, forestry, and hunting	5.3	5.4
Other	5.2	15.1
Share of crops and livestock from others	1.9	2.6
Rent received from land and other properties	0.1	0.5
Rental value for owner-occupied house	0	6.6
Interest and dividends	0.0	0.2
Profits from sale of stocks and bonds	0	0.0
Pension and retirement benefits, etc.	0.6	1.6
Backpay and proceeds from insurance	0.0	0.1
Gifts, support, assistance, and relief	1.9	2.5
Net winning from gambling and sweepstakes	0.2	0.4
Inheritance in cash or converted to cash	0.3	0.4
Others	0.1	0.1

Source: Republic of the Philippines, National Statistics Office, computer tapes.

Table 5.11   Distribution of Rural Families and Income in the Philippines by Source of Income, FIES 1985 (percentage)

Main Source of Income	Families	Income	Average Income (Pesos per Year)
Wages and salaries	32.71	33.98	22,719
Agricultural	12.92	9.81	16,615
Nonagricultural	19.79	24.16	26,705
Entrepreneurial activities	50.70	47.02	20,288
Crop farming and gardening	33.16	28.38	18,719
Livestock and poultry raising	1.07	0.96	19,720
Fishing	6.50	5.20	17,489
Forestry and hunting	0.84	0.59	15,439
Wholesale and retail trade	5.54	6.96	27,489
Manufacturing	1.74	2.00	25,058
Commodity, social, recreational, and personal services	0.59	0.86	31,753
Transportation, storage, and communication services	0.86	1.63	41,331
Mining and quarrying	0.31	0.32	22,667
Construction	0.05	0.07	32,339
Entrepreneurial activities, no economic classification	0.04	0.07	32,891
Other sources of income	16.58	19.00	25,064
Net share of crops, fruits, vegetables, livestock, and poultry from other households	2.47	2.39	21,177
Cash receipts, gifts, and other forms of assistance from abroad	3.67	8.96	53,432
Cash receipts, support assistance, and relief from domestic sources	3.29	2.08	13,812
Rental from nonagricultural lands, building spaces, and other properties	0.11	0.15	28,965
Pension and retirement, workman's compensation, and social security benefits	0.77	1.09	31,100
Dividends from investment	0.01	0.02	42,379
Imputed rental value of owner-occupied dwelling units	0.88	0.80	19,689
Net receipt from family sustenance activities	3.67	1.96	11,677
Goods and services received as gifts	1.61	1.25	17,035
Other sources of income	0.07	0.06	19,285

Source: Republic of the Philippines, National Census and Statistics Office. *Family Income and Expenditure Survey,* computer tapes, 1985.
Note: Average annual income for rural families is P21,875.

employing 1 to 3 workers represented 64 percent and 71 percent, respectively, of all such enterprises. This clearly indicates the relative smallness of establishments in the rural areas.

Linkages Between Agriculture
and the Rural Nonagricultural Sector

Linkages between agriculture and the rural nonagricultural sector can go both ways. The agriculture-to-industry linkages can be classified into consumption, backward, and forward linkages. These linkages are commonly exemplified by the significant association between income in agriculture and nonagricultural employment and income. In the other direction, the industry-to-agriculture linkage is based on the hypothesis that nearby industrial and urban growth reduces the imperfections in both factor and product markets faced by agriculture and thereby raises farm income per worker (Ranis, Stewart, and Reyes, 1990).

Several studies have been undertaken to investigate the magnitude of these linkages in the Philippines, particularly those of the first type, in terms of the effect of agricultural growth on nonagricultural employment and income. The most recent efforts include those by Ranis, Stewart, and Reyes (1990) and Ranis (1990). The results of the various studies on the magnitude and nature of these linkages have been summarized in Ranis, Stewart, and Reyes (1990).

1. The linkage effects from additional agricultural output are very substantial, even where policies are not especially conducive to promoting them. In the Gapan area of Nueva Ecija province (Central Luzon), increases in agricultural productivity of 5.5 percent per annum (1961–1967) and 8.2 percent per annum (1967–1971) were accompanied by annual increases of 8.2 percent and 9.0 percent in nonagricultural employment (Gibbs, 1974).
2. Rural nonagricultural employment is dominated by consumption-linkage activities. This is also supported by aggregate data presented earlier in this chapter for areas where most of the rural nonfarm employment occurred in trade and services.
3. Increases in agricultural output are accompanied by high increases in all types of linked activities.
4. Among production-related activities, forward linkages are of much greater significance for absolute employment and employment expansion than backward linkages.
5. The ranking of linkages in terms of employment derives partly from the labor intensity of the different types of activities.

As for the industry-to-agriculture linkage, the studies of C. Luna (1982) and E. Pernia and V. Hermoso (1983) provide some evidence on the positive effects of this type of linkage on agricultural productivity. Ranis, Stewart, and Reyes (1990) likewise found the effects of a linkage indicator like roads to be positive for agricultural productivity in Bicol.

Table 5.12   Distribution of Rural Families and Income in the Philippines by Source of Income, FIES 1988 (percentage)

Main Source of Income	Families	Income	Average Income (Pesos per Year)
Wages and salaries	37.07	41.87	31,431
Agricultural	13.35	10.52	21,933
Nonagricultural	23.72	31.35	36,778
Entrepreneurial activities	47.89	43.10	25,042
Crop farming and gardening	29.64	24.08	22,602
Livestock and poultry raising	1.20	1.23	28,539
Fishing	6.49	4.93	21,149
Forestry and hunting	0.63	0.50	22,019
Wholesale and retail trade	5.46	7.26	37,020
Manufacturing	1.69	1.82	29,840
Commodity, social, recreational, and personal services	0.94	1.09	32,168
Transportation, storage, and communication services	1.11	1.53	38,429
Mining and quarrying	0.36	0.32	24,390
Construction	0.27	0.25	26,114
Entrepreneurial activities, no economic classification	0.10	0.10	28,044
Other sources of income	15.04	15.03	27,804
Net share of crops, fruits, vegetables, livestock, and poultry from other households	2.16	1.70	21,851
Cash receipts, gifts, and other forms of assistance from abroad	4.08	7.49	51,033
Cash receipts, support assistance, and relief from domestic sources	3.72	2.33	17,428
Rental from nonagricultural lands, building spaces, and other properties	0.19	0.25	36,615
Interest from deposits and loans[a]	0.07	0.07	29,261
Pension and retirement, workman's compensation, and social security benefits	0.81	0.97	33,283
Dividends from investment	0.02	0.01	16,565
Imputed rental value of owner-occupied dwelling units	0.56	0.46	22,716
Net receipt from family sustenance activities	1.81	0.81	12,472
Goods and services received as gifts	1.56	0.91	16,228
Other sources of income	0.06	0.03	16,254

Source: Republic of the Philippines, National Census and Statistics Office. *Family Income and Expenditure Survey,* computer, 1988.
Note: Average annual income is P27,826.
[a]Not covered in the 1985 survey.

Further, the distance from the nearest urban center and the presence of modern establishments were found to be significantly and positively related to agricultural productivity.

Observations from Laguna: A Microlevel Case

This section provides a picture of the evolution and growth of nonfarm activities at the micro level. It also provides evidence to support the macro observations made in the earlier sections.[4]

Village Characteristics

The area of study is a village in Laguna, a province located south of Manila. Irrigation systems are relatively well developed in this province so that rice production can be practiced in both wet and dry seasons in most paddy fields. The village is one of the thirteen *barangays* (villages) in the municipality of Pila. It is located in a coconut grove surrounded by paddy fields. It is about 2 kilometers from a larger town (with a population of around 77,000 in 1989) and about 120 kilometers from Manila. The village had a population of 816, belonging to 156 households. The dominant occupation of the population was rice farming. The coconut grove covered an area of 19.7 hectares, with 6.1 hectares owned by the villagers and 13.6 hectares owned by absentee landowners. The total rice area cultivated by villagers in 1974, 111.5 hectares, declined to 91.6 hectares in 1987, reflecting the fact that a sizable amount had been transferred to nonvillager cultivation. Indeed, absentee landlords were common, with more than 80 percent of paddy fields owned by nonvillagers.

In 1966, the village had a population of 66 households (composed of 392 people). This grew to 156 households (816 people) in 1987. The village had an annual population growth rate of 3.5 percent, which was above the national average. From the mid-1960s to the end of the 1970s, the village population growth rate was above 4 percent—roughly a quarter higher than the national average. In the 1980s, the growth rate slowed to 2.2 percent. The unusually high rate of population growth resulted from both high birthrates and in-migration to the village. The deceleration in population growth rates in the 1980s was caused by falling birthrates and the out-migration of more educated villagers, which was facilitated by the improvements in the highway system, especially toward the end of the 1970s.

Rice farming is the major occupation of the people and the chief source of their work and income. The introduction of new, high-yielding rice varieties, coupled with increased application of fertilizers and chemicals and better irrigation facilities, brought about significant increases in agricultural production. Practically all the farms use the new seed varieties. Paddy yields per hectare increased by 60 percent from the mid-1960s to the mid-1980s. Further, there was no significant difference in average yield between large and small farmers. In 1987, 84 percent of the adult male population and 35 percent of the "economically active" adult females were engaged in rice farming. A majority of the farms are small, with the average size having fallen from 2.6 hectares in 1966 to 1.7 hectares in 1987. In 1966, 70 percent of the households were farmers, and 30 percent were landless workers. By 1987, this apportionment had almost completely reversed: Some 34 percent were farmers, and the proportion of landless households had increased to 66 percent. Size distribution of farms has become more unequal, an observation consistent with that for the whole country. In 1966, 13 percent of the farmers were cultivating farms of 1 hectare or less, accounting for 3 percent of the land area. About 7 percent had farms of 5 hectares or over, covering 16 percent of the total rice area in the village. In 1987, the proportion of small farms increased to 26 percent, accounting for 8 percent of the total area, and 6 percent of farmers were operating farms of 5 hectares or more, accounting for 22 percent of the total land area. Over four-fifths of the paddy fields were owned by absentee landlords, with most of them living in nearby areas.

Village Nonagricultural Activities

The increase in the number of landless laborers—a result of the relative scarcity of land, of land reform regulations that effectively abolished subtenancy contracts, and patterns of land ownership consolidation associated with indebtedness—released labor for nonfarm work. This is clearly evident in Tables 5.13 and 5.14, which give the occupation of the economically active male and female populations in the village. In 1974, the major occupations of 7.7 percent of the economically active males were outside agriculture. By 1987, this had risen to 11 percent. The share of landless male workers doing nonfarm work increased from 0 percent in 1974 to 10.9 percent by 1987. Among the economically active females, 8 percent were working outside of agriculture in 1974, as were 28 percent in 1987.

Similarly, nonagricultural income rose from 8.1 percent in 1974 to 36 percent in 1987 (Table 5.15). The bulk of the increase was shared proportionately by small farmers and landless workers. This suggests that nonagricultural income had an equalizing effect on income distribution and that its growth helped offset the growing inequality in agricultural income.

Using more intensive data from a smaller subsample of households, the figures in Table 5.16 reveal similar patterns. Village households experienced a sharp decline in rice income as shares of total income, falling from 43 percent in 1975–1976 to 25 percent in 1981–1982. This was matched by increases in nonrice agricultural production, from 14.5 percent to 18 percent, and nonagricultural income, from 43 percent to 57 percent. Changes in shares of output, value added, and employment followed similar movements—a falling share of rice, a rising share of other agriculture, and a sharply rising share of nonagriculture.

Table 5.13 Occupations of Economically Active Male Population (13–65 years old) in an East Laguna Village, 1974, 1980, and 1987 (number and percentage)

	1974			1980			1987		
	Total	Farmer	Landless	Total	Farmer	Landless	Total	Farmer	Landless
Number of persons	151	99	52	197	87	110	272	114	158
Major occupation (percent)									
Rice farming									
Self-employed	47.0	71.7	0.0	26.0	58.6	0.0	20.9	50.0	0.0
Hired	18.6	0.0	53.8	45.7	9.1	74.6	47.8	15.8	70.9
Duck raising	15.2	6.1	32.7	2.5	1.2	3.6	1.1	1.8	0.6
Fishing	0.0	0.0	0.0	1.0	0.0	1.8	2.2	0.0	3.8
Tricycle	0.0	0.0	0.0	0.5	1.2	0.0	1.5	0.9	1.9
Vendor	0.7	0.0	1.9	0.5	1.2	0.0	0.4	0.0	0.6
Buy and sell	0.0	0.0	0.0	0.0	0.0	0.0	7.0	0.0	0.3
Quack doctor	0.7	0.0	1.9	0.0	0.0	0.0	0.0	0.0	0.0
Carpentry	1.3	0.0	3.9	2.5	1.2	3.6	0.0	0.0	1.9
Salaried worker	3.3	4.0	1.9	6.1	8.0	4.6	6.2	6.1	6.3
Schooling	11.9	16.2	3.9	13.2	19.5	8.2	15.5	21.9	10.8
None	1.3	2.0	0.0	2.5	1.2	3.6	2.6	3.5	1.9
Total	100.0	100.0	100.0	100.0	100.0	100.0	100.0	100.0	100.0
Minor occupation (percent)									
Rice farming									
Self-employed	4.0	6.1	0.0	3.6	8.0	0.0	na	na	na
Hired	16.6	14.1	21.2	7.1	10.3	4.5	na	na	na
Duck raising	15.2	17.2	11.5	10.2	9.2	10.9	na	na	na
Cattle raising	0.0	0.0	0.0	0.5	1.1	0.0	na	na	na
Fishing	0.7	0.0	1.9	15.7	14.9	16.4	na	na	na
Tricycle	1.3	2.0	0.0	4.1	6.9	1.8	na	na	na
Vendor	0.0	0.0	0.0	0.5	0.0	0.9	na	na	na
Quack doctor	0.0	0.0	0.0	0.5	1.1	0.0	na	na	na
Carpentry	0.0	0.0	0.0	10.7	13.8	8.2	na	na	na

Source: Data from Hayami (1987: Table 16).
na = not available.

Table 5.14 Occupations of Economically Active Female Population (13–65 years old) in an East Laguna Village, 1974, 1980, and 1987 (number and percentage)

	1974			1980			1987		
	Total	Farmer	Landless	Total	Farmer	Landless	Total	Farmer	Landless
Number of persons	161	106	55	176	80	96	251	107	144
Major occupation (percent)									
Rice farming									
Self-employed	11.8	18.0	0.0	3.4	7.5	0.0	1.2	2.8	0.0
Hired	7.5	0.0	21.8	15.9	5.0	25.0	13.2	2.8	20.8
Duck raising	1.2	0.9	1.8	10.8	13.8	8.3	3.2	6.6	7.0
Sari-sari store	3.7	4.7	1.8	5.7	8.7	3.1	5.6	7.5	4.2
Vendor	0.6	0.0	1.8	0.0	0.0	0.0	3.6	3.7	3.5
Dressmaking	0.6	0.9	0.0	3.4	5.0	2.1	3.2	3.7	2.8
Handicraft	0.0	0.0	0.0	0.6	0.0	1.0	0.0	0.0	0.0
Rice-milling	0.0	0.0	0.0	0.0	0.0	0.0	0.4	0.0	0.7
Quack doctor	0.0	0.0	0.0	0.0	0.0	0.0	0.4	0.0	0.7
Maid	0.0	0.0	0.0	2.3	0.0	4.2	3.5	2.8	4.2
Salaried worker	3.1	4.7	0.0	2.8	3.7	2.1	4.8	8.4	2.0
Overseas worker	0.0	0.0	0.0	0.0	0.0	0.0	1.6	1.9	1.4
Schooling	11.2	13.2	7.3	17.6	23.8	12.5	11.9	16.8	8.3
None (household)	60.3	57.6	65.5	37.5	32.5	41.7	47.4	43.0	50.7
Total	100.0	100.0	100.0	100.0	100.0	100.0	100.0	100.0	100.0
Minor occupation (percent)									
Rice farming									
Self-employed	13.7	20.8	0.0	1.7	3.8	0.0	na	na	na
Hired	18.6	15.1	25.4	9.1	3.8	13.5	na	na	na
Duck raising	8.1	10.4	3.6	9.1	10.0	8.3	na	na	na
Sari-sari store	0.0	0.0	0.0	1.7	2.5	1.0	na	na	na
Vendor	0.0	0.0	0.0	1.7	1.2	2.1	na	na	na

Source: Data from Hayami (1987: Table 16).
na = not available.

Table 5.15   Source of Total Income in a Laguna Village, 1974 and 1987
(percent of total)

	1974			1987		
	Rice	Other Agriculture	Nonagriculture	Rice	Other Agriculture	Nonagriculture
All households	77.8	14.1	8.1	50.1	13.9	36.0
Large farmers	86.3	6.9	6.8	53.1	22.9	24.0
Small farmers	74.5	18.0	7.5	51.5	13.5	35.0
Landless	58.8	28.5	12.7	45.9	9.1	45.0

Source: Data from Ranis (1990: Table v.6).

Table 5.16   Shares of Income, Output, and Employment in a Laguna Village,
1975/76 and 1981/82 (percent)

	1975/76			1981/82		
	Rice	Other Agriculture	Nonagriculture	Rice	Other Agriculture	Nonagriculture
Income	42.6	14.5	42.9	24.9	18.0	57.1
Output	81.1	18.3	0.7	62.5	28.7	8.8
Value-added	87.3	12.2	0.6	74.3	25.7	4.1
Labor days	76.6	15.8	7.6	43.2	24.4	32.4

Source: Data from Ranis (1990: Table v.7).

Looking more closely at the time-allocation behavior of family labor, the proportion of time in terms of workdays spent on nonfarm activities significantly increased from 1975–1976 to 1980–1981 among all types of households (Figure 5.1), especially among the households of larger farms and of landless workers (Figures 5.2, 5.3, and 5.4). For the households associated with large farms, this was probably made possible by hiring workers to do the farm work, thus releasing people in the household to take on nonfarm work. The landless workers seem to have had little choice. The combination of mounting population pressure and the fact that the land-rental market was almost completely inactive due to land reform regulations has made it very difficult for landless laborers to ascend the so-called agricultural ladder, even to become tenant farmers. Further, improved roads and better transport facilities enabled the people to travel to nearby towns where nonfarm work is available. Finally, although some degree of seasonality is still evident in the allocation of time for nonfarm work, the overall picture suggests an increasing commitment to nonfarm work, shown by the significant reduction in the gap between the proportions of time allocated for farm and nonfarm work.

Figure 5.1 Monthly Workdays Spent on Nonfarm Activities in a Laguna Village, All Households

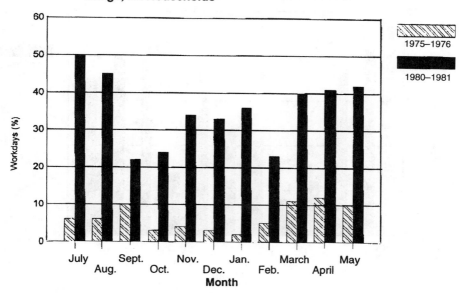

Figure 5.2 Monthly Workdays Spent on Nonfarm Activities in a Laguna Village, Large Farm Households

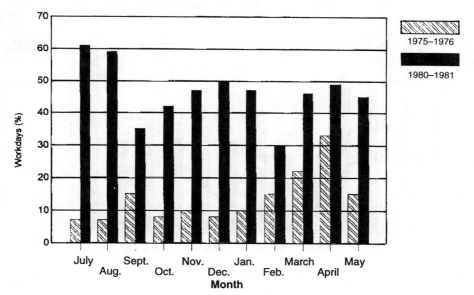

Figure 5.3 Monthly Workdays Spent on Nonfarm Activities in a Laguna Village, Small Farm Households

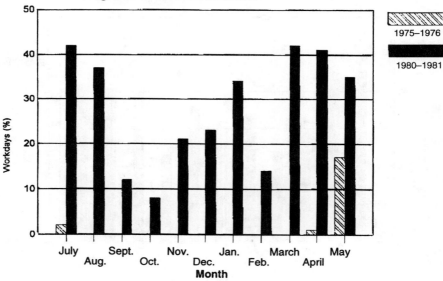

Figure 5.4 Monthly Workdays Spent on Nonfarm Activities in a Laguna Village, Landless Households

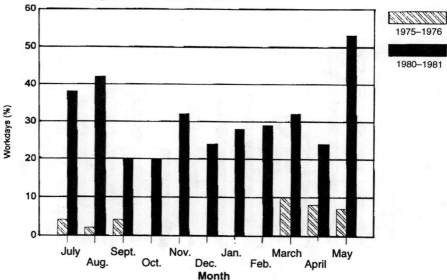

Conclusion

This chapter has traced the evolution of the rural nonfarm sector in the Philippines and examined its changing structure over time. The analysis focused on both macro and micro settings, the latter being a case study of a village where data permitted an evaluation of the growing importance of nonfarm activities in the structure of rural incomes and income distribution.

The rural sector in the Philippines has remained relatively large, with more than 50 percent of the total population still residing in rural areas. It has also maintained its subsistence character: Farm sizes have declined further, landlessness has increased, average rural incomes are still well below national poverty lines, and estimated underemployment rates have remained fairly high. Meanwhile, macroeconomic and sector-specific policies have been biased against the rural sector in general and agriculture in particular, and land reform programs have only benefited a small number of Filipino peasants. If, indeed, there were real increases in agricultural incomes and productivity, particularly in limited areas like Central Luzon and Southern Tagalog, these increases were not systematically associated with any changes in land tenure or ownership but were more often the result of the farmers' increased access to credit, irrigation, transportation, and HYVs.

The analysis of the micro case revealed characteristics consistent with the general observations on the rural sector as a whole. For example, the village has also been experiencing greater landlessness due to increased population pressure and land reform regulations, decreasing farm size, and more unequal size distribution of farms. This situation has released labor for nonagricultural activities both in the village and in nearby towns. On the whole, nonfarm income in the village rose from 8.1 percent to 36 percent of total income in just five years. The average income of large farmers increased significantly because a growing share of land rent accrued to them. The relative income position of the landless workers would have deteriorated if not for the marked increases in nonfarm work performed by the landless. Also of significance was the increased participation of females in a range of nonfarm work activities, such as retail trade (sari-sari stores), vending, dressmaking, domestic services, and office work (usually in government). This increased commitment to nonfarm work was aided by the development of stronger linkages through modern highway systems and transportation facilities.

Although the overall structure of the Philippine economy is most notable for its continuity since the 1960s, there is evidence of change within the rural economy. The basic dimensions of this change include declining farm size, worsening farm size distribution (especially in the export sector), stagnant productivity growth, and the increasing role of nonagricultural income in total rural household incomes. Undoubtedly, the rise of nonagricultural rural employment opportunities has moderated the deterioration of income distribution within rural areas. However, this must be evaluated against evidence that overall levels of poverty within the Philippine rural sector are deepening.

Stagnant productivity and income growth in agriculture can hardly serve as a productive "push" for transitions to nonagricultural labor. How, for example, can such households finance the labor transitions involved in moving outside the agricultural labor markets? At the same time, in the Philippine case, a historically weak industrial sector with no tradition of labor-intensive expansion hardly offers a promising "pull."

The Philippines faces a daunting challenge to find productive work for the over 750,000 new rural workers who enter the labor force each year. At this point, what work is found is more likely to be nonagricultural than agricultural, and it is increasingly likely to be found by women rather than men. However, there is crucial and disturbing evidence that little of the work that is found is especially productive—particularly in areas farther away from major cities and transportation arteries. Under these circumstances, the growth of nonfarm employment in the rural Philippines is more a change of omens than an omen of change: It is a "new" indication of the real costs of sluggish industrialization, stagnant agriculture, and a political economy averse to fundamental structural change.

Notes

Dr. Reyes was a research fellow at the Philippine Institute for Development Studies. She was assisted in preparing a draft of this chapter by Ma. Teresa Sanchez. Tragically, Dr. Reyes passed away shortly after completing the first draft. Bruce Koppel helped to bring the chapter to its final form, hopefully maintaining Dr. Reyes's original intentions.

1. There are, however, serious questions about the reliability of productivity data. These questions reflect concerns about oversampling of farms and farmers who are in more accessible areas and who, in recent years, were the clients of various government programs. Such data served program-evaluation purposes (and their links to donor funding), as well as more generic sectoral-monitoring objectives. Upland and marginal producers, who actually account for one-third to one-half of all areas, and farmers tended to be undersampled. Because the yields in the less-than-optimal environments tend to be low, the general sense is that Philippine commodity production data are biased upward, despite a record of low productivity and low productivity growth. For example, see the review by David et al. (1990).

2. There are several different types of tenancy. In cash-rent tenancy, a fixed amount of money is paid to the landowner as rental for the land worked by the holder. In a share-of-produce tenancy arrangement, a share of the harvest is paid to the landowner as rental for the land worked by the holder. Under a fixed-amount-of-produce arrangement, a specific quantity of crops is agreed upon by both landowner and tenant; the tenant or renter is obliged to deliver to the landowner the quantity of produce agreed upon, whether or not he or she gets any harvest

from the land. There are other forms, as well, including various combinations of the arrangements mentioned here, and a few cases of rent-free tenancy.

3. The definitions used by the Department of Trade and Industry were adopted in the survey: Small—total assets of 500,000 to 5 million pesos and an employment size from 10 to 99; Cottage—total assets of 50,000 to 500,000 pesos and an employment size of less than 10; Micro—total assets of less than 50,000 pesos.

4. This section draws heavily from Hayami, Mariano, and Bambo (1989) and Ranis and Stewart (1987).

References

Anderson, D., and M. Leiserson. 1980. "Rural Nonfarm Employment in Developing Countries," *Economic Development and Cultural Change*, Vol. 28, No. 2 (January), pp. 227–248.

APST (Agricultural Policy and Strategy Team). 1986. *Agenda for Action for the Philippine Rural Sector* (College, Laguna: University of the Philippines at Los Baños, Agricultural Policy Research Program and Philippine Institute for Development Studies).

Bautista, R. 1971. *Dynamic of an Agrarian Model with Z-Goods*, Discussion Paper No. 714 (Diliman, Quezon City: School of Economics, University of the Philippines).

Castillo, Gelia. 1979. *Beyond Manila: Philippine Rural Problems in Perspective* (Ottawa: Canada: International Development Research Center).

Choe, Y., and F. Chen Lo, eds. 1986. *Rural Industrialization and Non-Farm Activities of Asian Farmers* (Seoul: Korea Rural Economics Institute).

Chuta, E., and C. Liedholm. 1979. *Rural Nonfarm Employment: A Review of the State of the Art*, Michigan State University Rural Development Paper No. 4 (East Lansing: Michigan State University).

Clarete, Ramon. 1985. *Debt Crisis, Trade Liberalization, and Agricultural Policy Reforms: The Philippines* (Honolulu: East-West Center).

Clarete, Ramon, and James Roumasset. 1983. *An Analysis of the Economic Policies Affecting the Philippine Coconut Industry* (Manila: Philippine Institute for Development Studies).

Crisostomo-David, C., and R. Barker. 1972. "Growth Rates of Philippine Agriculture, 1948–1969," *Philippine Economic Journal*, Vol. 9 (first semester), pp. 88–148.

DAR (Department of Agrarian Reform). 1989. *Developing the Countryside: A Strategy* (Manila: Vera-Reyes).

David, Cristina. 1983. *Economic Policies and Philippine Agriculture*, PIDS Working Paper 83–02 (Manila: Philippine Institute for Development Studies).

David, I.P., A. Nenette, C. Mendoza, and David C. Besa. 1990. "Evaluation of Philippine Corn Statistics," *Journal of Philippine Development*, Vol. 17, No. 1, pp. 33–66.

de Dios, Emmanuel, ed. 1984. *An Analysis of the Philippine Economic Crisis* (Quezon City: University of the Philippines School of Economics).

Deshpanade, S., and L. Deshpanade. 1985. "Census of 1981 and the Structure of Employment," *Economic and Political Weekly*, Vol. 20, No. 22 (June 1), pp. 969–972.

Fabella, Raul. 1985. "Rural Nonfarm Activities in the Philippines: Composition, Growth and Seasonality," in Swapna Mukhopadhgay and Chee Peng Lim, eds., *Development and Diversification of Rural Industries in Asia* (Kuala Lumpur: Asia-Pacific Development Center).

Gibb, A. 1974. "Agricultural Modernization, Nonfarm Employment and Low-level Urbanization: A Case Study of a Central Luzon Subregion of the Philippines" (Ph.D. dissertation, University of Michigan).

Government of Korea. 1981. *Korea Statistical Yearbook* (Seoul: Economic Planning Board).

Haggblade, S., Peter Hazel, and James Brown. 1989. "Farm-Nonfarm Linkages in Rural Sub-Saharan Africa," *World Development*, Vol. 17, No. 8, pp. 1173–1201.

Hayami, Yujiro. 1987. *Kasugpong in Central Luzon: "Indianization" of the Philippine Rice Bowl?* Department of Agricultural Economics Research Paper 87–22 (Manila: International Rice Research Institute).

Hayami, Yujiro, Esther B. Mariano, and Luisa M. Bambo. 1989. *Rice Harvesting in Central Luzon and Laguna Revisited*, IRRI Research Papers (Manila: International Rice Research Institute).

Hymer, Stephen, and Stephen Resnick. 1969. "A Model of an Agrarian Economy with Nonagricultural Activities," *American Economic Review*, Vol. 59, pp. 493–506.

James, William E. 1983. "Settler Selection and Land Settlement Alternatives: New Evidence from the Philippines," *Economic Development and Cultural Change*, Vol. 31, No. 3, pp. 571–586.

Kilby, P., and C. Liedholm. 1986. *The Role of Nonfarm Activities in the Rural Economy*, EEPA Discussion Paper No. 7 (Cambridge, Mass.: Harvard Institute for International Development).

Koppel, Bruce. 1987. "Agrarian Problems and Agrarian Reform: Opportunity or Irony?" in Carl Lande, ed., *Rebuilding a Nation: Philippine Challenges and American Policy* (Washington, D.C.: Washington Institute Press), pp. 157–187.

———. 1992. "Between Ballot and *Balut*: Emerging Issues in Philippine Labor Markets and Industrial Labor Relations," in Chung-hoon Lee and Fun-koo Park, eds., *Emerging Labor Issues in Developing Asia* (Seoul: Korea Development Institute), pp. 98–143.

Koppel, Bruce, Hirohisa Kohama, Akira Takahashi, and Toru Yanagihara. 1988. *Japan-U.S. ODA Cooperation: Perspectives from India, Indonesia and the Philippines* (Honolulu: East-West Center).

Ledesma, Antonio. 1982. *Landless Workers and Rice Farmers: Peasant Subclasses Under Agrarian Reform in Two Philippine Villages* (Manila: International Rice Research Institute).

Liedholm, C. 1988. "The Role of the Nonfarm Activities in the Rural Economies of the Asia-Pacific Region," paper presented at a conference on "Directions and Strategies of Agricultural Development in the Asia-Pacific Region," Taipei, Taiwan, January.

Luna, C. 1982. "Agricultural Productivity and Urbanization in the Philippines" (master's thesis, University of the Philippines).

Mangahas, M. 1986. "Rural Employment Creation in the Philippines and Thailand," in Asian Development Bank, ed. *Rural Employment Creation in Asia and the Pacific, Papers and Proceedings of the ADB and ILO's Regional Workshop in Rural Employment Creation, Manila, November 24–28* (Manila: Asian Development Bank).

Medalla, F. N.d. "Off-Farm Incomes of Farm Households in the Philippines" (Mimeographed). Manila, Philippine Institute for Development Studies.

Montes, Manuel F. 1991. "The Philippines: In Search of Internal Dynamism in the Development Process" *Journal of International Economic Studies*, Vol. 5, pp. 97–118.

NEDA (Republic of the Philippines National Economic and Development Author-ity). 1989. *Philippine Statistical Yearbook* (Manila: NEDA).

Oshima, H. 1984. *The Significance of Off-Farm Employment and Incomes in Post-War East Asian Growth*, Asian Development Bank Economic Staff Paper No. 21 (Manila: Sian Development Bank).

———. 1987. *Economic Growth in Monsoon Asia: A Comparative Study* (Tokyo: University of Tokyo Press).

Pernia, E., and V. Hermoso. 1983. "Some Aspects of Urbanization and Agricul-tural Productivity," in Ernesto Pernia, Cayetano Paderanga, and Victorina Hermoso, eds., *The Spatial and Urban Dimensions of Development in the Philippines* (Manila: Philippine Institute for Development Studies).

Pernia, Ernesto, Cayetano, Paderanga, and Victorina Hermoso. 1983. *The Spatial and Urban Dimensions of Development in the Philippines* (Manila: Philippine Institute for Development Studies).

Ranis, Gustav. 1990. *The Dynamics of Rural Development: Theory and Applica-tion,* Discussion Paper No. 608 (New Haven, Conn.: Economic Growth Cen-ter, Yale University)

Ranis, Gustav, Frances Stewart, and Edna Angeles-Reyes. 1990. *Linkages in De-velopment: A Philippine Case Study* (San Francisco, Calif.: International Cen-ter for Economic Growth).

Reyes, Edna. 1987. "The Structure of Rural Household Income and Its Implica-tions on Rural Poverty in Bicol, Philippines," *Journal of Philippine Develop-ment*, Vol. 14, No. 2, pp. 302–320.

Reyes, E., E. Milan, and M.T. Sanchez. 1989. "Employment Productivity and Wages in the Philippine Labor Market," PIDS Working Paper 89–03 (Manila: Philippine Institute for Development Studies).

Shand, R.T., ed. 1986. *Off-Farm Employment in the Development of Rural Asia*, Vols. 1 and 2 (Canberra: Australian National University, National Centre for Development Studies).

Shih, J.T. 1983. "Decentralized Industrialization and Rural Nonfarm Employment in Taiwan," *Industry of Free China*, Vol. 60, No. 2 (August), pp. 1–20.

Thiesenhusen, W. 1990. "Recent Progress Toward Agrarian Reform in the Philip-pines" (mimeographed). Manila, Philippine Institute for Development Studies.

Tidalgo, Rosalinda P., and Emmanuel F. Esguerra. 1984. *Philippine Employment in the Seventies* (Manila: Philippine Institute for Development Studies).

USAID (United States Agency for International Development). 1981. "Household Poverty Profile Bicol Region (Region V)," (Mimeographed). Manila, USAID.

World Bank. 1978. *Rural Enterprises and Nonfarm Employment* (Washington, D.C.: World Bank).

———. 1985. *The Philippine Recent Trends in Poverty, Employment and Wages* (Washington, D.C.: World Bank).

6

Transformations in the Thai Rural Labor Market

Nipon Poapongsakorn

This chapter analyzes the effects of structural transformation on the rural labor market and nonagricultural employment in Thailand. The first portion describes performance and structural change in the Thai economy during the past three decades. The second part analyzes transformations in rural labor markets. Nonagricultural activities and rural employment issues in rural areas are discussed in the third part. The conclusion offers an agenda for future research.

Economic Performance and Structural Change

The Thai economy has been growing steadily throughout the past three decades (Table 6.1). Even in the early 1980s, when there was a worldwide recession, the Thai economy still managed to grow at a moderate rate of about 4 percent, while many Asian countries experienced zero or even negative growth rates.[1] The Thai economy has achieved record economic growth since the second half of 1986, characterized by surging exports, an investment boom, and a large influx of foreign private capital. Thailand had a narrowing fiscal deficit that turned into a surplus after 1987. Though the trade and current account deficits remained, debt service as a percentage of exports was stabilized well below 20 percent.[2]

Although agricultural sector growth has been quite impressive during the last three decades, as can be seen in Table 6.1, the rate has always been lower than the growth rate of the overall economy. As a consequence, the share of agriculture in the Thai economy has systematically declined, while the share of industrial activities has systematically grown (see Table 6.2). In 1988, the GDP share of the agricultural sector was only 17 percent, compared to almost 40 percent in 1960. The manufacturing sector share increased to 24 percent in 1988. However, the agricultural labor force still constitutes the largest share of the total labor force (i.e., 64 percent in 1988). This is quite a high figure by international standards (World Bank, 1986), although it is somewhat exaggerated because it is based on

167

Table 6.1   Growth Rates of Real GDP and Its Components in Thailand, 1950–1989 (percent)

	GDP	Agriculture	Industry[a]	Services[b]
1950–1960	4.5	2.7	5.7	6.2
1960–1970	8.0	5.2	11.5	8.6
1970–1980	6.9	4.2	10.0	7.3
1980–1989	6.5	3.6	7.1	7.2
1980–1986	5.4	4.3	5.3	6.0
1987–1989	10.8	5.9	12.3	10.5

Sources: National Economic and Social Development Board, *National Income of Thailand* (Bangkok: NESDB), various years.
Note: The growth rates are obtained by fitting a log-linear least squares time trend.
   [a] Includes mining, manufacturing, construction, electricity, and water supply.
   [b] Includes transportation and communication; wholesale and retail trade; banking, insurance, and real estate; ownership of dwellings; public administration; and defense services.

Table 6.2   Shares of Major Sectors in GDP in Thailand, 1960–1988 (current market prices, percent)

	Agriculture	Industry[a] All	Manufacturing	Services[b]
1960	39.8	18.6	12.5	41.7
1965	34.9	22.7	14.2	72.5
1970	28.3	25.3	16.0	46.4
1975	31.5	24.8	18.7	43.7
1980	25.4	28.5	19.6	46.1
1985	16.8	34.0	22.1	49.2
1986	16.5	34.3	23.3	49.2
1987	16.1	34.7	23.9	49.2
1988	16.9	35.1	24.4	48.0

Sources: National Economic and Social Development Board, *National Income of Thailand* (Bangkok: NESDB), various issues.
   [a] Includes mining, manufacturing, construction, electricity, and water supply.
   [b] Includes transportation and communication; wholesale and retail trade; banking, insurance, and real estate; ownership of dwellings; public administration; and defense services.

data from the peak agricultural season when labor demand in the agricultural sector is at the highest level. But even if the dry season figure is used (Table 6.3), the agricultural sector still accounts for almost 60 percent of total employment.[3] Overall, Thailand has experienced rapid structural change, moving from an agricultural economy to an industrial economy that is distinctly export-oriented.

The incidence of poverty as measured by the proportion of the population living below the poverty line has substantially declined. The percentage of poor in the total population fell from 57 percent in 1963 to 24.7 percent in 1981 but increased to 31 percent in 1986 as a result of a slump in the prices of most agricultural products (Meesook, 1979; World

Table 6.3 Total Employment and Share by Major Sectors in Thailand, 1960–1988

	Agriculture		Industry		Services		Total	
	No.	%	No.	%	No.	%	No.	%
1960	11,334	82.3	585	4.3	1,853	13.5	13,772	100
1970	13,202	79.3	976	5.9	2,474	14.9	16,652	100
1980	16,499	70.5	2,378	10.6	4,426	18.9	23,300	100
January								
1971	12,322	74.3	1,390	8.4	2,879	17.4	16,591	100
1976	8,644	62.6	1,971	14.3	3,200	23.2	13,816	100
1981	9,280	53.4	3,016	17.4	5,084	29.3	17,380	100
1986	13,597	57.9	3,689	15.7	6,195	26.4	23,481	100
1988	14,264	56.6	3,874	15.4	7,050	28.0	25,188	100
August								
1971	13,260	78.2	1,013	6.0	2,678	15.9	16,964	100
1976	14,167	74.5	1,611	8.5	3,231	17.0	19,014	100
1981	17,422	71.6	2,380	9.8	4,519	18.6	24,325	100
1986	16,794	65.9	2,940	11.5	5,754	22.6	25,488	100
1988	17,789	64.4	3,251	11.8	6,599	23.9	27,639	100

Sources: National Statistical Office, *Population Census 1960, Population and Housing Census 1970* (Bangkok: NSO); National Statistical Office, *A Report of the Labor Force Survey,* Round 1 (January–March, 1971–1988), Round 2 (July–September, 1971–1983), and Round 3 (August, 1984–1988) (Bangkok: NSO).

Bank, 1985; Pinthong, 1990). However, over the same period, there was an increase in income inequality. The Gini coefficient increased from 0.414 in 1963, to 0.429 in 1969, 0.451 in 1976, 0.437 in 1981, and 0.50 in 1986 (Meesook, 1979; Krongkaew, 1988; Hutaserani and Jitsuchon, 1988). The income share of the richest 10 percent increased from 33.4 percent in 1976 to 39.2 percent in 1986, and that of the poorest 10 percent decreased from 2.43 percent to 1.8 percent over the same period.

Among the most prominent factors that account for the nation's economic growth have been the nation's ability to take advantage of an abundant supply of land and cheap energy, its efficient industrialization policy, its sound macroeconomic management and political stability, its avoidance of large public sector projects, and its reliance on the private sector to make investment decisions (Siamwalla and Setboonsarng, 1987: 14–15; Meesook et al., 1988: 3.13–3.43; World Bank, 1989: 50–55). Thailand has also successfully managed its external debt and has taken advantage of opportunities in the international economy.

Growth in the Agricultural Sector

The respectable growth of the agricultural sector shown in Table 6.1 has been made possible by the ability of the smallholder to exploit the open land frontier. The outward orientation of the agricultural sector enabled incremental output to be marketed abroad. Total cultivated acreage per worker rose from 4.83 rai per worker in 1961 to 6.33 rai per worker in 1985 (one rai equals 0.16 hectare). Moreover, the size distribution of agricultural holdings has remained unchanged over the entire postwar period, despite the relatively rapid growth rate of the agricultural labor force.

The Thai farmers' response to growing demand in the world market was to increase the agricultural production surplus, despite several negative policy measures that heavily taxed farm incomes. Income from agricultural exports enabled the economy to maintain a fixed nominal exchange rate at 20 to 21 baht per dollar in the 1954–1981 period (Siamwalla and Setboonsarng, 1987: 14). As a consequence, inflation was held to a low rate.

Over the 1961–1985 period, gross agricultural crop value increased by 4.6 percent per annum. This was the consequence of increases in: (1) the number of agricultural workers (up by 48 percent), (2) the cultivated land area (up by 61 percent), (3) the average years of school completed (up 57 percent), and (4) the average size of farm capital stock (up by 9 percent). Using the growth accounting method, a Thailand Development Research Institute (TDRI) study found that 60.6 percent of the increase in the crop value during the 1961–1985 period was explained by increases in labor productivity, 11.2 percent by increases in the land-to-labor ratio, 12.7 percent by increases in schooling, 2.4 percent by increases in the capital stock, and −1.1 percent as a result of declines in crop prices (TDRI, 1987: 37). The study essentially found that growth in the agricultural sector can be explained by increases in agricultural productivity per worker made possible by the availability of land, improvements in educational attainment, government expenditure on irrigation and research, and other capital improvements. Now that the land frontier has already closed, further productivity improvement and growth will have to come from other sources. Intensification of production, both in terms of human and physical capital, is the new alternative to land expansion.

Structural Change in the Agricultural Sector

There have been three major characteristics of structural change in the Thai agricultural sector: commodity diversification, slow shifts of rural labor to employment outside of agriculture, and the emergence of agricultural labor shortages in the Central Region.

Although rice production has steadily increased, its relative role in the economy has significantly declined as new upland crops began to be cultivated in growing amounts. The expansion of maize production occurred in the late 1950s and early 1960s, followed by kenaf in the mid-1960s (though kenaf expansion was quickly reversed). Cassava and sugar boomed at the end of the 1960s. These crops are now important export commodities and major sources of livelihood for millions of farmers. Fishery and livestock products, especially chicken, have also become important since the 1970s. However, given the fact that most countries subsidize the agricultural sector, the outlook for Thai exports of upland crops is not very good. Indeed, the only products with healthy future prospects are fruits, vegetables, and cut flowers (Siamwalla and Pinthong, 1986).

Several factors prompted this crop diversification. First, the rice premium and other rice export restriction measures, which negatively affected the return to land used for rice production, induced farmers to switch to other products (Loohawenchit, 1977). Second, road construction that connected Bangkok with the Northeast in the 1960s allowed farmers to expand agricultural production into upland areas in response to world demand (Koomsup, 1973). Finally, medical advances in malaria control enabled farmers to settle down and clear forest lands that were suitable for upland agriculture.

Although the agricultural growth rate has been quite satisfactory, it is lower than the growth rates of other economic sectors (Table 6.1). Similarly, productivity per worker in agriculture is much lower than that of other sectors. The low share of agricultural product in the GDP, combined with a very high share of agricultural labor in the total labor force, indicates a very large differential in productivity between sectors. Hence, most farmers have to supplement their on-farm income by working off-farm. The slow structural shift in the percentage of agricultural employment can be seen in Table 6.3. Between 1971 and 1988, the employment share of the agricultural sector declined from 78 percent to 64 percent. This phenomena has not yet been fully understood, but a tentative explanation can be advanced.

Oshima (1987) has argued that the monsoon winds have imposed the distinctive seasonality of wet rice agriculture in Southeast Asia. Farming methods and institutions have been developed by Asians to cope with the seasonal patterns of rainfall and humidity defined by the monsoon. High concentrations of rain in a few months have resulted in relatively small farm sizes (about 20 to 25 rais per family) because work must be done quickly by family labor. It is extremely difficult for Asians to adopt the capitalistic farming methods that arose from the agricultural revolution in the West because the kind of work required on the Asian farm cannot be done well by low-paid wage workers. Moreover, it is difficult to draw labor out of the agricultural sector for two reasons, which will be discussed later. To attract labor for year-round industrial work, the factories have to pay high wages to compensate workers for forgone food production.

Until the mid-1980s in Thailand, the availability of new lands to be cleared probably accounted, in large part, for the slow rate of decline in agriculture's share of the labor force. Although the growth rate of the agricultural labor force was 2.65 percent per year between 1971 and 1985, the availability of land on the frontier helped maintain the size distribution of landholdings and cultivated area per worker. Because most Thai farmers employ family labor and own most of their land and capital, they do not reduce their level of production in response to a price reduction. When output prices drop, the returns to these inputs can fall to accommodate the drop in revenue. In other words, they reduced their cost of production by accepting lower returns to their own factors of production. Moreover, some of these factors are fixed, and some factors even have zero sunk cost (e.g., their stock of farming knowledge). Therefore, the farmers can put up with a continuous decline in their real standard of living by producing the same output.

Although there are a large number of rural-to-urban migrants, it can be so costly and risky to migrate to work in the urban areas that the net return from doing so may be lower than that from farming. This point is only a conjecture, and further research would be necessary to confirm or reject such a hypothesis. But in any case, there are two more reasons why rural residents are reluctant to migrate to the cities. The first is the availability of forest land that can be cleared and occupied. The second is that much of the newly settled land (usually former forest area) remains untitled, and someone must remain on the land in order to retain any family claim to it.

The third structural change in the agricultural sector was caused by labor shortages, especially in the Central Region, resulting from the irrigation projects and land consolidation policy first introduced in the Upper Chao Phraya River Delta of the Central Plains in 1969–1970. Although irrigation and land consolidation projects have allowed farmers to engage in multiple-cropping, they have also resulted in labor shortages because the planting periods are uniformly dictated by fixed water delivery schedules. Consequently, labor shortages in the peak season became so severe that mechanization and other less labor-intensive farming methods, such as the seed broadcasting technique, became feasible. And like the increase in the agricultural real wage rate, employment practices and institutions have also begun to change, as I will discuss further.

Growth and change in the agricultural sector has not occurred without cost. As crop production expanded on newly cleared land, the amount of forest area has declined, causing a drop in the output of the forestry subsector and increasing ecological problems. Another serious problem is the transfer of real resources out of the agricultural sector. Although the government has provided general infrastructure (e.g., roads, irrigation, and research) that benefits farmers, it has also employed pricing policies to keep down the domestic prices of agricultural products. Moreover, industrial protection policies and exchange rate policies have negatively affected the domestic prices of agricultural products. Some 32,750 million baht (at 1972 prices) were transferred out of the agricultural sector during the 1967–1984 period. In terms of income distribution effects, government interventions resulted in lower incomes for farmers, and rice farmers, especially those who had marketable surpluses, suffered the most. The beneficiaries of interventions that reduced domestic food prices were mainly the urban rich and middle-income consumers (Siamwalla and Setboonsarng, 1987).

Industrialization Policy

The primary explanation for the growth of the manufacturing sector, especially in the early period of industrialization, has to be protective government policies. Compared to farmers who have had to endure heavy agricultural export taxes, those in the manufacturing sector have enjoyed high rates of effective protection, financed, in part, by the resources extracted from agriculture (Christensen, Dollar, Siamwalla, and Vichyanond, 1992).

After the failure of economic nationalism and the fall of the Plak Phiboon government in 1957, the Sarit Thanarat government pursued a growth-oriented policy by promoting private investment, building up physical infrastructure, and giving first priority to the manufacturing sector. During the first two development plans (1961–1966 and 1967–1971), an import-substitution strategy was adopted. Investment incentives (in terms of tax holidays and import duty exemptions) and tariff protection were granted to selected large-scale import-substituting industries. Akrasanee's (1973) study found that high rates of protection for the manufacturing sector supported the growth of import-substitution industries with limited growth potential and high domestic resource costs at the expense of export industries with lower domestic resource costs.[4]

However, import-substituting industrialization was leading the economy into structural difficulties. Large amounts of imported raw materials and capital goods were required by the protected industries, resulting in widening deficits in the trade balance. Growth stagnated once the domestic market for consumer goods was saturated, and the protected industries failed to generate backward linkages and employment. The contribution of the import-substituting industries to the growth of demand for manufacturing output declined from 29.4 percent in 1966–1972 to 7.7 percent in 1975–1978 (World Bank, 1980). Then, in response to criticisms by Thai technocrats, the government announced an export-promotion policy in 1972. In addition to the exemption from export duties and business taxes for export products, there were other incentives offered, including tax exemptions for imported material inputs and imported products to be reexported.

As a result of the commodity boom in 1973–1974, there was a rapid expansion of exports, including processed goods. During the 1970–1980 period, manufactured exports grew in real terms by 19.3 percent per year. Export growth slowed down significantly between 1980 and 1985, largely due to the world recession in the early 1980s and depressed commodity prices. With recovery of the world economy under way after 1986 and with a long period of political stability in Thailand, the Thai economy achieved an impressive record of economic expansion during the second half of the 1980s and into the 1990s. Significant changes have occurred in trade and investment. Merchandise exports have surged by an average of more than 25 percent per annum since 1986, indicating a long-term shift in the Thai economy toward a greater manufacturing export orientation. The export boom was, in large part, caused by the 30 percent depreciation of the real exchange rate and the ability of Thai exporters to diversify their markets and improve product quality. Strong economic growth in Thailand has led to the current expansion of private investment, at an annual rate of 25 to 30 percent. Sharp increases in private foreign investment have resulted in the sudden appreciation of property values and stock prices.

Although small-scale and rural industries have received government support since the third plan was enacted, the previous promotion policy of the Board of Investment had discriminated against small-scale firms and small investment projects. However, in 1987, the promotion criteria were revised, and the biases against small firms were reduced, principally by revising the minimum investment requirements and by reducing exposure to corporate income taxes. Firms locating further away from the Bangkok metropolitan region now also receive more generous promotional privileges. However, past policy biases were not the only factors responsible for the failure of rural industry development. Other problems that constrained the growth of rural industry included business taxes that discouraged the use of subcontracting by downstream firms, lack of efficient infrastructure and business services, credit constraints, and small firms' lack of marketing and information technology.

It is important to recognize that significant policy biases persist. Although export industries benefit from the incentives provided by the government, their continued success depends on the effort of individual firms because they have to compete in the international market (Meesook et al., 1988). On the other hand, the protection of import-substituting industries creates high social costs and inefficient enterprises that enjoy comfortably high economic rents. These industries remain a strong vested interest group in the modern Thai economy.

Adjustments in the Rural Labor Market

Since Thailand was opened to free trade by the Bowring Treaty of 1855, Thai farmers have responded vigorously to the opportunities that international trade presents. There were seasonal labor shortages in peak seasons, but it was not until the late 1960s that a serious labor shortage began to emerge in the Central Plains. Several important factors account for this.

First, as already mentioned, the flexibility of the planting period and hence the abilities of agricultural households to make independent decisions on labor allocation and demand were sharply reduced as irrigation expanded in the 1960s and 1970s and as water delivery was increasingly placed on a fixed, areawide, and externally determined schedule. Second, a rapid decline in the population growth rate since the 1970s resulted in a slowdown of labor force growth, apparent by the later 1980s. Third, a large number of teenagers in the villages of the Central Plains have migrated to Bangkok and other urban areas. For example, a study (Kongkaew, 1990) of a village in the Central Plains in 1989 found that out of the 707 living children in 177 households, only 44.6 percent were still living in the village. Some 8.5 percent had moved to other villages, where they were still engaged primarily in agricultural activities, and 46.9 percent had moved to urban areas and were no longer engaged in agricultural work.

The Central Plains region has not been the only area to experience labor shortages. The Southern region has had to import labor from other areas to fill employment requirements throughout the year. The economy of the South is dominated by rubber production and mining, both of which are year-round activities. Fisheries, which operate nine to ten months a year, are also found extensively in the upper parts of the Southern region.

Finally, the unusually rapid economic growth during the 1988–1991 period has generated a large increase in manufacturing employment. As more rural teenagers move to urban areas to fill these new positions, a labor shortage is now felt in the agricultural sector in every region. Sugarcane plantation owners, for example, complain that their contract workers are being "poached" by urban labor recruiters, and Burmese and Cambodian laborers are being smuggled into Thailand to work on farms and on fishing boats.

Faced by higher real wage rates, farmers began to revise their labor demand. This section of the chapter will identify the pattern of changes in on-farm labor demand. However, changes in labor demand are not the only means of adjustment. Farmers can still rely upon certain labor market devices to solve their labor shortage problems (e.g., recruitment methods and employment contracts); this is the second issue in this section. The third issue is the adjustment of the farmers as suppliers of labor in response to the heavy implicit tax burden they bore in the form of low farm-gate prices for their agricultural products, particularly rice. The fourth issue is an analysis of why Thai farmers do not send their children to secondary schools but choose, instead, to invest in on-the-job training in nonagricultural jobs.

Wage Movements and Determinants of Wage Rates

Before discussing labor demand adjustment, it is necessary to understand the pattern of wage movements that signal labor market conditions. Unfortunately, rural wage rate data are not systematically collected. The longest and most systematic series data are those on the average wages collected by the Labor Force Survey since 1977. The data are obtained from a household survey. Therefore, in assessing labor market conditions, it is necessary to rely upon several data sources, which may not be entirely consistent with one another.

Table 6.4 shows that from 1965 to 1972, nominal and real wages were very stable. After 1972, they increased significantly as a result of the commodity boom in the early 1970s. Prices of major agricultural products, especially rice and sugar, were much higher in real terms than in the 1960s. Moreover, the increase in labor demand was caused by an expansion of double-cropping in the Northern Chao Phraya irrigation area. In the Northeast, the cassava boom caused rapid expansion of the cultivated area, which, in turn, increased the demand for labor. The data obtained from the Labor Force Survey are shown in Table 6.5. Before the fall in the agricultural-nonagricultural terms of trade in 1981, real wages remained very stable. The decline in prices of agricultural products in the 1981–1985 period resulted in a lower real wage rate. After 1985, the agricultural price index increased again, and so did the rural wage rate. For example, data from a survey of one Northern village confirm that the reference wage rate jumped significantly in the 1974–1975 and 1985–1986 periods, when there were significant increases in agricultural prices (Fuangfa, 1990). In effect, the agricultural wage rate is strongly related to the prices of the agricultural products. This wage behavior is consistent with marginal productivity theory.[5] But several other factors also influence agricultural wage rates.

Seasonal factors. Rice farming in monsoon Asian countries is characterized by a high labor demand and labor shortages during some brief intervals, particularly during the harvesting season. The data in Table 6.6 show that wage rates during the peak harvesting season are 10 to 50 percent higher than during the transplanting period. But the differences in Table 6.6 are not entirely the result of seasonal shifts in labor demand. Because the harvesting and transplanting wages are calculated on a piece-rate basis, some of the differences stem from work performance and variations in the hours of work. For example, data from the Ministry of Agriculture in 1978 revealed that the seasonal variation of wages in operations carried out mainly in the off-season is 10 to 20 percent below that for harvesting operations (World Bank, 1983: 109). Seasonal variation of wages is also observed in the operation of other agricultural products. For instance, the

Table 6.4 Farm Wage Rates on the Central Plains in Thailand, 1965–1976

| | Wage Rate (per day) | |
	Nominal	Real[a]
1965	10.0	10.0
1967	10.0	9.2
1970	12.0	10.4
1972	12.6	10.6
1975	25.0	13.6
1976	30.0	15.6

Sources: Data from Bertrand and Squire (1980).
  [a] 1965 prices, deflated by the consumer price index for the Central Region obtained from the Bank of Thailand. One baht = US$0.05.

Table 6.5 Rural Wage Rates in Thailand's Agricultural Sector, 1977–1988

| | | | Both Sexes | | Agricultural Price Index[b] | Terms of Trade[c] |
	Male	Female	Nominal	Real[a]		
1977	—	—	—	—	181.8	1.14
1978	—	—	—	—	193.4	1.10
1979	—	—	—	—	220.9	1.17
1980	—	—	—	—	247.4	1.16
1981	—	—	—	—	250.3	1.06
1982	—	—	—	—	233.8	0.93
1983	1,129.6	940.3	1,036.3	391.2	264.9	1.09
1984	1,271.5	1,123.9	1,199.9	506.7	236.8	0.91
1985	1,106.2	970.4	1,040.5	481.0	216.3	0.81
1986	1,120.4	976.4	1,052.7	458.3	229.7	0.84
1987	1,170.5	972.5	1,077.4	419.4	256.9	0.92
1988	1,262.4	1,061.9	1,165.5	394.1	295.7	1.00

Sources: National Economic and Social Development Board, *National Income of Thailand,* various issues; National Income Account Division; National Statistical Office, *Labor Force Survey Tape,* Round 2 (July–September, 1983), Round 3 (August, 1984–1988).
— indicates not available.
  [a] Deflated by consumer price index of the whole kingdom.
  [b] 1972 prices.
  [c] Agricultural price index divided by nonagricultural price index.

daily wage rates for planting upland crops (e.g., corn, cassava, cotton) are 12 to 50 percent below the wage rate for harvesting (Table 6.7).

Gender. Table 6.8 shows that the male wage rates in all but one region are 3 to 16 percent higher than the female wage rates. In the South, where labor force participation among Muslim women is the lowest, the wage differential is as large as 50 percent. Although the average wages of females tend to be lower than those of males, the former are usually hired

Table 6.6 Wage Rates for Rice Farming in Selected Thai Villages, 1971–1990
(baht per day)

Regional Location of Sample Villages and Year	Transplanting	Harvesting
Upper North region		
1971–1973	15–20	25–30
1974–1975	30	35–36
1978–1979	40	40–45
1985–1986	45	50
1988–1989	50	55–60
Northeast region		
1989	25–30	30–40
Lower North region		
1989	40	40–60
Western Central region		
1989	40	45–60
Central region		
1988–1989	na	105–120
1989–1990	90–112	135–165

Sources: Harnvajanawong (1991); Kongkaew (1990); Thongprapa (1990); Charonchi (1990); Fuangfa (1990); Chompoopa (1990).
na = not available.

for relatively light work. When both female and male workers are hired to perform the same tasks on a piece-rate basis, the wage rate is identical, implying that there is no wage discrimination against women in casual agricultural work. These tasks include transplanting, weeding, and harvesting.

Nonpecuniary factors. Each agricultural task differs in its degree of difficulty. There are at least two ways to differentiate the wage rate. First, those who perform a difficult task may receive the same wage as they would for an easier operation, but their employer will provide employees engaged in difficult work with a free meal. For example, the normal daily wage rate in the Northeast in 1989 was 30 baht. In addition to 30 baht, those who are hired to do weeding and cassava root-digging will also receive a free lunch. The second method is simply to pay different wage rates. For example, data from a village in the Central Plains reveal that there are three wage rates for paddy harvesting: 80 baht, 100 baht, and 120 to 150 baht per rai for the harvesting of three different kinds of paddy. The first two types of paddy are grown in upland circumstances; the third one, called *kao nak*, is grown on flat plains. The wage rate for work on *kao nak* is the highest because working conditions in a flooded and muddy field are more difficult, but the yields are also greater. It should be noted that the harvesting time for the third type also coincides with the period of highest

Table 6.7   Daily Wage Rates for Upland Crop Activities in Thailand, 1989
(baht per day)

Crop and Region	Planting	Weeding	Harvesting (peak season)
Corn			
Lower North	35	60	60
Western Central	50	—	56–105
Cassava			
Northeast	—	25–30+meal	30+meal[a]
			100[b]
Lower North	—	—	100
Western Central	50–60	50	100
Cotton			
Western Central	38–45	—	40–81

Sources: Compiled from various village studies (Charonchi, 1990; Chompoopa, 1990; Thongprapa, 1990).
— indicates not available.
[a] Daily wage rate.
[b] Transformed into an eight-hour daily rate from the piece-rate basis.

Table 6.8   Average Wages (in baht) of Male and Female Agricultural Workers in
Thailand, 1979 and 1987

	1979[a]		1987[b]	
	Male	Female	Male	Female
North	23.1	24.5	39.3	34.5
Northeast	20.6	20.3	35.6	34.5
South	—	—	80.2	52.2
Center	31.7	27.4	52.0	44.7
Whole kingdom	—	—	46.8	38.9

Sources: National Statistical Office, *Labor Force Survey Tape,* Round 3 (August 1987);
World Bank (1983: 110).
— indicates not available.
[a] Wage rate per eight-hour day classified by occupation. Data from World Bank (1983).
[b] Derived from the monthly wage rate by assuming that workers work twenty-five days
per month. Data classified by industry. Data from National Statistical Office.

demand for labor. Therefore, the high wage rate is also influenced by this
seasonal factor. In the Central Region, the wage (piece) rate for harvesting
paddy on the flooded field is higher for similar reasons. In addition, workers face the risk of being bitten by poisonous snakes.

Transportation cost.   When there is not enough hired labor within one village, farmers hire workers from other villages. Because their wage rate is
the same as that received by residents, the employer must bear the cost of
transporting the nonvillage workers. Otherwise, imported workers will

receive a higher wage rate (Chompoopa, 1990). It should also be noted that the wage rate is higher in the provinces that are closer to Bangkok (Table 6.6). One reason is because most rice harvested in these areas is transported to Bangkok for urban consumption or export; thus, the harvest has a higher cash value. Another reason, as indicated earlier, is that workers closer to Bangkok can consider employment in Bangkok's burgeoning manufacturing and construction sectors.

Mechanization and Method of Production

The theory of induced innovation predicts that changes in relative factor prices will induce a new method of production that economizes on the expensive factor of production (Hayami and Ruttan, 1971). E.O. Heady (1949) also argued that changes in relative factor prices would result in mechanization and technical change. In this section, evidence is presented to support the hypothesis that rising costs of labor will lead to farm mechanization and adoption of methods of production that are less labor intensive. When such adjustments in demand are not readily feasible, farmers will, instead, adjust their labor supply.

Mechanization. A number of studies report evidence of a significant expansion of mechanization processes in the Central Plains (World Bank, 1983: 62–70). An extensive land consolidation program and decreased flexibility in timing agricultural activities with double-cropping have contributed to the increased wage rates in the Northern Chao Phraya. This is why the degree of mechanization as measured by tractor horsepower is highest in that area. In a 1980 cross-sectional analysis, Nongluck Jongsuwat (1980) found that the more widespread use of small, two-wheel tractors in the Central Plains area was due to the relatively high agricultural wage rate there.

Mechanization can, therefore, help to reduce the cost of production because it economizes on labor utilization and time, compared to using bullock power (Issavilanon and Watlanijchariya, 1989). This is why the Central Plains, which has the highest rate of mechanization, has the lowest labor use per hectare in price production (Bot and Gooneratne, 1982: 105–106). Sriboonchitta (1975) showed that there was a difference of 500 man-hours of labor use for 40 rai of rice between tractor and buffalo farms in land preparation and 800 man-hours in threshing. For these reasons, mechanization has been rapidly adopted in the Central Plains and the North. For example, in 100 percent of the rice-growing area in the Central Plains and more than 80 percent of the irrigated areas in the North and Northeast, tractors were used for land preparation in 1986. Tractors are now also very popular for land preparation on rubber farms because the cost is approximately half that of hired labor. Rising wage rates are also the main reason for adopting the cutting machine to harvest sugarcane on the large plantations of the West Central Plains (Manarangsan and Kaewthep, 1987).

Rice threshing has also become mechanized very rapidly in the Central Plains as a result of the large proportion of labor costs in the total cost of threshing and the shortage of labor (Rasanand, 1977). Renu Pathanopas (1980) found that the total cost of threshing 1 ton of paddy by using bullocks was 192 baht—93 percent of which was labor cost. On the other hand, if a threshing machine was used, the cost was much lower. This is largely a result of reduction of labor use, from 22 man-hours when a buffalo is used to 2.7 man-hours when of a threshing machine is used. As a consequence, threshing machines have become increasingly popular in the Central Plains. Another study confirmed that a higher wage rate would increase the propensity to use tractors (Jongsuwat, 1980). In fact, the elasticity of substitution between labor and tractor power is found to be close to unity (0.97) (Montreevat, 1983).

Choices of technique. An increase in labor cost also has an impact on the choice of the technique used—broadcasting or transplanting—in rice production. Although transplanting requires 40 to 45 percent more labor than broadcasting, the former also gives a higher yield. Therefore, the choice of technique will be determined by the location and availability of family labor. When the wage rate increases, it will no longer be profitable to use the transplanting method. A survey by the Ministry of Agriculture found that the ratio of sample farmers transplanting rice declined from 90 percent to 81 percent in the North and from 67 percent to 61 percent in the Central Plains between 1970 and 1973. One study of the East Central Plains region found that most farmers (87 percent) used the broadcasting method because it cut the cost by almost one-third and because it was difficult to find and hire labor in Chachangsao Province, where good nonfarm employment opportunities existed (Lokaphadhana, 1976).

A higher wage also induces farmers to shift toward another type of cultivation, in which sprouted seeds are broadcast into the fields and the water level is increased in line with the growth of seedlings. It should be noted that this method is only popular in the Central Plains, where the farmers have low capital costs, because the technique is more capital-intensive than the transplanting and broadcasting methods.

Recruitment and Contracts

Labor shortages in some periods may compel the farmer employer to recruit workers from outside the village. Sometimes, employers must travel several hundred kilometers to find such workers. In other cases, poor farmers who want jobs will contract with employment brokers. The recruitment process is generally an informal one, but some degree of formality is also observed. As the need for hired agricultural labor increases, the recruitment process is gradually evolving into employment contracts.

Recruitment and teams of hired labor. Recruiting workers from other villages is widely practiced in rice and sugarcane harvesting operations. Occasionally, paddy transplanting also requires labor from outside the village. The farmer employer (usually a female) will normally visit some of her friends in other villages and ask them to recruit a number of workers by promising to pay a certain wage rate.[6] In the case of rice harvesting, the employer will make a contract a few days in advance and inform her contact person of the number of workers needed and of the date that they will be picked up. For sugarcane cutting, the employer has to pay a visit 1 to 2 months before the harvesting season (Table 6.9). Most of the time, both the rice and sugarcane employers will have to give advance money to the team leader who, in turn, will distribute the money to team members. The amount of money received by each sugarcane employee is 500 to 2,000 baht. Some team members may decide not to take any advance money, but those who do receive an advance are morally obligated to do the work. The employer will deduct the employees' debt from their wage income without any interest on the advance money.

The scheme is, in fact, a labor *forward contract* (Tables 6.9 and 6.10). This form of contract arises because there is a labor shortage in the harvesting season. Thus, the employer is willing to book labor in advance by lending the money at no interest. Having enough workers is crucial to preventing huge losses caused by delays in harvesting. In the case of sugarcane, failure to deliver the agreed quota of sugar to the sugar mill means a loss of quota rights to sell sugarcane to the factory. From the employees' viewpoint, the labor contract offer is attractive because they do not have to pay interest on the money. By contracting in advance, they will be certain to get jobs for a known period of time, thus reducing job-search costs. Moreover, the employees also economize on negotiation costs because contract negotiations are the responsibility of the team leader (or the broker).

The team leader receives a return for service as a broker. In the sugarcane business, the leader may receive 50 to 100 baht per worker recruited plus some other benefits, such as the privilege to borrow money from his or her boss (with interest). The team leader for rice harvesting receives 1 to 2 baht per worker. The rice broker's fee is lower than that for the sugarcane broker because the number of working days differ. The employer is responsible for providing free transport service for all workers; he or she also provides shelter, water, a stove, and a few other necessary items for guest workers, who will have to bring their own rice. Each team typically consists of 10 to 30 workers. The sugarcane-cutting team is relatively

Table 6.9 Labor Forward Contracts

	Rice	Sugarcane	Cassava
Operation	Harvesting and handling Transplanting	Cutting and handling	Root pulling
Occupation of team leader	Rice farmer	Rice farmer	Trader or vehicle owner
Origin of workers	Everywhere within 150 km	Northeast	Northeast
Advance payment with no interest	A few hundred baht	500 to 2,000 baht	None
Period of work	2 to 4 weeks	4 to 16 weeks	2 to 4 weeks
Group size	10 to 30	15 to 50	5 to 30
Payment basis	Piece-rate	Piece-rate	Piece-rate
Leader fee	1 to 2 baht per worker	50 to 100 baht per worker	None

Sources: Compiled from various village studies (Harnvajanawong, 1991; Kongkaew, 1990; Thongprapa, 1990; Charonchi, 1990; Chompoopa, 1990; Fuangfa, 1990).

Table 6.10 Classification of Contracts and Main Reasons for Their Existence

	Reasons	Example
Future contract (team)		
Forward contract	Shortage of labor and information cost reduction Price-risk allocation	Rice harvesting Sugarcane cutting Cassava digging
Tied contract	Shortage of labor and seasonal pattern of income cash flow	Tok Raeng
Form of hired labor		
Exchange labor	Shortage of labor	Rice harvesting
Hired labor	Shortage of labor and high cost of enforcement	All agricultural operation
Basis of payment		
Daily rate	Quality shirking	Weeding Harvesting in small fields
Piece-rate	Quality shirking and low cost of quality supervision	Harvesting

larger (about 15 to 50 workers) because the size of the harvested area is much larger in sugar crops than in rice crops. Most workers will have a few family members accompanying them, and most of the team members are relatives or close friends of the team leader. If any of the team members become ill and can no longer work, the team leader has the responsibility of finding others to replace them.

These workers receive the same wage rate as the local workers. Because they receive some fringe benefits, their actual wage rate is slightly higher. Most of the tasks are paid on a piece-rate basis. For example, the wage rate for paddy harvesting in the Central Plains is 80 to 160 baht per rai. The reward for sugarcane cutting is 30 to 40 baht per bundle (each of which contains 10 to 15 stems). The wage rate for loading the sugarcane bundles onto the truck is 20 baht per ton.

Labor recruitment through team leaders results from high information costs in the labor market. Despite this, it is fascinating to observe that both the employer and the employees, who live far away from each other and do not know each other, can successfully develop an information network and employment link. And although the network is an informal one, it is highly efficient. Of course, some employers may have friends or acquaintances in other villages thought to have an available supply of labor, and they will work this contact. Most others, however, hire an employment broker for the first contract to recruit workers on their behalf. After the first contract, these employers will go back to the same person in the same village. If that person is not available, another team member can be contacted and asked to be the new team leader. Moreover, many employees also introduce their farmer friends who want to hire workers to the villagers. Thus, workers from the same village have a tendency to work in the same province. The team leader will, in turn, contact the villagers whom he or she knows best. Workers who are known to shirk or be difficult to manage will not be selected. This explains why the size of the team is relatively small (10 to 50 workers). Moreover, workers from the same village tend to work in the same area because they will be persuaded and given job information by their friends. At the same time, many employers also take their friends who want to hire workers to visit the same village, and they introduce them to the villagers. Several studies found that most villagers in one village who go to work on the sugarcane farms will go to the same district (Panpiemras and Krusuansombat, 1985; Thongprapa, 1990).

It should also be noted that most, if not all, sugarcane workers are from the Northeast. The paddy harvesting season in the Northeast ends just before the sugar mills open, and after rice harvesting, Northeasterners do not have any additional on-farm work. Also, the Northeastern farmers are the poorest and have to accept jobs that people from other areas do not prefer. Sugarcane cutting, for example, is an extremely harsh job, involving backbreaking labor. On the other hand, workers in rice-harvesting operations come from every part of the country. Poor farmers who live in the Southern area, where the harvesting season comes late, will go North for harvesting work. When it is time to harvest the rice crop in their villages, farmers from the Northern villages who have already completed their rice harvest will be hired to harvest paddy in the South.

There are a few problems with this employment network. Sometimes, a team leader, who has received the advance money from the employer, runs away, and the employer has to recruit a new leader. Then, too, if team members who have already received advances go to work with another employer, the team leader must take full responsibility. This phenomenon happened during the sugarcane harvesting season in the Central West in 1990 because there was an increased labor demand in the Lower North. Employers in the latter region offered higher wage rates to attract the workers. A third problem is that some employers may not be satisfied with the quality of work of the contracted team. In this case, they will tend to go to other villages in the following season, where they may have to begin the search process all over again.

Cassava diggers. Another type of team employment observed in Thailand involves cassava digging. Here, the main employer is not the cassava farmer but the cassava trader or truck owner. In the 1970s, cassava was mainly grown in the Northeast, but cassava cultivation has since spread to the North and to the Central Plains, where there is usually a labor shortage. However, the nature of the labor shortage in cassava-digging operations is different from that in harvesting or transplanting activities for rice: The latter must be done almost simultaneously across many farms, but there is no fixed date for cassava harvesting. It may be dug out when it is six months old or when it is sixteen to eighteen months old. Farmers should, therefore, have no labor problem.

However, 90 percent of cassava is exported under a voluntary export restraint system, and the Ministry of Commerce has thus set up a quota-exporting system that sets a ceiling on exports for each period. Consequently, the domestic price of cassava fluctuates wildly, shooting to a peak when exports are allowed and falling to a floor when the export quota for that period is fulfilled. For this reason, the price risk is very high, and it is the cassava trader who takes the risk. Prior to the harvesting period, he or she will offer to buy whole crops from the cassava farmers. The trader will make an offer after inspecting the cassava field. When the contract is agreed upon, the trader will harvest the product with a team of workers from the Northeast. If the cassava price remains too low, the trader will delay harvesting the crop. Because there is an agreed deadline for harvesting the entire crop, if the trader fails to meet it, he or she must compensate the farmers for their opportunity cost of using the land.

Traders speculate on price increases, and they will make purchasing contracts with many farmers. A trader, therefore, needs to recruit large numbers of workers from the Northeast because he or she must be able to finish harvesting the contract crop before the prices go down (Table 6.10). Moreover, there are economies of scale in harvesting and marketing cassava. The process of recruitment is similar to that for rice-harvesting workers, except that the cassava workers may work for only a short period.

Tied contract. In some villages where there are ample job opportunities in the agricultural sector, one observes the highest percentage of landless workers living in the village. In certain cases, landless families account for 20 to 30 percent of all village households (Chompoopa, 1990; Harnva-janawong, 1991)—much higher than the national average of 10 percent. However, during the peak season, the total village supply of labor still falls short of demand. Therefore, the employers have to make future arrangements with the workers. At the same time, landless workers do not have jobs in the dry season, and the annual cash income of the landless worker is typically not enough to get through this lean period, especially if there is an emergency in the household. Because their need for cash can be solved by borrowing from the rich farmers, who also need their labor, both sides gain by entering the so-called *tok raeng* contract (Table 6.10). In this case, the employment contract is tied to the credit contract. The employer will provide needed cash advances to the landless workers; they, in turn, will have to repay their debt by working on the employer's farm. The rate of interest charged by the employer is about 5 percent per month. But the high interest rate is not the result of labor market monopsony. Rather, it is dictated by the imperfect credit market (Poapongsakorn and Netayarak, 1989).

In some technologically stagnant villages, the landless workers borrow paddy from the employers. In certain villages, employment brokers provide credit to the landless workers and, in return, ask them to provide labor services to other farmers with whom the brokers have contracted (Chompoopa, 1990).

Exchange labor and hired labor. In Thailand, the numbers of rural wage laborers increased slowly because there was abundant new land on the frontier until the 1980s and because the population growth rate rapidly declined after 1970. Therefore, landless rural labor as "a class" is not a problem (Bot and Gooneratne, 1982). However, many farm owners and farm tenants have become part-time hired laborers as a result of changes in technology and the development process. The traditional form of exchange labor has rapidly disappeared and been replaced by hired labor. The pace of change has occurred most rapidly in the Central Plains, starting in the early 1970s, and in the Upper North, in the late 1970s. By the late 1980s, there was almost no exchange labor except in remote and technologically stagnant villages.

The reason for such an institutional change appears to be the high opportunity cost of continuing traditional arrangements in the presence of new and more profitable technology. Irrigation and modern seed varieties allow multiple-cropping, leading to a highly concentrated labor

requirement during short periods of time. Because every farmer has to perform each operation simultaneously, labor demand cannot be met by family and exchange labor with neighboring farmers. In the traditional system,
farmers grow different types of native seeds according to locational factors
and conditions. All the work did not have to be done at the same time, so
exchange labor was possible. This is no longer the case. Also, there are
more off-farm employment opportunities outside the village than before.
Under these circumstances, the exchange labor system cannot survive because some workers who owe labor services to other families may be unable to provide timely farm work or they may shirk in their efforts, resulting in delays in cultivation and high costs of contract enforcement. Data
from the Northern villages reveal that the percentage of exchange labor on
owner-cultivated fields declined sharply, from 30 percent of holdings in
1980 to 10 percent in 1981 (Ganjanapan, 1989: 116).

It is interesting to note that during the period in which institutions
were changing, there was a transitory system of exchange labor in the
Upper North. After the introduction of multiple cropping in northern villages, Ganjanapan (1989) found a new type of contract that compensated
workers with a percentage of the crop harvested. Known as *chang roi
thon*, this contract featured the participation of hired laborers in a network
of exchange labor on behalf of the employer, recruiting others to participate in the network. The wage rate was 13 to 15 percent of the crop harvested for harvesting operations or 18 to 20 percent for a combination of
transplanting and harvesting, compared with 33 to 50 percent under cus-
tomary sharecropping practices.

However, the system quickly disappeared, giving way to the hired
labor system, and there are interesting reasons for its rise and fall. *Chang
roi thon* is a hybrid form of traditional exchange labor and hired labor. Although a large number of farmers who adopted multiple-cropping were
kept busy during short periods of transplanting and harvesting, there were
still, in the same village, other farmers who did not practice multiple-cropping. The implicit wage rate of *chang roi thon* was, at the time, attractive
to these farmers. From the employers' view, the system reduced enforcement costs because they did not have to closely monitor the work. The system allowed the farmer-employers more leisure time without reducing output because their employees had incentives to select good coworkers and
monitor them. Because leisure is a normal good (i.e., one for which the
quantity demanded increases when income is higher), it is not surprising to
find that the system was more popular among rich farmers.

Yet there were several difficulties with *chang roi thon*. Some landowners had cheated by substituting low-priced glutinous rice for the
higher-priced nonglutinous crop harvested. Moreover, the cost of contract
enforcement for employees was very high. Also, the employee had to recruit other workers as exchange helpers, and as labor shortages became

more severe and more job opportunities arose outside the village, it was hard to recruit enough helpers without providing more incentives. And *chang roi thon* employees had complained about the high cost of serving lunch to recruited exchange helpers.

Basis of payment: Piece-rate and time-rate contracts. Daily wage labor is the most common form of hired labor observed.[7] The time-rate payment system will be adopted first in those activities in which quality shirking is difficult to monitor (e.g., in chemical or fertilizer application). When traditional labor arrangements begin to disappear, the wage system for most activities will be established on a time-rate basis. On the other hand, where effort shirking is easily monitored by inspection, a piece-rate system will be chosen; quality shirking is the major problem encountered under the piece-rate system. Finally, in more specialized activities, a piece-rate system with teamwork will be used because it can further reduce the excess burden (or waste) associated with the use of hired labor by lowering the supervision cost. Decentralization of supervision lessens both effort shirking and quality shirking (Roumasset and Uy, 1980).

The data in Table 6.11 are derived from six villages covered in TDRI's employment study. Only two villages, which have surplus rice production and thus commercialized and specialized production of rice, report that they use the piece-rate payment system for transplanting and harvesting operations. However, a daily wage (time-rate) system for harvesting work is also found in these two villages. Daily wages are adopted in lower-yield paddy fields or in areas of low-yielding, shallow-water rice. (Such rice is appropriate on elevated land that has insufficient water for high-yielding varieties). In other villages, the time-rate payment system is used because farm size is relatively small and farmers are producing mainly for their own consumption. Because these farmers also work closely with the hired labor, the cost of supervision is low. The village studies reported various tactics that farm employers used to control their employees' pace of work.

Cassava digging is compensated on a piece-rate basis because most employers in this sector are cassava traders. They do not have time to supervise all employees because, as traders, they buy the whole cassava crop of many farms at the same time and must finish the harvesting job rapidly or risk a decrease in the cassava price. For supervisory work, all the trader has to do is check the amount of cultivated output against the estimated output and inspect the field. Moreover, quality is not critical in cassava digging, and the piece-rate system provides sufficient incentives for the workers.

The two villages in the TDRI study that produce corn have adopted the same system of wage payments. Seeding is paid on a daily basis because the employer wants to make sure most seeds will grow at the same rate. In all cases, the employer will work side by side with his or her

Table 6.11   Characteristics of Thai Villages and Wage Payment Methods

	Villages from					
Items	Nakorn Swan (LN)	Lopburi (C)	Uthai-Thani (UC)	Kon-Kaen (NE)	Udon (NE)	Lampoon (N)
Main occupation	Rice and upland crop	Rice	Cassava	Rice and gem cutting	Rice	Rice and off-farm employment
Multiple-cropping	No	Yes	No	No	No	No
Rice surplus	Yes	Yes	No	No	No	No
Landholding size	Large	Large	Small	Medium	Small	
Labor contract type						
Rice						
Harvesting	P	P	T	T	T	T
Transplanting	P	P	T	T	T	T
Cassava digging	P	—	P	—	P	—
Corn						
Seeding	T	—	T	—	—	—
Harvesting	P	—	P	—	—	—
Weeding	P	—	T, P	—	—	—
Sugarcane cutting	P	—	—	—	P	—

Sources: Charonchi (1990); Chompoopa (1990); Fuangfa (1990); Harnvajanawong (1990); Kongkaew (1990); Thongprapa (1990).
— indicates no activity reported.
C = Central.
LN = Lower North.
N = North.
NE = Northeast.
P = Piece-rate.
T = Time-rate.
UC = Upper Central.

helpers. On the other hand, corn harvesting and weeding, as well as sugarcane cutting, are paid on a piece-rate basis to give employees an incentive to work harder and for longer hours. It is also very easy for the employer to check the output performance of each worker by simply looking at the size of the output. It should be noted that piece-rate payments in sugarcane cutting have encouraged some workers to take stamina-enhancing medicine that may damage their health in the future.

Adjustments of Labor Supply

David Feeny (1982) has argued convincingly that in the prewar period, Thai underdevelopment was largely attributable to the ruling elite's lack of interest in investing in productivity improvement projects in the agricultural sector. In the postwar period, policy discrimination against the agricultural sector and in favor of the urban-industrial sector explains the poverty of the farmers. Moreover, even though the government has pursued irrigation and agricultural research projects that have led to productivity improvements, the average agricultural productivity is still extremely low. Hence, it is not surprising to find that poverty is highly concentrated in the agricultural sector. For these reasons, farmers have had to adjust their patterns of labor supply in order to increase income and provide for the consumption needs of their households. They may migrate to work outside the village or even outside the country, and farmers are increasingly inclined to take up nonagricultural jobs. Investment in development of new job skills is another choice. Such changes may, in turn, lead to shifts in production patterns on the farm itself.

Shifts in production patterns. Throughout the postwar period, rice and rubber export taxes and export quotas lowered the farm-gate prices of rice and rubber. Low prices for outputs, coupled with the protection of the domestic fertilizer industry, reduced the private returns to farm crop production. The discriminatory taxes on rice and rubber, as well as development of roads and infrastructure, stimulated crop diversification into maize, cassava, and kenaf production (Feeny, 1982). It is difficult to qualify the effects of specific taxes on crop diversification, but it is likely that discrimination against rice led to some social costs. In addition, part of the resources poured into nonrice production could possibly have been more efficiently used in rice production in the absence of an export tax.

Expansion of upland crops was made possible by the availability of unused land on the frontier. The encroachment into forest lands has had two opposing effects. The first is the negative effect on the environment for the forest area shrank drastically from 55 percent of total land in 1960 to less than 25 percent in 1987. The second effect is that the availability of unused land has helped maintain the standard of living of the poor families.

Internal migration. Between 1960 and 1970, rural-to-rural migration accounted for the largest stream of permanent migrants because the availability of forest land allowed people to move from densely populated rice-growing areas to thinly populated, upland crop-growing areas. The proportion of rural-to-rural migration in total migration declined from 62.6 percent between 1965 and 1970 to 52 percent between 1975 and 1980. The decline is a result of the gradual exhaustion of the land frontier. The second largest migration stream, rural-to-urban, has increased. In the poorest region, the Northeast, the number of rural-to-urban migrants was greatest, totaling more than 110,000 between 1975 and 1980.

Aside from permanent migrants, there are also large numbers of seasonal migrants from rural areas. Unfortunately, there are no reliable data on the magnitude of this type of migration. One study estimated that in 1981, there were about 366,000 seasonal agricultural jobs (such as sugarcane cutting) that attracted rural migrants. Another group of at least 122,000 temporary migrants moved from the rural areas to seek jobs in Bangkok (Panpiemras and Krusuansombat, 1985: 331). The main reasons for migrating are the lack of employment opportunities in villages during the dry seasons and inadequate income.

Most migrants to Bangkok receive information about job opportunities prior to their departure—information supplied by friends and relatives who have already worked there. Only a quarter of migrants venture on their own to search for jobs in Bangkok. And yet, they can easily obtain casual work. As a result, the unemployment rate among migrants is less than 2 percent. However, the information prospective migrants receive is not perfect. One study found that significant numbers of potential seasonal migrants do not migrate because they lack job information. Thus, the rate of seasonal migration is reduced by a lack of information (Sussangkarn, 1987).

Studies indicate that almost 60 percent of seasonal migrants failed to remit money back to their villages, and 30 percent remitted less than 500 baht each time. Migration, therefore, does not seem to improve the living conditions of the migrants' families beyond providing temporary relief from the hardship of poverty (Panpiemras and Krusuansombat, 1985: 337). Moreover, migrants also experience numerous social problems. For example, many rural parents send their children to work in urban factories or even to Bangkok's notorious bars and massage parlors, and these young migrants often end up living in the urban slums. Indeed, the number of slums in Bangkok increased from 361 areas in 1960 to 1,020 areas in 1985, and the total slum population now exceeds 1 million. Many children in the slums do not have proper household registration and, hence, cannot attend school in Bangkok. A large number of teenagers become drug addicts, and some eventually become criminals.

Overseas migration. Job opportunities in the Middle East and, more recently, in Asia and Europe, with relatively high wage rates, encouraged Thai rural laborers to venture abroad. The number of overseas migrants jumped from 293 persons in 1973 to 118,957 in 1988. The expansion of overseas migration primarily reflects the activities of both Thai workers and employment agencies; the government did not play any direct role in international labor migration until after 1980. More than 85 percent of these overseas workers are farmers and relatively young. The most significant fact is that about half of the overseas migrants come from the Northeast. Out-migration is concentrated heavily in some villages of certain provinces, such as Udonthani and Nakorn Ratchasima (Poapongsakorn and Sangthanapurk, 1989).

The heavy concentration of migrants results in severe labor shortages in those villages. A careful two-village study by Poapongsakorn and Sangthanapurk (1989) in the district of Udonthani looked at the adjustments in several markets caused by out-migration. As expected, the loss of family labor due to emigration led to the use of hired labor and increased labor inputs from those left behind. It also led to the renting out of land to other families. The amount of rice production on the farms belonging to the migrants' families was seriously affected by emigration, but the impact on the total village production appeared to be very small (less than a 2 percent reduction) because the nonmigrant families responded by increasing their output.

Income and land distribution in the village with heavy emigration improved after remittances were received. Conversely, land distribution in the village with few migrants worsened because returning migrants from other villages began to purchase land in the poorer villages with low levels of out-migration. Land transactions also increased in the village with more out-migration, not so much because of increased incomes among the migrants but rather because of the need to raise capital to finance emigration. These land sales, however, were not large enough to affect land prices.

As noted, the expansion of international labor migration has been facilitated principally by private employment agencies and brokers. Many villagers report being cheated by employment agents, leading, in some cases, to the loss of their land; about 49 percent of returned overseas labor migrants in the study villages reported they had been cheated at least once (Nipon and Hongpha, 1990). And there are social problems, as well, when a husband goes abroad for a long time, as suggested by a popular saying: "Losing the land when going abroad and losing a wife when coming back."

Investment in Human Capital

There is a paradox in the Thai educational system. Most Thais long for higher education, and almost half of those who finish upper secondary school will go on to university education. However, the overall enrollment in secondary education continues to be low. For 1987, it is estimated that 30 percent of all secondary-school-age children were, in fact, enrolled in school, compared to 68 percent in the Philippines and 94 percent in South Korea. Clearly, there has not yet been a transformation in the secondary education sector comparable to the transformation in the structure of the Thai economy. But this should not, perhaps, be surprising, considering that Thailand was only able to offer universal compulsory primary education in the 1970s. In fact, although the nation launched a program of 7 years of compulsory education in 1960, it was not until 1977 that this became a reality. By that time, the government had made progress in addressing problems of inadequate educational facilities and a corresponding lack of teachers.

Farmers realize the benefits of primary education for basic numeracy and literacy enables them to read the instructions on fertilizer, pesticide, and insecticide bags. One study found that farmers with primary educations had higher productivity than those with no formal education (Jamison and Lau, 1982), which helps explain why rural parents are willing to send their children to primary school. However, many farmers still do not see the benefit or relevance of secondary education. Even if they or their children migrate to the cities, the labor-intensive industries in which they are most likely to find work require only that they have rudimentary skills that can be learned on the job in a few days. Moreover, those who have completed primary school earn the same minimum wage rate as those who went on to secondary school. Even if better-educated workers become self-employed, one study (Sussangkarn, 1987) indicates that their earnings do not significantly differ from those of less-educated people.

Farmers know that if they are going to send their children to secondary schools, they must make a commitment to finance them through a university education.[8] However, university entrance depends on passing entrance examinations, and secondary schools outside the cities often cannot adequately prepare students for these exams. Added to all this, farmers have to hire workers to do work that could have been done by their students. Consequently, both direct and indirect costs of postprimary education are too high for many farmers (Chutikul, 1989).

Yet this does not mean that farmers do not invest in educating their children. For example, village studies show that richer farmers in the Central Plains will send their male children to vocational schools, teacher colleges, and military and police schools. (Vocational and military educations only require a few years of study.) Most female children are sent to take short courses in hairdressing and dressmaking after they finish primary school, and girls from poorer families who cannot afford such formal education often become apprentices of beauty parlor operators or female dressmakers.

Most rural children and teenagers who do not go to secondary school and who migrate to work in the cities acquire skills through various on-the-job experiences. This method of learning by doing is obviously a substitute, although an imperfect one, for secondary education, designed to increase the supply of semiskilled and skilled workers. Meanwhile, concerns are rising that Thailand will not be able to sustain its high growth rate if it fails to significantly increase enrollment in secondary schools.

Transitions in the Rural Labor Markets

Thai rural labor markets are in a transitional stage. Traditionally, demand for rural employment is dictated by the seasonality of agricultural labor demand. Off-farm employment during the slack season is viewed as an opportunity for the family to supplement its income. However, there are reasons to believe that Thai rural labor markets are now less dominated by agricultural seasonality than by the demand for nonfarm employment that draws labor away from the farm. As a result, nonagricultural employment has increased from an estimated 3.8 million (or 27.3 percent of total rural employment) in 1977–1978 to 6.6 million (or 31.3 percent of total rural employment) in 1987–1988.

If seasonal employment in the nonagricultural sector were predominantly caused by large numbers of agricultural workers becoming available during the slack season, then the nonagricultural wage rate should be lower than that of the peak period of agricultural labor demand. However, data in Table 6.12 show that for rural men between the ages of fifteen and fifty-nine who were privately employed in manufacturing, average monthly wages were higher during the slack season than during the peak season in all but the Central Region. Wages for private employees in construction were higher during the slack period for every region but the North, and wages in commerce were higher in the dry season in the Central and Southern regions. These data, although hardly conclusive, do suggest that seasonal variation in the overall demand for labor in nonagricultural industries is more important than seasonal growth of surplus agricultural labor in influencing the character of the rural labor market (Chutikul and Thosaguan, 1989).

Moreover, not only has the share of agricultural employment in total employment decreased but the absolute number of females employed in the agriculture sector has also been declining since 1985. By contrast, the rapid growth of labor-intensive industries has resulted in a major increase in the demand for young female workers. During the 1974–1979 period, a large majority of the increase in male and female employment (80 percent and 87 percent, respectively) in the dry season occurred in the agricultural sector. Between 1981 and 1988, only 61 percent of the increase in female employment was in the agricultural sector, compared to 74 percent for males.

Nonagricultural Activities in the Rural Economy

The persistence of significant levels of rural poverty in Thailand is mainly caused by a range of policy biases against the rural sector and by the dominance of low-productivity rural employment. Many studies show that expansion of nonagricultural employment is one of the most promising ways to alleviate rural poverty. There are problems, however, in applying this expectation to rural Thailand. First, most nonagricultural activities are located in urban centers. Seasonality, limited market size, and high transportation costs limit the extent of rural (as compared to urban) industrialization. Second, although many nonfarm employment opportunities do

Table 6.12 Average Wage for Privately Employed Thai Males (ages 15 to 59) by Industry, 1986 (baht per month)

Nonmunicipal Areas	Agriculture		Manufacturing		Construction		Commerce	
	R1	R3	R1	R3	R1	R3	R1	R3
Central	1,182	1,470	2,501	2,760	2,426	2,148	2,208	2,129
South	1,806	1,710	2,155	1,974	2,935	2,213	3,203	2,165
North	904	na	1,590	1,271	1,890	2,545	1,515	3,958
Northeast	1,268	na	1,639	1,403	1,949	1,527	1,566	3,322

Source: World Bank (1989: Table 5.1). Reprinted with permission.
R1 = Round 1 (February).
R3 = Round 3 (August).

exist in rural areas, the growth rate of such employment has been severely constrained by the slow growth of agricultural income.

Extent and Significance of Rural Nonfarm Activities

Table 6.13 shows the extent of rural nonfarm activities. In 1975–1976, roughly one out of five rural households specialized in nonfarm activities. Although there are variations in the definitions of household type, it is clear that the number of rural nonfarm households had rapidly increased to almost one in four by 1986. Available information reveals that the richer regions, such as the Central East, have a larger number of nonfarm households than the poorer regions.

The nonagricultural rural sector employed about 5.55 million in 1987–1988. This represents about 24.3 percent of the total rural employment in the peak agricultural season. Manufacturing employment accounted for 6.4 percent, and the construction, commerce, and transport sectors employed 1.9 percent, 7.3 percent, and 1.4 percent, respectively. Seasonality also characterized rural employment in manufacturing, construction, and commerce. During the dry season, when agricultural employment declined by 3.5 million, nonagricultural employment increased by 1.14 million.

Table 6.13   Percentage of Rural Nonfarm Households in Thailand, 1975/76, 1981, and 1986

Area/Household	1975/76	1981	1986
Municipal	14.8	16	20.9
Sanitary			
Farm	6.5	—	2.7
Nonfarm	5.8	—	6.1
Rural			
Farm	60.3	58[a]	45.6
Nonfarm	12.6	26[a]	24.7
Total[b]	100.0	100	100.0

Sources: TDRI (1987: p. 21); World Bank (1983: p. 36).
— indicates no data.
[a] Sanitary areas and villages are combined.

Nonagricultural income accounted for an increasing percentage of total income in rural areas. It jumped from 35 percent in 1975–1976 to 46 percent in 1986 (Tables 6.14 and 6.15). Furthermore, the poor had more diversified sources of labor income. Table 6.15 shows that higher proportions of the total income of poor farmers came from off-farm sources, as

Table 6.14   Sources of Income of Agricultural Households in Thailand, 1975/76 and 1986

Sources of Income	1975/76		1986	
	%	Baht	%	Baht/Month
Total income	100.0	1,623.2	100.0	2,665.7
Agriculture	65.3	1,060.1	54.2	1,443.2
On-farm	56.7	920.8	26.9	716.4
Off-farm[a]	8.6	139.3	27.3	726.8
Nonagriculture	34.7	563.2	45.8	1,222.3
Wage	18.0	292.8	9.2	245.2
Other[b]	16.7	270.4	36.6	977.1

Sources: TDRI (1987: p. 75); World Bank (1983: pp. 41–42).

[a] Agricultural off-farm income in 1975/76 includes rents from hiring out animals, farm equipment, land and living quarters, and wages. In 1986, only wages are included.

[b] Other nonagricultural income in 1975/76 consisted of sale of nonraised animals, off-farm crops, and homemade goods, as well as transfer income, interest, and other sources (such as mining). In 1986, it included salary and wages for hired work, profit, transfer income, and property income.

compared to rich farmers. Poor nonfarmers, on the other hand, earned a higher proportion of their income from farming than their rich nonfarm counterparts. The evidence suggests that income from secondary sources is an option forced on the poor more by necessity than by opportunity (TDRI, 1987: 20). One fact to support this interpretation is that poor farmers have to work much harder than rich farmers by taking on all kinds of available jobs outside the agricultural sector. Table 6.16 reveals that females and males in the low-income villages work about 1,755 and 1,812 hours per year, respectively. In contrast, in well-off villages, they work only 1,560 and 1,548 hours, respectively. Poor villages and poor regions also have a higher proportion of nonagricultural income (Akrasanee et al., 1983; World Bank, 1983). The data in Table 6.15 also show that diversity in income sources seems to have increased. Such diversity may be viewed as a reaction to increased hardship rather than a desirable structural shift (Siamwalla, 1991).

As a result of the monsoon, agricultural income is subject to wide seasonal and yearly fluctuations, resulting in negative cash flows during the dry season and positive flows during other months. For example, data from Kasetsart University Rural Off-Farm Employment Assessment Project indicate that the cash flow in richer villages fluctuates more than the flow in poorer villages.

Factors Affecting the Existence of Rural Industry

To understand the factors explaining the existence of nonfarm activities in rural areas, it is first necessary to characterize these activities.[9] The

Table 6.15 Percentage of Income from Different Sources in Rural Households in Thailand, 1975/76, 1981, and 1986

Income Groups	1975/76[a] Farm	Off-farm Wages	Off-farm Other	1981[a] Farm	Off-farm Wages	Off-farm Other	1986[b] Farm	Off-farm Wages	Off-farm Other
Rice									
Rich	73	11	16	63	4	32			
Medium	70	16	14	28	36	36			
Poor	65	13	22	49	9	42			
Nonrice									
Rich	65	10	24	58	7	36			
Medium	58	16	26	53	11	36			
Poor	52	17	31	41	16	43			
Nonfarm									
Rich	4	43	52	2	49	49			
Medium	5	47	48	4	42	55			
Poor	3	48	49	5	47	49			
Agricultural household									
Quintile 5 (richest)							61	4	35
4							63	4	33
3							58	8	36
2							50	12	38
1 (poorest)							48	12	40
Nonagriculture									
Quintile 5 (richest)							16	33	51
4							12	32	56
3							8	34	58
2							4	38	58
1 (poorest)							1	34	65

Sources: TDRI (1987: p. 74) and Siamwalla and Setboonsarng (1987: p. 21).
[a] Rural households.
[b] All households.

Table 6.16   Average Work Hours of Active Rural Workers in Thailand, Classified by Income Level, 1980–1981 (per year)

| Village Type | Farm | 1980 | | 1981 | | Total (Hours) |
		Nonfarm (Hours)	Nonfarm (%)	Nonfarm (Hours)	Nonfarm (%)	
Low-income						
Male	650	753	41.6	428	23.6	1,812
Female	565	345	19.7	844	48.1	1,755
Medium-income						
Male	941	272	16.4	443	27.0	1,662
Female	730	400	27.1	345	23.4	1,474
High-income						
Male	770	235	15.2	543	35.1	1,548
Female	640	585	37.5	335	21.5	1,560

Source: Akrasanee et al. (1983: 40).

most visible types of manufacturing found in rural areas are: (1) rice mills, tin mining and processing, sugar refining, and those involving a weight-reduction process for bulk shipments like tapioca pellets; (2) those producing raw materials for construction, such as bricks and cement blocks; and (3) industries that use perishable raw materials (such as canned fruits, vegetable oil, fish products, and frozen seafood) and cold storage. Most of the factories are small- and medium scale, with the exception of sugar mills and ore-processing plants, which are subject to economies of scale. For the first two types, transportation cost is the key factor explaining their location in the rural area. Both transportation cost and the perishable nature of the product are crucial in the third category.

Many small rice mills (more than 30,000) and small factory houses that produce highly perishable foods purchased almost daily by households are also found everywhere in the country. The former are located in almost all villages in the North and the Northeast. In the Central Plains, only medium- and large-scale rice mills are found because the transport system is very good and a large number of farmers are specialized in rice production. These farmers do not store the paddy but instead sell it all right after the harvest and buy rice for consumption from middlemen; this is cheaper than storing the paddy and paying a rice mill to process it for future consumption. In the North and the Northeast, most households store their own paddy because transportation costs make purchased rice more costly than keeping rice in storage. The small factories that produce highly perishable products, such as noodles, meatballs, fishballs, and pickles, are mostly located in the suburbs of cities and towns. Their products are in daily demand, and transportation costs are high. However, advances in technology, which make it possible to preserve noodles and some food products by dehydration, have allowed some manufacturers to expand their scale of production and locate their plants at the point of minimum transportation cost. Services constitute another important category of nonfarm rural activities. Examples include grocery stores, noodle shops, tractor and motorcycle repair shops, gas stations, tailors, and barbers.

Backward and forward linkage of the agricultural sector. The steady expansion of the export-oriented agricultural sector has greatly stimulated the growth of metal workshops, agricultural machinery manufacturing, and other input-supplying activities, such as the production of livestock feed. The agricultural machinery industry evolved out of traditional blacksmithing. The invention of new or locally adapted machinery designs often followed from the suggestions of customers dissatisfied with imported machines or because spare parts were unavailable (Loohawenchit, 1980).

The emergence of medium- and large-scale feed factories in rural areas is a response to the expansion of the livestock sector. Livestock demand itself has increased with the growing per capita income and expanding foreign demand. Feed factories tend to be located near livestock farms, which are, of course, the main users (Poapongsakorn, 1980). Animal feed production requires the use of grain and fish meals, and these raw materials come from different locations. Maize comes from the Lower North and the North, but fish meal and soybean meal must be imported. It should be noted that most modern animal feed factories are capital intensive and employ only a handful of operators, supervisors, and quality-control workers. For example, some factories in the high-labor-cost area of the eastern seaboard have mechanized the loading process.

The expansion of the agricultural processing industries just described is also the result of the growth in the agricultural sector. And agricultural growth is driven by the Thai farmers' response to domestic and world demand. Expansion of the agricultural sector also generates forward linkages to the transportation sector, which explains why transport workers make up a particularly important proportion of the nonagricultural labor force in the Upper Northeast and the South.

Agricultural income. The expansion of the agricultural sector increases the income of the majority of Thais, and this, in turn, creates demand for goods and services produced in both the urban and rural areas. Casual observation shows that when the prices of agricultural products go up, sales of durable and nondurable goods also increase—goods like radios, television sets, garments, light trucks, motorcycles, bicycles, liquor, cigarettes, tractors, and water pumps. The growth of village grocery stores is also consistent with the rising-income hypothesis. Moreover, sales of the village grocery stores tend to increase in the peak agricultural seasons when farmers do not have time to process food from their own farms (Chompoopa, 1990; Charonchi,

1990). This explains why sales activities are the most important nonfarm activities in terms of employment share (30 percent).

Data from village studies and field visits reveal that most villages have at least one retail shop. Villages with higher agricultural income can accommodate more grocery stores, food stalls, motorcycle and tractor repair shops, gas stations, and so on (Charonchi, 1990; Thongprapa, 1990; Harnvajanawong, 1991). These enterprises are often established by people who obtain nonagricultural skills while working in the cities and then return to their rural homes.

The hypothesis that there is a demand linkage between the agricultural sector and the output of the manufacturing sector is consistent with the findings of a study by Ammar Siamwalla (1991). He found that a 1 percent increase in agriculture and mining income induces an increase in manufacturing output of about 0.20 percent. This is accounted for primarily by the fact that agricultural processing accounts for 10 to 15 percent of manufacturing value added.

A more direct approach to ascertaining the influence of demand linkages is to look at the behavior of rural consumers in response to an increase in their income. Available data from the household expenditure surveys indicate that as rural income rises, there is a change in consumption patterns from food to nonfood, nondurable to durable goods, and traditional to higher-value-added goods produced in both the urban and rural areas. Regional income elasticities computed from 1986 data are found to be greater than 1 for most goods in the following categories: alcoholic beverages, housing materials, fuel and lights, minor equipment, vehicle parts, musical instruments, reading materials, and miscellaneous items used for festivals and ceremonies. Food, tobacco, cloth and clothing, drugs and medicines, and personal care items have elasticities between 0 and 1 (Grandstaff, 1989). Because most of the items are produced in urban areas but typically sold in rural areas, increasing rural income will certainly boost sales activities and, to some degree, rural employment. To the extent that goods are produced in the rural area, higher income will stimulate rural nonfarm activities.

Another approach to test the linkage hypothesis is to look at the marginal budget shares for various categories of goods and services. Siamwalla (1991) found that as income increases, the marginal budget share going to food declines 27 percent for poor families and 7.6 percent for rich families. Rural people, therefore, spend relatively little extra money on food. Siamwalla also found that most of the demand linkages from an increase in rural income accrue to service suppliers (especially for transport and shelter) in the local area.

Urban demand. Urban consumer demand has a powerful effect on the spatial distribution of agricultural activities,[10] especially the production of livestock, milk, fruits, and vegetables. It also influences the pattern of non-farm activities. A survey conducted by the Ministry of Agriculture and Co-operatives in 1978 and 1979 shows that farmers in the provinces adjacent to Bangkok had the highest proportion of income from the nonagricultural sector. This implies that farmers were able to sell homemade goods to urban consumers if they were close to the market. The goods produced and sold included items like homemade Thai desserts and preserved food products.

Effect of seasonality. As a result of highly concentrated monsoon rains in a narrow period, the pattern of rural labor utilization is characterized by peak demand in the wet season and low demand in the long dry season. In the wet season, agricultural work has to be finished quickly, and all the family labor must be fully utilized. Nonfarm activities in rural areas must follow a pattern of labor utilization that does not conflict with the utilization pattern of the agricultural sector. Because capital is scarce and non-farm capital equipment will tend to be idle for most of the wet season, nonfarm activities must have a very low capital intensity, as is commonly observed in rural areas. Examples of these activities include subcontracted garment work, silk production, and production of artificial flowers for export. One of the most fascinating nonfarm activities is the rapidly emerging gem-cutting work in Northeastern villages, which requires an investment of only 3,200 baht for cutting equipment (Kongkaew, 1990). In 1989, 28 of 36 households in one village of Khon Kaen were in this occupation. However, they still cultivated their ricefields and even stopped cutting gems in the harvesting season, despite the fact that net income from gem cutting was higher than that from rice production.

The background of gem-cutting activities in this area can be explained as follows. Cut gems are typically used for domestic jewelry decoration and export. In previous times, the activities were performed in Bangkok, where laborers from the Northeast went to be trained. But with rising labor costs in Bangkok, some Northeastern gem cutters found that it was more profitable to do the job in the village and sell the cut gems to the jewelry stores or middlemen. These Northeasterners then began to invest in gem-cutting production in their home villages. Such villages must have electricity and good road conditions so that transactions in the nearby towns can be conducted fairly often. The entrepreneur usually relies upon family labor, though other villagers who are eager to become gem cutters can also pay the entrepreneur for the training, which lasts one to three months; the training fee is 500 to 1,000 baht for the first month. Because skill can be rapidly acquired, the number of gem-cutting households rapidly increased from 2 to 28 within three years.

Limited extent of the market. Perhaps one of the most important factors limiting the growth and scope of rural nonfarm activities is the extent of the rural market. Rural villages are small, ranging in size between 50 and

1,000 households, with an average size of only 200 households. Village size is limited by the amount of cultivable land. When there is no longer any vacant land in the village, residents migrate to the land frontier and settle in a new village. Because the rate of settlement has been very rapid and the rural sector has not been considered as the top priority in terms of development budgets, infrastructure is usually lacking. Road conditions are poor, and many villages cannot be accessed in the rainy season. For these reasons, most nonfarm activities fail to expand because their size and growth are limited by the extent of the market. For example, the size of provincial industries tends to be larger if they are Bangkok oriented or export oriented. On the other hand, the provincial industries that mainly serve the rural market tend to be small (Chintayarangsan, 1989).

Conclusion

Despite the heavy export taxation on specific crops that has resulted in a net resource transfer out of the agricultural sector, agricultural performance throughout the postwar period has been respectable. With abundant unused land on the frontier and the increased export orientation of the sector, Thai farmers have vigorously and successfully exploited the opportunities through land expansion and crop diversification. But because farm-gate prices are low due to the export tax and because agricultural productivity is low, low incomes and even poverty are widespread in the rural areas. The farmers have no choice but to adjust by migrating internally, working abroad, diversifying their crops, and working in other nonfarm activities as a last resort.

At the same time, the agricultural sector has also benefited from some government development projects, especially road construction, irrigation investment, land consolidation, and the development and diffusion of high-yield seeds. As a result, multiple-cropping has become possible, and severe labor shortages have begun to emerge in the Central Plains and some parts of the Northern region. The dynamic farmers moved quickly to solve the labor shortage via farm mechanization and adoption of less labor-intensive techniques of production. Employment contracts and labor market institutions have also gradually evolved to cope with the problems associated with labor shortages, information needs, and monitoring costs. These adjustments are possible because there is little government intervention in the agricultural sector, apart from the export tax on specific crops, protection of the fertilizer and fish meal industries, and import quotas to protect soybean production. The growth of the agricultural sector is a major factor in the emergence and growth of rural nonfarm activities and employment. If growth is positive, backward and forward linkages appear and help generate higher-productivity nonfarm jobs. If agricultural growth is weak, the result is not only a slowdown in the growth of high-value-added nonfarm activities but also a push for poorer farmers to seek employment in low-productivity nonfarm jobs. Growth in agriculture is, therefore, the key. Rural poverty cannot be eliminated as long as agricultural productivity is low.

Notes

1. In 1985, Hong Kong, Singapore, Malaysia, and the Philippines had negative real GDP growth rates. Indonesia grew at only 2.5 percent, while Thailand grew at 3 to 5 percent (Asian Development Bank, 1991: 278).

2. Asian Development Bank (1991: 297–306).

3. The World Bank has argued that the Thai Labor Force Survey may be overstating the size of agricultural employment (World Bank, 1989: 191–193).

4. This led to the view that the growth-oriented policy was designed for the benefit of those who controlled the political machinery and for urban big businesspeople who controlled economic resources (Feeny, 1982: 117; Meesook et al., 1988: 5–48). After his death, it was disclosed that Sarit's cash holding was well over 2,000 million baht. A few families who owned the local banks and had close connections with the military, as well as the political leaders, also prospered through the industrial-promotion policy (Meesook et al., 1988).

5. One may argue that wage rates do not reflect labor market conditions because hired labor represents only 10 percent of all agricultural labor. However, the argument ignores the fact that most rural household owners, as well as tenants, become part-time hired laborers during the transplanting and harvesting periods.

6. It is interesting to note that even after the contract is agreed upon, an employee who finds another job at a higher wage can freely terminate the contract or can renegotiate for better terms.

7. In fact, exchange labor is a sort of daily in-kind payment labor.

8. Studies have found that primary education has the highest rate of both social and private return and that college education has the second-highest private return. Secondary education has a lower private rate of return than primary and college education, but it has a higher social return than a college education (Blaug, 1971; National Education Commission, 1989).

9. The section draws from a World Bank study (1983) and recently completed village studies by Chompoopa (1990), Charonchi (1990), Thongprapa (1990), Kongkaew (1990), Fuangfa (1990), and Harnvajanawong (1991).

10. One recent study (Greenberg, 1991) finds that the spatial distribution of agricultural activities in five provinces around Bangkok is significantly affected by the large influx of factories into the provinces. Significant improvements in transportation and exorbitant land prices in Bangkok are considered the principal factors responsible for this.

References

Thai Publications

Angsumalin, Sarote. 1989. "Finance and Credit with Industrial Development in Rural Industry," paper presented at the seminar on rural industry, organized by the Thailand Development Research Institute Foundation, Chon-Buri, August 19–20.

Charonchi, Patchaneebun. 1990. *Rural Employment Study: A Case of Ban Tapklay Village, Uthaithanee Province*, research report of the Rural Labor Market Project (Bangkok: Thailand Development Research Institute).

Chasombat, Pradith. 1989. "Regional Industry Labor Market," paper presented at the seminar on rural industry, organized by the Thailand Development Research Institute Foundation, Chon-Buri, August 19–20.

Chompoopa, Narong. 1990. *Rural Employment Study: A Case of Nongsonghong Village, Nakornsawan Province*, research report of the Rural Labor Market Project (Bangkok: Thailand Development Research Institute).

Fuangfa, Piachumpa. 1990. *Rural Employment Study: A Case of Ban Thungyao Village, Lampun Province*, research report of the Rural Labor Market Project (Bangkok: Thailand Development Research Institute).

Harnvajanawong, Rasamee. 1991. *Rural Labor Market: A Case of Ban Lard Village*, research report of the Rural Labor Market Project (Bangkok: Thailand Development Research Institute).

Issavilanon, Somporn, and Saran Wattanijchariya. 1989. *Acceptance of New Rice Production Technique and Differences of Wage Rate and Land Rent in Various Regions of Thailand*, research report, Faculty of Economics and Management, Kasetsart University.

Kongkaew, Ngaoslip. 1990. *Occupation and Employment in Pornsawan Village*, research report of the Rural Labor Market Project (Bangkok: Thailand Development Research Institute).

Krongkaew, Medhi. 1988. "Economic Development and Income Distribution of Thai People," *Bulletin of the Economic Society of Thailand*, No. 1, pp. 35–52.

Manarangsan, Somphob, and Kanoksak Kaewthep. 1987. *The Sugar Industry in Thailand* (Bangkok: Asian Study Institute, Chulalongkorn University Press).

Panyasawatsuthi, Chaiyooth, and Sakon Waranyuwattana. 1990. *Rural Small Enterprises: A State of Knowledge*, research report, Faculty of Economics, Thammasat University, Bangkok.

Pinthong, Chirmsak. 1990. "Thai Economy: Unfairness and Lack of Balanced Development," *Thammasat Economic Journal*, Vol. 8, No. 1 (March), pp. 1–42.

Poapongsakorn, Nipon. 1990. *Resource Management for Investment in Education*, report submitted to Ministry of Education, February.

Siamwalla, Ammar. 1987. "The Future of Agriculture in Thailand: How Do We Ask the Question?" *Bulletin of the Economic Society of Thailand*, No. 1.

Siamwalla, Ammar, and Direk Pattamasiriwat. 1990. "Migration of Population Analysis from Population and Housing Census: 1970," unpublished paper of Thailand Development Research Institute.

Siamwalla, Ammar, and Chirmsak Pinthong. 1986. "Economic Prospects for Thai Agriculture in the Future," paper presented to the Ninth Symposium on Directions of the Thai Economy in the Next Decade, Faculty of Economics, Thammasat University, Bangkok, February 13–14.

Tambunlertchai, Somsak. 1989. "Pictures of Industrial Development in the Regions," paper presented at the seminar on rural industry, organized by the Thailand Development Research Institute Foundation, Chon-Buri, August 19–20.

Thanapornpan, Rungsan. 1985. "Economics of Rice Premium: Frontier of Knowledge," research report presented to the Thai Kadhi Institute, Thammasat University, Bangkok, June.

———. 1988. "The Role of Government in the Development Process of Thailand and the Response of the People," paper presented to the seminar on "State and the Response of People to the Thai Development Process," Center for Social Development Studies, Faculty of Political Science, Chulalongkorn University, January 30–31.

Thongprapa, Surattana. 1990. *Rural Employment Study: A Case of Ruangchai Village, Udonthanee Province,* report submitted to Thailand Development Research Institute, April.

Wiboonchutikula, Paitoon. 1989. "The Household Demand for Goods Produced by Rural Industry," seminar on rural industry, organized by the Thailand Development Research Institute Foundation, Chon-Buri, August 19–20.

English Publications

Akarasanee, Narongchai. 1973. "The Manufacturing Sector in Thailand: A Study of Growth, Import Substitution and Effective Protection, 1949–69" (Ph.D. dissertation, Johns Hopkins University).

Akrasanee, Narongchai, T. Tangon, S. Tambunlertchai, P. Chasombat, and Y. Chalamwong. 1983. *Rural Off-Farm Employment in Thailand* (Bangkok: Industrial Management Consultants).

Asian Development Bank. 1991. *Asian Development Outlook 1991* (Manila: Asian Development Bank).

Bertrand, Trent, and Lyn Squire. 1980. "The Relevance of the Dual Economy Model: A Case Study of Thailand," *Oxford Economic Papers,* Vol. 32, No. 3 (November), pp. 480–511.

Biggs, Tyler, Peter Brimble, and Donald Snodgrass. 1990. "Rural Industry and Employment Study: A Synthesis Report," paper prepared for the Thailand Development Research Institute.

Binswanger, Han P. 1972. "Induced Innovation: A Critical Review of the Theory and Conclusion from New Evidence," staff paper, (Department of Agricultural and Resource Economics, University of Minnesota).

Blaug, Mark. 1971. *The Role of Return to Investment in Education in Thailand* (Bangkok: National Education Commission).

Bot, Kees, and Wilbert Gooneratne. 1982. "Labor Absorption in Rice Cultivation in Thailand," in Wilbert Gooneratne, ed., *Labor Absorption in Rice-based Agriculture* (Bangkok: Asian Employment Programme, ILO), pp. 69–116.

Chaisakul, Samart, Chuta Manasphaibool, and Mikimasa Yoshida, eds. 1989. *Thailand's Economic Development in the 1980s* (Tokyo: Institute of Developing Economics).

Chintayarangsan, Rachain. 1989. "Industrial Structure and Interindustry Linkages," paper presented at the seminar on rural industry, organized by the Thailand Development Research Institute Foundation, Chon-Buri, August 19–20.

Christensen, Scott R., David Dollar, Ammar Siamwalla, and Pakorn Vichyanond. 1992. "Institutional and Political Bases of Growth-inducing Policies in Thailand," paper prepared for the conference on "The Role of Government and East Asian Success," Honolulu: East-West Center and the World Bank, November 19–21.

Chulasai, Luechai, Suwarat Bhekasut, and Thongchai Shusuwan. 1986. "Family Labor, Hired Labor and Employment Linkages in Rural Thailand," in S. Hiroshima and M. Muqtada, eds., *Hired Labor and Rural Labor Markets in Asia* (New Delhi: ARTEP), pp. 151–175.

Chutikul, Sirilakasana. 1989. "Equity Concerns in the Development of Human Resources in Thailand with Particular Reference to Education," paper presented to the USAID-TDRI workshop on "Human Resource Problems and Policies," Hua Hin, Thailand, February.

Chutikul, Sirilakasana, and Vachareeya Thosaguan. 1989. "An Economic Assessment of the Guest Worker Phenomenon in ASEAN: The Thai Perspective," paper prepared for the workshop on "Guest Workers in ASEAN," Institute of Development Studies, Singapore, October.

Feeny, David. 1982. *The Political Economy of Productivity: Thai Agricultural Development, 1880–1975* (Vancouver: University of British Columbia Press).

Ganjanapan, Anan. 1989. "Conflicts over the Development and Control of Labor in a Northern Thai Village," in Gillian Hart, Andrew Turton, and Benjamin White, eds., *Agrarian Transformations: Local Processes and the State in Southeast Asia* (Berkeley: University of California Press).

Grandstaff, Somlakrat W. 1989. "The Role of Demand in Provincial Industry," paper presented to the seminar on rural industry, organized by the Thailand Development Research Institute Foundation, Chon-Buri, August 19–20.

Greenberg, Charles. 1991. "The Bangkok Metroshadow Region" (Ph.D. dissertation, University of British Columbia).

Greene, B. 1970. *Rate of Adoption of New Farm Practices in the Central Plains, Thailand,* research paper, Department of Agricultural Economics, Cornell University, October.

Hart, Gillian. 1984. *Agrarian Labor Arrangements and Structural Change: Lessons from Java and Bangladesh,* Working Paper of the World Employment Programme Research, ILO, WEP10–6/WP65, March.

———. 1986. *Power, Labor and Livelihood: Process of Change in Rural Java* (Berkeley: University of California Press).

Hayami, Yujiro, and Masao Kikuchi. 1981. *Asian Village Economy at the Crossroads* (Tokyo: University of Tokyo Press).

Hayami, Yujiro, and Vernon W. Ruttan. 1971. *Agricultural Development: An International Perspective* (Baltimore, Md.: Johns Hopkins University Press).

Heady, E.O. 1949. "Basic Economic and Welfare Aspects of Farm Technological Advance," *Journal of Farm Economics,* Vol. 31 (May), pp. 293–316.

Ho, Robert, and E.C. Chapman, eds. 1973. *Studies of Contemporary Thailand* (Canberra: Australian National University Press).

Hongladarom, Chira. 1981. *Labor Contracts in Thai Agriculture: A Preliminary Investigation,* Discussion Paper Series No. 84 (Bangkok: Faculty of Economics, Thammasat University).

Hutaserani, Suganya, and Somchai Jitsuchon. 1988. "Thailand's Income Distribution and Poverty Profile and Their Current Situation," research report, Thailand Development Research Institute Foundation, Bangkok, December.

Ishikawa, Shigeru. 1978. "Labor Absorption in Asian Agriculture," a report submitted to Asian Regional Programme for Employment Promotion, International Labour Organization, June.

Islam, Rizwanul, ed. 1982. *Rural Industrialization and Employment in Asia* (New Delhi: International Labour Organization Asian Employment Programme).

Jamison, Dean To, and Lawrence Lau. 1982. *Farmer Education and Farm Efficiency* (Baltimore, Md.: Johns Hopkins University Press).

Jayasuriya, S.K., and R.T. Shand. 1983. *Technical Change and Labor Absorption in Asian Agriculture: An Assessment,* Development Studies Center Occasional Paper No. 35 (Canberra: Australian National University).

Jongsuwat, Nongluck. 1980. "Productivity Growth and Farm Machinery Adoption in Thai Agriculture" (master's thesis, Faculty of Economics, Thammasat University).

Kawsaard, Mingsan, ed. 1981. *Industrialization and Rural Employment in Thailand* (Chiang Mai, Thailand: Chiang Mai University).

Komata, S. 1976. "Labor Problems of Double-Cropping at the Chanasutr Land Consolidation Project" (master's thesis, Faculty of Economics, Thammasat University).

Koomsup, Praiphol. 1973. "Trade Protection and Industrialization in Thailand: A Case Study of the Textile Industry" (master's thesis, Faculty of Economics, Thammasat University).

Koppel, Bruce, and John Hawkins. 1988. "The Future of Work in Rural Asia: Implications for Education, Policy and Research," Memorandum for Discussion (East-West Center Resource Systems Institute, Honolulu).

Krongkaew, Medhi. 1985. "Agricultural Development, Rural Poverty and Income Distribution in Thailand," The Developing Economies, Vol. 23, No. 4 (December), pp. 325–346.

―――. 1988. "The Development of Small- and Medium-Scale Industries in Thailand," Asian Development Review, Vol. 6, No. 2, pp. 70–95.

Lokaphadhana, Tipaporn. 1976. "Economic Comparison of Broadcasting and Transplanting Dry Season Rice in Thailand" (master's thesis, Faculty of Economics, Thammasat University).

Loohawenchit, Chesada. 1977. "A Dynamic Multi-Crop Model for Thai Agriculture with Special Reference to the Rice Premium and Agricultural Diversification" (Ph.D. dissertation, Princeton University).

―――. 1980. "The Farm Machinery Industry in Thailand," paper presented to a seminar on "ASEAN Comparative Study of the Development of Labor Intensive Industry," Pattaya, Thailand, October, 28–31.

Manoopimoke, Supachit. 1989. "Choice of Rice Production Technique in Thailand 1880–1940" (Ph.D. dissertation, Agriculture and Resource Economics, University of Hawaii).

Meesook, Oey Astra. 1979. Income, Consumption and Poverty in Thailand, 1962/63 to 1975/76, World Bank Staff Working Paper No. 364 (Washington, D.C.: World Bank).

Meesook, Oey Astra, Pranee Tinakorn, Chayan Vaddhanaphuthi, and Rangsan Thanapornpon. 1988. The Political Economy of Thailand's Development: Poverty, Equity and Growth, 1850–1985, paper prepared for the World Bank (mimeographed).

Ministry of Agriculture and Cooperatives. 1976. Chao Phraya Irrigation Development Project October 1975–September 1976: Annual Report No. 3 (Bangkok: Ministry of Agriculture and Cooperatives).

Montreevat, Sakulrat. 1983. "Power Input Utilization and Substitution in Thai Rice Product" (master's thesis, Faculty of Economics, Thammasat University).

National Education Commission. 1989. Costs and Contributions of Higher Education in Thailand (Bangkok: Charoenpon Press).

Onchan, Tongroj, ed. 1985. "Rural Industrialization and Employment Generation: A Study of Regional Industries in Thailand," report for the ILO-ARTEP, July.

Oshima, Harry T. 1983. Off-farm Employment and Incomes in Post-war East Asia, research monograph, Development Studies Center.

―――.1987. Economic Growth in Monsoon Asia: A Comparative Survey (Tokyo: University of Tokyo Press).

―――. 1989. "Strategic Processes in Monsoon Asia's Economic Growth," preliminary draft in author's possession, forthcoming.

Panpiemras, Kosit, and Somchai Krusuansombat. 1985. "Seasonal Migration and Employment in Thailand," in Theodore Panyoto, ed., Food Policy Analysis in Thailand (Bangkok: Agricultural Development Council), pp. 303–344.

Pathanopas, Renu. 1980. "The Economics of Rich Threshing Machines in Thailand: A Case Study of Chachoengsoa and Suphan Buri Province" (master's thesis, Faculty of Economics, Thammasat University).

Poapongsakorn, Nipon. 1980. "The Animal Feed Industry in Thailand," paper presented to the seminar on "ASEAN Comparative Study of the Development of Labor Intensive Industry," Pattaya, Thailand, October 28–31.

Poapongsakorn, Nipon, and Prayong Netayarak. 1989. "Regional Variation in Interest Rates in Thailand," research report prepared for the Asian Development Bank and the Thailand Development Research Institute, Bangkok.

Poapongsakorn, Nipon, and Hongpha Sangthanapurk. 1989. "Consequences of Overseas Contract Labor Migration on the Rural Economy: The Case of Two Northeastern Villages," report submitted to the Asian Regional Programme on International Labour Migration, International Labour Organization, September.

Rasanend, Sriaroon. 1977. "A Survey of the IRRI Axial Flow Thresher Efficiency Compared with Traditional Methods of Threshing," research paper, Faculty of Economics and Business Administration, Kasetsart University.

Roumasset, James, and Joyotee Smith. 1981. "Population, Technological Change, and the Evolution of Labor Markets," *Population and Development Review*, Vol. 3 (September), pp. 401–419.

Roumasset, James, and M. Uy. 1980. "Piece Rates, Time Rates and Teams: Explaining Patterns in the Employment Relation," *Journal of Economic Behavior and Organization* (December), pp. 343–360.

Setboonsarng, Sunantar. 1987. "Supervision Cost, Transaction Cost and Rural Labor Markets," research monograph, Yale University, New Haven, Conn.

Siamwalla, Ammar. 1991. "Land Abundance, Agricultural Growth and Some of Its Consequences: The Case of Thailand," paper presented to the International Food Policy Research Institute Conference on "Agriculture on the Road to Industrialization." Taipei, September 4–7.

Siamwalla, Ammar, and Suthad Setboonsarng. 1987. *Agricultural Pricing Policies in Thailand: 1960–1985* (Bangkok: Thailand Development Research Institute).

Silcock, T.H., ed. 1967. *Thailand: Social and Economic Studies in Development* (Canberra: Australian National University Press).

Small, L. 1972. "An Economic Evaluation of Water Control in the Northern Region of the Greater Chao Phraya Project of Thailand" (Ph.D. dissertation, Cornell University).

Sriboonchitta, Songsak. 1975. "The Private Cost of Using Tractors Versus Buffaloes: A Case Study of Farming in Cha-Choeng-Sao Province" (master's thesis, Faculty of Economics, Thammasat University).

Sukharomana, Supachat. 1982. "The Impact of Farm Power Strategy in Thailand," in John Farrington, Fredrick Abeyratne, and Gerard J. Gill, eds., *Farm Power and Employment in Asia* (Bangkok: Agricultural Development Council), pp. 139–160.

Sussangkarn, Chalongphob. 1987. "The Thai Labor Market: A Study of Seasonality and Segmentation," paper presented to the Macroeconomic Research Conference, TDRI, Cha-Am, Thailand, October 17–18.

———. 1988. "Elementary Education in the Thai Economy and the Role of Nonformal Education," paper presented to the Ministry of Education seminar on "Alternative Education for Primary School Leavers," July.

———. 1989. "Structural Changes and Income Distribution in Thailand," paper presented to the international symposium on "Making Economies More Efficient and More Equitable Factors Determining Income Distribution," Tokyo, November 27–29.

Tambunlertchai, Somsak, and Chesada Loohawenchit. 1980. "Labor-intensive and Small-scale Manufacturing Industries in Thailand," paper presented at the seminar on "ASEAN Comparative Study of the Development of Labor-intensive Industry," organized by ILO, Patlaya, Thailand, October 28–31.

———. 1985. *Rural Industries in Thailand* (mimeographed), research report of the Faculty of Economics, Thammasat University, Bangkok.

TDRI (Thailand Development Research Institute). 1987. "Productivity and Competitions in Thai Agriculture," paper presented at the 1987 TDRI Year-end Conference on "Efficiency and Competition in the Thai Economy," Cha-Am, Thailand, November 28–29.

———. 1989. "Human Resource Problems and Policies," workshop presented at Hua Hin, Thailand, February 24–25.

Thongsri, Sornchai. 1974. "Economic Evaluation of Manual and Mechanical Land Clearing and Preparation: A Case Study of Rubber Replanting in Songkhla" (master's thesis, Faculty of Economics, Thammasat University).

Turton, Andrew. 1978. "The Peasantry of Thailand: Scientific and Social Revolution," *Comparative Studies in Society and History,* Vol. 20, No. 4, pp. 16–30.

———. 1989. "Thailand: Agarian Bases of State Power," in Gillian Hart, Andrew Turton, and Benjamin White, eds., *Agrarian Transformations: Local Processes and the State in Southeast Asia* (Berkeley: University of California Press).

Usher, D. 1966. "Income as a Measure of Productivity: Alternative Comparisons of Agricultural and Non-Agricultural Productivity in Thailand," *Economica,* Vol. 33, No. 132 (November), pp. 430–441.

Wattananukit, Atchana, and Teerana Bhongmakapat. 1989. "The Impact of the External Sector on the Thai Economy and Its Determinants," paper presented at the 1989 Year End Conference "Thailand in the International Economic Community," organized by the Thailand Development Research Institute, December.

Wongsanggaroonsri, Anuwat. 1982. "Farm Mechanization, Production and Labor Requirements" (master's thesis, Faculty of Economics, Thammasat University).

World Bank. 1980. *Thailand: Industrial Development Strategy in Thailand* (Washington, D.C.: World Bank).

———. 1982. *Thailand: Program and Policy Priorities for an Agricultural Economy in Transition,* Report No. 3705a-TH (Washington, D.C.: World Bank).

———. 1983. *Growth and Employment in Rural Thailand,* Report No. 3906-TH (Washington, D.C.: World Bank).

———. 1985. *World Development Report 1985* (Washington, D.C.: World Bank).

———. 1986. *Thailand: Growth with Stability—A Challenge for the Sixth Plan Period.* Report No. 6030-TH (Washington, D.C.: World Bank).

———. 1989. *Thailand Country Economic Memorandum: Building on the Recent Success—A Policy Framework,* Vol. 1, Report No. 7445-TH (Washington, D.C.: World Bank).

7

Rural Development
and Nonfarm Employment in Java

Tadjuddin N. Effendi and Chris Manning

The impact of rapid rural economic change and agricultural modernization in rural work on Java has been an issue of considerable interest among researchers and policymakers in Indonesia over the past twenty years.[1] This is particularly true because of the high levels of poverty and land scarcity, which have long forced households to seek income outside agriculture to make ends meet.[2] Rural nonfarm work in Java has been discussed in recent literature mainly in the context of two major themes. The first concerns the high incidence of rural poverty, emphasizing survival strategies adopted by rural households in the light of extreme pressure on scarce agricultural land. The second theme emphasizes marked and increasing inequalities between poor and better-off households as a consequence of the larger landowners' abilities to channel surplus income from agriculture into higher-earning nonfarm activities (White, 1986). Thus, a high and rising proportion of rural households involved in nonfarm work is not necessarily an indicator of general economic progress or improvement in income distribution. Indeed, a range of studies suggest quite the opposite.

The actual outcome in particular communities and regions is likely, however, to depend on local and national political, social, and economic structures and their interaction and evolution over time. In this chapter, we emphasize changing national and regional circumstances as key determinants of patterns of rural nonfarm work and their impact on rural socioeconomic structure in Jatinom, one subdistrict of Central Java. We will argue that although rural poverty and growing inequalities are clearly discernible in Jatinom, they have not been the only processes at work. Nonfarm work has been extremely varied in terms of activities undertaken and participants involved. In part, this is related to specific regional circumstances, and partly, it is the result of the effects of fluctuating patterns of national economic growth, beginning with the oil boom period in the 1970s.

As in other parts of Java, the state has played a major role in influencing the pattern of rural economic change in Jatinom. We also argue, however, that the state's major impact has been its support for general diversification of the rural economy, although it has also facilitated rural elite access to new income-earning activities.

Most of the empirical analysis for this chapter is based on a census of nonfarm enterprises in one subdistrict in Java and a household survey conducted in three villages in the subdistrict from March to October 1989.[3] We have chosen the much-neglected service sector as a major focus. As with research on other Asian countries, much of the research on rural nonfarm work in Indonesia has tended to concentrate on manufacturing, despite the relatively limited impact and often highly region-specific nature of rural manufacturing activities (Islam, 1987). In the case of Java, this emphasis is clearly misplaced. Macro data and village studies suggest that trade and services both account for more rural jobs than manufacturing and that these sectors, together with construction and transport, have made a substantial contribution to rural employment and income growth in recent years. Perhaps more important, all these activities have close linkages with growth in agricultural output, and they received a stimulus from expenditure generated by incomes earned in agriculture and manufacturing.

The next section examines the growth of nonfarm employment in Java since the 1970s and presents some national- and provincial-level data on the changing rural employment structure in the context of the national economy's rapid expansion and diversification. The third section indicates how, after a long period of economic stagnation following the disintegration of the colonial economic structure in 1942, Jatinom has experienced rapid economic growth and substantial changes in consumption patterns over the past fifteen years. In the fourth and fifth sections, we examine the implications of these developments for rural nonfarm work in Jatinom, focusing on the linkages between rural economic change and patterns of growth in service sector enterprises and on characteristics of enterprise owners and households involved in service sector activities.

Macroeconomic Change, Labor Processes, and Rural Nonfarm Employment Structure

Since General Suharto came to power in 1965, Indonesia has experienced rapid economic growth and structural change.[4] The rise in international oil prices in 1973 and again in 1979 and the huge increase in public revenues generated by the oil sector facilitated a decade of government-led economic expansion. Both the manufacturing and service sectors—especially those supported directly by the expansion of government spending, such as construction—grew very quickly. Much of the manufacturing was concentrated on Java, where the infrastructure was most developed and the labor supply was relatively abundant. Unlike many other oil exporters, Indonesia gave special attention to agriculture and especially rice production in the context of achieving national self-sufficiency, and this sector also experienced quite rapid growth by Third World standards (Booth, 1990). Rural development was also supported by substantial programs of rural infrastructure development, in particular the extension and rehabilitation of irrigation, the extension of rural roads, and the provision of social infrastructure through special primary school and health-center building programs. By the mid 1980s, the goal of rice self-sufficiency had been achieved, primary school enrollments on Java had risen to close to 100 percent, and rural road networks, served by small minibus operators, extended within relatively easy reach of almost all villages in Java.

From the early 1980s, economic growth was much slower due to both the world recession and a substantial decline in the real price of oil; this finally forced the government to make significant cuts in development spending, including rural public works programs, in the mid-1980s (Sundrum, 1988). Rice production growth, which had been concentrated on Java primarily through increased productivity, also began to slow substantially after the achievement of rice self-sufficiency. Despite a move toward agricultural diversification—horticulture, livestock, and poultry in particular—there is evidence that rural economic conditions took a turn for the worse on Java beginning in the mid-1980s. National expenditure data suggest that after a decade of decline, the incidence of rural poverty may have begun to increase in the period 1984–1987 (Booth and Sundrum, 1989).[5] After several years of quite strong growth in the first half of the 1980s, real wage rates appear to have declined in both rice and estate agriculture, beginning around the middle of the decade (Jayasuriya and Manning, 1990).

National labor force statistics document some of these changes. They show a fairly substantial decline in agriculture's share in total employment, especially on land-scarce Java (from 65 percent in 1971 to just under 50 percent in 1985). By far the largest increment in total employment was in services, transport, and construction, particularly during the intercensal period 1971–1980, although manufacturing employment also grew rapidly. Despite the location of much of the new service sector employment in and around major cities, new jobs in this sector were nevertheless quite widely dispersed throughout Java in the 1971–1980 period (Jones, 1984). In contrast, new manufacturing growth in the same period was heavily concentrated in relatively capital-intensive industries producing for the domestic market in large- and medium-scale establishments in and around Java's major cities, in particular in the urban connurbation areas of Jakarta and, to a lesser extent, Bandung in the west and Surabaya in East Java.[6] This pattern of "urban bias" in new job creation in manufacturing—and, indeed, in nonagricultural employment generally—appears to have intensified in the slower growth period of 1980 to 1985 (Manning, 1988). The division of labor markets into distinct urban and rural segments has become increasingly blurred, however, as a consequence of much more intensive transportation links and an apparently marked increase in the incidence of commuting and circular migration between rural and urban areas (Hugo, 1978, 1984; Manning, 1987).

Table 7.1 provides a broad picture of employment change by sector in rural Java and rural Central Java (the region from which our case study was chosen) between 1971 and 1985. As might be expected, the decline in the share of agricultural employment was much lower than that for the region as a whole, although the national-level statistics almost certainly understate the extent of nonfarm work in rural areas.[7] Among males, construction and transport recorded the largest increases in employment share outside agriculture, particularly transport since 1980. Among females, trade and service sector employment growth were most significant. Wage work in government activities such as teaching and health care was particularly marked among females in the service segment. For males and especially for females, the share of total rural employment in manufacturing declined quite substantially. The patterns of change in Central Java were similar to those for Java as a whole. The share of female nonagricultural employment, especially in manufacturing, was substantially higher in Central Java than in other provinces, a pattern frequently attributed to the high levels of rural poverty and land scarcity and also the high rates of female participation in the Central Java labor force.

What major factors are contributing to these changes? In prime rice-growing regions, the backwash effects of new technology—most notably, the introduction of the sickle and the *tebasan* contract system of rice harvesting—and associated changes in work contracts were the major factors leading to an increase in job search activities outside agriculture in the 1970s.[8] Poor and landless households were marginalized as a consequence of a decline in wage labor opportunities in rice and the tendency for these to be increasingly allocated to more prosperous farming households or for new wage contracts to reduce labor earnings.

Several village studies conducted in the late 1960s and early 1970s provided detailed evidence of the significant contribution that petty trade and highly labor-intensive home industries (such as mat and string weaving and coconut sugar production) made to household incomes, especially among the poor and landless.[9] Reliance on these activities can be viewed, in part, as a response to seasonality in labor demand, particularly in wet-rice agriculture.[10] More importantly, however, it should be seen as a manifestation of the high and increasing levels of landlessness and near landlessness associated with population pressure and the maldistribution of land (and wealth) in many rural communities. A high proportion of rural households tended to be engaged in long hours of work for extremely low returns per hour in rural nonfarm labor. The returns from this rural nonfarm work were often substantially lower than those for wage work in rice, the major source of income for the rural poor (see, for example, White, 1976).

Table 7.1 Percent of Employment Shares by Sector, Rural Java and
Central Java, 1971–1985

Gender and Sector of Activity	All Java			Central Java		
	1971	1980	1985	1971	1980	1985
Male						
Agriculture	73	65	65	70	68	68
Nonagriculture	27	35	35	30	32	32
Manufacturing	23	21	21	30	23	24
Construction	8	13	14	6	15	15
Trade	31	25	26	28	22	23
Transport	7	8	11	7	8	11
Services	30	31	27	29	30	26
Other[a]	1	2	2	—	2	1
Female						
Agriculture	66	57	62(?)	56	54	56(?)
Nonagriculture	34	43	38	44	46	44
Manufacturing	38	32	31	44	37	35
Trade	46	46	49	45	46	48
Services	15	20	19	11	16	16
Other[b]	1	1	1	—	1	1

Sources: Indonesia Central Bureau of Statistics, *Population Census 1971: Series C* (Jakarta, 1973); *Population Census 1980: Series S2* (Jakarta, 1984); *Intercensal Population Survey, 1985* (Jakarta, 1988).
Note: The 1985 SUPAS appears to have provided a more careful enumeration of family workers than both censuses; this probably contributed to the upward trend in the agricultural share of employment among females in particular in the period 1980–1985.
— indicates not available.
[a] Includes mining and public utilities.
[b] Includes mining, public utilities, transport, and construction.

A second development identified around this time was the increasing propensity of larger farmers to recycle profits earned in rice farming into new nonagricultural activities. Several authors found that surpluses earned from application of the new rice technology tended to be increasingly reinvested in profitable nonfarm enterprises, first in agroprocessing (rice hulling) and later in transport and trade (Gunawan et al., 1977 and 1979; Husken, 1979 and 1989). Although there apparently are strong differences between villages and regions, it seems clear that new nonfarm activities have often exacerbated the already quite substantial rural income inequalities derived from agriculture (White, 1986; White and Wiradi, 1989). They were supported, moreover, by direct and indirect state support for rural elites (Hart, 1986).[11]

Thus, low-income nonfarm activities proliferated among the poor as a "survival" strategy to compensate for a lack of agricultural employment opportunities, alongside the "accumulation" strategies adopted by larger farmers (White and Wiradi, 1989). However, demand-induced (rural) non-farm work and urban-based nonagricultural jobs associated with spending from the oil boom began to make a much greater contribution to employment among poorer households during the middle to late 1970s.[12] One contribution to the change was the spread of rural public works programs—roads, schools, health-care centers, and associated construction activities. A second element was the growing engagement of rural households in urban jobs through commuting and circular migration. This was partly stimulated by the growth of opportunities to earn income in self-employed work, construction, and manufacturing in and close to major urban areas; it was also stimulated by a transport "revolution" marked by the spread of urban-rural minibus services in rural Java. Both these developments meant a substantial broadening of job opportunities for many of the rural poor. New work in construction, transport, trade, and modern manufacturing was frequently much better remunerated than agricultural wage work. The wages of some groups (especially young females in manufacturing) were low and irregular, and older, less mobile persons tended to remain dependent on (an often declining) traditional, low-wage jobs in their villages (Mather, 1983; Wolf, 1986; Sawit, Sri Hartoyo, and Saefudin, 1985).

Several studies have suggested that the main stimulus to rural incomes came from urban rather than rural work and that linkages between the green revolution and rural nonfarm work were weak (Collier et al., 1982 and 1988; Manning, 1987). Increased incomes were mainly spent on imported or urban-produced consumer durables. Although rural trade flourished, there was little encouragement for rural manufacturing growth, a situation exacerbated by the backwash effects of new, urban-based industries on traditional manufacturing.[13]

These new activities have been described as "consolidation" strategies on the part of lower- and middle-income households, although some argue that many of these new jobs, taken in response to increases in labor demand, did not significantly improve household economic status (White and Wiradi, 1989). Some village studies (particularly in West Java) found, however, that incomes rose and consumption patterns changed quite substantially among poor and middle-income households primarily in response to involvement in new nonagricultural jobs (Saefudin and Marisa, 1984; Sri Hartoyo and Makali, 1984; World Bank, 1985; Collier et al., 1988). Most studies of nonfarm employment have concentrated on the interaction between agricultural and nonagricultural employment and income growth in regions of Java where irrigated rice cultivation (often combined with sugarcane) predominates as a smallholder crop. Here, access to agricultural land has long been the major determinant of rural economic and social status. In large areas of rural Java—supporting around a quarter to a third of the rural population—dryland cultivation predominates, agricultural land is more evenly distributed, and, consequently, land is much less significant as an indicator of economic status. Many poorer upland agricultural regions in the south and along the central mountain chain have experienced high rates of permanent and circular out-migration as residents search for income opportunities in urban areas. In these regions, remittances from urban areas and increasingly intensive economic interaction with rapidly growing lowland agricultural areas have been major determinants of rural economic change.

The distribution of nonagricultural work in rural Java in the mid-1980s reflected a wide range of employment situations, covering both the survival strategies of poorer marginalized households and new income-earning opportunities created by demand expansion and public sector spending in rural areas (Table 7.2). Overall, compared with agriculture, nonagricultural jobs involved a smaller proportion of older, less educated, and family workers and a higher proportion of females. High-status activities, including teaching and government administration, were heavily dominated by males. Relatively new jobs mainly employing younger males were also found in services (in motor repairs and welding, for example), construction, and transport.

In contrast, many young females with relatively little schooling were concentrated in low-wage manufacturing industries—especially the rapidly growing textile industry, batik, and cigarettes. Women also dominated mainly self-employed and family worker involvement in foodstalls, market trade, and low-wage basket and mat weaving (from bamboo). But on average, this group tended to be older and less educated than their counterparts in large-scale manufacturing.

From our study of service industries in one subdistrict in Java, it is not possible to draw definitive conclusions regarding the pattern and change of rural nonfarm work on the island as a whole; nor can we resolve some of the unsettled issues discussed earlier. Village studies all show that there is substantial variation in the pattern of nonfarm work and its impact on incomes and equity from region to region and even between communities located in the same districts and subdistricts.[14] Issues regarding the economic and social impact of service sector work are discussed in the specific context of Jatinom, highlighting factors that have influenced the growth of services in the past twenty years and their impact on the distribution of work within the subdistrict. Before turning to nonfarm activities in the region, we first look at some aspects of the political and economic history of the region and its role in the rich and diversified regional economy of Klaten district.

Table 7.2 Some Characteristics of Workers in Selected Nonagricultural Occupations, Rural Java, 1985

Occupation[a]	Percent of All Nonagricultural Workers	Age		Gender	Schooling[b]		Work Status	
		Percent <25	Percent 50+	Percent Female	Percent <Primary	Percent Secondary+	Percent Self-employed[c]	Percent Family Workers
Professional, managerial, and clerical								
Primary teachers	3.3	23	3	39	0	100	0	0
Government officials	1.9	5	24	5	13	54	0	0
Sales								
Shop assistants, etc.	1.8	30	17	39	41	18	48	17
Stalls/hawkers, etc.	32.5	19	21	59	65	6	81	14
Services[d]								
Servants	3.1	53	14	91	68	2	0	21
Hairdressers	0.2	13	37	32	43	15	82	0
Masseurs	0.7	3	7	78	82	12	80	0
Tailors	2.5	44	6	63	29	17	55	5
Motor repair workers	0.6	33	7	2	27	36	33	6
Welders, etc.	0.4	34	8	3	36	25	26	3
Bricklayers	4.3	28	10	2	48	9	17	2
Carpenters	2.9	14	19	0	55	6	31	1
Drivers	2.9	22	4	0	25	36	33	1
Becak drivers	2.5	16	8	0	68	3	87	0

Manufacturing								
Textile making	2.5	41	13	64	54	12	36	9
Batik making	0.9	39	17	86	69	11	24	5
Rice milling	0.7	33	15	25	56	11	12	8
Sugar production	2.2	21	21	62	75	5	35	49
Cigarette production	0.6	53	5	95	57	3	2	0
Furniture making	0.6	22	16	7	56	6	44	10
Tile and brick making	2.4	34	15	35	64	6	31	25
Mat, basket weaving	2.4	27	32	77	81	17	64	32
All Nonagriculture	38.1	26	16	41	52	9	46	11
Agriculture	61.9	24	25	35	70	4	46	34

Source: Indonesia Central Bureau of Statistics, *Intercensal Population Survey 1985*, data tapes.

a Main occupation in the past week.

b Completed schooling.

c Self-employed includes those managing family enterprises.

d Tailors, motor repairmen, welders, bricklayers, carpenters, drivers, and becak drivers usually classified under production workers according to ISCO codes.

The Subdistrict Setting

Location and Characteristics of the Subdistrict

Jatinom is a subdistrict of Klaten district, located in the south central part of Central Java. It lies about 10 kilometers from Klaten (the district capital), 28 kilometers from Boyolali, and 30 kilometers from Solo and Yogyakarta (two major cities in Central Java), and about 100 kilometers from Semarang (the capital province of Central Java). This area lies on the hill slopes straddling the lowland wet paddy areas in the south Klaten and the hilly region of Boyolali in the north.

Jatinom consists of eighteen villages (*kalurahan*). The household survey indicates that a high proportion of the agricultural land area is dry fields—more than twice the area devoted to wet-rice cultivation.[15] The crops most commonly grown in this area are dry field crops, such as cassava, corn, chili, and peanuts. The area is also endowed with good livestock resources, such as dairy cattle and goats.

The total population of the district in 1989 was just over 50,000. It has experienced relatively slow population growth in recent years, with an average annual increase of 1.5 percent per annum in the period 1985–1989.[16] The success of the family planning program and out-migration have contributed to this figure. However, in 1988, population density was 1,405 persons per square kilometer, which was higher than the total Java figure of 755 per square kilometer in 1985. The household survey suggests that the proportion of landless households was around 50 percent. This figure was in the middle of the range in terms of the proportion of landless households found in various studies of rural Java as a whole, although landlessness was much higher in Jatinom's main areas for growing wet rice (*sawah*).[17] In *sawah* areas in Jatinom, the proportion of landless was about 80 percent, whereas it was 40 percent in the dry field areas.[18]

The average amount of land owned by landowners was very small (just over 0.2 hectares), and only 1 percent of all households owned 0.8 hectares of land or more, accounting for under 10 percent of the total land owned in the village. Thus, land was generally more evenly distributed than in many other regions of Java, a fact that can be partly attributed to the land redistribution that occurred in the early 1950s (see our later discussion) and the absence of a significant trend toward land concentration in the predominantly dry land areas since then. The main roads that connect this area to nearby cities like Klaten, Boyolali, Solo, Salatiga, Yogyakarta, and Semarang are in good condition. This allows easy access and cheap travel by buses and minibuses to and from this district. Although the roads within the district are not in as good a condition as the main roads, they are wide enough to be used by four-wheel vehicles. This has led to a close integration of Jatinom subdistrict with the economies of the rich rice-growing area of Klaten and urban areas nearby. This integration has stimulated the expansion of the economic activities that had stagnated before the mid-1970s.

Social and Economic Background

In the period 1942–1976, the Jatinom economy was much less diversified than it is today. The most prominent feature of this period was social disturbance, which affected economic conditions. As in other parts of rural Java during the colonial period, the plantation economy dominated activities in this area (Bryant, 1973). Before 1942, for instance, one of the biggest sugarcane factories of Central Java was located in Jatinom. During that time, commercialization in terms of agricultural activities, especially through employment of wage labor, had spread to this area. During the Japanese occupation (1942–1945), however, the plantation economy no longer functioned. To support Japan's war efforts, the Japanese military forced the farmers to plant food crops, cotton, and caster oil (Kartodirjo, 1982). Between 1945 and 1949, the cultivation of cash crops practically ceased as the Indonesian army controlled Jatinom, a situation that continued until the late 1950s. In the same period, social unrest occurred in this district. Major disturbances broke out against Chinese traders, and one major anti-Chinese protest movement was accompanied by destruction of the sugarcane factory (Daldjoeni, 1973: 3).[19]

Partly as a result of these disturbances, the Jatinom economy began changing in the early 1950s from a plantation economy to a subsistence economy. Subsistence farming became the major activity after the land that had formerly been cultivated by the private companies was taken over by the local government. Each landless household was given 0.2 hectares of land.[20] But, after the government controlled the local social movements, the farmers still could not cultivate land efficiently. Prior to the 1965 army coup, this region was one of the centers of Communist Party activities in Central Java. Land taken over from the plantation companies became a major issue in the party's political strategy, and political action by the party discouraged farmers from cultivating land intensively.[21] After the Communist Party was banned in 1966, Jatinom subdistrict was under close government control until 1975, and during this period, outsiders were not allowed to enter some Jatinom villages without government permission. These conditions had a negative impact on the economic activities of the area, and in this era, many people experienced considerable poverty.[22]

The period after 1976 was the starting point of much more rapid economic change in Jatinom. The opening up of some villages previously closed to outsiders was one important factor contributing to this development. By that time, the government was also involved in rural development programs, especially improving rural roads and building rural infrastructure.

Better roads facilitated public transport, such as the buses and minibuses that connected Jatinom to other regions or cities. Commercial and service activities within the district increased significantly toward the mid-1980s, by which time considerable agricultural diversification had taken place. The introduction of dairy cattle in 1976 was sponsored by the local *kabupaten* (district) government, and a few larger farmers began planting orange trees after 1979. Both activities provided a stimulus to the rural economy. Agricultural diversification also included the production of vegetables for the market. The increased demand for agricultural products of the area came not only from urban areas but also from nearby lowland rice-growing areas in Klaten, and it was associated with increasing income generated from rice production.

Commuting and circular migration also increased, involving many traders, government employees, and other laborers who worked outside this area (see Table 7.3). The proportion of traders who commute is relatively high compared with other occupational groups. Most of them sell agricultural products to markets in rural towns of the rice-growing areas or nearby urban areas. They buy and sell vegetables or fruit in the Jatinom market in the morning and return home in the afternoon. Among government employees and wage labor in manufacturing, the proportion engaged in circular migration is also relatively high. As in other regions of Java, government employees (teachers and army officials) and wage laborers in manufacturing who work in large cities like Semarang, Solo, and Salatiga are involved in circular migration to reduce the housing and education costs of their children. Circular migration in particular increased after 1976 (Table 7.4).

Table 7.3   Incidence of Commuting and Circular Migration in Jatinom, by Primary Activities

Primary Activities	Percent of Total Labor Involved in		Total Number of Workers
	Commuting	Circular Migration	
Government employees	42.2	25.0	64
Traders	51.9	8.5	129
Service workers	29.3	14.4	167
Manufacturing laborers	14.0	24.6	114
Total	33.5	16.7	474

Source: Jatinom Household Survey, 1989, conducted for this chapter.

Data on the first year in which individuals in the household sample worked outside the village give an indication of the increasing labor mobility since 1976 (Table 7.4). This suggests that the integration of the economy of this area with the urban and rural towns has contributed to rural employment, especially nonfarm employment, both within and outside Jatinom.

Income and Consumption

A comparison of the net income from traditional crops (such as rice, cassava, and corn) with the new crop (orange) gives a general picture of the substantial agricultural diversification in Jatinom (Table 7.5). It is apparent that net annual farm incomes from cassava and corn and even from rice were much lower than the income from oranges.[23] As in the case of rice, a few large farmers were first involved in orange farming, but this spread rapidly to smaller farmers in subsequent seasons. Similar patterns also occurred in cattle activities, with richer households sharing their cattle with

Table 7.4   Incidence of Commuting and Circular Migration in Jatinom, by Primary Activities and Periods

Primary Activity	Commuting			Circular Migration		
	Before 1976 (%)	After 1976 (%)	Number	Before 1976 (%)	After 1976 (%)	Number
Government employees	59.3	40.7	27	6.3	93.7	16
Traders	43.3	56.7	67	9.1	90.9	11
Service workers	38.8	61.2	49	29.2	70.8	24
Manufacturing laborers	18.7	81.3	16	0.0	100.0	28
All samples	42.1	57.9		11.4	88.6	
Total number	67	92	159	9	70	79

Source: Jatinom Household Survey, 1989, conducted for this chapter.

Table 7.5   Farm Structure and Inputs-Outputs per Annum in Jatinom

	Rice	Cassava	Corn	Orange
Farm structure				
Cultivated area (ha)	0.2	0.2	0.2	0.2
Type of field	wet	dry	wet/dry	dry
Length of cultivation (months)	3.5	6	2.5/3	12
Inputs-outputs per annum				
Inputs (rupees)	290,000	30,000	149,486	450,000
Value of output (rupees)	675,000	160,000	394,000	1,575,000
Net farm income (rupees)	385,000	130,000	244,514	1,125,000

Source: Case study of selected households in Jatinom, 1989, part of the survey conducted for this chapter.

the poorer households in exchange for labor within a neighborhood. In the case of orange growing, the new crop almost certainly had much less impact on economic differentiation within the village in comparison with commercialization in many rice-growing areas because land was initially much more equally distributed.

The contributions of dry field activities and cattle to household incomes have increased significantly in recent years. The household survey suggests that dry field activities contributed about 23 percent and cattle contributed around 35 percent to household incomes in Jatinom in 1989. This movement toward diversification appears to have been a general trend in Java, even in major wet-rice-growing areas. For example, a resurvey of Sriharjo in Yogyakarta in 1989 revealed that in 1970, the dry field and cattle activities contributed almost nothing to household incomes, whereas they contributed some 15 percent in 1989 (Singarimbun and Effendi, 1989).

Extra income has offered more options, in terms of food purchased as well as other consumption needs. Most villagers are able to meet daily needs, and quite a large number could afford consumer goods such as motorbikes, television sets, tape recorders, and radios. During the 1980–1989 period, the recorded number of all these goods grew significantly in this district (see Table 7.6).

Table 7.6   Number of Durable Goods Owned in Jatinom, 1980–1989

	1980	1989
Car/minibus	56	25
Motorbike	57	2,512
Television	150	650
Radio[a]	628	1,540

Source: The district office record, 1980 and 1989.
[a] This figure is also certainly a gross underestimate because some residents failed to report ownership for fear of having to pay taxes. Almost every household in the subdistrict owns a radio.

The purchase of consumer goods increased after 1980. The survey of 400 households suggests that the proportion of households buying consumer durables rose quite substantially in the periods 1980–1984 and 1985–1989 (Table 7.7). Data on the source of money for buying consumer goods suggest that a high proportion was derived from income from livestock, oranges, off-farm work, and wage/government employment (Table 7.8). The income source for the purchase of expensive consumer goods tended to come mainly from off-farm work, especially trade and work in urban areas, whereas agriculture income tended to be allocated to lower-

Table 7.7 Year of the First Purchase of Consumer Durables, Jatinom, 1989

	Before 1970 (%)	1970–1979 (%)	1980–1984 (%)	1985–1989 (%)	Total (%)	Number
Minibus	8.3	—	25.0	66.7	100	12
Motorbike	1.2	14.8	42.0	42.0	100	81
TV (color)	—	—	28.6	71.4	100	14
TV (black and white)	4.0	10.1	21.2	64.7	100	99
Tape recorder	9.6	8.7	34.8	46.9	100	115
Radio	12.4	21.9	38.8	26.9	100	242

Source: Jatinom Household Survey, 1989, conducted for this chapter.

Table 7.8 Sources of Income for Purchase of Consumer Goods in Jatinom

	Income from Oranges or Livestock (%)	Income from Off-farm Work (%)	Income from Salary and Pension (%)	Remittances (%)	Number
Car/minibus	16.7	83.3	—	—	12
Motorbike	30.9	39.5	24.7	4.9	81
TV (color)	14.3	50.0	35.7	—	14
TV (black and white)	28.3	40.4	29.3	2.0	99
Tape/tape recorder	39.1	28.7	26.1	6.1	115
Radio	42.1	29.7	25.3	2.9	242

Source: Jatinom Household Survey, 1989, conducted for this chapter.
— indicates not available.

value goods (radios, recorders) and to motorbikes.[24] The extra income from oranges and livestock was also spent to rebuild houses or build new, more modern ones. However, this constituted a third priority in the spending of income derived from oranges.[25] More than half the household sample rebuilt or built their houses from 1985 to 1989.

The foregoing has indicated the increasing ability of households to buy consumer durables and build new houses as one indicator of increased prosperity in Jatinom. We now turn to the impact that economic change has had on nonfarm employment, with specific reference to the service industry and the demand for the services of repair workers, middlemen, construction workers, and others.

Rural Economic Change, Nonfarm Employment, and Work in Services

In the preceding sections, we discussed the very substantial changes that have occurred in the national and regional economies and have had an impact on Jatinom over the past twenty years. These have included the closer integration of economies on the national, regional, and village levels marked by more intensive trade and transport links and labor migration. A second key element has been agricultural modernization and diversification, specifically the boom and bust of the orange industry and the growth of the beef and dairy industries. A third element has been the influx of capital, including employment supported by the public sector, incomes from outside Jatinom (especially through the banking sector, both public and private), and spending on rural infrastructure, especially roads, educational, and health facilities. We also described the quite substantial changes in consumption patterns that have occurred in Jatinom in association with these developments.

This section assesses the impact of these developments on rural nonagricultural work, with specific reference to service sector activities. The major question dealt with here is the extent to which changes of the national, regional, and local economies have induced a transformation of rural work patterns in services. To what extent have new, more skilled, and capital-intensive activities provided work, especially for younger, more educated entrants to the work force? To what extent have women participated in new employment activities? And how much diffusion of new job opportunities has occurred within a rural community where control of land is a much less important source of differentiation among classes than in predominantly wet-rice-growing communities?

We begin with a description of the structure of rural nonfarm and services sector work in Jatinom, followed by a discussion of the characteristics of workers engaged in service activities and the contrast between newer activities and those that were established in Jatinom a decade or more prior to the survey. The nonagricultural sector of Jatinom in 1989 consisted primarily of small-scale, self-employed activities in trade and services. Close to half of the 2,600 rural nonagricultural enterprises were engaged in predominantly self-employed service activities (broadly defined to include construction and transport), and approximately 40 percent were in trade (Table 7.9). Despite its close linkages with the plantation economy in the 1930s, manufacturing accounted for a very small proportion of total nonagricultural work. This can be attributed to the relative stagnation and isolation of the rural economy during the first three decades after independence, in contrast to several lowland areas of Klaten district that are well known for their thriving rural textile and metalwork industries. There is no indication, moreover, that agricultural diversification and the incomes generated by new agricultural activities had a significant impact on manufacturing activities in the region. Both manufactured producer and consumer durables are almost entirely supplied from towns and cities outside Jatinom. Besides a small number of blacksmiths and metalworking enterprises already in operation in the 1960s, manufacturing

Table 7.9 Characteristics of Enterprises by Nonfarm Sector, Jatinom, 1989

Characteristic	Industry	Trade	Services
Number of firms	156	1,142	1,293
Entirely self-employed (%)	8.3	73.5	74.6
Employed family labor (%)	49.4	16.6	12.1
Employed wage labor (%)	42.3	9.9	13.3
>5 workers (%)	6.4	0.9	1.5
>10 workers (%)	1.9	0.2	—
Total employment	656	1,640	2,306
Total number of wage employees	237	263	405
Ratio of firms to number of households	.01	.10	.12

Source: Jatinom Enterprise Survey, 1989, conducted for this chapter.

activities consisted mainly of household food processing and tile and brick making enterprises that marketed their products locally. Manufacturing activities, in turn, provided little stimulus to trade and service activities within Jatinom.

Rural trade activities, on the other hand, have flourished since the mid-1970s, with close to one-third of all enterprises being established in the period 1976–1985 and a further 10 percent since 1985. Notably, many new enterprises engaged in the trade of nonagricultural products marketed from Klaten and nearby towns have emerged in the past fifteen years. In general, the marked growth in the number of trade establishments can be attributed to increased trade in both agricultural and nonagricultural products within the subdistrict and to and from nearby towns. As in other regions of Java, trade activities involved a high proportion of less-educated females, especially among market and street traders (over 80 percent of whom were females).

The 1989 survey records just under 1,300 service activities and businesses in Jatinom subdistrict, defined for the purposes of this study to include personal services (repair, hairdressing, brokering, and art and entertainment activities), business and community services, foodstalls and hawkers, construction workers, and transport workers. Around 30 percent of all activities were located in the subdistrict center (population 3,500), and the remainder were situated in the various village centers and along the feeder roads that link the villages of Jatinom with the subdistrict center (Table 7.10). Table 7.10 also shows that 40 percent of all activities were already in operation when the government dropped restrictions on the free movement of goods and persons between parts of the subdistrict and surrounding areas in 1975; a further 40 percent began in the following ten years, spanning the national oil boom period and the advent of significant agricultural diversification in the region. The balance began in the more difficult times of national budget stringency, slower overall growth in agriculture and especially the rice sector growth, and—important from a local perspective—in the years following the collapse of Jatinom's orange industry in 1986.

Table 7.10   Firm Characteristics of "New" Services and All Service Activities, Jatinom, 1989 (percentages)

Characteristic	Percent of All Services
Established before 1976	40
Established 1976–1985	41
Established 1986–1989	19
Located in subdistrict town	30
Ever obtained bank credit	14
Owner-operator attended formal courses	15
Employed wage labor	13
Located in owner's house	32
Main source of household income	43
Gross earnings:	
< Rp1,000/day	32
> Rp5,000/day	15

Source: Jatinom Enterprise Survey, 1989, conducted for this chapter.
Note: Number of firms = 1,293.

According to a range of criteria, the large bulk of establishments were small-scale, self-employed, and household enterprises that drew relatively little on modern sector services for skills and capital. Thus, most operators had never obtained bank credit (over 70 percent depended on their own or family capital) nor attended the plethora of private and government-sponsored courses offered for typists, drivers, and small industry in recent years. Relatively few employed any wage labor, and around one-third of all activities were located in the owners' or operators' own houses (see Table 7.11). Only in just over 40 percent of cases did service activities represent the major source of household income: Nearly one-third of all operators reported gross daily incomes of less than Rp1,000 in the week prior to the survey (approximately $0.70—less than the male daily agricultural wage), and only 15 percent reported gross earnings of Rp5,000 or more.[26]

Table 7.11   Distribution of Service Sector Activities and Sex and Age of Service Operators-Owners in Jatinom, 1989

	Total (No.)	Total (%)	Female (%)	Age < 30 (%)	Age 50+ (%)
Personal services	504	40	30	22	29
Repairs/maintenance	178	14	3	34	30
Bicycle	61				
Radio/TV/clock	35				
Motorcycle	23				
Car/truck	10				
Shoe/umbrella	19				
Furniture/carriage	16				
Other	14				
Tailors	126	10	67	38	20
Brokers/middlemen	81	6	25	3	47
Art/decoration	72	6	50	24	18
Puppeteer (*dalang*)	18				
Bridal preparation (*rias pengantin*)	18				
Rent of party/music equipment	13				
Other	23				
Barbers	17	1	0	6	71
Hairdressers	9	1	100	22	11
Other	31	2	17	13	47
Construction workers	433	33	4	17	24
Transport owners-operators	147	11	27	17	26
Gasoline sellers	44	3			
Truck/minibus owners	40	2			
Carriage/becak drivers	25	3			
Other	38	3			
Foodstalls/hawkers	127	10	60	20	27
Noodles/satay/soup (*soto*) sellers	89	7			
Snacksellers	22	2			
Other	16	1			
Community and business services	81	6	67	7	56
Healers/masseurs	44	3			
Doctors/midwives	12	1			
Bus agents	12	1			
Other	13	1			
All service activities	1,293	100	26	19	28

Source: Jatinom Enterprise Survey, 1989, conducted for this chapter.

An extraordinarily wide range of service sector activities provided employment in Jatinom in 1989. The diversity reflects the proliferation of new activities in the 1970s and 1980s that overlay more traditional activities and characterized the rural economy from the 1950s. Close to 75 percent of all service sector activities were in personal services (40 percent) and in construction activities (33 percent), the latter primarily involving self-employed bricklayers and carpenters (Table 7.11). Among personal services, largely male-operated repair activities predominated, including a mixture of "modern" repair activities (on motorcycles, cars and trucks, TVs, radios, clocks and watches) and more traditional activities, which included repair of bicycles, shoes and umbrellas, and furniture and carriages. The second major category of personal services involved tailors and wearing-apparel outworkers, relatively evenly balanced between females and male self-employed workers.

One surprisingly large group of personal service activities involved a substantial number of (mainly male) brokers and middlemen. Many of these were engaged as go-betweens in transactions, particularly for the purchase of secondhand consumer goods like motorcycles, television sets, and radios and for providing village consumers with information on prices and quality. A similar proportion of activities involved art and decoration, which, like repairs, featured a mix of newer activities (for example, renting of music equipment) and more traditional activities (such as those of puppeteers [dalang]). The final two major categories included transport owners and operators and (predominantly female) foodstall operators and hawkers. The former consisted mainly of gasoline sellers and truck and minibus owners and drivers—occupations that have sprung up with the intensification of transport links, especially in the 1980s. Foodstall workers and snacksellers, most operating in the subdistrict town and along the main road from Klaten, mushroomed during the 1980s.

The very significant growth of service sector activities in the 1980s can be surmised from data on the year in which such activities were established in Jatinom (Figure 7.1). Close to half of all activities and a much higher proportion of foodstalls and transport-related activities began operations in the 1980s, with a significant percentage operating from 1985 onward. The one major exception was construction workers, a considerable proportion of whom had begun work in the industry by the mid-1970s. Many of these people were engaged in work stimulated by the expansion of public expenditure on roads, schools, and other buildings in both urban and rural Java areas in the 1970s. They returned to Jatinom during the less buoyant years of public sector expenditure in the 1980s and were engaged mainly in building and repairing houses in Jatinom and nearby rural areas—work that was primarily stimulated by the growth in local incomes associated with agricultural diversification.

Increased spending on consumer durables in particular has induced demand for a second round of service activities, many of which are located in close proximity to consumers' village areas rather than in the district or subdistrict town.[27] Motorcycle, clock and watch, and other repair shops and brokers with knowledge of prices and quality in many purchases of

Figure 7.1 Establishment of Service Activity in Jatinom

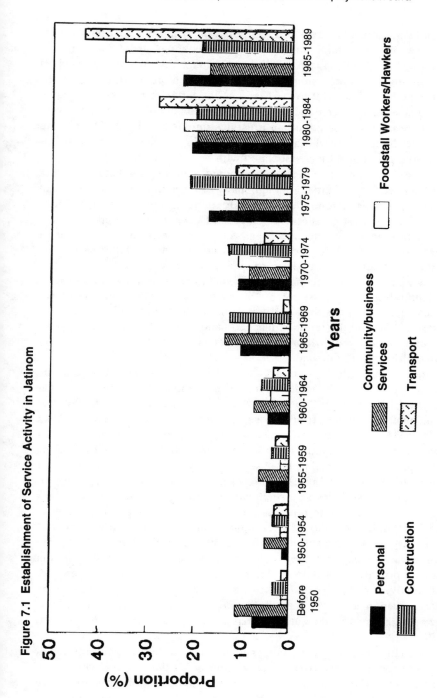

Source: Jatinom Service Survey, 1989, conducted for this chapter.

secondhand consumer goods are good examples. Construction workers employed in the building and repair of houses are another. But increased incomes have also been spent directly on a range of new services, such as hairdressing, film processing, and photocopying, more of which tend to be centralized in the district town. Many of the latter activities have grown in response to greater expenditure on a national village and life-cycle ceremonies, as well as the urban lifestyles imitated by local officials and better-off households who attend the increasing number of government-sponsored public meetings associated with new development projects.

Three additional points should be noted regarding the nature of work in the services sector. First, although many of the activities are quite recent in origin, especially minibuses, a considerable proportion involve enterprises that have long been established and have accumulated sufficient capital to branch out into new areas. For example, some bicycle repair shops now also serve motorcycles, the owner leaving the latter part of the business to a better-educated son or other relative. Many of the new activities were reported as secondary, however, to agricultural and other non-agricultural pursuits. Most notable here is the involvement in small businesses such as hairdressing and tailoring by the wives and daughters in better-off households (farmers, teachers, and local officials in particular), the large majority of whom reported service activities as a secondary source of household income.

Indeed, the quite low proportion (44 percent overall) of operators who reported services as the major source of household income indicates that activities described here do not mark a clear break with past patterns of supplementing income from various off-farm work. It is noteworthy that there was little overall difference among male or female operators of newer activities compared with those in more established services in terms of the proportion reporting their service activity as the major source of household income. And it also is worth noting that a higher proportion of those reporting services as a secondary source of income reported *other nonfarm* activities, not farming, as the major source. Government employment was important among other major sources of nonfarm income, but so, too, were trade and service activities other than those in which the respondent was engaged. It seems clear that sources of capital accumulation were not primarily based on land nor, indeed, on the salaries from and access to government officials in this region. This is in sharp contrast to the patterns seen in some of the predominantly lowland, wet-rice-growing villages studied by various authors during the 1970s (Hart, 1986; Husken, 1989).

Second, many recently established activities reflect a search for a subsistence income on the part of many households that are still very poor. Workers in tiny foodstalls, hawkers, market porters, and sanddiggers are examples of these. In addition, older, less mobile persons continue to be engaged in "traditional" activities; they are traditional healers (*dukun*), masseurs, gamelan players, and the like.

Finally, it is important to stress that although many younger people have left Jatinom to seek income in the towns (and many have also returned), village-based services were of much greater significance in this region than is implied in studies of West Java, in particular in the early and mid-1980s (Collier et al., 1988; Manning, 1987). A much more varied pattern of service sector growth in this area can be explained by the earlier date of other surveys, the much greater attraction that employment opportunities in Jakarta held for younger people, and the more decentralized pattern of manufacturing growth in Central Java, in particular the region of Klaten.

New and Old Service Sector Activities

One of our hypotheses was that more recently established service sector activities would differ from older activities in a range of criteria. It was expected that activities induced by the expansion of consumer demand during the 1980s would tend to attract more-educated persons, receive more support from the state, and provide higher incomes than many of the activities that had begun one or more decades earlier. To some extent, this hypothesis was confirmed, but there were some important exceptions. Newer activities consisted of a hierarchy of work in services, including some jobs involving better-off households, larger amounts of capital, and greater inputs of skill; others were much more akin to relatively unskilled jobs taken as part of the "survival" strategies adopted to meet minimum consumption needs.

These patterns are indicated by data for a selection of older and newer activities—the former established, for the most part, in the 1960s and 1970s, and the latter mainly beginning operations in the 1980s (Tables 7.12 and 7.13).[28] Activities begun in the 1980s tended to involve more-educated persons. In part, this reflects the need for skills that require a higher level of formal schooling, such as those in car, motorcycle, and television repair. In part, it reflects the generally higher level of education of the younger people who were entering the labor market and taking up some of those activities in the 1980s. Nevertheless, in several newer activities, such as selling gasoline and snacks, there is little need for formal education, and quite a high proportion of operators had not completed primary school (Table 7.12).

These involved in newer activities did not, however, show a greater tendency to acquire skills through formal courses run by private or public bodies. Only among TV, radio, and watch and clock repair workers was there a significant proportion of persons who had attended formal courses, mainly held in the nearby cities of Klaten and Solo. Among those pursuing

Table 7.12   Education and Formal Training of Enterprise Owners in Jatinom
(percent of owners)

				Skill Acquisition		
	Number	Gender Mainly	< Primary School	Secondary School +	Formal Schooling	Apprentice
Schooling mainly begun in the 1960s/1970s						
Healers/masseurs	44	F	96	2	39	—
Construction workers	433	M	56	2	4	23
Brokers	71	M	52	7	5	—
Carriage/becak drivers	25	M	48	4	8	—
Barbers	17	M	41	—	—	12
Puppeteers (*dalang*)	18	M	33	11	44	33
Tailors (male)	42	M	19	14	52	24
Schooling mainly begun in the 1980s						
Snacksellers (*ratengan*)	22	F	73	5	—	—
Gasoline sellers	44	M	41	23	9	—
Minibus/truck owners	40	M	15	28	17	5
Motorcycle repairmen	23	M	13	61	9	30
TV/radio repairmen	35	M	11	40	40	17

Source: Jatinom Enterprise Survey, 1989, conducted for this chapter.
— indicates none.

Table 7.13   Enterprise Characteristics of Selected Service Activities in Jatinom
(percent of activities)

Activity Reported as the Major Source of Household Income	Major Income Source	Gross Income		Ever Received Bank Credit
		<Rp1,000	>Rp5,000	
		(per day/last week)		
Activity mainly begun in the 1960s/1970s				
Healers/masseurs	16	23	14	5
Construction workers	33	4	9	7
Brokers	38	30	34	19
Carriage/becak drivers	44	64	—	1
Barbers	47	100	—	—
Puppeteers	33	—	83	—
Tailors (male)	79	2	5	5
Activity mainly begun in the 1980s				
Snacksellers	36	77	1	—
Gasoline sellers	14	71	14	21
Minibus/truck owners	33	33	68	55
Motorcycle repairmen	61	48	—	26
TV/radio repairmen	74	23	—	26

Source: Jatinom Enterprise Survey, 1989, conducted for the chapter.
— indicates none.

older activities, on the other hand, quite a substantial proportion of highly skilled puppeteers, tailors, and healers or masseurs also took formal courses. About half of all puppeteers had attended the government-run school for *dalang* in Solo, and many traditional healers were obliged to attend government courses to be able to continue their trade. Tailors, conversely, generally attended privately run courses, which had extended to Jatinom subdistrict by the 1980s and were common, as were a plethora of other private sector courses held in nearby cities.

Similar to patterns of involvement in formal courses, there was no marked contrast between newer and older activities in terms of apprenticeships. Almost all the more skilled activities involved some participation in apprenticeships (*magang*), and this has clearly remained an important means of acquiring skills despite the growth in vocational training programs in Jatinom and surrounding areas.

Although the income data provide only a crude indicator of returns to labor, it seems clear that returns to newer activities were not significantly higher than to older activities. Quite a large proportion of selected activities that began operations in the 1980s earned gross daily incomes of less than Rp1,000 (Table 7.13). Only a significant percentage of colt and truck owners (68 percent) earned daily incomes of Rp5,000 or more. Activities begun in the 1960s and 1970s showed quite a wide range in incomes. All barbers and two-thirds of becak and carriage operators, all relatively unskilled jobs, earned incomes of less than Rp1,000, and most tailors and construction workers earned between Rp1,000 and Rp5,000. However, a significant proportion of other activities produced incomes of Rp5,000 or more, most notably the highly skilled *dalang* (83 percent). In general, there is no indication that these incomes were lower on average than those of the newer activities.

It might be expected that the low incomes of many service operators could be explained by the fact that their activities constituted secondary income sources and that farming or other nonfarm activities were the main source of income for the individuals and households involved. To some extent, the survey data support this proposition but only for the activities begun in the 1960s and 1970s. Among these, only a majority of tailors (79 percent) reported income from services as their major income source (see the first column in Table 7.13). In all other activities, including relatively highly paid *dalang*, a minority of persons reported services as their main income source—ranging from a low 16 percent of healers and masseurs to 47 percent of barbers. Surprisingly, among the newer activities, a high proportion of relatively more-educated but lower-income repair workers reported services as their major source of income. This was in contrast to the relatively high-income minibus and truck operators, the large majority of whom acknowledged services as a secondary income source. These data do not, in general, support our hypothesis that an increase in local spending had a significant impact on drawing labor out of agriculture and other low-income activities.

Thus, three principal groups of service operators can be identified. The largest group consisted of landless and near-landless persons who earned only a relatively small proportion of their income from a range of activities—for example, construction work, becak and carriage driving, and snack selling. For these individuals, service sector work represented an opportunity to gain some additional income as part of a survival strategy. Their principal sources of income came from both agriculture and other nonagricultural activities, especially petty trade. Many were older males, and frequently, they were the major family breadwinner.

A second group consisted mainly of female foodstall owners, younger males engaged in repair activities, and tailors; for them, services tended to be a major source of income. Incomes were not significantly higher than for the first mentioned group, for whom services were a supplementary source of household income. But within the household, many in this group were secondary workers who supplemented the earnings of the household head. Finally, there was a smaller group of individuals from better-off families who channeled income into services as part of an accumulation strategy. This group consisted primarily of larger traders, salaried local officials and teachers, and more prosperous farmers mainly working with cattle, oranges, and, to a lesser extent, rice. As in lowland areas of Java, favored service activities among this group were investment in minibuses and trucks to meet the growing demand for commercial vehicles, female-operated beauty salons (hairdressing), larger car and truck repair activities, foodstalls operations, and moneylending. Service activities were considered a secondary activity for this group, although in some cases, incomes earned in services were comparable to or even greater than those made in their reported principal activity.

Among this latter group, a significant proportion of service sector entrepreneurs were able to develop new businesses through access to credit from government and private sector banks established in Jatinom during the 1980s. Thus, for example, over half of all commercial minibus and truck operators received bank credit for their businesses, compared to some 20 or 25 percent of those in other new service activities and a much smaller proportion in almost all service activities begun in the 1960s and 1970s (Table 7.13).

Newer service activities tended to be concentrated among the latter two groups, and most of these were stimulated by the upsurge in trade and transport in Jatinom in the 1980s. Although incomes were not necessarily higher in these activities, a much greater proportion of younger and more-educated persons participated in them than in other service activities. The overall impact of these activities on economic welfare within the subdistrict depends, however, on their contribution to household income among various strata within the community. We take up this subject in the following section.

Service Sector Work and Household Income

Thus far, the discussion has focused on the characteristics of service sector owners and operators and the nature of work in this sector, based on a survey of service sector establishments. The contribution of these activities to household income is evaluated based on a random sample of 400 households from three villages in Jatinom, which were selected according to dominant agricultural type and proximity to the subdistrict center.[29] The largest proportion of respondents (31 percent) gave farming as their principal source of household income, followed by individuals in service enterprises (19 percent); government employment, including village officials (14 percent); trade (12 percent); and livestock raising (11 percent). Among those giving farming as their principal source of income, land- and non-land-based agriculture were the major contributors to total annual household income, whereas farm laboring was insignificant (Figure 7.2).[30] However, the figure also shows that agriculture accounted for a relatively small proportion of total income among the other groups for whom farming was *not* reported as the major source of household income, except in the case of village officials and government sector workers (including teachers). Allocations of land to village officials (*bengkok*) mainly helped account for the latter.

Total average household incomes did not vary substantially among the four groups distinguished in Figure 7.2, although income earned by households whose major source of income was in nonfarm activities, especially in trade and services, was slightly higher than for the other groups. The fact that village officials and government workers did not earn significantly more than other groups within the village can be partly attributed to the lower quality of much of the *bengkok* land allocated to village officials, especially in the predominantly dryland agricultural areas of Jatinom, as compared to many of the lowland, wet-rice-based agricultural regions of Java.[31] Thus, in general, government officials in this area did not constitute a rural elite to anything like the same extent as has been suggested was the case in many lowland villages in Java in the 1970s and 1980s (Hart, 1986).

Average incomes were higher among the larger landowners (0.5 hectares and above), and income from agriculture was a major contributor to the household incomes of this group (Figure 7.3). But the difference in average incomes between the larger landowners and the landless was quite small. Moreover, in contrast to generalizations drawn from experience in several lowland, wet-rice-based areas of Java, *absolute* incomes earned

Figure 7.2 Mean Household Income by Activity and Landowning Class in Jatinom

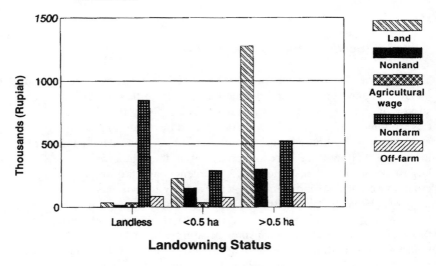

Source: Jatinom Household Survey, 1989, conducted for this chapter.

Figure 7.3 Mean Household Income by Activity and Landowning Class in Jatinom (households with majority of income from services)

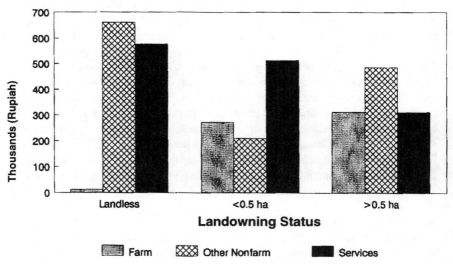

Source: Jatinom Household Survey, 1989, conducted for this chapter.

Figure 7.4 Mean Household Income by Activity and Landowning Class in Jatinom (household heads engaged in services)

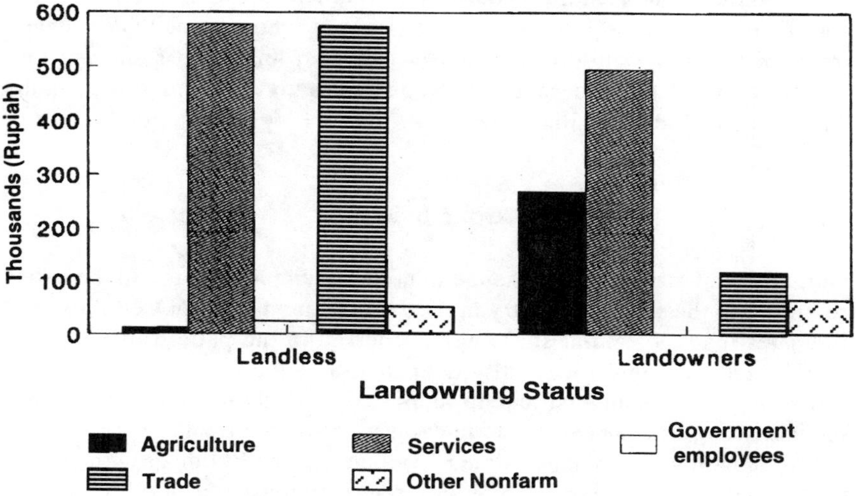

Source: Jatinom Household Survey, 1989, conducted for this chapter.

outside agriculture were not closely correlated with farm size.[32] Figure 7.3 shows that average annual incomes earned in nonfarm activities were significantly higher among the landless households than among landowners with less or more than 0.5 hectares of land in Jatinom.[33] A combination of factors, several of which we have already alluded to, have contributed to this pattern. These include the low quality of agricultural land in many parts of Jatinom, the importance of non-land-based agriculture, and the increased opportunity for earning incomes in nonfarm activities. Richer households in Jatinom have generally not used agriculture as a basis for accumulation and have not found agricultural land an attractive form of investment. This applies, in particular, to a small number of interlinked families engaged in wholesale trade who have replaced Chinese traders driven out of the subdistrict in the early years of independence. As in urban fringe areas, which are becoming increasingly common on Java as urbanization proceeds apace, there is evidence of a breakdown in the close nexus that had been observed between landowning class and economic status in earlier decades.[34]

A similar pattern is also shown for the seventy-four families engaged in service activities who were covered in the household survey (Figure 7.4). Income from services was higher among those who owned no land than among those who owned some land. Among the former, trade was a major source of household income, and other sources were relatively insignificant. In contrast, for landowners (most of whom owned quite small tracts of land), agriculture was the second most important source of income, followed by trade and other nonfarm activities undertaken both within and outside the village.

Conclusion

Our survey of structure and change in nonfarm employment, with specific reference to the service industry in the Jatinom subdistrict in Central Java, indicates that substantial shifts have occurred in the pattern of nonfarm work since the region was fully opened to outside contact in the mid-1970s. Agricultural diversification supported by government programs and the increasing trade between and integration of Jatinom with the rich, rice-based economy of lowland Klaten have encouraged both growth in incomes and increased expenditure on a range of consumer goods. This, in turn, has stimulated demand for new service, construction, and transport activities: in vehicle repair, brokering, house repair and construction, and more intensive minibus services linking the subdistrict with major urban centers close to Jatinom.

Relatively few of these new activities are supported directly by the state or "modern sector" institutions. Most capital—in the majority of cases, still in very small amounts—continues to be generated by households, and most skills are learned through informal channels. Self-employed and family enterprises predominate, and relatively few service activities employ any wage labor. Thus, although many activities provide new services, they do not represent a sharp break with past patterns of nonfarm activity in the type or scale of nonfarm work. The state can claim it has made some contribution to stimulating change through the introduction of dairying cattle, improvements in rural roads, and support for educational expansion in the subdistrict. But many of the developments must be attributed mainly to innovative and fiercely competitive private sector activity, developed in response to new income-earning opportunities outside agriculture.

We have argued that a broad range of service activities can no longer be typified as pure subsistence-oriented searches for income to meet basic physical needs. At the same time, though there is now a much wider choice of occupations than there was in the mid-1980s, returns to labor are still very low in most service activities. Earnings may have grown in real terms, but the increases have not been enough to significantly impact the living conditions of the majority of poorer households. It is more likely that the main stimulus to family incomes may have come not through increased average returns to labor but through higher utilization of labor in cash-earning activities, especially the involvement of more females in off-farm work.[35]

We have only looked at some preliminary data on the relationship between socioeconomic class and involvement in nonfarm work. But the data clearly show that control over agricultural land is not a major source of investment in nonfarm work in Jatinom, contrary to the findings of studies conducted in the agriculturally more prosperous lowland areas of Central Java. The role of local officials in accumulating capital is not altogether clear from the data presented in this chapter. Our tentative conclusion is that although the officials represent an important group involved in investment in nonfarm work, there are now greater opportunities for middle-income groups to accumulate capital *without* access to land, regular salaries, or preferential treatment by the state.[36]

What conclusions can be drawn about the future of work in Jatinom, especially with regard to the service sector? The population has obviously taken advantage of a considerable range of employment opportunities that have emerged in the service sector over the past decade, in response to agricultural diversification, public sector spending, and a consequent intensification of trade and transport linkages. In contrast to studies that suggest that agricultural growth has had little impact on employment opportunities in trade or related activities, it is clear that both trade and service sector employment have grown rapidly in recent years partly in response to new opportunities created by the income generated in agriculture. With respect to employment creation in the agricultural sector, our data lead to the same conclusion as that Joan Hardjono reached, based on a village study conducted in West Java in the early 1980s. She suggested that though "greater crop diversification might increase farm incomes, it will not increase labor absorption" (1985: 74). But the opposite would appear to be more appropriate in evaluating the effect of agricultural diversification on nonfarm employment. Much more work is now available than in the past—stimulated mainly by consumption rather than production linkages with agriculture—but incomes remain very low in most nonfarm activities.[37]

We also agree with Benjamin White (1986: 61) that it would be "rash" to believe that what has occurred is a dynamic pattern of rural nonfarm employment creation resulting from agricultural growth. Many of the new jobs in services and trade have been stimulated by income generated by government expenditure, either on salaries of teachers and officials or on rural construction, or from incomes returned to the subdistrict from jobs created in urban areas. However, recent experience suggests that there are opportunities for further agricultural diversification and income creation, chiefly in non-land-based agriculture (such as milk and beef production). Incomes created in these activities are likely to result in a further spread of work in services and trade for both males and females.[38]

But in the foreseeable future, the excess supply of laborers competing for work in rural nonfarm activities in Jatinom will continue to hold returns at a low level. Significant improvement in incomes for the majority of the population without access to capital or physical resources will depend on the more-educated younger generation being able to take advantage of still relatively limited opportunities for more skill-intensive employment in modern sector work outside Jatinom. In the longer term, more sustained and widespread growth in living standards will have to await substantial labor absorption in nonagricultural activities outside Jatinom; this would create conditions of relative labor scarcity and bring about a general increase in returns to labor in both farm and nonfarm activities. There is little evidence that Jatinom was close to such a turning point in 1989.

Finally, to what extent can one generalize from these findings to other regions of Java? Certainly, restrictions on mobility into the region before 1976 meant that some of the changes in both agricultural and nonfarm work patterns were more abrupt than in many other parts of Java. Also, some important differences were noted in the relationships between agricultural and nonfarm growth in Jatinom and those observed in lowland paddy regions.[39] Jatinom is, nevertheless, typical of a large part of the area along the central and southern mountain slopes of Java, all in close proximity to major urban centers. We see no reason to expect a significantly different pattern of nonfarm—especially service sector—change in many of these areas.

Notes

Collection of the field data for this chapter was supported by a grant from the United Nations Fund for Population Activities. The entire field research effort was given very substantial moral and material support by the Population Studies Centre at Gadjah Mada University.

1. We use the term *nonfarm* to denote all nonagricultural work located in rural areas.

2. During the Dutch colonial period, low-wage, labor-intensive industries (such as batik, weaving, and *kretek* cigarettes) played an important role in rural employment in certain regions, and females have been reported as being heavily involved in trade activities. See, for example, Sitsen (1942) and de Vries (1985) for a description of these patterns in the 1930s. In the early 1970s, Java had one of the highest proportions of rural nonagricultural employment among Third World countries (Jones, 1983).

3. The enterprise survey involved a full census of all enterprises and individuals engaged in manufacturing, trade, and services in the subdistrict.

4. See especially Booth and McCawley (1981), Sundrum (1986), Warr (1986).

5. Any judgment on whether poverty declined in Java over this period depends partly on the choice of the price deflator.

6. A rather different pattern was observed in Central Java, however, where manufacturing employment has tended to be much less concentrated around the major cities. Low-wage, traditional industries (such as the production of *kretek* cigarettes, batik, and weaving) have been major sources of nonagricultural employment—many of them drawing on a rural-based, female labor supply.

7. The data in Table 7.1 refer only to major sources of employment, and there is a tendency for rural people to give farming as their principal activity even though a substantial share of income and work may be derived from the nonagricultural sector. According to the 1985 SUPAS data, 55 percent of rural households earned some income from outside agriculture, and for 27 percent of households, nonagricultural activities were the only source of household income.

8. See especially White (1979), Collier (1981), and Hart (1986).

9. See especially White (1976), Hart (1978 and 1986), Gunawan, Hurmanaf, and Sawait (1977 and 1979), and Rozany, Gunawan, and Sri Hartoyo (1979).

10. See especially Hart (1986, Chapter 6).

11. It is argued that village political elites, who are frequently also large landowners, are supported in new investment activities through patronage links with government officials outside the village. This is manifested in their easier access to government-subsidized credit, licences, and the like.

12. See especially Collier et al. (1982), Saefudin and Marisa (1984), Soentoro (1983), World Bank (1985), Rietveld (1986), and Manning (1987 and 1988).

13. Examples of this are the replacement of bamboo-based matt and string weaving by plastics and traditional batik by batik printing (White, 1986).

14. Of no less importance is the rate of economic change and the discontinuities in national and regional economic fortunes, which make comparisons of the findings of various microlevel studies particularly hazardous.

15. The household survey was conducted in three villages. The village samples were chosen according to the land use type, the dominant agricultural pattern, and the distance from rural town center.

16. The comparable figure for rural Java was 1.81 per annum in the period 1980–1985.

17. For example, Hart's (1986) study in a village in the northern part of Central Java found that the landlessness rate was 49 percent. Collier et al. (1988: 23), from a study of seven villages of Central and East Java, found that the proportion of landless ranged from 50 to 66 percent. See also White and Wiradi (1989).

18. Among landowners, the percentage of households and land owned was much less equally distributed in upland than in lowland areas in Java (Wiradi and Manning, 1984; Hart 1986).

19. From 1930 up to 1945, Chinese traders dominated economic activities. Since then, they are much less active in this area.

20. Selosoemardjan (1984: 104) notes that similar distributions occurred in rural areas around this time. All of the crops cultivated by plantation companies were destroyed by the farmers, who changed to crops such as rice, cassava, and corn. These crops were more consumption-oriented than market-oriented, and production was unable to meet even local demand for food. As a result, many people suffered food shortages during the slack season. The social movement called Merbabu Merapi Complek (MMC), against the Indonesian army, rose up in 1950, and this also disturbed the agricultural activities of the district. Thus, the distrust and disruption influenced economic activities and hindered the economic development of Jatinom.

21. Communist Party campaigners argued that the farmers should support party activities; if not, the land that had been taken from the plantation companies

would be taken back by the government. This issue was related to land reform policy in 1960.

22. This area was classified as one of the poor subdistricts of Klaten district (Indonesia Department Dalam Negeri, 1983).

23. It should be noted, however, that most of the farmers cultivate the oranges mixed with cassava, corn, or vegetables. The oranges can be considered as a source of cash income, whereas cassava, rice, corn, and vegetables are grown for home consumption or local markets.

24. Most households bought cheaper, secondhand motorbikes and TVs from brokers or middlemen. Government employees, on the other hand, bought new motorbikes and TVs because they have access to bank credit.

25. According to the village head (lurah), priorities in the spending of income from oranges can be divided as follows: (1) buying TVs, tape recorders, and radios; (2) buying motorbikes; (3) repairing houses or building new ones; and (4) purchasing gold or other items that allow the (male) household head to take an extra wife! However, in the fifth harvest in 1986–1987, most of the oranges were destroyed by a virus.

26. It should be stressed that the income figures refer to gross, not net, incomes and hence are partly an indicator of scale. For many of the smaller service activities (those of bicycle repair workers, barbers, tailors, construction workers, and drivers), the two figures differ little, as the value added is primarily in the form of labor inputs. They do diverge quite substantially, however, in some of the more "modern" activities, such as hairdressing (beauty salons), and motorcycle and auto repair and for owners of minibuses, for which materials and power constitute a considerable proportion of total costs.

27. This contrasts, for example, with relations between the district town and its hinterland in one region of rapid agricultural change in South India (Harris, 1981).

28. In both groups, two-thirds or more of activities were begun in the 1960s–1970s period and in the 1980s, respectively.

29. One village was a predominantly wet-rice-growing community located close to the subdistrict town. In the other two, orange growing and dairying were the major sources of agricultural income, respectively, and both were located some distance from the subdistrict center.

30. These income data are based on responses to questions regarding the net income from each of the major income-earning activities undertaken by household members over the twelve-month period prior to the survey, which was conducted from March to October 1989.

31. A second explanation is related to the fact that many teachers who were young and recently appointed to fill vacancies in newly established primary schools were at the lower end of the government pay scale.

32. White (1986) has suggested that one important feature of income distribution in rural Java is the higher absolute incomes earned in nonfarm activities by larger landowning households who engage in accumulation strategies by investing the profits from farming in nonagricultural pursuits.

33. It should be noted that this pattern persists if the same data are examined for landless households excluding village and other government officials.

34. See especially Rietveld (1986) and Schrevel (1989) for a discussion of these changing patterns in other areas of Java.

35. This is consistent with the macrodata, which show marked increases in the rates of labor force participation by rural females in the 1980s.

36. The extent of vertical mobility between various income classes is a subject still to be examined.

37. See Effendi (1991) for an analysis of the income and employment effects in trade and industry.

38. One important feature of the cattle industry is that resources controlled by the poor are increased through arrangements that provide for a division of livestock offspring between better-off owners and the poorer households entrusted with caring for the cattle. See Effendi (1991).

39. Even in the latter, however, it is becoming increasingly difficult to see a clear relationship between land controlled and economic status. See, for example, Schrevel (1989).

References

Booth, Anne. 1990. *Agricultural Development in Indonesia* (Sydney: George Allen and Unwin).

Booth, Anne, and Peter McCawley. 1981. "The Indonesian Economy Since the Mid Sixties," in Anne Booth and Peter McCawley, eds., *The Indonesian Economy During the Suharto Era* (Kuala Lumpur: OUP), pp. 1–22.

Booth, Anne, and R.M. Sundrum. 1989. *Employment Trends and Policy Issues for REPELITA V* (Jakarta: International Labor Organization).

Bryant, Nevin Arthur. 1973. "Population Pressure and Agricultural Resources in Central Java: The Dynamics of Change" (Ph.D. dissertation, University of Michigan).

Collier, William L. 1981. "Agricultural Evolution in Java," in Gary E. Hansen, ed., *Agricultural and Rural Development in Indonesia* (Boulder, Colo.: Westview Press), pp. 147–178.

————. 1987. "The Economic and Social Transformation of Rural Java," memo for the United States Agency for International Development, Jakarta.

Collier, William L., et al. 1982. *Accelerating Rural Development in Java: From Village Studies to a Macro Perspective of Rural Java,* Occasional Paper No. 6 (Bogor, Indonesia: Rural Dynamics Study, Agro-Economic Survey).

————. 1988. *Employment Trends in Lowland Javanese Villages* (mimeographed) (Jakarta: United States Agency for International Development).

Daldjoeni, N. 1973. "Sejarah Sosial Ekonomi: Suatu Aktiva bagi Pembangunan Daerah Klaten," *Cakrawala*, Majalah Penelitian Social, No. 2 th VI, September–October, pp. 137–151.

de Vries, Egbert. 1985. *Pertanian dan Kemiskinan di Jawa* (Jakarta: Gramedia).

Effendi, Tadjuddin Noer. 1991. "The Growth of Rural Non-farm Activities at the Local Level: A Case Study of Causes and Effects in a Subdistrict of Upland Central Java (Ph.D. dissertation, Flinders University, Adelaide).

Gunawan, Memed, et al. 1977. *Penyediaan dan Kebutuhan Tenaga Kerja di Sektor Pertanian: Tahap II 1976/77* (Bogor, Indonesia: Rural Dynamics Study, Agro-Economic Survey).

Gunawan, Memed, Rozany Nurmanaf, and M. Husein Sawit. 1979. *Penyediaan dan Kebutuhan Tenaga Kerja di Sektor Pertanian: Tahap IV, 1978/79* (Bogor, Indonesia: Rural Dynamics Study, Agro-Economic Survey).

Hardjono, Joan. 1985. "Employment for Rural Women: A Case Study in West Java," *Prisma*, Vol. 37, pp. 68–77.

Harris, John. 1981. "Agriculture/Non-Agriculture Linkages and the Diversification of Economic Activity in Rural Asia," paper presented to the Workshop on the Green Revolution in South and Southeast Asia in Perspective, Department of Human Geography, Research School of Pacific Studies, Australian National University.

Hart, Gillian. 1985. "Structural Change and Labor Mobility in Rural Java," in Guy Standing, ed., *Labor Circulation and the Labor Process* (London: Croom Helm), pp. 46–88.

———. 1986. *Power, Labor and Livelihood: Processes of Change in Rural Java* (Berkeley: University of California Press).

Hugo, Graeme. 1978. *Population Mobility in West Java* (Yogjakarta, Indonesia: Gadjah Mada University).

———. "Structural Change and Labour Mobility in Rural Java, in Guy Standing, ed., *Labour Circulation and the Labour Process* (London: Croom Helm) pp. 46–89.

Husken, Frans. 1979. "Landlords, Sharecroppers and Agricultural Laborers: Changing Labor Relations in Rural Java," *Journal of Contemporary Asia*, Vol. 9, No. 2, pp. 140–151.

———. 1989. "Cycles of Commercialization and Accumulation in a Javanese Village," in Gillian Hart, Andrew Turton, and Benjamin White, eds., *Agrarian Transformations: Local Processes and the State in Southeast Asia* (Berkeley: University of California Press), pp. 303–331.

Indonesia Department Dalam Negeri. 1983. *Penentuan Daerah Miskin Propinsi Jawa Tengah* (Jakarta: Indonesia Department Dalam Negeri).

Islam, Rizwanul, ed. 1987. *Rural Industrialisation and Employment in Asia* (New Delhi: ARTEP-ILO).

Jayasuriya, Sisira, and Chris Manning. 1990. *Agricultural Wage Growth and Rural Labor Market Adjustment: The Case of Java, 1970–1989*, Working Paper in Trade and Development (Canberra: Research School of Pacific Studies, Australian National University).

Jones, Gavin W. 1983. *Structural Change and Prospects for Urbanization in Asian Countries*, Papers of the East-West Population Institute No. 88 (Honolulu: East-West Center).

———. 1984. "Links Between Urbanization and Sectoral Shifts in Employment in Java," *Bulletin of Economic Studies*, Vol. 20, No. 3, pp. 120–157.

Kartodirjo, Suyatno. 1982. "Revolution in Surakarta 1945–1950: A Case Study of City and Village in the Indonesian Revolution" (Ph.D. dissertation, Australian National University).

Makali, and Sri Hartoyo. 1978. "Perkembangan Tingkat Upah adan Kesempatan Kerja Buruh Tani di Pedesaan Jawa," *Prisma*, Vol. 7, No. 3, pp. 33–45.

Manning, Chris. 1987. "Rural Economic Change and Labor Mobility: A Case Study from West Java," *Bulletin of Indonesian Economic Studies*, Vol. 23, No. 3, pp. 52–79.

———. 1988. "Employment Creation in Rural Java: Lessons from the Green Revolution and Oil Boom," *Population and Development Review*, Vol. 14, No. 1, pp. 47–80.

Mather, Celia. 1983. "Industrialization in the Tangerang Regency of West Java: Women Workers and the Islamic Patriarchy," *Bulletin of Concerned Asian Scholars*, Vol. 15, No. 2, pp. 2–17.

Naylor, Rosamond. 1990. "Wage Trends in Rice Production in Java: 1976–1988," *Bulletin of Indonesian Economic Studies*, Vol. 26, No. 2, pp. 133–156.

Riddle, Dorothy. 1986. *Service-led Growth* (New York: Praeger).

Rietveld, Piet. 1986. "Non-Agricultural Activities and Income Distribution in Rural Java," *Bulletin of Indonesian Economic Studies*, Vol. 22, No. 3, pp. 106–119.

Rozany, Nurmanaf, A., Memed Gunawan, and Sri Hartoyo. 1978. *Penyediaan dan Kebutuhan Tenaga Kerja di Sektor Pertanian: Tahap III 1977/78* (Bogor, Indonesia: Rural Dynamics Study, Agro-Economic Survey).

Sabolo, Yves. 1975. *The Service Industries* (Geneva: ILO).

Saefudin, Yusuf, and Yuni Marisa. 1984. *Perubahan Pendapatan dan Kesempatan Kerja*, Rural Dynamics Series No. 26 (Bogor, Indonesia: Agro-Economic Survey).

Sawit, Husein M., Yusuf Saefudin, and Sri Hartoyo. 1985. "Activities Non Pertanian Pola Musiman dan Peluang Kerja Rumah Tangga di Pedesaan Jawa, " in Mubyarto, ed., *Peluang Kerja dan Berusaha di Pedesaan* (Yogjakarta, Indonesia: BPFE).

Schrevel, Aart. 1989. "Akses Tanah Sebagai Indikator Pendapatan Rumah Tangga Pedesaan," *Prisma*, Vol. 18, No. 4, pp. 38–51.

Selosoemardjan. 1984. "Land Reform di Indonesia," in Sediono M.P. Tjondronegoro and Gunawan Wiradi, eds., *Dua Abad Penguasaan Tonah* (Jakarta: Gramedia), pp. 103–111.

Singarimbun, Masri, and Tadjuddin Nur Effendi. 1989. "Pekerjaan Non-Farm dan Kemiskinan di Pedesaan: Studi Kasus di Miri, Sriharjo dan Jatinom," Population Studies Center, Gadjah Mada University, Yogyakarta, Indonesia.

Sitsen, Peter H.W. 1942. *Industrial Development of the Netherlands Indies,* Bulletin 2 (New York: Netherlands Indies Council, Institute of Pacific Relations).

Soentoro. 1983. "Penyerapan Tenaga Kerja Luar Sektor Pertanian di Pedesaan," in Faisal Kasryno, ed., *Prospek Pembangunan Pedesaan di Indonesia*, Rural Dynamics Series No. 23 (Bogor, Indonesia: Agro-Economic Survey), pp. 169–239.

Sri Hartoyo, and Makali. 1984. *Perubahan Pola Pengeluaran Rumah Tangga di Pedesaan Jawa*, Rural Dynamics Series No. 28 (Bogor, Indonesia: Agro-Economic Survey).

Sundrum, R.M. 1986. "Indonesia's Rapid Economic Growth: 1968–81," *Bulletin of Indonesian Economic Studies*, Vol. 22, No. 3, pp. 40–69.

———. 1988. "Indonesia's Slow Economic Growth," *Bulletin of Indonesian Economic Studies*, Vol. 24, No. 1, pp. 37–72.

Warr, Peter G. 1986. *Indonesia's Other Dutch Disease: Economic Effects of the Petroleum Boom*, Working Papers in Trade and Development 86/2 (Canberra: Department of Economics and National Center of Development Studies, Australian National University).

White, Benjamin. 1976. "Production and Reproduction in a Javanese Village" (Ph.D. dissertation, Columbia University).

———. 1979. "Political Aspects of Poverty, Income Distribution and Their Measurement: Some Examples from Rural Java," *Development and Change*, Vol. 10, No. 1, pp. 91–114.

———. 1986. *Rural Nonfarm Employment in Java: Recent Developments, Policy Issues and Research Needs* (Jakarta: ILO-UNDP).

White, Benjamin, and Gunawan Wiradi. 1989. "Agrarian and Non-Agrarian Bases of Inequality in Nine Javanese Villages," in Gillian Hart, Andrew Turton, and Benjamin White, eds., *Agrarian Transformations: Local Processes and the State in Southeast Asia* (Berkeley: University of California Press), pp. 266–303.

Wiradi, Gunawan, and Chris Manning. 1984. *Landownership, Tenancy and Sources of Household Income*, Rural Dynamics Series No. 29 (Bogor, Indonesia: Agro-Economic Survey).

Wolf, Diane Lauren. 1986. "Factory Daughters, Their Families and Rural Industrialization in Central Java" (Ph.D. dissertation, Cornell University).

World Bank. 1985. *Indonesia: Policies for Growth and Employment* (Washington, D.C.: World Bank).

8

Rural Nonagricultural Activities in China: Assisting or Impeding Agriculture?

Yok-shiu F. Lee

China is in the midst of a rapid rural employment transition. The rural economy is shifting from the predominantly agricultural employment structure of the past to a more industrial occupational structure. Because about 80 percent of the Chinese population still reside in rural areas, tracing rural occupational changes in China will greatly enhance our understanding of that country. In contrast to the Soviet Union, which managed to reduce agriculture's share of total employment from 71 percent to about 50 percent within twelve years after the start of its First Year Plan (Riskin, 1987: 4), China is still largely rural—with 87 percent of its labor force engaged in agriculture in 1978—almost three decades after the introduction of state economic planning (*ZGNCTJNJ 1985*: 224).

From the start of rural reforms introduced between late 1978 and 1986, China's rural nonfarm sector, as measured by the output value of township enterprises,[1] has multiplied rapidly, at an average rate of 28 percent per annum (*RMRB*, 1987, July 31). In 1989, its output value was equivalent to 58.0 percent of the entire output value of the rural sector, and the output value of its industrial component accounted for 28.1 percent of the nation's total industrial output value (*ZGJJNJ 1990*: III-10, III-11). As shown in Table 8.1, the proportion of rural labor force (not counting those in designated towns) engaged in nonagricultural activities has increased steadily from 10.3 percent in 1978 to 20.8 percent in 1989.

Unprecedented in China's economic development experience, the tremendous growth of the rural nonfarm sector since 1978 has been received with mixed reactions in different quarters. Supporters point to the surging economic significance of the rural nonfarm sector. They emphasize the important role of rural nonfarm enterprise in providing added employment and earning opportunities to the rural surplus labor, in allocating parts of their profits to improve the social welfare of the peasants and to subsidize agriculture, and in enhancing the tax revenues of the state (*RMRB*, 1987, August 12). Critics, on the other hand, charge that rural

Table 8.1 Sectoral Composition of the Rural Labor Force in China, 1978–1989

	1978	1979	1980	1981	1982	1983	1984	1985	1986	1987	1988	1989
Total[a] (thousands)	306,378	na	318,359	326,723	338,665	346,898	359,676	370,651	379,898	390,004	400,667	409,388
Agriculture[b]	274,883	na	287,787	296,464	300,624	305,011	302,972	303,515	304,679	308,700	314,557	324,405
Nonagriculture[c]	31,495	na	30,572	30,259	38,041	41,887	56,704	67,136	75,219	81,304	86,110	84,983
Total (percent)	100.0	na	100.0	100.0	100.0	100.0	100.0	100.0	100.0	100.0	100.0	100.0
Agriculture[b]	89.7	na	90.4	90.7	88.8[d]	87.9	84.2	81.9	80.2	79.1	78.5	79.2
Nonagriculture[c]	10.3	na	9.6	9.3	11.2[d]	12.1	15.8	18.1	19.8	20.9	21.5	20.8

Sources: 1978, 1979–1984: calculated by the author using data in *ZGNCTJNJ 1985:* 224; 1985: calculated by the author using data in *ZGNYNJ 1986:* 152–154; 1986: calculated by the author using data in *ZGTJNJ 1987:* 135–136; 1987–1989: calculated by the author using data in *ZGNCTJNJ 1990:* 224.

na = not available.

a Contrary to the broad definition of the rural nonfarm sector that I have adopted, the available figures being used here do not include labor in designated towns. However, because the labor force in designated towns is largely engaged in nonagricultural activities and because village-to-town migration is strictly controlled, the omission of the labor force of designated towns in this table should not weaken my argument.

b Agriculture here refers to crop cultivation, forestry, animal husbandry, sideline production, and fisheries and does not include state farms.

c Nonagricultural activities include township and village industries, construction, transportation, commerce, food services, education, health and social services, research, government, migrant contract work in urban areas, and others.

d The 1982 Population Census produced a slightly different set of figures for the sectoral composition of the rural labor force: agriculture, 87.8 percent; nonagricultural, 12.2 percent (Ho, 1986: 34). These figures may be more accurate. However, to preserve the consistency of the figures in the table, I did not use the 1982 Population Census figures.

nonfarm enterprises are unduly competing with state factories for raw materials and other inputs that are in short supply, that rural factories are polluting the countryside, and that rural industries are diverting meager resources away from farming, thus impeding long-term agricultural growth (*RMRB*, 1987, August 12).

Of the controversies surrounding the rapid increase of rural nonfarm activities in the People's Republic, in this chapter I will focus on the following research question: To what extent and in what manner is agricultural development being assisted or impeded by rapid expansion of rural nonfarm enterprises? Agriculture requires close scrutiny because its growth or decline will influence the future course of rural nonfarm development, and it will have a fundamental impact on China's overall development strategy. The future of the rural nonfarm sector itself also depends greatly on its performance in the context of national development policy, as well as its effect on agriculture's long-term growth prospect.

Major Argument

The major argument of this chapter is that the success of the growth of rural nonfarm activities in China has aggravated a number of secondary problems and sometimes created new ones. By almost all accounts, township enterprises have succeeded in bringing more jobs and higher income to the peasants. Even though underemployment still exists and actually remains a major concern in the less-developed regions, the expansion of township enterprises is regarded as an expeditious solution to the problem of rural surplus labor in the economically more advanced areas.

The contents of national policy statements on township enterprises indicate that the central government is equally concerned with these issues: rural surplus laborers, agricultural development, and the retention of rural labor in the countryside. Local cadres, however, now appear less concerned with agriculture, partly because their control over farming was diminished after the communes were abolished and partly because agricultural production has steadily improved since the introduction of the household responsibility system. At present, they are more interested in running the township enterprises, through which, with some exceptions, they often can control the distribution of the profits. Beginning in 1984, peasants were formally authorized to run their own nonfarm enterprises. Driven by enthusiasm for pursuing personal wealth, individual and other types of noncollective enterprises mushroomed in many parts of the advanced regions and in some parts of the less-developed areas.

At the local level, extra budget revenues (for local authorities) and added incomes (for the peasants) are becoming the primary reasons for initiating rural nonagricultural enterprises. One of the larger societal goals—

agricultural development—is, more through inadvertence than design, sacrificed for immediate gains in local employment and earning opportunities.

From the perspective of economic development, agricultural growth is unduly impeded as rural nonfarm activities (industrial production in particular) capture the peasants' energies and deflect their interests away from farming. Nonfarm enterprises are commanding more attention and a better allocation of resources because both the local officials and the peasants find them financially more rewarding than cultivation. The improvement in per capita agricultural productivity in the early 1980s has not advanced further, in part because peasants who now receive nonfarm income work their fields halfheartedly and are not keen to produce more than enough to feed their own families. The amount of agricultural inputs, such as fertilizer, has declined, and in some extreme cases, farmland has been left fallow or even abandoned altogether. The plan to institute mechanized, large-scale farming has encountered obstacles because the program of farmland consolidation has received very little support from the peasants. With a few exceptions, therefore, the gains in added employment, incomes, and local revenues are obtained at the expense of agricultural stagnation.

Objectives of Township Enterprises

There are two major policy objectives of township enterprises: to subsidize agriculture and to help prevent excessive rural-to-urban migration (*GWYGB*, 1984: 146–155). Guided by the principle "to subsidize agriculture by industry" (*yi gong bu nong*), the township enterprises are expected to help modernize the agricultural sector through (1) the increased construction of agricultural infrastructure, (2) the provision of agricultural machinery, and (3) the provision of services related to agricultural production. Guided by the principle "to leave the land [*li tu*] but not to leave the rural areas [*bu li xiang*] ," the policymakers expect the township enterprises to help retain the rural labor in the rural areas through the provision of nonagricultural jobs for surplus and displaced farmers and the development of rural market towns (*GWYGB*, 1984: 146). The discussion here will focus on the first objective.

From the perspective of the central government, one of the overriding concerns in developing the rural nonfarm sector is the modernization of agriculture. The central planners believe that the modernization of the agricultural sector requires the placement of surplus and displaced labor and the accumulation and investment of huge amounts of capital. They also believe that township enterprises, which have some close ties to the farmers and agriculture, can effectively contribute to efforts to satisfy these two requirements.

With regard to the placement of surplus and displaced labor, the central planners conclude that the modernization of agriculture primarily entails mechanization. As a result, surplus laborers would have to be removed from the agricultural sector to increase productivity. With little prospect of easing the strict control of rural-to-urban migration in the future, nonagricultural jobs would have to be created in the rural areas. Accordingly, the planners project that township enterprises would need to provide employment for about 40 percent of the rural labor force by the end of the century (*Beijing Review*, 1984, No. 50: 19). They also believe that the township enterprises would concentrate in small market towns; thus, they call for the planned development of such towns (*GWYGB*, 1984: 148). Thus, the growth of the township enterprises is, in a sense, a major economic impetus for the development of the small towns.

With regard to the accumulation of capital, the central planners assert that expansion in the size of arable land has more or less reached its limit. The further development of agriculture depends primarily on raising labor productivity, which, in turn, demands huge amounts of capital investment. The policymakers believe that the township enterprises could assist the state in providing a major portion of the capital needed for agriculture's modernization. Their belief is based upon the fact that the commune and brigade enterprises have made considerable contributions toward agriculture in the past. With those enterprises steadily growing in the early 1980s and with the cooperative and individual enterprises beginning to prosper at the same time, the central government must have felt confident that the combined strength of the collective and private enterprises would be able to shoulder a major part of the burden to modernize agriculture.

Subsidizing Agriculture

Township and village enterprises have, indeed, helped reduce the state's burden by allocating some of their after-tax profits to subsidize agriculture directly. That subsidy comes in three forms: purchasing farm machinery, investing in farmland infrastructure, and giving monetary aid to poor production teams. For instance, between 1979 and 1982; township and village enterprises allocated 8 billion yuan of their profits to subsidize agriculture, a sum of money that was equivalent to 73 percent of the central government's investment in agriculture during these years (Zhang Zhuo-yuan, 1985: 64). Then, between 1981 and 1984, around 5 billion yuan of township and village enterprises profits were diverted to the agricultural sector, an amount that was three times the state's investment in agriculture in the same period (*RMRB*, 1985, December 7).

As early as 1978, however, the level of financial subsidy that township and village enterprises extended to agriculture began to diminish notably. In 1978, 30.0 percent of township and village enterprises profits were used to subsidize agriculture. By 1988, only 4.5 percent were used for this purpose (Table 8.2).

The profits of township and village enterprises were also allotted to fulfill two other nonreinvestment purposes. First, in 1982, up to 19.5 percent of the enterprises profits were distributed as extra income to those team members who continued to work on the farmland. Such profits were not used for this purpose in 1978 and 1979, but data are insufficient to establish the exact point when this became routine practice. Nevertheless, by 1985, the share of profits assigned to this purpose had dropped to 3.6 percent.

Second, the share of profits allocated to collective welfare—which includes rural highway, schools, theaters, market town infrastructure (Zhang Zhuo-yuan, 1985: 64)—has grown gradually since 1978; by 1987, 16.6 percent of township and village enterprises profits were used in this way (Table 8.2). In certain more developed areas, these profits have become the major financial source for the construction of undesignated towns (Wu Da-qian and Wu De-fu, 1984: 34). Between 1977 and 1981, for instance, township and village enterprises profits accounted for 85 percent of the total infrastructure investment for undesignated towns in Shanghai's rural counties (Gong Jie-min and Xiong Shi-ping, 1983: 46).

What are the major reasons for these temporal changes in the distribution pattern of the profits of township and village enterprises? First, the decline in the level of support for agriculture is primarily a result of the demise of the commune and its many functions. An important function of the commune was to channel rural resources toward the collective agricultural sector. Irrigation equipment and farm machinery, for example, were purchased by the commune to be used on its collectively owned farmland. However, with "decommunization" coming as a natural and necessary consequence of the household contract responsibility system (Shue, 1984), the collective's role in providing communal services was diminished. The level of financial subsidy that went from township and village enterprises into agriculture was accordingly reduced over the years.

Second, the distribution of some township and village enterprises profits to team members who continue to work on the farmland is basically a strategy to provide this group with an additional wage to augment their lower and unstable farming income. This is intended to minimize the income gap between farming and nonfarming jobs within the same rural community and thus to alleviate the negative impacts that a big income gap may have on the morale and the output level of the farm workers (*RMRB*, 1985, October 8).

Third, the increase in the amount of profits slated for collective welfare was due to two major factors. The demise of the commune and the post-1979 nationwide campaign on constructing small towns must have greatly influenced the local cadres to commit a larger proportion of the township and village enterprises profits into improving or building the market town infrastructure. Moreover, the transfer of enterprise ownership from the commune to the township government has helped facilitate such a priority shift on the part of the local cadres. Local cadres must also have recognized the prospering township and village enterprises as a new source of local finances. Different kinds of "management fees" or "mandatory contributions," previously imposed upon the peasants by the local cadres, are now being levied against the township and village enterprises. Some enterprises even had reportedly been forced to make "contributions" that exceeded their earnings (*RMRB*, 1985, December 14). To be sure, this decision to shift the burden from the agricultural sector to township and village enterprises is a calculated effort to avoid a deterioration of the output level of agriculture. This same concern underlies the decision to provide a stable basic income to team members who hold farming jobs.

From the point of view of many local cadres, distributing the profits of township and village enterprises to the peasants as extra income and turning toward township and village enterprises—rather than the peasants—for "mandatory contributions" serve the same goal: to appease the peasants and to maintain the output level of agriculture. For them, both of these methods of using the profits are valid forms of "subsidizing agriculture."

Such interpretations of subsidizing agriculture, however, may have obscured the original intentions of the central policymakers. Formerly, subsidizing agriculture meant using township and village enterprise profits to purchase farm machinery, to invest in farmland infrastructure, and to subsidize the poor teams. The thrust of these activities was to improve the long-term production capacity of the agricultural sector. Now, however, subsidizing agriculture may mean distributing township and village enterprises profits directly to the peasants. The primary effect of this financial subsidy is an increased income level for some peasants. Most of this extra income, however, has gone into personal consumption rather than into productive investment in agriculture (Wang Dai and Zhu Gang, 1986: 24). As a result, the long-term production capacity of the agricultural sector has been greatly impaired (Xu Yun-quan, 1985: 1; Gu Song-nian and Yan Ying-long, 1985: 59). Dispersing profits of township and village enterprises directly to the peasants is, therefore, a temporary remedy that closes the income gap between farm workers and nonfarm workers but will actually prolong and aggravate many problems existing in the farm sector.

In Jiangsu Province, for instance, the state of the irrigation system and farm machinery has reportedly deteriorated since the advent of decommunization, seriously hampering the further development of agriculture (*RMRB*, 1986, February 17). This apparently has prompted the central and provincial governments to urge local authorities to emphasize investment in agricultural machinery and farmland infrastructure over giving profits

Table 8.2. Distribution of Net Profits of Township (Commune) and Village (Brigade) Enterprises in China, 1978–1988

	1978	1979	1980	1981	1982	1983	1984	1985	1986	1987	1988
Total net profits (billion yuan)	8.80	10.45	11.84	11.28	11.55	11.78	12.87	17.13	16.10	18.78	25.92
Reinvestment	3.09	4.06	4.70	4.30	4.76	5.06	6.10	7.94	8.03	10.00	13.82
Assist agriculture	2.64	2.69	2.27	1.70	1.43	1.36	0.66	0.88	0.69	0.85	1.16
Purchase farm machinery	1.15	1.13	0.91	0.70	0.53	0.41	na	na	na	na	na
Farmland infrastructure	1.18	1.17	0.94	0.80	0.71	0.72	na	na	na	na	na
Aid to poor teams	0.31	0.39	0.42	0.20	0.19	0.23	na	na	na	na	na
Distribute to team members[a]	—	—	na	na	2.25	1.70	0.64	0.62	na	na	na
Collective welfare[b]	0.40	0.49	0.68	0.70	0.94	1.14	1.57	1.98	2.40	3.12	2.64
Market town infrastructure	na	na	na	na	na	na	na	na	0.30	0.41	na
Education	na	na	na	na	na	na	na	na	0.66	0.92	na
Other welfare	na	na	na	na	na	na	na	na	1.44	1.79	na
Others	2.67	3.21	4.19	4.58	2.17	2.52	3.90	5.71	4.98	4.81	8.30

Total (percent)[c]	100.0	100.0	100.0	100.0	100.0	100.0	100.0	100.0	100.0	100.0	100.0
Reinvestment	35.1	38.9	39.7	38.1	41.2	43.0	47.4	46.4	49.9	53.2	53.3
Assist agriculture	30.0	25.7	19.2	15.1	12.4	11.5	5.1	5.1	4.3	4.5	4.5
Purchase farm machinery	13.1	10.8	7.7	6.2	4.6	3.5	na	na	na	na	na
Farmland infrastructure	13.4	11.2	7.9	7.1	6.1	6.1	na	na	na	na	na
Aid to poor teams	3.5	3.7	3.5	1.8	1.6	2.0	na	na	na	na	na
Distribute to team members[a]	—	—	na	na	19.5	14.4	5.0	3.6	na	na	na
Collective welfare[b]	4.5	4.7	5.7	6.2	8.1	9.7	12.2	11.6	14.9	16.6	10.2
Market town infrastructure	na	na	na	na	na	na	na	na	1.9	2.2	na
Education	na	na	na	na	na	na	na	na	4.1	4.9	na
Other welfare	na	na	na	na	na	na	na	na	8.9	9.5	na
Others	30.3	30.7	35.4	40.6	18.8	21.4	30.3	33.3	30.9	25.6	32.0

Sources: 1978–1979: ZGNYNJ 1980: 366; 1980–1981: ZGNCTJNJ 1985: 190; 1982: ZGNYNJ 1983: 83; 1983: ZGNYNJ 1984: 124; 1984: ZGNYNJ 1985: 181–182; 1985: ZGNYNJ 1986: 228–230; 1986: ZGNYNJ 1987: 289–290; 1987: ZGNYNJ 1988: 318–319.

— indicates not applicable.

na = not available.

[a] "Team members" here refers to those who have remained in farming jobs, not the peasant workers.

[b] Collective welfare includes rural highways, schools, theaters, and market town infrastructure (see Zhang Zhuo-yuan 1985: 64).

[c] Details may not add to totals due to rounding and, for 1980 and 1981, incomplete data.

directly to the peasants and in the interest of improving agricultural productivity (*RMRB*, 1987, March 23, and 1986, April 26).[2]

Problem of Farmland Consolidation

In addition to using profits from township and village enterprises to subsidize agriculture, the central policymakers are also looking to the development of rural nonfarm activities to help develop the agricultural sector in another manner. By permitting and actually urging those who are less efficient in cultivation but otherwise skillful in nonfarm trades to give up their land, planners hope to see a consolidation of farmland into the hands of fewer but more efficient farmers. When smaller pieces of farmland are consolidated into larger parcels, agricultural productivity can be raised through the use of agricultural machinery and other large-scale farming techniques.

It is very rare to see an entire household leaving the land, however. In almost all instances, it is the able-bodied members of a family who leave farming for nonfarm jobs (Mei Tai-he and Ding Zhao-xiang, 1984). The reality is that although many rural laborers may entirely give up farming for nonfarm employment, very often they retain their title to parts or all of their contracted farmland. They usually ask their non-"*li tu*" family members and relatives to help cultivate their land. During the busy harvesting and planting seasons, they may temporarily leave their nonfarm positions to return to work alongside their families in the field (Field notes, 1985). In the rural areas, therefore, a substantial number of households are concurrently involved in agriculture and industry or other trades. A 1984 study of four villages in Wujiang County, a more developed part of Jiangsu Province, for example, showed that between 44.3 percent and 69.7 percent of the households in four villages were concurrently engaged in farm and nonfarm activities (Zhang Yu-lin, 1986b: 181–182).

To explain this issue further, we need to understand that for distribution purposes, farmland is divided into three categories: (1) food grain fields (*kouliang tian*), (2) responsibility fields (*zeren tian*), and (3) fodder fields (*siliao tian*). Food grain fields are distributed on a per capita basis to each household, and the products from these fields are retained by the households for their own consumption requirements. Responsibility fields are assigned to each household, according to the number of able-bodied laborers in each family. The output from these fields is what the peasants are obligated to produce for the state. Fodder fields are distributed to those households who keep livestock (Wang Guo-xiang, 1986: 21).

It is obvious that each household will try to obtain as many food grain fields as possible to ensure an adequate food supply for everyone in the family. For reasons discussed later, many rural laborers are trying to contract as little responsibility land as the state will allow, and almost all rural households keep some livestock and thus receive a share of the fodder land. Therefore, one of the inevitable consequences of distributing land in this fashion is the tendency to equalize the share of land contracted by each household. According to several Chinese researchers, this phenomenon has been observed on a widening scale in the rural areas (Wang Guoxiang, 1986: 21; Yang Yi, 1985b: 2).

Two Major Tendencies

Two major unintended consequences of rural nonfarm development have arisen in rural China: (1) the tendency of more and more individual rural laborers and households to be concurrently engaged in farm and nonfarm work, and (2) the tendency to equalize the share of land contracted by each household (Dong Han-ying, 1986: 52).

These are, of course, contrary to the original intentions of the central planners, who wanted to encourage an exodus of the less-efficient workers from the land into the rural nonfarm sector and a consolidation of larger pieces of farmland into the hands of fewer but more efficient producers. The planners envisioned a division of labor in the rural areas, where farmers and nonfarm workers would both increase their productivity through specialization and commercialization, but the current situation indicates that they apparently did not fully anticipate the concerns of the peasants. They have also failed to consider thoroughly the policy's implications for the rural sector and agriculture. The relevant question here is this: Why does a rural worker who has a full-time nonfarm occupation still want to maintain a share of the farmland?

Some analysts believe that the traditional conservatism of the peasants has prevented them from giving up their contracted farmland, which many consider their private property (Mu Hong-tao, 1985: 7). Although this may be true, there are several real economic concerns that heavily influence a rural worker's decision to keep a piece of farmland, while at the same time opting for a nonfarm job.

First, a rural laborer who works in the rural nonfarm sector is, in almost all instances, a peasant-worker who is required by law to maintain his or her agricultural household status. This means that he or she is not entitled to receive subsidized commodity grain and other subsidized urban rations from the state. Thus, to ensure an adequate and stable food supply, the peasant-worker naturally wants to keep a share of the food grain land.

In the last several years, food grain has once again become available on the market. One might expect that because the peasant-workers can now buy their food grains from the market, their need for farmland will diminish. In some localities, "market grain supply certificates" were issued to the *li tu* peasants as a way to guarantee their food supply (Chinese Communist Party Yunnan Province, 1983: 62). The problem, however, is that the supply of market grain is often unreliable, and the price is more than double that of the state's commodity grain (Mu Hong-tao, 1985: 7). This only reinforces the peasant-workers' determination to hold on to their land.

Second, a claim to part or all of his or her contracted farmland insures a peasant against any unexpected downturns in nonfarm endeavors. The peasant-workers are fully aware that the rural nonfarm sector, unlike the state sector, does not guarantee stable income or yearlong employment. Therefore, they are naturally conservative and are reluctant to sever all of their ties to the land (Wang Guo-xiang, 1986: 22–23; Xu Jing-yong, 1984: 55).

Third, the non–*li tu* members of a household are generally capable of cultivating the extra land kept by the *li tu* members. They do not consider the extra land unmanageable. This is because one result of the equalization of land distribution is a low land-to-labor ratio. The average size of land contracted by each household is currently recorded at about 8 mu, which is a comparatively low figure by both world standards and China's own (Liu Gang, 1986: 7). Therefore, even though the non–*li tu* members are usually the elderly, the women, and the young, they are still able to attend to the farming needs of the entire household (Shan Yong-tang et al., 1984: 37; Yang Yi, 1985a: 40). In other words, maintaining additional shares of the land is not a great extra burden on the family members of the *li tu* peasants. Peasant-workers and their families as well do not see any disadvantage in retaining shares of the land.

Fourth, subsidies derived from the profits of rural industries had previously been diverted to the agricultural sector to help it develop. Since the establishment of the household responsibility system, these subsidies have been distributed to the peasants according to the size of their contracted responsibility land. Although farming the responsibility land represents a drain on the peasants' resources, the financial subsidies, in many circumstances, have turned farming into a marginally profitable business (Chen Sheng, 1986: 33). Thus, the first three factors explain the motivations behind the *li tu* peasants' determination to keep their food grain land, and the last factor explains their decision to keep their responsibility land.

All of these factors have effectively persuaded the *li tu* peasants to hold on to their shares of the land. As a result, two unintended consequences for the agricultural economy have emerged. One is that the average household is now primarily interested in small-scale, self-sufficient production. That is, each household works on several small pieces of farmland, and its production is primarily geared toward satisfying the food consumption needs of its members. Another unanticipated consequence is that an overwhelming majority of the rural households are now concurrently engaged in farm and nonfarm work. In many cases, nonfarm work has become the primary source of income for the rural households.

Effects on Agriculture

The two unanticipated tendencies in the agricultural economy have had several negative effects on agriculture. First, with small and scattered parcels of land contracted by different households, economies of scale in agricultural production are not realized. Because land is not being consolidated into the hands of full-time producers, the condition needed for the mechanization, specialization, and commercialization of farm production is not achieved (Chen Sheng, 1986: 33; Sun Han, 1986: 10). According to one analyst, if the size of a household's farmland is less than 20 mu, then the investment cost of using a small tractor alone is about 150 yuan per mu (Liu Gang, 1986: 7). Considering the fact that the average household works on about 8 mu of land and that the land is made up of small pieces scattered in different locations (*RMRB*, 1987, October 23), such a cost figure means that agricultural mechanization is entirely out of the question for the majority of the farming households.

Second, the satisfaction of their own consumption needs has become the top priority of most agricultural producers. They are increasingly disinterested in fulfilling their obligations for the state's grain procurement quota (Yang Yi, 1985a: 40). This may stem from the traditional mentality of self-sufficiency characterizing the small-scale producer, as some people have suggested (Wang Guo-xiang, 1986: 23), but it is more likely that the decline in producing and supplying commodity grain to the state is the result of rural households and laborers concurrently engaging in farm and nonfarm work. In areas where the rural nonfarm sector has flourished, proceeds from farm activities may constitute only 10 to 20 percent of a rural household's total cash income (Yang Yi, 1985a: 40).

For many peasant-workers, farming has become a "sideline" business and a secondary income source (Huang Huan-zhong and Sun Xin-ya, 1986: 46). Because many peasants now derive their primary income from outside agriculture, the immediate objective of farming thus becomes that of fulfilling their own consumption requirements. As a result, peasants' interests in cultivation and their investment in agricultural production have both declined. In some localities, farmland has even been partly or totally abandoned by peasants who find nonfarm work substantially more lucrative (Liu Rong-qin, 1987: 46; Shi Fu-yuen, 1986: 18–19). A study of Langfang Region, Hubei Province, showed that 5 percent of the region's farmland were abandoned and that about 20 to 50 percent of the rural households were neglecting their farming duties (Cao Meng-jiao and Liu Zong-xiao, 1987: 32).

Third, there is a noteworthy characteristic now commonly found in households that are involved in both farm and nonfarm activities. Because it is generally the male adult and the more skillful, able-bodied laborers who are hired away by rural nonfarm enterprises, agricultural growth inevitably suffered as the average level of competence of the remaining non–*li tu* agricultural work force declined (Xiong Cheng-jia, 1986: 57; Liu Fu-chen and Guo Wei-guo, 1985: 18).

Finally, there is an alarming phenomenon that is closely linked to the previous argument. One of the original goals of the central planners was to see a consolidation of land into the hands of skillful, full-time farmers, but increasingly, even this group of specialized rural laborers has begun entering the nonfarm sector (Li Jian-de, 1986: 35). On the one hand, they realize that they possess the knowledge and skills to make an occupational transition as well as secure a much higher return from nonfarm work. In many areas, rural laborers can double or even triple their earnings by switching to construction or mining jobs (Zhao Hing-han, 1986: 27; Cheng Lu, 1987: 85). On the other hand, they see persistent obstacles in consolidating more farmland into their hands than they have anticipated. For a majority of these skillful peasants, the logical conclusion is, therefore, to join their neighbors and enter the rural nonfarm sector.

In conclusion, many peasants have only nominally left their land: Rural workers may have taken up nonfarm positions, but they have not given up their land. This has greatly hindered one of the higher objectives of rural nonfarm development—the consolidation and transfer of farmland to specialized farmers. Because land continues to be evenly distributed among most households and because most households are concurrently engaged in farm and nonfarm work, the implications for agriculture are largely discouraging.

Problem of Farmland Subleasing

The extremely low rate of farmland subleasing has been documented in several instances. A survey study in Ezhou City of Hubei Province reported that in 1983, only 3 percent of the city's agricultural land was subcontracted, involving only 5 percent of all the agricultural households (Wang Xing-long, 1984: 24). In Bangshan Commune, Longhai County, Fujian Province, out of a total of 1,695 specialized rural nonfarm households, only 9 had subleased their land to other farmers (Xu Jing-yong, 1984: 55). Another survey conducted in Gudianzi Township of Jilin Province recorded that in 1983, when farmland subleasing was first practiced, only 7 households out of a total of 5,965 were involved in such an activity. A year later, in 1984, the number of households that had subleased their land jumped to 36, which was still a very small part of all the households in that township (Zhao Jun-xiang, 1985: 40).

The hesitation of full-time farmers to accept more land has also been recorded in two survey studies. In 1985, a survey of 100 rural households in Xiaoshan County, Zhejiang Province showed that only 1 percent of those interviewed were willing to lease more land from the others (Wu Zhihua and Meng Zhi-xian, 1985: 54). In 1986, a survey of 173 rural households in Fengci Township, Nanhai County, Guangdong Province, reported that only 2 percent of those questioned were willing to take on more land. Only 8 percent in the same study said that they were willing to sublease their land, and an overwhelming 90 percent expressed no interest in either reducing or expanding their landholdings (Li Zhong, 1987: 46).

Before I discuss the reasons behind the reluctance of the full-time farmers to accept more land, it is instrumental to understand the prevailing arrangements of farmland subcontracting. There are basically two kinds of arrangement: subcontracting without compensation and subcontracting with compensation.

Under the first kind of arrangement, the leaseholder turns over his or her land to the lessee with only one condition: The lessee will fulfill all the obligations as specified in the original contract between the leaseholder and the government. In general, this means that the lessee will meet the state grain procurement quota and pay taxes to local authorities, as prescribed in the original contract. Aside from this requirement, the lessee does not have to compensate, in any manner, the original contractor (Lu Hou-da and Chen Hong-er, 1984: 9).

The second kind of arrangement—subcontracting with compensation—requires the lessee to fulfill extra requirements. In addition to the terms of the original contract, the lessee will have to compensate the original leaseholder in three major ways:

1. Compensation by supplying foodstuffs. The lessee will either guarantee to supply low-priced food grains or ensure the supply of a specific amount of food grains, free of charge, to the original leaseholder. The latter may also sometimes request an additional supply of other agricultural products, such as fresh vegetables (Lu Hou-da and Chen Hong-er, 1984: 9).
2. Compensation by paying cash. The lessee will turn over a part of his or her extra income derived from the transferred land to the original leaseholder. In one study conducted in Gudianzi Township of Jilin Province, the original contractors took 26.4 to 51.3 percent of the lessees' income (Zhao Jun-xiang, 1985: 41).
3. Compensation by contributing labor. In some instances, certain households that are short of able-bodied laborers may keep only parts of their land and sublease the rest. The lessee, in this case, will help the original leaseholder to cultivate that part of the land that is still kept by the latter (Li Zhong-xian, 1985: 38). The available data show that an overwhelming majority of those households that are willing to sublease their land have asked for some forms of compensation from the lessees (Zhao Zhi-yuan et al., 1985: 46).

In 1985 in Yingshan County, Shanxi Province, for instance, close to 90 percent of all the land subleasing cases involved compensation (Li Zhong-xian, 1985: 37). Moreover, the majority of the leaseholders would lease out parts but not all of their land. It should also be made clear that leaseholders are not relinquishing the legal title to their contracted land. They are only transferring to the lessees, usually on an annual basis but sometimes on a seasonal basis, the right to cultivate the land (Li Sheng-wen, 1987: 39).

Why do most land transfer cases require compensation? Most lease-holders, for a variety of reasons, are not keen on subleasing their land. One of the major reasons is that they want to assure themselves a stable and inexpensive supply of food grains from their own property. Because the subleased land is, to the leaseholders, an important source of low-cost food grains, it is understandable that, in almost all instances, the lessees are asked to guarantee the former an inexpensive or sometimes free food supply (Li Zhong-xian, 1985: 37; Zhou Qi-ren et al., 1985: 15). The leaseholders may also require compensation because they want to recoup their previous investment (in infrastructure, fertilizer, etc.) in making the land productive.

There are, to be sure, ongoing debates on the extra nature of this kind of compensation because it has a clear connection to sensitive issues like exploitation and land ownership. Supporters for this kind of arrangement point out that such compensation greatly facilitates the process of transferring farmland. Moreover, because the arrangement has to be a mutual agreement and both parties must gain from it, supporters believe the practice should be sanctioned and extensively promoted (Zhao Zhi-yuan et al., 1985: 46: Li Zhong-xian, 1985: 38). Critics, on the other hand, are quick to challenge the legitimacy of this type of compensation. They question whether such compensation constitutes a form of exploitation by the lease-holders and whether the compensation should go to the collective, which is the legal owner of agricultural land (Zhao Jun-xiang, 1985: 42–44).

Although the legitimacy of compensation in land subcontracting is an important issue to analyze, to go further into it is beyond the scope of this chapter. The relevant question here is: Why are full-time farmers unwilling to increase their landholdings?

It is natural to believe that most farmers are not interested in leasing more land because they refuse to shoulder the burden of compensation. What is intriguing here is that even when the leaseholders are willing to sublease their land without asking for compensation, it is still very difficult to find someone who would agree to take on more land (Yang Yi, 1985a: 40).

In this regard, it is pertinent to recall that when someone subcontracts a piece of land from a leaseholder "without compensation," the former still must satisfy the latter's tax obligations to the central and local authorities. The lessee will fulfill the grain procurement quota to the central government, and he or she will pay local taxes and other fees to the local officials (Wu Xiang-yu, 1986: 27). Thus, the main obstacle that discourages full-time farmers from acquiring additional land, even when compensation is not demanded, is that the economic burden of these government levies has outweighed the gains from cultivating a larger farm.

The amount of a peasant's tax payment is, by and large, calculated on the basis of the size of his or her farmland (Zhou De-zheng et al., 1984: 18). If one acquires more land, one's tax assessment also increases, regardless of whether one's income has actually become larger or smaller. Compared with the fixed income tax rate of the nonagricultural sector, the progressive land tax in the agricultural sector thus makes large-scale production very unattractive to full-time farmers. To them, farming more land simply translates into bearing a higher but unjustifiable financial burden.

That burden has two major components: (1) a low state grain procurement price, despite rising production costs (*RMRB*, 1987, November 14), and (2) the rising level of local levies. First, although most inputs into agricultural production have become more expensive since 1980, the state's grain procurement price has not been raised high enough to fully cover the increased cost of production (*RMRB (OE)*, 1986, January 6; Zhang Wen-hui, 1986: 58). For instance, in 1986, when it cost 0.26 yuan to produce 1 jin of grain in Yunnan Province, the state procurement price was set at 0.162 yuan per jin. Grain cultivation has, therefore, become a marginally profitable or even money-losing business. Farmers mandated to sell their grains to the state were, in effect, forced to take heavy losses (Hai Zuo-liang, 1986: 61).

Low prices for agricultural products have also led to a larger income gap between full-time farmers and nonfarm rural workers. The income per workday for the former in 1985 was estimated at 4.9 yuan, but the corresponding figures for the latter ranged from 8.4 yuan (for sideline and commercial undertakings) to 15.0 yuan (for industrial and transportation activities) (*RMRB (OE)*, 1986, May 12). Earnings from nonfarm jobs could double and even triple those of full-time farming positions. An inevitable result is the refusal of almost all farmers to subcontract more land from their nonfarm neighbors (Li Sheng-wen, 1987: 40; Li Wei-wu, 1985: 24). For many in the villages, it makes more economic sense to become a part-time farmer and also to engage in some sort of more lucrative nonfarm activity. In many areas, nonfarm pursuits have actually become the most important economic undertaking for many peasants, who look upon farming with much less enthusiasm and give it a much lower priority (Chinese Academy of Agriculture, 1986: 30–33).

The second major component of the financial burden is the rising level of local taxes. In many localities, types and rates of taxes have increased repeatedly since the early 1980s, sometimes well beyond the limits set by the central and provincial authorities. A study in Gucheng County of Hubei Province revealed that in 1985, there were nineteen different kinds of local taxes imposed upon the peasants, up from only five types of taxes in 1982 (Pan Wen-hui, 1986: 20–21).

Moreover, peasants are often forced to finance local highway construction, small-town infrastructure development, and educational and recreational facilities, all of which are supposedly the responsibilities of various local government offices (Pan Wen-hui, 1986: 21, Zhan Qing-lan and Fu Quan-de, 1986). Such demands are particularly serious in areas where collective enterprises are underdeveloped and local officials see peasants as their only major source of revenues.

In a nutshell, because local taxes are determined by the size of a farmer's landholdings and because these taxes have rapidly risen in the last several years, many farmers have lost interest in subcontracting more land from those who want to give up their land (Yu Shi-zhen and Chen Qiao-nan, 1985: 59).

It is apparent that one major way to convince the peasants to undertake large-scale cultivation is to reduce their economic burden. A logical solution would be to mitigate the two major components of the burden by increasing the procurement prices for grains and reducing local taxes (Zhu Ji-yu, 1986: 18). In reality, however, state prices and local levies prove to be very difficult to modify. Instead, the most commonly adopted strategy is to use the profits from rural nonfarm enterprises to augment the farmers' income. These profits are also used to finance some of the local expenditures, thus relieving part of the farmers' tax obligations (Cheng Chun-dao, 1986: 43; Ye Yen-yu, 1984: 15).

For instance, in 1985 in the township of Luyang, Kunshan County, Jiangsu Province, full-time farming households were given a subsidy of 20 yuan per mu for the extra land that they leased. In addition, they were exempted from paying the labor expenses for using collectively owned agricultural machinery and were promised favorable terms in the provision of agricultural inputs and related services (Chen Gen-xiang and Xu Ruen-quan, 1986: 43). To be sure, such a practice is only feasible and has only been reported in areas with well-developed rural nonfarm enterprises that can provide the necessary financial sponsorship (*RMRB*, 1987, May 23).

Although this subsidy has lured some peasants into farming larger tracts of land, such a practice is not without shortcomings. It is true that this arrangement has facilitated the concentration some farmland, but the long-term productivity of the agricultural sector may, at the same time, have been greatly compromised. The problem here lies with the fact that the subsidy can only lure the peasants to accept more farmland; it cannot induce them to sustain, much less improve, the productivity of the land that they have leased (Yang Yi, 1985a: 40). This is because most subcontracting agreements run on a short-term basis (one to two years). Consequently, the lessees do not have any compelling reason to enhance the fertility of the land beyond the duration of the agreements. The results are a reduced application of fertilizer and other inputs, minimal attention to the condition of the leased land, and a rapid deterioration of the farmland's long-term productive capacity (Zhao Jun-xiang, 1985: 44).

An examination of the problem of farmland subleasing reveals a major obstacle standing in the way of agricultural development. Even when the migrants are willing to give up their land, the rising level of the land tax burden has effectively discouraged the more efficient farmers to sublease more land and engage in large-scale production. The current practice of using profits from rural nonfarm enterprises to augment the full-time farmer's income can only lure the peasants to increase their landholdings nominally. However, without raising the price levels of agricultural products and revising the land tax system, income subsidy alone will not prompt the farmers to increase yields or to invest in making the land more productive.

Conclusion

The major lesson of this chapter is that the development of the rural nonfarm sector and even the out-migration of rural workers to the small towns do not necessarily and automatically lead to a rural division of labor that permits a higher concentration of farmland in the hands of the more efficient producers. Higher prices for farm products and lower agricultural taxes may be more effective in stimulating the farmers to increase their productivity. However, both of these options require some basic restructuring of the national pricing and taxation systems, which are not prone to quick adjustments.

To break the link between the peasant migrants and their land is an even more delicate and difficult task. One possible solution is to grant migrants nonagricultural household status. Only after their economic security has been guaranteed would they be willing to give up their land. However, this means that Chinese planners will have to rethink the overall rural and urban development strategy and revamp the household registration system.

Another possibility, which requires much less monumental work, is to design a different policy that will actively encourage the grouping of small pieces of farmland into larger tracts to permit large-scale production. This policy would no doubt require a reaffirmation of the collective interests above that of the individual. Because local officials would be able to draw on the experience of the former collective system, they might be more receptive to this solution to the farmland subleasing problems.[3] A third strategy is to introduce a land market mechanism. However, because this entails the free sale of farmland among the peasants, it would be looked upon with skepticism by hard-line politicians.

The second major conclusion of this chapter is that the relationships between productive utilization of agricultural land and the transformation of rural labor relations are subject to a variety of macro and micro forces that can significantly influence the characteristics and outcomes of these relationships. Among the most important macro forces influencing relationships between changing patterns of land utilization and patterns of differentiation in the rural labor force are policies affecting land use, taxes, public investment, and small-town development, as well as the state's continuing need to manage relationships between land use and nonfarm work. Among the micro forces of special importance are a variety of local processes and opportunities for generating nonfarm work, for maintaining connections to the land through different forms of intrahousehold division of labor, and for modifying the impacts of state policies and directives by influencing local administrative arrangements.

The question that remains is how and at what costs productive nonfarm employment growth in rural areas can be sustained in the context of a stagnant agriculture. Stated differently, the question is: What are the probable social characteristics of the growth of nonfarm work in a context of part-time and low-productivity agriculture? It is too soon, for example, to see definitively which forms of stratification in rural labor relations are likely to last and which types of households are most likely to benefit. Indeed, these questions suggest that the future of China's rural transformation has hardly been determined.

Notes

I have received useful comments from Bruce Koppel, John Hawkins, and William James in revising this chapter. Valuable suggestions on an earlier draft of this paper were given to me by Karen Polenske, Tunney Lee, Shwu Chen, and Casey Hammod. Angelina Lau helped prepare and revise the manuscript in an efficient and pleasant manner.

1. Township Enterprises are mainly rural industries, but they include construction, commercial, transport, and other nonfarm enterprises run by local authorities at the township, town, and village levels, as well as by the peasants themselves.

2. In this respect, provincial officials in Jiangsu Province are the most vocal (Sun Han, 1986; Chen Sheng, 1986; Wu Rong and Li Peng, 1986: 15; Shi Fu-yuen, 1986: 21). Central authorities have also pleaded with local officials to reduce the burden placed on township and village enterprises in financing small-town construction for the same reason—to make sure there is adequate investment in agricultural infrastructure (*RMRB*, 1985, July 22 and July 29).

3. In August 1987, *People's Daily* reported on a successful program of consolidating farmland initiated by local officials in Beijing Suenyi County (*RMRB*, 1987, August 12A). Only one month later, however, *People's Daily* printed a com-

mentary that criticized the consolidation of farmland through administrative coercion (*RMRB*, 1987, September 14).

References

Periodical and Serial Publications in Chinese Language

GWYGB	*Guowuyuan Gongbao*
	(State Council Circular)
RMRB	*Renmin Ribao*
	(People's Daily)
RMRB (OE)	*Renmin Ribao*
	(People's Daily, Overseas Edition)
ZGJJNJ 1990	*Zhongguo Jingji Nianjian 1990*
	(China's Economics Yearbook 1990)
ZGNCTJNJ 1985	*Zhongguo Nongcun Tongji Nianjian 1985*
	(Statistical Yearbook of China's Rural Sector 1985)
ZGNCTJNJ 1990	*Zhongguo Nongcun Tongji Nianjian 1990*
	(Statistical Yearbook of China's Rural Sector 1990)
ZGNYNJ 1980	*Zhongguo Nongye Nianjian 1980*
	(Statistical Yearbook of China's Agriculture 1980)
ZGNYNJ 1983	*Zhongguo Nongye Nianjian 1983*
	(Statistical Yearbook of China's Agriculture 1983)
ZGNYNJ 1984	*Zhongguo Nongye Nianjian 1984*
	(Statistical Yearbook of China's Agriculture 1984)
ZGNYNJ 1985	*Zhongguo Nongye Nianjian 1985*
	(Statistical Yearbook of China's Agriculture 1985)
ZGNYNJ 1986	*Zhongguo Nongye Nianjian 1986*
	(Statistical Yearbook of China's Agriculture 1986)
ZGNYNJ 1987	*Zhongguo Nongye Nianjian 1987*
	(Statistical Yearbook of China's Agriculture 1987)
ZGNYNJ 1988	*Zhongguo Nongye Nianjian 1988*
	(Statistical Yearbook of China's Agriculture 1988)
ZGTJNJ 1987	*Zhongguo Tongji Nianjian 1987*
	(China's Statistical Yearbook 1987)
ZGTJNJ 1989	*Zhongguo Tongji Nianjian 1989*
	(China's Statistical Yearbook 1989)

Other References

Beijing Review. 1984. No. 50, p. 19.

Cao Meng-jiao and Liu Zong-xiao. 1987. "Langfang diqu shixing shidu guimo jingying de diaocha" ("A study of large-scale production in the Langfang region"), *Zhongguo nongcun jingji (China's rural economy)*, Vol. 1, pp. 32–36.

Chen Feng. 1985. "Xiaochengzhen de jianzhi wenti" ("On the question of designation of small towns"), *Chengshi guihua (City planning review)*, Vol. 2, p. 63.

Chen Gen-xing and Xu Ruen-quan. 1986. "Kunshanxian luyangxiang jiating nongchang de diaocha" ("An investigation of family farms in Luyang township, Kunshan County"), *Jingji wenti tansuo (Inquiry into economic problems)*, Vol. 8, pp. 41–43.

Chen Sheng. 1986. "Cong fenpei shang 'yigong bunong' zhuanbian wei shengchan zhong 'yigong jian nong'" ("A shift from 'using industry to assist agriculture' as a distributive measure to 'using industry to construct agriculture' as a production strategy"), *Nongye jingji wenti (Problems of agricultural economics)*, Vol. 3, pp. 33–35.

Chen Wei. 1985. "Lueshu woguo renkou yu gengdi guanxi de maodun jiqi houguo" ("A discussion of the contradictory relationship between population and farmland in our country"), *Renkou yanjiu (Population research)*, Vol. 5, p. 21.

Cheng Chun-dao. 1986. "Anhuxiang zenyang jianshao zhengtian nongmin de fudan" ("How Anhu Township reduced the burdens of the peasants"), *Jingji wenti tansuo (Inquiry into economic problems)*, Vol. 4, pp. 42–43.

Cheng Lu. 1987. "Lun woguo liangshi shengchan jinyibu fazhan wenti" ("A discussion on the problem of further developing our country's food grain production"), *Jingji dili (Economic geography)*, Vol. 2, pp. 83–87.

Chinese Academy of Agriculture. 1986. "Guanyu nongmin dui chonglian di kanfa di wenti" ("On the problem of the peasants' attitude towards grain cultivation"), *Nongye jingji wenti (Problems of agricultural economics)*, No. 8, pp. 30–33.

Chinese Communist Party Yunnan Province. 1983. "Chengjiang xian xiancheng di yige deicai" ("An investigation of the county seat of Chengjiang County"), *Jingji wenti tansuo (Inquiry into economic problems)*, No. 5, pp. 60–63.

Cui Gonghao. 1985. "An investigation of our cities' characteristics and their development strategy," in *Research on Urban Development Strategy* (New China Publishing Society), pp. 146–163.

Cui Qinglin. 1986. "Chengxiang xietiao fazhan yu nongcun renkou liuxiang" ("Coordinated urban-rural development and the transfer of rural population"), *Caijing kexue (Science of finance and economics)*, Vol. 1, pp. 52–56.

Dong Han-ying. 1986. "Tudi jingying guimo yu nongye jijiehua" ("Scale economics of farmland production and agricultural mechanization"), *Zhongguo nongcun jingji (China's rural economy)*, Vol. 8, pp. 50–53.

Field notes. 1985. Notes prepared by author during a field study of rural nonfarm enterprises in Taishan County in Guangdong Province in the summer of 1985.

Gong Jie-min and Xiong Shi-ping. 1983. "Heli shiyong shedui gongye lirun, cujin jiaoqu nongcun jingji quanmian fazhan" ("To rationally use the profits of commune and brigade enterprises, to promote development of suburban village economy"), *Caijing yanjiu (Study of finance and economics)*, Vol. 1, pp. 45–50.

Gu Song-nian and Yan Ying-long. 1985. ("Development of researches in the economic theory of rural enterprises"), *Jingji yanjiu (Economic research)*, Vol. 5, pp. 55–61.

Hai Zuo-liang. 1986. "Zhongliang tieben de wenti jidai jiejue" ("The problem of subsidized production of grain needs to be resolved"), *Jingji wenti tansuo (Inquiry into economic problems)*, Vol. 5, p. 61.

He Peijin and Zhang Pingyong. 1985. "Fazhan xiaochengzhen jingji de zhongyao buzhou" ("Important steps to develop the small town economies"), *Zhongguo nongcun jingji (China's rural economy)*, Vol. 4, pp. 31–35.

Ho, Samuel P.S. 1986. *The Asian Experience in Rural Nonagricultural Development and Its Relevance for China* (Washington, D.C.: World Bank).

Huang Huan-zhong and Sun Xin-ya. 1986. "Tiaozheng nongcun chanye jiegou yu hongguan zhidao" ("To reform the rural occupational structure and a macro-level policy direction"), *Jingji yanjiu (Economic research)*, Vol. 2, pp. 43–46.

Li Jian-de. 1986. "Nongye tudi jingying de jizhong yu duice" ("The consolidation of agricultural land and its strategy"), *Jingji yanjiu (Economic research)*, Vol. 4, pp. 33–35.

Li Sheng-wen. 1987. "Qianxi nongcun tudi zhuanbao" ("An analysis of the sub-leasing of farmland"), *Caijing kexue (Science of finance and economics)*, Vol. 2, pp. 39–41.

Li Wei-wu. 1985. "Hubei nongcun chanye jiegou gaige de chubu shexiang" ("A preliminary thought on Hubei's rural occupational transition"), *Jianghan luntan (Jianghan forum)*, Vol. 7, pp. 23–27.

Li Zhong. 1987. "Zhujiang sanjiaozhou nongye jingying xingshi de xianzhuang he fazhan qushi" ("On the current state and the trend of development of agriculture in the Pearl River delta"), *Guangdong shehui kexue (Guangdong social sciences)*, Vol. 1, pp. 45–54.

Li Zhong-xian. 1985. "Tudi youchang zhuanbao wenti chutan" ("A study of the problem of farmland subcontracting with compensation"), *Nongye jingji wenti (Problems of agricultural economics)*, Vol. 9, pp. 37–39.

Liu Fu-chen and Guo Wei-guo. 1985. "Jiangzhe diqu nongcun laodongli zhuanyi tanxi" ("An analysis on the transformation of rural laborers in the Jiangsu-Zhejiang region"), *Renkou yanjiu (Population research)*, Vol. 6, pp. 17–19.

Liu Gang. 1986. "Qiwu shiqi nongye jijiehua fazhan chuxi" ("An analysis of agricultural mechanization during the Seventh Five-Year plan period"), *Zhongguo nongcun jingji (China's rural economy)*, Vol. 7, pp. 5–8.

Liu Rong-qin. 1987. "Nongcun gongye fazhan le yinggai zenyang duidai nongye?" ("How to treat agriculture when rural industries have developed?"), *Zhongguo nongcun jingji (China's rural economy)*, Vol. 4, pp. 45–49.

Lu Hou-da and Chen Hong-er. 1984. "Yetan chengbao tudi de zhuanrang" ("A discussion on the transfer of leased farmland"), *Zhejiang Xuekan (Zhejiang academic journal)*, Vol. 2, pp. 7–12.

Mei Tai-he and Ding Zhao-xiang. 1984. "Yingdang guli nongmin 'litu bu lixiang'" ("Should encourage the peasants 'to leave the land, but not the rural areas'"), *Nongye jingji wenti (Problems of agricultural economics)*, Vol. 11, pp. 27–29.

Mu Hong-tao. 1985. "Nongcun jinyibu gaige suo mianlin de tudi wenti" ("To further reform the land problem in the countryside"), *Zhongguo nongcun jingji (China's rural economy)*, Vol. 11, pp. 7–10.

Pan Qionglin. 1985. "Zailun nongcun shangping jingji de fazhan" ("To further discuss the development of rural commercial economy"), *Hunan shida xuebao (Journal of Hunan Normal University)*, Vol. 2, pp. 39–41.

Pan Wen-hui. 1986. "Jianqing nongmin fudan" ("Reduce peasants' burdens"), *Zhongguo nongcun jingji (China's rural economy)*, Vol. 3, pp. 20–22.

Riskin, Carl. 1987. *China's Political Economy* (New York: Oxford University Press).

Shan Yong-tang et al. 1984. "Shilun woguo nongye laodongli youli de jiben quxiang jiqi yiyi" ("A discussion on the trends and meanings of the transformation of our country's rural laborers"), *Jingji wenti (Problems in economics)*, Vol. 12, pp. 35–37.

Shi Fu-yuen. 1986. "Jingji fada diqu shifou cunzai nongye weisuo xianxiang" ("Is agriculture deteriorating in the more developed areas?"), *Zhongguo nongcun jingji (China's rural economy)*, Vol. 5, pp. 16–21.

Shue, Vivienne. 1984. "The new course in Chinese agriculture," *The annuals of the american academy of political and social science*, Vol. 476, pp. 74–89.

Sun Han. 1986. "Nongye shidu guimo jingying he shixing 'yigong bunong' de tan suo" ("Scale economics of agricultural production and a discussion on implementing the policy of 'using industry to assist agriculture'"), *Nongye jingji wenti (Problems of agricultural economics)*, Vol. 2, pp. 9–13.

Wang Dai and Zhu Gang. 1986. "Nongcun jingji fazhan yu tudi jizhong jingying" ("Rural economic development and the consolidation of farmland"), *Zhongguo nongcun jingji (China's rural economy)*, Vol. 3, pp. 23–25.

Wang Guo-xiang. 1986. "'Juntianhua' shi fazhan nongcun shangpin jingji de yida zhang'ai" ("An equal distribution of farmland is an obstacle in developing agrarian commercialization"), *Zhongguo nongcun jingji (China's rural economy)*, Vol. 5, pp. 21–24.

Wang Xing-long. 1984. "Xianjie duan nongcun tudi zhuanbao wenti qianyi" ("A discussion of the problem of farmland subcontracting"), *Hongqi (Red flag)*, Vol. 8, pp. 24–28.

Wu Da-qian and Wu De-fu. 1984. "Suzhoushi xiao chengzhen jianshe chutan" ("An inquiry of small town development in Suzhou"), *Shehuixue tongxun (Sociology bulletin)*, Vol. 3, pp. 27–34.

Wu Rong and Li Peng. 1986. "Yi gong jian nong shi fadadiqu fazhan nongye di xindujian" ("To rely on industry to build agriculture is a new strategy to develop agriculture in more developed region"), *Zhongguo Nongcun Jingji (China's rural economy)*, No. 3, pp. 12–15.

Wu Xiang-yu. 1986. "Nongmin fudan de jixianzhi" ("The limit of peasants' burden"), *Zhongguo nongcun jingji (China's rural economy)*, Vol. 4, pp. 27–28.

Wu Zhihua and Meng Zhi-xian. 1985. "Nongcun jingji wenti minyi diaocha" ("An investigation of the people's opinion on the rural economy"), *Nongye jingji wenti (Problems of agricultural economics)*, Vol. 11, pp. 54–56.

Xiong Cheng-jia. 1986. "Litu bu lixiang de tifa butuo" ("The proposal 'to leave the land, but not the rural areas' is not appropriate"), *Nongye jingji wenti (Problems of agricultural economics)*, Vol. 1, pp. 57–58.

Xu Jing-yong. 1984. "Cujin zhuanye fengong fazhan shangpin shengchan" ("Promote specialization and division of labor, develop commercialized production"), *Zhongguo jingji wenti (China's economic problems)*, Vol. 4, pp. 53–57.

Xu Yun-quan. 1985. "Yituo fada xiangzhen gongye tuijin xiandai nongye fazhan" ("To rely on township industries to push forward agricultural modernization"), *Nongye xiandaihua yanjiu (Research of agricultural modernization)*, Vol. 6, pp. 9–12.

Yang Yi. 1985a. "'Shi guodu moshi haishi mubiao moshi?'—Xi 'litu bu lixiang' [Xia]" ("An analysis of 'to leave the land, but not the rural areas'—Is it a transitional model or an ultimate aim? [Part II]"), *Zhongguo nongcun jingji (China's rural economy)*, Vol. 11, pp. 37–42.

————. 1985b. "'Shi guodu moshi haishi mubiao moshi?'—xi 'litu bu lixiang' [Shang]" ("An analysis of 'to leave the land, but not the rural areas'—Is it a transitional model or an ultimate aim? [Part I]"), *Zhongguo nongcun jingji (China's rural economy)*, Vol. 10, pp. 1–3.

Ye Yen-yu. 1984. "Xiangzhen qiye yu nongye fanfan" ("Township enterprises and agricultural development"), *Jianghan luntan (Jianghan forum)*, Vol. 11, pp. 12–16.

Yu Shi-zhen and Chen Qiao-nan. 1985. "Yao yunxu tudi zhuanxiang shiyong" ("Should allow land-use conversion"), *Nongye jingji wenti (Problems of agricultural economics)*, Vol. 4, p. 59.

Zhan Qing-lan and Fu Quan-de. 1986. "Qiantan jianqing nongmin fudan de tujing" ("A discussion on how to reduce the peasants' financial burden"), *Zhongguo nongcun jingji (China's rural economy)*, Vol. 10, pp. 24–26.

Zhang Wen-hui. 1986. "Guanyu dinggou liangjia wenti de jianyi" ("A proposal on how to solve the problem of grain prices"), *Jingji wenti tansuo (Inquiry into economic problems)*, Vol. 5, pp. 58.

Zhang Yu-lin. 1986. "The shift of surplus agricultural labour force at different levels," in *Small Towns in China* (Beijing: New World Press), pp. 171–195.

Zhang Zhuo-yuan. 1985. "Fazhan xiangzhen jingji, jiasu shehuizhuyi xiandaihua jianshe" ("To develop the township economy, to accelerate Socialist modernization"), *Study materials for economists*, Vol. 2, pp. 63–68.

Zhao Jun-xiang. 1985. "Yetan tudi youchang zhuanbao" ("A discussion on farmland subcontracting with compensation"), *Nongye jingji wenti (Problems of agricultural economics)*, Vol. 9, pp. 40–44.

Zhao Hing-han. 1986. "Jiage gaige zhong yao fangzhi gongnony chanpin dafudu lunfan zhangjia" ("Guard against spiral inflation of industrial and agricultural goods during price reforms"), *Tianjin shehui kexue (Tianjin social sciences)*, Vol. 2, pp. 25–27.

Zhao Zhi-yuan et al. 1985. "Dui shahexian zai chanye jiegou tiaozheng zhong jiejue tudi zhuanbao wenti de diaocha" ("A study of the problem of farmland subcontracting in Shahe County undergoing occupational transition"), *Nongye jingji wenti (Problems of agricultural economics)*, Vol. 9, pp. 45–47.

Zhou De-zheng. 1984. "Guanyu wosheng zhuanyecun qingkuang de chubu diaocha" ("A preliminary study of specialized villages in our province"), *Zhongzhou xuekan* (Zhongzhou academic journal), Vol. 1, pp. 14–19.

Zhou Qi-ren et al. 1985. "Tudi zhuanbao de diaocha, he chubu fenxi" ("A study and analysis of farmland subcontracting," *Village, economy, society*, Vol. 3, pp. 10–16.

Zhu Ji-yu. 1986. "Dangqian woguo tudi wenti jiqi duice" ("The land problem in our country and its solution") *Zhongguo nongcun jingji (China's rural economy)*, Vol. 3, pp. 16–19.

9

Development or Deterioration? Understanding Employment Diversification in Rural Asia

Bruce Koppel and William James

A key step in interpreting the significance of nonfarm employment in rural Asia is to assess when and whether the appearance and growth of this form of employment differentiation is an indicator of economic and social development—associated with diversified and increased sources of income for rural households and with the relative liberation of these households from dependence on agrarian social and political relations. Conversely, it is vital to determine if this differentiation is symptomatic of processes of deterioration—in economic welfare, in social mobility, and in the distribution of political power.

In the first chapter, we identified two fundamental conceptual problems that must be addressed in order to evaluate the causes and consequences of employment differentiation in rural Asia, specifically the evolution of differentiation along lines away from agrarian modes of production.

1. First, it is essential to improve our understanding of relationships between diverse local processes of socioeconomic and political change in rural Asia and the growth and exercise of state power and its influence on rural Asia. How are these micro and macro processes interrelated and with what consequences for employment diversification and class differentiation in rural areas?
2. Second, it is especially essential to improve our understanding of the theoretical significance of nonfarm employment in rural areas. Should such employment be understood primarily in relation to processes of agrarian differentiation (which has been the predominant perspective) or in relation to processes of urbanization (which is really another way of reaffirming the agrarian metaphor as the paramount perspective on rural socioeconomic processes)? Or are distinctive theoretical connections needed, connections, for example, that would not limit nonfarm employment in rural areas to a residual outcome of agrarian (implicit in the term *nonfarm*) processes?

In this chapter, we will review what we see as the principal conclusions that can be drawn from the country studies with regard to these two issues. For these purposes, our discussion will be organized around three themes: (1) macro-micro relationships, (2) the emergence of "new" economies, and (3) a reassessment of the East Asian model.

Macro-Micro Relationships

The studies confirm both the reality and diversity of macro-micro relationships as a context for understanding employment differentiation. The diversity, long apparent to Asian specialists, is important to acknowledge, especially given the residual allegiances to orientalism and related forms of essentialism that can still be found in Asian studies and the dedication to universality found in several disciplines. The challenge of explaining the diversity draws attention to the limits of existing conceptual frameworks for understanding agrarian change and rural transformation, a point developed in Chapter 1. However, this does not imply that any broader explanations are infeasible. Across the diversity discussed in this volume, several interesting and important themes do appear. These themes will all require further research, but the studies do suggest some important possibilities about their significance.

First, it is important to note that macro forces that traditionally have attracted the most analytical attention—the roles of the state; macroeconomic development strategies; the impacts of foreign investment, external debt, and other indicators of incorporation into the world capitalist system; and patterns of urbanization and regionalization—all appear in the studies, and clearly, all are relevant. Similarly, at the micro level, the studies lay out evidence of a range of familiar conditions and processes—including the effects of population pressure and restricted access to land on the political economy of agrarian labor relations, both increasing and declining agricultural productivity and their effects on rural household survival strategies and polarization processes within rural communities, and the sources and consequences of community politics and factionalism.

Second, attention is given to the relationships between macro and micro processes, most notably between the nature of urbanization and industrialization processes and the political economy of agrarian relations; between the roles of foreign capital and markets and community labor allocation; and between processes of state development and local-level processes of class formation. As seen, for example, in the chapters on Bangladesh, India, Malaysia, the Philippines, and Thailand, these patterns and relationships have a fundamental bearing on the prospects for productive employment generation in both the rural and urban sectors, as well as on the causes and consequences of employment differentiation in rural areas specifically.

However, the studies also illustrate that conventional unilinear and top-down understandings of macro-micro relationships in rural employment differentiation are not only too simplistic, they may also be fundamentally misleading. In several cases, we see much more interactive processes, in which the impacts of macro forces are not simply modified in some way by micro-level processes, rather, fundamental characteristics of these macro-forces are actually derived from the interplay of micro-level forces. This interactiveness and, in particular, what can be called polycentric initiative within macro-micro relationships is a consequence of a variety of vertical linkages—some old and some new—that have developed to organize macro-micro relationships in rural Asia.

In some cases (e.g., China, Indonesia, the Philippines, and Thailand), these vertical linkages are embodied in the evolution or persistence of regional market systems and political economies that do not simply intermediate between macro and micro forces but that also establish relatively independent arenas for economic exchange and political discourse. In other cases (e.g., Bangladesh, India, and Malaysia), the vertical linkages between macro and micro processes are being institutionalized in the form of emerging gender, class, and territorially based affiliations. These linkages are still tentative but appear to be closely related to evolving claims of cultural and political representation. However, what is especially crucial is that these claims are generally contested. In fact, different local, regional, and national actors are contending for preeminence and legitimacy.

Both cases—evolving and persistent regional systems and new and contending arrangements for organizing macro-micro relationships—draw our attention to potentially significant discontinuities in macro-micro relationships affecting rural Asia. These discontinuities could, in turn, have very crucial implications for the significance of nonfarm employment differentiation in rural areas. For example, several of the chapters raise important questions about our understandings of rural households and communities. In studies of rural Asia, however, it is not unusual to hear that, in reality, rural communities are not the solidary social units sometimes portrayed. But the drift away from unity is not simply a story of political and social factionalism within essentially agrarian relations, nor even of the intrusion of capitalist relationships into a kinship-based hierarchy. Rather, on occasion, the drift appears to be a more fundamental diversification of the premises of legitimate power within the community. What is important here is that this differentiation within many rural communities is the immediate playing field for employment differentiation.

Similarly, the question of discontinuities in the changes characterizing the rural household opens some important new doors. The picture of the household as a minifirm, allocating labor and other resources in response to a unitary capital accumulation and welfare maximization function, is challenged in several chapters. The challenge is not to the reality of the residential household but to the virtually exclusive affiliative priority for broader sociopolitical purposes often assigned to the residential household. We see, instead, a variety of old and new affiliative foci—kinship, work group, age group, gender group, ethnicity, class, political party, community—and importantly, each in many ways is contesting for priority, not merely a role. It is this process of contesting that creates a fluid situation in many cases for the status of the household as the prime unit of analysis in political and social mobilization. Here again, we need to recognize that employment differentiation unfolds in this disputed context.

It is also important to recognize, however, that there are important continuities operating as well. Although these function particularly at the micro level, they have important implications for the evolution and consequences of macro-micro linkages. In the case described by Miriam Sharma, for example, a development strategy was premised on the existence of continuities in relationships between hierarchies based on the organization of the household and hierarchies based on gender. In other cases, the presence of important continuities has a significant implication for how we interpret the political economy of employment differentiation. The rise of nonfarm wage labor in all the cases studied here clearly does not have equivalent political significance. A major reason for this is that employment differentiation does not represent a totally clean break with the ideology of existing agrarian social relations. This is not equivalent to conceding that the differentiation is a derivative of agrarian differentiation; rather, it suggests that whatever the causes of nonfarm employment differentiation, this differentiation is embedded in differing ways in an agrarian context. This context, in turn, though experiencing some of the discontinuities noted earlier, also experiences important continuities—in cultural norms, in forms of political legitimacy, and in accepted patterns of capital accumulation. An important implication here is that, in many instances, the differentiation remains more embedded in the ideologies of agrarian relations—especially as they relate to questions of power—than in the actual dynamics of agrarian differentiation processes. This point is well illustrated by Gillian Hart's Malaysian analysis, where the points of contention between differing claims for representation and initiative relate more to attempts to challenge ideological continuities rather than political economy discontinuities.

What is especially interesting in this regard is that when the continuities and discontinuities in the sociopolitical significance of rural communities and households are considered in relation to the changing roles of the state, an important and fundamental issue arises. State aggrandizement has been documented for each of the countries discussed in this book. However, as several of the studies suggest (e.g., those on Malaysia and Thailand), the composition and orientation of the state is considerably more dynamic than the more static and deterministic traditional pictures have suggested. The states are characterized by important concerns for control, regulation, extraction, and legitimation, but these are unevenly institutionalized and, in practice, may be more characteristic of evolving processes of state-society interaction instead of settled, institutionalized designs for that interaction. Often, for example, claims of legitimation exceed institutionalized capacities for independent regulation—a point that is especially clear in the Philippine case. Similarly, for state roles in extraction, it is increasingly clear that the position of the state in relation to both domestic and international nonstate actors is more tentative and contested than might have been previously thought—again, a point that is particularly well illustrated by the Philippine case.

Against this background, a fundamental crisis in welfare and legitimation appears to be unfolding. As the rural community and household lose their solidarity and their primary claims on allegiance, they are also losing their abilities to serve as the principal sources of social security and normative stabilization. This has consequences both for social welfare and for processes of political legitimation at the macro level. At the same time but in different ways across countries, the state has proposed itself as the provider of social security and, through its increasing focus on legitimation (through appeals, for example, to ideologies of nationalism and statism), as the guidepost for normative stabilization. This point can be seen most clearly in the chapters on China and Malaysia, but it is significant in different ways in other chapters, as well.

However, the state's ability to actually provide these functions of social security and normative stabilization is questionable. As the closing pages of Miriam Sharma's chapter illustrate vividly, the splintering of the rural household and community and the limited capacity of the state to substitute for certain key functions that household and community have played means that important spaces for socioeconomic and political innovation are opening. But with the opening of these spaces—the product of macro-micro relationships—come risks. Old local elites may be resanctified. New local elites may successfully arise. Nonfarm employment differentiation is unfolding precisely in this increasingly contested space. At the least, this strongly suggests that assessments of the significance of nonfarm employment in rural Asia must be set in the context of these complex processes of both construction and deconstruction, of articulation and disarticulation.

At a minimum, this means that relationships between structure and agency in explanations of employment differentiation in rural areas must be handled very carefully indeed. Much more attention is needed on the explication of polycentric initiative in macro-micro relations and in the evolution and consequences of different patterns for institutionalizing these relationships. Concluding his study of political change in a northern Vietnamese village, Hy V. Luong (1992: 232) offers an example of what this kind of self-conscious deconstruction can illuminate:

In the final analysis, the Vietnamese revolution involved a dynamic interplay between local tradition and capitalist imperialism in the colonial context. In the encounter between the two systems, the persistence of the noncapitalist labor reserves in north and central Vietnam did not merely contribute to capitalist accumulation. It also provided ideological and organizational support for the anticolonial resistance. In the long run, the encounter between the Vietnamese tradition, on the one hand, and western colonialism and capitalist imperialism, on the other, both adversely affected capitalist accumulation and ushered in a new era in the indigenous social formation.

The Emergence of "New" Economies

In assessing the theoretical significance of nonfarm work in rural Asia, it is clear that research questions must move beyond some of the key assumptions routinely made in major conceptual frameworks about the composition and dynamics of agrarian and rural social structure and economic activity. For example, analysts cannot merely assume that certain employment relations (e.g., wage employment) uniformly mean that a capitalist economy is operating; they must strive for a more contextual understanding of what kinds of economic structures and relations are actually operating. Stated another way, analysts will need to consider how the economies are actually working, rather than assuming they belong to some broad classification with essentially predefined attributes. What, then, would an analysis of nonfarm employment need to encompass?

The studies in this volume address such issues as access to agrarian land, income and population pressures on wages and household welfare, the pull of urban and industrial development, and the growth of regional economies—central topics for most contemporary development theory focused on rural transformation issues. However, what also comes out very strongly from the studies is the juxtaposition of two processes that, though related to the central concerns of most theory, may also indicate other, distinctive concerns. Indeed, they raise the questions of whether and when nonfarm employment differentiation is associated with "old" economies (and economics) and when it is better associated with "new" economies (and economics).

The first process is the growth of a service economy in rural areas. The second is the feminization of rural nonfarm labor. The two processes are not necessarily related, nor are they new in terms of incidence. But it is important to recognize that these two processes together appear to be dominating—not simply characterizing—the growth of nonfarm employment in rural areas. This combination of prominence and juxtaposition has potentially important theoretical implications.

The growth of a rural service economy is an important outcome, but in some ways (for much development theory), it is also an anomalous one.

The service sector is seen, in many cases, as a tertiary sector that appears *after and under* agriculture and manufacturing—in terms of both sequence and developmental significance. From this perspective, the growth of a service sector in the context of a predominantly agrarian rural economy appears implausible, except for the most basic kinds of services (e.g., household services for the wealthy). Nevertheless, as seen especially in the chapters on Bangladesh and Indonesia, a complex rural service economy is appearing throughout the region. And in some ways, it is distinct from the employment growth in manufacturing in rural areas that has received more attention in assessments of nonfarm employment.

What is the significance of this service economy? Is it a rurally based service economy, or is it an essentially urban or national service economy in rural areas? Is this service economy an offshoot of the agrarian economy—something that might better be called off-farm rather than nonfarm employment? Is it a precursor of the urban economy—for example, through extension of the urban informal economy into rural areas? It is not clear whether there is or should be a uniform answer to any of these questions, but in weighing the conceptual significance of nonfarm employment in rural areas, we cannot ignore these questions and the significance of diversity. For instance, is wage employment in the service sector a case of proletarianization—a conclusion that might follow from the assumption that the service economy is a form of protocapitalism. Or are employment relations in the rural service sector a case of neofeudalism—a conclusion that might follow from the assumption that precapitalist agrarian relations dominate the service economy? The answer (which need not be limited to the proletarianization or neofeudalism choice) would appear to depend on what the nature of a specific service economy is, what the sociopolitical structure in which it is embedded is, and, at the least, how the service economy actually relates to both the agrarian and manufacturing sectors through both labor and capital markets.

The feminization of rural nonfarm labor is a second development. In one sense, this development has been far better documented than the first process. There is evidence in the literature and in the studies in this volume (e.g., the chapters on Bangladesh, India, and Malaysia) that the feminization of rural nonfarm labor may be highly correlated with recent growth of the rural service economy. Yet it is not clear that the two processes are interchangeable (i.e., that the growth of the rural service sector is the feminization of rural nonfarm labor) or that they are parts of some single larger process of gender-based employment differentiation.

In the Philippines and Thailand, for example, the two processes do appear to be closely related—that is, both the rural service economy and the gender characteristics of nonfarm and off-farm rural employment are significantly feminized. However, there are also clearly complex relationships between the "push" coming from processes of agrarian differentiation and the "pull" coming from nonagrarian sources in both urban and rural areas. For example, there is important evidence of the feminization of the urban service and manufacturing sectors in the Philippines and Thailand, especially in the more labor-intensive industries (e.g., textiles). These complexities can also be seen in the analyses of Bangladesh, India, and Malaysia, but there, the feminization of rural labor appears to be more closely related to fundamental processes of social mobilization and political differentiation in rural areas. The growth of rural service economies is not unrelated, but it appears, at least in part, to be the result of distinct processes of economic differentiation.

The studies explore reasons for the feminization of rural labor that are independent of the service economy. These primary reasons are tied to issues addressed earlier in this chapter, in the section on macro-micro relationships. They include the weakening solidarity of rural communities and households—a development that holds both promising and problematic implications for rural welfare generally and for the legitimacy of existing rural power relationships in particular. In some instances, factors like the changing characteristics of the community and the household, as well as factors such like narrowing access to land, stagnant growth in agricultural productivity, and increased mobility facilitated by access to transportation and education, have increased the possibilities for breaking preexisting forms of kinship-based and gender-based stratification.

What the studies indicate, in many cases, is that gender stratification in terms of the division of labor may be breaking. There is evidence of increasing female occupational mobility. The question of the status of kinship-based stratification is less certain, caught up as it is in the changing significance of the rural household. Moreover, it is not always clear whether high levels of female participation in nonfarm employment differentiation reflect a form of liberation or whether, quite the reverse, feminization of rural nonfarm labor reflects a process in which the burdens for household survival are being placed inordinately on the shoulders of women. Indeed, the studies point out that though traditional gender-based divisions of labor may be weakening in terms of what work women do, the gender-based hierarchies that govern relative autonomies of choice in labor allocation are not necessarily weakening at the same pace. However, it is precisely the latter that are being contested.

Here again, we must be wary of simple conclusions and formulas. In the studies in this volume, the answer appears to be that in some cases, the feminization of rural nonfarm labor may potentially be a form of liberation; in other cases, it may well be a continuing and more intensive reproduction of existing stratification arrangements. The studies are less certain about the trajectory of the service economy. But here, too, the analyses suggest that in some circumstances, the service economy—whatever its origins and linkages—may be a vehicle of transition between an agrarian economy and an industrial one. In most cases, however, the rural service economy is seen as problematic in terms of employment conditions and relations.

Moving beyond the need to examine the relationships between these two processes more carefully, a careful assessment of the theoretical significance of nonfarm work in rural areas cannot ignore the principal arenas in which this differentiation plays out. When we discussed macro-micro relationships, we suggested that this was a context for employment differentiation—a context that needs to be both theorized and documented on its own merits. Here, we come to a similar conclusion. Processes of feminization of rural labor and processes associated with the emergence of a service economy in rural areas may be very logical extensions of existing differentiation processes in agrarian or national economies. But it is also possible that the emergence of service economies in agrarian settings and the feminization of nonfarm labor indicate important discontinuities in relationships between the evolution of rural social structure and processes of agrarian differentiation, to cite one example. Service economies must be better documented and better theorized, and as part of that project, a better understanding of the theoretical significance of nonfarm employment is likely to follow.

It should also be pointed out that the outcomes of such an understanding would have significant implications for the design and management of policies and programs to improve the status of women and the productivity of rural employment. Miriam Sharma's case study is especially instructive in this regard. An intervention (Operation Flood) was designed, in part, to strengthen the economic independence of rural women, but the policy was driven more by external normative expectations than by a real understanding of the political dynamics of gender-based labor differentiation in rural communities. More generally, the studies suggest that it is important to understand the structures and processes through which specific patterns of nonfarm labor differentiation are unfolding before considering well-intentioned processes of intervention. For instance, as implied in the chapters on Bangladesh, India, and Malaysia, there are important issues associated with the question of whether additional institutions are needed to ensure that rural women are strengthening their autonomy rather than their dependence.

New Economies or New Economics?

The suggestion that the growth of the service economy in rural areas and the increasing feminization of rural nonfarm labor are "new" economies may appear to be an exaggeration. It undoubtedly is if the implication is that these two processes are without historical antecedents or that they necessarily represent absolute discontinuities with previous forms of economic organization and relations in rural areas. However, the characterization of these processes as "new" has important heuristic value. We should not underestimate the degree to which the major perspectives in development studies have imposed dichotomous interpretations on complex and diverse processes of employment differentiation, multiple forms of specialization, and the changing composition and significance of local institutions.

The studies in this volume all point to complex processes that are the causes, contexts, and consequences of patterns of nonfarm employment differentiation. These processes are oriented to service sector occupations, workplaces, and employment relations, and they are strongly characterized by high levels of female participation. The studies suggest that though individual elements of these processes may not constitute new economies, the processes *together* may reflect new economics. Two broad characteristics, in particular, of these new economics can be noted.

First, reiterating a point made earlier about the emerging welfare crisis as both households and the state lose their capacities to ensure social security and normative stabilization, is the feminization of rural labor. As illustrated most vividly in the chapters on India and Malaysia, rural women are not simply playing larger roles as income earners through participation in nonfarm work; their load in terms of unpaid family labor may be growing as well. In effect, in the thinning domain created by the weakened roles of the household, community, and state, responsibilities for household reproduction, family security, and normative coherence are increasingly falling on females. As the India and Malaysia studies illustrate, this is independent of levels of agricultural performance, and it reflects broader processes of institutional change—including, in the Malaysian case, diversification activities by men. On the other hand, as suggested in the chapters on Bangladesh, China, the Philippines, and Thailand, stagnant or declining agricultural incomes certainly create conditions that place extraordinary pressures on rural women to both maintain core agricultural and family activities and provide outside income. Clearly, these processes associated with the feminization of rural labor demonstrate considerable diversity, and it is this diversity that suggests that we are facing new economics.

Second, the studies suggest that these economics will be significantly characterized by complex macro-micro relationships and by the emergence of diverse intermediate forms of sociopolitical mobilization, cultural representation, and economic organization. For example, the Bangladesh, Malaysian, and Philippine studies show how macroeconomic goals, adjustments, and biases influence the allocation of rural resources—land, labor, and capital—but also how these regimes are, themselves, influenced by the changing organization of power in rural areas. The chapters on China and the Philippines indicate how processes of circular rural-urban migration both caused and were caused by patterns of industrialization, by the distribution of service sector opportunities, and by the characteristics of agricultural performance and agrarian relations. The chapter on Indonesia illustrates how interrelationships between a national political economy and local processes of employment differentiation and resource allocation can be influenced by political economies that operate at an intermediate level.

To understand the theoretical significance of nonfarm employment generally—and to understand the relationships between nonfarm employment, inequality, and poverty—it is essential to reorient conceptual attention to these broader macro-micro relationships and to an understanding of the structures and relations in which nonfarm work is embedded in terms of their actual political economies, cultural motifs, and social processes.

Agrarian Transformation, Work, and the East Asian Model

Discussions about the incidence and significance of employment differentiation in rural Asia have been strongly influenced by interpretations of the development experiences of Japan, Korea, and Taiwan. Not surprisingly, the economic successes in these countries have spawned numerous analyses seeking to identify the reasons for such successes. These analyses have paid substantial attention to processes of rural transformation and industrialization. Subsequently, many analysts have been tempted to hold out the experiences first of Japan, then of Taiwan and Korea as blueprints or models, of sorts, in terms of the "stages of development" through which other parts of Asia presumably would (or could) pass. They are also seen as models for the choice and sequencing of economic policies during the course of economic development—supposedly, to ensure that the passage is smooth.[1]

Given the variety of development experiences throughout Asia, particularly the variety of conditions under which *apparently* similar development processes are unfolding, it is arguable whether there is a viable common analytical framework within which to examine East, Southeast, and South Asia. Indeed, there are strong reasons to question even the presumed homogeneity of the experiences in Japan, Korea, and Taiwan (Koppel, 1993). Hence, it is an oversimplification to refer in any narrow sense to an "East Asian model," especially for purposes of interpreting employment differentiation in the rest of rural Asia. Nevertheless, can an examination of prominent aspects of the varied development experiences in Japan, Taiwan, and Korea provide some instructive points for understanding rural development trajectories elsewhere in Asia? Given the popularity of the East Asian model, in particular, as a basis for exploring the significance of nonfarm employment in South and Southeast Asia, it is important to seriously consider this question.

The Argument for an East Asian Model

What follows is a stylized summary of the argument for an East Asian transformation model and for its reproducibility in other parts of Asia. Far-reaching redistributive land reforms in the late 1940s and early 1950s preceded the rapid postwar industrialization of Japan, Korea, and Taiwan. The land reforms ultimately created a relatively equitable distribution of rural assets and a unimodal pattern of land distribution, characterized by small owner-operated farms. A focus on agriculture (rather than an industrialization "pull" strategy) was, to a significant extent, necessitated by the scarcity of other natural resources that could be exploited to generate foreign exchange and drive economic recovery. The unimodal pattern meant that gains from the diffusion of technological improvements (e.g., better rice varieties) and the improvement of land infrastructure (e.g., irrigation) were spread among many farm households. The rapid postwar growth and industrialization of Japan, Taiwan, and Korea are explained, in part, by their success in raising agricultural productivity and rural incomes.

Although growth in agricultural productivity was, in one sense, a consequence of agrarian reform, in another sense, it was also an important reason why the reforms could be successful. Gradual improvement in agricultural technology and infrastructure and, especially in Japan, the prior evolution of a technology support system responsive and even accountable to independent farmer associations laid a firm foundation for sustained growth in productivity. Moreover, an important theme in the evolution of technologies and technology choices was the intensive demand for and supply of inputs, which compensated for the limited supplies of agricultural land and improved the productivity of labor inputs into agriculture (Hayami, 1964 and 1967; Hayami and Ruttan, 1970; Ohkawa, Johnston, and Kaneda, 1969).

Land reform, which actually occurred in Japan in several steps before and during World War II, and the postwar fiat that has received the most attention took place against the background of this established production support system. The postreform growth in agricultural production, labor productivity, and farm incomes stimulated the development of positive linkages between agriculture and other sectors. Initially, these linkages took the form of increased demand for agricultural inputs and services. As both rural incomes and farm productivity rose, demand for consumer goods also grew, as did savings and investment. The savings and investment financed various types of nonagricultural development, including higher education and off-farm labor mobility for family members. With the rise of agricultural labor productivity and the increasing demand for nonagricultural goods and services by farm households, farm household members became involved in nonagricultural employment in order to supplement family income.

Some important differences among the three cases should also be noted. Japan not only initiated its growth process much earlier than either Korea or Taiwan, it was also vastly different in terms of population size and growth. Population growth in Japan had been a little more than 1 percent since before the turn of the century, and from the 1950s on, it has continued to decelerate (Ito, 1992: 17). The slower growth of population meant there was less pressure to expand food production rapidly (except during the war years, when the need to produce food was one of the factors leading to the 1943 land reform). Agricultural technology was advanced enough that rice yields in Japan during the Meiji era were already higher than in most Asian countries in the 1960s. In the 1950s, Japan was well ahead of Taiwan and Korea in science and technology, education levels, and industrial capabilities, and over 80 percent of its exports were manufactured goods by 1955. Agriculture required a smaller proportion of investment in Japan, which had already achieved a high savings rate and had well-established fiscal capabilities. Furthermore, Japan's postwar political stability and external security were underwritten by the United States, and it was under less immediate danger from an external threat than either Taiwan or Korea. By 1960, agriculture accounted for only 13 percent of GDP, and less than a quarter of Japan's work force was employed in agriculture, compared to half or more in Korea and Taiwan. Japan also had a far larger internal market, and its manufacturing industry could be developed through import-substitution and domestic demand growth for a longer period. With smaller and poorer populations, Taiwan and Korea did not have large internal markets, and in general, they started out in weaker positions than Japan.

The new government on Taiwan faced immediate, pressing problems of high inflation, low savings, an absence of any industrial base, and a cutoff of trade with its major sources of supply and markets (namely, Mainland China and Japan). It overcame each of these immediate threats and focused efforts on stimulating agricultural production to feed a population that had increased almost overnight by one-third and that was growing at an annual rate of over 3 percent. The nationalist government on Taiwan moved quickly to institute land reform and to curb inflation (Myers, 1991). The early emphasis on land reform, on improvements in agriculture infrastructure, and on diffusing technology rapidly to small, family-operated farms paid off. Not only did increased output meet the demand of a growing population, it also was sufficient to obviate the need for farm imports; after a short period, production spilled over into exports. Unlike Japan, which already had a formidable manufacturing base for the development of exports, Taiwan had negligible industrial capacity in the early 1950s, possessing only food-processing and sugar-refining facilities. In the 1950s, over 90 percent of Taiwan's exports consisted of agricultural products and processed agricultural goods.

Taiwan began to turn outward with trade liberalization, and unification, and devaluation of the exchange rate in 1958. By that time, agricultural development had contributed to an improved savings rate, a healthier tax revenue base, a greater export capacity, and wider internal markets. The unimodal pattern of agricultural development in Taiwan maximized positive intersectoral linkages and stimulated industrial growth. Once Taiwan's industrialization turned outward, dramatic growth in off-farm employment occurred because of the boom in the export of labor-intensive, manufactured products—textiles, clothing, and various resource-based manufactures (James, Naya, and Meier, 1989: 31–39). Farmers could readily substitute machinery for labor in farm operations for they now had adequate incomes, skills, and savings to do so (Ho, 1979). Meanwhile, farm households could divide their time between farm and factory employment. The phenomenon of part-time farming began to emerge, as it had earlier in Japan.

Korea was even poorer than Taiwan in the immediate postwar years. The conflict on the Korean Peninsula ended in a stalemate in 1953 and left the Korean republic in devastation. Korea had a larger population (about 20 million) than Taiwan but even less of a functioning industrial and infrastructure base. Its savings rate was lower than Taiwan's and, as late as 1960, was only 1 percent of GDP. Its tax system and financial sector were similarly underdeveloped. Although Korea introduced agrarian reform quickly, in other respects it lagged behind Taiwan in agricultural and industrial development. In the early 1960s, agriculture still accounted for a far larger share of its GDP than did industry, including manufacturing, utilities, and construction. In contrast, industry superseded agriculture in share of GDP for Taiwan by 1960. Even as late as 1970, 50 percent of Korea's labor force was engaged in agriculture, compared to only 37 percent in Taiwan and 19 percent in Japan.

Korea was late in introducing improved rice varieties in comparison to Taiwan. It experienced its most rapid period of agricultural production growth in the 1960s, when it began to introduce improved varieties in earnest. The strong growth of agriculture in the 1960s coincided with Korea's reorientation of industry to export markets. Agriculture and other primary goods, which contributed over 80 percent of exports in 1960, contributed less than 10 percent in 1970—reflecting the surge of Korea's manufacturing exports. Its agricultural growth more nearly paralleled its industrialization drive, rather than preceding it. Nonetheless, the preconditions for success in attaining high growth in agricultural production and productivity were established in earlier decades. These included an educated peasantry, rural infrastructure, and experience with higher use of farm inputs like fertilizer. Incentives to improved agricultural productivity were likewise slower to be introduced in Korea than in Japan or Taiwan. However, when the exchange rate and other pricing reforms were introduced in Korea in the early 1960s, the response was even more dramatic than it had been in Taiwan. By the mid-1970s, Korean rice yields were even higher than in Taiwan.

The positive interactions of agricultural development and industrialization in Korea were evident in the 1960s and 1970s. The linkages between the growth of manufactured exports and the emergence of off-farm employment opportunities were significant but not to the same degree as they were in Taiwan (Fujita and James, 1990). There are rather substantial differences between Korea's and Taiwan's paths out of poverty. Even with the urban real estate and stock market booms of the late 1980s, Taiwan maintained a more equitable distribution of income and wealth than Korea. Taiwan's pattern of industrial development, like its agriculture, was based on small- and medium-sized, family-owned enterprises. In contrast, Korea concentrated its resources into large industrial conglomerates, the *chaebols*. Economic power has been more unevenly distributed in Korea than in Taiwan or Japan and is reflected in a less equitable distribution of income. Other important differences in the Korean experience are its lower household and domestic savings and its greater reliance, through the 1970s, on external financing of investment. The considerably larger external debt of Korea, as compared to Taiwan, is related directly to its choice of heavy industrial investments and its lower domestic savings in the 1970s.

The Lessons According to the Argument

The importance of agricultural development for a successful transition to an industrial economy is underscored by the experience of most developing Asian countries. Without a prior and sustained period of agricultural growth that is reasonably broad based, industrialization tends to stagnate. Developing Asian economies that initially concentrated resources on industrial investment and biased macroeconomic policies against agriculture have ended up with less industrial development than others that first emphasized the growth and expansion of agriculture and ancillary activities in rural areas and that kept policies more or less neutral.[2] For example, both India and the Philippines adopted import-substitution industrialization strategies with policies strongly biased against agriculture in the 1950s (Power and Sicat, 1971; Mellor, 1976). The average annual real GDP growth rate of India was 4 percent during the Second Five-Year Plan (1956–1960), which concentrated government efforts on heavy industry. Subsequently, real growth during the third plan (1961–1965) fell to 2.2 percent per annum. In the Philippines, growth declined from about an 8 percent annual average rate in the period 1950–1956 to less than 5 percent from 1956 to 1970. In contrast, in Taiwan, where agricultural development was emphasized in the 1950s, real economic growth expressed as an average annual rate accelerated from 7.6 percent in the 1950s to almost 10 percent in the 1960s (Ranis, Fei, and Kuo, 1979; Kuo, 1981).

Over a longer period of time, the rate of structural transformation from an agricultural-based economy to an industrial-based one has been most rapid in Asian countries that have struck a balance between agricultural development and promotion of industry. Japan, Taiwan, and Korea have achieved the highest shares of industry in GDP and have done so most expeditiously, followed by Malaysia and Thailand. In contrast, in the Philippines and Burma, industrial shares in GDP have stagnated or even declined over the entire period. In India and Indonesia, industrial GDP shares increased very slowly between 1960 and 1970, but with more favorable agricultural development performances, the industrial sector share rose sharply thereafter (Glassburner, 1985; Vyas and James, 1988).

A substantial body of literature, both theoretical and empirical, has evolved, providing analytical underpinnings and persuasive evidence for the relationships mentioned earlier (e.g., Hsieh and Lee, 1966; Johnston and Kilby, 1975; Johnston and Mellor, 1961; Ho, 1979; Ohkawa and Rosovsky, 1973; Lee, 1971). The focus has been on the contributions agricultural development can make to overall economic development. This literature identifies potential linkages between sectors that can transmit the impulses of growth. As agriculture develops and is commercialized, it expands the supply of wage goods to other sectors, provides increased raw material inputs, and potentially contributes savings that can be reinvested in raising agricultural productivity further or in nonagricultural productive assets. It can also save or earn foreign exchange to finance the importation of capital goods and other inputs. And as farm incomes rise, the market for goods and services produced by other sectors increases. These distinct contributions may receive varying emphases, according to specific conditions and priorities (Myint, 1975; Hayami and Ruttan, 1985).

Do the Lessons Apply to Other Parts of Asia?

Landlessness and persistent rural poverty are characteristics of large areas in South and, to a lesser extent, Southeast Asia. Agricultural land per capita varies widely between and within countries. However, with the exceptions of Malaysia and Indonesia's outer islands, there is little additional land available for intensive agriculture. The distribution of landholdings also varies widely, but in much of the region, land ownership is far more concentrated than it was in East Asia—a point with significant implications for the political economy of agriculture and the feasibility of reforming that political economy. Nowhere in South or Southeast Asia (outside of Vietnam) has redistributive land reform been enacted effectively on a scale anything near that seen in East Asia. Moreover, in Southeast Asia (and also, to some degree, in South Asia), plantation agriculture, mining, and logging provided alternative sources of foreign exchange and government revenue. The presence of natural resource wealth and plantations, coupled with an uneven distribution of agricultural land, created a much different institutional and political environment for the introduction of new agricultural technology and infrastructure for small-farm cereal production in South and Southeast Asia than in Japan, Korea, or Taiwan.

In South and Southeast Asia, the high-yielding varieties of rice seeds and associated capital inputs (such as chemicals, fertilizer, irrigation, and farm machinery) were often introduced into an environment where access to land, credit, and other resources was significantly uneven and biased in favor of large commercial farmers and landowners. The absence of a uni-modal distribution of farms and a high incidence of tenants and landless rural labor meant that the introduction of new production technologies, even if widely diffused across small and large farms alike, could widen rural inequalities. The commercial risks involved in financing and applying HYVs frequently meant that they were adopted earlier by larger farms, rather than small farms, thereby widening inequalities. In the worst case, in which successful adoption of HYVs was limited to larger commercial farms and political power and economic power became more concentrated, there was a danger that additional polarization would occur. For example, the profitability of modern varieties could (and did) induce landowners in South and Southeast Asia to expand their holdings and increase the ranks of landless rural workers and submarginal peasants by replacing tenant farmers with hired wage laborers.

The widespread adoption of inward-looking industrial and trade poli-cies, together with later and more limited efforts to improve agricultural production, meant slow growth in productive nonagricultural employment, particularly in manufacturing. In terms of the patterns of industrial devel-opment, labor absorption by modern industry has been less pronounced in South and Southeast Asia than it was in East Asia at a similar level of in-dustrial sector shares in GDP. The industrialization process in many South and Southeast Asian countries has been overly capital intensive; in addi-tion, it has made inefficient use of capital investment. Once available arable land had been brought into cultivation, rural landless labor began to spill over into the tertiary (services) sector. Thus, the abnormal expansion of marginal employment in services that is seen in many urban settings in South and Southeast Asia is a manifestation of the poverty problem, rather than a sign of economic growth and development.

To explore these points further, we examine two cases: the Philippines and Thailand.

The Philippines. The Philippines stood out as one of the most industrial-ized developing countries in Asia in 1960. It had a high literacy rate and some of the highest school enrollment rates in the region. However, sub-sequent decades have seen almost no change in the sectoral composition of GDP (Koppel, 1992). The shift in the pattern of employment has mainly been toward an abnormal expansion of services employment as the rural poor increasingly engage in marginal activities in the informal services sector.

The Philippines adopted import-substitution policies in the 1950s and sustained high economic growth during that decade. However, it also pursued policies strongly biased against agriculture (Power and Sicat, 1971; Bautista, 1986). The result was repeated balance-of-payments difficulties, excessive reliance on external borrowing, and slower growth in the subsequent decades. Protected manufacturing industries failed to create much employment, which meant that agriculture had to absorb much of a rapidly growing labor force.

During the late 1960s, rice HYVs were adopted in the Philippines, and agricultural growth rose. Policies to improve agricultural incentives and to introduce land reform in the early 1970s seemed to brighten the country's prospects. However, the actual implementation of land reform fell far short of the target (Koppel, 1987). Macroeconomic policies important for maintaining agricultural incentives were relaxed or reversed. The exchange rate remained overvalued, inflation increased, and caution in fiscal policy gave way as external borrowing rose during the period leading up to the debt crisis in 1983. Though agricultural product grew at an average rate of better than 4 percent, agriculture could no longer easily absorb increments in a fast-growing rural labor force. Manufacturing and other industries employed 13 percent of the labor force in 1960 and the very same percentage in 1987; the share employed by agriculture declined from 60 percent to 45 percent over the same period. Services had to absorb the difference. The absolute numbers of rural poor have mounted, and in 1988, it was estimated that 54 percent of all rural families were impoverished (Balisacan, 1993). Moreover, poverty incidence in the rural Philippines is almost as severe among small cultivators as it is among the landless. Unless broad-based agricultural growth, coupled with an expansion of labor-intensive manufacturing, occurs, rural poverty will worsen for population growth remains extremely high (over 2.8 percent annually).

The failure of the industrial sector to generate employment and the weak linkages from agriculture to industry have reduced the positive effects that growth in one sector can have on the other. Indeed, the benefits of agricultural growth have been concentrated among wealthier farmers and landowners, while real agricultural wages have declined. The capital-intensive nature of Philippine industries also means that the dividends of limited industrial growth have largely been enjoyed by industrialists and, relatively speaking, laborers in protected industries. The patterns of domestic demand that have been generated in the process have not stimulated development of internationally competitive, labor-intensive industries.

As employment has stagnated, unemployment has grown, and international labor migration has become an increasingly important feature of the

Philippine economy. A very high proportion of households in the Philippines report that remittances and other forms of financial assistance as real wages have continued to decline. It is clear that even during periods of apparent economic growth, the Philippines follows a pathway divergent from those traversed by Japan, Korea, and Taiwan.

Thailand. In lieu of redistributive land reform, Thai peasants were allowed to occupy and clear forests to develop farms in Thailand. This process was, for a period, an effective means of providing agricultural land to those who otherwise would have become landless, and it helped to explain consistent growth in aggregate agricultural productivity. The availability of extra land well into the 1970s prevented, in part, the emergence of large numbers of tenants and landless rural workers and limited the fragmentation of existing farms. Consequently, Thailand's agriculture is now characterized by owner-operated farms of modest size.

Thailand's industrial structure has systematically shifted from agriculture to manufacturing. However, it is important to understand the basic characteristics of this change. Growth in manufacturing has been financed principally by expropriation of resources generated in agriculture (principally through taxes on rice exports) and, more recently, by a boom in foreign direct investment (FDI), especially from Japan. This FDI has been concentrated in Bangkok and its environs. Regional inequality between Bangkok and the rest of the country (particularly the poor Northeast) is exceptionally high in Thailand. The Northeast has the largest agricultural share in gross regional product; it also has the lowest agricultural productivity. Peasant laborers from the Northeast migrate to the Central Plains to harvest rice and engage in construction and other trades in the dry season for there is little irrigation—hence, opportunities for on-farm work in the Northeast at that time are limited.

The increase in FDI has accelerated the growth of manufactured exports, and manufacturing employment has likewise increased. But to date, it does not appear that this is exclusively a labor-intensive pattern of export-oriented growth. Less-skilled labor is not being absorbed rapidly into the new enterprises. Rather, better-skilled and better-educated laborers are in demand. However, this trend is not definitive. There has also been a significant growth in female employment, especially in the textile industry where an estimated 85 percent of the labor force is female.

All this brings increasing concerns that the recent growth boom will generate extreme distributional inequalities, rather than open a relatively egalitarian growth path as occurred in East Asia. The investment-led growth has been constrained by shortages of adequately skilled workers and mid-level technical personnel. Secondary school enrollment ratios have been low in Thailand, and drop-out ratios are high, particularly in rural areas. The problem is most serious in the Northeast. Real wage increases in categories of skilled and technical workers reflect the supply situation. In the future, the growth of more labor-intensive and outward-looking industries in regions beyond Bangkok and its immediate out-skirts—industries that can link up with existing export-oriented indus-tries—will be a crucial element in determining whether Thailand will advance along a more equitable growth path. The alternative may be an economy characterized by wide inequality between regions and between an urban-based elite of the skilled and highly educated and a rural-based underclass of unskilled and less-educated workers, principally female.

Consequently, despite the rate of structural change in Thailand's GDP, employment has remained concentrated in agriculture. This seems not to have resulted in widespread poverty mainly because population growth has fallen to less than 2 percent per annum and agricultural incomes have con-tinued to grow at nearly 4 percent per annum. Only about 10 percent of the labor force was primarily employed in industry in 1987, and over two-thirds of the labor force was reported to be primarily engaged in agriculture. Ser-vices constitute an unusually low share of total employment (21 percent in 1989), despite the fact that they accounted for almost half of GDP.

There are problems with the data showing continued high agricultural employment shares.[3] Data on manufacturing employment as a percentage of total are likely to be more accurate for it is fairly easy to enumerate em-ployees in manufacturing establishments. But the numbers engaged in in-formal, largely service-oriented activities may be understated.[4] Hence, the highly aggregated data available do not give us a very accurate picture of what is really happening in rural labor markets. The large absolute in-crease in agricultural employment implied by the figures on labor force share, given the continued growth of the rural labor supply, seems im-plausible. This is an important point because the high agricultural em-ployment share coexists with institutional changes that seem to economize on labor in agricultural operations.[5] Of course, increased cropping inten-sity and/or expansion of the area sown could somewhat offset the effects of shifting from transplanting to broadcasting seed, mechanizing land preparation, harvesting and threshing, and enforcing contracts that require harvesting labor to provide other crop cycle services without additional pay. However, it is also likely that households with low levels of assets like land are pushed as much as they are pulled into nonfarm employment. Consequently, although the directions of change appear, on the surface, to mimic those seen in Japan, Korea, and Taiwan, closer examination sug-gests the dynamics are quite different.

Implications for the Development Studies Debate

The discussion of the East Asian "model" illustrates several fundamental issues in conceptualizing the significance of employment differentiation in rural areas. On one side is the idea that all materially similar employment is economically and technologically equivalent. By materially similar, we refer to the broad occupational characteristics, such as agriculture, service, manufacturing, and transport, that relate to the sector in which the work takes place. This approach essentially considers employment differentiation from a macro perspective. The categories it uses reflect concerns about differentiation in the composition of economic activities in the aggregate. From that macro basis, it maintains an interest in evaluating technical and economic efficiency by focusing on aggregate labor productivity indicators, capital-to-labor ratios in sectors and industries, and assessments of appropriate wage rates. This sometimes prompts interest at the micro level in the characteristics of efficient work specialization and job standardization in specific industries.

This approach has been valuable in examining the changing composition of national economic activity and its relationships to the changing composition of the labor force, the changing distribution of labor productivity, and the broad impacts of macroeconomic policies on investment and savings. The analyses generated from this perspective have had important influences on policy debates about rural employment promotion. The approach has been naive, however, in using the narrow platform of techno-economic equivalence as a basis for claiming to understand the broader social and political dimensions of changing work relationships and what they mean for and reveal about the evolution of economic organization in rural areas. Indeed, most often, the assumption is that economic organization in rural areas can be described either in terms that are consistent with those used for aggregate economic descriptions or as historical anomalies that will eventually be transformed into patterns that are consistent.

On another side is a conception of rural work as a very complex and profoundly contextual social phenomenon. This tends to promote a distinctively micro emphasis that, though it does not deny the possibilities or utilities of comparative analyses, is not driven by a need to make aggregate generalizations. This approach is sensitive to broader processes of social adaptation and learning that underlie (and can both facilitate and constrain) specific patterns of rural economic development. However, it focuses on the forms and consequences of those processes in individual settings more to illuminate the dynamics operating in those settings than to establish the universality of the processes.

This approach has been valuable in exploring the dynamics of employment diversification processes in specific settings and assessing how these processes relate to characteristics of agrarian organization and land use; population growth and demographic change; patterns of community organization and capital accumulation; and, in some cases, the impacts of state activities, such as land use restrictions, wage policies, and infrastructure investments. However, this perspective has been naive in discounting the significance of what amount to economic and technological "imperatives" in rural employment diversification and in frequently assuming that multidimensional rural work roles must somehow be internally consistent. The latter problem can lead to an underestimation of the discontinuities that diversification is introducing. This is illustrated by community development and appropriate technology strategies as pillars of rural employment policy. Employment that is quite compatible with existing work roles and labor skills can be generated. Left out of focus, however, is the enormously important issue of whether and at what rate broader technological and economic changes are making obsolete the nexus between the "traditional" rural community and "traditional" rural work roles and labor skills.

An example of the difficulties inherent in balancing these approaches is provided by the proposed East Asian model. Increasing recognition of diversification in rural Asia has drawn attention to interpretations of economic development experiences in the region's most economically advanced countries—Japan, Korea, and Taiwan. Based on these interpretations, some conclude that the most important transition occurring in the structure of Asia's rural employment is a shift from an agrarian to a nonagrarian base. The analysis of this shift in East Asia has lent support to the proposition (and expectation) that agricultural development, by increasing farm incomes, creates favorable conditions for the expansion of productive nonagricultural rural employment and the reduction of rural income inequalities (Ho, 1986; Oshima, 1983).

The question, however, is whether these propositions adequately account for what has happened in Japan, Korea, and Taiwan. And whether or not they do (Bradford, 1986), should the propositions (and the expectations they generate) be applied to other parts of Asia? For example, a description of economic development in China's southern Jiangsu Province, northern Zhejiang Province, and the Pearl River Delta of Guangdong Province concludes:

> All three regions share particular advantages which cannot be easily replicated elsewhere. These include well-developed transport systems and access to urban or external markets; higher starting base incomes from traditional agriculture to finance the first stage of industrial development, and a relatively skilled and educated rural workforce, including large numbers of rural-origin workers employed in nearby cities, which leads to technology transfer when workers return to their villages (Delfs, 1987: 79).

These characteristics are not common to rural Asia, nor are they necessarily sustainable even within the fast-growing regions of China (Hawkins and Koppel, 1991), a point developed by Yok-Shiu Lee in his chapter in this volume. Throughout most of rural Asia, development policy regimes frequently discriminate against agriculture. High rural population pressures on agricultural resources and major patterns of agrarian organization and change (such as the increasing concentration of land ownership and the volatility of monocultural commodity production systems) are frequently associated with the perseverance of rural poverty and inequality. There are indications that as much as half the rural labor force already seeks some income from off-farm sources (Table 1.5), and there is evidence of declining growth in per worker income in agriculture (Table 1.6). All these factors are interacting in dynamics that frequently appear to be quite different from those described in East Asia's experience. Diversification of employment and income sources by rural households is being driven, in many cases, by *declining* abilities to maintain standards of living based only on agrarian activities—in terms of both levels of income and forms of consumption.

Conclusion

What is the meaning of employment differentiation in rural Asia? When does it represent a trajectory of development, and when does it describe a trajectory of deterioration? The answer is not simple. Though there are important continuities with the past that can make answering the question a form of extrapolation, there are also very significant discontinuities that can make extrapolation risky. A major challenge is understanding when we are looking at continuities and when we are faced by important discontinuities. Shelley Feldman puts it well in a note to her chapter in this volume (p. 127, note 11).

> Research on the nonfarm sector has often grown out of the need to diversify income earning among those dispossessed of landed property. Although forms of income diversification may be stimulated by the need to replace agricultural production with nonfarm work, processes to alleviate poverty, diversify income, or devise income-earning strategies are not synonymous because each may generate a different pattern of labor market participation and restructure the economy in diverse ways. Moreover, nonfarm employment has an independent historical trajectory that should not be equated with the ways in which nonfarm employment interfaces with changes in agricultural production.

There is little question that a shift is occurring in the composition of employment in rural areas of Asia. In many cases, this shift is not a recent development, but the scope and composition of diversification processes often have contemporary implications that suggest the processes are qualitatively different than those that may have existed previously. At the least, what these differentiation processes suggest is that an increasing proportion of rural labor relations are not connected directly or exclusively with traditional agrarian processes; rather, they are associated with more complex socioeconomic relationships in which agrarian processes may be only one part. One very important implication is that employment generation, enterprise formation and expansion, labor skill acquisition, and occupational choice and mobility are occurring in a socioeconomic context that is in significant transition. Important dimensions of rural life are being contested—and not simply by external forces. The result is not simply diversity of forms—which most analysts appear prepared to accept, albeit often as entries in classifications that deny the impact of diversity—but also a significant diversifying of meanings. This presents a challenge that conventional development studies on rural employment issues in Asia are not completely prepared to face.

A good portion of the existing theoretical debates on rural labor processes continue to be cast in neo-Marxist or liberal economic molds—molds that fundamentally insist on the standardization of processes, structures, and significances associated with work diversification generally and with the rise of rural nonagricultural wage employment specifically. However, as seen in the seven country studies and the discussion of the limits of the East Asian "model," the complexity and variability of the changing work situation in rural Asia strongly suggest that existing theoretical debates across the rural social sciences about these processes should be reoriented. What is strongly needed is a significant dose of grounded theory development that responds to the specific contexts of rural Asia, certainly more than a continued defense of what amounts to highly stylized forms of theory confirmation.

In the course of developing such a grounded theory, three points in particular, are likely to attract special attention. The first point involves confronting several compelling questions. What, under various circumstances, is the socioeconomic and political significance of nonfarm work in rural areas? When is it best understood as a by-product of agrarian differentiation? And when are other (although possibly related) processes more directly present—processes such as agrarian incorporation into a wider political economy, attendant processes of class formation and gender stratification, and the possible emergence of forms of economic activity that lie between the classic urban-rural dichotomy.

The second point involves recognizing that the processes and incidence of nonfarm work in rural areas are likely to be manifested in a variety of forms and institutional arrangements. What these forms and arrangements are and what their socioeconomic and political significance are will be key issues. Recognizing and assessing these issues will most likely require seriously challenging some of the central metaphors that have been used to conceptualize rural labor processes. One example is the (re)emergence of a neo-Weberian tradition in political sociology. Writers in this tradition are making progress in overcoming problems of reification, functionalism, and teleology that have plagued both Marxist and liberal economic analyses (e.g., Bourdieu, 1977; Giddens, 1981; Scott, 1985; Willis, 1977). From these roots, there are possibilities for more basic paradigmatic change. It will be especially important to problematize morphological continuities in rural labor processes, looking beneath these for content and contextual sources of discontinuities in the meanings of apparently similar institutional arrangements.

The third point entails confronting the complex issues of articulation among particular processes associated with nonfarm work in specific rural areas and wider processes of economic incorporation, social mobilization, state development, and the (de)politicization of structural change. Attention will need to move beyond a preoccupation with macro-micro analyses as assessments of the impacts of one level on the other to an examination of the sociopolitical processes that constitute the linkages between macro and micro processes. This implies, in turn, a rejection of a priori assumptions about the unidirectionality of influence in these relationships.

Notes

1. There is, for instance, an ongoing debate in Japanese academic circles on whether Japan's experience can provide a model for the rest of Asia. See, e.g., Ohkawa (1980); and Ohkawa and Johnston (1969); and Ohkawa, Johnston, and Kaneda (1969). There is also an abundant literature on the East Asian development experience, including Lau (1986) and Vogel (1991).

2. Neutral policy in this context means that the terms of trade are not deliberately turned against agriculture. This also implies that expenditure, credit, exchange rate, and other policies should be framed so they are not severely biased against agriculture.

3. It is well established that services tend to be rather labor intensive, on average. Hence, if one adjusts the Thai data by making the assumption that Thai services are at the average labor-output ratio of the rest of the Southeast Asian services sectors, services would account for about 40 percent of the labor force in Thailand; this would cause a downward adjustment in agriculture's share of employment to 47 percent.

4. This may be especially true of migrant seasonal workers seeking temporary jobs in urban areas.

5. In Thailand, farmers have begun to use small tractors and other labor-substituting farm machinery on a widespread basis.

References

Balisacan, A. 1993. "Agricultural Growth, Landlessness, Off-Farm Employment, and Rural Poverty in the Philippines," *Economic Development and Cultural Change*, Vol. 41 (April), pp. 533–562.

Bautista, R.M. 1986. *Domestic Price Distortions and Agricultural Incomes in Developing Countries* (Washington, D.C.: International Food Policy Research Institute).

Bourdieu, Pierre. 1977. *Outline of a Theory of Practice* (Cambridge: Cambridge University Press).

Bradford, Colin I., Jr. 1986. "East Asian 'Models': Myths and Lessons," in John P. Lewis and Valeriana Kallab, eds., *Development Strategies Reconsidered* (Washington, D.C.: Overseas Development Council), pp. 115–128.

Delfs, Roben. 1987. "Lesson from Sunan," *Far Eastern Economic Review*, Vol. 137 (June 4), pp. 78–80.

Fujita, N., and W.E. James. 1990. "Export-Oriented Growth of Output and Employment in Taiwan and Korea, 1973/74–1983/84," *Weltwirschaftliches Archives*, Vol. 126 (Winter), pp. 737–753.

Giddens, Anthony. 1981. *A Contemporary Critique of Historical Materialism* (Berkeley: University of California Press).

Glassburner, B. 1985. "Macroeconomics and the Agricultural Sector," *Bulletin of Indonesian Economic Studies*, Vol. 21 (August), pp. 51–73.

Hawkins, John, and Bruce Koppel. 1991. "Special Economic Zones and Education in China: Bold Reform or Timid Experiment?" in Irving Epstein, ed., *Chinese Education: Problems, Policies, and Prospects* (New York: Garland Publishing), pp. 172–195.

Hayami, Yujiro. 1964. "Demand for Fertilizer in the Course of Japanese Agricultural Development," *Journal of Farm Economics*, Vol. 46 (November), pp. 776–779.

———. 1967. "Innovations in the Fertilizer Industry and Agricultural Development: The Japanese Experience," *Journal of Farm Economics,* Vol. 49 (May), pp. 403–412.

Hayami, Yujiro, and Vernon W. Ruttan. 1970. "Factor Prices and Technical Change in Agricultural Development: The United States and Japan, 1880–1960," *The Journal of Political Economy,* Vol. 78 (September–October), pp. 1115–1141.

———. 1985. *Agricultural Development: An International Perspective,* 2d ed. (Baltimore, Md: Johns Hopkins University Press).

Ho, Samuel P.S. 1979. "Decentralized Industrialization and Rural Development: Evidence from Taiwan," *Economic Development and Cultural Change*, Vol. 32 (October), pp. 77–96.

———. 1986. *The Asian Experience in Rural Nonagricultural Development and Its Relevance for China* (Washington, D.C.: World Bank).

Hsieh, Sen-Chung, and Teng-Hui Lee. 1966. *Agricultural Development and Its Contribution to Economic Growth in Taiwan* (Taipei: Chinese-American Joint Commission on Rural Reconstruction).

Ito, T. 1992. *The Japanese Economy* (Cambridge, Mass.: MIT Press).

James, William E., S. Naya, and G.M. Meier. 1989. *Asian Development: Economic Successes and Policy Lessons* (Madison: University of Wisconsin Press).

Jeffrey, Patricia. 1982. *Frogs in a Well: Indian Women in Purdah* (London: Zed Press).

Johnston, B., and P. Kilby. 1975. *Agriculture and Structural Transformation* (London: Oxford University Press).

Johnston, B., and J. Mellor. 1961. "The Role of Agriculture in Economic Development," *American Economic Review*, Vol. 51 (September), pp. 566–593.

Koppel, Bruce. 1987. "Agrarian Problems and Agrarian Reform: Opportunity or Irony?" in Carl Lande, ed., *Rebuilding a Nation: Philippine Challenges and American Policy* (Washington, D.C.: Washington Institute Press), pp. 157–187.

———. 1992. "Between Ballot and *Balut*: Emerging Issues in Philippine Labor Markets and Industrial Labor Relations," in Chung H. Lee and Park Fun Koo, eds., *Emerging Labor Issues in Developing Asia* (Seoul: Korea Development Institute), pp. 98–143.

————. 1993. "Land Policy Problems in East Asia: Understanding the Past and Moving Towards New Choices," in Bruce Koppel and Dai Young Kim, eds., *Land Policy Problems in East Asia: Toward New Choices* (Seoul: Korea Research Institute for Human Settlements), pp. 3–47.

Kuo, S. 1981. *The Taiwan Success Story* (Boulder, Colo.: Westview Press).

Lau, L.J., ed. 1991. *Models of Development* (San Francisco, Calif: Institute for Contemporary Studies Press).

Lee, Teng-Hui. 1971. *Intersectoral Capital Flows in the Economic Development of Taiwan* (Ithaca, N.Y.: Cornell University Press).

Luong, Hy V. 1992. *Revolution in the Village: Tradition and Transformation in North Vietnam, 1925–1988* (Honolulu: University of Hawaii Press).

Mellor, J. 1976. *The New Economics of Growth: A Strategy for India and the Third World* (Ithaca, N.Y.: Cornell University Press).

Myers, R.H. 1991. "The Economic Development of the Republic of China," in L.J. Lau, ed., *Models of Development* (San Francisco, Calif.: Institute for Contemporary Studies Press), pp. 13–64.

Myint, H. 1975. "Agriculture and Economic Development in the Open Economy," in L. Reynolds, ed., *Agriculture in Development Theory* (New Haven, Conn.: Yale University Press), pp. 327–354.

Ohkawa, Kazashi. 1980. *Dualistic Development and Phases: Possible Relevance of the Japanese Experience to Contemporary Less Developed Countries* (Luxemburg, Austria: International Institute for Applied Systems Analysis).

Ohkawa, Kazashi, and Bruce F. Johnston. 1969. "The Transferability of the Japanese Pattern of Modernizing Traditional Agriculture," in E. Thorbecke, ed., *The Role of Agriculture in Economic Development* (New York: National Bureau for Economic Research, Columbia University Press).

Ohkawa, K., and H. Rosovsky. 1973. *Japanese Economic Growth: Trend Acceleration in the Twentieth Century* (Stanford, Calif.: Stanford University Press).

Ohkawa, Kazashi, Bruce F. Johnston, and Hiromitsu Kaneda, eds. 1969. *Agriculture and Economic Growth: Japan's Experience* (Tokyo: University of Tokyo Press).

Oommen, T.K. 1984. *Social Transformation in Rural India: Mobilization and State Intervention* (New Delhi: Vikas Publishing House).

Oshima, Harry T. 1983. *The Transition to an Industrial Economy in Monsoon Asia*, Asian Development Bank Staff Paper No. 20 (Manila: Asian Development Bank).

Power, J.H., and G. Sicat. 1971. *The Philippines: Industrialization and Trade Policies* (New York: Oxford University Press).

Ranis, G., J. Fei, and S. Kuo. 1979. *Growth with Equality: The Case of Taiwan* (New York: Oxford University Press).

Scott, James. 1985. *Weapons of the Weak: Everyday Forms of Peasant Resistance* (New Haven, Conn.: Yale University Press).

Vogel, E. 1991. *The Four Little Dragons: The Spread of Industrialization in East Asia* (Cambridge, Mass.: Harvard University Press).

Vyas, V.S., and W.E. James. 1988. "Agricultural Development in Asia: Performance, Issues, and Policy Options," in S. Ichimura, ed., *Challenge of Asian Developing Countries* (Hong Kong: Nordica Press).

Willis, Paul. 1977. *Learning to Labour* (Hampshire, United Kingdom: Gower Publishing).

Acronyms

ASEAN	Association of Southeast Asian Nations
BRDB	Bangladesh Rural Development Board
BSCIC	Bangladesh Small and Cottage Industries Corporation
CLT	Certificate of Land Transfer
EEC	European Economic Community
EP	Emancipation Patent
FDI	foreign direct investment
FIES	Family Income and Expenditure Surveys
GBP	Grameen Bank Project
GDP	gross domestic product
GNP	gross national product
HYV	high-yielding varieties
IFAD	International Fund for Agricultural Development
ILO	International Labor Organization
IRDP	Integrated Rural Development Program
JKKK	Jawatan Kuasa Kemajuan Kampong
LDC	less-developed country
MADA	Muda Agricultural Development Authority

NEDA	National Economic and Development Authority
NEP	New Economic Policy
NGO	nongovernmental organization
NIEs	newly industrialized economies
NIP	New Industrialization Policy
NORAD	Norwegian Development Assistance, Ministry of Development Cooperation
PAS	Partai Islam
TDRI	Thailand Development Research Institute
UMNO	United Malay National Organization
USAID	U.S. Agency for International Development

The Contributors

Edna Angeles-Reyes was a fellow at the Philippine Institute of Development Studies, where she focused on the analysis of economic development issues in the Philippines. Her publications included "The Structure of Rural Household Income and Its Implications on Rural Poverty in Bicol, Philippines," which appeared in the *Journal of Philippine Development* (1987).

Tadjuddin N. Effendi is a professor of economics at Gadjah Mada University in Jogyakarta, Indonesia, where he specializes in issues of population and economic development.

Shelley Feldman is an associate professor in the Department of Rural Sociology and the director of the Program on Gender and Global Change at Cornell University. She has published widely on rural development issues in Bangladesh. Her recent works include *Unequal Burden: Economic Crises, Persistent Poverty, and Women's Work,* which she coedited in 1992, and "Contradictions of Gender Inequality: Urban Class Formation in Contemporary Bangladesh," in *Gender and Political Economy: Explorations of South Asian Systems,* Alice Clark, editor (1993).

Gillian Hart is an associate professor in the Department of City and Regional Planning at the University of California at Berkeley. Her publications include *Power, Labor and Livelihood* (1986) and *Agrarian Transformations: Local Processes and the State in Southeast Asia,* which she coedited in 1989.

John Hawkins is dean for international studies and overseas programs and professor of comparative education at the University of California at Los Angeles. He has published many works on education and human resource development, with a focus on China.

William James is a senior fellow in the Program on International Economics and Politics at the East-West Center in Honolulu. Among his numerous publications on economic development issues affecting the Asia Pacific region are *Economic Development: Economic Successes and Policy Lessons* (1989) and *Foundations of India's Political Economy: Towards an Agenda for the 1990s* (1992).

Bruce Koppel is vice-president for research and education at the East-West Center in Honolulu. He has published extensively on Asian development issues. His work has appeared in journals such as *Economic Development and Cultural Change*; *Development and Change*; and *World Development*. His most recent books are *Induced Institutional Innovation and International Agricultural Development: A Reassessment* (1994) and *Land Policy Problems in East Asia: Toward New Choices* (1993).

Yok-shiu F. Lee is a fellow with the Program on Environment at the East-West Center in Honolulu. His research and publications emphasize issues of regional and urban development, especially in China and Southeast Asia.

Chris Manning is a professor of economics at Australian National University, Canberra. Focusing on issues of human resource development, especially in Indonesia, his publications have appeared in journals such as *Population and Development Review* and the *Bulletin of Indonesian Economic Studies*.

Nipon Poapongsakorn is a professor of economics at Thammasat University in Bangkok, Thailand. He has published widely on Thai economic development issues in articles and monographs appearing in Thailand and elsewhere in Southeast Asia.

Miriam Sharma is a professor of anthropology at the University of Hawaii, Manoa. Her works on Indian agrarian development issues have been published in numerous journals, including the *Economic and Political Weekly* and the *Journal of Peasant Studies*.

Urmila Vanjani is an instructor in the sociology of development at the Rajasthan Institute of Public Administration in India, Jaipur.

Index

About the Book

Previous analyses of employment diversification in rural Asia have been strongly influenced by two assumptions—that the principal forms of diversification are all within agriculture, and that the emergence of nonfarm employment connotes the emergence of "positive" economic development. Questioning these assumptions, this book is the result of a three-year comparative and cross-disciplinary examination of the dynamics and significance of nonfarm work in rural Bangladesh, China, India, Indonesia, Malaysia, the Philippines, and Thailand.

The authors document the complex connections between macro and micro processes of employment diversification in rural areas, giving special attention to the growth of a service economy, the relationship between employment diversification and the changing organization and performance of agriculture, and the impact of employment diversification on the social and political roles of women. A major contribution is their assessment of the conditions under which employment diversification does—and does not—appear to be "developmental."

George Logan

of Philadelphia

GEORGE LOGAN in 1805

By Gilbert Stuart

courtesy the Historical society of Pennsylvania

George Logan

of

Philadelphia

FREDERICK B. TOLLES

NEW YORK

OXFORD UNIVERSITY PRESS

1953

Printed in the United States of America

TO

HENRY J. CADBURY

SCHOLAR, HUMANITARIAN, PEACEMAKER LIKE LOGAN
BUT A BETTER QUAKER

This is the second book ever written about George Logan. The first — a 'little memoir . . . sacred to the virtues of his heart and to his domestic worth' — was begun within a few months of his death in 1821 by Deborah Norris Logan, his widow, and published many years later, long after her own death. Deborah Logan's *Memoir* is an affecting tribute to a dead husband, a charming monument of wifely devotion. It is that and much more. For Deborah Logan, in addition to being a delightful woman and a devoted wife, was a gifted writer, and her book is a little gem of early American biographical literature. Moreover, Deborah had the instincts of a historian; she was an assiduous collector and preserver of documents, a pious guardian of historical traditions, a sharp-eyed, retentive observer of her own stirring times. Her 'little memoir' is an indispensable source of information about her husband and about his time, the first half-century of the American Republic.

A wife can be a man's best biographer or his worst. Deborah was both. On the one hand, she knew and recalled incidents that no other person could have known. She could remember vividly that day in 1787 when General Washington had come to call at Stenton, their lovely mansion outside Philadelphia — how he had dandled her three-year-old boy on his knee, held her baby in his arms, admired her husband's agricultural improvements. Writing in the 1820's, she could still see in her mind's eye the ruffles and the 'elegant topaz ring' that Thomas Jefferson had worn when he had come to Stenton fresh from the court of Louis XVI. She and she alone vouches for the story of Benjamin Franklin's helping Adam Smith compose *The Wealth of Nations;* she had heard it from her husband, who had it straight from Dr. Franklin himself. She gives us one of our best accounts of the hysterical days of 1798, those days of distrust when self-appointed committees of Federalists shadowed prominent members of the opposition such as George Logan and Vice-President Jefferson himself on the assumption that any opponent of John Adams's administration was probably an agent of revolutionary France. For all these touches, the biographer of George Logan and the historian of the early Republic must be grateful.

On the other hand, the likeness that Deborah created is scarcely a speaking image, an adequate picture of the man. She was too close to him for that. Of George Logan the pioneer in scientific farming she tells us almost nothing. Of George Logan the pamphleteer, the political economist, the literary antagonist of Alexander Hamilton, nothing. Of George Logan's role in the Pennsylvania legislature — in a day when state legislatures were supreme and Pennsylvania truly the 'keystone state' — nothing. Of Logan the abolitionist, the champion of popular education, the early advocate of 'internal improvements,' nothing. Of Logan the Senator, trusted lieutenant, then disenchanted critic of President Jefferson, the unsuccessful peacemaker of 1810, next to nothing.

Because Deborah scanted or neglected these aspects of his career, and overemphasized one dramatic incident, George Logan is today known — where he *is* known — as a 'busybody,' a 'meddler,' a 'great fool,' [1] who took it upon himself in 1798, when war with France was imminent, to set out on a private 'peace mission' to Paris. His mission was not without its importance — it resulted in a law, still on the books and known as the 'Logan Act,' which makes all such adventures illegal; and it gave John Adams, by his own testimony, one of the bits of data on which he based the most momentous and statesmanlike decision of his life — the decision to restore diplomatic relations with revolutionary France and spare the young American nation a disastrous war.

Quite apart from this episode — about whose usefulness and propriety opinions will continue to differ, as they did in his own day — George Logan's career was a rich and notable one. It sheds new light on the beginnings of scientific agriculture in the United States. It shows us one of the channels through which the democratic convictions of Benjamin Franklin were perpetuated and made operative in the next political generation. It illuminates the origins of the faith we call Jeffersonian Democracy. It gives us a clue to Pennsylvania's role in the growth of Anti-Federalism or Democratic-Republicanism as a political force — and in the subsequent dissipation of that force through internal schism. It affords us a new vantage point from which to watch the unfolding Presidency of Thomas Jefferson. And finally it yields us some new sidelights on Franco-American and Anglo-American relations in the critical years of our nation's infancy.

But primarily this is a book about George Logan, not about his times, his 'historical significance,' or — God save the mark — his 'impact.' I have tried to keep myself out of the book, to see things, as far as possible, through Logan's eyes, to refrain from coming obtrusively upon the stage with Olympian judgments, judgments made after the fact with the wisdom of hindsight. I have adopted this method, at the risk of appearing biased and uncritical, for artistic reasons, because my effort is to present a man as he was, to convey, as far as may be, some sense of how it felt to be George Logan.

This does not mean that I abdicate the historian's responsibility to formulate critical judgments about his subject. Such judgments are implicit in what I have said above of my reasons for thinking Logan's story worth telling. Indeed they are implicit in my having written the book at all. But there are further judgments — not all favorable to my subject — which my conscience as a historian and a biographer compels me to pronounce.

George Logan was 'not a great man'; his views were 'limited.' This frank judgment comes from one of his own Senate colleagues,[2] but I accept it. Not that his mind was limited in breadth or scope or range. On the contrary, with something of the wisdom of the learned man that 'cometh by opportunity of leisure,' he combined the earthy common sense of the man that 'holdeth the plough . . . that driveth oxen . . . and whose talk is of bullocks.' No, the limitation of his mind came from a condition inherent in its very workings, a peculiar rigidity, a cramped quality, a doctrinaire character, alien to the minds of the really great men — the Franklins, Jeffersons, Madisons — of his era and of his acquaintance.

Paradoxically, this man so doctrinaire in his thinking, this man who too often put theory before fact, logic before experience, could be utterly inconsistent, almost perversely illogical in practice. Consider for a moment some of his inconsistencies: a Quaker and a peace-lover, he was disowned by the Society of Friends for bearing arms; a man ready to risk everything to prevent war, he opposed Jefferson's substitute for it, the Embargo; a zealous advocate of temperance, he objected to a tax on whisky stills; an opponent of slavery in the United States, he favored leaving the independent Negroes of Santo Domingo to Napoleon's tender mercies; the advocate of a diminished state, he was among the first to favor building roads and canals, establishing universities, abolishing slavery, all by federal power; a fervent Francophile in the 1790s, he was an equally fervent Anglophile in the next decade; a callow Tory in 1775, he stood forth a few years later as a fierce patriot, a last-ditch defender of the Revolution; a bold radical under Washington and Adams, he led a conservative retreat under Jefferson.

In the face of these bewildering reversals one might be tempted, as John Quincy Adams was, to write Logan off as one of those wispy, volatile creatures who 'float in uncertainty,' [3] veering now this way, now that, with each wind of doctrine, each tug of sympathy, each puff of popular sentiment. Would a really first-rate mind, one asks, be found on opposite sides of so many important questions? On the other hand, it is only fair to point out that greater men than Logan have sometimes lacked absolute consistency in public life: again the names of Franklin, Jefferson, and Madison come to mind. Circumstances alter cases — in politics perhaps most of all — and in a rapidly changing world perfect consistency is hardly to be counted among the cardinal political virtues.

This is, of course, simply a way of saying that for some of Logan's seeming inconsistencies — which I have purposely and unfairly set out in the most glaring light — there is an explanation rather favorable to his good sense, his warm heart, and his states-manship. To take one example, he hated war at least as much as Jefferson did, but to his tender spirit an embargo calculated to kill women and children by slow starvation did not seem more humane than a war in which soldiers killed each other with guns. Or to take another example, he opposed power in the national government when it was being used to promote special privileges for a few moneyed men, but he welcomed it when it could be used for the benefit of the whole people. But I will leave it to the reader to determine how far Logan's inconsistencies were real and worthy of censure, how far they were merely ostensible or actually indicative of a praiseworthy flexibility.

There is one further remark to be made, however, before I pass from this aspect of my subject. It contains a paradox, but it does, I believe, explain much of Logan's seemingly wayward po-litical conduct. Like his friend John Randolph of Roanoke, George Logan of Stenton was fundamentally a conservative throughout his life. At heart and by inheritance he was an aristo-crat, a country gentleman, who longed to preserve in America the rural society in which he had grown up in eastern Pennsylvania — a society characterized by rough equality of status, widely diffused prosperity, and all but unbroken peace. Land to him was the only real wealth; hence his attraction to Physiocratic doctrines. Those who labored on the land, the American yeomen, whom he came more and more to idealize, were to him, as to Jefferson, God's chosen people. The smoking factories of the coming industrial order threatened to spoil his agrarian Eden. The new middle class, the *parvenu* bankers and entrepreneurs, the false aristocracy of 'paper and privilege,' were parasites, men of contracted souls, bent on destroying his yeoman democracy and raising a new feudal society on the backs of grimy, down-trodden mill operatives.

In the first years of the Republic, Alexander Hamilton, with his ambitious financial and manufacturing schemes, seemed the princi-pal enemy, for Hamilton was using the new government to bestow special privileges on this false aristocracy. A few years later, Hamilton and the other Federalists appeared ready to jeopardize peace and prosperity by their unholy zeal for a French war.

Against such antagonists Logan grew bitter and shrill; his words had a radical sound; he consorted with 'jacobins' and talked a heady, revolutionary language.

With Jefferson's peaceful 'revolution of 1800' accomplished, it looked for a moment as if the agrarian paradise of Logan's vision were secure. But scarcely had his own state, Pennsylvania, been rescued from city nabobs than it fell into the hands of city demagogues, men such as William Duane, who were ready to corrupt the democracy at its source. Even Jefferson and Madison, whom the people had called to preside over them, threatened the nation's peace and harmony with their risky experiments in economic warfare, their unnecessary war with England, their postwar concessions to the parasitic businessman.

Logan's devotion to his agrarian ideal was doctrinaire, yes; by the end of his life he was clearly fighting for a lost cause. But at least in this respect he 'obeyed at eve the voice obeyed at prime.' The George Logan who in 1818 was still quoting Jefferson's *Notes on Virginia,* with its paean to the sturdy yeoman farmer, was more consistent than most men in public life — almost as consistent, indeed, as Alexander Hamilton.

By temperament, and heritage too, Logan was a conciliator, a moderator between extremes, a harmonizer of differences. There is paradox and inconsistency even here, for Logan had a temper that he could not always control; he often wrote and talked like an intransigent; and in personal relations he antagonized almost as often as he mollified. Still, his deepest instincts were those of a peacemaker. As a legislator in Pennsylvania he steered a middle course and tried to reconcile political opposites. In 1798 and again in 1810, when his country was on the verge of war, he made desperate, impulsive, no doubt imprudent efforts to bring the parties to the quarrel together, to seek agreement before it was too late. In the confusion of Pennsylvania politics after the Jeffersonian triumph, he tried to win support for a middle course between the extremes of demagogic republicanism and mercenary federalism. Was it a residual Quaker faith in the potential goodness of all men that led him always to look for common ground on which men could come together, where they could recognize the good in each other and the evil in the passions that kept them apart?

George Logan, to sum up, was not the wisest, the most prudent, the most consistent of men. He was naïve, impulsive, humorless, often wrong-headed. But he had something that the wise, the prudent, and the consistent do not always have. He had goodness. He was not a simple man, but he had simple goodness. And simple goodness among men in public life is not so common that we can afford to despise or overlook it when we come upon it.

Surely in the capacious American pantheon there is a niche for George Logan — not among the demigods, the Washingtons, Franklins, Jeffersons, Madisons, but on a lower range, perhaps alongside his friends Benjamin Rush and Joel Barlow. My effort in this book is to fill that niche — to dust off the figure so lovingly carved by Deborah Logan, to take a few inches off the pedestal on which she placed it, to bite more deeply into the stone, create a more recognizable human likeness, and make the most of the play of light and shadow that gives life to the inert material of biography.

F.B.T.

The Huntington Library
San Marino, California
July 1953

ACKNOWLEDGMENTS

The shape and texture of this book owe more to J. H. Powell of Philadelphia than anyone — except Mr. Powell and myself — could possibly know. The book is not as good as he wanted it to be, but the fault is mine, not his. I am grateful to two other good friends, John Robert Moore of Indiana University and Edmund S. Morgan of Brown University, for reading parts of the manuscript. Their comments were invariably helpful, though, of course, they bear no responsibility for the flaws that remain. Whitfield Bell, Jr., of Dickinson College was especially generous in sharing with me the results of his explorations in the libraries of the University of Edinburgh. The kindness of Sanford W. Higginbotham of the University of Mississippi and S. K. Stevens of the Pennsylvania Historical and Museum Commission enabled me to read Dr. Higginbotham's *Keystone in the Democratic Arch: Pennsylvania Politics, 1800–1816* in galley proof. I shall always remember the encouragement given me by the late Charles F. Jenkins of Philadelphia in the preparation of this book.

An author must depend on his friends for certain indispensable services, on institutions for others. I am deeply grateful to the Trustees of the Huntington Library for a fellowship that enabled me to write this book under conditions scholars dream about. Grants from the Swarthmore College Faculty Research Fund and the Penrose Fund of the American Philosophical Society helped greatly with the initial research and with the writing of the first draft.

When I think back over the libraries in which I have worked, I think of them not merely as the institutions that housed the books and manuscripts I needed, but as places where people were generous and helpful and unfailingly patient — even when, many months later and many miles away, I bothered them with importunate and troublesome requests for information I should have obtained for myself when I was there. I cannot name them all, but I cannot fail to mention Barney Chesnick of the Library Company of Philadelphia; Dorothy G. Harris and Lyman W. Riley of the Friends Historical Library of Swarthmore College; John Nickalls and Muriel Hicks of the Library of the Society of Friends, Friends House, London; Eleanor Melson of the Department of Records of Philadelphia Yearly Meeting; Gertrude Brincklé of the Historical Society of Delaware; Meredith Colket of the Columbia Historical Society, Washington, D.C.; Mary Rhoads Fox of the C. J. Marshall Memorial Library of the University of Pennsylvania — and, most especially, R. Norris Williams, 2nd, and the staff of the Historical Society of Pennsylvania.

Portions of this book have already appeared in the *William and Mary Quarterly,* the *Pennsylvania Magazine of History and Biography,* and the *Proceedings of the American Philosophical Society.* I wish to thank the editors of these journals for permission to reprint material from their pages.

CONTENTS

LIST OF ILLUSTRATIONS

George Logan
of Philadelphia

＊

I. STENTON

GEORGE LOGAN lived all his life in one house. It was a great mansion called 'Stenton,' and it is still standing, in a decayed sort of grandeur, in the northern part of Philadelphia. Noisy factories, gaunt warehouses, grimy rows of tenements crowd round it now, but in Logan's time it stood in the midst of golden wheatfields, green meadows, and rolling pastures. The oaks and pines, the sycamores and hemlocks that shaded its broad lawns were already large when George Logan was born in 1753. He planted new trees, and they were huge and old by the time he died, sixty-seven years later. Some of those years — exciting, fateful years — he spent in the capitals of the Atlantic world, in Edinburgh, Paris, London, Washington. But always he came back to Stenton, to its security, its serenity, its peace. He was a Logan, a Logan of Stenton.

Actually, he was the first Logan to be born in the great house. Grandfather Logan, who had built it in 1728, had lived there in his long old age. A year and a half after his death, his eldest son, William Logan, having 'deliberately considered [his] station,' and 'concluded in favor of a country life,' had moved out from Philadelphia with his wife Hannah, his two sons, James and William, and his little daughter Sarah.[1] Hannah Emlen Logan was great with child. On 9 September 1753, less than four months after the family moved into Stenton, she gave birth to a son and named him George, after her own father.

3

For the first seven years of his life, George knew only the little world of Stenton. It was a good place to grow up. Grandfather had built the mansion solidly, amply, sparing nothing to make it comfortable. Old James Logan had been a Quaker, the secretary and trusted friend of William Penn. Also he had accumulated a great fortune as a fur merchant. Stenton imaged its builder's qualities. It reflected Quakerism in its sedate simplicity, the plainness of its doorway, the total absence of ornament, the honest, straightforward design. It bespoke the opulent trader in its very scale and solidity, its massive chimneys, rising from a flat-topped, hip roof, its rich-textured brickwork, its high-posted rooms, wainscoted to the ceiling. George grew up surrounded by simple elegance, elegant simplicity.

What delighted a boy growing up at Stenton were the curious nooks and crannies with which the house abounded, reminders of Grandfather's crotchets. They were capital places for hide-and-seek — the secret panel in the dining room, the dark tunnel to the barn, the narrow passageway to the attic bedrooms. Every room had its fireplace. On a winter evening, George could sit on the hearth, listening to the crackle and roar of the flames, watching their ever-shifting shapes and colors, shivering a little at the fantastic shadows they threw on the wainscoted walls, puzzling out the stories from Scripture painted on the tiles.

Sometimes he was allowed to go into the great library, which stretched across the entire front of the house on the second story. Once this room had held Grandfather's huge black-letter folios, his quartos and octavos in strange tongues, his scientific treatises, full of abstruse formulas. Most of the books were gone now — Grandfather had given his library to the City of Philadelphia. But the smell of books, the aroma of scholarship, still clung to the room. Everyone spoke with respect and a little awe of James Logan's vast learning. A small boy could not but wonder what kind of man his grandfather had been.

There were always guests in the great house. 'Public Friends,' Quaker ministers traveling 'in the love of the gospel,' regularly stopped at Stenton. They found its comfort grateful and refreshing after nights spent under the stars and long arduous days in the saddle. Whenever a 'public Friend' arrived, Hannah and William Logan would gather the children and the servants together in the parlor for a solemn religious 'opportunity.' It was not easy to sit still, to be kept indoors, when there were so many things to do outside. It was always a relief when the visitor finally arose and broke the silence, preaching in an unmelodious sing-song. A small boy could make little sense of the exhortations to 'dig deep,' to 'center down,' to 'keep close to the root.' But it was exciting to hear new voices, to see new faces. And what stories the visiting Friends could tell, after the general shaking of hands which announced the end of the little meeting in the parlor — stories of storms at sea, bears and wildcats in the American forests, floods and snowstorms along the road, stories of disputes with unfriendly Baptists and Presbyterians in New England or North Carolina.

George could barely remember the visits of Catherine Payton and Mary Peisley. Stenton had been a rendezvous for these two frail but hardy English Quakeresses as they had traveled, separately or together, up and down the colonies, from Charles-Town in South Carolina to Casco Bay in the Province of Maine.[2] Then there had been the great Samuel Fothergill with his booming voice, his commanding presence, his grave, dignified manner. He too had been at Stenton when George was very small. But George remembered Samuel Fothergill because, soon after his coming, Father had gone away and stayed nearly four months. He was accompanying the English Friend, Hannah Logan explained, in his travels through New England. Father had come back from that journey shaking his head over the decline of Quakerism in the eastern provinces. He reported 'refreshing seasons' at some meetings, but in general he had found 'Truth . . . at a low ebb in those parts.'[3]

William Logan had a poor opinion of New England anyway; it was an 'ironbound country,' its fields so stony that a Pennsylvania farmer would not consider them worth owning, 'much more clearing and fencing.'[4] Father had strong feelings about the southern provinces, too. Often George heard him tell the story of the southward journey he had once made with Cousin Jemmy

Pemberton. They had gone all the way to Frederica, Georgia, on the very edge of Spanish Florida. That had been eight years before George was born, but William Logan still spoke with feeling of the 'miserable' towns, the 'mean' inns with their drafty chambers and 'stinking' beds, the 'nasty' food. As for the people, he had found them 'indolent and lazy,' but, withal, 'very kind to strangers.' But the trip had not been all hardship. Father still recalled with gusto that evening in North Carolina when the two Quakers had met with 'a canoe of fine fish, just caught, and had drum, boiled for supper, very well, and afterwards like gentlemen refreshed ourselves with a glass or two of good Madeira wine.' But, he always added, they had brought the wine with them from Philadelphia; the southerners did not know the virtues of good Madeira.[5]

It was from his father and the guests who came to Stenton that little George got his first pictures of the world outside. Some of the guests brought glimpses of a world very different from that of the traveling Friends. Indians — Delawares, Shawnee, Mingo — were part of George's boyhood. They came in groups of twenty and thirty, as they had done since Grandfather's day, and squatted in the Stenton woods. Sometimes they stayed a whole year. They shot rabbits and squirrels, and the wild pigeons that darkened the sky in their flight. They made baskets and ladles and simple things of wood to sell. Surprisingly, they made 'tolerably good fiddles.'[6] Little George spent hours playing with the dark-skinned children, listening to the stories of their elders, learning the immemorial lore of the forest.

From his father George learned more about Indian life. William Logan often traveled unarmed on the frontier, for the Delawares and the Shawnee knew him and trusted him. Was he not James Logan's son? And had not James Logan been the personal representative of William Penn, whom they called Onas? William Logan regularly went to attend the Indian treaties at Lancaster and Easton; and when Pennsylvania's halcyon decades of peace came to an end — an Indian war broke out when George was three — Father was one of those Friends who tried to call back the old days of mutual trust and agreement between white man and red. With other Quakers he organized the Friendly Association for Regaining and Preserving Peace with the Indians by Pacific Measures. He gave generously to provide clothing and presents for the confused and angry Delawares.

One day when George was ten, a large number of peaceable 'praying Indians' came flocking in from the country, seeking refuge in Philadelphia. The 'Paxton Boys,' Scots-Irish frontiersmen, had massacred twenty of their brethren at Conestoga. By order of the governor, they were taken to barracks in the Northern Liberties, not far from Stenton. But a regiment of Highlanders was stationed there, and they refused to share their quarters with the aborigines. So the Indians were sent, shivering with fear and cold (for it was December) to the islands in the Delaware. Finally, New York offered them a haven, and it was William Logan who sped them on their way, traveling with them as far as Trenton.[7] Logans of Stenton knew the Indians. They neither feared nor scorned them. Little George learned from his father to accept them naturally. They were fellow human beings; they deserved respect and sometimes they needed compassion.

George also learned from his father to love and respect the soil. William Logan was a good farmer. On his five hundred acres he grew wheat, rye, oats, Indian corn — Pennsylvania's staple crops. But he experimented too. He read the new agricultural writers, tried out their methods, and made careful notes on the results. 'Memoranda in Husbandry on My Own Plantation,' he headed these notes.[8] He was growing flax, hops, and turnips years before most farmers knew the value of such crops. To diversify his forage, he planted new varieties of grass. He sent to England for sainfoin and vetch seed. The Reverend Jared Eliot sent him fowl meadow-grass seed from Connecticut. The fragrance of mown hay was always in the air at Stenton in summer.

At other seasons there were different scents, and George learned to love them all — the rich smell of the black earth when Matthew Potter, the hired man, turned the furrows in the spring and fall, the pungent odor of the smokehouse, where the great hams and sides of bacon hung, the warm scent of the cattle and sheep in their winter stables. There were plenty of animals on the farm. On New Year's Day 1756, William Logan took inventory of his livestock: eight horses and mares, twenty-three horned cattle, forty-two sheep, eight pigs.[9] It was a large number, a considerable wealth on the hoof. Farming was William Logan's calling. '[I] am determined, if kind Providence bless me with my health,' he had written, soon after moving to Stenton, 'to spend the remainder of my days here, and make what improvements I can in husbandry.' [10]

Every autumn the Logan family went over the river to attend the country fair at Burlington, New Jersey. For a farmer like William Logan it was a serious occasion — a time for trading livestock, selling produce, discussing crops and politics. But for a small boy it was a bright and happy holiday, a glorious chance to get lost in the crowd of country people, to consume too many cakes and tarts, to admire the fat hogs and powerful oxen, to watch — when Father was not looking — the horse races.

Uncle John Smith, who lived in Burlington, was always there. Always in his stiff way he was disturbed by the confusion and hubbub of the fair, 'the various accidents and squabbles, such as breaking of earthenware by horses and carriages running over it, quarreling for the best stalls, and breaking limbs and necks of the riders at the horse race.' But Uncle Smith had a Quaker's eye for business. Shrewdly he examined the quantities of desirable English manufactures on display, for he had once been an importer of dry goods and hardware himself. Whimsically, he observed 'the spirit and intrepidity of many of our young beaux, who at the expense of their coppers, showed their hearty regard for our own manufactures, by treating themselves and their sweethearts with the various sorts of cakes, tarts, and custards, on the stalls occupied by some ancient females.'

All the country folk from both sides of the Delaware were there, decked out in their once-fashionable wedding clothes, now donned only 'for fairs and other extraordinary times.' It was an agreeable crush, the whole week, though Uncle Smith regretted the unrestricted sale of rum. Vendors, he observed, were artful, and used 'many provocatives, particularly fiddlers,' to entice 'the silly, unthinking youth' to taste 'the bewitching poison and many probably to love it for ever after.'[11] The Logans of Stenton mingled easily, naturally, with the other country families. Social differences meant little at Burlington Fair. The farmers knew William Logan as a farmer, and — since this was Quaker country — they knew him as a Friend.

Burlington Fair came only once a year, but Quaker meeting came twice each week. Regularly, on First Day and Fifth Day, William and Hannah Logan bundled the whole family into the coach and took them to the stone meetinghouse in Germantown. There George sat through the long silence alongside Billy, Sally, and Charles (the youngest Logan). The benches were hard, and it was impossible to keep from fidgeting. But presently his wandering thoughts would be captured by the voice of a ministering Friend, filling the plain little room with its strange music. A child could make little of the speaker's words, but the sound was awesome and the serene faces of the ministers and elders in the gallery gave him a sense that all was well. After meeting there was the long line of coaches and teams at the shed to inspect, the other children to see and talk with, the meaningless, amiable remarks of adults to endure. And there was the long drive home to dinner.

Quarterly and Yearly Meetings were great occasions in a Quaker household. When Yearly Meeting came round in September, the whole Logan family moved into Philadelphia or over to Burlington for a week. For the older Friends it was a time of solemn deliberations, sober fellowship, and hearty dinners. For the younger ones there was the excitement of a great concourse of people, the chance to see all the young cousins. And, in Philadelphia, there was the possibility of a visit to the ships lying in the Delaware — Cousin James Pemberton's or Uncle Isaac Norris' ships, just in from Madeira or Curaçao or Bristol or Rotterdam. For a small boy those ships were evidence of a great world lying beyond Philadelphia, beyond Pennsylvania and New Jersey, beyond the American Provinces.

But for the most part George Logan's world during his first seven years was bounded by the Germantown Road and the York Road. A boy could be forever busy at Stenton. He could stand in the poplar field, between the great barn and the Germantown

Road, watching the harvest hands at work. He could race with his brothers through the spruce-tree pasture to fetch the cows in for milking. He could fish for trout in Wingohocking Creek, sail boats in the millpond, watch the leaves and twigs swirling through the millrace. Stenton was a good place in which to grow up.

When he was eight, George, with his brothers Billy and Charles, was put to school in Philadelphia under the care of Robert Proud. William Logan paid £10 per year for their tuition and a further sum for firewood.[12] Young Robert Proud was a Yorkshireman, only recently come to Philadelphia to be Latin Master at the Friends Public School. He glowered at his pupils through beetling eyebrows, over a high Roman nose. He was precise, demanding, humorless, and hard, a petty, pedantic man, lonely in his bachelorhood, hungry for wealth. Robert Proud hated being a schoolmaster; he resented his lowly station. And so he tyrannized in his classroom over the sons of the rich and high-born, longing hopelessly for a place in the world of their parents. Grimly he forced them to learn; glumly they learned. Under his harsh direction, boys at the Friends School lisped their Latin verbs and Greek paradigms, wrote original verse in the ancient tongues, read Plutarch and Virgil and Tully, all the improving authors, and some — Juvenal and Horace and Ovid — whom Quaker parents thought not so improving.

Pupils at Friends School were mostly young Quakers, but there was a sprinkling of Anglicans, Presbyterians, Baptists, even Roman Catholics. George's schoolmates were the children of the merchant princes of Philadelphia. There was Charley Pemberton, son of Israel Pemberton, who was called 'King of the Quakers.' There were the Fisher boys, Miers, William, and Jabez Maud, whose parents were intimate with the Logans. There was Joseph Richardson, son of the wealthy silversmith. There were Joseph Wharton, Samuel Coates, and Henry Drinker — indeed at Friends School was all the wealth and position even so egregious a snob as Robert Proud could wish.

George spent six years under the shadow of Proud's ferule, six years of hard, unremitting mental discipline. At seven o'clock in the morning he was in the schoolhouse at Fourth and Chestnut streets, and there he stayed till late afternoon, except on Fifth-Day and First-Day mornings, when he went with the other boys to worship in the meetinghouse next door. Every evening there was 'some lesson or version' to be done. The Overseers of the school felt themselves responsible for the boys' moral health as well as for their mental development, and the evening lessons were calculated 'to wean them away from so eager a desire for unprofitable amusements.' [13]

Rules were strict at the Quaker school. Pupils were expected to use invariably 'the plain language of the singular number to one person.' They must be careful 'never to utter any rude or uncivil expression, nor to call their schoolmates or others by any nickname or term of reproach.' In their infrequent 'hours of leisure,' they must 'avoid ranting games and diversions, and every occasion of quarreling with each other.' And young Friends must remember that they were a 'peculiar people.' The Overseers decreed that 'none shall at any time play or keep company with the rude boys of the town, but shall converse, as much as they can, with their own schoolfellows, and shall live in harmony and friendship together.' [14]

Robert Proud was not a man to evoke young George's affection, nor was Friends School as pleasant as Stenton. But James Logan's grandson respected learning, even in an unhappy, overbearing man like Proud. And what he taught, Proud taught well — the tough discipline of Latin grammar and prosody, the intricacies of Greek syntax, the rudiments of mathematics. It was a gentleman's education — and a good one — that George Logan got at his hands.

When George was fourteen, his father decided it was time for him to finish his education in England. William Logan himself, as a boy, had gone to Bristol, where his father James Logan, and *his* father before him, had been teachers at the Friends School. There was another reason aside from family tradition for sending the boys away. Philadelphia was growing fast — too fast, the Stenton farmer thought — and losing its Quaker purity. It was full of temptations, likely to set even the most piously reared boy 'on the high road to destruction.' To let his sons remain 'where there is so much liberty allowed to almost all youth, and where there are more avenues to every kind of vice than in any other city, numbers excepted,' would, he feared, 'end in their ruin.' [15]

So off to England in 1768 went George Logan and his brother Charles, who was a year younger than he. John Hunt, a well-known British 'public Friend,' was returning home with a company of Quakers. He agreed to take charge of the Logan boys, convey them across the ocean, and see them well started in a Friends school. The long Atlantic crossing was high adventure, but its sequel was disheartening. George and Charles paused in London for a few days' visit with their older brother Billy, just commencing the study of medicine. Then they proceeded to Worcester, in the west of England, where John Hunt delivered them into the care of their new master, James Fell.

If Robert Proud was a mean-spirited snob, James Fell was a sullen misanthrope, far harder to endure. Gentleness and kindness were traits seldom found in eighteenth-century schoolmasters anywhere, but George Logan was especially unlucky in his teachers. James Fell had conducted the Friends school in Worcester for a quarter of a century, quite to the satisfaction of his Quaker employers. But when George came under his tutelage, he was an embittered, bewildered man, stunned by the loss of his wife.[16] He was as much a tyrant as Proud had ever been. Secretly, in his room, George wrote his first letter home to his sister Sally. 'I cant stay now to say mutch,' he scrawled hurriedly, 'for I am afear'd every Moment of Masters coming up, for he will not let one Letter go ought of the School without his knowing & so I am Afeard he will catch me.' [17]

George was homesick and unhappy at Worcester. He sat in his little room on Friar Street, one eye on the door, his ears straining for a sound of a heavy step on the stair, and he thought of Stenton, its green fields, its tall trees, its friendly hearths. To take his mind off his troubles, he composed some pious verses. 'O Lord,' he began,

> . . . direct me in my youthful days
> That I may keep thy holy laws and ways.

His rhythm limped badly, but before he reached the end he had managed to transmute self-pity into compassion for others who might be in worse case:

> O Lord that thou wouldst feed the poor with bread
> And that they may find a place to lay their head.[18]

This benevolence was not feigned. It was part of his nature. One day, while at school, George received a present from his sister Sally — a hand-knit purse containing a gold piece. It was the largest sum of money he had ever owned. But in a neighboring street there was a poor widow who had a lame son. In a burst of expansive generosity, George ran to her house and pressed the gold piece into her hand, telling her to use it to send her little boy to school.[19]

On such tender-minded lads as George and his brother, James Fell's truculent bullying bore harshly. Presently, word of their unhappiness reached the London Friends to whose care William Logan had entrusted them. A letter from Dr. John Fothergill, the older brother of Samuel Fothergill, informed the boys' father that, in view of James Fell's disturbed state of mind, they would 'reap no great benefit where they are.' [20] Sadly William Logan summoned them home; gladly they returned to Stenton, overjoyed to be released from their durance in Worcester.

George was now seventeen. More than anything else, he wanted to be a physician, to follow in Billy's footsteps and those of his old schoolmate, Thomas Parke, who was just graduating in medicine from the College of Philadelphia and setting off for Edinburgh.[21] It was natural for a young Friend to covet a medical career. Everyone knew the names of the great Quaker doctors, Fothergill and Dimsdale, in England, and Friends had laid the foundation of Philadelphia's medical pre-eminence in America. There was plenty of precedent in the family too, for Grandfather's brother, William, had been a famous physician in Bristol.

But brother Billy, fresh from Edinburgh, was already commencing the practice of physic in Philadelphia. One doctor in the family, William Logan felt, was enough.

Billy, five years older than George, was a high-spirited, lovable youth. He was given to melodramatic behavior, however, and had been something of a trial to his parents. On his voyage to Great Britain to complete his medical education, he had been shipwrecked on the Welsh coast, and his account to his parents showed how thoroughly he had enjoyed the calamity. The experience had been harrowing enough — 'the sea running mountains high, and rocks and breakers all round us' — but Billy had missed no chance to heighten its dramatic qualities. 'Seeing that we must die,' he wrote, 'I called all hands in the cabin, and we all joined in supplicating the Almighty to receive our dying souls into His mercy. . . . After some time spent in prayer, we took a most affectionate leave of each other, and I went to my berth and formed a sheet around me by way of shroud, and in much silence and, I hope, resignation, waited for the awful moment.' But resignation had presently given way to hope; he found a hencoop and resolved to cast himself into the sea and float ashore on it. Suddenly the wind ceased, and the ship's company found itself in the hands of rough men, wreckers and smugglers 'who live by rapine and plunder.' One of them took him to Swansea, where he found Friends who assisted him in reaching Bristol.[22]

After this adventure, Billy had matriculated at Edinburgh. His extravagant ways never ceased to distress his father. The boy needed watching, what with his 'openness of temper and heart, and his want of a sufficient knowledge of the true value and use of money.'[23] Dr. Fothergill, his medical mentor, agreed, after coming to know Billy: 'with great sensibility,' the Doctor wrote, 'he was too presumptuous, thought himself equal to any difficulties, and required still to be managed with great prudence and parental authority.'[24] Billy's headstrong, romantic nature had shown itself again in his clandestine match with the daughter of Dr. Portsmouth, a well-known English physician. The girl's father had forbidden him the house, but he had wooed her secretly, dressed in a servant's livery.[25]

George had all of Billy's 'openness of temper and heart.' But he was less impetuous, less mettlesome, a sober and considerate youth with strong inclinations to benevolence. Unquestionably, he would make a good physician. But William Logan was adamant; one doctor in the family was enough. So George was apprenticed to a merchant, the wealthy and pious Quaker John Reynell.

Friend Reynell had come to Philadelphia forty years before from Kingston, Jamaica. People still told the quaint tale of his last years in Jamaica, how he had been the sole surviving member of a once-flourishing Quaker community, how every First Day he had gone in solitary devotion to the meetinghouse, had sat down all alone to hold a regular Friends meeting, never missing, never joined by anyone else. Had he exercized himself, Quaker wags would always ask, in the vocal ministry in his Jamaica meeting? For forty years, John Reynell had prospered in Philadelphia. He had entered fully into the social life of the Quaker city. Benignly he presided over the Board of Managers of the Pennsylvania Hospital. Generously he gave of his wealth to charity; people said he regularly allotted one-third of his annual expenditures to the relief of the poor.[26] John Reynell was a model Quaker.

As an apprentice, George lived at his master's house on Front Street, ate at his master's table, and attended meeting with his master's family. He learned to keep accounts, write business letters, prepare bills of lading. He stood by the hour on the wharf, supervising the unloading of crates of earthenware, casks of nails, bolts of calico and oznabrig. He went on board the ships in the Delaware to oversee the stowing of flour and beef and barrel staves in the holds, to deliver John Reynell's final orders to the captains and supercargoes before the vessels weighed anchor. He dealt with customers in John Reynell's store on the waterfront.

But the life of business, so congenial to most Philadelphia Friends, was repellent to George Logan. He had no desire to be another John Reynell, wealthy as that worthy Quaker was. Friend Reynell, though strictly honest, was a close-mouthed man, a shrewd and subtle trader. 'In doing business,' he would advise his apprentices, 'be a little on the reserve, and observe well the person thou has to do with.' It did not pay to be too frank: 'Keep thy business to thyself,' was his advice, 'and don't let it be known who thou dost business for, or what sorts of goods thou ships off.' There were plenty of stratagems by which, without actual dishonesty, an astute merchant could enlarge his profits, and John Reynell confided them to his apprentices: 'If thou finds out a place where they sell cheap, keep it to thyself, for if thou ships off goods cheaper than others, it will increase business.' [27]

These precepts of silence and secrecy ran athwart George's open and candid nature. The prospect of a lifetime of moneymaking by such means was abhorrent. A physician's career still beckoned. Fortunately John Reynell, an old man now, was not often in his countinghouse, and George found himself with time on his hands. He made good use of his leisure.

Out at Stenton, in the great library that extended across the mansion's second story, was a magnificent collection of medical books. James Logan's brother, the Bristol physician, had recently left them to William Logan, his nephew and namesake. William Logan had little interest in them; ultimately they would find a place alongside Grandfather's books in the Loganian Library in Philadelphia.[28] But meanwhile they lay, unread, on the shelves at Stenton — unread, that is, until George Logan seized on them and began to devour them. There were six hundred volumes, and they covered everything a doctor needed to know — anatomy, surgery, physic, *materia medica*. George would have had to go far in the American colonies to find a richer collection. The little library at the Pennsylvania Hospital did not begin to compare with it.

Here were the medical classics — Galen, Avicenna, Paré, Vesalius, Harvey, Boerhaave. Here were the important recent treatises — the anatomical works of Morgagni and Alexander Monro *primus,* Lieutaud's *Physiology,* the discourses of Mead and Pringle and Van Swieten. Here were curious volumes like Arnaud de Villeneuve on rejuvenation and Albertus Magnus' treatise on cosmetics, *The Secrets of Women*.[29] Every time George went out to Stenton, he loaded himself with medical books and carried them into Philadelphia. In John Reynell's quiet countinghouse he sat poring over Galen and Hippocrates, pondering the aphorisms of Boerhaave, studying Sydenham's detailed clinical reports. The mercantile apprentice was bound to satisfy his hunger for a medical education. He even indulged in surreptitious practice. Disregarding his parents' wishes, he successfully inoculated himself against smallpox.[30]

In 1772, when George was not quite twenty, Billy suddenly died — gay, romantic, high-spirited Billy, who loved life so passionately. His young widow took their small son and hired maid home to England on the *Mary and Elizabeth* in company with John Woolman of New Jersey and a group of other Friends.[31] For George, Billy's death was a sad loss. The handsome, dashing young physician had been a boy's dream of what an older brother should be. George Logan sat sorrowfully now at his ledgers and daybooks. For three years more he struggled with the daily tasks at the countinghouse, preparing bills and invoices, listing cargoes, computing the profits on manifests the sea captains handed him, entering John Reynell's accounts current. He missed Billy's lighthearted laughter, missed the open fields and the great trees of Stenton. He spent as much time as possible poring over the medical books from Great-Uncle William's library.

Gradually George Logan's resolution took shape. Now that Billy had died, William Logan could have no further objection to his second son's studying the practice of physic. And now that a war was threatening to break out between the American colonies and the mother country, there was every reason why he should look favorably on the proposal. William Logan was a good Quaker, and as a Quaker was conscientiously opposed to both war and civil rebellion. What better provision could he make for his son in these dangerous times than to send him to Great Britain? There he would be remote from the scene of fighting. There he could devote himself to learning the humane art of healing while the other young men of his generation were condemned to learn the savage art of killing.

In May 1775, just a month after the first shots were fired on Lexington Common and at Concord Bridge, George Logan rode down to Chester with his parents, fondly bade them farewell, stepped on board the brigantine *Two Friends,* Captain Cary, and sailed for Britain. He was twenty-two years old; at that age he should have been long since established in his life work. Instead, he was bound for Edinburgh and three years as a student of medicine. He would follow in Billy's path, be another Dr. Logan of Stenton.

*

II. EDINBURGH AND PASSY

THE *Two Friends* dropped slowly down Delaware Bay and turned her prow toward England.

It was George's third ocean voyage; he was familiar with the long tedious days, the monotonous suspension of life for six weeks, and the discomforts of the Atlantic crossing. The first few days on shipboard were calm. After putting his cabin to rights, George had time to reflect on the 'dreadful situation' of his fellow Quakers in Pennsylvania, on the difficulties of neutrality in the struggle with the mother country.[1] Non-resistant Quakers were bound to be misunderstood, reviled by patriots and Tories alike.

But these reflections were presently brought to an end by a violent thunderstorm. The *Two Friends* wallowed in 'a high dis-agreeable sea,' heavy rains pelted down, the ship's cook was struck by lightning. George was confined to the gloom of the cabin, 'amidst the sighs, groans, and dejected countenances' of the other passengers — 'a truly horrid sight.' Ladies shrieked, and even gallant young men were dismayed when one wave, greater than the rest, poured down the hatchway and set boxes afloat in the staterooms.

Once out of the storm and through the Gulf Stream, the *Two Friends* made a steady, routine voyage. The Quakers on board held meetings for worship three times a week, and the younger ones held 'disputes generally three times a day.' Chief instigator of these arguments was Jabez Maud Fisher, George's old school-mate, whose brother Thomas had recently married Sally Logan.

19

Jabez was forever making outrageous statements, 'absurd asser-
tions . . . with respect to the situation of places and things he
has never seen.' He talked as if God had appointed him 'surveyor-
general of the whole globe.' When not occupied in deflating young
Jabez, George and his shipmates whiled away the time discussing
what they intended to do once they reached England.

On 20 May, they passed a mythical point in the sea known to
sailors as 'Mother Cary's.' Thereupon Captain Cary announced
that, having passed his mother's abode, they were now halfway to
their destination. Captain Cary was a garrulous bore, a trial to
his captive audience. 'He entertained us with the genealogy of his
family, etc., etc.,' George wrote, 'till we were glad to get rid of
him by giving him some rum.'

A few days later, the skipper speared a porpoise, and George
set down for his brother a detailed description of the eight-foot
monster. Having studied the beast first-hand, he decided he could
not credit Pliny's account of their leaping on shipboard by pairs.
The sailors commenced skinning the creature before it was dead,
and George writhed inwardly at the obscene sight. The porpoise
was 'terribly convulsed,' he noted, 'and in such agony that he made
a noise very much resembling the cry of a child.'

On 9 June, five and a half weeks after George had said goodby
to his parents at Chester, he heard the helmsman's cry of 'Land!
Land!' The dim outlines of the Lizard off their port bow told
them they were entering the Narrows, the long voyage almost
over. Next morning they were abreast of Eddystone Light, its
hundred-foot stone shaft towering high above the mountainous
waves that crashed on its base. The lighthouse was one of the
engineering marvels of the century, but George was more interested in the fate of the late keeper, whose story he related to his
brother in gruesome detail. During the recent fire, the keeper had
somehow swallowed a large quantity of molten lead from the
lantern. He had lived for ten agonizing days with an eight-ounce
lump of lead in his stomach, thus demonstrating, the young medical student pointed out, the fallacy of the notion that molten lead
could not enter the stomach without causing instant death.

Passing the Isle of Wight, George discovered another bit of

curious lore for his brother's edification. The celebrated Nancy Dawson, one-time belle of London and Dublin, and heroine of the street-ballad 'Nancy Dawson was a Whore,' had married a farmer, retired to this island, 'and become a notable honest wife.'

Near Beachy Head the brigantine was becalmed. George and his young friends, craving exercise, rowed Captain Cary three miles against the tide to a French fishing smack. All the while they endured the skipper's garrulities. They exchanged American tobacco for plaice, herring, and mackerel, and the sailors entertained them with gay French songs.

Anxious to reach London without delay, George and three other passengers left the *Two Friends* a few miles below Dungeness and boarded a Dover cutter, which quickly left the slow-moving brigantine far astern. Coasting swiftly under the 'romantic and stately' chalk cliffs, they soon docked at Dover. A hearty meal of lamb and green peas at the 'King's Head,' a hasty sightseeing tour of Dover Castle, and George was flying over the gravel road in the London coach. Arriving before nightfall, he was 'joyfully received' by members of the London Quaker community, and by the great merchant-banker David Barclay, to whose special care his father had commended him.

Like many another American medical student before him, George went early next morning to Harpur Street in fashionable Bloomsbury, to wait upon Dr. John Fothergill. The famous Quaker physician received him 'in such a manner as had more the appearance of a tender father than a transient friend.' Fothergills and Logans had always been closely tied. Years before, Dr. Fothergill had translated Grandfather's experiments with Indian corn from Latin and published them in England. His younger brother Samuel, the Quaker minister, had been at Stenton in George's childhood. Dr. Fothergill had already seen Billy Logan through his medical studies, and had taken a fatherly interest in the two younger lads during their dismal experience at James Fell's school.

Good Doctor Fothergill, sixty-four years old now, had always shown a special partiality for Americans. Among his trans-

Atlantic friends he numbered the mercantile Pembertons, Israel and James, the botanical Bartrams, John and William, most of the leading physicians in America, including young Dr. Benjamin Rush, and the brilliant Dr. John Morgan. His most rewarding American friendship, however, was with Benjamin Franklin. Twenty-five years before, he had paid the then unknown colonial the compliment of writing a preface to his book on electricity. Franklin, long used to his friend's goodness, avowed he could scarcely conceive that a better man than Fothergill had ever lived. Recently, Fothergill and Franklin had engaged with Friend David Barclay in a prodigious effort to reconcile Britain and the American colonies. Their proposals had been conceived in equitable, statesmanlike spirit, addressed to calm and rational minds on both sides of the Atlantic. But few minds were calm and rational in 1775, and the well-meant effort had ended in failure. Dr. Franklin had set sail for Philadelphia in March, arriving there only a few days after George Logan had left for England.

Over the breakfast table Dr. Fothergill told George that he meant to have taken him into his own family but for the serious illness of his sister Ann, upon whom the care of the Harpur Street household fell. Since George needed a period of medical apprenticeship before he went to the University, Fothergill recommended him to Dr. R. C. Sims, a Quaker physician of Dunmow in Essex.[2]

Having seen a bit of London society, even though it was only the sober Quaker community, George was loath to leave it behind. He set out for Dunmow with no relish, as if bound on an exile. The little Essex village was a market town of some fifteen hundred souls. It was less than forty miles from London, but far enough to make him feel, when he arrived, that he was utterly isolated from the great world. 'It is a properer situation for an anchoret,' he grumbled, 'than a human being who has the least taste for a social life.'

Rustication, however, had to be accepted. For, as he wrote his brother philosophically, he was about to learn 'the first rudiments of the noblest profession on earth.' He made his financial arrangements with Dr. Sims — seventy pounds for a year's board and instruction [3] — and commenced his first steps in the art of healing. Dr. Sims was a dispensing physician; he set George to work at once mastering the *materia medica* and compounding prescriptions. Sometimes George accompanied the doctor on his rounds, absorbing fragments of that medical wisdom that comes only from the long experience of a practicing physician. But most of the time he applied himself to textbooks, determined to qualify for matriculation at Edinburgh, foremost center of medical learning in all the world.

By winter he was so full of his studies that they overflowed into the letters he wrote faithfully every month to Charles. He assisted Dr. Sims at a post-mortem on a local citizen killed in a brawl by a blow in the solar plexus. He studied Dr. Fothergill's account of a recent influenza epidemic, and sent his own observations up to the Doctor. He composed a technical explanation — in Latin, to impress Charles — of the proper procedure in blood-letting.

But even the most conscientious medical student, buried though he was in the Essex countryside, could not overlook the momentous political events transpiring at London and at home. Letters from Philadelphia told him of preparations for defense going forward there, 'the rich . . . removing out into the country,' cannon mounted to command the river approaches to the city, five or six new men-of-war fitting out, a hundred fire rafts building, 'several chevaux de frise sunk in suitable places' in the Delaware (these latter, his correspondent told him, had already proved their efficacy by wrecking a shallop and a brig owned by Philadelphians).[4]

His reactions are those of a loyal subject of the King. The sheriffs of London hold a meeting of freeholders at Mile-End to discuss the American war. The gathering is disorderly and ends to the 'disgrace and chagrin of the patriots and to the pleasantry and despicability of the nation.' The King addresses Parliament on the measures he proposes for putting down the rebellion. George copies out the monarch's words at length and adds a monitory note: 'Your own good sense will satisfy you what the Americans may expect next summer.' London newspapers publish letters, intercepted in the post, written by certain prominent ringleaders of the revolution. These documents, George reports, 'have opened the eyes of many in England, and been the greatest real disadvantage to America of anything whatever.'

Occasionally he allowed himself a holiday from his studies. In April, he strolled out to the site of Dunmow Priory, where in earlier days a flitch of bacon had been bestowed annually upon any married couple who had lived together for a year without quarreling. Another excursion took him to Colchester, famous for its Roman wall, its Norman castle, and its succulent oysters. But despite these interludes, he was glad when his year with Dr. Sims was up, and he could get on more directly with the business of becoming a physician.

In August 1776, he left Dunmow, and spent nearly a month in London, satisfying his appetite for social life after long famine. Then he set out on a two-months' tour of the west of England, with Edinburgh his ultimate destination. Everywhere he went he made notes on local agriculture — the fertile, chalky soil near Basingstoke, the fat, fleecy sheep in Hants, the neat enclosures in Wiltshire, the double plows used by the farmers around Worcester. Though medicine was his chosen career, George was a Logan of Stenton, never far in heart from the fields and woods of his home, never slow to study the art and science of farming.

Never slow to study the high fashion, either, the elegant world of tinsel and silk so new to a Quaker youth. Bath he pronounced 'one of the most superb and magnificent cities in the world.' He wandered around the fantastic spa, gazing at the elegant fops, the ladies in their sedan chairs, the elaborate mansions in the Queen's Square and the colonnaded Circus, mansions, he commented, in which 'magnificence, elegance, and convenience are united in the highest degree.' He went to the Pump Room, tasted the waters, and listened to the 'excellent band of music.' He looked into the King's and Queen's Baths, and found that 'the ladies and gentlemen go in promiscuously, not being distinguished in the water but by their headdresses, the gentlemen wearing their hats and the ladies their bonnets.' Of the efficacy of the waters he took a somewhat skeptical view. Perhaps they cured real ills and itches; but, he concluded, two thirds of those who flocked to the spa came simply 'to alleviate an unsurmountable itch for pleasure.'

From Bath he went to Bristol, on a visit of filial piety. Here at Bristol, his grandfather had first met William Penn; here his great-uncle William, the physician, had lived. Bristol was a city of the sea, full of meaning to any American. But Bristol was also a city of the slave trade, where new fortunes were rising even now from the traffic in human misery. George Logan was disappointed at the city's narrow, ill-paved, dirty streets, the 'incommodious' houses. 'The inhabitants,' he wrote with a touch of disdain, 'seem near an half century behind any of their neighbors in civility and good breeding, particularly among the lower class of people, who certainly measure their greatness and independency by their in- civility to strangers.'

Turning north, he passed through the neat, rolling fields of Gloucestershire, and revisited Worcester, the scene of his un- happy schooldays. Near Manchester he came upon the system of canals the Duke of Bridgewater, founder of British inland naviga- tion, had constructed to transport coal from his mines at Worsley to Manchester and Liverpool. Logan marveled at the ingenious aqueducts and tunnels. He admitted that the canals had been 'of the greatest advantage to the nation' but tempered his admiration of the Duke's enterprise with some dismay that a peer of the realm should dabble in trade, underselling his less fortunate neigh- bors.

Liverpool he found delightful. With its fine harbor facilities, he predicted, it would soon outstrip Bristol in commerce. At Preston his careful eye took in 'the greatest number of handsome, well-dressed women' he had seen in any town of its size in Eng- land. He was susceptible to other kinds of beauty too. He com- posed rapturous descriptions of the scenery in the Lake Country. The road from Windermere was 'the most romantic road you can imagine . . . between two ridges of mountains, from the tops of which you constantly see a number of small cataracts . . . which must look excessively grand after heavy rains.'

As November began, he arrived in Edinburgh, his goal ever since leaving Pennsylvania. The first thing to strike him as a weary, dusty traveler entering the city was the wretchedness of the inns, 'the chambers of which,' he complained, 'are dirty and comfortless and the beds very paltry.' The picturesque 'old town' of Edinburgh itself, with its narrow wynds and dark closes, he found inconvenient and malodorous, 'really worse than I had any idea of.' The general filth was occasioned by the scarcity of water, he learned, and the lack of privies. A city in which the inhabitants were not 'accommodated with *temples,*' in which there were no underground drains, seemed medieval to a Philadelphian. After a rain the streets were unspeakable. Writing to his brother, George could do justice to them only by quoting Swift's 'Description of a City Shower':

> Now from all parts the swelling kennels flow,
> And bear their trophies with them as they go:
> Filth of all hues and odors, seem to tell
> What street they sailed from by their sight and smell. . .
> Sweepings from butchers' stalls, dung, guts, and blood,
> Drowned puppies, stinking sprats, all drenched in mud,
> Dead cats and turnip-tops come tumbling down the flood.

He found lodging on the southside of Cowgate, near George Square, just outside the old city walls. Here he had a fine view of the sun-drenched, wind-swept meadows, where on Sundays one might meet some of the 'finest, genteelest women in the world,' seeking escape from the close confinement of the city.

It was a Periclean era in the Scottish capital. George found himself walking the same pavements with Adam Smith, David Hume, Lord Kames, William Robertson — the literary, philosophical, theological giants of the day. But brilliant as the city's literary constellations were, it was her medical luminaries that had drawn Logan to the Athens of the North. Alexander Monro *secundus,* whose former pupils already numbered in the thousands, Joseph Black, discoverer of 'fixed air' (carbon dioxide) and latent heat, William Cullen, the greatest medical teacher of the age — these men, George knew, had made Edinburgh what it was — 'the first university in Europe for medicine.'

The town was thronged with medical students, collected, as Benjamin Rush had observed a few years earlier, 'from several parts of the continent of Europe, as well as from every part of the British empire.' [5] In Logan's time came students from Lisbon and Rotterdam, from Antigua, Jamaica, and Barbados, from the American mainland, from England, Ireland, Scotland, and Wales.[6] George was the only Philadelphian there at the moment. This was unusual, for in the past quarter of a century a constant stream of young men from the Quaker City had flowed through the University. These men, returning home as physicians, were making Philadelphia the Edinburgh of America.[7]

Outwardly, like much of the rest of Edinburgh, George found the medical college unimpressive, 'a poor irregular pile of building.' But when he went inside to hear the professors give their introductory lectures — Cullen warm and engaging, Black judicious and instructive, Monro eloquent and learned [8] — his disappointment melted away. He knew he had come to the right place.

During his first year, George studied anatomy and surgery.[9] With three hundred other students he went daily to the anatomical theater to attend the lectures of Dr. Monro. The famous son of a famous father, Monro had been teaching anatomy at the University for eighteen years. His manner was dignified, his language forceful, his delivery emphatic. He was the orator of the Medical Faculty.[10] Unfortunately, George remarked, Monro possessed a large fortune. This had 'lulled his genius asleep.' He did little new or original work, and contented himself with repeating his lectures 'nearly verbatim as he did fifteen years ago.'

In physiology, George thought, Monro was unexcelled for 'perspicuity and strength of argument.' But when he came to the practical parts of anatomy and surgery, so indispensable to a physician, he was 'too great a philosopher to enter so minutely into his subject as the demonstrative part of it requires.' Moreover, cadavers for dissection were hard to come by in Edinburgh, owing to 'the prejudices of the Scotch.' Indeed, one of the Doctor's rivals declared that in Monro's class, 'unless there be a fortunate succession of bloody murders,' not three subjects were dissected in a year. 'On the remains of a subject fished up from the bottom of a tub of spirits, are demonstrated those delicate nerves which are to be avoided or divided in our operations; and these are demonstrated once at the distance of 100 feet!' [11]

The first year at Edinburgh passed swiftly. Every morning George went to the anatomical theater to hear Monro. Every afternoon he met with a group of his fellow students to compare notes and write out a full transcript of what the doctor had said. Each week he spent several evenings at meetings of the undergraduate societies. These societies, organized and conducted entirely by students, were an indispensable supplement to the formal medical training at Edinburgh. There were three of them — the Chirurgo-Medical, the Physico-Medical, and the Medical Society. George joined them all. At their weekly meetings, he wrote, the students discussed the 'doctrines and opinions of great men' — their teachers included — 'with diffidence and candor.' Some undergraduates professed to feel that time spent at the meetings was wasted, that 'few of the members understand the subjects on which they debate,' that 'the undigested matter they threw out tends more to perplex than to increase medical knowledge.' [12] Not so George Logan. He 'received as much improvement' from the student societies, he wrote his brother, 'as from any one professor.'

Near the end of his first year, he read a paper on dyspepsia before the Chirurgo-Medical Society. He ascribed the ailment to such causes as grief, anxiety, lack of exercise, and hard drinking. 'Dejection of spirits,' he wrote, 'is a symptom that requires the greatest attention from the humane practitioner, who, in this case, should employ the advantages he has received in a polite liberal education, in making rational remarks, which might soothe the dejected mind of the patient.' He prescribed exercise and fresh air. Proudly, he sent a copy of his paper to Charles, asked him to show it privately to Sally's husband, Thomas Fisher. Tom needed 'a little advice respecting [his] neglecting to use sufficient exercise.'

He followed his own prescription and found time in the midst of his studies for relaxation and exercise, for strolling about the old city and the romantic Scottish countryside. Tiring of his books one day, he climbed up to Edinburgh Castle, impregnably perched on its high rock. He pronounced it far more impressive 'for excellence and grandeur of situation' than any castle he had ever seen. On the other hand, Holyrood House struck him as 'miserably situated in a low damp place at the bottom of the High Street.' He drew a rough sketch of the palace for his brother and noted its curiosities — the state bed of Mary Queen of Scots, the bloodstains of her murdered secretary, David Rizzio, which obstinately resisted scrubbing, the portraits of scores of Scottish kings, which were 'nothing extraordinary.'

Not since he had left Stenton at the age of eight had George been so content with life. The dreams he had dreamed in John Reynell's counting room were all coming true. But toward the end of the spring term, he had a rude shock. He opened a letter from Stenton one day to read the melancholy news that William and Hannah Logan had both died during the winter. It was, he wrote his brother, 'an irreparable loss.' Suddenly he realized that he stood in a new relation to the world. At twenty-three he was the head of the family, the inheritor of Stenton. The responsibility of being a Logan came down on him with crushing force. 'The eyes of mankind,' he solemnly told Charles, 'are attentively engaged in observing whether, now left unrestrained, we give ourselves up to licentiousness and debauchery, or whether, influenced by the best of principles, we consecrate our time in rendering every possible service to our fellow creatures and our country.'

To settle his mind after this sudden blow, he went with another medical student for a five-day ramble into the countryside north and west of Edinburgh. At Kenmore on Loch Tay they were invited to a Highland wedding feast. The menfolk, George reported, soon became fuddled with whisky and fell to quarreling — though since they quarreled in Erse, he could not tell what it was about. George loved the Highlanders, relished their hospitality, their bravery, and their pride. Yet he could not help but see that their native character was fading away as the clans disintegrated. The chiefs, having lost their power, were seeking to uphold their dignity by raising rents to extortionate levels, making virtual slaves of their tenants. Highland men, George recorded, were too proud to work and left all the labor in the fields to the women — which was the reason, he concluded, that he saw no handsome girls in the Highlands.

Back in Edinburgh after his brief holiday, George applied himself to anatomy and surgery with a new determination to train himself for 'rendering every possible service' to his fellow creatures and his country. Monro's lectures gave him a solid theoretical grounding. But still he felt that he knew the human body only as a transparent ghost on Monro's charts or a gobbet of discolored flesh held up by the professor in the anatomical theater. Actual practice in dissecting was what he needed now. He went to Dr. Cullen for advice. Cullen was easily the greatest man in medicine, not merely in Edinburgh but in the whole world. But he was always ready to bestow a favor on an American, especially a protégé of Fothergill. He gave George a letter of introduction to his old friend Dr. William Hunter, who conducted a famous anatomy school in London.[13]

It was hot when George reached the capital early in September. Dr. Hunter advised him to wait for cooler weather before starting his work in the dissecting room, so George made a short excursion to Bristol. Friends in Bristol welcomed him. They remembered old Dr. William Logan, who had practiced medicine there for nearly half a century. Why should not young George plan to settle among them and take up the old doctor's practice? It was a flattering invitation and a tempting one. But George thought of Stenton and Philadelphia, of his responsibilities there, of his old schoolmates and friends. He told the Bristol people he was not ready for such a decision. After three days he went back to London to attend Dr. Hunter's Anatomy School in Great Windmill Street, just off Piccadilly Circus.

Dr. Hunter was a fine, courtly gentleman, generous and patient with his pupils.[14] He preferred to teach his art rather than practice it, he said — for 'the influence of a teacher extends itself to the whole nation and descends to posterity.' [15] Nevertheless, he still practiced as a man-midwife. For years he had been Physician Extraordinary to Queen Charlotte, having, as he put it, 'sole direction of Her Majesty's health as a child-bearing lady.' [16] His fame was at its peak when George came to his school. The Baskerville Press had just published his *Anatomy of the Gravid Uterus,* the great work on which he had spent thirty years.

Hunter provided an ample supply of cadavers for his pupils by claiming the corpses of felons and paupers. But he had to ask the students to be discreet, not to discuss their work with outsiders, 'especially with respect to dead bodies.' [17] In the foul-smelling anatomical rooms in Great Windmill Street, students spent hours every day bending over their cadavers, dissecting, making anatomical preparations, practicing operations, developing their manual skill, increasing their knowledge of the human body. In the afternoon they listened to Dr. Hunter's daily lecture. Then, to relax and drive the noxious vapors of the laboratory out of their heads, they went to Drury Lane or Covent Garden. The London theater was in the doldrums in the autumn of 1777. Garrick had just retired and no one had emerged to take his place. But even a routine London performance was a revelation to a young Quaker who had seen only the unpolished productions of the Philadelphia and Edinburgh stage.

Late in November, George was back in Edinburgh. He repeated Monro's course, listening with new understanding after his two months' work with scalpel and forceps. He also studied midwifery, botany and the 'Institutes' or theory of medicine, in addition to attending the clinical lectures at the Royal Infirmary. These courses were all given by lesser men on the faculty, competent men, he wrote Charles, but 'not so much esteemed' as Monro, Cullen, and Black.

Dr. James Gregory, who taught the 'Institutes,' was a brilliant, witty, irascible young man, whose poor health alone, George wrote, prevented him from shining as brightly as his elders on the faculty. Nevertheless, he was a character; he habitually came into the lecture room with a stout cane over his shoulder, and he never removed his hat. Dr. John Hope, who occupied the chair of botany, was allowed by the University to charge the students only two guineas instead of the three exacted by the others: 'yet such is his meanness,' George observed bitterly, 'that he will take three guineas not only the first but the second year if any gentleman should do him that honor to attend him' — as George himself was to do. The professor of midwifery was Dr. Thomas Young, who had inaugurated the teaching of obstetrics at the University twenty years before. His students had the benefit of practical instruction at the Lying-In Hospital on the upper floor of the Royal Infirmary.[18]

Outside the classroom George gave a great deal of time to the Medical Society. It was the oldest and most important of the student organizations. Six undergraduates had founded it in 1734. By Logan's time it was a flourishing institution. It had just built a new hall of its own, and was in the process of acquiring a royal charter. George had become a member, along with seven others, on 7 December 1776, a little more than a month after his arrival in Edinburgh.[19]

The Society met every Saturday evening at its new hall in Surgeon's Square. At every meeting someone was required to 'give in' an aphorism of Hippocrates and elaborate on it. ('Acute diseases come to a crisis in fourteen days,' it might be. Or, 'In summer, purge by preference upwards, in winter downwards.' Or again, 'If a woman be going to have a male child, she is of good complexion; if a female, of a bad complexion.') The debates were enlightening, George felt, and the Latin language was 'spoke with great fluency and ease.' (A more sophisticated contemporary, Sylas Neville, had a different view: 'Very little is generally said,' he wrote superciliously, 'and such Latin!') [20]

At every meeting someone presented a written answer to a query proposed at a previous session. These papers required careful preparation. They were circulated in advance among the officers and certain other members, whose responsibility it was to 'impugn' them. Logan was given the question 'What substances contain fixed air?' His conclusion was that 'there are few substances in nature which do not contain some proportion of it.' He could cite the great Dr. Joseph Priestley, who had actually measured the amounts of carbon dioxide in Madeira, six-year-old port, hock, Tokay, champagne, and cider.

A little later, in January 1778, George took his turn at presenting a 'case.' He diagnosed it as confluent smallpox, a particularly virulent form of the disease. He paraded his learning. The Greeks, he wrote, had known nothing of smallpox. It had been left for the Arab physicians Rhazes and Avicenna to recognize it, describe it accurately, and prescribe the proper cold regimen. Early European doctors had aggravated the malady, killing their patients with hot, stifling treatments. By the 'indefatigable industry and good judgment' of Thomas Sydenham the old plan had been revived and Helvetius, Friend, and Boerhaave had subsequently made 'several good observations on the nature and cure of the disease.' Still, he had to acknowledge, medicine was 'entirely ignorant' of the cause of smallpox. He recommended giving the patient Peruvian bark, putting him on 'a thin and cooling diet' of vegetables, fruit, and milk, and keeping him 'constantly exposed to a circulation of fresh air.' [21]

For a young man with a keen taste for a social life, Edinburgh was a paradise. Young ladies of family in the Scottish capital were 'perhaps the finest and most accomplished women in Europe' — so declared the worldly-wise young Quaker from Philadelphia. True, they were rather too fond of showing themselves in public places and in the streets, 'where their walk, looks, and negligence of behavior occasions most Londoners to take them for women of pleasure.' But perhaps there was some excuse for this forward conduct in the coldness and insensibility of the menfolk, 'who do not possess the least spark of gallantry and therefore require all the art the ladies are mistresses of to attract their attention.' George was beginning to shed Quaker strictness. He could remark without disapproval that 'a Scotch lady has no objection to a genteel *double entendre.*'

He could not, however, conceal his disgust for the crude, debauched habits of the Edinburgh men, who 'pay their devotions to Venus,' he wrote Charles, 'at some of the dirtiest brothels you can imagine.' Still, their boorishness had its advantages. At theaters, assemblies, and racecourses, Scottish men were so preoccupied with cards and bottle that University students had an open field. All one had to do at the assembly room was to make it known that one was a gentleman, and the reserve of young Scottish ladies soon melted.

The Edinburgh theater was wretched. So low was the taste of the townfolk that they were more pleased 'with the narrow limits of a Scotch song or a Scotch anecdote than with the most masterly piece of Italian music or finest character in Shakespeare.' George had seen a whole house rocking with laughter at the 'low and despicable character' of Sir Archy MacSarcasm in Charles Macklin's *Love à la Mode;* and a country dance or reel was universally preferred to the stately and decorous measures of the minuet. Most inexplicable of all was the devotion of the Scots — even men of seventy or eighty — to the game of golf. It was a strange pastime, he wrote, which consisted in 'the dexterity of driving a hard ball with the fewest number of strokes of a bat into a hole at a considerable distance over a rough common.'

One spring day George made a special pilgrimage to the ancient village of Restalrig on the Firth of Forth. There he saw the ruined castle of the Logans, from whom his own family claimed descent. The last Logan of Restalrig — 'ane godles, drunkin, and deboshit man,' according to a contemporary [22] — had been attainted of treason in 1609 for conspiring against King James. Nevertheless, there was pride in George's words as he wrote to Charles of the castle of 'your ancestor.'

During the summer vacation, he made an excursion into the northern Highlands. He crossed the Firth of Forth between Leith and Kinghorn, passing the bleak island of Inchkeith, formerly the place of banishment for all persons in Edinburgh afflicted with venereal disease. 'It is very fortunate,' observed the fledgling doctor to his brother, 'that no such law exists at present; otherwise the city would be nearly depopulated.' At Ury, seat of the Barclay family, he was warmly welcomed by Robert Barclay, great-grandson and namesake of Penn's friend, the Quaker theologian, and cousin of David Barclay of London. This Barclay was a great farmer. Though he wrote but little, his experiments were well known; and the other Scottish agriculturists called him 'our great master.' [23] He entertained George and his companion with generous hospitality, showed the young man from Stenton around his splendid estate, whose improvements, George averred, were 'equal to any in the neighborhood of London.' Passing by Culloden Moor, scene of the great Jacobite defeat of 1746, the young Pennsylvanian noted with a touch of nostalgia that its planting had 'almost the appearance of an American forest.'

The third was the crowning year at Edinburgh. George sat at the feet of two illustrious scientists and teachers, Dr. Joseph Black and Dr. William Cullen. Black, who occupied the chair of chemistry, was known all over the scientific world as the discoverer of 'fixed air,' or carbon dioxide. Since becoming Professor of Medicine and Chemistry at Edinburgh, he had restricted his private medical practice, abandoned original research, and concentrated upon teaching. He lectured in a low, fine voice, so clearly and distinctly that no one in his large class missed a word. His language was simple, succinct, and pure. Often he paused in the middle of a sentence, seeking the exact word, the lucid phrase. He illustrated his lectures with experiments.[24] Still, Logan had much the same feeling about Black's lectures that he had about Monro's — they were 'more calculated for the physician as a philosopher than as a practitioner.' It was Edinburgh's vice, this philosophizing tendency — and its great virtue. It gave the student a sense that all science was one, that law was continuous and pervasive in the physical universe.[25]

The celebrated Cullen was another philosopher in the guise of a physician. But above all else, he was a teacher, this tall, awkward, kindly man who had been on the Medical Faculty for twenty years. His American students all rhapsodized over him. Thomas Parke called him 'that shining oracle of physic,' and Benjamin Rush declared that he would not have missed his lectures for ten thousand pounds.[26] Cullen lectured sometimes as long as four hours a day, speaking rapidly and extemporaneously, drawing easily upon a capacious memory, laying out facts in orderly arrangement, holding his students' attention by the vivacity and force of his illustrations, the amazing ingenuity of his arguments.[27]

George Logan sat rapt at Cullen's lectures. Faithfully, he

memorized Cullen's classification of diseases under its four rubrics
— *pyrexiae,* or fevers, *neuroses,* or nervous diseases, *cachexiae,*
or maladies resulting from bad bodily habits, and *locales,* or local
ailments. Cullen was the great nosologist, the classifier of human
ills, the Linnaeus of medicine. But he not only classified, he also
systematized. Impatient with traditional trial-and-error medicine, he sought to discover the 'proximate causes' of all diseases,
and upon these 'to establish a more scientific and decided method
of cure.' For after all, he told his students, 'when many new facts
have been acquired, it becomes requisite that these should be incorporated into a system.' In developing his own system, he asserted, 'I flatter myself that I have avoided hypothesis, and what
have been called *theories.'* [28] George was not so certain about this
point. He was full of admiration for Cullen as a teacher, but he
refused to be swept off his feet. Unlike Rush and Parke, he was
not ready to accept the master's grand system without further
experience and study.

You know [he wrote to his brother] he has established a new theory of
medicine; but like all other great men, I am afraid he is too fond of this child
to make it of long continuance. As the Boerhavians accounted for every disease of the body from a vitiated state of the fluids, so, on the other hand, Dr.
Cullen refers them to a vitiated state of the nervous system. Both these
opinions have their merits and demerits: wherefore it is necessary for a
student to attend several universities, and not too early to form his opinion.

During his last year at Edinburgh, George was deeply involved
in the affairs of the Medical Society. On 27 January 1779, he was
chosen president, the first under the new royal charter, and the
first American ever elected to the office.[29] This honor, he later
told Charles, he prized more highly than the M.D. degree itself.

Like everyone else, the president was expected to read papers.
Conscious that all eyes would be upon him, George stayed up late
for nights preparing a long essay on gastritis. He seized this opportunity to develop some of the ideas he had put forward in his
earlier paper on dyspepsia. He was more sure of himself now,
bolder about challenging the authorities, freer in throwing out
original suggestions.

Gastritis was caused, he explained confidently, by 'a defect of vital principle in the stomach.' But what *was* the 'vital principle,' that mysterious immaterial force which sustained all life? No one knew. The great Cullen seemed to hint that it might be found in the nervous system. But George was skeptical. The snail, he pointed out, was equipped with an elaborate set of nerves, while the leech, so far as anyone could tell, had none at all. Yet no one would contend that the sluggish snail had more vitality than the tenacious leech. No, the 'vital principle' remained a mystery. The physician could only perceive its defect and treat conditions arising from its weakness.

If a patient were far gone with gastritis, Logan suggested, he might be given 'fixed air' — carbon dioxide — to lessen the pain in his stomach. 'Fixed air,' Professor Black's great discovery, had its uses in medicine, but it was no panacea; to suppose it was, 'or that it is the *vinculum nat[urae]*, as some of its advocates have fondly asserted,' was an opinion 'too ill grounded to require refutation.' [30] So much for the enthusiastic claims of Black's disciples.

Never had George been busier or happier than he was in the spring of 1779, his last few months in Edinburgh. Every week he presided over meetings of the Royal Medical Society. Every day he listened to the lectures of Black and Cullen. Every night he prepared for his final examinations and sweated over his thesis.

The final steps to the M.D. at Edinburgh extended over three months.[31] In March there was a preliminary examination, conducted privately at the house of one of the professors. It was designed to test the student's skill in Latin as well as his general knowledge of medicine. The next step was to submit a thesis to preliminary scrutiny and revision by a faculty member.

George's thesis was on poisons (*de Venenis*). As he sat down to frame his opening definition, he was grateful for the hours he had spent in Robert Proud's classroom perfecting his Latinity. '*Venenum,*' he wrote, '*est quicquid exigua copia in corpus receptum, corporive admotum ad vitae actiones aut delendas pertinet.*' (A poison is anything that, taken or forced into the body in small quantity, tends to hinder or destroy the vital forces.) There were

two kinds of poisonings, he continued: those that attacked the
fluids (as cantharides, arsenic) and those that affected the general
nervous system (snake venom, hydrophobia). For the former he
would prescribe the orthodox treatment — emetics and cathartics; for the latter, stimulants or sedatives, as required. The subject was confused, difficult. He mustered such authorities as he
could — Redi, Tozzi, Mead, Home, his own teacher Monro
secundus. He reported examining a drop of snake poison through
a microscope and finding it crystalline in form. Beyond this there
was little to be said. Logan's thesis was brief; it embodied no
startling conclusions. But it was a competent study, modest in its
claims, workmanlike in its construction, and Dr. Cullen endorsed
it with his *perlegi.*

Early in May Logan presented himself before the Faculty for
a rigorous public examination in anatomy, chemistry, *materia
medica,* practice, and theory. Bewigged and gowned, the examin-
ers sat in the library — Cullen and Black, Monro and Gregory,
surrounded by the lesser men. Each successive examination was
a solemn, awesome, memorable ceremony. Twelve days after his
first ordeal, he appeared before his masters again to explain and
illustrate an aphorism of Hippocrates and answer a question on
medicine. Another twelve days and he was standing once more
in the library, this time to discuss two case histories and answer
questions on them. Meanwhile, he was seeing his thesis through
the press, correcting proofs, composing a florid dedication to
David Barclay, his patron, and to the memory of James Logan,
his illustrious grandfather. The slim pamphlet finally came from
the University printer, and he had the satisfaction of seeing his
name — *Georgius Logan Pennsylvaniensis* — on the title page of
his first published work.[32]

Graduation day was 24 June 1779. Candidates for the medical
degree assembled in the Guard Hall to meet the Principal and the
professors. Then they trooped across to the Public Hall, where
their professors examined them, one by one, on their dissertations. It was little more than a formality, this public defense of the
thesis. As soon as it was over, the candidates withdrew, donned
doctors' gowns, and returned to sign the oath. (Logan, as a

Quaker, was allowed to sign a *sponsio* or affirmation.) Now came the crowning moment, when the Principal, William Robertson, celebrated throughout the Western world for his historical works, his theological prowess, and his classical style, stepped forward and, in the name of the University, bestowed upon them the degree of Doctor of Medicine.

It was late in the afternoon when Logan came back to his lodgings. In a glow of excitement, he sat down and wrote to Charles that he had just received 'the highest title . . . which this or any other university has in its gift.' He was now George Logan, M.D.

At the age of twenty-five, Dr. Logan was at last entitled to practice 'the noblest profession on earth.' But there was still much to learn in Europe. His medical training must be crowned by attendance at the anatomical lectures in Paris. His education as a gentleman would not be complete without the experience of the Grand Tour. And, though he did not know it when he left Edinburgh at the end of June, a new phase of his education — his political awakening — was about to commence.

He packed up his belongings, said farewell to his Edinburgh friends, and set out for London. He traveled in a wide circle, taking in Glasgow, Dublin, and Wales on the way. After a brief pause in London to see his friends, he crossed the Channel to Holland, spent the summer and autumn seeing Germany and Italy, and arrived in Paris in time to attend the anatomical lectures in the winter.[33]

Soon after arriving in Paris, George drove out to Passy to pay his respects to a distinguished fellow Philadelphian. Passy was the temporary home of Dr. Benjamin Franklin, Minister Plenipotentiary of the United States to the court of Louis XVI. In this 'neat village on high ground, half a mile from Paris,' the Doctor held his extraordinary court. Seventy-six years old, painfully afflicted with gout, dressed always in a plain brown coat, with a fur collar in cold weather, leaning on a crabtree stick and wearing his bifocal spectacles, he was waited on by the 'noblesse and learning' of Europe and surrounded by a bevy of adoring French ladies who doted on his simplicity and his homeliness.[34]

At once the old Philadelphian made the young man feel at home. George went out to Passy often to visit the wonderful old man, to bask in the mellow sunset glow of his wit and wisdom. He had the freedom of Franklin's study; frequently he took breakfast there and spent the morning in endless talk. They had much to talk about, the old sage and the young doctor, half a century his junior. Franklin had known old James Logan, George's grandfather, well, and had often been at Stenton discussing science, letters, and politics with him. With Logan's English friends, Dr. Fothergill and David Barclay, he had participated in a last-minute effort to stave off the rebellion of the colonies. He had once been in Scotland with Black and Cullen and Monro, and he remembered the visit as 'six months of the *densest* happiness' he had ever experienced.[35]

One of Franklin's visitors, while George was at Passy, was Dr. Jan Ingenhousz. This learned Dutchman, formerly court physician to the Empress Maria Theresa, was almost as versatile as his host. He worked in chemistry, electricity, botany, the physics of heat, and had made important contributions in each field. A young man fresh from Edinburgh found no lack of stimulating scientific conversation at Passy.[36]

But the one inescapable topic of conversation in the Franklin household was, naturally, politics. The war in America was dragging, in spite of a French alliance that the old Doctor had negotiated. New York was still in British hands, a recent attempt to retake Savannah had failed, the value of American currencies was plummeting, war weariness was overtaking the new nation. Franklin was tired too, plagued by gout and a steady flow of drafts from Philadelphia that strained his government's dubious credit. But he never lost faith in the ultimate success of the American cause, in the rights of man, the achievement of freedom.

A simple incident that occurred while George was in France made an indelible impression on his mind. At dinner with Franklin one day, he met an American named Adair who, hearing that his host was having trouble procuring Madeira, offered to send him a few dozen bottles from his own private stock. Adair and Logan drove back to Passy in the same coach that night; subsequently the two exchanged visits. One day, George called at Adair's lodgings and was told by a servant that his friend had disappeared mysteriously. Presently, it became known that he was confined by *lettre de cachet* in the Bastille on suspicion of having sent poisoned wine to the American minister. The charge was groundless. As soon as Franklin heard of it, he had the American released. In later years, Dr. Logan was wont to say that this incident had given him his first distaste for arbitrary power, his first glimmering of the 'blessings and benefits of a free constitution, where the rights of every individual are placed under the protection of the laws.' [37] It was his first lesson in the realities of politics.

In April 1780, Logan made his way to London. He bore letters from Franklin to Fothergill and Barclay, the two men to whom he had brought letters of introduction when he had landed in England nearly five years before.

He carried other letters too. He acted as courier for John Adams, who had recently arrived in France to open peace negotiations with Great Britain. At Adams' request he sought out Thomas Digges, a Maryland merchant and a secret agent for the United States. He delivered to Digges a copy of the new Constitution of Massachusetts, largely Adams' handiwork. The copy was defective, George wrote to Adams, 'that part respecting the upper house being lost.' Nevertheless, Digges had shown it to members of both houses of Parliament. They were 'much pleased with the liberal and just principles on which it was founded,' George reported. He also arranged for Adams to be supplied regularly with the political prints as they appeared in London.[38]

George Logan could not leave England without sending Franklin a note on the state of political opinion there. His language no longer bespoke the callow Toryism of his Dunmow days. He was an American patriot now. The Whig opposition was daily gaining strength, he wrote, and 'American affairs have an agreeable aspect.' He had just paid a visit to Franklin's friend, David Hartley. Hartley, he reported, was still working for peace, still persistently challenging the ministry on its American policy. 'America,' George concluded, 'has only to pursue the plan of conduct which she has commenced with so much reputation.' [39]

Having said his farewells to his two good friends, Fothergill in England and Franklin in France, Logan sailed for home. He had been away five years. His medical education, the object of his coming to Europe, was completed. His political education was just beginning.

*

III. MASTER OF STENTON

STENTON, when George Logan reached it in the fall of 1780, was a sad picture of desolation and decay. Windows in the great house were broken. The sheds and stables were empty and silent. Scarcely a cow or a pig was to be seen. Gardens and fields were choked with weeds. For four years, ever since William Logan's death, the estate had been masterless and neglected, while armies marched through it completing the destruction. From the old housekeeper, who had stayed in the mansion through the terror and the loneliness, from the tenant, who had tried with small success to keep the farm in production, from Charles and Uncle James, who had occasionally ridden out from the city to inspect the estate, young Dr. Logan pieced the story together.

In August of 1777, General Washington's forces, moving south from Jersey to meet Howe coming up from Chesapeake Bay, had marched down the Old York Road and bivouacked at Nicetown, a few miles away. Washington, with twenty staff officers and their servants, had taken up quarters overnight on 23 August at Stenton. They had bought a sheep from the tenant and dined on it. The General 'appeared extremely grave and thoughtful, and was very silent.' After dinner he had issued orders for the troops to be paraded through Philadelphia to encourage the fearful and rally the disaffected in the threatened city.[1]

A few weeks later, General Howe, having routed Washington at the Brandywine, had encamped the main body of his troops about a mile northwest of the Logan place. He too used the mansion as headquarters. From Stenton he had sent a force into Philadelphia under Cornwallis to occupy the city. From Stenton on 4 October he had directed the bloody battle that swirled all day around Judge Chew's house, two miles up the Germantown Road. People recalled Howe as 'a fine large man,' who looked remarkably like Washington. He had walked abroad 'in plain clothes in a very unassuming manner.' [2]

During the occupancy of two such gentlemen as Washington and Howe, the great house and farm had fared reasonably well. But after they left, no one could protect it from plunder and forage by detachments of both armies. It narrowly escaped burning, the fate that befell John Dickinson's nearby mansion, Fairhill. Orders had gone out from British headquarters in November 1777 to fire a number of houses along the Germantown Road in retaliation for damages inflicted by American raiding parties. Seventeen dwellings went up in flames that day.

Stenton was saved by the resourcefulness of the aged housekeeper. Two redcoats, torches in their hands, had hammered on the door, ordered her to remove her private belongings immediately. They had orders from Colonel Twistleton to burn the house, they said. They disappeared around the corner looking for straw to kindle the blaze. Just then, a British officer rode up the avenue of hemlocks, sabre in hand, looking for deserters. With a straight face the old woman told him she had just seen two of them going to the barn to hide in the straw. Off he spurred, shouting: 'Come out, you rascals, and run before me back to camp.' [3]

The ready wit of an old servant had prevented complete disaster. But in the next three years slow decay and casual marauders did their work, and the huge old mansion slumped into ugly ruin.

To be the principal inheritor of the great Logan estate, George found, was not to be a man of wealth. The mansion house was his, with the barn, stables, and two hundred acres of orchard, woodland, and meadow. There was a town lot in Philadelphia and scattered parcels of land in Bucks and Chester Counties and in New Jersey. Stenton itself — buildings and lands — was valued at £1600. But it would take money to repair the house and stables,

to put the fields back into cultivation, and he had little of that —
only 'piles of utterly depreciated paper currency.' Inflation was
rampant; the thousands of pounds in 'old paper money' that
Thomas Fisher, Sally's husband, turned over to him as executor
of William Logan's estate were worth no more than £125.[4] For
the moment, George could not even borrow money with his lands
as security. Sadly, he turned his back on the old mansion, took
quarters in Philadelphia, and commenced his medical practice.
Some day, with good fortune, he would be able to restore his patri-
mony, settle down in a Stenton nobly reconstructed. Meanwhile,
he must earn a living by his profession.

Still, he could not let the great house go unoccupied. The war
still dragged on at the south, and the news was bad. 'The British
arms,' he wrote to Dr. Franklin, 'are still sullied with the greatest
barbarity and cruelty.' Charleston had fallen, Cornwallis had put
Gates's militia to flight at Camden. Refugees from the Carolinas
were arriving in Philadelphia every week. Logan threw himself
into a work of mercy, 'procuring the means for the genteelest reception of those worthy few who have been banished from
Charleston.'[5]

Robert Morris, recently appointed Superintendent of Finance
in the new Confederation government, was organizing the relief
effort. Morris was the richest man in Philadelphia, the most
powerful individual in America. Logan, impressed by his energy
and his masterful manner, offered his services. Morris proposed
to raise funds for the refugees by a lottery. He knew that the
Quakers held a testimony against such schemes. Still, he hoped
somehow to tap their wealth, to enlist their well-known philanthropy. He made a special application to them for a loan at five
per cent interest, and encouraged Logan, as head of a prominent
Quaker family, to press the matter with them.

George visited all the leading Friends, hoping, he told Franklin,
to persuade them to 'do something worthy the profession they
make of universal charity to mankind.' He waited upon the elderly
John Reynell, his former master; he visited James Pemberton,
his father's old friend; he saw Nicholas Waln, Owen Jones, Samuel Emlen, Jr., all the 'weightiest' Friends in Philadelphia. They

all gave him the same answer. They felt the deepest sympathy for the Charleston exiles. But the 'sorrowful calamity' of war, of revolution had impoverished them. Harassed by confiscatory laws, persecuted as suspected Tories, burdened with the relief of their own poor, they had lost, they said, 'the capacity for the exercise of benevolence.' [6]

Logan was discouraged by their response, although he understood their plight. He too was hard pressed for ready money. But he had woodlots at Stenton and a great empty house to offer. He promptly set laborers to work cutting firewood and hauling it into the city for the poorer refugees. And he put the mansion at the service of the 'worthy few.'

Three aristocratic Southerners, the cream of South Carolina's patriotic gentry, accepted Logan's hospitality — Colonel Charles Cotesworth Pinckney, his younger brother Thomas Pinckney, and their brother-in-law Edward Rutledge. All three were on parole, awaiting exchange as prisoners of war. Tall, spare Thomas Pinckney was nursing a leg that had been shattered by a musket ball at Camden. The other two had been captured at the fall of Charleston. All three had distinguished Revolutionary careers behind them; Rutledge had signed the Declaration of Independence, the elder Pinckney had commanded a regiment at the sieges of Savannah and Charleston. With their families they numbered ten persons, a sizable company. But Stenton — even a dilapidated Stenton — could accommodate them all in reasonable comfort, even in a certain tattered elegance. For Logan it was a way of carrying on the family tradition of benevolence, of hospitality — at the same time serving the new republic. [7]

A Logan had duties to the republic of letters too, and George quickly shouldered them. In its little brick building on Sixth Street, the great Loganian Library, Grandfather's noble gift to the people of Philadelphia, was moldering away from disuse and neglect. Since William Logan's death no new books had been added, and the building had been closed to the public. Dust filtered in from the street, settled thick on the editions of Cicero, Sallust, and Menander, Tasso, Racine, and Milton, Boyle, Newton, and Huygens — all the rare and learned works that old James Logan had imported from Europe before George was born.

The young man had always been taught to revere his grand-father's 'great and memorable name,' a name that, as he had written to Charles from Edinburgh, had 'outlasted the short date of human life,' and would be 'transmitted down to posterity.' Now that he was Hereditary Librarian of the Loganian, he had a responsibility to see that it answered, even in a wartime Philadelphia, the purposes of its foundation.

He was shocked at the state of the library as he saw it in 1780, and set about at once to rehabilitate it. Only two of the Trustees, to whose care James Logan had originally committed the library, were living — George's Uncle James and Benjamin Franklin. Uncle James had inherited little taste for books, but George knew he could count on Franklin's interest in any project for the intellectual welfare of Philadelphia. He wrote to his new friend for advice.[8] It was just half a century since young Franklin himself and his tradesmen friends had first turned to James Logan for help in starting their library company. Franklin would not be likely to overlook the coincidence or to withhold his aid.

Philanthropy, generous hospitality, the encouragement of learning — these were the avocations of a gentleman. It was pleasant to act the gentleman, but Logan knew that he must face the urgent problem of making a living. And that, in Philadelphia in 1780, would not be easy. The city had never recovered from the British occupation. Provisions were scarce and dear, money was plentiful but valueless, business stood still, social life was demoralized. There was plenty of sickness, plenty of call for a physician's services, but little ability to pay his fees. It was a bad time for a young doctor to start a practice in Philadelphia.

For a while, one could live on the excitement, the mental stimulation that came from practicing 'the noblest profession on earth' in the Quaker city. For Philadelphia was America's Edinburgh, her doctors the ablest, most celebrated physicians in the New World. There was the venerable Dr. John Redman, a kindly old man who had been treating patients in Philadelphia before George was born. There was the vain and elegant Shippen, brilliant but quarrelsome, who taught anatomy, surgery, and midwifery at the University of Pennsylvania, and his colleague, Dr. Adam Kuhn, a lantern-jawed, dogmatic Pennsylvania Dutchman who had studied botany with Linnaeus. There was Dr. Benjamin Rush, only a few years older than Logan, but already near the head of the profession. And there were able men of Logan's own age — Tom Parke, who had been just ahead of him at the Friends Public School and later at Edinburgh, portly Dr. James Hutchinson, who had played an honorable part in the war, inoculating thousands of soldiers against smallpox at Valley Forge and fighting in the line as a volunteer when his medical services were not needed.

Perhaps there were too many doctors in the city. A Philadelphia doctor's life was rewarding in the intellectual and humanitarian senses, but hardly in the material. When he became discouraged, young Dr. Logan often thought of the Bristol Friends and of their invitation to him to settle and practice among them. He even made plans to go to Virginia and take a ship for England.[9] He had been happy in the British Isles, and, even though patriotic sentiments were awakening in him, he was not yet unreservedly, irrevocably an American. Still he stayed. The principal reason was Debby Norris.

Debby was a Quaker girl whom George had always known. He had seen her often at meeting, had taken her for granted. She had been only fourteen, an awkward schoolgirl in Anthony Benezet's classroom, when he had left Philadelphia. But now, at nineteen, she had flowered into a lovely, talented woman. Everyone admired her. 'For the united charms of mind and person,' wrote one of her school friends in her diary, 'I don't know such another.' [10] A visiting French nobleman, the Marquis de Barbé-Marbois, meeting her at tea, pronounced her 'beautiful as an angel.'

George had spent enough time in the assembly rooms of Edinburgh to develop a sophisticated eye for beauty in women. But, like the Marquis, he found Debby utterly captivating in her white Quaker cap and unpowdered hair, her simple gray satin gown. He was enchanted by her fresh complexion and soft features, her modest air, and her animated conversation. Behind her Quaker primness, Debby was something of a flirt. The Marquis had been charmed — and not a little surprised — when, all the seats in the room being occupied, Mademoiselle Norris had shyly invited him to sit with her in a chair obviously made for only one.[11]

With all her beauty, her elegance, her cultivated mind, Debby was a strict, 'consistent' Friend. People noticed that young Dr. Logan began to dress more plainly, to attend meeting more regularly than when he had first come back from Edinburgh and Paris. They noticed, too, how often he called at the great four-story brick mansion on Chestnut Street, near the State House, where Debby lived with her widowed mother. Debby had many suitors, but it was soon clear that George was the favorite.

The romance was a subject of gossip at Philadelphia tea tables, for everyone knew that a quiet Quaker feud had been going on between the Logans and the Norrises for thirty years. Debby's grandfather, Isaac Norris, had been an intimate friend of old James Logan, his associate in business, his ally in politics, and a fellow bibliophile. Debby's uncle, also named Isaac, had married George's Aunt Sarah. The coolness between the two families had started when old James Logan had brusquely refused to give his second daughter, Hannah, in marriage to Charles Norris, young Isaac's brother. Charles Norris had found another wife, and Debby was their daughter.[12]

All Philadelphia Quakerdom knew of the thirty-year estrangement. All Philadelphia Quakerdom turned out on 6 September 1781 to see the quarrel ended, the two houses reunited. On that day, the great brick meetinghouse on High Street was full of gray bonnets and broad-brimmed hats, murmurous with the rustle of satins, the suppressed whispers of children. Presently, a hush settled over the assembly. There was a period of silent worship. Then, at the head of the meeting, the two young people arose and took each other by the hand. The man was short, plainly clothed, handsome, easy and assured in his bearing. The girl was dressed in 'neatest elegance.' 'True tranquillity,' noted one of her friends, 'reigned throughout her countenance.'[13]

The young man spoke the familiar Quaker marriage formula:

'In the presence of the Lord and of this assembly, I, George Logan, take thee, Debby Norris, to be my wife, promising through the Lord's assistance to be unto thee a loving and faithful husband until death shall separate us.'

It was the girl's turn now. She spoke in a clear voice that everyone in the great meetinghouse could hear: 'In the presence of the Lord and of this assembly, I, Debby Norris, take thee, George Logan, to be my husband, promising through the Lord's assistance to be unto thee a loving and faithful wife until death shall separate us.' [14]

They sat down again, and the wedding certificate was brought. They signed it.

George Logan
Debby Logan

They were man and wife.

Silence settled down again, until the voice of a minister arose, offering a religious exhortation, a prayer for the couple's spiritual well-being. Silence again, then meeting 'broke,' and all the Friends crowded round to sign the certificate and offer their good wishes to the bride and groom. One of Debby's schoolmates went home to write to a friend: 'The doctor . . . must be entirely insensible to every delicate and refined sentiment if he does not feel the most tender attachment for her; she is indeed a lovely girl.' [15]

Not many months after his marriage Dr. Logan came to an important decision. He decided to abandon medicine in order to move out to Stenton and take up the life of a farmer. Not that he was unsuccessful as a doctor; on the contrary, he was finding himself 'as busy as generally falls to the lot of young practitioners.' [16] But Debby was great with child in the summer of 1783, and the prospect of supporting a family in a city still plagued by inflation was discouraging. At Stenton there would be no need to worry about fees. He could draw on the wealth of his broad fields, his lush meadows, his fruitful orchards. All this belonged to him as a Logan, and he had come to realize that he belonged to Stenton.

Even during his Edinburgh years, he had felt the strong pull of country life, especially when he had visited the Scottish estates of Lord Kames and Robert Barclay, had inspected their improvements, seen how the 'new husbandry' that they practiced was remaking British agriculture. Stenton was his now; the lovely, ravaged mansion, the wasted fields, the unproducing soil all called for their master. George could resist no longer. The change would mean giving up medicine, giving up the chance to take his place beside Shippen and Rush in Philadelphia's medical galaxy. But the farmer's calling was older than the physician's — older and just as noble, just as ennobling. At Stenton, Logan told himself, he could put his scientific training to use for the benefit of his countrymen as fully and as effectively as by prescribing pills and setting broken legs in the city.

For Debby, the change would be rather a wrench. Stenton was all of six miles from Chestnut Street, and the road between was one of the worst in America — muddy, rutted, thronging with traffic. Debby loved the mild pleasures of Philadelphia Quaker society — the round of teas, the literary conversations, the skating parties, the coming and going of Friends at Yearly Meeting time. Stenton would be a kind of exile from all that. But her friends had already noticed an alteration in Debby. 'It seems,' wrote one, 'she is perfectly domestic, stays much at home, and employs her mind in the useful study of family affairs, contrary to my expectations.' [17] Debby would miss Philadelphia, but she was prepared for the responsibility of being mistress of Stenton.

There were endless labors awaiting them at the old place. The mansion must be restored, refurnished. The gardens must be won back from a wilderness of weeds. Sheds and stables must be rebuilt, the millrace reconstructed and the mill put into working order, fences mended, orchards pruned, fields ploughed and made ready for cultivation. While Dr. Logan worked out-of-doors supervising the farm hands, Debby saw to the cleaning and refurbishing of the great house. She found little time to pine for the social joys of Philadelphia.

The hard work bore fruit. The mansion began to recover its old air of comfort and simple elegance. The fields grew green with clover, golden with wheat. The stables and barnyard teemed with life. 'In a little time,' Debby recalled later, 'the improved state of [the] farm attracted general notice.' [18] Visitors who had seen the estate in ruins were amazed at the transformation: 'the place has undergone a great alteration since first I knew it,' wrote Susanna Dillwyn; ' 'tis one of the sweetest places I know in this country.' [19]

Dr. Logan rounded out his holdings, restoring the estate to its original size by buying the parcels of land that had gone to Charles and Sally. Charles had married and gone to Virginia to live on his wife's plantation. Sally's husband, Thomas Fisher, was a merchant in Philadelphia; they kept only a few acres for a summer house. Now Stenton was a unit again.

The farm stretched from Fisher's Lane on the north to Nicetown Lane on the south, from the Germantown Road on the east to the Old York Road on the west — a huge, rolling, barony of four hundred acres, surrounded by busy thoroughfares.[20] Wingohocking Creek bisected it, flowing placidly through the meadows, turning the great stones in the mill. Outside the gates, heavy wagons lumbered by, carrying produce to town. Drovers urged their noisy herds of cattle and swine to market. Stagecoaches dashed along the Old York Road, bound for Philadelphia, Trenton, New York. Stenton was one again, but it was no longer the quiet place it had been in James Logan's day, or even in William's. It seemed more like a spot on a travel map, a way station in restless America.

There was plenty of activity within the gates too, as the farm came back to life. Debby was constantly busy with household tasks until November 1783, when her first child, a son, was born. She returned to Philadelphia, to her mother's house, for her lying-in, but soon she was back at Stenton with her baby, whom she had named Albanus. If she had been busy before, she was busier than ever now. Aside from caring for the baby, she wrote to a friend, there was always 'homespun work to do . . . linseys and clothes to make, pickles and preserves to attend to.' [21]

It was Dr. Logan's dream to make the farm self-sufficient, an industrial as well as an agricultural unit. Household manufacturing with him was an article of the true republican faith, a moral and political duty. It distressed him to see American women, now that the war was over, deserting their spinning wheels and looms to buy the cheap British textiles that were flooding the market. With Governor Livingston of New Jersey he was ready to cry: 'To your homespun, my fellow citizens. Have the patriotism to disappoint both Gaul and Albion in their arts to drain your every copper for their trifles and baubles.' [22]

Fortunately, Debby fell in with her husband's enthusiasm for household manufactures — at least to the extent of outfitting him with clothes of her own making. The sociability connected with domestic industry pleased her — 'the agreeable interchange of visits' with other farmers' wives, 'the beneficial emulation, and the harmless pride with which we exhibited specimens of our industry and good management to each other.' [23] Dr. Logan preached unceasingly what his wife practiced. Ladies who visited Stenton were likely to be treated to a homily calculated to inspire them with the 'laudable ambition of spinning their own clothes.' That was Susanna Dillwyn's experience when she came to visit Debby. The doctor, she reported, had recently attended a wedding, attired all in homespun 'except the bit of cambric which ruffled his shirt.' Debby herself, she noted, did not take to these patriotic austerities — 'she was clad like other people.' [24]

Logan's faith in the virtues of homespun extended to the product of the 'ingenious mechanic,' who spun yarn and wove cloth 'in his own shop, for his own emolument.' [25] Those who were not as fortunate as he, who did not have a clever wife to spin and weave for them, should at least, he thought, patronize local handicraftsmen rather than buy imported textiles. He encouraged Debby to furnish employment to their poorer neighbors by giving out flax and wool to be spun into yarn, and he looked kindly upon the weavers and other independent artisans of Germantown. To propagate this gospel, he needed a pulpit and a congregation, so he formed the Germantown Society for Promoting Domestic Manufactures. He was president and leading spirit of the organization, and the principal author of its constitution, which bound each member to appear at the annual meeting in May 'clothed in the manufactures of his country, if not inconvenient to himself.' [26]

In the evenings, while Debby worked at her spinning wheel, Dr. Logan studied the new English farming methods — studied them as intently as he had studied medicine, eager to put science at the service of human welfare. He spent hours in his library with the books of Arthur Young, 'Turnip' Townshend, Lord Kames, and William Marshall — men who were transforming the British countryside, introducing new crops, eliminating wasteful methods of cultivation, doubling, tripling the yields of ancient, worn-out farms. He began to dream of bringing these innovations to America, adapting them to local conditions, discovering new ways of making agriculture more efficient, more productive.

His father had dreamed that dream before him. When George was only a baby, William Logan had read the English writers on country matters. He had been full of admiration for Tull and Bradley and Miller. Still, he had felt (as he wrote to Jared Eliot, the Connecticut agriculturist) that English methods did not 'altogether agree with our climate.' So, as a result, he had carried on experiments of his own at Stenton.[27]

George Logan resolved to make his father's dream come true. With Stenton as his laboratory, he would domesticate the English reforms, Americanize them, appropriate them for the benefit of his own countrymen. Agriculture in the middle states needed improvement; of that there was no doubt. True, there were a few enlightened gentleman farmers in the neighborhood of Philadelphia who, like himself, had read the English writers and were using English methods. There were the neat, industrious Germans in the hinterland, whose great barns, tidy farmyards, and fat fields spoke of sound farming practices brought over from the Old World. But by and large, as he traveled about through Pennsylvania and New Jersey, Logan saw farmers using the inefficient methods of their grandfathers, wearing out the soil, neglecting their livestock, wasting precious manure, letting their stables and fences fall into disrepair. The very fertility of the soil, its prodigal bounty, was a constant temptation to improvidence. Logan could only agree with a late anonymous writer who had observed that the farmers of the middle states were 'the greatest slovens in Christendom.' [28]

That same writer — some thought it was Arthur Young — had thrown out a challenging suggestion to the 'gentlemen of Philadelphia and its neighborhood who are lovers of agriculture.' Why should they not 'form themselves into a society,' he had asked, hold monthly meetings, offer bounties and premiums for improvements in husbandry? Within a few years, such a body could 'alter the face of things . . . introduce a better system of rural economy and be . . . of infinite service to their country.' [29]

Since 1775, when that suggestion had been made, the 'gentlemen of Philadelphia' had had their minds fixed on more pressing matters — on winning a war and establishing independence. But peace had come now and independence was a fact. The improvement of American farming took on a new aspect, a new urgency. Patriotism demanded that Americans look to their agriculture, that they make their farms the equal of British farms — and common sense dictated that they do this by appropriating and improving British methods.

Oddly, it was a Marylander, John Beale Bordley, who issued the call to the gentlemen of Philadelphia. A lawyer and provincial politician before the Revolution, Bordley was now a gentleman farmer, living on his model farm at Wye Island on the Eastern Shore. He had just published a little pamphlet on crop rotation, showing how the 'Norfolk system,' celebrated by Arthur Young, could be adapted to Maryland.[30] The apathy of Eastern-Shore farmers discouraged him. He looked to Philadelphia, to 'men of property and education, not tied down by professional engagements or local prejudice,' for support in his campaign for better farming.[31]

Bordley invited twenty-three gentlemen to dine with him at a Philadelphia tavern on 11 February 1785. Logan was among the guests. He found himself in a distinguished company — the intellectual and social elite of the Quaker city. Dr. Rush was there, slender, well-dressed, self-assured, interested in every movement for the good of the city and of mankind. So was Dr. Kuhn with his guttural accent, his pompous manner, his gold snuffbox, and gold-headed cane. The leaders of the Philadelphia bar were there — jovial Richard Peters, who spiced his conversation with outrageous puns, James Wilson, who was occupying his great legal mind these days with land speculations. But the majority of Bordley's guests were businessmen — merchants, bankers, land speculators like Robert Morris, his partner, Thomas Willing, Samuel Powel, Henry Hill, George Clymer.[32] Some of these men of wealth maintained country houses outside the city, where they played at being farmers. Except for Bordley himself, Logan, the youngest of the group, was the only man who devoted his whole time to farming.

The gentleman sat down to a good dinner. Afterward, over the wine glasses, Bordley broached his plan for a society dedicated to the improvement of husbandry 'within the states of America.' Pleasantly replete and glowing with wine, the guests responded with enthusiasm. They set 8 March 1785 as the date for the first formal meeting of the Philadelphia Society for Promoting Agriculture.

Meetings were held weekly at first at Patrick Byrne's tavern, 'The Sign of the Cock,' on Front Street. Later, they became monthly and were held at Carpenter's Hall. At the second meeting, it was decided that the Society should publish selected 'memoirs and observations' on agricultural topics, and that it should offer annual prizes for original essays and accounts of actual experiments.[33] New members were admitted nearly every month — men such as Dr. John Morgan, the tired, bitter, prematurely aged man who had founded the medical school at the College of Philadelphia; General Thomas Mifflin, late president of the Continental Congress; Timothy Pickering from Massachusetts, another Revolutionary veteran, who was planning to settle as a farmer on the wild lands west of the Susquehanna; John Dickinson, Debby's cousin, just now President of Pennsylvania.

Dr. Logan was a regular attender, hopeful of finding support for his ideas on reform. In January 1786, he was appointed to a committee to discuss a proposal of great interest to him — a plan to send for a 'skilful English farmer, acquainted with the best improved modes of husbandry in England.' The Society would settle this Englishman on a plot of land near Philadelphia and encourage him to carry on experiments to determine 'the practicability and usefulness of those modes' in Pennsylvania.³⁴ Logan favored the scheme; he was eager to learn all he could about the latest innovations in English farming. But the Society had no funds to support such a project, and it came to nothing.

This was discouraging, but Logan had his own plans. He would make Stenton a model farm. He would carry on experiments there, practice the English mode of agriculture in full view of every traveler along the Germantown Road and the Old York Road. Townshend of Raynham, Bakewell of Dishley, Barclay of Ury — these men, by their example and their writing, had pioneered the reform of British agriculture. Why should not Logan of Stenton play a similar role in America?

Late in the summer of 1785, after the harvest was in, Logan made a trip to New England to study the practice of agriculture and the state of society there. Debby, left behind with little Albanus, found the great house suddenly cheerless and lonely. One night she wrote disconsolately to her brother, 'it was extremely dark — it rained and the wind blew high; I could not sleep for a great while for the apprehensions it raised in my mind. I imagined the worst that could befall me and wept at the idea.' She missed her girlhood chums, almost regretted moving from the city. 'Society,' she knew, was 'the best cordial for low spirits.' A feeling of self-pity came over her, and she complained that people in Philadelphia had forgotten her face — 'not that it is handsome,' she added quickly; 'it has lost all pretensions of that distinction, if it ever possessed them.'

She whiled away the time until the Doctor's return by reading *The Princess of Cleves,* Madame de La Fayette's interminable tale of the French court in the days of Mary Stuart. Little Albanus, not yet two, did his best to keep her spirits up: 'He is a most lovely boy,' she wrote fondly, 'quite of the equestrian order,

for he makes everything serve for a horse, and rides about continually.' [35] Still, she missed her husband badly and longed for
his return.

Meanwhile, Logan was spending several days on Nantucket
Island. Accustomed to Philadelphia's neat gridwork of streets,
he found the houses 'strangely jumbled together in the most irregular manner.' He noted the decline of the whale fishery, and
attributed it to the loss of the English market since the Revolution. The most enterprising inhabitants, he found, were leaving
the island. Some were going to Nova Scotia to resume their whal-
ing as British subjects, others to upper New York state, to the new
town of Hudson, still others to North Carolina to become farmers. The island was still redolent of whale oil and Quaker piety,
but its great days, he thought, were over.

At Dartmouth on the mainland, the Reverend Samuel West
told him about Dighton Rock and its mysterious hieroglyphical
scratches. President Ezra Stiles of Yale, said Mr. West, was convinced that they were made in ancient times by westward-sailing
Phoenicians. Skeptical, Doctor Logan paid a visit to the rock himself and sketched the characters. They were nothing but 'the
scrawl of some Indians,' he concluded, for 'the figures are made
after their rude manner and the woman appears to have a child at
her back, a method of carrying children known to no European
nation.'

He inquired about the constitution of Massachusetts. He knew
it as an instrument on paper, for he had discussed it with its principal author, John Adams, in France. But how was it working in
actual practice? All the reports he heard were favorable. John
Adams seemed to have given his state 'the best form of government of any in the union.' Pennsylvania's elaborate constitution,
with its twelve-headed executive, its single-chamber Assembly,
its cumbersome Council of Censors, suffered, Logan thought, by
comparison.

On the way to Providence, Rhode Island, Logan was struck, as
his father had been thirty years before, by the poverty of New
England's stony soil, so different from the rich loam of Stenton.
Trade at Providence was thriving, he found, but Newport, 'once

the pride and glory of the state,' was 'verging fast to ruin.' 'With all their mock virtue and regard for the liberties of mankind,' the merchants of this Quaker town had just fitted out several vessels for the slave trade. 'How different,' he observed, 'the employ of the honest Quakers of Nantucket.' [36]

Late in September, Dr. Logan cut short his travels and hurried back to Pennsylvania. The annual elections for the state Assembly would take place early in October, and Logan's name stood on the ballot. The people of Philadelphia County could not forget how old James Logan had dominated Pennsylvania politics for half a century as personal representative of William Penn and defender of his interests. They recalled how his son had sat on the Provincial Council for twenty-five years, the last symbol of Penn's 'holy experiment.' For a Logan of Stenton, public office was almost a birthright. Young George Logan, they told themselves, had shown himself a good farmer, an educated gentleman, a benevolent, public-spirited citizen. Why should he not represent them at the State House? On 11 October 1785 they elected him to the legislature on the Republican, or conservative, ticket.

*

---

iv. FARMER in POLITICS

THERE was an unusual stir in the streets of Philadelphia on 29 October 1785, a holiday feeling among the people. George Logan was aware of it as soon as he drove out the Stenton gate that morning and started down the Germantown Road, past Fairhill Meeting, past the Rising Sun Tavern. Throngs of country people were heading for the city, dressed in their Sunday best. Logan drove along Front Street, turned up Chestnut, the crowd becoming denser as he passed the Norris mansion, Debby's old home, and approached the imposing brick State House with its high cupola. He made his way through the press of people, entered the building, and took his seat in the Assembly Chamber, the room where, ten years before, the Continental Congress had declared American independence.

Promptly at eleven o'clock, the doors opened and the twelve members of the Supreme Executive Council trooped in. At their head, leaning on a colleague's arm, was old Dr. Franklin. Full of years and honors, he had come back to Philadelphia from France barely a month before, hoping to live out his few remaining years in tranquillity. But his fellow Pennsylvanians would give him no rest. ('They have eaten my flesh,' he complained mildly, 'and seem resolved now to pick my bones.' [1]) Philadelphia had elected him to the Council as the only man who could command the respect and support of radicals and conservatives alike. Now the Council and Assembly, voting jointly, proceeded to make him President of Pennsylvania. Only one vote was cast against him.

The House adjourned, and Logan, with the other members, went outside to form a procession to the Court House, where, according to tradition, the election would be proclaimed. It was an imposing little parade. First in line were the constables with their staves, then the sheriffs with their wands. Next marched the Judges and the public officers — the Prothonotaries, the Marshal of the Admiralty, the Wardens of the Port of Philadelphia, the Collector of Customs, the Naval Officer, the Secretary of the Land Office, the Master of the Rolls and Register of Wills. Then, hobbling along on the arm of Vice-President Charles Biddle, came President Franklin, corpulent, stricken in years, racked by gout and stone. Then the other Councilors, 'two and two,' followed by the Sergeant-at-Arms with the mace, the Speaker of the Assembly, General Thomas Mifflin, and all the members of the legislature in double file, Logan walking with the rest. The Provost and Faculty of the University of Pennsylvania in their gowns, the militia officers in their uniforms, added touches of color. A miscellaneous rout of citizens brought up the rear.

The little procession moved along Fifth Street, turned down High (or Market Street, as people were beginning to call it). Mechanics, artisans, farmers with their wives and children, lined the streets and filled the Court House Square. Balconies and upper-story windows were crowded with well-dressed ladies and portly gentlemen. Everyone was out to see the parade, for Dr. Franklin was Philadelphia's most distinguished figure and one of the first citizens of the world.

From the Court House balcony came the cry, 'Silence, under pain of imprisonment.' It was the High Sheriff with his long wand. The crowd grew quiet. In a loud voice, Samuel Bryan, Clerk of the Assembly, proclaimed 'His Excellency Benjamin Franklin, Esquire, President of the Supreme Executive Council of the Commonwealth of Pennsylvania, Captain-General and Commander in Chief in and over the same.' Cannons roared, the bells of Christ Church, St. Peter's, and Gloria Dei rang out. Small boys set off squibs, and the people 'expressed their satisfaction by repeated shouts.' The ceremony over, members of the procession straggled back to the State House. Logan and the other Assemblymen and Councilors offered their congratulations to the new President. It was a taxing ordeal for an old man. Franklin confessed himself 'very much rejoiced' when he could finally sit down and rest in his own house across the street.[2]

George Logan had been a member of the Assembly just two days when he took part in this little pageant. The legislature had barely organized itself, but already one could forecast the character of the coming session. The day before its two factions had united on Franklin as President, they had divided sharply over the choice of Speaker. Logan's party, the Republicans, had put up George Clymer, a prosperous Philadelphia merchant with a history of stout patriotism and devoted public service during the Revolution. The opposing party — the Constitutionalists — had supported General Mifflin. His Revolutionary record was not, perhaps, impeccable, but he was a great favorite with the radicals of the back country. Logan knew both candidates, saw them often at meetings of the Agricultural Society. As a Republican he had voted for Clymer. The speakership had gone to Mifflin, but the vote had been close — thirty-three to twenty-nine. The parties were almost evenly balanced, radical Constitutionalists and conservative Republicans dividing the house between them. Clearly, neither group would have its unobstructed way in this session.[3]

Nevertheless, leaders of Logan's party were confident. They sensed that the spirit of the time, the mood of the citizenry, was with them. The war was over; officially it had been over for two years, actually for four. People yearned for the fruits of peace — stability, prosperity, a respite from strenuous exertions, austerities, and democratic experiments. The work of the radicals had no doubt been necessary; they had overthrown the old provincial order, written a new, democratic state constitution, and kept the spirit of revolt alive through desperate years. But surely the time for revolutionary ardor was past. The Constitution of 1776 was showing serious flaws, moreover; it was too 'popular,' it opened the way to mob rule, to irresponsible attacks on property, to reckless finance. It was time to revise it, time to curb the excesses of democracy and give the government back to men of substance, education, and sound financial views. This was the mood of 1785, and it gave the Republican leaders grounds for confidence.

True, the Constitutionalists had come back into power briefly the previous year, and had shown themselves still fertile in mischief. They had set the printing presses rolling, had struck off a hundred and fifty thousand pounds in paper money. Powerful men such as Robert Morris and Thomas Willing had publicly opposed this inflationary measure. As officials of the Bank of North America, they had refused to accept the bills. The radicals had promptly declared war on the Bank and sworn to destroy it. This monopoly, this 'enormous engine of power,' they had cried, was dangerous to public safety, destructive of republican equality. Its charter must be revoked. James Wilson, defending the Bank with vigor and superb ability, had pointed out that, since Congress had chartered the institution in the first place, the Pennsylvania Assembly was powerless to touch it. The radicals had brushed this argument aside. 'We are not bound by any terms made by Congress,' Jonathan Dickinson Sergeant, the radical Attorney-General, had shouted. 'Congress are our creatures.' The blow, when it fell, had been quick and deadly. On 13 September 1785, just a few weeks before the new election, the Assembly had annulled the Bank's charter.[4]

But the radicals had gone too far. The Republicans, having swept Philadelphia and the eastern counties in the October elections, were strong enough now to challenge them on nearly equal terms. As George Logan looked about him in the Assembly Chamber, his eyes rested on some of the ablest, most substantial men in Pennsylvania. There sat Robert Morris, founder of the Bank of North America and its heaviest stockholder, no longer Superintendent of Finance but involved in vast financial operations of his own. There sat George Clymer, Morris's close associate, and Irish-born Thomas FitzSimons, wealthy merchant and Director of the Bank. Chester County had sent a solid delegation of Republicans, led by General Anthony Wayne, whose handsome aquiline features could not conceal the contempt he felt for the radicals. Their imbecile Constitution, he had said, was 'not worth defending.'[5]

With men of this caliber upholding their cause, Republicans might well be confident. But the radicals had their formidable spokesmen too, and Logan came to know them all — tough, rowdy debaters, shrewd parliamentarians, Scots-Irish frontiersmen suckled on Calvin and the Bible, weaned on whisky and Indian-fighting. Robert Whitehill of Cumberland, John Smilie of Fayette, and William Findley of Westmoreland were their great champions. General Mifflin, the Speaker, was one of their men too. Accustomed to command, he presided over the Assembly like a martinet, maintaining rigid order and decorum, permitting no whispering or moving about while the house was in session. Even General Wayne had to obey.[6]

The Republicans did not wait long to reopen the Bank question. Letters appeared in the newspapers defending the Bank of North America, demanding its recharter. Some of the letters were signed 'Common Sense' — a pseudonym that stirred memories of another struggle, only ten years behind. If Tom Paine — for everyone knew the letters were his — was on the side of the Bank, it could hardly be the dangerous monster, the undemocratic monopoly that its opponents pictured.[7] Franklin too was known to be on the Bank's side. Petitions with hundreds of signatures flooded in, attacking the late Assembly's high-handed action in revoking the charter. A committee dominated by Republicans, with George Clymer as its chairman, looked into the record of the previous session; 'precipitancy, prejudice, and partiality' was its verdict.

The issue was before the house once more. Grimly, the radicals prepared their position. Smilie, Whitehill, Findley (all inveterately suspicious of all things Philadelphian) were resolved that the colossus on Chestnut Street that they had once brought down should not rise again. But the Bank had able advocates in this Assembly — well-dressed, well-heeled Philadelphia gentlemen, officers and stockholders in the institution, eager to see it operating again under a Pennsylvania charter.

Logan was disinterested. He had bought three shares of Bank stock in 1784 but had sold out soon after. He was prepared to listen to the arguments on both sides and make up his mind 'according as he should be convinced.'[8]

The debate commenced late in March 1786. Philadelphians of all classes crowded into the galleries to listen. 'No subject of debate that has been agitated before the legislature of Pennsylvania,' reported Tom Paine, 'ever drew such crowded audiences as attended the House during the four days the debate lasted.' [9] The westerners, anxious to bring the matter to a quick vote, insisted on short adjournments. 'They scarcely allow us time,' complained Morris, 'to take a comfortable dinner and glass of wine, before we are obliged to return to the charge.' [10]

Logan listened intently as the Constitutionalists took the offensive. The Bank, they charged, was oppressive and rapacious, it withdrew specie from circulation, locked it up in the vaults on Chestnut Street, made it difficult for farmers to borrow money. The Republicans counterattacked: the Bank, they maintained, actually increased the amount of money in circulation by paying out its profits in dividends; moreover, it made available for loans funds that would otherwise be kept in merchants' chests and cash drawers. But the Bank was irresponsible, retorted the westerners, it was autocratic, a closed corporation of wealthy men, an entity inconsistent with republican institutions. It could only end by creating a schism, a sectional and class division in the state. 'Like Hamburgh and Dantzick,' they insisted, Philadelphia would not only 'promote monopolies, but have its foundation placed in the principles of monopoly and aristocracy.' [11]

The debate soon descended to personalities. Smilie branded Paine as an 'unprincipled author, who lets out his pen for hire.' Morris, who only a little while before had accused Findley of unethical land-jobbing, called for 'more delicacy' in mentioning individuals. His friend Clymer reminded the house of an earlier argument by Findley: that though the repeal of the charter might have been overly hasty, the end (defeat of the Bank) justified the means. This doctrine, said Clymer, had been laid to the Jesuits. 'But I find there may be Jesuits out of the Roman Church.' Then with a shrewd thrust at his Calvinist opponents: 'It is not taught by any Presbyterian synod that I know of.' But the westerners were quick at the riposte too. Morris complained that not even an angel from heaven could make a westerner see reason. Whereupon

Whitehill remarked that if an angel should argue as Morris had done, 'I should regard him as a fallen angel.' [12]

In the midst of this undignified wrangling, George Logan stood up in his place. He was sorry, he said, 'to see that the gentlemen opposed to the bank, instead of answering the arguments made use of on the other side, had recourse to personalities.' The opponents of recharter, he believed, had not made good their charges against the Bank. Especially, they had misrepresented its effects on the farmers' welfare. There were, he said, 'two modes by which the interests of agriculture could be promoted; by a loan office, and by the bank.' The loan office was already in existence. Established by the previous Assembly in response to clamors from the west, it was authorized to expand the currency by issuing fifty thousand pounds in bills of credit. Logan approved this measure. 'By enabling the farmer to borrow money for the improvement and cultivation of his lands, [it] greatly advanced his interests.' But the Bank was also useful to the country people. It furnished the merchants with money, and thereby 'procured a ready sale for produce.' Tom Paine had pointed this out. Logan knew it was true. As a farmer, he had actually 'experienced the good consequences of it.' [13]

It was a brief speech, quiet, temperate, undramatic, in strong contrast to the rancorous harangues that had preceded it. It showed the Assemblymen and the visitors in the gallery what kind of man this newcomer was — a moderate among extremists, a conciliator amidst angry men. They knew he was an easterner, and an 'aristocrat' to boot; but now they knew he was also a farmer, able to speak for the country people quite as faithfully, quite as effectively, as Findley or Whitehill or Smilie. He had been elected as a Republican, but obviously this was no rabid partisan, no rigid conservative who, in the same breath, could support Robert Morris's Bank and speak a good word for the radicals' favorite institution, the loan office.

The vote was taken late that afternoon. It went against the Bank. Recharter would have to wait until the Republicans could control the house. But Assemblyman Logan had found his role in politics. By temperament, no less than by training, he was marked out as a moderator, a peacemaker — above all, a spokesman for the farmer.

Logan spent the summer of 1786 at Stenton. A farmer had no excuse for idleness. There were a thousand details to see to. A sheepfold had to be repaired, the mill dam needed cleaning out, a new pair of oxen must be broken to the yoke. And always there were the recurrent duties of seedtime and harvest. Moreover, he was now beginning to sow new crops, use new fertilizers, try out new modes of raising young stock, and he must spend hours in the barns and fields supervising his experiments and recording the results.

Deborah was busier than ever. She was expecting her second child in autumn. There were extra clothes to be made and special preparations for her first lying-in at Stenton. The baby was born early in October, another son. They named him Gustavus. Now there were two boys to grow up on the old estate where George Logan and his father before him had spent their childhood.

The birth of Gustavus diverted Logan's attention from the elections that fall. But the Republicans carried all the eastern districts and he was re-elected easily. When the new Assembly convened, late in October, George found his party in the majority. The recharter of the Bank was assured. Logan favored it up to the last moment. Suddenly, just as the bill was about to pass, he swung over to the opposition.[14] His colleagues naturally expressed surprise. But he had been listening to his neighbors, his constituents. Many of them, he found, distrusted the Bank, fearing that it might abuse its financial power. Earlier, Logan had dismissed the charge of monopoly as a mere bugbear conjured up by envious, demagogic radicals. Now it began to trouble him. A charter was a grant of exclusive privileges. It might, after all, be restrictive of liberty and unfair to potential competitors.

Later in the session he had a chance to voice his new-found opposition to monopoly. A petition came before the house from two men seeking leave to build a floating toll bridge over Neshaminy Creek, just a few miles northeast of Stenton. Logan knew the place well, knew how convenient the bridge would be to the farmers of Bucks County — but, it was argued, there was already one chartered bridge across the stream. A second would interfere with the exclusive privileges granted to its proprietors by the legislature.

The sanctity of charter rights no longer seemed so important to Logan as the right of the farmer to carry his produce to market without having to pay excessive tolls. Earnestly he 'warned the legislature of establishing monopolies.' The existing bridge was a monopoly 'because it gave a superiority to one party over the other.' It was an elementary principle that he stood on : 'The more bridges, the better the traveller would be accommodated.' [15] Only eighteen months ago, he had rejected a similar argument in the case of the Bank that the borrower would be better served if he had 'two shops to go to.' George Logan's political education was proceeding apace.

Dr. Franklin was one of his teachers. Franklin's house — a three-story brick mansion between Market and Chestnut Streets — was only a few steps from the State House. Logan formed the habit of stopping there on his way to or from the Assembly to pay his respects. He often found the Doctor, as others did, sitting hatless under the mulberry tree in his garden, 'a short, fat, trunched old man in a plain Quaker dress, bald pate, and short white locks.' [16] Logan usually stayed longer than he intended, listening, as he had once done at Passy, to the Doctor's ceaseless flow of wise and witty talk.

Franklin took him into his book-lined study, urged him to read the French *économistes* — Mercier de la Rivière, Le Trosne, Turgot, all the disciples of Quesnay. He recommended Adam Smith's *Wealth of Nations* and related how, in London before the Revolution, Smith used to bring the uncompleted manuscript to him, chapter by chapter, for criticism.[17] He recalled his early days in Philadelphia, remembered how George's grandfather had befriended him, had shared his books and scientific knowledge with an obscure young tradesman. He told George of a copper mine that James Logan had once owned in Lancaster County, how it had a spring whose waters were so heavily impregnated with copper that a knife-blade dipped in it would come out heavily coated.[18] Franklin never ran out of anecdotes, and each one was a lesson in moral or natural philosophy.

The house in Franklin Court was, in short, a splendid school of science, history, and politics — the best in America. George Logan made the most of it. Franklin, for his part, relished the company of young men, found 'an agreeable society' among the grandchildren of his contemporaries.[19] He had seen most of his own generation go to their graves. He knew that in the eyes of the middle-aged men — Robert Morris's friends — who now dominated politics, he was suspect, thought to be a little unsound, a little radical. Everyone was respectful, of course. After all, he was an elder patriot, a brilliantly successful diplomatist, a savant of universal renown. Still, as Debby Logan heard a Philadelphia politician remark one day, 'it was by no means "fashionable" to visit Dr. Franklin.' [20]

George Logan belonged to the 'fashionable' party. Franklin, because he had helped write the democratic Pennsylvania constitution of 1776, was claimed by the radicals. But party labels meant little more to the younger man than they did to the older. Logan was finding the conservatism of Morris and Clymer distinctly uncongenial. And Franklin, whatever might be whispered of him, was no irresponsible demagogue; neither was he a doctrinaire radical. Indeed, he was busy, in this summer of 1787, working behind closed doors at the State House on a new and more conservative constitution for the United States, which would replace the Articles of Confederation. Franklin did not approve every detail of the Federal Convention's work, but he sympathized with its general aims.

It was well into September 1787 before the new frame of government was finished and Franklin could speak freely of it to his young friends. On the seventeenth of the month, thirty-eight tired men finally set their signatures to the completed document and adjourned to the City Tavern for dinner. There they toasted the work of their hands and said their farewells. They had been laboring steadily for four long months, sweltering through the soggy heat of the Philadelphia summer, tormented by flies, suffocating in the white-paneled Assembly Chamber behind closely guarded doors.

Next morning, 18 September, the Assembly moved back into its chamber — it had been meeting temporarily in another room — and took up its regular order of business. Dr. Logan made a brief speech that morning against a bill that would permit aliens to hold land in Pennsylvania. The debate was desultory. Everyone knew that more important business impended.

Promptly at eleven, Dr. Franklin entered the room with the other Pennsylvania delegates to the Convention — Clymer, Fitz-Simons, Mifflin, Robert Morris, Gouverneur Morris, Jared Ingersoll, James Wilson. Logan knew them all well. Indeed, four of them were members of the Assembly. All except Mifflin were stanch conservatives — Federalists, as they now preferred to be called. Franklin addressed the Speaker: 'Sir, I have the very great satisfaction of delivering to you and to this honorable house the result of our deliberation in the late convention. We hope and believe that the measures recommended by that body will produce happy effects to this commonwealth, as well as to every other of the United States.' [21] He handed a printed copy of the proposed constitution to the Speaker.

Now at last the people could have a sight of the Convention's handiwork, for the people must decide — the people of nine states, at least — whether to accept it or not. It would be the Assembly's duty to call a convention in Pennsylvania. Everyone knew there was a hard struggle ahead. The country people, the westerners especially, were suspicious, apprehensive, touchy. And Pennsylvania's decision was critical. Her adhesion was absolutely necessary if the new government was to have a chance of success.

George Clymer, one of the framers of the new instrument, proposed to allow the opposition no time to organize. He moved that a ratifying convention be called at once, even though Congress had not yet requested the states to act. George Logan concurred; he had evidence that the people in his district, at any rate, were ready. On 22 September he presented a petition from 249 inhabitants of Lower Dublin and Oxford Townships, praying that measures be taken to adopt the new constitution. On the morning of 28 September — this Assembly about to expire and still no official request from Congress — he voted with his party to call a convention.[22] Now there remained only the task of setting a date for the election of delegates before the Assembly could adjourn.

The radicals were alarmed; they were desperate. Matters were being settled altogether too rapidly. They scented a plot. They had voted as a block against calling a convention. But their votes were no longer sufficient to restrain the Republicans. They had to employ other tactics. They held a hasty caucus at noon and agreed to boycott the afternoon session, thus preventing a quorum. They had used this stratagem before and to good effect. But the Republicans were more numerous now and more confident. They refused to be trifled with. When they returned at four in the afternoon to find nineteen seats vacant, they sent the Sergeant-at-Arms out to round up the absentees. He returned and reported; he had found them at the house of Major Boyd, a notorious radical, but they had refused to stir. Angrily, the house adjourned.

Early the next morning, an express from New York brought a resolution from Congress, calling upon the states to hold ratifying conventions. This strengthened the Republicans' hand. Now they had a legal basis for their proceedings. But still the radicals stayed away from the State House. The roll call showed there were two short of a quorum. It was the last day on which the Assembly would sit. Action was imperative. The Sergeant-at-Arms went out again. Once more he came back empty-handed.

Meanwhile, a mob of citizens had collected in the State House yard — a Republican mob, made up of respectable gentlemen indignant at the radicals' effrontery. Captain John Barry was one of them, his Irish blood boiling. A Revolutionary veteran, only recently returned to the countinghouse from the quarter-deck of the frigate *Alliance,* Barry knew how to deal with mutineers. He took command of the crowd, and they rushed down the street to Major Boyd's house. At the mob's approach, many of the delinquent legislators made off down the back alleys, but Barry and his crew laid hands on James McCalmont and Jacob Miley, dragged them off to the State House, pushed them into the Assembly Chamber, and barred the exit. Hugh Henry Brackenridge later celebrated the incident in ribald verse:

> It seems to me I yet see Barry
> Drag out McCalmont . . .
> . . . and also Miley
> Was taken from an out-house slily
> To constitute with him a quorum
> For he, it seems, was *unus horum*.[23]

McCalmont was a fiery Scots-Irishman from Franklin County. When he discovered that he was officially counted present, he begged to be excused. The Speaker asked the Clerk to read the rules of the Assembly. Every member who did not answer the roll call, it appeared, was liable for a fine of two shillings sixpence, or five shillings if there were no quorum without him. Thereupon McCalmont thrust his hand into his pocket, took out some loose silver, addressed the Speaker: 'Well, sir, here is your five shillings, so let me go.' [24] The radicals in the galleries roared with laughter.

Speaker Mifflin restored order. Members commenced to debate the metaphysical question of whether the gentleman from Franklin County was present or not. The humor of the situation was lost on George Logan. He was impatient with this quibbling, anxious to get on with the important business before the house. He rose to his feet and launched into an elaborate exposition of the advantages that would flow from the adoption of the new constitution. But everyone present, except the unhappy McCalmont and his colleague Miley, was already convinced and needed no further urging. In any case, the merits of the constitution were not before the house. The Doctor was requested to confine himself to the question. Annoyed at being cut off in mid-flight, he announced that, in his view, the member from Franklin County was undoubtedly present, and sat down.[25]

Members called for the question. McCalmont made a dash for the door, but he was held in the chamber by main force until it was duly voted to hold an election for a ratifying convention on the first Tuesday in November, a bare month away. Dr. Logan voted with his party and rode back to Stenton content that he had done his part toward providing the country with an adequate general government. Perhaps this constitution was not perfect, but Dr. Franklin at least believed the nation was unlikely to get a better one. If it was good enough for Franklin, Logan was satisfied with it.

The regular October balloting in 1787 drew little notice. The pending fight over the new government occupied everyone's attention. The Republicans, under the name of 'Friends to the Federal Constitution,' swept the elections for the Assembly in the east. Logan's constituents — the farmers of Philadelphia County, the weavers of Germantown — sent him back to the legislature for the third time.

One of his colleagues in this session was Richard Peters, lately a delegate to the Congress at New York. The Peters were old friends of the Logans. Richard Peters' father had been a protégé of old James Logan and his successor as Provincial Secretary. The younger Peters was a lawyer by profession. Between sessions of the court he lived comfortably at Belmont, his elegant country seat overlooking the Schuylkill. There he busied himself, as Logan did at Stenton, with agricultural experiments. The two men often saw each other at meetings of the Agricultural Society.

Peters was a noted wit, an incorrigible punster. His friend Logan — austere, sober, humorless — was fair game. Then, too, lawyer Peters could never resist a jibe at a medical man. Not even the dignity of the Assembly Chamber could restrain him. His opportunity came early in the new session, when Logan rose to defend a memorial from the College of Physicians in Philadelphia, in which the doctors, at Benjamin Rush's instigation, deplored the excessive use of spirituous liquors within the state and prayed for measures to keep it in bounds. They submitted a horrifying catalogue of diseases — dropsy, epilepsy, palsy, apoplexy, melancholy, madness — to which overindulgence could lead.

Dr. Logan was on his feet immediately, praising the College for its patriotic and disinterested plea — disinterested because it was obviously to the physicians' advantage to encourage drinking, since it led to so many profitable ailments. If there was humor in the remark, it was unintentional. But nothing could keep Logan's colleagues from treating the matter lightly. One member proposed that the petition be committed to the College, since it was obviously so much better informed on the subject than the Assembly. Speaker Mifflin ruled this suggestion out of order. If the physicians had asked leave to bring in a bill, he granted, the house might have referred the matter to them. Peters had been waiting for this opening. Let the physicians bring in a bill? He would never approve of that. 'I have already smarted severely,' he said, 'under very long ones of their bringing in.' The house roared with laughter. The doctors' memorial was dismissed, in spite of Logan's earnest protest that it was a 'serious matter and deserved serious consideration.' [26]

The legislators, however, had plenty of serious matters to deal with at this session — among them the reform of the penal laws. In 1786 the Assembly had enacted a new criminal code — by contemporary standards a remarkably mild and humane one. But the Quaker city was full of philanthropic men eager to soften still further the impact of the law. They objected to the notion, embodied in the existing code, that 'continued hard labor, publicly and disgracefully imposed' was the best means of reforming the criminal. Shaven heads, 'infamous dress,' iron collars with heavy cannon balls attached, guards armed with swords and blunderbusses — all this, argued the philanthropists, did little to reform the lawbreaker. They recommended more private, even solitary labor, the segregation of hardened criminals from first offenders, the elimination of strong drink from prison rations.[27]

Logan heartily agreed with part of this program. Certainly, liquor should be kept from the convicts. And it was atrocious, he thought, that 'young men of dangerous dispositions' should be herded together with 'men who will conduct them rapidly to the last pitch of destruction.' But Logan disagreed with his fellow Quakers on the value of imprisonment as a means of regeneration. The notion 'that the most wicked should live, in order to become better, and be prepared for a blessed eternity' was to him a sentimental fallacy, 'an unnatural combination of religious tenets with political principles.' [28]

On this issue Dr. Franklin was a better Quaker than Logan. In February 1788, he urged the Assembly to amend the penal laws in such a way as 'to render punishment a means of reformation and the labor of criminals of profit to the state.' [29] Speaker Mifflin appointed Logan to a committee to study the working of the present code. Always a conscientious committeeman, Logan was dissatisfied with the cursory official investigation. He made his own private inquiry, plied the jailer at the Walnut Street Jail with questions, visited the prison and found it 'a hell upon earth,' a place of unspeakable filth where 'persons of all characters and colors, crowded together, oppressed by their misery, their dirt, and their despair . . . exist in a fermentation of smothered rage, and groan or imprecate the most horrid curses as often as they breathe.' [30]

The committee recommended reforms designed to improve conditions. To Logan palliatives were useless, indeed pernicious. He felt bound to submit a minority report and defend it on the floor. His prescription was radical in its bluntness, shocking in its harshness. It was nothing less than a return to the bloody, vindictive code of pre-Revolutionary days which punished felonies by death and lesser crimes by whipping, branding, mutilation, the pillory, the ducking stool. There was little or no provision for imprisonment in the Doctor's scheme. He had discovered, he said, that it cost the state three times as much to support criminals as it received from their labor. This support came from the pockets of honest, law-abiding citizens. Moreover, the jailer had told him that the new system, far from improving the manners and morals of the offenders, had made them 'ten times worse.' Under the present law, Logan concluded, 'the worst of rogues are maintained at a heavy charge to the public, without producing any good consequences whatsoever.' [31]

Logan's colleagues were appalled. The Doctor was always preaching benevolence as 'the only foundation to insure the happiness of ourselves or the prosperity of our government.' [32] And what he preached he practiced. Everyone knew him as the most gentle, most humane, most kindly of men.

Only his closest friends realized that Logan was a profoundly troubled man these days, disturbed and baffled by the deterioration of manners, the rapid changes, the political unsettlement, all the dislocations that were racking society in Pennsylvania and the other states in 1788. As a country man, a farmer, he was especially shocked by what he saw every day on the streets of Philadelphia — the vice, the crime, the many evident signs of moral laxity. Perhaps, he began to feel, these things were inseparable from the rise of great cities. Perhaps Philadelphia — the bustling metropolis of merchant, banker, manufacturer — was a portent, a symptom of the kind of cancerous growth that might corrupt and eventually destroy the rural America that Stenton symbolized. Bewilderment, vexation, and anxiety had led Dr. Logan to prescribe radical social surgery. The same inquietude of spirit was driving him to his books in search of a philosophy that might unravel his perplexities, confirm his diagnosis, perhaps quiet his troubled spirit.

Logan spent long evenings in the great high-ceilinged library above the parlor, reading hard in Locke and the English writers on natural law, in Adam Smith, Turgot, and the French Physiocrats. Deborah learned that she must not interrupt when she saw him poring over Bishop Cumberland's thick quarto *Treatise of the Laws of Nature,* making notes on *The Wealth of Nations,* puzzling out the French of the *économistes.* He seemed to find clues there, answers to the problems that harassed him. Soon he began setting his thoughts down on paper, reading them aloud for Debby's criticisms, giving them, with her help, a literary polish. Then one day — the day the Assembly started debating the penal laws — he took his first essay to Philadelphia with him and left it at the office of Daniel Humphreys on Spruce Street, near the old drawbridge over Dock Creek. Humphreys was editor of the *Pennsylvania Mercury and Universal Advertiser.* Three days later, the essay appeared in the columns of the *Mercury,* over the signature 'Cato.' [33]

The pseudonym was inevitable. The name of the great Roman Censor was almost a household word at Stenton. Grandfather Logan had once translated (and young Benjamin Franklin had printed) the soliloquy on old age that Cicero had put into the mouth of Cato the Elder. And every young Logan was brought up on the *Moral Distichs* (also translated by Grandfather and printed by Franklin) that had long been ascribed to Cato. The grandson of James Logan was not likely to forget how the Censor had lived through a time of social convulsion much like his own, how he had preached an austere ideal of civic virtue, how he had harked back to an earlier, simpler, agrarian civilization, upholding pure republican manners in the midst of civic decay and moral degeneracy.

'The more we become acquainted with the occurrences which take place in the growth and decline of nations,' Logan began his article, 'the more we shall be convinced that things are equally connected in the moral as in the physical system of this world.' This was the teaching of Bishop Cumberland and of the Physiocrats — the men whose works he had been devouring at Stenton. 'A universal complaint prevails,' he went on, moving from abstract principle to current reality, 'respecting the distresses of the people, and the deranged situation of our public affairs.' Some blamed the officers of government. Others declared the people obstinate and ignorant, 'incapable of governing themselves, or acting for their own good.' That indeed was the refrain Logan heard daily in the Assembly Chamber from his Republican colleagues — Clymer, FitzSimons, even his friend Peters. It was the attitude that, according to Dr. Franklin, had dominated the Federal Convention.

Such a view of human nature, such a betrayal of the Revolutionary faith was not acceptable to Logan. 'I believe our present calamities,' he wrote, 'cannot be attributed to any innate depravity of the American character.' The mischief lay in 'the selfish Machiavellian principles,' the pessimistic notions that man is 'naturally inclined to evil,' that he has 'such an aversion to his fellow creatures, as to be at all times prepared for their destruction.' John Locke and Benjamin Franklin had taught Logan otherwise. 'With man,' he declared, 'all is education; by his nature he is neither good nor evil, but is constantly engaged in seeking his own happiness.'

The pursuit of happiness . . . already Americans were forgetting their Declaration of Independence. But Logan was just beginning to appreciate it, to make its philosophy his own. 'Impress on the minds of mankind this solid truth,' he exhorted, *'that the only true source of our happiness is to promote the happiness of our neighbors,'* and almost overnight, 'we should . . . observe a change for the better, not only in our public but private affairs.' [34] Quakers had always known that; Logan had always known it instinctively. But he had to rediscover it in his reading, find it formulated as a principle of philosophy.

Benevolence was the favorite doctrine of Cumberland and the English moralists. It was the clue Logan had been seeking. He developed the idea in a second essay. 'The Supreme Being of the Universe has undoubtedly placed man in this world to be happy and to promote the happiness of his creation.' Benevolence was not just a 'good moral idea, only proper to be taught in the schools of philosophy.' It was 'a practicable principle,' the foundation of the only real and lasting happiness and prosperity of individuals or states.[35]

The law of universal benevolence, however, did not cancel the claims of justice. Justice, indeed, was its inescapable corollary. No one in society has the right to injure another, Logan wrote, 'for society is established to ensure the happiness of every individual, and is only useful when it promotes justice amongst its members.' An unjust man 'breaks the chain which unites him with neighbors: he becomes the enemy of all, and therefore subjects himself to be injured by the combined force of those with whom he is united.' Logan was bringing his argument around to the problem that had sent him off on this philosophical quest — the problem of crime and punishment.

In the moral economy, rights and duties were reciprocal, interdependent. This he had learned from the French writers, the Physiocrats. He pursued their logic relentlessly, with a curious doctrinaire heartlessness. As society's right over individuals depends on the happiness it procures for them, so 'it becomes the duty of such society to remove those persons from amongst them who, by their unjust and violent conduct counteract this great end.' Therefore — he brought his argument temporarily to rest on the issue of the moment — 'the alteration of the Penal Laws of Pennsylvania cannot be supported as a just measure.' To compel the honest and industrious to support the worthless and profligate is contrary to reason and nature, 'however plausible it may appear in theory to draw a revenue from the labor of convicts to repair the injury society may have sustained by their outrage.' [36]

Logan's hours in the library, his sober reflections on the times, his conversations with Franklin had convinced him that society has its laws, as irrefragable as the physical laws he had learned from Black and Cullen. This realization, this revelation gave him a new assurance — and a new message. He found himself speaking more often in the Assembly now, and more freely. A new intensity, a new conviction lay behind his words. His colleagues could not help but notice it.

A week after his outburst on the penal laws, he was on his feet again. A group of Philadelphia businessmen had lately formed a Society for the Encouragement of Manufactures. Certain members of the Assembly were interested in this scheme for promoting industry in Pennsylvania. Thomas Mifflin was president of the Society, George Clymer a vice-president. Tench Coxe, an intense young Federalist whom Logan often saw at Franklin's house, was its leading spirit. The Society wished the Assembly to prohibit the transportation of industrial machinery out of the state.

Logan opposed the measure. Such a statute, he declared, 'would do more harm than good.' He favored postponement as 'the most decent way to get rid of the bill.' Not that he was unsympathetic to manufacturers and mechanics. He wished every encouragement given to such valuable citizens, 'but he would not make them the principal object of legislative patronage.' Agriculture, he affirmed dogmatically, was 'the first and most important pursuit.' If gentlemen were so eager to encourage American industry, let them do as he did — let them use and wear American manufactures exclusively. But let them not interfere — the voice was Logan's, but the doctrine was that of Adam Smith and the Physiocrats — let them not interfere with the laws of the market. [37]

Up rose William Robinson, Jr., another Republican from Philadelphia County. He could not conceal his surprise at Logan's objections. 'Has he not always addressed you on such occasions

with language the most pathetic, and a high degree of concern?'
Robinson's tone was mocking, malicious. 'Oftener did not the
Roman Senate house ring with *delenda Carthago* than these walls
with *cherish and nurture the interest of the farmer and mechanic.*
When we were about to encourage the manufacturer by laying a
protecting duty on such articles as were fabricated amongst us,
did we not hear the cry of Germantown stockings vibrate incessantly from his lips?' [38] The sarcasm was not lost. Logan *had*
supported bills to protect the local knitting interests. But that had
been before his conversion to the doctrines of Adam Smith and
the Physiocrats.

At the end of March, the Assembly adjourned for the summer.
Logan turned back with relief to the life of a farmer. But still he
found time to write, to share with the readers of the *Mercury* his
new-found philosophy — to conduct, as it were, his education in
public.

Six states had now ratified the new constitution, Pennsylvania
among them. The air was still full of controversy, the columns of
the newspapers crammed with observations on the nature and
authority of government in general and of the proposed new government in particular. Cousin John Dickinson's 'Letters of Fabius'
were appearing in Humphreys' *Mercury,* alongside Logan's Cato
letters.

Logan's problem was to reconcile freedom with order, equality
with authority, the Declaration of Independence with the proposed new constitution. It was the oldest problem of politics, but
for Logan it was a new, fresh challenge. His starting point was
the great Declaration. In his fourth essay he quoted its words:
'that all men are created equal; and that they are endowed by their
Creator with certain unalienable rights: that among these are
life, liberty and the pursuit of happiness. That to secure these
rights, governments are instituted among men, deriving their just
powers from the consent of the governed.' Logan accepted these
propositions as axiomatic. But he was aware that his friends were
using other language these days. They talked of the need for vigor
and authority in government, of the natural inequality of men and

the desirability of distinctions, even hereditary distinctions, in rank.

George Logan of Stenton bore Pennsylvania's most patrician name, but he set himself unequivocally against the aristocratic principle. 'The advantages any individual procures to his neighbor ought to be the only cause of distinction in America.' Not that a democratic society had no place for authority. On the contrary, 'in every well-regulated government, a part of the citizens are entrusted with the authority of the whole, and this subordination is well founded, as it has the general happiness of the people for its object.' Civil authority originates in a compact 'founded in nature,' an engagement by the sovereign power 'to govern well, to do nothing injurious to our persons, liberties or properties . . . to protect us from all oppression and injury,' and by the governed 'to honor and to obey the just commands of such rulers.' If the sovereign power is 'influenced by selfish, partial, or unjust principles, the obligation of the citizens becomes null and void.' Logan advised Americans, in a word, to view the proposed federal constitution in the light of the principles of 1776.

'An apparent neglect of these salutary and equitable principles, the encouragement of the agreeable, instead of the useful arts; the sacrifice of agriculture to commerce, the seeking of foreign aid, instead of deriving it from resources within ourselves, and a neglect of the public finances, are causes which threaten the destruction of our boasted equality.' He was not arguing for equality of wealth, 'but only that . . . no one citizen should be rich enough to buy another, either by largesses or sumptuous entertainments.' [39]

By June, Cato was bestowing praise on the Pennsylvania Constitution of 1776, the instrument whose 'popular' features the Republicans had been trying for a dozen years to eliminate or modify. 'Of the different forms of government existing in the world,' he wrote, 'the inhabitants of Pennsylvania have adopted one the most honorable, and at the same time, the most agreeable to nature and to the equal division of property amongst us.'

If his Republican colleagues grimaced at that, they smarted at what followed. Cato-Logan now assumed his role as *censor morum*. He charged the distresses of the times to the rich Philadelphians, their 'vanity and ostentation,' their 'love of parade,' of 'idle amusements and dissipation.' 'Like an epidemic disorder,' he fulminated, 'this folly and luxury' have pervaded the whole state to the ruin of many families and the demoralization of society. 'Our government,' he proclaimed sternly, 'should not encourage wealthy and idle characters amongst us.' Indeed, 'an idle wealthy man is frequently the greatest bane to a republican government.' Opulence and luxury had one sure effect: 'to render us insensible to the distresses of our fellow citizens.' [40]

No one could accuse Logan of idleness or extravagance. Those who knew his life at Stenton found it comfortable, gracious, idyllic — but always simple, almost Spartan, never ostentatious. If his attitude toward criminals seemed heartless, readers of the Cato letters could ascribe it to the doctrinaire social theory within which his thinking was temporarily imprisoned.[41] They knew him as a naturally tender-hearted man, never insensitive to genuine human distress when he saw it. And he saw much suffering and poverty in his travels about the Pennsylvania countryside during the summer of 1788. Times had never been worse for the farmers. Wheat barely brought five shillings the bushel in Philadelphia.[42] It hardly paid to take it to market. The ordinary farmers' plight was Logan's too in a measure — though at Stenton he was cushioned as they were not. Their distress weighed heavily on his mind when the legislature reassembled in September.

A bill to enforce the collection of taxes came before the house. It would give the tax collector authority to distrain upon the goods of delinquents — to seize a cow, a spinning wheel, a bed, if necessary, to make up the unpaid tax. In the last resort, the collector could commit the offender to prison without bail until the tax was paid. Logan found all this irregular, distasteful, needlessly harsh. He kept silence, however, until the bill reached its third reading. When he finally took the floor, members were aware of a new urgency in his voice, a new vehemence in his language. The bill was oppressive, he began; it was arbitrary and without precedent.

He could not support a bill that took power from the local magistrate and placed it in the hands of the tax collector, 'a person that is not known in the Constitution.' All this smacked of tyrannical rule, of despotism. It was 'directly contrary to every idea on which free governments are founded.'

But this was not his only objection. He warmed to his subject. Members, he said, must take account of the times. Conditions were critical in the country regions. Misery and want were widespread. Soberly, Logan told the Assembly: 'Since I have had the honor of a seat in this house, I have never felt the anxiety on any occasion that I do at present.' He described what he had seen on his travels — fields lying uncultivated, crops unharvested, farms going to ruin. To make matters worse, the Hessian Fly, the deadly insect that had crossed the Delaware from the Jersey side two years before, threatened to ravage the wheat crop again.

If this time should be chosen to enforce the collection of taxes — he spoke slowly, deliberately — 'it will either be productive of a revolution, or your citizens will silently leave a country which they find devoted to extreme oppression.' Just the other day, in Bucks County, he had learned 'with poignant concern' of more than a score of families migrating to the Niagara country. In view of the low price of land, the house had recently granted speculators a stay in the collection of taxes. Logan grew indignant now; his voice trembled with emotion. 'And shall the honest, industrious, hard-working husbandman, on whom all our prosperity depends, receive less indulgence from the legislature than the gentlemen of *Philadelphia,* who hold large tracts of land unoccupied and unproductive?' [43]

He sat down, conscious of cold, hostile stares from the Philadelphians. The debate went on. Finally, someone called for the question, and the law passed. Logan's distrust of the city politicians deepened.

Later in the session, just before the Assembly expired, he heard the Republican leaders discussing a matter of transcendent interest — the question of who should represent Pennsylvania in the upper house of the new Congress. The ninth state — New Hampshire — had ratified the Constitution, and a federal government was actually being organized. At first, the city men supported George Clymer for one of the two seats in the Senate. Then they shifted to a stronger man — the redoubtable Robert Morris.

Everyone understood that a westerner, a man acceptable to the farmers, should have the second seat. The name of William Maclay had often been mentioned. No name could have pleased Logan more. Maclay was a dour and crusty Scotsman, a veteran of the French and Indian War and the Revolution, a colleague of Franklin on the Supreme Executive Council. Everyone knew him for his austere and unbending manner, his incorruptible honesty — and his caustic tongue. But perhaps, some said, he was a little too outspoken. Besides, he could be a little tiresome, always harping on republican simplicity and purity of manners, always harking back to the ideals of the Revolution.

On second thought, the party leaders dropped Maclay, put forward John Armstrong, Jr., a less thorny, less independent, more manageable man.

Logan was disgusted. Maclay was a man whom the farmers could trust, a genuine patriot, a republican of the classical mold. There was little support among the rural members for Armstrong. The day before the election, it was clear that he could not command a majority vote. Quickly, the Federalists turned back to Maclay. For all his independent spirit, his 'republican' manners, he was assumed to be 'highly Federal,' well disposed toward the Constitution and the new government.[44] Logan had the honor of putting Maclay's name in nomination on 1 October, and the satisfaction of seeing him elected by sixty-six votes — almost twice as many as Morris, the other successful candidate, received.[45]

Maclay reciprocated the respect that Logan felt for him. Though he was habitually chary of praise, notoriously captious by nature, he spoke of Logan with genuine warmth. 'This is really a worthy man,' he was to write in his diary. 'I think he holds the first place in point of integrity.' Maclay had watched Logan's legislative career closely. He honored the young man for his refusal to form 'a coalition with the city interest.' He applauded his firm attachment to 'the rural plans and arrangements of life and the democratic system of government.' [46] In Maclay's view there were too few men of Logan's stamp in public life.

Logan's attachment to rural life and rural interests pleased his constituents too. In October 1788, they returned him for his fourth term in the Assembly. His health was poor that fall, however, and he did not take his seat until spring.

When he finally did rejoin the house, he found it debating an old issue — one on which he held strong views. Every year since he had entered the legislature, there had been petitions for the licensing of theatrical productions in Philadelphia. The source of the petitions was Lewis Hallam, a veteran actor and manager of a troupe that had been playing up and down the American coast for thirty years. Every year his petitions had been denied. Quakers had joined hands with western radicals to keep stage plays out of the city. The Federalists — those who were not Friends — were determined that Philadelphia should have its theater. Why should they be deprived of the civilized pleasures that gentlemen enjoyed in New York and London? The stage, they argued, was not the 'great corruptor of mankind,' as the Quakers contended, not a decadent luxury, as the radicals maintained. It was 'the great Mart of Genius.' Indeed, it was 'a natural and necessary concomitant of our independence.'

George Logan had been a theater-goer himself in his Edinburgh and London days. But his views had changed since then. The objections he now felt arose only incidentally from his religious training. Theatrical exhibitions, Logan felt, encouraged immorality. Moreover, they tended to undermine the purity of republican manners. The testimony of the most enlightened men — Plutarch, Sir Matthew Hale, Archbishop Tillotson, Lord Kames, the Continental Congress — could be cited against them. But above all — he was back on a favorite theme — no legislature should countenance public amusements at a time when so many were in actual distress. Logan voted with the radicals against granting Hallam's request. The measure passed over his protest. [47]

The Federalists were carrying all before them now, riding a

conservative tide that was reaching flood proportions in Pennsylvania. They restored the charter of the old College of Philadelphia, whose faculty and trustees had been tainted with Toryism during the Revolution. They called a convention to revise the state Constitution of 1776, to lop off its democratic excrescences. Logan supported the first of these measures only half-heartedly and tried unsuccessfully to bury the second by postponing it to an indefinite future.[48] He had never been a good party man. He had always been too independent, too prone to follow his own judgment wherever it might lead. It was leading him now down another road from the one his party was taking. For the Federalists — the old Republicans — it was obvious that the Revolution was over in Pennsylvania. For George Logan it was just beginning.

He was relieved when the Assembly recessed for the summer of 1789. His experiments at Stenton were beginning to yield results, and he busied himself observing, recording, reporting them.[49] For the moment, it seemed, he could serve the farmers better by helping them become better farmers than by pleading their cause in a hostile Assembly dominated by city politicians.

He had little heart for legislative work in the short autumn session of the legislature. Under the old state Constitution — now about to fall, just as Logan was beginning to appreciate its virtues — no one could serve more than four consecutive terms in the Assembly. It was a sound democratic principle. Logan was not sorry when his legislative service came to an end in October 1789.

He still drove regularly into Philadelphia during the winter and the following spring. Dr. Franklin was dying — slowly, painfully. There was little that one could do to ease his agony. But when one owed a man as much as Logan owed Franklin, one could at least watch by his bedside, read to him when the pain subsided, cool his brow when the fever was on him.

Death came on the night of 17 April 1790. Three days later, a solemn cortege moved through the streets of Philadelphia. Slowly it passed from the State House across Market Street to Christ Church burying ground on Arch Street. All the leading citizens walked in the procession. Twenty thousand people watched it, while muffled bells tolled the passing of Philadelphia's greatest man. Citizens carried the coffin, taking the place of the city watchmen. George Logan was one who performed this last service for his friend.[50] As he helped to lower the body into the grave, he knew he could never forget the political lessons he had learned from Benjamin Franklin.

___

V. 'THE BEST FARMER IN PENNSYLVANIA'

THE FARMERS of Philadelphia County knew George Logan well. He often stopped to talk with them as he drove by their farms, proudly showed them his latest improvements when they brought grain to be ground in his mill. They knew him as a good farmer and a successful one — even if he was forever trying out strange new ideas that he got from books. They knew him, too, as their faithful spokesman in the Assembly, defender of their interests against the city bankers and merchants. They admired and trusted him. But they were a little in awe of him. They had always stood in awe of the Logans of Stenton.

One day in the summer of 1788, George Logan invited his neighbors to dinner at the great house. Some of the guests were gentlemen-farmers like Logan himself. Most of them were simple countrymen, uncomfortable in their Sunday clothes, ill at ease in the grandeur of Stenton. The Doctor met them at the door, dressed in plain homespun. Debby was by his side, eager to set them at their ease. They all sat down to a simple, bountiful meal. Afterward, they found out why they were there. Dr. Logan had a plan to lay before them. Why should not the Philadelphia County farmers organize their own agricultural society? [1]

They knew, most of them, about the Philadelphia Society. A few of them, with Logan, were members. The Society was still holding meetings, though attendance was beginning to fall off. But there was no vitality, Logan told them, in an agricultural society whose members were not really farmers. Moreover, the Philadelphians had no interest in the farmer's moral welfare.

Only a few months ago, Logan had read them a paper against the universal custom of giving strong drink to harvest hands. The practice of handing out 'these poisons,' he had declared, could have only one effect — 'the certain destruction of the morals, the liver, and the property of our fellow citizens.' His own men no longer had rum at harvest time. Instead, they were given 'small malt beer' of Debby's own brewing. The results had been gratifying; he had just 'finished a very extensive harvest without any accident, drunkenness, or disorder, and with an alacrity and neatness which I never before experienced.' He had hoped the Philadelphia Society would join him in promoting this reform.[2] The merchants and lawyers, dram-drinkers all, had listened politely. They had even directed that the paper be printed.[3] But there the matter had rested. And when he had taken up the same topic a few weeks later at the State House, speaking on the memorial from the College of Physicians, several of these same gentlemen, members of Assembly, had made jokes, had laughed him down. No, there was little good to be expected from the Philadelphia Society. Its members did not understand the farmer's problems. They were not even friendly, he had begun to suspect, to the farmer's interests.

What the farmers must do, then, was clear; they must form their own societies, organize by counties. Logan proposed to begin, this evening, in Philadelphia County. His guests fell in with his scheme, elected officers, and settled upon a regular time and place for meetings. A few weeks later, on 4 August 1788, they approved a constitution. The second article read: 'No man shall be eligible as a member but a farmer.' [4]

Now Logan had a forum. From it he could reach not only the farmers in his neighborhood but also a wider audience. He began to prepare reports on his experiments at Stenton; he regularly read them before the Philadelphia County Society for Promoting Agriculture, and then, with the society's approval, published them in Mathew Carey's monthly *American Museum* or Eleazer Oswald's *Independent Gazetteer*. Carey and Oswald were Philadelphia's two most enterprising editors. They were also bitter enemies who had faced each other on the dueling ground. Characteristically, Logan befriended them both — and thereby assured himself the widest possible public for his agricultural papers.

Mathew Carey was a peppery Irishman who had been at Passy, working in Franklin's print shop, when Logan was there. He had only recently landed in Philadelphia, but already his *American Museum* had more than 850 subscribers, mostly in the middle states, but some as far away as Massachusetts or South Carolina, and a few in Europe.[5] It was the most successful magazine that had appeared in the United States. Like most publications of its kind, the *Museum* was largely a collection of reprinted pieces on politics, history, religion, or almost any topic. Logan's essays were among the few original contributions.

Colonel Oswald was an Englishman who had fought on the American side in the Revolution. He had distinguished himself as an artillery officer at Ticonderoga, Quebec, and Monmouth, and his editorial methods showed the marks of his artillerist training. He had been publishing the *Independent Gazetteer* since 1782. He resented Carey's intrusion as a competitor. An exchange of insults had led to an exchange of pistol shots early one morning on the Jersey shore, and Carey still limped about Philadelphia with Oswald's bullet in his thigh. Oswald and Carey — one a Republican, the other a Constitutionalist — scarcely spoke to each other, but Carey's magazine was always open to Logan, and people were soon saying that Oswald's paper too was 'at his devotion.'[6] He used them to propagate the gospel of better farming.

Logan's own farm bustled with activity these days. The stables and barnyard were full of livestock. The Doctor spent hours out there, experimenting with new feeds, supervising the shearing of his lambs, weighing his hogs, comparing the performance of oxen and horses at the plough. Pennsylvania farmers — he said it again and again — paid too little attention to livestock husbandry. In particular, they were 'too negligent of their young stock of every kind.' This neglect was wasteful, foolish, inexcusable. Experience had convinced him that 'a stricter attention to the raising of our cattle and stock of all kinds, would give us a breed on our farms equal to any in the world.' At the same time, it would 'add greatly to our wealth and that of our country.' [7]

Farmers, he had found, were too ready to follow traditional methods in raising their young stock. Everyone thought that pigs would fatten best if you turned them into a rich clover field with the sow. That was the way it had always been done. Logan put this folk belief to the test. He put three pigs with the sow into a clover field 'with the advantage of shade, a fine spring of water to drink or wallow in at pleasure,' and fed them 'the common wash of the kitchen.' He kept four others in a dark stable, on clean straw, fed them as much skim milk as they could drink. The results of his experiment contradicted the traditional belief. At the end of three weeks, the pigs that had run loose in the sunshine weighed less than those kept in the stable.[8] It was time, Logan decided, for Pennsylvania farmers to change their methods.

Logan had radical ideas about raising calves too. He had found his clue in Arthur Young's *Annals of Agriculture,* which he read eagerly, month by month, as it came from England. The Duke of Northumberland, he had learned, was no longer feeding valuable whole milk to his calves; instead, he gave them skim milk thickened with treacle and ground linseed cake. The expense, the Duke reported, was only a third of the cost of new milk. Arthur Young had tried the Duke's formula, without success. Logan proposed to adapt it to American conditions by substituting Indian meal for linseed cake, and to try it at Stenton.

He chose two calves of the same age for his experiment. One he fed on cow's milk three times a day. To the other he gave skim milk with two or three handfuls of corn meal stirred in. Every morning and evening he 'crammed' the second calf with 'two boluses of the size of a hen's egg made with Indian meal, linseed oil, and an egg.' After a few weeks, he found the second calf heavier and superior in every respect. He encouraged other American farmers to adopt his practice. If they would only raise their male calves to the age of five or six weeks, instead of destroying them at birth, they would find in the veal and the hides a new source of income.[9]

He urged farmers to take more pains with their sheep. The scrawny creatures that straggled, pathetically untended, about the woods on most Pennsylvania farms, looking more like goats than sheep, their scanty fleece matted and caked with mud, produced a few pounds of wool a year — enough for the farm family's barest needs. No one ate mutton in Pennsylvania and it could not be salted or smoked for export. But the wool, Logan pointed out, could be made profitable to the farmer and to the country. To increase the yield from his own sheep, he tried shearing some of them twice a year. Another group, his controls, he clipped only once. The results surprised him. The total clip from the first group was nearly twice as heavy as that from the second. The staple, to be sure, was shorter, but the fleece was fine, thick, unmatted. The success of this experiment gave him special pleasure, for an increased wool production meant more household manufacturing, and household manufacturing was with him an article of the pure republican faith. Ultimately it might mean that American hatters could shake off their dependence on Great Britain. And this, wrote the Doctor, 'is a great national object.' [10]

Behind everything Logan wrote lay some patriotic or moral consideration — even when he discussed the relative merits of horses and oxen. The slow-moving ox was disappearing from Pennsylvania farms; the handsome, powerful Conestoga horse was proving itself faster, more adaptable, more efficient. But Logan clung to his oxen. He could cite practical, economic reasons. Oxen were cheaper to feed, less susceptible to disease. They had more power 'at a dead weight.' Their yokes, bows, and chains cost less than the elaborate harnesses that horses required. Moreover, their dung made better manure, and they yielded valuable leather, tallow, and beef when their working days were over. But Logan had another reason for preferring the ox. Most farmers, he suspected, kept horses for fear of being thought old-fashioned. 'Do you not work and toil one half of the year at least,' he challenged them, 'to support your *gallant, sightly* teams of horses?' He himself kept but two horses, superannuated beasts, one lame, the other blind. They grazed peacefully in the 'butterfly pasture' while lumbering oxen did the work on Stenton farm.[11]

There was another matter concerning livestock that Logan wanted to bring to the attention of his neighbors — and, he hoped, of American farmers everywhere. They all grew Indian corn, ground it into meal, and fed the blades to their cattle. But the stalks were generally left standing in the fields through the winter, in unkempt rows, snow settling around them, until they finally rotted and fell to the ground. To Logan this was sheer waste. Cornstalks 'certainly contain a great quantity of farine substance,' he told the Philadelphia County Society, 'and therefore must be highly nutritive.' [12] At Stenton he always cut and fed them to his cattle, and the cattle thrived. He urged his neighbors to follow this example.

Debby, her hands full with the two boys and the management of the household, had little time for the outdoors and the experiments going on in the fields and barnyard. She was no reformer in any case, no crusader like her husband. Her taste ran to flowers, which she grew for their gay colors, their fragrance, their sheer loveliness. But the Doctor saw a use even for her flowers. Every farmer, he thought, should keep a 'herd' of bees, should let them browse in the fields and gardens and make honey. This would reduce the American farmer's dependence on imported sugar — a most desirable result. Moreover, the beehive was an admirable school of political economy.

He looked into the literature of beekeeping, read Columella, Virgil, the modern French writers. The ancient Sicilians, he learned, had been in the habit of transporting their bees great distances to Hybla in search of forage; the Egyptians in Cleopatra's time had shepherded their swarms from pasture to pasture along the Nile in boats; apiarists in France carried their hives about in carts. The Pennsylvania farmer would not, he thought, follow any of these practices; he should fix the size of his swarm, therefore, by the amount of pasture available in his own fields.

It was possible, he had read somewhere, to extract the honey without destroying the bees. He made the experiment with the aid of his neighbors Shoemaker and Lukens, but found the bees unco-operative. It distressed him to have to kill the creatures, for he was a tender-hearted man. He took comfort in reflecting that the life of the bee was short at best, that the swarm would pass a hungry winter once its communal larder had been rifled.

It pleased him to contemplate the social life of the bee. The little insects exemplified everything he believed about the good society. With apologies to Virgil, he developed this theme and applied it to the contemporary scene in an address before the Germantown Society for Promoting Domestic Manufactures. The beehive, he said, was 'a school to which numbers of people ought to be sent; prudence, industry, benevolence, public spiritedness, economy, neatness and temperance, are all visible among the bees.' The 'little animals' formed a body politic 'intimately united and perfectly happy,' all its members unselfishly working for the common good.

'Let us compare human societies to this,' he said, 'and they will appear altogether monstrous.' He was back on a familiar refrain. Cato the Censor was looking over the shoulder of Columella. Necessity, reason, philosophy, all recommended society 'for the commendable purposes of material aid and benefits; but a spirit of selfishness destroys all; and one half of mankind to load themselves with superfluities, leave the other destitute of common necessaries.' [13] Let Philadelphia, he implied, look to the beehive.

The reform of animal husbandry was important, urgent, and necessary. But it did not go to the root of the farmer's problem. Logan continued to read Arthur Young, William Marshall, Lord Kames, the other great British farmers. What was the key, the central core of their new system? Was it clover, was it crop rotation, was it fertilizer? It was all these things in conjunction, he concluded, for each required, each presupposed, each depended upon the other. No clover, no livestock; no livestock, no manure; no manure, no clover. It was a baffling circle, but Logan was not discouraged. He would attack it at all points. He had begun with livestock, had urged the farmers to raise more cattle and sheep and to raise them more carefully. Now he addressed himself to the problem of clover — for the substitution of clover in place of unproductive fallow, he sometimes thought, was close to 'the very heart of the improved system of English husbandry.'[14]

Ever since his father's time, the main obstacle to widespread cultivation of clover in America had been the difficulty and expense of obtaining seed.[15] One day in the summer of 1789, Logan heard of a new method of extracting seed from clover tops. He heard it from Judge Henry Wynkoop of Bucks County, who had learned of it in New York, where he was representing his district in the First Congress. Logan had just been elected to the Bucks County Agricultural Society, and he often saw Wynkoop at its meetings.[16]

The New York farmers, Wynkoop told him, extracted seed by fermenting their clover tops in water. As soon as the tops were dry, they threshed the seed out easily. Logan had seen Pennsylvania Dutch farmers thresh out timothy seed in this manner. He was anxious to share the suggestion with his neighbors. Even before trying it himself, he recommended it as an experiment to the members of the Philadelphia County Society. If the method were successful, he told them, they would at last have a cheap and simple means of procuring selected clover seed; they would no longer have to rely on sweepings of haymows full of useless chaff and pernicious weed seeds.

An available supply of clover seed would enable Pennsylvania to appropriate one of the major reforms in English agriculture. But Logan cautioned his neighbors against expecting wonders from clover alone. The real value of clover would appear only when it was associated with other crops in a suitable rotation. In a year or so, he promised them, his own experiments on crop rotation would be completed, and he would have advice to give them on that important subject, too.

Meanwhile, he reminded them, clover would not grow without fertilizer, natural or artificial. He urged them to keep their cattle penned during part of the year, to collect the manure, and to lavish it on their hard-worked fields, twenty cartloads to the acre, every seven or eight years. Pennsylvania farmers, he said, were altogether too improvident, too careless of the soil's fertility, 'too much in the habit of depending on the annual decay of weeds, arising in a course of years from their worn-out fields for the principle source of nourishment to their crops.' [17]

Manure — Logan dwelt endlessly on this theme — was one of the most valuable products of any farm, and most farmers squandered it, letting their cattle roam the pasture all year round. Others let the precious fertilizer collect uselessly in great mounds outside their barns until finally it was necessary to move the buildings.[18] Logan was aware that in preaching the virtues of manure, he was setting himself against formidable obstacles — not only the dead weight of local tradition and inertia, but also the redoubtable authority of the great Jethro Tull, first of the English scientific farmers. Still, he never ceased urging the American husbandman to utilize the neglected riches of his stables and barnyard for the good of his soil.

Even if the farmer jealously husbanded the precious dung from his flocks and herds, Logan realized, he would still have insufficient fertilizer for his tired land. If he lived near a town or city, he could haul manure from livery stables by wagonloads to spread on his fields. If he lacked this resource, he was still confronted by the stubborn circle — for more manure he must have more livestock, but more livestock demanded more clover, and to grow more clover, he must have fertilizer. To Logan it was obvious that there was only one way to break the circle — to introduce artificial fertilizer on a large scale. His father had started on a search for artificial 'manures.' William Logan had spread lime and soap ashes on the Stenton fields with good results.[19] George Logan carried on the quest.

His reading in Arthur Young told him that marl, 'the grand fossil manure of Norfolk,' had been the starting point of the great revolution in English husbandry. As he traveled through the countryside on both banks of the Delaware, he kept his eyes open for beds of marl — 'squankum,' the New Jersey farmers called it.[20] From roadside ditches and old gullies in Bucks, Montgomery, Northampton counties, in East and West Jersey, everywhere he went, he dug samples and brought them back to Stenton for experiment. Near Buckingham Meetinghouse, not twenty-five miles from his own farm, he saw some marl that had been dug from a well. The substance was easily recognized 'by its being of an unctuous, slippery nature.' 'When dug out of the pit,' he noted, 'the spade cuts it like so much hard soap'; crumbled into small pieces and put into the fire, 'it will crackle like oyster shells.' Using these tests, any farmer could recognize it. If he found any substance that resembled marl he should try it on his fields. 'Should it even not answer, the lost labor or expense would not be great.' [21]

The artificial fertilizer that completely captured Logan's fancy, however, was gypsum (plaster of Paris). Jacob Barge, one of the few genuine dirt farmers in the Philadelphia Agricultural Society, had been using it for years on his garden plot in the city. He had obtained it first from Germany. There, so the story went, its value as a fertilizer had been discovered accidentally by a plasterer, who noticed that the path by which he returned from work every day was growing luxuriantly in clover, while the fields on both sides remained bare. He attributed the odd phenomenon to the dust that shook from his clothes as he walked, and he began sprinkling waste plaster on his truck garden with surprising results.[22] Judge Richard Peters and a few other progressive farmers near the city had taken notice of Barge's practice and begun plastering their own fields.

There was no more enthusiastic devotee of land plaster in Pennsylvania than George Logan. Ever since 1785, people driving along the Germantown Road in springtime had blinked in disbelief when they passed Stenton and saw his fields covered with a dazzling blanket of white, as though by a sudden, belated snowfall. Once Logan had learned the magic of gypsum, he delighted to play tricks with it in order to advertise its startling qualities. He got this idea, as he did so many others, from Benjamin Franklin.[23] He traced initials and words on his fields with plaster in April. By midsummer he could watch astonishment come over the faces of his visitors when they saw the letters standing out boldly in grass of a deeper green, a greater height and luxuriance, than that around it.

Debby could never forget the pleasure her husband had taken in showing these 'beautiful experiments' to General Washington. It had been in the summer of 1787. Washington had come up to

Philadelphia from Mount Vernon to preside over the Constitutional Convention. One memorable First Day in July, he had ridden out to Stenton to escape the oppressive heat, the pestering flies, the tense political atmosphere of Philadelphia. Daniel of St. Thomas Jenifer, a close friend and a delegate from Maryland, had come with him.

Washington was in a genial, expansive mood. He recalled his last visit to Stenton — that gloomy day, ten years before, when he had paused on the way to his bloody defeat at the Brandywine, just before the bitter winter at Valley Forge. But all that was a memory now. He passed the day, Debby remembered later, 'in the most social and friendly manner imaginable.' He was gallant to his hostess, he bounced three-year-old Albanus on his knee, took baby Gustavus in his arms and caressed him 'in the most endearing manner.'

There had been only one jarring note, one domestic tiff, to mar the occasion. Knowing her husband's preference for simple 're-publican fare,' Debby had ordered a Spartan meal to be served, consisting of beef, potatoes, and small beer. But she could not resist the temptation to prepare with her own hands an elaborate and tasty dessert. When it was served — so at least the story ran as it passed into gossip — the Doctor 'got up in a passion,' declared that 'he never suffered them things, such trumpery, on his table,' and to poor Debby's bitter mortification, ordered the lovely confection away.[24]

But that was the only untoward incident in a shining day. Proudly, Dr. Logan conducted his tall, stately guest about Stenton farm. They examined the young stock in the stables. They rode through rolling pastures, through fields rich with wheat, timothy, clover, corn, flax. With boyish delight, Logan led Washington to the top of the hill behind the mansion and showed him his dramatic demonstration of the efficacy of land plaster, the green words inscribed on his fields. The General was full of praise for everything he saw. Later he declared himself 'a friend to gypsum,' even though his own land at Mount Vernon was too 'stiff and cold' to respond to it.[25]

Praise from the greatest farmer, the greatest man, in America was praise indeed. Logan was heartened to keep on with his experiments. He found that gypsum from Nova Scotia, brought down by water from the Bay of Fundy, was quite as satisfactory as French gypsum, and much less costly. Its action on clover and grass was immediate, he observed; on grain it was slower, but equally potent. It resisted weathering, remaining in the soil for several years, so that one dressing fertilized several successive crops. Logan drew together all his conclusions in October 1789, added some observations on the chemical structure of gypsum, marl, other calcium fertilizers, and submitted a long report to the county agricultural society.[26]

Logan's was not the only voice lifted in praise of land plaster. His friends Peters, Wynkoop, and Bordley, joined the chorus. Soon, wherever Logan rode in the springtime — up the Old York Road into Bucks County, west along the Lancaster Road, south into Chester County — he saw fields white with gypsum, stretching away on both sides of the road. Later in the season, the same fields were verdant with clover. 'Clover and plaster husbandry' transformed the agriculture of southeastern Pennsylvania. Farmers were raising more livestock than ever before; they were fertilizing their fields and reaping more abundant harvests.[27]

For all this no small share of the credit was Logan's. Already farmers were coming to him for advice; already they looked upon him as an authority, an oracle. His improvements at Stenton, the rich green fields, the superior stock, the obvious success of his novel methods had overcome the skepticism his neighbors had once felt toward his 'book-farming.' Within a very few years he would be known as 'the best farmer in Pennsylvania, both in theory and practice.'[28]

Logan's most ambitious experiments, the ones for which he expected to be remembered, however, dealt with crop rotation. Scientific crop rotation, involving clover and other 'artificial' grasses, was the basis of Norfolk's leadership in English agriculture. The founders of the Philadelphia Agricultural Society had read deeply enough in Arthur Young to know that. Their first premium, announced back in 1785, had been offered for a course

of crops to be worked out 'agreeably to the English mode of farming,' but adapted to Pennsylvania conditions. No one had yet
claimed the premium — a piece of plate worth two hundred dollars. Dr. Logan's heart was set on winning it.

Soon after he had moved out from the city — even before the
Agricultural Society had organized — he had commenced what
was to be a long and tedious series of experiments designed to
discover the rotation most suitable for his locality.

He laid his plans carefully, systematically. He divided his fields
into fourteen experimental plots, from one to fifteen acres in size.
In each plot he sowed a different succession of crops. His object
was clear and comprehensive: to develop for his region a rotation
that would provide the largest number of cash crops and the greatest amount of fodder, and one that would at the same time preserve the soil in the best condition and distribute the farm work
most evenly through the growing season.

Year after year, he planted his fourteen fields, manured and
plastered them, ploughed, harrowed, and cross-ploughed them.
He made the necessary allowances for wet seasons and light soils,
and kept meticulous notes on all his results. Finally, in December
1790, at the end of seven years, he concluded the experiments, reviewed his observations, and sat down in his library to draw up
a report for the Philadelphia Society.

He described each experiment separately, in full detail, noted
the condition of the soil, the type of fertilizer used, the yield per
acre. Then he put forward his own preferred rotation, the one he
had fixed upon after seven years of steady experiment and observation:

1. Indian corn
2. Potatoes and flax
3. Wheat
4. Winter barley, followed by buckwheat with
   clover and timothy
5. Clover (two crops for hay)
6. Clover (one crop for hay and pasture)
7. Pasture
8. Wheat
9. Winter barley

'This plan,' he wrote confidently, 'constitutes my present mode of farming, and the success attending it leaves no room to doubt of its superior advantages.' It fulfilled all the basic conditions he had laid down for it. And it had further advantages. It made use of Indian corn, whose virtues as a fodder crop he had already demonstrated. It gave the farmer each year a crop of potatoes, part of which he could feed to his stock. It would encourage household manufacturing by producing an annual crop of flax, 'a valuable article too much neglected by our country.' [29] A hundred and twenty acres of wheat, barley, clover, and timothy 'would enable a farmer to winter fifty head of stock, besides sheep,' and this, with a proper system of barnyard management, 'would give him every year five hundred loads of good manure.'

Dr. Logan set down his pen, read over what he had written. It was clear, concise, cogent; it certainly fulfilled the conditions that the Philadelphia Society had set for its premium. Yet he was dissatisfied. The seven years during which he had worked on this problem had also been years of education in political realities. He was no longer the same George Logan he had been when he had commenced his experiments seven years ago. Experience at the State House had convinced him that no rotation of crops, no system of husbandry, however scientific, would solve the farmer's problems and make him a prosperous, self-respecting member of society unless the government were conducted on just and enlightened principles. Merchants, bankers, speculators, moneyed men — the new aristocracy of the countinghouse — were crowding out the old landed families, were corrupting government, prostituting it for selfish ends, enriching themselves at the expense of the people, the great mass of farmers. And some of the worst offenders sat in the meetings of the Philadelphia Society for Promoting Agriculture.

Society for Promoting Agriculture . . . Logan thought of its leading members — Morris, Clymer, FitzSimons, Henry Hill, Tench Francis, Samuel Powel — sitting over their ledgers, calculating their profits from the farmer's distress. The irony was too bitter. He took up his pen again. His rotation, he wrote was not designed for a poor, degraded peasantry, 'but for an independent yeomanry — such as our American farmers ought to be — gentlemen cultivating their own estates.' Such a yeomanry could never flourish under an oppressive businessmen's government 'directed by the wretched principles of fiscality.' History, the experience of every nation, proved it. He turned to the philosophical French traveler Pierre Poivre, favorite of the Physiocrats, for evidence. The Malabars, the Siamese, the Malayans, Poivre had reported, were poverty-stricken on the richest land in the world because of unjust and tyrannical laws, while the Chinese, 'governed as one family and submitting to the laws of reason,' were a flourishing people. The Frenchman concluded — and Logan agreed — 'in every country in the world, the state of agriculture depends solely upon the established laws and customs of the country.'

The experience of France — just now bursting the bonds of the old regime — should be even more instructive to the gentlemen of Philadelphia. Agricultural societies had long existed there, offering premiums, encouraging innovations, and yet — Logan chose his words carefully — 'owing to the nature of that government, and the dissipated manners of the Court, by which the whole country was infested, agriculture has been for many years in a languishing situation.'

The implication was obvious. But Dr. Logan made it explicit, unmistakable. 'Where is the encouragement to agriculture in this country,' he demanded, 'oppressed with the most ruinous system of indirect taxation and commercial regulations, and overwhelmed with scenes of parade, extravagance, and dissipation?' He laid down his pen with a feeling of satisfaction. Let the Philadelphians ponder on that!

He wrote out a fair copy and delivered the paper to the officers of the society on 20 December 1790 — the last day on which manuscripts could be submitted for the premium. Three weeks later, at a stated meeting, his paper was read. After the reading, there was a frigid silence. Someone moved that it be referred to a committee for further consideration. John Beale Bordley was named chairman of the committee. Bordley was a gentleman-farmer like Logan himself, a close student of English husbandry, thoroughly devoted to rural pursuits. Logan had visited his model farm on Wye Island in Maryland, and knew him to be a genuine and progressive farmer.[30] But the others — Jacob Hiltzheimer, prosperous livery-stable keeper, Henry Hill, opulent wine merchant, George Clymer, wealthy banker, leader of the conservatives in Pennsylvania politics. What could be expected from such a committee?

The committee was to report at the Society's next regular meeting on 8 February. The day came, and no member of the committee appeared at the meeting. Indeed, aside from Samuel Powel, the President, only two members of the Society attended — Tench Francis, Cashier of the Bank of North America, and Logan's old professional colleague, Dr. Samuel Powel Griffitts. They met only to adjourn. Eight days later, the Secretary managed to collect fifteen members and a meeting was held. The committee's report was read. It was brief. Dr. Logan's experiments did not 'altogether come up to the object of the Society.' They were not in accord with 'the English mode of farming.' Therefore they did not merit the premium. On the other hand, they were not wholly without value, and the committee recommended that they be published.[31]

Logan was incensed. Not 'agreeable to the English mode of farming'? Bordley certainly knew better; he of all men knew that the core of the English system consisted chiefly in 'substituting a crop of clover in place of an unproductive fallow' — just as Logan had done in his rotation. Bordley must have allowed himself to be overridden by the others. But the others — what did they know about English husbandry, or any other kind except the husbandry of dollars, of stock certificates, of six per cent government bonds?

For ten days Logan nursed his indignation. Then he laid all the evidence before the people, publishing his experiments and the committee's report in Oswald's paper. The farmers must not be deceived 'by the *pompous,* but *empty* declarations of the Philadelphia Agricultural Society.' There were only two possible explanations of the episode, he wrote. Either 'the gentlemen who composed the committee are totally unacquainted with the foundation of that improved method of English husbandry which the Society proposed as a pattern — or . . . they have been totally inattentive to the experiments submitted to their consideration.'

With this indignant outburst, George Logan washed his hands of the Philadelphia Agricultural Society and the mercantile aristocrats who composed it. To his essay in the *Independent Gazetteer*, he attached a 'motto' that represented his final disillusionment with agricultural societies composed of merchants and city men, his new conviction that the farmer must look to political action to safeguard his rights : '*Could the Philadelphia Society, instituted for the laudable purpose of promoting Agriculture, influence the government of the United States, to establish a free, unlimited and unrestricted commerce, it would tend more to improve the Agriculture of our country than all the premiums in their gift.*' [32]

✳

VI. AGRARIAN DEMOCRAT

COVERED with dust, the Assistant Marshal rode up the avenue of hemlocks to the great house, and dismounted. The year was 1790; the Assistant Marshal was gathering data for the first federal census. Dr. Logan was always at Stenton these days, puttering about the barns and stables behind the mansion, or supervising the hired hands in the fields. The Assistant Marshal found him, and politely proceeded to put the questions required by law.

How many free white males of sixteen years and upward on the place? Four, the Doctor said. And four under sixteen. He gave his answers brusquely, suspiciously, annoyed by this invasion of his privacy. How many free white females? the census-taker persisted. Dr. Logan bridled. He refused to answer. The census act, he spluttered, was an arbitrary law — undoubtedly the precursor of a poll tax.

The Assistant Marshal was surprised. Patiently he started to explain that the Constitution directed Congress to make an enumeration of the country's inhabitants. It was 'a damn rotten Constitution,' the Doctor burst out wrathfully. And as for Congress, they were 'a set of aristocratic rascals and Washington at their head.' The census-taker stood by, astonished, as the Doctor, railing on, declared that 'he wished the Constitution overset.' Was he prepared, then, for a civil war? Yes, said Logan; if there were no other way to set aside the Constitution, he was ready for revolution, and if it came tomorrow, he would draw his sword in the cause.

Stiffly the Assistant Marshal took his leave. For such talk as this, he announced, he could bring Logan before the District Court at York. He turned and walked off. The threat had a chastening effect — a federal marshal was not to be trifled with. Abruptly, the Doctor called after the departing official. His wife was free to do as she pleased about giving the names of the females, he cried. Deborah, who took her politics less seriously, gave the names cheerfully, treating the officer 'with her well-known affability.' [1]

George Logan had become convinced, after less than a year's observation of the new federal government, that the country was in the hands of merchants and speculators, countinghouse statesmen bent upon enriching themselves at the expense of the farmers. America was an agrarian nation; the overwhelming majority of her citizens were farmers. But they were falling prey to 'the partial views of interested men.' At first, Logan had favored the new strong Constitution, but as one national measure succeeded another, as Alexander Hamilton's program began to reveal its contours, as President and Congress became more and more 'federal,' more and more given to innovations, the Doctor grew alarmed, then angry. The Constitution was a class charter, he concluded, a license to merchants and moneyed men to reduce the farmer to servitude.

By February 1790, the new government having been in operation less than a year, Logan was already using incendiary language. He looked forward, he told the Philadelphia County farmers and later the readers of Oswald's paper, to the time when 'the patriotic exertions of the real friends of America shall be blessed with success — when our government shall be so organized that the cultivation of the land shall constantly tend towards its best possible state.' [2]

It was strong language for a Quaker, this revolutionary talk, this heady blustering, these threats to draw his sword. It scarcely comported with the Friends' doctrine of non-resistance. But ever since his return from Europe, George Logan had been sitting loose to the religion of his fathers. To Debby's sorrow, few

Friends drove out to Stenton now, and George never went with her to First Day meeting. Presently the Overseers — a reverend group of Quaker officials who kept a watchful eye on the 'dress and address' of members — reported his persistent absences to Philadelphia Monthly Meeting. His neglect of meeting-going was not the only cause for complaint, the Overseers added. There was an even more serious offense — Dr. Logan sometimes 'appeared in a military way.' The Overseers had gone to him, treated him in a loving manner, but he had told them he desired 'to be no longer considered as a member' of the Religious Society of Friends.

Friends were hesitant to take action against a Logan of Stenton, whose family history was so closely entwined with William Penn's 'holy experiment.' Committee after committee of weighty Quakers was sent out to Stenton to try to change his mind. Logan received them all graciously, but he 'appeared fixed in his sentiments, and unlikely to take the advice of [the] meeting.' His case dragged on from month to month, so reluctant was the meeting to cast him off. But finally, in January 1791, it was agreed, in accordance with Quaker practice, to issue a testimony against him.

George Logan [the document read] having been educated and made profession amongst us, the people called Quakers, hath departed from our peaceable testimony against wars and fightings by associating with others in bearing of arms; and on being tenderly treated with on account thereof, persists in vindicating the same, professing himself not convinced of the necessity of adhering to our said Christian principle, and desiring no longer to be considered a member among us. We therefore testify that he hath separated himself from us, and disown him from retaining any right of membership in our religious community; desiring nevertheless he may be so favored with the fresh extendings of heavenly regard as that, through a conformity thereto, he may become renewed in the spirit of his mind, and unite in the support of our Christian testimony.[3]

The clerk of the meeting made no record of exactly what his military activity was. In point of fact, it was very slight. George Logan was no soldier. His bold rebellion against the 'peaceable testimony' of Friends led him to do nothing more aggressive than join the militia — which he considered his civic duty. Soon, he was captain of a troop of horse. But during the Whisky Insurrection, when the militia was called up, he resigned.[4] He would not bear arms against the country people. Never again did he engage in military activity, nor could he approve of those who did. In his later years, Deborah tells us, 'he thought all war unlawful to a Christian except that which was strictly of a defensive kind.'[5]

George Logan did not — nor could he — turn his back completely on his Quaker inheritance. He never joined any other religious body. Indeed, in later life he often went to meeting with Debby, who remained a faithful and consistent Friend. He could not slough off habits of thought and action ingrained in him by his Quaker upbringing. What his disownment did mean was his decisive turning away from the conservative political philosophy of the Philadelphia Friends. The Quaker merchants, the landed families of Friends, the old established leaders, were aristocrats. The thought of violent revolution repelled them — and not just because of their religious scruples. By and large, the Quakers of Logan's set were federalists hearty in their support of Washington, Hamilton, and the new, strong government. Logan was a 'traitor to his class' when he cast his lot with the opposition.

There was, to be sure, no organized party of opposition at this moment, either in the nation or in Pennsylvania. But there was, especially in the country districts, a pervasive though inarticulate dissatisfaction with the course the new federal government was taking. George Logan set himself to the task of working with this unrest, shaping it, molding it, giving it clear outlines and tough, hard substance. He worked in emotions and ideas — emotions he felt in himself, ideas he borrowed, for the most part, from others. What emerged in the end was not merely a rationale for opposition to the stockjobber's mean and calculating spirit, but a vision of America as an agrarian republic, a nation of free farmers living in equality and brotherhood.

During its first year and a half, the federal government sat in New York. Logan at Stenton presently found himself writing long letters to old Senator Maclay, encouraging that sturdy, upright republican to resist every federal measure, to speak out for sim-

DR. JOHN FOTHERGILL
BY (Thomas?) Cook
Courtesy the Huntington Library

DR. ALEXANDER MONRO secundus
BY James Heath after Raeburn
Courtesy the New York Public Library

DR. WILLIAM CULLEN
BY C. Elliot after W. Cochrane
and V. Green
Courtesy the New York Academy
of Medicine

DR. WILLIAM HUNTER
BY J. Thornthwaite
Courtesy the Huntington Library

LOGAN'S MEDICAL MENTORS

STENTON MANSION

A recent photograph. From *Portrait of a Colonial City*

by Harold D. Eberlein and Cortlandt Hubbard, Lippincott, 1939

plicity and honesty in government, for justice to the farmer, and for the curbing of greed.[6] When the government moved to Philadelphia, at the end of 1790, Logan could see it operating close at hand. What he saw he did not like.

What he saw he took to be the subversion of the principles of the Revolution, the overthrow of Franklin's ideals, the undermining of the agrarian way of life, the emergence of a new aristocracy, battening on speculation and special privilege. All these evils, it seemed to him, stemmed from one source, the administration. Under the firm hand of Alexander Hamilton, with the approval and encouragement of President Washington, the administration was surrendering government to the city merchants, the traders, the manufacturers, the wealthiest citizens in the nation. Hamilton's design stood revealed in his long 'Report on Public Credit,' issued in January 1790. He called for funding the entire national debt at face value. The debt had been drained in the first instance from men of small property. It was to be met by taxes paid by the same men of small property. But the certificates of indebtedness had accumulated in the hands of a few rich men, men who planned to grow still richer by using them in speculative enterprises. The new aristocrats of paper and credit, men such as Robert Morris, George Clymer, Thomas Willing — men Logan had known all his life — were gathered in the Federal Court. Around Lady Washington and the President-General swirled a glittering and extravagant social life, the antithesis, Logan felt, of republican simplicity. The nation was being led into paths of corruption and effeminacy, as had the older countries of Europe. The gains of the Revolution were in jeopardy.

Early in 1790, Logan sat down at his desk in the great library at Stenton, and sharpened his pen. He would fight Hamilton's program, idea for idea, fact for fact, in newspaper and pamphlet. Oswald's *Independent Gazetteer* was 'at his devotion,' [7] and Oswald had built up a strong rural circulation. He was as anxious as Logan to stop the flow of federal measures, and restore the ideal of the free citizen-farmer. Dr. Logan, the agricultural writer, was one of his regular contributors; gladly he now opened his columns to Dr. Logan, publicist and author of the Cato letters.

Logan was determined to leave no part of the federal citadel unscathed. His first target was one of the outlying bastions, the Tariff and Tonnage Acts of July 1789, enacted before Hamilton had come into the government, but expressing his views. Logan urged the farmers to seek the repeal of 'all laws restricting the commerce of the country, and particularly those laws which subject strangers, who visit our ports, to higher duties and greater expenses than our own citizens.' Free trade, he argued, would foster competition among nations abroad for America's agricultural surplus, and 'the greater the price a farmer procures for his produce, the greater will be the net proceeds of his annual labor; and consequently, the greater will be the profit to the state.'

This argument, that the farmer's profit was the nation's gain, Logan put forward as the polar principle of political economy. Agriculture was the only source of 'real' wealth, he urged. Therefore the only just and equitable tax was a direct impost, 'confined to a certain proportion of the net proceeds of our farms.' Tariffs and tonnage taxes violated this rule; they lowered the farmer's income by raising the cost of the imported manufactured goods he must buy. The farmer's rights, he insisted, must not be 'sacrificed to the interest of local merchants.' [8]

The excise tax, with which Hamilton proposed to meet the interest on the national debt, was a second violation of America's agrarian economy. Against this threat Logan directed a volley of five newspaper essays — 'Letters' he called them, 'to the Yeomanry of Pennsylvania.' He sought a wider audience, sought to carry the battle to the enemy by securing a city circulation. So he offered the letters to Andrew Brown, publisher of the *Federal Gazette*. Brown was a conscientious editor, a fair and just man. Everyone liked him. But Brown was also thoroughly Federal, a mouth for Hamilton's voice. He read Logan's 'Letters,' acknowledged that they were well written, but declined to print them. Instead, he hurried off to New York in panic to report to Hamilton. Maclay, who saw him there, declared that he 'really never saw any man have more the appearance of fright upon him.' [9]

Logan gave up his attempt to reach a wider public, and the letters appeared in Oswald's paper between 13 March 1790 and

8 January 1791. Later, Oswald published them as a pamphlet under the title *Letters Addressed to the Yeomanry of the United States: Shewing the Necessity of Confining the Public Revenue to a Fixed Proportion of the Net Produce of the Land; and the Bad Policy and Injustice of Every Species of Indirect Taxation and Commercial Regulations.* Logan chose to hide his identity behind the phrase 'a farmer,' the pseudonym that John Dickinson, his wife's kinsman, had made famous thirty years before. Most of Logan's political writings were to be signed in this way, though his authorship was widely known, or suspected.[10]

In these letters Logan emerged as a theorist of agrarian democracy — one of the earliest philosophers of what came to be known as Jeffersonianism. The ideas he expressed were not original; like those of the Declaration of Independence, they were the more effective for being in common currency. They came chiefly from three sources — John Locke, Adam Smith, and the French *économistes*. To all these writers he had been introduced by Benjamin Franklin, and something of Franklin's spirit hovered over the essays.

Like any other eighteenth-century philosopher, the 'Farmer' grounded his argument upon the laws of nature. These laws are simple and evident, he declared. 'They have their foundation in the reciprocal duties men owe to each other, and their rights arising from such duties.' Turgot, Quesnay, every French agrarian, had said as much. It was the business of government to support natural law.

Having laid his foundation, he came quickly to the point. It was the right and duty of American farmers to procure a system of statutory law 'favorable to [the] divine science' of agriculture — law under which their property, 'after having once contributed to the support of government by an equal direct tax, would become perfectly free, without being subject to unjust commercial regulations.' [11]

Lawyers, he charged, had done their best to confuse the citizen. They had involved the rights of man in 'a labyrinth of error,' much as the clergy had befogged the simple religion of Jesus. But the essential axioms of political economy were beautifully few and simple. Thanks to the writings of 'a few enlightened men in France' — Dr. Logan glanced up at the treatises of Quesnay, Turgot, Mercier de la Rivière, Le Trosne, on his shelves — they could be set down in plain words:

1st. The earth is naturally fruitful.

2nd. The earth is not sufficiently productive for the support of civil society without cultivation.

3rd. The earth is the only source of those things necessary to the existence of men.

4th. The earth being the only productive fund, the cultivation of the earth is the only productive employ.

5th. Every other kind of work which has for its object the preparation, alteration, or transport of such productions may be more or less necessary, but they are not productive.[12]

George Logan, at his mahogany desk in his book-lined study, saw no reason why all farmers should not devote their leisure time, as he did, to the study of political economy. It was a science, he wrote, which 'brings us near to God himself, by engaging us to promote the general prosperity and happiness of mankind.' [13] Let the farmers but master its simple principles, and they would never sacrifice their rights to 'the ambition and avarice of a few.' Vigilance was the more needful, because the country was 'just at the commencement of a new and important era,' when too many Americans, "infatuated with the false principles of the government of Great Britain,' were 'anxious to adopt her wretched system of policy.' [14]

The Doctor's language showed that his temper was rising. But he made an effort to suppress it. Political economy, after all, was a science, and in science conclusions flowed logically from premises. His series of axioms led him straight to the favorite fiscal device of the followers of Quesnay — the *impôt unique,* the single, direct tax on land. The *impôt unique* was the fantasy of the Physiocrats, the central doctrine to which all their thinking led, and to which few could follow them. Franklin had never swallowed the *impôt unique;* neither had Jefferson. Both had too much experience of the world to think a government could be run on a single, general tax. But George Logan accepted it. He was not concerned with experience; he was concerned with logic. It was logical, from Physiocratic premises, to reach Physiocratic conclusions.

'As all the private and public wealth of a country arises from the land,' he wrote, 'the revenue necessary for the support of government can only be derived from the proprietors and farmers.' Therefore, every indirect tax, such as an excise on spirits, must finally flow, however circuitously, from the same source. Indirect taxes and all forms of commercial regulation contained a 'hidden poison' that had proved to be the downfall of many nations by destroying the liberty of the citizens. Therein, Logan hinted, lay the cause of Egypt's decay, and Greece's, and Rome's.

Indirect taxes, he explained, 'are obscure in their operation, and devoid of all order and proportion. The money raised by a direct tax passes immediately into the public treasury, whilst an indirect tax, upon articles of consumption, requires a great expense to support a host of revenue officers. A direct tax, being confined to a just proportion of the net produce of your farms, can never be oppressive, whilst an indirect tax, preying upon the gross produce of your farms, will destroy the means of future cultivation.' 15

Dr. Logan thought of Hamilton's excise, and his ire rose again. Even now, he warned his readers, 'Congress is establishing a system of finance, founded in deception, which has never been pursued by any government but to the oppression of the great body of the people.' Do not let yourselves be lulled into a perilous lethargy, he adjured the farmers, by the machinations of place-seekers. 'Come forward, tell your servants in Congress that it is you who must feel the effects of their Machiavellian politics . . . tell them that you are willing to pay a just proportion of the annual produce of your land into the public treasury, but that the remainder shall be left free at your own disposal.' 16

No longer could he repress his feelings, no longer dwell in the cool, serene realm of natural law, of Physiocratic dogma. He was aroused, and he must arouse the yeomanry.

How long [he asked the American farmers] will you suffer yourselves to be duped by the low cunning and artifice of half-informed lawyers and mercenary merchants? Are these characters to be the dictators of a free people? Are you to have no laws, no regulations, but through their influence or by their authority? Certainly you have not wrested the power from Great Britain to place it in the hands of these men. As you value your own prosperity and that of your children, look well to the present moment: a dangerous aristocracy is forming, which if not crushed in the bud, will destroy your liberties forever.[17]

The age was corrupt and impure. Logan thought of the Federal Court, of President Washington's Tuesday levees, of John Adams's fondness for titles, of Mrs. William Bingham's sumptuous soirees. These were strange sights to a free people — a people too ready 'to connect the dignity of government with the parade and extravagance of its officers.' Greedy merchants, 'citizens of the world . . . who know no country but their coffers of gold,' were carrying all before them. The independent yeomen, the bulwark of the nation, 'the most valuable class of citizens,' were losing their birthright — freedom.[18]

Nor did the excise tax exhaust the villainies, the 'low cunning and artifice' of the new aristocracy. He had neither space nor energy left to do more than mention the other evidences of their 'Machiavellian politics.' Congress had just authorized an increase in the standing army from 700 men to the alarming total of 1216. The liberties of the yeomen, Logan warned, were safe only so long as they resisted all efforts to saddle them with standing armies. A well-regulated militia was the safest defense of a republic: 'Those who experience the labor of acquiring property will ever be the best defenders of it.' [19] Was he not himself, at this very moment, sacrificing his right of membership in the Society of Friends to that principle?

The Tariff and Tonnage Acts showed clearly that Congress was substituting 'the interest of the local merchant . . . for the general interest of the country, as depending on a free, unlimited commerce.' Freedom of commerce had, after all, been one of the objects of the revolt against Great Britain. And yet American legislators were now imitating the British Navigation Acts, though Britain herself, Logan maintained, had never reaped any real benefit from them.[20]

And finally, Logan said, the funding of the public debt — the core of Hamilton's system — was a dishonest, potentially disastrous scheme for enriching the merchants at the expense of the farmers. But that was a subject in itself, and Logan, anxious to bring his letters to a close in order to set them before the public in pamphlet form, could not do it justice now. So he left it, content for the moment with the observation that 'public credit, which our politicians esteem of the greatest importance to government, should be regarded as the most unjust and ruinous importation of modern times.' [21]

The erstwhile Quaker, grown hardy on the strong diet of revolutionary doctrine, ended his tract with a covert threat of violent rebellion. 'Under every government,' he wrote, 'the *dernier ressort* of the people is an appeal to the sword : whether to defend themselves against the open attacks of a foreign enemy, or to check the insidious encroachments of domestic foes . . .' [22]

He had written in anger, in resentment; the master of Stenton's many acres was flailing out at the new aristocracy of lawyers and merchants whose power and wealth lay not in land but in paper, in government securities, in accounts receivable, in promises to pay. By writing as 'A Farmer,' by directing his letters to the 'yeomanry,' he had tapped deep reservoirs in the American consciousness. Those words called up an emotional response such as only the most powerful myths evoke. He had given incisive utterance to the vague stirrings of unrest among the farmers. He had begun to build a platform on which they could stand.

Logan saw that the farmers could make their stand, could defend their rights, only by organizing on a national scale. The means lay ready at hand, in the local agricultural societies of which he was so zealous a promoter. In his mind's eye he saw a network of farmers' societies spreading over the countryside, linked together by committees of correspondence, like those committees of patriots who had engineered the Revolution. No longer, however, was their purpose to be merely the encouragement of agricultural reform. 'In the present situation of public affairs,' he wrote, 'it is highly proper that the yeomanry should have stated meetings in every part of the United States, not only for promoting agricultural knowledge . . . but to stimulate and encourage each other to support their rights *as men.*' [23]

He broached this scheme in a series of letters ostensibly addressed to some 'gentlemen of Virginia' who had asked for advice on the formation of agricultural societies. For these letters he found a new publisher, one who promised to command a nation-wide audience. Philip Freneau, the editor of the *National Gazette,* was a poet, a thin, bandy-legged, slightly stooped man, whose melancholy steel-gray eyes still seemed to be seeing the horrors of the British prison ship to which he had been condemned during the Revolution. He had recently come to Philadelphia to edit the *National Gazette,* with the backing of Thomas Jefferson, who gave him a clerkship in the State Department. Everyone recognized his paper as the leading anti-Federalist organ. It was being read up and down the Atlantic seaboard. Old Sam Adams was promoting its circulation in Massachusetts. James Madison was soliciting subscriptions in Virginia, and Aaron Burr was singing its praises in New York.[24] What more likely agency for achieving Logan's ambitious design?

On the surface, the six letters to the Virginians were devoted to Logan's old enthusiasm — the improvement of agriculture. He offered the constitution of the Philadelphia County Society as a model for imitation, he made some characteristic observations on the virtues of homespun, he reprinted his experiments on crop rotation. But his new obsession with politics forced its way through, as he wrote of the 'insidious chicane of financial regulations,' and insisted that every agricultural society 'should also be regarded as a political society' to protect the rights of the farmers.[25]

Meanwhile, the Federalist program continued to unfold. On 5 December 1791, Hamilton laid before Congress his long, tightly packed 'Report on Manufactures.' The elaborate preamble might have been written as an answer to Logan's *Letters.* There Hamilton set forth the arguments of those who contended for agriculture as 'not only the most productive, but the only productive species of industry.' Then he set out to refute them. In deference to the great mass of Americans who lived on farms, he admitted that on various counts husbandry had 'a strong claim to pre-eminence over every other kind of industry.' [26] The Secretary followed this introduction, however, with a masterly case for protective duties, navigation laws, bounties, and similar mercantilist devices, all designed to encourage manufacturing.

Already, the energetic Secretary announced, a well-capitalized society was forming 'for prosecuting, on a large scale, the making and printing of cotton goods.' [27] This was a reference to the Society for Establishing Useful Manufactures (the 'S.U.M.'), a grandiose scheme to create a great industrial plant in Paterson, New Jersey. William Duer, a wealthy entrepreneur and close associate of Hamilton, was 'Governor' of the Society, and Hamilton himself had probably drafted the charter. It was a remarkable charter in any case, conferring generous privileges and exemptions. The Society was to have exclusive jurisdiction over an area of thirty-six square miles, the right to exercise eminent domain, freedom from taxation — temporary so far as its lands and buildings were concerned, perpetual with respect to its goods and chattels — and exemption of its employees from personal taxes and militia duty.[28]

Neither the 'Report' nor the charter for the industrial venture across the Delaware escaped Dr. Logan's watchful and, by now, suspicious eye. The design was clear. Give Hamilton his way, and he would change the face of America, desecrate Logan's agrarian paradise, enslave its happy, independent yeomen. In its place he would substitute a ravaged landscape of smoke-belching factories, peopled by sooty, cheerless mill hands and opulent, arrogant industrial magnates. To Logan such a prospect was abhorrent. Grimly, he set to work on a second blast against Mr. Secretary Hamilton's nefarious plans.

A new series of 'Letters to the Yeomanry' began appearing in Oswald's *Independent Gazetteer* in February 1792. Freneau promptly picked them up and reprinted them in the *National Gazette*. Again Oswald put them together into a pamphlet, and on 21 August, he and five other booksellers were advertising *Five Letters Addressed to the Yeomanry of the United States: Con-*

taining Some Observations on the Dangerous Scheme of Governor Duer and Mr. Secretary Hamilton, to Establish National Manufactories.[29]

Logan opened his new 'Letters' by quoting from the Declaration of the Rights of Man and of the Citizen, promulgated in 1789 and prefixed to the new French Constitution. That was what the United States needed, he roundly declared — an adequate Bill of Rights, one which would 'clearly and unequivocally dictate to the legislature its duty and to the people their rights.' [30] Such a guaranty, he asserted, would have saved the country from being saddled with the four monstrous evils perpetrated by Alexander Hamilton: the mercantile regulations, the funding system, the Bank, the Excise Law.

The same spirit of arbitrary power that had dictated these infringements of natural right, he went on, now threatened to interfere in the occupations of the mechanic and the manufacturer. This was flying in the face of the best principles of political economy and the sacred rights of mankind, as expounded by Adam Smith in his *Wealth of Nations.* Hamilton and his associates, with the aid of the New Jersey legislature, were bent upon securing special privileges. Special privileges could end only in the creation of an aristocracy in America.

Men were not really equal, Logan admitted. They differed in virtue, in talent; perhaps they must always differ in fortune. But government must not be allowed to aggravate economic inequality. This was exactly what the New Jersey legislature, under the influence of 'artful and designing men,' had done. 'Is it reasonable,' he demanded, 'is it just, that a numerous class of citizens, whose knowledge in mechanics and manufactures [is] not less necessary for the support of their families than useful to their country, should be sacrificed to a wealthy few, who have no other object in view than to add to their ill-gotten and enormous wealth?' [31]

Logan was aroused now. 'The preference of partial to general interests,' he proclaimed, 'is . . . the greatest of all public evils.' In his wrath he left the high ground of political abstraction. It was power that menaced the farmer, concentrated economic power. 'The accumulation of that power which is conferred by wealth in the hands of the few,' he wrote, 'is the perpetual source of oppression and neglect of the mass of mankind.' The power of the wealthy, he added, is increased 'by their tendency to combination, from which number, dispersion, indigence, and ignorance equally preclude the poor . . .'[32] This was a new note. American agrarianism had hitherto lacked this kind of analysis, this frank facing of the facts of economic power, this realistic picture of the average farmer.

Logan turned, as always, to history for proof. Whenever lawmakers had interfered in the daily occupations of citizens, the results had been pernicious. From Greek history and Roman, from Louis XIV's France and George III's England, from his books on Holland and Siam, from all the pages of Stenton's library, the Doctor drew examples to buttress his faith in *laissez faire*. The whole history of policy could be summed up by the words of an old French merchant; asked by Colbert what the king should do to encourage commerce, he had replied simply: 'Let us alone.'[33]

The success of American manufactures would not depend, Logan was sure, on financial regulations or legislative interference. It would come from the patronage and encouragement of patriotic citizens. The Doctor was not unsympathetic to the development of American manufacturing — so long as its growth was natural, not forced by the grant of special privileges. Opposition to American industry came from merchants engaged in the carrying trade — 'a powerful and increasing . . . interest.' For his own part, Logan favored making the United States as self-sufficient as possible.[34]

But as a good Physiocrat, he believed in perfect freedom of trade. He took as his own the favorite maxim of the *économistes*, '*Faire le bien c'est le recevoir.*' Tariffs merely invited retaliation, he said. They led ultimately to the stagnation of commerce and the loss of markets for surplus agricultural produce. Free trade, not artificial stimulation of the home market, was the answer to the farmer's needs.

Logan ended by reminding the yeomanry that they formed nine-tenths of the American people. They had never sought 'partial privileges.' Their only demand was a just one — 'a free unrestricted sale for the produce of their own industry,' and security from arbitrary laws that infringed their natural rights by enriching another part of the community at their expense.[35] It was the issue of the American Revolution all over again, Logan believed. He appealed to the yeomanry to stand once more for the exhilarating principles of 1776. Those principles had been temporarily 'suppressed by the influence of avarice and ambition.' But they were destined to appear again, he told the farmers, 'with additional lustre, reflected from the glorious Revolution of France.' [36]

Just before his *Five Letters* went on sale in the Philadelphia bookshops, Logan made another attack on the Paterson enterprise. The occasion was a meeting of the Germantown Society for Promoting Domestic Manufactures, and the audience included a good number of stocking weavers and other artisans. Only a few weeks earlier, Logan had read his charming essay on beekeeping before this society. But the address he made on 13 August 1792 was no bucolic discourse with literary embellishments. It was a fighting speech, the outburst of a man thoroughly alarmed, thoroughly angry.

He began by exposing, one after another, all the special privileges that Hamilton and Duer had secured for their enterprise. How, the Doctor asked the artisans, could they expect to survive against 'a combination of rich men enjoying the particular patronage and protection of government'? Vehemently, Logan denounced the slavish dogma 'that government has the whole property of citizens under its command, and that every law enacted by the legislature ought to be obeyed.' Had the workingman forgotten the doctrine of 1776 — that free men should oppose every attempt by government to violate their natural rights?

Into his peroration the Doctor poured all his apprehensions, all his indignation, all his wrath. His hearers sat in startled attention.

'The ambition and avarice of some men are never to be satisfied.' (The stocking weavers nodded their agreement with the laird of Stenton.) 'A few such characters have been for some time bending the whole power of the United States to promote their own private views of ambition and wealth.' (Yes, there was no question about it; Hamilton, Duer, and their friends were going too far.)

'Not content with the honorable name of citizen, they wish to introduce distinctions of rank; not content with enjoying at their ease every advantage which our country can afford, or their wealth procure, they desire to interfere in the occupations, and to curtail the enjoyments of their fellow citizens.' (The Germantown craftsman knew about class distinctions; he felt them every time he walked down Chestnut Street in Philadelphia. And now the aristocrats were reaching into the poor man's pocket, meddling with his livelihood.) 'They act as if they wished to bring the whole wealth and power of the country under their feet.'

The audience was following every word now, and waiting for the climax. It came. 'May the early opposition of the people of America to the unjust measures of these deluded men — may the glorious and blessed light of the French Revolution, aided by the writings of the friendly clubs in England, tend to convince them of their errors, and bring them to regard the rights of men in every occupation as sacred.'

The stocking weavers had not expected this kind of talk from the Quaker gentleman who owned the great mansion on the Germantown Road. They left the meeting disturbed, excited, their minds on fire. And Logan? He was tasting the dangerous delight of knowing that he had stirred men's feelings, molded their thought, stiffened their wills.

Soon Logan's views on Hamilton's manufacturing schemes were in everyone's hands, on everyone's lips. By order of the Germantown Society, his inflammatory address appeared in Mathew Carey's *American Museum* and in Freneau's *National Gazette.* John Fenno, Hamilton's *protégé,* quickly reprinted it in the official Federalist organ, the *Gazette of the United States,* so that Logan's former friends in Philadelphia could see to what dangerous lengths his incendiary philosophy was carrying him.[37]

Later in the year, as the people prepared to go to the polls,

Freneau's paper carried extracts from the *Five Letters,* and Carey reprinted them in full.[38] The pamphlet itself was advertised steadily in the anti-Federalist press until after the November elections. Its circulation was not confined to Pennsylvania. In September, Alexander Hamilton had a letter from Major Pierre Charles l'Enfant, the French engineer, who was supervising the works at Paterson: 'A pamphlet of this day come in my hand,' wrote the Frenchman, 'containing some observations on Mr. Secretary H. by a farmer.' [39] Logan's 'Letters to the Yeomanry' had penetrated to the very heart of the enemy camp.

Not only farmers but city people, businessmen and workers, were reading the *Five Letters* and the Germantown address, discussing them, quoting them, arguing over them. Rebuttals and defenses filled the columns of the Philadelphia papers for weeks.[40] Agrarian discontent, agrarian philosophy, had found a spokesman in the middle states. The opponents of the Society for Useful Manufactures, Logan their spearhead, contributed to the collapse of Duer and Hamilton's scheme by drying up its sources of capital. Their vigorous campaign forestalled the incorporation of similar societies. Agrarian democracy was killing off Hamilton's 'Report on Manufactures,' before Congress could act on it.[41]

In attacking corporations on behalf of the farmer, Logan had drawn from the reservoir of American democratic folklore two powerful myths. First, the symbol of the yeoman farmer himself — a symbol he had exploited before and would exploit again. And second, he appealed to the widespread popular sentiment that all corporations were 'monopolies,' 'aristocracies,' destructive of the social compact. This sentiment flourished in the rural districts and among the city artisans alike — wherever the doctrines of the Revolution retained their potency. This fear of the chartered corporation had little basis, perhaps, in reason or experience. But its roots went down into the emotional subsoil of American democracy.[42]

Stenton in these days was becoming a regular meeting-place for the opponents of the federal administration. The men who gathered under Logan's lofty trees were, like their host, inheritors of Benjamin Franklin's spirit, of his zest for science as well as his zeal for democracy. On a given day the circle might include the celebrated astronomer David Rittenhouse, the corpulent physician Dr. James Hutchinson, lawyer Alexander James Dallas, and Franklin's grandson 'Benny' Bache, the mettlesome editor of the *General Advertiser,* an anti-Federalist organ. On Stenton's broad lawns these men could speak freely of their distaste for the federal measures, their distrust of the federal leaders.

The central figure in the group was usually Thomas Jefferson, the Secretary of State. Jefferson often rode out to Stenton to escape from the tensions of official Philadelphia, where he was uncomfortably yoked in Washington's cabinet with his great opposite, Alexander Hamilton. There were few enough havens in which he could find congenial refuge. It was well known in Philadelphia that the only gentlemen who entertained him were Logan, Rittenhouse, and Charles Thomson, the former secretary of the Continental Congress.[43]

When he had first come out to Stenton, fresh from his diplomatic mission to Versailles, Jefferson had been dressed as a French dandy, Debby recalled, in 'a suit of silk, ruffles, and an elegant topaz ring.' Soon, however, he adopted 'a more republican garb,' influenced, perhaps, by the Doctor's example. Deborah always relished his conversation. His judgments of men and measures were temperate and restrained, she thought. Still, she wished he would show a little more reverence for General Washington.[44]

Her husband had no reservations. Jefferson was a fellow spirit — a farmer to whom he could proudly show his fat livestock, his latest experiments, his fields of golden wheat; a political philosopher with whom he could share his fears of Federalist excesses, his theories of agrarian politics, his dreams of a democratic America. He and Jefferson could spend hours together, happily discussing the design of plows. For years Jefferson had been covering sheets of paper with figures, trying to work out the mathematical formula for the perfect moldboard. To his surprise he found that Logan, working as a practical farmer, had already designed a plow that fitted his specifications perfectly. He ordered one made for his Virginia friend James Madison. Jefferson had talked with all the progressive Pennsylvania farmers about the rotation of crops, but he got more sound information on that subject from Logan, he told his son-in-law, 'than from all the others put together.' [45]

They made an odd pair as they walked about the farm — Jefferson tall, gangling, informal, with the easy bearing of the Virginia gentleman; Logan short, precise, intense, with something still of Quaker primness in his manner. But they had much in common, much in addition to their interest in farming, their love of letters and science, their aristocratic backgrounds, their simple 'republican' tastes. Logan's life at Stenton was the life Jefferson longed to lead at Monticello; Logan's fears of Federalist designs were Jefferson's fears; and Logan's philosophy of an agrarian America was Jefferson's philosophy. But the Doctor had what Jefferson lacked; not being a prisoner of office, he had freedom to speak out.

The two men often talked long and earnestly. They had much to talk about in the winter and spring of 1793. Washington had just been re-elected President, as everyone had expected, as indeed everyone wanted. But this meant that Hamilton and his henchmen were secure for four more years. Their schemes for 'national manufactories' might founder (Duer had recently gone bankrupt, dragging many down with him), but the main pillars of the Federalist structure remained — the funding system, the assumption of state debts, the Bank.

Jefferson and his friends were convinced that there was 'a corrupt squadron of voters in Congress at the command of the Treasury.' [46] The anti-Federalists demanded that the Secretary make full reports on his fiscal operations. Reluctantly Hamilton complied, producing, after prodigious labor, a series of reports, sophisticated in argument, studded with figures. Jefferson's partisans scanned these bewildering masses of statistics and were rewarded. They discovered in them grounds (minor, technical grounds, but grounds none the less) for the charge they had been making all along — that Hamilton was carrying things with a high hand in the Treasury. They introduced resolutions of censure. In the dying days of the Second Congress, battle was joined. The Federalists voted the resolutions down — but only after a bitter fight.

Partisan warfare was raging — in the papers of Fenno and Freneau, in the halls of Congress, in the coffee houses and taverns — wherever Federalist and anti-Federalist collided. Everywhere the issues were the same — the public debt and the Bank, Hamilton's two great creatures.

In the midst of this strife George Logan rounded out his attack on the Federal program by publishing his third series of 'Letters to the Yeomanry.' He had written them rapidly during the debate on Hamilton's official conduct, and Freneau printed them as fast as they came from his pen. They were in the booksellers' shops in May 1793 under the title *Letters Addressed to the Yeomanry of the United States, Containing Some Observations on Funding and Bank Systems.*

'The present rulers of the United States call "PEACE, PEACE!" — but there is no peace.'

So Logan commenced his most eloquent tract, his most cogently argued agrarian essay. Peace was the product of social good will, of public integrity, of decency and order. 'Peace reigns where justice reigns, but where this is not made the foundation of a government and of laws, confusion must ensue.'

Justice was not the foundation of the new Constitution, Logan complained. It owed its existence to a selfish faction — to 'the influence and artifices of a few men, who had taken advantage of the distresses of the country, and who had largely speculated in the certificates given for services rendered by the most meritorious citizens.' [47] The farmers and soldiers of Revolutionary America had little dreamed, as they fought to free themselves from British commercial regulations and indirect taxes, that the 'corrupt British system of finance and politics' would be forced upon them by their own government — that the property they sacrificed when their country was attacked would eventually find its way into the pockets of speculators.

It was Hamilton who had betrayed the people. It has been asserted, Logan wrote, 'by a person who hitherto has been suffered

to assume too great a degree of authority in the government' —
no one could mistake the reference — that a public debt is a public
blessing. This was cant. It was economic inanity, inconsistent with
nature, unsupported by facts. Hamilton's 'long reports on finance,
by fatiguing the memory, confound the judgment, and force his
readers into such a labyrinth of error that the clue of decision has
not length enough to reach the extensive mazes of a wandering
imagination.' [48]

There was but one rule of justice for individuals and for society, Logan declared. The principle of bankruptcy ought to be
applied to governments. The individual bankrupt, after dividing
all his property among his creditors, was declared free and clear
of all further indebtedness. So should it be with governments.
Often it was done in practice, by inflating the currency. American
soldiers and farmers had received two shillings sixpence in the
pound for their certificates when the government was actually in
a state of bankruptcy. This discharged the indebtedness. But now
the speculators, to whom in their distress the poor yeomen and
artisans had assigned their certificates, were permitted to receive
face value from the government. It was atrocious. By this means,
the original creditors and all their posterity too became hewers
of wood and drawers of water to a moneyed interest — largely a
foreign moneyed interest at that.

Banks and public credit could only end by aggravating inequality among the people. National credit — the shibboleth of Federalism — was a modern invention by which the property and labor
of posterity were mortgaged to satisfy the debts contracted by
the present generation. It was unjust, it was criminal, it was a
flouting of natural right: 'The present generation, even to preserve its own existence, has no right to infringe on the property
of posterity.'

To enforce this point Logan borrowed one of Thomas Jefferson's favorite themes — the notion that 'the earth belongs to the
living.' Indeed Jefferson, unable to speak out publicly because of
his position in Washington's cabinet, may have 'inspired' Logan
to take this line against Hamilton's policies. In his third letter the
Doctor contended that since the earth belongs to the living, since

the dead have neither power nor right over its fruits, 'we have
. . . only to determine what length of time a law made by one
generation can continue in force without violating the rights of
their successors.' [49] From a study of Buffon's tables of mortality
— undoubtedly Jefferson's study, not his own — he derived the
conclusion that nineteen years was the longest period over which
the representatives of a nation could validly extend a debt. Beyond that time a public debt violated the natural rights of the new
generation.

To this theory of political generations, he added an argument
based on history. He sought to show, by examples drawn from
Blackstone and Adam Smith, how funding systems had wrecked
Genoa, Venice, the United Provinces, and threatened even Great
Britain herself. He capped these historical illustrations by listing
the particular evils rising from funding systems: poverty, especially in farming areas, where the tax burden fell most heavily;
subjection to foreign capitalists; idleness and extravagance on the
part of the security-holding class. Such a system, almost unaided,
had caused the overturn of the French monarchy. Was not this a
horrid enough example to make the upholders of funding — those
friends of monarchy — stop and reflect?

Turn to Adam Smith, he told his readers, and to the exponents
of the 'heaven-born French philanthropy' for sound policy, for
right thinking on these great issues. He cited other books — Tom
Paine's *Rights of Man*, Joseph Priestley's *Lectures on History
and General Policy*, Arthur Young's *Annals of Agriculture*,
Catherine Phillips's *Considerations on the Causes of the High
Prices of Grain and Other Provisions*.[50] These were his authorities, the sources of his radicalism — Paine, the old firebrand of
the American Revolution, now defender of the French; Priestley,
radical in politics as in religion, whom persecution would presently
drive from England to America; Arthur Young, energetic promoter of the 'new agriculture'; Catherine Phillips, the 'benevolent
Quaker,' who had been a guest at Stenton in the Doctor's childhood, and who believed in translating religion into social action.
These books he recommended to his readers.

But George Logan himself was no longer dependent on books

and other men's ideas, no longer merely the thrall of a doctrinaire philosophy. What his own eyes had seen in Philadelphia was enough to convince him that a counter-revolution had all but swept away the glorious fruits of 1776:

To satisfy the ambition of one class of men and the avarice of another [he wrote], the Americans have submitted to a second revolution, by which they have bartered their domestic rights, liberty, and equality for the energy of government and the etiquette of a court. After having wrested the sceptre from the hand of the British tyrant, they have suffered it to be assumed by a monied aristocracy, where it will be found more oppressive and injurious to the people.

But Logan could still be optimistic, for he still believed in the essential goodness and political wisdom of the people — the simple yeomen on their farms, the independent artisans in their shops, the real America that lay beyond and around and above the aristocrats of the Federal Court.

The more a nation is compact and the power of government left in the hands of the people, the more we shall find that love for the public good, that general esteem for virtue, and that disinterestedness which are held in light estimation by the supporters of a grand and extensive empire, where public counsels and emoluments of the state are wholly in the hands of the few, and where the people are neglected, despised, and oppressed.[51]

George Logan, wealthy master of Stenton, heir of the most aristocratic tradition in Pennsylvania, had identified himself irrevocably with the common people, the people who were forgotten on Chestnut Street, in Congress Hall, in the Treasury Office, at Mrs. Bingham's soirees. In three years of writing — bitter, angry, petulant writing, writing that was often incendiary and sometimes eloquent — he had set forth a coherent philosophy of agrarian democracy. Now the battle for democracy was entering a new phase. It was time to lay down his pen, to go out from Stenton, to act.

***

VII. DAYS OF TERROR

OLD FRIENDS who remembered the polished young doctor just back from Europe, the austere, conservative Assemblyman, the sedate, Quakerish gentleman-farmer, could only wonder at Dr. Logan these days, at his frenzied activity, his undignified behavior. He seemed like a new, strange man, a creature possessed, 'hurrying through the country' — so the newspapers described him — 'like a Bedlamite escaped from the cell, brawling in every tavern against the government . . . vilifying the character of the majority of Congress, pasting up . . . handbills with the specious words *liberty, property,* and *no excise,* and endeavoring to excite disturbances and tumult in opposition to a law of the land.' [1] People on Chestnut Street shook their heads. A Logan of Stenton become a fanatic political colporteur, a reckless fomenter of trouble, a demagogue? It was unaccountable.

More unaccountable yet, the Doctor consorted daily with dangerous radicals from the west, with disreputable incendiaries from the city, men of no family, no property, and no principles — except the old, exploded principles of equality and liberty and 'popular' government. Why last year, Philadelphians said, his name had appeared in the papers along with those of notorious democrats such as Blair McClenachan, David Rittenhouse, Dr. Hutchinson. He had allowed a 'committee of correspondence' made up of anti-Federalist politicians to propose him as a presidential elector for Thomas Jefferson.[2] Like any back-country demagogue, he was publicly referring to the discredited state Constitution of 1776 —

now happily discarded — as the 'late excellent constitution,' and speaking of Philadelphia's leading citizens — old family friends of the Logans and Norrises — as an 'aristocratic junto,' a sinister cabal.[3] It was not only unaccountable, it was positively shameful.

What a trial for poor Debby to be married to such a man, people said. And yet, when her old friends drove out to Stenton — infrequently now — they found her as serene, as cheerful, as content as ever, eager to discuss the latest books, proud to display the products of her loom and spinning wheel, her lovely gardens, her family of boys (there were three now, since the birth of Algernon Sidney in 1791). Apparently she was oblivious to the sad change that had come over her husband. Either that or she was putting up a brave front.

But Debby knew there was nothing unaccountable, nothing inconsistent in her husband's behavior. She might remonstrate gently with him over his restless activity, his ceaseless coming and going. She might wish for him that tranquillity, that inner peace and calm that she found in the silence of the Friends' meeting, but she knew her husband better than the fashionable people on Chestnut Street did. She knew that in his mind he was only upholding the doctrines of 1776 — Franklin's doctrines — against what seemed to him a new tyranny, a counter-revolution. As a Quaker she knew that if he had a burning 'concern' within him, she could not, she must not, stand in his way. Now she knew he could no longer be satisfied to sit in his library, composing philosophical letters to the yeomanry. He must go out among the farmers, stir them up, inflame them, organize them — not in academic societies to promote agriculture, but in action groups to protect their rights as men, to mount guard in defense of their liberty and their property.

George Logan found the yeomen ready. Hamilton's excise had stirred resentment and anger among the farmers of the Monongahela country, far to the west. It was an invidious, an intolerable tax, they said, and it was aimed directly at them. For they grew one staple crop — Indian corn — which they regularly converted into whisky. Only in that form was it profitable to transport across the Alleghenies to market. By placing an excise on distilled liquors the Federal government was interfering directly with their livelihood, taking bread from their mouths. When Federal revenue agents actually started coming over the mountains to collect the tax, the farmers began reaching for their long rifles.

Logan had opposed the excise from the beginning. His reasons, drawn straight from the Physiocrats, were already in print. He had even persuaded the Germantown Society for Promoting Domestic Manufactures to pass resolutions declaring the whisky excise 'a dangerous violation of our natural and inalienable rights.' [4] But he realized now that his pamphlets were too philosophical, his resolutions too feeble for the frontier farmers. He must speak directly, simply, trenchantly — above all, loudly — if he was to catch their ears. In May 1793 he boiled his arguments down to a handbill and distributed it among the yeomanry.

This excise, shouted the broadside, was 'THE FAVORITE SYSTEM OF ARISTOCRATS, BY WHICH UNEQUAL TAXES ARE DRAWN FROM THE LABORIOUS PART OF THE COMMUNITY.' It was 'a British system of finance.' Things British, Logan knew, were not loved in the west. The Revolution was still remembered there, Redcoats were even yet manning posts on American soil. Furthermore, this excise was an indirect tax. It smacked of deception, of secrecy, mystery. It was a subtle means to drain money from the people without their knowledge or consent.

A final question struck directly on the westerners' land-hunger, on their resentment of eastern speculators: 'What must be thought of the justice of the government of the United States that demands an oppressive tax from a farmer for the privilege of making the best use of the produce of his own labor, whilst it demands nothing from the wealthy proprietor of fifty thousand acres of land?' Logan urged the newly formed Democratic Societies to organize opposition to the iniquitous tax.[5]

The Democratic Societies, just struggling to birth, were the first tentative centers of organized opposition to the Federalists. They were anxious not to alienate possible supporters. To be found urging resistance to law might be fatal. They declined to take up Logan's challenge.[6] Pusillanimous, the Doctor thought them. But *he* was not timid. He would become an agitator himself. And so the summer of 1793 found him riding tirelessly through the countryside, scattering his fiery handbills everywhere, to the astonishment and disgust of his former friends in Philadelphia.

From a man in Logan's frame of mind perfect consistency was hardly to be expected. Even while he was fighting for the western farmers against Mr. Hamilton's excise, he was preparing to attack another project of the 'aristocrats' — also hatched in Philadelphia but calculated in this case to benefit the farmers inestimably. The back-country people needed good roads in order to transport their wheat, flour, and whisky, their cattle, sheep, and hogs to market in Philadelphia. Philadelphia needed the farmers' products for consumption and for export. If no roads were built, those products — Pennsylvania's real wealth — would find their way down the Susquehanna valley to Baltimore.

Robert Morris and the Philadelphia businessmen understood this very well. Back in 1789 they had formed the Society for Promoting the Improvement of Roads and Inland Navigation, with an ambitious program to link the rivers of Pennsylvania in a great network of waterways. Canals were to be supplemented by improved roads.[7] The canal scheme came to little, but the notion of building a toll road on the new principles of the Scotch engineer, McAdam, caught the imagination of Thomas Mifflin, Governor of Pennsylvania. He recommended it to the Assembly, and in 1792 the Philadelphia and Lancaster Turnpike Company was chartered, with authority to sell stock.

When the books were opened on 4 June 1792 at the State House, a riot almost took place, so great was the rush for shares. All Philadelphia was 'infected with the turnpike rage,' one observer commented. 'The quiet Quakers, who attended for the purpose of joining in the subscription and encouraging the road, finding such an uproar, withdrew.'[8] Organization was completed in July, and construction began the following spring on what was to be the first, and for many years the best, long turnpike in the United States.

No such 'exclusive charter' could be granted to a corporation in Pennsylvania without arousing George Logan's suspicions. To his jaundiced eye, the whole scheme looked like another plot set on foot by the associated forces of money and privilege. The very fact that the company's president was William Bingham was enough in itself to insure Logan's hostility. For Bingham — the elegant, opulent Bingham, banker, shipper, real-estate baron, high-born, high-married Bingham whose mansion on Third Street was the hub of Federalist social life — was the very personification of the forces that Logan blamed for corrupting American life.

On 17 May 1793, shortly after construction on the turnpike began, the Doctor took the chair of a public meeting at the Prince of Wales Tavern. The meeting considered 'the late unjust and arbitrary laws by which a few wealthy men are incorporated and empowered to violate the rights of their fellow citizens.' Resolutions were passed. The first proclaimed every citizen's right to be protected by the government in the full enjoyment of his life and property. The second declared the act incorporating the turnpike company, and endowing it with the power of eminent domain, unjust and dangerous — unjust because it took the property of citizens without their consent, dangerous because it opened the way to unlimited future infringements of property rights.

The meeting empowered Logan and Edward Heston to act on its behalf — to crystallize anti-turnpike sentiment and organize an effective opposition. Heston was a Revolutionary veteran, a former state Senator and Judge of the Court of Common Pleas. He was a man people would listen to. A gentleman-farmer like Logan, he had an ample estate along the proposed route of the turnpike. He shared Logan's agrarian philosophy, his concern for the farmer's prosperity. He had often been heard to say that 'he should be happy to know every human being as comfortably situated as himself.' [9] Heston and Logan were instructed to prepare an address to the people of Pennsylvania, and then to organize protest meetings of property owners along the proposed right-of-way. These meetings in turn would appoint delegates to a grand protest meeting to be held three weeks hence at Nathan Levering's tavern on the Ridge Road.

The newspapers carried an account of the meeting at the 'Prince of Wales.' They also printed the address. Turnpike promoters, Logan and Heston charged, were animated by 'the sordid desire of private gain' rather than zeal for the public good. They cited Blackstone — 'a considerable law character in England' — in support of the absolute right of property.[10] Logan's concern for landed rights, his suspicion of the moneyed class, his hostility to anything that savored of special privilege or monopoly ran through every word of the address.

Publication of the proceedings at the 'Prince of Wales' brought a swarm of attacks down upon Logan's head. The ablest, most scurrilous, signed himself 'A Friend to Improvements.' He was a stockholder in the company, he said, and denied that the law had any particular rich men in view, since no names were mentioned and the books had been open to the public. He threw back the charge of cupidity by pointing out that Logan and other eastern farmers had every selfish reason to obstruct the progress of the road in order to avoid competition with the farmers of the Lancaster region.

The 'Friend to Improvements' also charged Logan with citing sentences from Blackstone out of context. If the Doctor read his medical books in the same fashion, he observed, he might find himself prescribing a glyster of fishhooks instead of calomel or rhubarb for a child afflicted with worms. 'In one passage of the Testament, we are told that "Judas hanged himself"; in another it is commanded "go thou and do likewise." Tack them together, Doctor, and few will regret your following the precepts.' [11]

The turnpike controversy kept Philadelphia aroused and entertained for several weeks.[12] At a local protest meeting held in Germantown in June, Logan helped draft a petition which was diligently circulated through the county.[13] But by the time of the grand conference on the Ridge Road, Logan's attention and that of everyone else had been diverted elsewhere. For on 16 May, Citizen Edmond Charles Genêt had arrived in Philadelphia.

Early in 1793, Logan and all other enthusiastic Philadelphia republicans were exulting with Hugh Henry Brackenridge that

'Louis Capet has lost his *caput.*' Debby's reaction was quite otherwise. To her, the French news was 'very melancholy.' She was 'extremely afflicted for the fate of the royal family.' Strong in her Quaker faith, she prayed for inward peace, for freedom from the violent emotions of the day: 'Happy are those,' she wrote, 'who in times of such distractions can witness a calm in their own minds and retire as into a safe retreat from the conflicting passions of the world.' [14]

Her husband, however, wanted no such calm mind or safe retreat in these exciting days. As Jefferson said, 'all the spirit of 1776' was rekindling.[15] Dr. Logan thrilled to the Declaration of the Rights of Man and of the Citizen, he marveled at the Constitution of 1791, he found the Revolution in France exhilarating, inspiring, awesome. Republican France seemed as strong in freedom as republican America seemed corrupt. If he did not go dancing the *Carmagnole* or singing *Ça ira* with the mob in the streets, it was perhaps because his enthusiasm for the Revolution was intellectual, not emotional. But it was none the less intense.

The spirit of France in America was approaching a climax in 1793. It reached its crescendo in Philadelphia when Citizen Genêt arrived, the Minister of the new French Republic. Logan did not attend the banquets and public demonstrations with which Francophiles feted the handsome young Minister — he was 'not fond' of such functions.[16] But he was much in the Minister's company, and in June he aligned himself unmistakably with Genêt's partisans by joining the *Société française des amis de la liberté et de l'égalité,* a Philadelphia society imitative of the Jacobin Clubs in France. Mostly it was made up of native Frenchmen or Santo Domingans. Logan was one of the few American-born members.

The society's avowed object was to propagate the revolutionary principles of liberty and equality. Specifically, the purposes were to correspond with the Jacobin Clubs, to aid French republicans in the United States, to seek to improve commercial relations between the two countries, in short, 'to serve any cause that may interest the French republic in general and the French patriots in particular.' [17]

Logan saw Genêt often at meetings of the *Société française.*

The two men worked together on a revision of the society's constitution. Presently the Doctor was dining with Genêt in Philadelphia, entertaining him at Stenton.[18] The little circle of anti-Federalists that regularly gathered under Logan's lofty trees welcomed the Frenchman into their midst. For a time his presence added a special *bouquet* to the heady wine of their discussions on liberty and equality.

Debby even grew accustomed to hearing herself addressed as *citoyenne* Logan — it was preferable at least to the barbarous term 'citess' which the American Jacobins affected. She found the French Minister 'very pleasing in his address and manners,' noted that he retained his 'good humor and gentlemanly demeanor' even when bested in an argument.[19]

At first there were few arguments. Logan and his friends had captured a lion and they made the most of him, exulting in his reports from Paris, nodding their agreement with his criticisms of the Federalist administration, sympathizing with his exasperation over President Washington's studied coolness. Jefferson took special note of Genêt's remark that 'Colonel Hamilton had never in a single instance addressed a letter to him as the Minister of the *Republic* of France, but always as the Minister of France.' [20]

But there was a limit to tolerance, even for the most ardent friends of France. The young man's official behavior became more and more overbearing. Jefferson presently found it necessary to remonstrate with him, to complain of his recklessly undiplomatic behavior in fitting out privateers in American ports. It violated the declared neutrality of the United States. Genêt replied that his country was engaged in a desperate struggle to keep alive the great principles in which France, and America too, believed. In these circumstances, he said, he could not observe all the nice diplomatic amenities.

Long afterward, Deborah recalled the scene vividly. Rising from his chair on the broad lawn and taking in Stenton's quiet grounds with a gesture, the brilliant, glittering youth from the youngest republic exclaimed: 'Well, gentlemen, if my country were once happily settled in peace and the enjoyment of her rights as yours is now, I would sit under my own vine and trees as you do, but I would disclaim political disquisitions altogether.' [21]

Yet young Genêt was outrageous — soon everyone saw it. He could not take advice, he was strangely insensitive. He grossly insulted even his friends. For all his gallantry, he behaved with deplorable crudeness. One by one, his supporters, Logan among them, forsook him, lest he 'sink the republican interest' and drag them all down with him.[22]

The Genêt furor lasted only a summer. It passed when the Minister overreached himself, and with it passed the high tide of the French frenzy. But some, even some intelligent Quakers, insisted that it had required a providential intervention in the form of the yellow fever to avert 'a fatal revolution of government.' The plague came just as Genêt faded. It carried off two of the Minister's warmest supporters, Dr. Hutchinson and Jonathan Dickinson Sergeant.[23]

Dr. Logan's mind, certainly, was distracted from politics by the appalling epidemic, which struck Philadelphia in mid-August. The fever came, no one knew whence; it spread, no one knew how; it was cured, when it *was* cured, no one knew why — though there were as many theories as doctors. Wealthy merchants who had summer houses in the country fled in terror from the stricken city. Those who could not flee were at the mercy of the fever; they died by scores every day, later by hundreds. In the end, deaths were more than five thousand.[24]

The doctors were magnificent, trudging wearily from patient to patient, but they were far too few and they could never agree on the proper treatment. The great weight of Dr. Benjamin Rush's prestige was behind a heroic, and often disastrous, course of bleedings and purgings. Others, like Dr. Jean Devèze, who had known the fever in the West Indies, favored simple measures and gentle medicines, designed only to assist nature in fighting off the disease.

George Logan could not forget that he was a trained physician. He had not practiced his profession these ten years, but his strong sense of duty sent him every day into the plague-bound city. Deborah made no attempt to conceal her anxiety. The Quaker in her knew he must go, but the wife would have him stay in the safety of Stenton. Every day, as he set off for the fever-ridden city, she prayed fervently for his preservation. Meanwhile, she kept the great house odorous with garlic as a defense against infection. The children went barefoot that summer, for she did not dare send to town for new shoes.[25]

Like the other doctors, Logan had his own ideas on how to manage yellow fever cases. And like other doctors, he gave his ideas to the newspapers. Characteristically, he favored a course midway between the extremes — between the opposing methods of Devèze and Rush. He rejected the West-Indian treatment. It had never succeeded, he said, in the islands. Still, he agreed with Dr. Devèze in prescribing only mild emetics and cathartics. Mercury and jalap, as recommended 'by our worthy citizen, Dr. Rush,' made the best purgative, but they should be used in moderation, not in the massive, murderous doses that Rush prescribed. And Rush's relentless bloodletting, by which he weakened patients already wasted by fever, and his 'great purge,' was unwarranted, contrary to the best medical authority, 'as well ancient as modern.' [26]

Rush was not a man to take criticism, even Logan's polite demurrers, calmly. Besides, his nerves were raw from his exhausting labors in the city. He knew perfectly well that his old friend Logan was working devotedly among the sick. Nevertheless he made gratuitous and biting remarks about men who wrote treatises on yellow fever 'in their closets for the instruction of men who have gained a knowledge of it at hourly risk of their lives for four or five weeks.' [27] Later, a card appeared in the papers from 'the physicians of Philadelphia engaged in attendance on those laboring under pressure of disease,' sarcastically inviting Logan to join them in active service 'instead of insulting their understandings and distracting the public mind by giving vain advice.' [28]

Soon afterward, Logan received an official request which showed that he enjoyed a full measure of public confidence as a physician. The request came from the committee of citizens that had volunteered to maintain the city's services when the municipal government had disintegrated in terror. The committee wanted him to investigate the lazaretto at Bush Hill, recently reorganized under the direction of the merchant Stephen Girard and placed under the medical care of Dr. Devèze. Bush Hill, where the mild West-Indian regimen was in effect was 'the inescapable refutation of Rush's enthusiastic claims' for bleeding and the 'great purge.'

Dr. Logan found the hospital clean, with no offensive smell, the sick well accommodated. Girard and his associates, he reported, deserved the thanks of all Philadelphians. Moreover, Logan had followed the physicians in their rounds, and pronounced their practice 'rational and consistent with the nature of the disease.' [29] He had come, finally, to accept the West-Indian treatment, the treatment, incidentally, which enlightened physicians would adopt a century later.

The fever did not release the shuddering city from its grip until the first frosts came, early in November. For George Logan and his friends, it was a relief to be able to turn once again to politics after this nightmarish interlude. Though he had had no political object in view in fighting the plague, his humane and heroic efforts as a physician had undoubtedly enhanced his popularity with the common people.

When they heard, next spring, of his extraordinary kindness to a young hired hand sick with the smallpox, they said to one another that this was only what they had come to expect of the good Doctor. The laborer was a lad just arrived in the neighborhood from the western part of the state. Dr. Logan knew nothing of his background or circumstances, but hired him to help with the spring plowing and planting. The boy boarded with the family at Stenton, but lodged with relatives near by. One day, after working for a week, he failed to appear. Dr. Logan made inquiries, learned that he was lying ill with a fever. Going straightway to the house of the boy's relatives, he examined him and diagnosed the case as confluent smallpox, the most virulent form of the disease, and one of which he had made a special study at Edinburgh. When he spoke the dread word 'smallpox,' the boy's kinsfolk rushed out of the house in panic, lest they take the infection.

To Dr. Logan there was only one thing to do. He bundled the boy up, had him carried to Stenton, put him to bed in one of the chambers of the great house. He stayed by the patient's bedside, administering Peruvian bark and supervising his care and diet until the lad finally recovered. Word presently reached the boy's father in the west. He drove to Stenton, Debby later recalled, 'with a fine team of horses and every appearance of substantial circumstances.' It turned out that the boy had left home in a moment of rebellious pique. The father, after profuse thanks to the Doctor, took him back. Reports of the case spread to Philadelphia, and physicians came out to Stenton for a supply of the variolous matter with which to inoculate their own patients.[30] Ordinary people heard the story, and their hearts grew warm toward the good master of Stenton.

Logan had not joined the Democratic Society of Pennsylvania when it formed in the spring of 1793. Naturally he shared its sympathy with popular aspirations at home and abroad, but he found it timid, irresolute, cautious, when the times required bold, unhesitating action. In January 1794, however, he swallowed his misgivings and became a member.[31] Perhaps the Democratic Societies — they were spreading from Philadelphia into every state — might be made rallying points for the effective, concerted, nation-wide political opposition he had been waiting for.

At this very moment, the Society was making ready for a fight on the long-smoldering issue of commercial policy and neutral rights. The British, at war with revolutionary France since February, had imposed cramping restrictions on American shipping. To Logan's friends, the administration's apparent acquiescence was simply new proof of hopeless subservience to Great Britain. James Madison of Virginia had rebelled, had proposed that Congress meet the British Orders-in-Council with stiff retaliatory measures.

Like most pronouncements on foreign affairs, Madison's resolutions had domestic political ends in view. They furnished an occasion for renewed attack on Hamilton's 'paper system' as dependent upon the favor of the liberticide British government.[32]

JOHN RANDOLPH OF ROANOKE
By Gilbert Stuart
Courtesy the National Gallery of Art
(Mellon collection)

ABRAHAM BALDWIN
By E. Leutze after Robert Fulton
Courtesy the Historical society
of Pennsylvania

GOUVERNEUR MORRIS
By Ezra Ames
Courtesy the New-York Historical
society, New York city

JAMES ROSS
By Thomas Sully
Courtesy the Pennsylvania Academy
of the Fine Arts

LOGAN'S CONGRESSIONAL COLLEAGUES

DEBORAH NORRIS LOGAN in 1822

BY Charles Willson Peale

courtesy commissioners of Fairmount Park

It was at this point that the Democratic Societies entered the fight. They organized a powerful propaganda machine, hoping to overcome the Federalists' control of the greater part of the press. The Philadelphia Democratic Society, strategically located at the seat of the national government, naturally played a commanding role in this campaign. It held meetings every week, sometimes at the German Lutheran schoolhouse on Cherry Street, sometimes at the University of Pennsylvania on Mulberry Street, only a few squares from Congress Hall and the offices of the federal government. The Society soon developed into a well-oiled 'electioneering engine.' [33]

By joining this incipient political machine, George Logan added still another tie to the Philadelphia democrats. They, for their part, lost no time in putting his pen to work. With Dallas, Bache, and young Peter DuPonceau, he drafted a letter of fraternal greeting to the French National Convention. Appointed to the Committee of Correspondence, he was kept busy writing out resolutions expressing satisfaction with the course of events in France, and praising Minister James Monroe for his expressions of open sympathy with the Revolution, complaining of British infringements of neutral rights, and protesting the appointment of a well-known Anglophile, John Jay, as Minister to London. The committee gave copies of the resolutions to the newspapers, sent them out to other societies up and down the coast and in the back country. It was exhilarating, satisfying work. At last, Logan could feel, something was being done to weld together the elements of opposition, to build up democratic solidarity throughout the nation.[34]

Something was being done — but not enough. Members of the society were still too timid, too cautious. In May 1794, they allowed the committee to publish a set of strong resolutions against new excises; but in July, when news reached Philadelphia of riots in the west, they pulled back, condemned the action of the Whisky Boys as 'an outrage upon law and order,' and appealed to the westerners to pay the tax. Disgusted, Logan followed Blair Mc-Clenachan, the society's burly and gouty president, out of the room in protest against this skittishness.[35] He could scarcely believe his ears when, in November, President Washington made a gratuitous attack on the 'self-created' popular societies for having fomented the rebellion. The Doctor knew the societies were innocent — entirely too innocent for his taste. And the imputation that they had no right to exist in a free country was an offense against Americans, even against man.

But the treaty that John Jay brought back from England at the very end of the year was an even greater offense. As Logan read it, he could see only concession after damaging concession. Far from protecting the right of Americans to trade freely with France, Jay had tacitly agreed to let the British seize any French property they might find in American ships. Was there no limit, then, to the lengths the 'monocrats' in their mercenary frenzy would go to placate William Pitt and protect Hamilton's financial system? To Logan, Jay's treaty seemed a base betrayal of his country's traditional friendship with France, a violation of Franklin's treaties of 1778, a virtual alliance with the late enemy. It looked to him as if the federal administration, not content to have stifled republicanism at home, was bent on joining the counter-revolutionary pack in Europe to throttle it there.

Other men shared his concern. James Monroe, in Paris, felt quite as Logan did. Monroe was a democrat and a Francophile after the Doctor's own heart. He had often been a guest at Stenton during his years in the Senate. Upon his appointment as Minister, he and Logan had playfully agreed to meet in Paris, to drink exhilarating draughts of revolutionary idealism at its undefiled source.[36]

Monroe had arrived in France as American Minister just five days after the fall of Robespierre. He found the government in confusion, the impersonal guillotine at its bloody work, liquidating the 'republic of virtue' it had once served. Monroe was not the most discreet of diplomats. He allowed himself to be given a demonstrative public reception; he made a fervid speech in reply, and was kissed on both cheeks by the President of the National Convention. To Federalists at home, this was highly unneutral behavior. Republicans, however, could counter by asking whether

John Jay had been strictly neutral when he had kissed Queen Charlotte's hand in London.

Timothy Pickering, Washington's new Secretary of State, chose to keep Minister Monroe in the dark in regard to the progress of Jay's negotiations in London. In good faith Monroe assured the French government it had nothing to fear; Philadelphia, he was sure, would insist on complete neutrality, on commerce and friendship with all nations. When rumors of Jay's concessions finally reached Paris, Monroe found himself in a difficult, if not impossible, position — left high and dry by his own government, discredited and reviled by the French.

The hapless envoy sat down and poured out his frustrations and embarrassments, his hopes and fears, in a long letter intended for Logan and his other friends in America. Affairs in Europe, he wrote, had borne until lately a favorable aspect. Recent political and military events promised an early and happy consummation of the Revolution. But the first, unverified reports of the Anglo-American treaty had 'operated like a stroke of thunder and produced upon all France amazement.' If the treaty turned out to be as favorable to England as rumor had it, relations between the sister republics would certainly suffer. The United States would have thrown away a favorable opportunity for a new understanding with her erstwhile ally. And with French fortunes in the ascendant everywhere in Europe, it was to the interest of all nations 'to stand well with this republic.' 'Upon every principle,' Monroe concluded, 'it were greatly to be regretted if America should lose in any degree the ground upon which she hath heretofore stood in the estimation of her ally.' [37]

Monroe made copies of this letter and dispatched them to five influential, strategically situated anti-administration men at home — Logan and John Beckley in Pennsylvania, Jefferson in Virginia, Aaron Burr and Robert R. Livingston in New York. To Logan he suggested publishing the letter anonymously in Bache's *Aurora*. If Logan approved, he would engage to send him regular news letters 'whereby the community at large may be more correctly informed of the progress of the Revolution than they heretofore have been or can be from the English prints.' [38]

Unhappily, the copy addressed to Logan, with its covering letter, was intercepted and brought to Secretary Pickering's attention. The administration was eager for an excuse to recall its wayward minister. This letter was just what it had been looking for. The Cabinet met and decided to lay Monroe's note to Logan before the President. 'A minister,' they argued, 'who has thus made the notorious enemies of the whole system of the government his confidential correspondents . . . cannot be relied on to do his duty. . . .' [39] Washington agreed, and recalled Monroe from Paris.

A national election was impending in the autumn of 1796. Logan and the other 'notorious enemies' of the administration in Pennsylvania made the most of Jay's unpopular treaty to crystallize Republican sentiment. It was the most effective campaign weapon they had yet found. Genêt, the excise, the Democratic Societies — all these issues had backfired, but the treaty proved a reliable vote-getter. There was no more political neutrality in Pennsylvania. From now on 'there were only known democrats [or Republicans, as Logan's friends chose to call themselves] and federalists.' [40]

Even the conservative Quakers, fearful of war with France if the Federalists stayed in office, supported the Republican ticket.[41] All but two of Pennsylvania's fifteen electoral votes went to Thomas Jefferson in November. To Logan the local returns were as hopeful as the national returns were discouraging. Democratic-Republicanism was at last an effective political force in Pennsylvania. But when he considered the country at large, John Adams's election — he received three more electoral votes than Jefferson — caused him grave forebodings. The party that was responsible for Jay's treaty, Logan feared, would not be satisfied until it had carried the nation into war with France.

On Christmas Day 1796, Debby Logan wrote to her mother, now living in Chester. She had no interesting news, she said, from the city, 'for Dr. Logan does not bring home anything scarcely but politics.' [42] The wave of anti-Federalism that swept Pennsylvania for Jefferson carried the Doctor into the state legislature. He saw

new faces as he took his seat once more in the Assembly Chamber
— but then, he looked about him with new eyes. He found himself
working closely with men he had once distrusted and disdained —
with old Constitutionalists such as John Smilie, who had opposed
the Federal Constitution when Logan had favored it, with new
men like Dr. Michael Leib, a perfumed and dandified physician
who was showing an astonishing ability to bring the German-
speaking community into the democratic camp.

National and international issues overshadowed local ones at
this sitting of the Assembly. Relations with France were steadily
worsening; the Federalists were becoming more and more intoler-
ant of opposition. In retaliation for Jay's treaty, the French Directory had loosed its corsairs upon American merchant vessels
with instructions to treat them 'as they shall suffer the English to
treat them.' [43] President Washington had sent Charles Cotesworth Pinckney, a stanch Federalist and defender of Jay's treaty,
to Paris in Monroe's place. The Directory refused to receive him,
bluntly telling him to get out of France before he was arrested.
Unfortunate, deplorable, most unmannerly, said the Republicans
— but what did the administration expect under the circumstances? This was the mood of Logan's party as it approached
the legislative session.

President Washington had recently published his valedictory
to the American people. In solemn language he warned them
equally against entangling commitments abroad and factional
politics at home. Everyone knew what was on the President's
mind — the foreign crisis, the flagrant efforts of the French Minister, Adet, to influence the recent presidential elections, the growing strength of the Republicans.[44] Governor Mifflin, opening the
Assembly, referred to the President's farewell address. Mifflin
was an old enemy of Washington and by this time a thorough Republican; still, he could express sincere regret at the President's
imminent 'retreat from public life.' For Washington was a potent
symbol of national unity. His retirement, coming at a time when
the French were openly, truculently, even if justifiably, dissatisfied
with American policy, might have lamentable consequences.
Mifflin closed his address with the hope that mutual confidence

could somehow be restored between the two republics and that
the 'ungenerous asperity of party spirit' could be assuaged.[45]

Republicans such as Logan were still smarting under Washington's pointed reference to 'the baneful effects of the spirit of
party.' They bitterly resented his insinuation that they were susceptible to 'the insidious wiles of foreign entanglements.' Behind
the Presidential address they recognized the hand of their old
enemy Alexander Hamilton. Here was a chance to put their re-
joinder on record. While the Assembly was debating its reply to
the Governor, Dr. Leib made a motion, seconded by Dr. Logan,
to add some new paragraphs.

In a tone of injured innocence, they declared their full unity
with the Governor in deprecating party spirit. 'A feeling so il-
liberal and unworthy [of] enlightened republicans,' they assured
him, would *never* show itself in their deliberations. They echoed
Mifflin's concern over foreign affairs, but gave the subject a different twist. 'In the lap of promised security,' they declared, 'danger
seems to menace us and that too from a nation in whom our best
affections centered.' Gratitude and principle dictated perpetual
harmony between the two sister republics. Any interruption of
that harmony 'ought to be deprecated by every friend to peace
and his country.' At the end, Leib and Logan came to the point:
'We hope that no untoward circumstance will arise that shall dissolve an alliance which contributed to the independence of the
United States.' [46]

It was an obvious maneuver to commit the House to the Republican position on foreign policy. The attempt failed. But
Logan did not give up. He was determined somehow to put the
Pennsylvania Assembly on record against the outgoing administration. A month later, he opposed a motion to draft a 'respectful
communication' conveying the Assembly's regrets at Washington's retirement. When the address was actually brought in by
a committee, he moved postponement. That tactic failing, he finally joined with twenty-six other intransigents and voted against
it.[47]

When the Doctor reported these maneuvers to Debby at night
in Stenton's peaceful, quiet atmosphere, they struck her as un-

necessary, unfruitful, undignified; moreover, they seemed to smack of ingratitude. To her the President was an awe-inspiring figure, endowed with supernal wisdom; he could do no wrong. But she kept still. Politics was something she did not pretend to understand. She left it to her husband, and busied herself with the needs of the growing boys, the spinning of homespun, the care of her gardens.

Washington retired in March 1797, and John Adams became President. The squat, rotund, irascible man from Braintree, whom Logan had known briefly in Paris, continued his predecessor's policies and retained his cabinet officers. The crisis with France deepened. Two days before Adams's inauguration, the Directory issued a decree, authorizing new spoliations against American shipping. Privately the President wrote to his son in Europe: 'America is not SCARED.' [48] Publicly he called upon Congress to create a navy and authorize the arming of merchant vessels, to build up the army and put the militia on a war footing. France, he blustered, must be made to realize 'that we are not a degraded people, humiliated under a colonial spirit of fear and a sense of inferiority.' [49] Still, he was willing to try negotiation once more. He appointed three envoys extraordinary — Pinckney, John Marshall, and Elbridge Gerry, an old friend from Massachusetts. The first two were Federalists, the last a Republican.

Late in June, before Marshall and Gerry sailed to join Pinckney, James Monroe came home from France. The disgraced envoy faced a chilly reception from his government, but he found a warm welcome at Stenton. Dr. Logan overcame his aversion to public demonstrations and got up a great testimonial dinner at Oeller's Hotel on Chestnut Street, almost under the shadow of Congress Hall. Vice-President Jefferson was there, with the entire anti-Federalist block in Congress. It was a bold defiance to the federal administration. The gathering passed resolutions heartily endorsing the Minister's conduct, declaring that he had done nothing in France for which any American needed to blush.[50] Monroe had much to tell the group that met at Stenton — of the progress of the Revolution in France, and his own humiliation at the hands of an unreasonable home government.

Other visitors came and went — adventurous, romantic men, members of an international freemasonry of revolutionary enthusiasts. Jean de Marsillac came one day, an amiable French Quaker who had tried to establish a model agricultural school in France. He brought with him a high-spirited young physician named Justus Erich Bollman, who had gallantly rescued the Marquis de Lafayette from an Austrian prison at Olmütz.[51] The swashbuckling Napper Tandy, a chieftain of the United Irishmen, came up from Wilmington, where he was living in exile, itching for a chance to return to Ireland and lead an insurrection against British rule.[52] Straight from his captivity in Russia came Tadeusz Kosciuszko, who had fought valiantly for freedom in America and later in Poland.[53]

A succession of French diplomats, ostracized in Philadelphia, came out to Stenton, and always found 'Dr. Laughan' willing to listen as they poured out their complaints against the Federalist government. As least one of them, Pierre Auguste Adet, took home with him a copy of Logan's pamphlet on the Bank and the funding system, with a cordial inscription by the author.[54] Two French emigrants, refugees from the Terror, occupied Wakefield Farm at the rear of the Logan estate.[55] Indeed Stenton, during these years, was a serene little outpost of the French Revolution on the edge of Federalist Philadelphia.

In Philadelphia itself, the atmosphere grew steadily more tense, more excited, and — for men of Logan's mind — more oppressive. The Federalists seemed hagridden with fear — fear of invasion from without, fear of insurrection within. Fear bred hysteria, and hysteria induced a fever of warlike emotion.

On 4 March 1798, the anniversary of his inauguration, President Adams received the first full dispatches from his envoys in France. He read them, then boiled with anger. The Directory had refused again to receive his mission. Talleyrand, their Foreign Minister, had added insult to injury by sending agents to the three American envoys with demands for *douceurs* and bribes as the price of recognition. It was intolerable. Adams laid the dispatches before Congress, gave them to the newspapers. Soon everyone knew about Messieurs X, Y, and Z, and their impudent attempts at blackmail. And everyone was quoting Pinckney's indignant 'No! No! Not a sixpence!' — usually in its more resounding version: 'Millions for defense, but not one cent for tribute.'

Overnight, a frenzy of war spirit swept the capital. Congress took steps to create a provisional army, authorized the capture of armed French vessels, discussed the abrogation of all treaties and commercial agreements with France. The wave of hysteria caught up many a lukewarm Republican. Those who resisted it became the objects of special legislation as enemies of the Republic. With an eye on radical Irishmen and Frenchmen such as those who were known to visit Logan at Stenton, Congress began discussing laws to intern or deport aliens. In the hope of silencing opposition editors such as Benjamin Franklin Bache, and political writers such as Dr. Logan himself, they broached laws to punish those who criticized the government.[56]

For the more excited Federalists, the process of legislation was too slow. They took their own informal security measures. They deputed vigilance committees to watch over the movements of such well-known Republicans as Thomas Jefferson, Vice-President of the United States. They did not overlook Logan. Wherever he went in May and early June, he was followed. One of his shadows was none other than Benjamin Rush, once his friend, his professional colleague, and a fellow member of the Democratic Society. It was a veritable reign of terror, 'a state of society,' Debby wrote later, 'destructive of the ties which in ordinary times bind one class of citizens to another . . . Friendships were dissolved, tradesmen dismissed, and custom withdrawn from the Republican party. . . Many gentlemen went armed . . .'[57]

Mobs marched in Philadelphia almost every evening. On 7 May 1200 young Federalists pinned black cockades to their hats and paraded through the streets to the President's house — Robert Morris's old mansion on High Street. John Adams received them in his elegant, chandeliered saloon. Afterward, some of the youths, inflamed with liquor, headed for Benny Bache's house, down High Street, near the market. They hammered on his doors and filled the night with catcalls and insults. Next evening, small patrols of men roamed the streets indiscreetly flaunting tri-colored French cockades. The Citizen Volunteers were called out to guard the Mint and the Arsenal. Troops of cavalry clattered through the streets.[58]

Four days later, on 12 May 1798, Dr. Logan startled a distraught and tense Philadelphia by making a bold appearance before the Tammany Society at its Columbian Wigwam on the Schuylkill. The Society of the Sons of St. Tammany had changed greatly since the days before the Revolution when it had been a select club for benevolent gentlemen such as George Logan's father. In the early 1790's it had passed into desuetude, from which it was resurrected as a political club in 1795 by some of Logan's friends, who, like him, found the Democratic Society too timid, too irresolute and vacillating. By 1798 it was a hive of radical Democratic-Republicans, mostly poor artisans recently landed from Ireland, full of passionate hostility toward England and vague intoxicating revolutionary doctrines from France.[59]

Logan's audience was composed of just such men as Congress was determined to deport as dangerous aliens. And his speech was just such a speech as the Federalists proposed to brand as seditious. The subject — 'The Natural and Social Order of the World' — sounded innocent enough. So did Logan's opening words — innocent and dull. Heated with whisky, drowsy in the close atmosphere of the Wigwam, the audience yawned as the Doctor spoke in his quiet voice of the order and regularity everywhere apparent in nature, of the infinite perfection of the heavenly bodies, of the subtle adaptations in the animal and vegetable creation. They shuffled their feet, muttering with impatience and boredom as he went on, citing Cumberland against Hobbes to prove that man was intended for society, invoking reason and revelation to support the perfectibility of man.

Though designed for perfection, he said, mankind was everywhere in misery. The Sons of St. Tammany pricked up their ears. Was the Doctor coming to the point? 'This degraded state of man has been affected by the executive magistrates of all countries; who have uniformly encroached on the liberties of the people, until such time as they filched from them their sovereignty, and reduced them to a state of wretchedness.' His listeners looked at each other. It was true, be Jasus, and Johnny Adams was as bad as George III.

'Wars created by ambitious executives have been undertaken more to their own aggrandizement and power than for the protection of their country.' True again. Just look at what Adams was up to. This farmer could hit the nail on the head, even if he was a gentleman.

'The people, involved in a state of abject misery by accumulated wrongs, and drove [sic] almost to a state of desperation, are comforted with a promise of eternal happiness by interested priests, who participate with the government in the plunder of its citizens.' It was to escape tyranny and oppression like this, said Logan, that immigrants had been coming to the American shore for a century and a half. It was to free herself from 'arbitrary regulations,' British regulations, that Pennsylvania and the other colonies, 'assisted by the blood and treasure of that brave and generous people, the French,' had fought a revolution.

The crowd in the smoky Wigwam exploded into cheers. Logan had said nothing explicitly seditious; he had not mentioned the Adams administration, William Pitt, or the French Revolution. But everyone, even the dullest bog-trotter just off the boat from Sligo, understood his innuendoes, knew perfectly well what he was talking about. It was a skillfully calculated climax.

Logan ended his speech with an appeal to his auditors as mechanics and artisans. They represented, he said, only one-twentieth of the American people. But they must see that their well-being was linked to that of the farmers who composed eighteen-twentieths. Neither group had any real interest in common with the remaining five per cent — the Federalist 'merchants, agents, etc,' who were intent on keeping wages down and discouraging small independent manufacturing enterprises. Let the farmers and mechanics unite, then, to uphold each other and protect the nation's independence.[60]

More cheers and tumult in the crowded, hazy, reeking Wigwam. Burly sons of Erin and St. Tammany surged up to the speaker's table, engulfing Dr. Logan's slight, aristocratic figure, filling their bumpers with whisky. Boisterously, they toasted the abstemious master of Stenton, toasted the glorious French Revolution, toasted the ultimate triumph of Democratic-Republican principles in America.[61]

It had been bold and dramatic, this uproarious defiance of the Federalist terror. For Logan it was a climax to five years of ceaseless political agitation. It was satisfying, encouraging, exhilarating. But he looked beyond the hubbub, the tobacco smoke, the whisky fumes of the Columbian Wigwam and saw a rapid, fateful drift toward war undoing all his efforts and those of his friends to create an effective democratic party of farmers and workers. Already the next desperate step was taking form in his mind. It would require no less courage, no less imagination, no less conviction, than his years of uncongenial agitation among the masses. This step he must take alone.

*

VIII. MISSION TO PARIS

STENTON in the spring of 1798 was as serene and lovely as ever, its fields burgeoning with wheat, barley, Indian corn, its uplands green with clover, the young stock frisking in the barnyard, the clear waters of Wingohocking Creek purling and tumbling into the millrace. But for once Logan could find no pleasure in this annual rebirth, this promise of domestic peace and plenty. The crisis with France cast its dark, ominous shadow over everything. At any moment, Logan feared, the wickedness and folly of the government in Philadelphia might plunge the country irrevocably into war.

He was not alone in his anxiety. The Quakers were alarmed and his fellow Republicans shared his apprehensions. Old James Pemberton, his father's friend, gave him a copy of a memorial that he and three other Quakers had sent to Congress. Convinced that peace was essential to the happiness and prosperity of the nation, 'and that war ought to be deprecated as the worst calamity that can befall us,' the Friends begged the legislators 'to preserve peace and harmony with all nations; and if possible to avert from America the destructive calamity of war.' [1] John Dickinson, Debby's cousin, had lived familiarly with crisis for a third of a century. But he too was gravely concerned. 'Never,' he wrote to Logan's friend Thomas McKean, 'was the happiness of a people more wantonly exposed to hazard.' [2] Even Benjamin Rush, Logan's unsuspected shadow, addressed him, somewhat hypocritically, as his 'friend . . . the early, the upright and the uniform

153

friend of his country,' and expressed his fears: 'Ah!' he wrote, 'What a storm impends our beloved country.'[3]

Every time Logan went into Philadelphia, every time he looked at the newspapers, he saw some new evidence of preparation for war. Late in May, the *Ganges,* first vessel in the new American navy, sailed from Philadelphia with orders to capture French privateers off the American coast. Shipyard workers along the Delaware labored feverishly to fit out two new frigates, the *Constellation* and the *United States,* so that Truxtun and Barry could put out to sea against the French. In Congress Hall an excited House of Representatives was debating bills to raise a provisional army of ten thousand men, to grant letters of marque and reprisal, to suspend all commercial intercourse with France.

There were rumors that Marshall, Pinckney, and Gerry had all but given up hope of reaching a settlement in Paris. On 5 June, John Adams confirmed these rumors. He laid before Congress the latest dispatch from France. Talleyrand and the Directory, it appeared, were still haughty, still unyielding. The three envoys were on the point of asking for their passports.[4]

To Dr. Logan this was a signal for action, desperate action. Surely something could be done to prevent a complete rupture, an irreparable break. Perhaps he should go himself to France, talk to the commissioners, somehow induce them to stay, to persevere in their efforts for agreement. Perhaps — who could tell? — some further opportunity would open before him once he reached France. He might even be able to talk to the Directors themselves, persuade them in their own interest, in the common republican interest, in the interest of humanity, to drop their arrogant tone and avert a disastrous war.

It was a mad scheme. People would call him quixotic, meddlesome, presumptuous, perhaps treasonable. Even Debby thought his project 'romantic.' Still, she knew that it was in the Quaker tradition, that in times of stress and danger, there had always been individual Friends willing to stand in the courts of the mighty, with no warrant but that of private conscience, to lay their concerns before the rulers of nations. As a wife Debby feared for her husband's safety and reputation; as a Quaker she knew she must not stand in his way.[5]

In order to travel through Europe, Logan knew he would need some kind of credentials. The American government did not issue regular passports, but officers of government frequently wrote out certificates of citizenship for Americans traveling abroad. Logan went to his friend the Vice-President for such a certificate. He breathed no word of his purpose in going to Europe, though Jefferson undoubtedly had some inkling. He simply asked for a letter of credence, and Jefferson gladly gave it. He had given similar letters 'to an hundred others,' he wrote later, when the propriety of his action was questioned, 'and they have been much more frequently asked and obtained by Tories than by Whigs.' [6]

> I, Thomas Jefferson [he wrote], do hereby certify that George Logan, the bearer hereof, who is about to visit Europe on matters of business, is a citizen of the commonwealth of Pennsylvania and United States of America, of one of the most ancient and respectable families of the said commonwealth, of independent fortune, good morals, irreproachable conduct, and true civism; and as such he is recommended to the attention of all those who, from principles of humanity, or a desire to attach to their country the respect of others, could interest themselves in seeing the protection and hospitality of their laws extended to a worthy and unoffending stranger placed under their safeguard. Given under my hand and seal, at Philadelphia, this 4th day of June, 1798.
>
> Th: Jefferson [7]

Logan had other preparations to make. He was obliged to sell two parcels of land in order to pay off his outstanding debts and raise funds for the voyage. He understood the temper of the Federalists well enough to anticipate a violent reaction when they should learn of his mission. In their rage they might even confiscate his property, take Stenton away from him and his family. Against this contingency, he executed a letter of attorney before Thomas McKean, Chief Justice of Pennsylvania. He gave Debby power to manage his affairs during his absence, and to sell Stenton, if necessary, to keep it out of his enemies' hands.

He could not preserve his secret from his friend McKean. The judge, a tall, stately man, Republican by political faith and a friend of France, listened intently. 'Thank God,' he exclaimed, when Logan had finished, 'that we possess one man who is capable and devoted enough to undertake this task.' He drank to the Doctor's success, drew up the power of attorney, and wrote out for him a second certificate of citizenship, stating simply that he was a native-born Pennsylvanian and a former member of the state legislature.[8]

From Létombe, the French consul in Philadelphia, Logan obtained two letters of introduction — one to Merlin, head of the Executive Directory, the other to Talleyrand, Minister of Foreign Affairs. All these preparations he made quietly, without even attracting the attention of the committee the Federalists had set to watch over him. On 12 June he stepped on board the *Iris,* a Dutch ship bound for Hamburg, and dropped down the Delaware on the first leg of his desperate journey in quest of peace.

Logan's absence was soon discovered. The Federalist press promptly scented a dangerous conspiracy. William Cobbett, the English-born editor of *Porcupine's Gazette,* led the baying pack. 'Recollect his connections,' he screamed in print, 'recollect that seditious Envoys from all the Republics that France has subjugated first went to Paris and *concerted measures* with the despots; recollect the situation of this country at this moment, and *tremble for its fate!*' Darkly, Cobbett hinted at further dreadful revelations yet to come. 'In the meantime,' he adjured his readers, 'watch, Philadelphians, or the fire is in your houses and the *couteau at your throats.* . . Take care: when your blood runs down the gutters, don't say you weren't forewarned of the danger.' [9]

Young Andrew Brown, who had inherited the *Philadelphia Gazette* from his father, was close at Cobbett's heels. He knew precisely what Logan's diabolical, treasonous purposes were. 'There cannot be the least question,' he wrote, 'but the Doctor, from his *inordinate* love of *French liberty,* and hatred to the *sacred constitution* of the United States, has gone to the French Directory, fraught with intelligence of the *most dangerous tendency to this country.*' Logan's 'abandonment of wife, children, relations, and country' was 'a species of conspiracy, most fatal to freedom, and abhorrent to humanity.' Could anyone doubt that his 'infernal design' was the 'introduction of a French army, *to teach us the genuine value of true and essential liberty* by re-organizing our government, through the brutal operation of the bayonet and guillotine?' Every American, wrote Brown solemnly, must now gird on his sword. 'The times are not only critical, but the secret of the Junto *is out. Their* demagogue is gone to the Directory for purposes *destructive of your lives, property, liberty, and holy religion.'* [10]

Congress was immediately apprised. Robert Goodloe Harper, once a Jacobin in South Carolina but now more Federalist than the Adams administration itself, stood up in the midst of debate on the Alien bill, and announced portentously that an event had taken place within the past few days which 'would lead to the discovery of a treasonable correspondence . . . of the most criminal nature' between certain Americans and the French government.[11]

A friendly Federalist warned Debby that the administration would send officers out to Stenton to search the house for treasonable papers. He advised her that if she knew of any compromising documents, she should destroy them. Politely, she thanked the gentleman for his solicitude, calmly assuring him there was nothing to hide. If a suspicious government chose to ransack Stenton, she said, its officers would find nothing incriminating — 'they would only have to regret that they had insulted a man of honor in his absence.' [12]

Again and again Republicans challenged Harper on the floor of the House to produce evidence for his charges of conspiracy. Edward Livingston of New York, the brilliant, witty idol of the democrats, taunted him, calling him 'A modern Theseus!' who claimed to have the clue that would lead through the labyrinth to the Minotaur's cave. But 'who the fair Ariadne is, who so kindly gave him the ball, he has not revealed; nor, though several days have elapsed since he undertook the adventure, has he yet told us where the monster lurks.' [13]

Lamely, Harper replied that he had not yet fully unraveled the plot. Still, its 'ramification' was so visible that he would be a traitor if he did not 'resist those attempts which are made to bind us hand and foot until our enemy comes upon us.' Later, he put the House on notice that he would have his proof 'at the beginning of next session,' if not before — not legal proof perhaps, but 'circumstances sufficient to influence opinion, to induce belief, to fix conviction in the mind.' For himself, he declared, he was already fully persuaded 'that France is not without a party in this country, engaged in a most criminal correspondence with her agents.' [14]

George Logan, the object of all these dark hints and innuendoes, was meanwhile enduring the tedium of a slow Atlantic crossing. The captain of the *Iris* was a cautious Dutchman who refused to take advantage of a favoring wind if it happened to blow after dark. Logan fretted at the delay. War might flare out before he could reach France.

Finally, toward mid-July, they sighted the Lizard. As they ran up the English channel, Logan could not help noting down in his journal that it was full of Danish, Swedish, and other neutral vessels, while ships flying the American flag were excluded by his country's 'mistaken policy' of 'relinquishing her neutral rights to Britain.' The *Iris* coasted past the chalk cliffs, which he had last seen nearly twenty-five years before. Now they were lined with soldiers and excavated for fortifications against invasion by Bonaparte's 'Army of England.' All this, Logan thought, was an unnecessary expense, as the town and harbor of Dover 'are not objects deserving the attention of an enemy.' [15]

On the evening of 22 July 1798, after nearly six weeks at sea, the *Iris* dropped anchor in the harbor of Hamburg. Early next morning, Dr. Logan went to the French legation. The *chargé d'affaires* informed him he had orders from Paris not to permit any American to cross the French frontier. Was the long journey, then, in vain? Someone told him that the Marquis de Lafayette, lately released from his long imprisonment in Austria and now living at Wittmold on the shores of near-by Lake Plon, was in Hamburg. Logan promptly waited on him, introduced himself, explained his concern.

Lafayette was, as always, delighted to see an American.

Eagerly he pressed Logan for news of the land that stood second only to France in his affections, the land to which he hoped to retire for the rest of his days. 'He said that he was sincerely attached to our country,' Logan wrote later to Debby, 'and had for some time viewed with great anxiety the misunderstandings which had taken place between the sister republics.' [16]

Lafayette had been out of favor in Paris since 1792. Still, he would try to intercede for Logan. Surprisingly, the name of Citizen Lafayette still carried some magic. The secretary of the legation agreed to violate his instructions and issue a passport. He justified his action on the ground that the letters from Létombe that Logan carried 'might have a tendency to restore friendship between the two countries . . . an event anxiously desired by France.' [17]

Logan left Hamburg on 28 July. On that day, William Vans Murray, American Minister to the Batavian Republic, at his listening-post at The Hague, picked up an interesting report. A 'Mr. Droghan' had arrived at Hamburg, with letters for Merlin and Talleyrand from Jefferson and others, letters calculated to prevent war. The faithful diplomat, a brilliant young Federalist from Maryland, relayed this intelligence to Secretary of State Pickering. 'Doubtless, sir,' he added, 'all this is a thing of charitable supererogation — yet there are times in which these eccentricities look suspicious.' Murray was puzzled to know who this 'Droghan' could be. Undoubtedly an Irishman, he speculated in a letter to his friend John Quincy Adams in Berlin. Perhaps it was the notorious Archibald Hamilton Rowan, ringleader of the Irish rebels, last heard of in America. In any case, it must be some 'deputy from the United Americans, who brings his "Erin go bragh" and his calumet to be offered at the shrine of the Directory.' [18]

Murray discovered who the mysterious traveler really was when news came that he had arrived at Amsterdam. It was none other than 'that incendiary physician,' that 'propagandist of sedition and philosophy,' that 'plaster of Paris philanthropist,' Dr. Logan of Philadelphia.[19] He promptly set a secret agent on the

Doctor's trail. By a stroke of luck, he reported, the agent, mistaken by Logan for 'one of his party,' got a sight of his papers. They were 'guardedly worded,' of course — 'friend of science and humanity — the gibberish of hypocrisy' — but they were actually signed by Jefferson and McKean! To be sure, Logan had admitted in the agent's hearing that if the French were to invade the United States, 'all parties would oppose them.' But he had added that he feared a war would destroy the Republican party.[20] All very interesting, the Minister observed, and undoubtedly treasonable.

Minister Murray sprang into action. 'Sorrowfully,' he requested the Dutch authorities to apprehend Logan at Rotterdam, hold him for questioning, find out *'who he is, from whence, whither going, what passports he has.'* Next he went to Pichon, the French secretary of legation at The Hague, and revealed what he knew of the 'plot.' 'If this Doctor be an authorized fanatic, which I believe him to be,' he explained to young Adams later, 'I thought it would break the project to let them know at once that *the whole* was discovered.' Besides, Murray himself was carrying on delicate negotiations with Talleyrand through Pichon, and he feared the Doctor's advent might upset them.[21]

Late at night on 6 August, Murray set off for Rotterdam. He would confront Logan himself, demand to know his business. But the Dutch authorities at Rotterdam had seen no sign of the Doctor. Disappointed, Murray concluded that he must have gone by another route. He returned to The Hague, put the American *corps d'observation* in Paris on the alert, then he sat down to justify — to himself and to his chief in Philadelphia — his drastic action in ordering the Doctor's arrest.

An unauthorized mission, even if the object was 'merely to avert war,' he argued in his report to Pickering, 'was in the greatest degree dangerous, as it would tend to foster the wishes of France to make use of a party in the United States at the expense of government, break in upon the effects which the idea of union and energy were certainly producing, and open a new source of influence.' Privately, Murray was not so sure of himself. Writing to his fellow diplomats, Rufus King in London and John Quincy Adams in Berlin, he acknowledged that his order for Logan's arrest had been a 'strong measure.' Did they think it was warranted? Adams had no doubt about it. He took an even graver view of Logan's mission than Murray did. It was 'the gauntlet of civil war' in the United States. After reflecting on the matter 'as coolly as possible,' the President's son had reached a conclusion: 'If it be so — *the gauntlet must be taken up.'* [22]

Logan, unwitting participant in the game of hide-and-seek, was peacefully gliding along a Dutch canal toward Antwerp in a *trekschuit,* a blunt-ended towboat, making notes on the condition of the soil and the state of agriculture in the rich lowlands through which he passed. Near Antwerp he came upon an encampment of seventy thousand Coalition troops, a solemn reminder of the military burden he was striving to save his country from. He rested at Antwerp, then passed, unmolested, through Brussels, Mons, Valenciennes, Cambrai, St. Quentin, to Paris. He arrived at the French capital on 7 August.[23]

His first act was to inquire for the American Commissioners. Marshall and Pinckney, he learned, had left months before. Gerry was at that very moment taking ship for home, with assurances from the French government of its desire for reconciliation. This last news was welcome. He had been sure the French would come to their senses. But Logan knew too that John Adams, the Federalist Congress, and probably most Americans, would be skeptical. Was there anything he could do to test the sincerity of those assurances, to give Americans an unmistakable pledge of French good will?

Fulwar Skipwith, the American Consul-General, told him that the Directory had recently laid an embargo on all American shipping in French ports, had thrown a number of American seamen into prison. Logan saw immediately what he must do — he must persuade the French authorities that their protestations of good will would carry conviction in America only if they were supported by deeds, that the prompt raising of the embargo, the release of the imprisoned sailors would do more to convince Americans than all the words, all the soft assurances, they could send across the Atlantic.

He talked with members of the American colony in Paris. There was Joel Barlow, a cheerful, friendly man from Connecticut, who had spent six years in France and been honored with French citizenship for his political writings. There was Robert Fulton, a former miniature-painter in Philadelphia, who was in Paris trying to interest the Directory in his newest invention, a 'plunging boat.' American officials were helpful — Fulwar Skipwith from Virginia, the Consul-General, Nathaniel Cutting, Consul at Le Havre, both appointees and friends of Jefferson. All these men were Republicans, anxious, as Logan was, to see the overhanging cloud of war dispelled. They had all seen too much of the French government to be sanguine of success. Still, they could not but wish Logan well in his venture.

Unexpectedly, Logan encountered a man who had been his guest at Stenton only a few months before — Tadeusz Kosciuszko, the Polish patriot, who was in Paris under the assumed name of Thomas Kannberg. Kosciuszko had come to France on an errand similar to Logan's, except that his mission actually had Thomas Jefferson's blessing. The kindly Pole 'warmly appreciated' Logan's motives, and 'approved of his design.' But like the others who knew the Directors, he warned Logan to put no faith in their promises 'unless they would immediately give a pledge of their sincerity by a removal of the embargo.' 24

Even the Federalist merchants and speculators in Paris encouraged Logan. Richard Codman of Boston felt that the Doctor had 'essentially served his country' by coming to France on his peace mission. These hardheaded businessmen could see, in any case, that he was serving their interests, for they well knew what a war between France and the United States would mean — the immediate confiscation of their property, the disruption of their lucrative trade. So they too encouraged him to carry his concern to the highest authorities.

Codman even wrote a memorial for him to present to Talleyrand, a memorial setting forth in highly compromising language the advantages to France of a more conciliatory attitude. Logan flatly refused to present the memorial on the ground that it would have 'too much the appearance of an official act.' 25

He did not hesitate, however, to present himself, as a private citizen, at the Hôtel Galiffet, the luxurious quarters of the Ministry of Foreign Affairs in the Rue du Bac. Consul Létombe's letter soon brought him before Talleyrand. The Minister regarded him coldly through sleepy eyes. They made a curious contrast — the subtle, cynical ex-Bishop of Autun, the skillful diplomatist who could serve any master and in so doing always served himself, and the ingenuous, forthright New-World idealist with his Quaker 'concern.'

Talleyrand listened while Logan spoke of the state of opinion in America, of the imminent danger of war, of the measures France could take to avert it. He accepted the gift of Logan's essay on crop rotation. He was all politeness — but he revealed nothing of what was in his mind, and he offered to do nothing more than introduce Logan to the Minister of the Interior, with whom he could discuss his nine-year rotation and the virtues of plaster of Paris.[26] Logan left the Hôtel Galiffet disappointed and perplexed.

Later, like his three official predecessors, he was favored by private visits from gentlemen obviously sent by Talleyrand to draw him out on the purpose of his mission. One of the visitors was Adet, the former French Minister to Philadelphia, whom the Logans had entertained at Stenton. These men were not seeking bribes, as Messieurs X, Y, and Z had done — Talleyrand had thought better of that approach, and in any case he knew that Logan had no access to public funds. They made strenuous efforts, however, to possess themselves of Létombe's letter to Merlin. Generously, they offered to convey it for him to the First Director. Shrewdly, Logan declined to give it up.[27]

It was clear that Talleyrand had no intention of allowing him to see the Directors. Very well, he would find another avenue to their presence. He introduced himself to Rutger Jan Schimmelpenninck, a friendly young Dutchman, who represented the Batavian Republic at Paris. The Dutch government, Schimmelpenninck told him, was anxious to see peace restored between France and the United States; it stood ready to use its good offices at any time as mediator. Heartened by this word, Logan unfolded his concern, explained what had brought him to Paris. To the Dutchman such impulsive, quixotic behavior was incomprehensible and Logan seemed undoubtedly a mere amiable enthusiast. Nevertheless, he offered to arrange an interview with Merlin.[28]

Meanwhile, on 19 August — only a few days after his apparently fruitless interview at the Hôtel Galiffet — Logan received another visitor from the Ministry of Foreign Affairs. It was La-Forêt, one of Talleyrand's *chefs de division*. He bore surprising news, gratifying news. As soon as he had gone out the door, Logan sat down and dashed off an excited letter to Skipwith, the Consul-General:

My Friend:

Citizen La Forest has been with me this moment to inform me from Monsieur Talleyrand, the Minister of Foreign Relations, that everything will be done according to our wishes, in evidence of which Captain Gardner will this day receive permission to sail, with whom I shall embark for America. Your presence in Paris is *immediately necessary*.

I am &c.

Your Friend,

Geo. Logan [29]

This was unexpected success. Here was assurance, straight from Talleyrand, that the embargo would be raised, the American sailors freed. Surely reasonable men at home would be persuaded now that the French were ready for peace. Still, Logan reflected, he had no tangible evidence, no documents that he could take home to satisfy the skeptics. And he had not yet seen Talleyrand's masters — the five powerful men who ruled France from the Luxembourg. He decided to postpone his departure, accept Schimmelpenninck's kind offer, and hold a conversation with Merlin.

The Dutch diplomat was as good as his word. He took Logan to the Petit-Luxembourg, introduced him to Merlin de Douai, the learned jurisconsult who occupied the highest political office in the French Republic. Merlin received them cordially, read Létombe's letter, and expressed a desire to talk privately with the American. He listened attentively while Logan set forth his views on the state of opinion in America.

It was not his concern, Logan began, to justify the conduct of his own country or to criticize that of France. At the root of the misunderstanding between the two republics, he was convinced, lay the vaulting ambition of William Pitt and the British Court. By intrigue and corruption Pitt was seeking to undermine the independent status of the United States. The British — Franklin had told him this, and Franklin surely knew — had never reconciled themselves to American independence.[30] Even now paid British propagandists such as William Cobbett were exploiting the early 'atrocities' of the French Revolution, and the more recent outrages of French privateers, to stigmatize 'every friend to France and republican principles' as an enemy of the United States. French policy was playing directly into British hands, helping Pitt drive a wedge between the two nations that had once been allies.

France, Logan went on, was not a mercantile nation, 'but more attached to the manly pursuit of agriculture.' Hence it was to her interest to respect neutral flags, to encourage competition in her ports. Only so could she expect to exchange her agricultural surplus advantageously for the products of other countries. 'No people,' he reminded Merlin, 'were so well calculated to assure these advantages to France as the citizens of the United States.' Consequently, Logan made bold to say, it behooved the French to respect the American flag, to cease molesting American shipping.

He followed this bit of advice with a warning. Should France so far forget the enlightened principles of her own Revolution as to violate the territory of the United States — his voice became grave — 'every citizen of our country would become her enemy.' The spirit of 1776, he concluded stoutly, would be promptly revived against any new threat to American independence, from whatever quarter it might come.[31]

Merlin returned a soft answer. France, he said, had no intention of interfering in the internal affairs of the transatlantic republic. She was mindful of the glory she had acquired in helping to create a free American nation. Never would she sacrifice that glory, never disgrace her own Revolution, by attempting its destruction.

As for the violation of neutral flags, she had been driven to it by England's example. But all this, he assured Logan, would shortly be corrected.[32]

The next day, 23 August, Logan was back at the Petit-Luxembourg, sitting down to dinner with Merlin and his family. Schimmelpenninck was there too, with the Minister from the newly proclaimed Cisalpine Republic, and several heads of government bureaus. The atmosphere was informal, friendly, relaxed. Between dessert and coffee, there was a round of toasts. First someone proposed 'The Republic of France.' Then 'The Batavian Republic,' 'The Cisalpine Republic.'

Boldly Logan asked leave to propose a toast. He would give them 'The United States of America, and a speedy restoration of amity between them and France.' Quickly Merlin interrupted, protested that he wished to give that toast himself. He did so, using Logan's very words. 'The company looked upon each other with surprise and pleasure,' the Doctor later told Debby, 'and, joining their glasses, drank the toast with the utmost hilarity and enthusiasm.'[33] And when Logan left the Petit-Luxembourg that day, he took with him actual copies of the decrees by which the Directory raised the embargo and ordered the American seamen set free.[34]

Soon the Paris newspapers were full of '*le brave Logan,*' the 'new American envoy,' the 'envoy of the patriotic party.' 'The intrigues of M. Pitt to foment war between the French and American republics are almost entirely thwarted,' exulted the *Bien informé* on 24 August. '. . . Logan dined yesterday with the President of the Directory . . . There is reason to expect a firm peace.'[35] 'It is virtually certain,' echoed the *Chronique universelle,* three days later, 'that war between the United States and France will not take place.' For a brief moment George Logan was the hero of Paris.

It suited the Directors that Logan should seem to have played a decisive role. Actually, they had never wanted outright war with the United States. To permit matters to reach that point, Talleyrand told them, would be to fall into 'an Anglo-Federalist trap.' It would only strengthen their real enemy, Great Britain, by making available a new reservoir of American sailors to man her navy. Moreover, it could wreck Talleyrand's grand scheme to revive the French empire in North America, for a declaration of war would almost certainly send American frontiersmen whooping into Louisiana before he could succeed in prizing that rich colony away from Spain. Besides, the Directors were deeply involved to the eastward now; Bonaparte, their brilliant, daring, young general was fighting in Egypt under the shadow of the Pyramids, the Turks were up in arms as a result, and a new formidable coalition of hostile powers was forming in eastern Europe.

No, Talleyrand and the Directors saw clearly that they had nothing to gain by tempting the Americans into war. Even before Logan's unexpected appearance in Paris, they had thought better of the embargo, had considered removing it and releasing the imprisoned sailors. Young Victor Du Pont, son of the great Physiocrat, had just come back from the United States to tell them that the Americans were aroused, angry, bristling with resentment; even the Republicans, he reported, were ready to resist any further aggressions. Then came Kosciuszko to confirm the report, and on his heels Dr. Logan himself, a prominent Republican, to give it emphasis. The cumulative effect of these reports stirred the government into action. Logan, having arrived at the crucial moment, became the pivot on which French policy swung around — at least for the public, the people of Paris.[36]

Paris under the Directory was a glittering, feverish city, masking its immorality, its parvenu vulgarity behind a façade of neoclassic smartness. Into such a city Logan came like a breeze from the New-World forests. Every literate Frenchman cherished a number of romantic conceptions of what the American should be — and Logan fitted not one but several of them. At first it was rumored that he was Logan, the famous Indian chief whose wild, untutored eloquence every intellectual knew from Jefferson's *Notes on Virginia*.[37] Later, when his real identity was known, he seemed to fit another stereotype, one that was familiar to every reader of Voltaire, Raynal, Brissot — the stereotype of the good Quaker. After all, he came from the City of Brotherly Love, his dress and manner were severely plain, his grandfather had been the personal friend of William Penn, he himself had known Benjamin Franklin, and his mission was peace. If the Parisians had not caught a noble savage, at least here was *le bon Quaker* incarnate.[38]

Logan spent three weeks in Paris. He had further interviews with Merlin, met other members of the Directory. He talked with 'zealous friends of America' such as Du Pont de Nemours, the Physiocrat, who was convinced that the *estimable* Doctor from Philadelphia, together with his own son Victor, had greatly promoted the cause of Franco-American peace.[39] Barlow and Fulton took him to one of Helen Maria Williams's famous dinner parties to meet the English literati who gathered there.[40] Logan visited the Louvre, the Jardin des Plantes, the National Institute. Everywhere, he studied the transformation that had come over the French capital since he had last seen it, before the Revolution. Everywhere he found changes for the better, everywhere order, regularity, prosperity — the municipal officers attentive to their duties, the laws respected, the streets lighted and cleaned as in Philadelphia, the shops open and business flourishing, not a beggar to be seen anywhere.

There was no longer any established religion in France. 'Every citizen is left at full liberty to worship God agreeably to the dictates of his own conscience.' He saw no sign that the Roman Catholic church was persecuted; he actually attended the celebration of Mass, 'the doors of the church being open for the free admission of any person.' He also attended the ceremonies of the Theophilanthropist cult and found them not unlike Congregationalist or Baptist services in New England. 'In one respect,' he added, 'this sect resembles the Quakers — every gifted brother has the liberty of preaching without any formal ordination.'

He visited sessions of the Council of Five Hundred and the Council of Ancients. 'The greatest order and regularity,' he reported, 'were preserved in their deliberations.' The Directors themselves he found to be able, conscientious public servants and exemplary citizens in private life. He was prepared to admit that some crimes had been committed in France's 'moment of revolutionary frenzy.' These, however, had been punished. 'At present,' Logan concluded, 'no government in Europe is more firmly established, more ably administered, or better calculated to promote the general happiness of its citizens than that of France.' [41]

On 29 August, Logan left Paris for Bordeaux to take ship for home. As he traveled down the valley of the Loire, he found the countryside everywhere prosperous, new farmhouses building, 'the cottagers, well clothed, [exhibiting] a pleasing appearance of happiness and content.' 'This numerous and heretofore degraded class of men,' he added with satisfaction, 'have received immediate advantage from the Revolution, whilst the privileged orders have been annihilated by its impetuous storms.' [42]

At Bordeaux he had to wait a week before his ship, the *Perseverance,* was ready to sail. He passed the time in writing letters, visiting the local châteaux, making notes on the famous Bordeaux vineyards, talking with the American merchants and ship captains.[43]

The masters of American vessels, now released from their long confinement in the river Garonne, presented him a grateful address of thanks. 'At an awful crisis,' they declared, 'when two great sister republics appeared to be on the eve of war,' he had stepped forward as 'the friend of both countries, like a true patriot, the friend of humanity,' to prevent 'that worst of all calamities.' They were fully convinced that it had been Logan's 'exertions and manly remonstrances' which had persuaded the French authorities to raise the embargo and set them free. 'Your disinterested conduct,' they told him 'merits the approbation and friendship of all your fellow citizens.' They wished him a short, pleasant passage and a warm welcome at home.

To this cordial address Logan returned a brief, modest reply. As a citizen of a free, independent republic, he said, he had considered it not only his right but his duty to do what he could for peace. The real credit, however, should go to the French government for its 'magnanimity and sound policy.' He hoped that his own government would be as benevolent and farseeing.[44]

Logan had a number of letters to write before he left French soil. To Merlin he recalled the substance of their several conversations and expressed the hope that the American government would take prompt steps 'to meet the friendly disposition' of the French. In a letter to his Dutch friend Schimmelpenninck he continued a conversation the two men had started in Paris on the virtues and defects of the American Constitution. From Consul Skipwith he had received a report that the French were at last taking measures to control their corsairs. He promptly wrote to La Revellière-Lépeaux, one of the Directors, to urge further steps in this direction, in order that 'the new order of things . . . may not be defaced by the horrid system of privateering.'

To Skipwith he sent a note of encouragement. He advised the Consul-General to keep pressing the Directory on the issue of privateers; this was the last real obstacle to peace. 'Give my respects to my good friends Barlow and Fulton,' he added. 'Tell them it is not the season for good men who have a proper idea of the importance of the French Revolution to be idle.'

And to Debby he wrote that he would soon be home, bringing with him the Directory's pledges of peace.[45]

Poor Debby, back at Stenton, needed every bit of comfort, every scrap of reassurance her husband could send her. The Doctor's long absence from home had been a time of deep trial. Naturally, she was anxious for his safety, fearful lest the Alien and Sedition Acts, passed just after his departure, should somehow bring him under a charge of treason. The Federalist press kept up its cruel sniping, its relentless stream of malicious insinuations. As if that were not enough, the summer was unbearably hot; the yellow fever returned to Philadelphia and spread to near-by Germantown. Debby had more than twenty refugees from the city under her roof, including her husband's uncle James and her own brother Joseph, who was desperately ill with the fever. But she could be philosophical about this extra burden of domestic cares; it 'was better for me,' she realized, 'than to be left in solitude.' [46]

The newspapers were obnoxious, poisonous. Cobbett, young Andrew Brown, the other Federalist editors missed no chance to slander her husband; they alternated between gross ridicule and hysterical alarmism. To spike their guns, she published parts of the Doctor's letter from Bordeaux, telling of the new decrees which he was bringing home, of the bright prospects for peace. Young Brown printed the excerpts with a sarcastic comment: this showed, he wrote, what sort of patriot Logan was, 'to sacrifice the liberty of [his] country to the insidious designs of an unprincipled foreign foe.' Cobbett, who never pretended to be a gentleman, did not spare even Debby herself. He proposed that when the Doctor landed, he should be promptly clapped into the pillory, his wife beside him. The adulation of the Republican journalists was hardly easier for Debby to bear — especially when they compared her with Madame de Roland, or cast her, with absurd incongruity, as Lodoïska to her husband's Louvet.[47]

The American 'reign of terror' was reaching a climax in the summer of 1798. Republican editors were being sent to prison for speaking lightly of the administration. Frenchmen, Irishmen, immigrants who had fled to America for freedom, were cowering and trembling lest they be momently deported. Debby feared that her hospitality to the two French *emigrés* at Wakefield Farm might be construed as a crime under the Alien Act. She had never shared her husband's ardent Republicanism, his enthusiasm for the French and their revolution; indeed she had never had any political beliefs. Still, she found herself 'under the ban of political excommunication.' Federalist families in Philadelphia — the people among who she had grown up — ostracized her, 'for it was said that those would be marked who should be seen to enter' the Stenton gates.[48]

One good friend she had, who stood loyally by her in her ordeal. Ten days after her husband's departure, just as the storm of abuse was reaching the peak of its crescendo, she was surprised and overjoyed to see Thomas Jefferson ride in through the rarely used gate on the York Road. The household was at tea when he arrived. He apologized for coming so late in the afternoon, but explained how he had had to take a circuitous route — by the falls of Schuylkill and along a back lane through Germantown — in order to shake off the spies who constantly watched his comings and goings.

The Vice-President was almost in despair over the hysteria of the times, the madness which had overcome Congress and most of the people. If anything were done to injure her, he said gravely, it would be proof to him that the last shadow of civil liberty was gone from America. He advised her, however, to be brave, to show the world her faith in her husband's innocence by appearing, unafraid and unashamed, in Philadelphia. A few days later, she acted on Jefferson's advice and went boldly into the city. It was a painful and disturbing experience. People who had known her from childhood told her rudely that they were surprised to see her, or, behind her back, confessed their astonishment that the wife of a traitor could be so 'gay and cheerful.' [49]

Cobbett soon got wind of Jefferson's visit to Stenton. He announced it to the public with his characteristic blend of misrepresentation and sly innuendo:

> It is said that JEFFERSON went to his friend Doctor Logan's farm, and spent three days there, soon after the Doctor's departure for France. *Quere:* What did he do there? Was it to arrange the Doctor's valuable manuscripts? [50]

As the time of Logan's expected return drew near, Debby could scarcely control her eagerness, her anxiety. From the rumors that were afloat she was fully convinced that the government intended to imprison him the instant he stepped on shore. His actual arrival was unexpected. It was early in November. The two Frenchmen who lived at Wakefield Farm had come back from Philadelphia late in the afternoon, saying that the *Perseverance* was in the Delaware, that the Doctor would undoubtedly land the next day.

Debby had put Algernon, the youngest boy, to bed, and was sitting in the dining room by the tiled fireplace, nursing the Doctor's favorite spaniel, which had been hurt while hunting with the older boys. Albanus and Gustavus were in the room with her, reading. They heard a step on the piazza. The wounded spaniel 'raised himself, and, instinctively knowing the sound, strove to get to the door.' The door opened, and they knew that the traveler had returned. 'There was an honest security in his manner,' Deborah recalled later, 'that at once banished all my fears from the machinations of his enemies.' [51]

But in Philadelphia, at this very moment, the printer of *Porcu-*

pine's Gazette was putting into type an announcement laden with the bitter distillate of William Cobbett's venomous sarcasm:

He is come!
He is come!!
He is come!!!

ENVOY LOGAN, THE PEACEMAKER, is come. The *Perseverance* is below, and Logan is very probably in — Germantown. It is reported that he is to make his public entry this afternoon, bearing in his hand an *Olive Branch,* and accompanied by his secretary of Legation — What a pity that *addled eggs* are so scarce.[52]

George Logan's peace mission was completed, but the campaign to discredit him by ridicule, vilification, and misrepresentation had just begun.

*

IX. REPORT on a MISSION

Dr. Logan barely paused to spend the night at Stenton. Next morning, before breakfast, he was off to Trenton, New Jersey. The federal government had moved its offices there temporarily, to escape the yellow fever. He had official dispatches for the Secretary of State from Consul Skipwith. With them were copies of the precious decrees of the Directory. And he had his own observations to report, his own conviction, based on private conversations with the Directors themselves, that the French wanted peace.

There was no time to lose. War preparations, he found, had gone forward at an alarming rate since he had left Stenton, barely five months before. The new navy was roaming the seas, taking prizes, hunting French men-of-war in the West Indies. General Washington had agreed to come out of retirement, to lead the new American army, the 'army of the black cockade,' with Alexander Hamilton his second in command. Even John Marshall, Debby told him, had been astonished at the extent of military preparations, the warlike atmosphere of the country, when he had returned from France in the spring.[1] Now in November, though the French, he was convinced, wanted peace, Logan feared that his own country might rush recklessly into a needless war. He must see the Secretary of State, the President, dissuade them from this wicked folly.

He stopped in Bristol for breakfast. There, by a strange chance, he fell in with Charles Cotesworth Pinckney, whose carriage had broken down. On his return from the XYZ mission,

Pinckney had been made a major general, ranking just below Washington and Hamilton in the 'army of the black cockade.' He was on his way to Trenton for a council of war. He was slightly embarrassed to see Logan. Still, he was a gentleman; he could not forget Dr. Logan's kindness to him when he had been an exile from South Carolina during the Revolution.

While tavern onlookers gaped and made audible comments, the two men sat down to breakfast together. Pinckney was friendly, expressing the greatest interest in Logan's report of his conversations with Talleyrand and the Directors. But when Logan offered him a ride to Trenton in his carriage, he declined politely. Nothing in his code as a South Carolina gentleman required him to be seen entering the temporary capital with so dubious, so incongruous, a companion.[2]

Logan drove on alone, crossed the Delaware River, and came into Trenton. He inquired at once for the office of Timothy Pickering, the Secretary of State. He had known Pickering for a dozen years. They had been fellow members of the Philadelphia Society for Promoting Agriculture back in the 'eighties. But Pickering, he knew, now regarded him as a 'notorious' enemy of the government. Besides, Pickering was one of Hamilton's men, hard at work within John Adams's official family to make his master's will prevail over the President's. At this very moment, he was deep in preparations to send General Hamilton's army into Spanish Louisiana and the Floridas on the first word of hostilities with France. He was not glad to see Logan.

Ushered into the Secretary's presence, Logan 'advanced with eagerness,' handed him the dispatches from Consul Skipwith, the copies of the French decrees. If he had hoped these documents would assure him a welcome, he was quickly disappointed. The Secretary glanced at the dispatches, then peered suspiciously at Logan through his spectacles. Coldly he remarked that he had already seen them. Joseph Woodward, a Boston Federalist and friend of Codman, whom Logan had met in Paris, had crossed the Atlantic on an earlier ship, carrying a duplicate set of dispatches from Skipwith.

But Logan had another card to play. He mentioned the Directory's latest decree, the one Skipwith had sent him at Bordeaux, just before he had started — an order restraining the French corsairs in the West Indies. Pickering was scornful. This decree, he said, was merely 'ostensible and illusory.' It would give no real relief to American commerce. Undismayed, Logan spread all his cards on the table. He reported everything he had learned of the French situation. He set his own conduct in full view. The Directory, he said, was friendly, was prepared to move as rapidly as possible to curb its privateers. It would take time, though, for the privateering interests were strongly ensconced in the two legislative councils.

Pickering's long saturnine face kept its look of skepticism and scorn. The country stood in imminent peril of invasion, the Secretary insisted. Preparedness was of the very essence. Logan agreed; it would do no harm to have the militia in good order. 'The militia, sir!' sputtered the Secretary of State, 'the militia never did any good to this country except in the single affair of Bunker Hill. We must have a standing army of fifty thousand men.' The Secretary showed his visitor to the door. 'Sir,' he said, as Logan left, 'it is my duty to inform you that the government does not thank you for what you have done.' [3]

Logan rode back to Stenton, saddened by what seemed like wilful blindness in the man who was entrusted with his country's foreign relations. He must find someone, someone in high place, who would see what was so plain to him — that the nation must not and need not take the disastrous plunge into war. The President was at Quincy and therefore inaccessible at the moment, but General Washington was in Philadelphia. He had arrived there from Mount Vernon on the same day that Logan had landed from France. He had come to discuss military plans with his Major Generals and with the Secretary of War. Logan decided to talk with him without delay. After all, they were old acquaintances. Washington had been his guest at Stenton; he and Debby had been entertained at Mount Vernon.[4]

On 13 November he went to Rosanna White's boarding house on Eighth Street, where the General was staying. The Reverend

Robert Blackwell, rector of St. Peter's Church, happened to arrive at the same time. A servant ushered them into the parlor, took their names upstairs.

The General was busy writing, his mind preoccupied with military problems. Should he send troops into the Spanish Floridas, in the event the French should occupy them? How many pieces of ordnance should he assign to each park of artillery? Did the French use pikes? Should he substitute a rose-colored cockade with a small tin eagle for the black cockade, which the British also wore? [5] These were serious problems, and he was annoyed at the interruption.

Logan and Blackwell waited below. Presently, the General descended, thin and worn from a recent attack of malarial fever, showing his sixty-six years, but still tall, stately, imperious, an imposing figure. He gave his hand to Blackwell, affected not to notice Logan. The Doctor, assuming that Washington did not recognize him, introduced himself. The General was 'backward' to take his hand — his 'polluted hand,' as a Federalist newspaper later described it — but finally, 'in a very cool manner and with an air of much indifference' did so. At the same time he asked the Reverend Mr. Blackwell to be seated.

After inquiring in a perfunctory way for Debby, Washington pointedly addressed all his conversation to the clergyman, returned only a curt 'Yes' or 'No' to 'the other.' (In the memorandum that he later made of this interview, Washington could not bring himself to write the Doctor's name.) He and Blackwell discussed the late calamitous epidemic of yellow fever. Courteously, Logan offered him several rooms at Stenton, should the disease return to the city. Washington 'thanked him slightly, observing there would be no call for it.'

Presently, Blackwell rose to take his leave. Washington moved toward the door, 'expecting the other would follow,' but Logan held his ground. He had seen Lafayette and his lady at Wittmold, he said; Lafayette had sent greetings to his old comrade-in-arms. Washington, wishing 'to get quit of him, remained standing, and showed the utmost inattention to what he was saying.' But the Doctor was determined to be heard. He spoke of the reasons that had induced him to go to France, of his hopes for reconciliation between the two nations. The General, a little more attentive now, observed caustically how singular it was that *he,* a private individual, should suppose himself able to accomplish what 'gentlemen of the first respectability . . . specially charged under the authority of the government' were unable to do. To this the Doctor modestly responded that he could only answer for his own conduct, not for that of the official commissioners.

Doggedly he continued with his story. Merlin, he said, had shown an unmistakable desire for friendship with the United States. This statement aroused Washington's ire. Logan, he declared, his loud voice heavy with sarcasm, had been more fortunate than the official envoys; *they* had not even been permitted to see the Directors. Furthermore, he pursued, if France was really sincere in her professions of friendship, let her repeal all her obnoxious decrees at once, put an immediate stop to her depredations, make full restitution for the injuries she had inflicted on American commerce. His face was flushed with anger now. So the Directors felt the Americans were hostile, did they? What stronger proof of the contrary could they ask than the patient way in which Americans had endured their 'outrageous conduct'?

Quietly the Doctor protested: the Directors had raised their embargo, they were making restitution of captured property. Washington broke in. This was 'a matter of no great importance,' he said. The number of American vessels affected by the embargo had been trifling. As for the 'hostile appearances' that the French complained of, they were purely measures of self-defense. Did the Directory look on Americans as worms, he asked, 'not even allowed to turn when tread upon?' No, the United States had 'borne and forborne' enough, more than enough. He 'hoped the spirit of this country would never suffer itself to be injured with impunity by any nation under the sun.' Logan hastened to reply: that was just what he had told Merlin — 'that if the United States were invaded by France, they would unite to a man to oppose the invaders.' [6] Washington made it plain that the interview was at an end.

As Logan stepped out of Rosanna White's boarding house onto

the street that November day, the atmosphere outside hardly felt icier than that he had just left. The prospect for peace looked dark.

But there was still the President. John Adams came down from Quincy toward the end of November, and Logan had a long conference with him on the twenty-sixth in the old Robert Morris house on Market Street. The President was unexpectedly gracious. He served tea to his guest, plied him with questions about the attitude of the French.

John Adams was a troubled man. At long last he was realizing that he had not been master in his own official household, that his cabinet ministers, 'panting for war,' were following Hamilton's bidding, not his. Slowly, painfully, he was beginning to grope for an independent line in foreign policy. In June he had announced to Congress that he would never send another diplomatic emissary to France without assurances that he would be 'received, respected, and honored as the representative of a great, free, powerful, and independent nation.' ⁷ But what if such assurances should now be forthcoming? Only lately he had had several intimations that they might be on their way. His old friend Elbridge Gerry had come to see him in Quincy, had told him that Talleyrand was genuinely anxious for peace. Letters from William Vans Murray at The Hague, from his own son John Quincy at Berlin, tended to bear out this report. Indeed, he had recently seen a letter from the Paris merchant, Richard Codman, a sound Federalist, giving Dr. Logan credit for fostering this new French attitude.⁸

And now here was Logan himself, to give him a personal report on the temper of the French government. Adams received him with mixed feelings. He knew Logan of old, knew him to be a Francophile, an outspoken anti-Federalist, a friend and supporter of Thomas Jefferson. Moreover, he believed him to be the author of an incriminating communication to Talleyrand, a letter suggesting, among other things, that the French should temporarily take a more moderate tone so that the Jeffersonians might capture the coming elections. Joseph Woodward had lately brought that story back from Paris, had actually brought a copy of the compromising document, along with Skipwith's dispatches and the decrees of the Directory.

Still, in spite of all this, Adams knew Logan to be a 'gentleman of fortune and education, and certainly not destitute of abilities.' There was no reason, he wrote later, 'to believe him a corrupt character, or deficient in memory or veracity.' Indeed, there were 'marks of candor and sincerity' in his narrative that persuaded him of its truth.[9]

Only once during Logan's recital did the President's well-known temper flash out. Logan told him he was convinced that the Directory would now receive a minister from the United States. Adams rose and exclaimed with a petulant gesture: 'Yes, I suppose if I were to send Mr. Madison or Mr. Giles or Dr. Logan, they would receive either of *them*. But I'll do no such thing; I'll send whom I please.' 'And whoever you do please to send,' replied the Doctor serenely, 'will be received.'[10]

Now, Logan could feel, he had done his duty toward his government. He had reported to the Secretary of State — and been shown the door. He had told his story to the nation's first citizen, the commander of its army — and been heard grudgingly, reluctantly, with cold hostility. Finally, he had unburdened himself to the President. John Adams, at least, had listened attentively, but had kept his own counsel, had dropped no inkling of what he intended to do. Now Logan had a further duty. He must let the people know — for America was still a republic, still ultimately responsible — in spite of Sedition Acts and 'reigns of terror' — to the majority will, to public opinion. His channels of communication with the people were only such as his party provided, but he made the most of them.

Soon after his interview with President Adams, he drove with Deborah down to Chester to pay his respects to his aged mother-in-law. From there they went on to Wilmington to visit Deborah's kinsman John Dickinson. It was a triumphal procession. 'When we met the stages,' Deborah recalled later, 'there was a general burst of welcome and congratulation.'[11] The public demonstrations sounded sweet to her ears after the ostracism, the opprobrium, the humiliation she had suffered only a few weeks before.

The Federalists kept close watch on Logan's movements. Colonel McLane, the Collector of Customs at Wilmington, sent Secretary Pickering a confidential report on the Doctor's actions in that 'hopeless sink of Jacobinism.' Logan, he reported, had been hobnobbing with the 'Directory' of the Delaware Jacobins, a group that embraced some very disreputable characters. Old John Dickinson was one. That 'piddling genius' — it was John Adams's own phrase — had penned the 'Farmer's Letters' against the Townshend Acts thirty years before, had served through the Revolution as a member of the Continental Army and the Continental Congress, had drafted the Articles of Confederation and helped write the Constitution, had been elected successively President of two American commonwealths, Delaware and Pennsylvania. But Dickinson was known to be a friend of France, and therefore a suspicious character. Dr. James Tilton was another. A brilliant physician, a masterly organizer and administrator of hospitals during the Revolution, he had recently declined a medical chair at the University of Pennsylvania. But he too sympathized with revolutionary France. Pickering would know what to make of Logan's association with men such as these.

The 'Jacobins' had called a meeting of their 'Council of Safety' at Tilton's house to hear Logan. The meeting was attended, Pickering was informed, by two grocers, a dry-goods dealer, a coachmaker, a silversmith, a printer, a tanner, a miller, and the proprietor of the Dover mail stage. Logan's purpose, the Collector reported, was 'to impress upon the public mind that peace was fully in the power of the Executive.' Next morning, the Doctor was overheard in a barber shop, criticizing the President. Obviously — McLane did not need to underline the point — he was violating the Sedition Act. It was even rumored that Logan had had an interview with Hamilton Rowan, 'the United Irishman and traitor.' [12]

No sooner had Logan returned from this brief excursion to the southward than he set off on a week's trip to New York. In the Republican strongholds of New Jersey, he was cordially received. A group of citizens in Morristown presented him an address congratulating him on his safe return, declaring that 'every lover of peace, every friend to the welfare of America, must view your disinterested endeavors to prevent a ruinous and destructive war with pleasure and approbation.' [13] In New York City the Republicans gathered on 19 December to hear the Doctor's report. The Federalist newspapers duly noticed the meeting and scattered dark hints that Logan had paid a visit to Genêt, now rusticating quietly under his own trees on Long Island, as he had yearned to do during his whirlwind days five years before.[14]

Meanwhile in Philadelphia, Logan's name was on everyone's lips. The Federalist editors, now that their quarry was actually come to earth, were in full cry. Cobbett kept up his shrill yelping, and a new voice was added to the pack. John Fenno, veteran editor of the *Gazette of the United States,* had died of yellow fever in September, but young John Ward Fenno was proving himself his father's equal in vituperation. Logan's mission, he bayed, was 'an unparalleled display of impudence, folly, and vice,' his boldness in waiting upon General Washington was 'unpardonable effrontery,' the Doctor himself was an 'agent of Mammon,' a 'poor addled cat's paw of our infamous Vice [-President].' [15]

The Republican press, on the other hand, exulted over Logan's mission, made him a popular hero. Even staid, conservative Quakers put aside their distrust of Logan's Republicanism to rejoice in his tidings of peace. Everyone knew the story of the Friend, a Federalist to boot, who, hearing a merchant denounce the Doctor for preventing war with France, retorted, 'Thee would not be so loud in thy declamation if thee had disposed of thy late importation of swords, pistols, muskets, and other implements of death.' [16]

Another Friend declared he was shocked to hear any member of his 'peaceable and meek society' complaining of Logan's conduct. 'What has friend Logan done?' he asked. 'Is the action evil? That is not even pretended. But he has done it without consulting friend Adams.' Did official approval, then, make an action right? 'Our society (in its principle at least) think not.' Every man, the good Quaker continued, should follow his inner leading. If Logan's course had truly been determined by the Light 'that lightens every man that cometh into the world,' he did right, and he would be enabled to bear the buffetings that would always be the lot of those who seek peace and pursue it.[17]

Thus the Federalist press howled and snapped at Logan's heels, the Republican papers jubilated and sang his praises. Meanwhile, Logan and his mission were topics of absorbing interest on the higher, more confidential levels of political discussion. Each of the national parties was eagerly planning how to exploit the incident for partisan advantage. At his Albemarle plantation in Virginia, James Monroe set down his thoughts in a memorandum for his friend Thomas Jefferson. To Monroe it appeared that Logan's embassy — 'I had like to have called it *mission,*' he interjected, 'for a heavenly one it seems to have been' — would be most useful to the Republican cause if Logan should tell 'the truth, or rather the whole truth' about it. Logan's steadfast denial that he had represented anyone but himself would avert from Jefferson and the party any imputation of intrigue. At the same time, his frank statement that he had been afraid the administration would involve the country in war, that he had gone to France to do what he could to prevent that calamity, would make it difficult to attack his enterprise without attacking his motive, which was peace.

Monroe went on to forecast what the administration's strategy would be. He had little doubt, he wrote, that the President would mention Logan's trip in his forthcoming message to Congress, and would do it, if he could, in such a way as to hurt the Republican cause. Adams might go further. He might even 'propose a law to prevent such interference or intriguing, as he will call it, between the citizens of the United States and foreign governments.' [18]

Monroe was clairvoyant. On 8 December, President John Adams stood before Congress, flanked on one side by Generals Washington, Hamilton, and Pinckney, on the other by the British and Portuguese Ministers, and delivered a message, written in large part by Pickering and Wolcott, the faithful friends of Alexander Hamilton. France, he said, had given the United States no reason to relax its defensive measures. The administration's policy would therefore be 'to extend and invigorate' these measures. General Hamilton's face could not conceal his pleasure. Still, the President went on — and it was John Adams speaking now — the door would remain open for a renewal of negotiations, provided this could be had on honorable terms.[19]

The Senate made a formal reply, commending the administration for its 'wise and manly policy.' Scornfully, it dismissed any French proposals for conciliation that might be transmitted by 'individuals without public character or authority.' Such proposals could be calculated only 'to separate the people from their Government, and to bring about by intrigue that which open force could not effect.'[20]

The President quickly picked up this hint. Perhaps he was prompted to it by his Hamiltonian advisers. At any rate, he was convinced, though mistakenly, that Logan had made treasonable proposals to Talleyrand. His reply to the Senate on 12 December included these ominous words: 'Although the officious interference of individuals without public character or authority is not entitled to any credit, yet it deserves to be considered whether that temerity and impertinence of individuals affecting to interfere in public affairs between France and the United States, whether by their secret correspondence or otherwise, and intended to impose upon the people and separate them from their government, ought not to be inquired into and corrected.'[21]

The gage was down. It was obvious that Logan's mission would be the central issue in this session of Congress, as the Alien and Sedition Acts had been in the last. The people of Philadelphia County, Logan's friends and neighbors, now took a hand in the affair. Four days before Christmas, there was a by-election in the County to fill a vacant seat in the state Assembly. It was barely a week since the President's scathing reference to Logan's 'officious interference.' Logan himself was still in New York. Unbeknownst to him, his friends put his name up for the vacant seat. He was elected by a resounding majority over Frederick Augustus Muhlenberg, a former Federalist Speaker of the national House of Representatives. 'The election of Dr. Logan,' crowed the *Aurora*, 'is the best reply which could have been given by the people to the president.'[22]

✳

---

x. 'LOGAN'S LAW'

Now George Logan had to sit at Stenton helpless while a hundred men in Congress Hall argued over his recent conduct, anatomized his motives, reconstructed his actions, impugned and defended his loyalty, heaped blame and praise, ridicule and honor on his shoulders. Though for weeks his name was not even mentioned, though there was no suggestion that he should be punished by law, he was as much the focus of attention as if he sat in the pillory on Chestnut Street to be pelted by Federalist Congressmen, taunted, hooted, and jeered at by the crowd. It lasted a month, this humiliating public ordeal. Through it all he had nothing to support him but Debby's faith and love, the valiant efforts of a handful of loyal Republican defenders, and his own clear sense of having done no wrong, of having done only what he had been impelled to do by his conscience, his devotion to peace, his love of his country.

It was the day after Christmas, just two weeks after the President's speech, when the debate commenced. Roger Griswold introduced the subject. Griswold was a prickly, combative Federalist from Connecticut. Not many months before, the whole country had been talking about his brawl on the floor of the House — literally on the floor of the House — with Matthew Lyon, a pugnacious Republican from Vermont. Solemnly, Griswold proposed that a committee should consider amending the Sedition Act in order to punish any person 'who shall usurp the Executive authority of this Government, by commencing or carrying on any cor-

185

respondence with the Governments of any foreign Prince or State, relating to controversies or disputes' between such governments and the United States.[1]

Immediately John Nicholas of Virginia sprang to his feet. Young, handsome, scion of an aristocratic and steadfastly Republican family, he was determined to smoke the Federalists out. If this resolution had a general object in view, he snapped, it was unnecessary. If, however, it was 'founded upon what had been seen in the public papers relative to the conduct of a certain gentleman who has lately been in France,' it was premature. The mover should wait until the President laid facts before the House.[2]

The gentleman from Virginia, retorted Griswold, mistook the purpose of the resolution. It had no reference to particular persons. Its object was general — to prevent a faction opposed to the administration from sending an agent to a foreign country to negotiate on its behalf. Piously, he added that he 'hoped no occasion would ever arise for bringing into operation a law of this kind.' Still, if it should, 'it would be well to be prepared to meet it.'[3]

Nicholas would not be shaken off. He did not know, he said, whether Griswold's reference to a 'faction' was directed toward a political group then existing in the country. But he felt free to say that if he had had any share in sending the gentleman in question to France — which he had not — he would not hesitate to confess it. He would not be 'ashamed or afraid to promote the peace of his country,' said Nicholas. If all individual efforts for peace are to be prohibited, 'how is peace to be procured,' he asked, since the President had declared negotiation at an end? He took a fling at the Federalists, the 'war party.' 'If . . . any individual or set of men were bent upon involving the country in war' the case, he said, 'would be very different.'[4]

There was no question about it now: the battle was on — even though no bill and no facts were before the House. Everyone had read the newspapers. Everyone knew about Logan's mission, everyone had made up his mind about its motives, its results, its political possibilities. John Rutledge, a South Carolina Federalist, promptly revealed his party's strategy: play upon the widespread fear of subversive activity, dilate on the sinister doings of revolutionary French agents, the unhappy example of the French satellites in Europe. Everyone knew, said Rutledge, how Holland had lost her independence. 'We know that the United Irishmen, who have deluged their country in blood, had their agents in France, who instructed the French army where to land, where to find pikes, provisions, and other necessaries, for their work of devastation.' [5]

The Republicans now sent their ablest champion into the field. Swiss-born Albert Gallatin still spoke with a thick foreign accent, though he had lived in western Pennsylvania for ten years. He talked slowly, calmly, reasonably, his one gesture an awkward perpendicular motion of his right arm, sawing the air. Conceivably, he began, the present resolution, as its mover insisted, had no reference to any recent occurrence. Still, he thought it doubtful that such a resolution would have been proposed 'unless a certain event had taken place.' Should they not wait, then, until they were in possession of the facts that the President had promised?

Granting, for argument's sake, that the proposition were really general and prospective in intent, Gallatin felt bound to point out that it was improperly, loosely drawn. How could the carrying on of a correspondence, the mere writing of a letter, be a usurpation of the President's authority? As it stood, the resolution could result in a bill which would prevent the owner of a ship that had been plundered by a foreign privateer from seeking to recover his property. Surely the gentleman from Connecticut — who represented a maritime constituency — did not intend that.

But there was still a more serious objection. Congress, said Gallatin, should deal only with cases of *criminal* correspondence, cases such as that which had occurred in his own native Switzerland, when individuals had actually called in French troops to overrun the country. He agreed with his colleague from Virginia that if, from a sincere desire of peace, a hypothetical citizen — for he lacked information, he said, on any actual case that might have taken place — should go to France and persuade her government to desist from aggressive measures, to cease its depredations, to discuss terms of accommodation, 'he saw nothing either criminal or improper in such a conduct, but the contrary.' [6]

Presently, Robert Goodloe Harper took the floor. Universally acknowledged as the leading Congressional orator, this reformed Jacobin, handsome, self-assured, powerful in debate, was the lion of Philadelphia society, the admiration of his Federalist colleagues. He held the floor for four hours,[7] laying about him with a fine disregard for Congressional amenities or the feelings of individuals. Perhaps, he began, the mover of the resolution did not have a 'particular and recent case' in mind. For his own part, he would make no secret of the fact that he *did* have such a case in mind. After all, it was from particular cases that general legislation usually arose. He had made up his mind about this case when it first came to light, six months earlier. He reminded his colleagues how he had called it to their attention then. He had considered this individual, from the moment of his embarkation, he said, 'as an agent employed and sent by a party in this country,' for it was obvious that no one would be so 'silly, so vain, so totally void of common sense' as to undertake such a mission purely on his own initiative.

Harper was omniscient. He could reveal in full detail the sinister motives behind the mission, the actual language of the interviews with the Directory. He proceeded to reconstruct the whole transaction, down to the last treasonable confidence, the last ominous counsel. The individual in question, he said confidently, had urged the French to slacken off a little in their offensive measures, make some appearance of conciliation, give the pro-French party in America a breathing-space, a chance to regain its lost prestige, so that in due course it could pave the way for the entrance of French troops. 'To have held other language under the circumstances,' Harper continued, 'would . . . have betrayed a degree of incapacity, of ignorance, and of childish simplicity, of which he could not suspect the contriver of this mission' — Jefferson, of course — 'nor even the agent employed in it.' The late 'embassy' in itself, had been 'a very silly affair'; yet if such interference were allowed to go unpunished, it could lead presently to the total subversion of government.

No Federalist, least of all Harper, the ex-Jacobin, could forego an opportunity to dilate upon the horrors of revolutionary Europe. He thanked Gallatin for bringing up the example of Switzerland. 'By whom,' he asked, 'were the inhabitants of that beautiful and happy country delivered up to pillage, slaughter, and a foreign yoke? By whom but her own profligate sons who, stimulated by a boundless and unprincipled ambition, chose, rather than not rule, to rule over a country plundered and ruined, and to hold a precarious power as the miserable vice gerents of a foreign despotism!' Harper paused, looked about meaningfully. 'Are there no persons of this description among us?' [8]

Gallatin was soon on his feet again, pointing out the dilemma in which Harper had caught himself. If the mission in question had been effective, he said, 'it would then appear that peace might have been made by our Executive.' If, on the other hand, it had had no effect, 'then there is no ground of complaint.'

If Harper could play the game of construing motives, so could Gallatin. Was it not logical to assume — since assumptions were the order of the day — that the Federalists had introduced this resolution 'to raise a clamor about foreign affairs, and to connect what the gentleman is pleased to call the French party in this country with the French government'? Only by raising such a clamor had they been able to put through the Alien and Sedition Acts, create a standing army, an army created, incidentally, 'not to repel an invasion, but, as it is now confessed, for the crushing of a faction at home.'

Gallatin's thin, sharp features were more animated now; his speech more rapid, more guttural. It was a new doctrine the Federalists were preaching — that because liberty had been abused in Europe, 'the old maxims of liberty and republicanism, which laid the foundation of our Revolution and of both our general and state constitutions and governments, are to be laid aside, at least for a while.' This, he said, was a betrayal of American principles. It was a doctrine of alarm. [9]

Now John Nicholas returned to the attack. Could it be, he asked, that the administration was being forced into a peace that it did not want? As for the 'particular case' that everyone was discussing so freely, he would remind the House that it still had no information about it. But the gentleman from South Carolina could 'always dive to the bottom of everything at once.' If his story of a treasonable conspiracy behind the recent mission was true, how did he explain the fact that none of the conspirators had made any use of its fruits? Had any member of the House recommended disarming? Quite the contrary. All were agreed on the necessity of defensive measures.

Harper had acknowledged, he went on, that 'fanatics of a certain religious persuasion' had often gone to great lengths to procure peace. How, Nicholas asked, did he know 'that the religious principles of that society may not have had some effect in a late transaction?' After all, the gentleman concerned had been educated as a Quaker, 'and although he did not now conform to their habits, he may still retain principles peculiar to that sect, which had been early instilled in his mind.'

The gentleman from South Carolina was afraid of subjugation by a foreign power. For his own part, Nicholas believed more mischief was to be feared in the United States 'from the votaries of despotism than from the votaries of France.' The cry of national unity was now being used to destroy the liberties of the people by silencing all opposition to the government.[10] This was the real mischief, the real danger. On this note Nicholas rested his case. The House heard one more speaker on the Federalist side, then adjourned, weary of so much oratory.

Next morning the debate went on. Abraham Baldwin, a moderate Republican from Georgia, rose to say that he was willing to have the matter committed, for he could not believe that any judicious committee would put obstacles in the way of sincere efforts to avert war. 'Monuments and altars,' he reminded the House, 'have been erected to peacemakers.' [11]

Now it was the turn of Harrison Gray Otis of Massachusetts to speak. He had been waiting impatiently to be recognized. Otis was a tall, elegant, fastidiously dressed patrician, a Harvard-bred aristocrat, who left no one in doubt concerning his capacity for eloquence and his contempt for the common people. He finally caught the Speaker's eye. The current state of relations with France, he began, was so nearly indistinguishable from war, that 'every defensive and cautionary measure' necessary in wartime was now in order, including measures to 'conceal' party divisions. Previous speakers had defended 'a late eccentric mission' on the ground that it had tended to promote peace. This, Otis proclaimed in his cultivated tones, was nothing but the old Jesuitical doctrine, 'new vamped and varnished by modern *illuminati*,' that the end justifies the means.

Otis did not wish to impute conspiracy to anyone. Still, it was strange indeed that the only persons privy to the secret departure should have been the Vice-President, the Chief Justice of Pennsylvania, and — Congressmen leaned forward in their chairs to catch the next name — Genêt.

Otis had created his sensation, retailing a canard he had picked up from Woodward, the Boston Federalist. It was now his turn to conjure up horrors. He did it with a difference. Not merely for himself and his associates was he alarmed. He feared for the fate even of those who opposed him. He well knew that 'when the confusion incident to French principles should overtake his country . . . friend and foe would be involved in promiscuous ruin. The same dagger that was whetted for his bosom would strike deep into theirs, the same hands that rifled his pockets would plunder their pockets, and the violence which beggared and enslaved his children would involve theirs in the same distress.' [12]

Otis took his seat and Harper sprang to his feet again. He denied flatly Gallatin's charge of the day before that he was in a dilemma. If peace could be had on honorable terms, the government, he was sure, would make peace. But never would it allow unauthorized individuals to usurp its sovereignty, even to make peace on terms it desired. In some quarters, he went on, the word *peace* had become a magic word, the abracadabra of American Jacobinism, but he was not bewitched by it. There were circumstances under which he would 'spurn at peace with disdain.' If peace could be had only by submission or the surrender of essential rights, then peace would be a curse rather than a blessing.

Before sitting down, Harper sought to take advantage of the

sensation Otis had created by his mention of the Vice-President. He threatened to read the now-famous letter to Philip Mazzei in which Jefferson had made uncomplimentary references to President Washington. This was too much even for Jonathan Dayton, the Federalist Speaker. He ruled it out of order.[13]

These loose aspersions angered Gallatin. He obtained leave to speak a third time. Harper's charge that the opposition was engaged in treason was founded, he declared, on nothing more solid than 'that gentleman's fertile imagination.' As for Otis's imputation that Gallatin defended the recent mission on Jesuitical grounds, he indignantly denied it: from his point of view the whole transaction, from beginning to end, had been innocent. Firmly, deftly, he parried the familiar charge that the Republicans were uncritical Francophiles, bent on subverting the American Republic.[14]

Nathaniel Macon of North Carolina closed for the opposition. Macon was no orator, but his simple dress, his 'republican' manners, his known integrity commanded respect. He objected to the hue and cry against the supposed 'French party.' Might it not as well be argued from the ubiquity of British capital and British subjects in the United States that there was a 'British party' in the country? What shocked him most was the implication that Thomas Jefferson was a party to a treasonable plot. He found it 'a little extraordinary' that Congress should be 'talking of an officer in our Government being a traitor.' Such insinuations could be designed only for one purpose — to create suspicion in the minds of the people. If any gentleman had proof of malconduct by the Vice-President, let him bring it forward. 'But if no such proof exist,' Macon concluded stoutly, 'it is a strange way of supporting the constituted authorities, thus to calumniate a man whom the people have thought proper to place in so high a station.'[15]

It was growing late. Tempers were fraying. The debate was wandering far from the proposal before the House. The question was called for. By a vote of 65 to 23, the matter was referred. When Speaker Dayton named the committee, no one could doubt what its report would be. He chose three of the ablest, most vigorous and influential Federalists in the House — Griswold, Thomas Pinckney of South Carolina, James A. Bayard of Delaware — and two relatively obscure Republicans — Abraham Baldwin of Georgia, conscientious, hard-working, but unspectacular, and Richard Dobbs Spaight of North Carolina, who had been in the Congress barely three weeks.[16]

Meanwhile the debate was attracting great public interest. Newspapers everywhere relayed it to an avid reading audience. The *Aurora* carried the proceedings in full, and the reader's eye was caught by an advertisement in a neighboring column of Dr. Logan's Tammany address of the previous May, now printed as a pamphlet. The Doctor's name had not yet been mentioned in Congress Hall, but it was on everyone's lips outside. To Federalists it was a byword, the evidence of Republican perfidy, though as Gallatin and Nicholas punctured the claims of conspiracy, it began to seem to some administration men that it would have been better to have ignored Logan's mission completely.[17]

Up in Connecticut, the Federalist wit Richard Alsop took a fling at Logan in a set of New Year's verses, which were widely circulated in other states. Repeating Cobbett's sly innuendo, he addressed Vice-President Jefferson:

> With joy we find thee rise from *coguing* [18]
> With Judge McKean and *'foolish Logan,'*
> And reeling down the factious dance,
> Send Deborah's husband off to France,
> To tell the Frenchmen to their cost,
> They reckon'd here without their host;
> Whilst thou, to smooth the ills of life,
> Held sweet communion with the wife.[19]

Congressmen quoted snatches from Alsop's verses on the floor of the House and sent many a reader scurrying to the poem to smack his lips over the references to the Doctor and his wife.[20]

Dr. Nathaniel Ames of Dedham, Massachusetts, a Republican, confided to his diary his sense of shock at the 'mean servility' of the pro-British 'war party.' Because Logan, going to France, had done 'more than the President with all his tiptoe envoys to avert war with sister Republic,' he wrote, the administration and its supporters in Congress were trying to conceal their mortification by giving his deeds the taint of crime. 'Nicholas, Gallatin, etc., as if divinely inspired, thunder against it with irresistible argument and reason . . . but argument is lost on Harper, Rutledge, and other tyrants or tools of tyrant power.' Dr. Ames's Federalist brother, the brilliant, bellicose Fisher Ames, had a different reaction to the speeches of Nicholas and Gallatin : 'The country where such abominations as they utter can be even tolerated,' he wrote to a friend, 'is to be tried and purified in the furnace of affliction.' [21]

On 7 January 1799 Griswold reported from committee a bill 'for the punishment of certain crimes therein specified.' Two days later, the debate reopened, the House sitting at first as a committee of the whole. The bill surprised many members by its broad scope. It provided a fine and imprisonment for any citizen who should 'without the permission or authority of the government of the United States, directly or indirectly, commence or carry on any verbal or written correspondence or intercourse with any foreign government, or any officer or agent thereof, relating to any dispute or controversy between any foreign government and the United States, with an intent to influence the measures or conduct of the government having disputes or controversies with the United States.' [22] Bayard of Delaware quickly proposed that the fine should be five thousand dollars, the term of imprisonment not less than six months or more than three years. Republicans suggested limiting amendments, but they were all beaten down.

Debate on the substance of the bill commenced on the tenth. Nicholas again led the attack. He took up the theme with which Macon had ended the previous discussion. The real object of the bill, he was convinced, was 'to excite suspicion and clamor' against all opponents of the party in power. But it went beyond that. By attaching a measure of guilt 'to all the friends of peace in this country,' it would 'excite a suspicion against any overtures of peace which may come from France, so that the Government may not be forced to meet them.' This, he hinted broadly, was precisely what the Federalists wanted. Had he not 'for six years past, been witness to the earnest desire which has existed in these gentlemen to create armies and navies?' More particularly, over the past three years, had he not seen 'with what pleasure they had viewed a state of things which afforded them plausible ground . . . for carrying their schemes into effect?' [23]

This was a home thrust. Bayard of Delaware, tall, florid, an able Federalist orator and one of the framers of the bill, sought to distract attention from it. What, after all, was the nature of the offense aimed at in the bill? It was 'separated only by a shade from treason.' The gentleman from Virginia had earlier stated that he would not have been ashamed to commit it. Bayard left his colleagues in no doubt as to the light in which he regarded John Nicholas.[24]

Robert Williams of North Carolina, a moderate, expressed his misgivings about the character of the bill. He had voted, he said, for the original resolution — to amend the Sedition Act so as to prevent the usurpation of the executive authority. Now he found himself confronted with an entirely independent bill 'for the punishment of certain crimes therein specified.' What, he wanted to know, was going on? Was it a repetition of an earlier maneuver by which the majority, after proposing merely to punish sedition, had ended by muzzling the press?[25]

Thomas Pinckney, a second member of the committee, rose to his feet to defend the bill. Veteran of the Revolution, former Governor of South Carolina, Minister to Great Britain and Spain, Pinckney was heard with respect. He defended the bill in sober, calm, rational language. An evil existed in the world — 'no less than an endeavor on the part of one government, by means of its diplomatic skill, to overset all the governments which do not concur with them in its mad career.' It was necessary to take measures to guard against this evil. Hence the bill before the House.

As for 'the gentleman lately in France,' Pinckney took a charitable view: probably he had not realized that his conduct was criminal. It was clear that Pinckney was speaking under some restraint. He explained that he 'considered himself as under obligation to that gentleman.' He had not forgotten the winter he had passed at Stenton, seventeen years before, an exile from his native South Carolina, wounded and sick after the battle of Camden. Nothing but what he conceived to be the public interest, he declared, could have induced him to have remarked upon 'a conduct which he considered as calculated to bring the greatest mischiefs upon this country, if not put a stop to.' [26]

(Across the ocean at The Hague, William Vans Murray, still vexed at having failed to nip the whole affair in the bud, read the debates and complained of the gentleness with which 'sweet Dr. Logan' was being handled. Pinckney's considerateness drew a derisive snort: 'I can by some pumping and working of my fancy,' Murray wrote to John Quincy Adams, 'find out the temper of mind that leads a lovesick green girl to sing the song "I pardon the treason, the traitor's so dear" but for a bearded politician in speaking of the very man who rendered a penal law necessary to be a subject of thanks! I can not skin fleas.' [27])

Late in the day, Harper created a fresh sensation. He knew the eyes of the nation were upon him. Perhaps he felt that his party's case needed a fillip. At any rate, he announced in solemn tones that he was now about to produce the evidence of a treasonable conspiracy that he had promised the House seven months earlier. He was going to read a document presented to the French Minister of Foreign Affairs by the individual whose guilty conduct the House had been discussing. A Republican interrupted, demanded to know by whom the paper was signed. Harper admitted that it bore no signature. Still he had 'reason to believe . . . it to have been presented to the French Government by an American citizen who was lately in France.'

Harper then proceeded to read by paragraphs a letter addressed to Talleyrand by one who described himself as 'a firm friend to the principles of the French Revolution, and well known as such in his own country, the United States of America.' He interlarded the paragraphs with elaborate explanatory glosses, caustic comments, oratorical flourishes. Members of Congress sat bolt upright in their chairs listening, the Federalists gleefully, the Republicans suspiciously, apprehensively.

Everything in the memorial fitted what they knew or believed about Logan. The writer commenced by deploring the differences which had arisen between the two republics, once firm allies. He spoke, he said, for 'all the principal characters in America famed for their sacred love of liberty in general' and their attachment to the French cause in particular. 'We all know what this jargon means,' observed Harper sarcastically, 'when translated into plain English.' He warned the Directory against further provocative acts, promised that any attempt at invasion would be resisted by a united people, urged the French 'by a great and magnanimous conduct to draw back those wandering affections, which intrigue and misunderstanding have estranged for a moment, and leave the true American character to blaze forth in the approaching elections.'

Harper paused significantly, while Congressmen caught their breath, looked at each other, or stared fixedly at their desks. Then he went on. This passage, he declared, 'discloses the cloven foot of the mission.' France, he took this to mean, should 'shorten sail for a while' so as to let the pro-French party in America recover its popularity and win the election of 1800. Then, presumably, the government would welcome the revolutionary troops with open arms.

The rest of the memorial contained specific advice to the Directory. It should revoke its embargo on American ships, liberate the imprisoned American seamen, send a Minister to Philadelphia or to a neutral city like The Hague to negotiate a settlement.

Harper ended on a note of triumph. This incriminating document, he said, made two things crystal clear: interference such as the bill under debate was designed to prevent had actually taken place, and its purpose had been 'insidious and destructive.' The peroration that followed was one of Harper's best efforts. He had been charged, he said, with seeking to excite alarm. He pled guilty. 'Shall I be asked why I wish to create alarm? Ask the sentinel who sees the enemy approach under the cover of night, why he creates an alarm.' Harper's voice, as he closed, was dramatic, portentous. 'I see, or think I see . . . the enemy attempting, by secret marches and ambuscade, to make a lodgment in our works, or take our camp by surprise; and believing this, my most sacred duty to

those who have placed me here to watch for their safety, commands me to give the alarm. . .' [28]

Harper had timed his speech perfectly. The House adjourned
with his ominous words still reverberating.

On the next morning, as soon as he could gain recognition, Gallatin was on his feet to renew his criticism of the bill's loose
phraseology and to answer Harper's sensational charges. He had
objected earlier that the bill, as written, would prevent a merchant
or ship-captain from recovering property from confiscation by a
foreign government, that moreover it would place a gag on harmless social intercourse with foreigners. Harper had denied this.
He had gone even further, had stated that if, after the bill became
law, he were invited to supper with Talleyrand, whom he had
known in America, and were asked for his opinion on the relations of the two countries, he would not hesitate to give it.

This was Gallatin's opportunity. He made the most of it. 'What
does this amount to,' he demanded, 'connected with what [has]
been said about the existence of a dangerous combination of men,
a French party in this country, and other expressions of the same
import?' Gallatin answered his own question. 'Does it not mean
that the law is to attach to a certain description of men, and not to
others? . . . If a man is a federalist, he will be innocent, but if
he is an anti-federalist he will be guilty.'

It was a shrewd hit. Gallatin followed it with another. Why, he
asked, do the French think they have a party in the United States?
Because the Federalists are constantly saying so on the floor of
the House and in the press. But is it not remarkable, he continued,
'that when a certain state paper was read to the House yesterday
. . . the crime appeared to be, that the writer had attempted to
show the French Government that they have *no* party here?' Republicans looked relieved as their floor leader deftly turned the
tables on Harper and the Federalists. Relentlessly Gallatin pursued his temporary advantage. 'Gentlemen think it perfectly innocent in themselves to invite further aggressions, nay, an invasion,
by assuring France that they have a party here ready to receive
them; and they hold it up as a crime that an individual should
have spoken of the unanimity of the people, and their determina-

tion to rally round their Government against the attacks of any foreign nation whatever. . .'

Gallatin now cast aside the cautious anonymity which had hitherto veiled every reference to 'the late mission.' 'A gentleman by the name of Dr. Logan,' he said, had called at his lodgings that morning. He had declared categorically that he was not the author of the memorial Harper had read, that he had not presented it or any other paper to Talleyrand. He had, to be sure, seen a copy of the document in Paris, indeed he had been asked by Richard Codman, the Boston merchant, to deliver it as from himself, but he had declined to do so. Relief, as from an intolerable burden of doubt, stood written on the faces of Republican members, while Federalists glowered and muttered to each other.

Gallatin could not resist a last fling at his discomfited opponents. 'The clamor which gentlemen have thought proper to raise about this paper,' he prophesied, 'when the public knows the fact, may recoil on themselves.' [29]

Next day, the *Aurora* carried a long address 'to the citizens of the United States,' signed by Dr. Logan. It was a circumstantial narrative of his recent visit to France. It ended with a carefully phrased denial of complicity with any party or individual: 'I did not go to France at the direction, at the request, or on the advice of any person whatever. I went for my own pleasure, with my own views, and at my own expense. I did not go or act as the agent, official or unofficial, of any man or set of men whatever.' [30] This frank and comprehensive statement was widely reprinted in other journals. A few days later, the papers carried another statement from the Doctor, in which he categorically denied Harper's charge that he had corresponded with Talleyrand. He ascribed the document which had been read in Congress Hall to Richard Codman, 'the friend and correspondent of Mr. Otis.' [31]

On 17 January, the bill was read a third time. Speaker Dayton, in his thunderous voice — always so surprising coming from such a gaunt, slender man — put the question: 'Shall this bill pass?' But it was not yet time for a final vote. Edward Livingston, the New Yorker, who had closed the debate against both the Alien

Act and the Sedition Act for the Republicans, had taken his seat
only a few days before; he had still to be heard from. He delivered
a long, eloquent, and learned speech against the bill. It was an
unnecessary, useless, foolish piece of legislation. By way of comparison, he cited a law of Henry VIII's time under which the
Bishop of Rochester's cook had been attainted of treason for
causing his master to die of indigestion and was ordered to be
boiled in his own pot.[32]

Harrison Gray Otis was determined that the opposition should
not have the last word. He accused Livingston of wilfully delaying a vote with his silly anecdotes. Then he brought up the by this
time famous memorial to Talleyrand again. He confessed what
he knew of it — that it was brought from Paris 'by a gentleman
by no means inimical to the supposed author of it and by him delivered to an individual of this country, as a copy of the identical
paper presented by a certain gentleman then in Paris to the Directory.' But it was really immaterial, Otis added, whether Logan
had presented it or not. What mattered was that he *could* have
done so. By the time he had taken his seat, Otis had made it plain
how little the case against Logan rested on the documentary evidence. Suppose Codman did compose the letter to Talleyrand, he
argued; perhaps he wrote it because he feared that Logan might
have 'presented something worse.' [33]

Otis had committed a serious tactical blunder. Federalists could
not but feel that he had cut much of the ground from under their
case. To John Dennis of Maryland it now appeared necessary to
arouse Congressional emotions with another burst of lurid
rhetoric. He brushed lightly over the 'recent transaction,' hurried
on to ring changes on a familiar Federalist theme. The ringleaders of the revolutionary movement in France, he declaimed, were
a set of 'atheistical philosophers, fanatical politicians, political
metaphysicians, and bloodthirsty Jacobins.' Their adherents in
other countries were 'an organized banditti, robbers, and assas-
sins, who like beasts of prey when all creation is at rest, make
from their fastnesses nocturnal excursions and plunder and destroy all who are opposed to their nefarious projects.' [34]

It was very late. After seven days of debate, gentlemen were
showing signs of fatigue and bad temper. There were loud calls

for a vote. But Gallatin claimed the floor for some final arguments. Why all the mystery over the exploded memorial? he demanded. 'The gentleman from South Carolina says an Eastern gentleman brought it from Paris, that he gave it to another gentleman, who sent it to an acquaintance of his in this city, who gave it to him.' Gallatin would dispel the mystery. He knew that the paper in question had been handed to several Federalist Congressmen in turn, that lacking proof of its authorship, none of them would have anything to do with it — until it came into the hands of Otis and Harper, 'the unofficial agents on this floor of their acquaintance, our Minister of Foreign Relations.'

The Pennsylvanian pounced on Otis's damaging concession that the memorial might not have been presented or even written by Logan, his bland insistence that this did not matter. 'What!' Gallatin cried, 'Can it be immaterial whether a paper which is produced to prove that a gentleman is the agent of a party in this country, was not written or presented by him, but written by a Federalist, the correspondent of the gentleman from Massachusetts?' [35]

This called for another flight of sanguinary rhetoric from the Federalist side of the house. As if loath to abandon the discredited memorial, Bayard attempted to show that it was at least 'the natural off-spring of the spurious envoy.' The passage in which the author described himself as a friend to the principles of the French Revolution gave Bayard his cue. What were the principles of the French Revolution? Solemnly, he named them over:

The annihilation of all religion . . . A despotism more violent and atrocious in its excesses than even the despotism of the most mad and brutal of Roman Emperors — a despotism which has shed oceans of blood and which racked invention in order to multiply its victims in a given time, which, not satisfied with the devouring guillotine, introduced *noyades* and *fusillades,* which plunged hundreds and thousands into eternity at once . . . the proscription of every man of wealth, for the purpose of seizing his property . . . the abolition of the liberty of the press . . . foreign conquest . . .

Such, proclaimed Bayard, are the principles of the French Revolution.

The memorialist, he went on, had spoken of the French people, of their having shed blood in the American Revolution. This, he submitted, was 'an absolute falsehood.' It was not the French people, it was that 'great friend of our country' Louis XVI, 'and next to him . . . the Queen of France,' victims of the present blood-stained rulers of France, to whom gratitude was due. And anyway, said Bayard, resting his case, the effect of French aid on the outcome of the American Revolution had been negligible.[36]

If Bayard could prolong debate, Nicholas could play at that game too. He rose up to point out inaccuracies and inconsistencies in Bayard's harangue. Tempers were snapping now. There were angry exchanges between Nicholas and Bayard, Nicholas and Otis. Calls for the question grew insistent. Finally, late at night on 17 January, the yeas and nays were taken. By a party vote of 58 to 36, the bill was passed.[37]

A few days later, it went to the Senate. The upper chamber met behind closed doors. No one except the Senators knew what was said there. There was little occasion therefore for public oratory; still, it is likely that Thomas Jefferson, sitting in the presiding officer's chair under portraits of Louis XVI and Marie Antoinette, heard himself implicated as an accomplice before the fact of treason, heard his loyalty as an American questioned, his integrity as a political leader impugned. When the bill came to a vote, only two Senators, Langdon of New Hampshire and Bloodworth of North Carolina, were recorded against it.[38]

On 30 January, John Adams signed the bill and 'Logan's Act' became the law of the land. It stands yet on the statute books as a warning to any citizen who might be moved, as George Logan was, to act upon a private 'concern' for peace. 'It is still perfectly legal, however,' two recent historians wryly comment, 'for any American citizen to do his utmost to stir up war with a foreign government.' [39] From time to time over the next century and a half, the 'Logan Act' — it is still called by his name — would be invoked in Congress and in the public press, usually for partisan political purposes. No one, however, has ever been convicted under it.[40]

The passage of 'Logan's Law' was a triumph for the party of the administration. Everyone understood the Federalists' strategy. 'The real views in the importance they have given to Logan's enterprise,' wrote Thomas Jefferson, 'are mistaken by nobody.' [41] If the Federalists could only identify Logan in the public mind as the agent of Jefferson, the tool of the 'French party,' if they could cover him with infamy or ridicule — either treatment promised to be effective, and the Federalists used both — they could undermine the opposition, weaken its popular support. By striking at Logan they could damage Jefferson.

But the Federalist strategy failed to produce the expected result; the excitement which the Federalists stirred up boomeranged. James Monroe foresaw this outcome. He was not disturbed, he wrote to Jefferson, by the clamor of the moment. 'The enterprise of Logan with its consequences,' he was confident, 'will not hurt any in his political sentiments, while the attempt to make it instrumental to that end will have its advantages. The ill humor shown by the head and all the members of the opposite party at an interference forbidden by no law, prompted by benevolent motives, and which was useful to the public is a circumstance which will tend to show the views of that party.' The longer the debate lasted and 'the greater the zeal of its friends,' Monroe felt, 'the better the effect, since at best it is legislating on an abstract principle against the force of a precedent showing the folly of the law.' [42]

John Adams himself played a crucial role in the drama that followed. For a quarter-century and more he had been on the stage of American politics, an indispensable figure — in the supporting cast. Now for once he rose to the stature of a tragic hero. He had been meditating his part for months, reflecting over the reports Gerry and Woodward had brought him from Paris, reading and rereading his letters from Murray and his son John Quincy, studying a recent letter that Washington had forwarded from Joel Barlow, pondering his conversation with Logan. Murray's latest dispatch had enclosed a letter from Talleyrand, in which the French Foreign Minister agreed to receive an American envoy, 'with the respect due to the representative of a free, independent, and powerful nation.' These were almost Adams's own words to Congress, his own conditions for a renewal of diplomatic relations.

Should he, could he accept this olive branch? He knew full well what it would mean — that Hamilton's friends in Congress, in his own cabinet, would never forgive him, that his action would split the Federalist Party in two, perhaps end its effectiveness as a political instrument, certainly foreclose his own political future. Still, it was a solemn thing to expose a young, disunited, unprepared nation to war with a great military power. John Adams decided to act.

On 18 February 1799, barely two weeks after he had signed the 'Logan Act,' he transmitted Talleyrand's letter to Congress. Along with it he sent a message which exploded in Congress Hall like a bombshell. 'Always disposed and ready,' he said, 'to embrace every plausible appearance of probability of preserving or restoring tranquillity,' he nominated William Vans Murray as Minister Plenipotentiary to negotiate with the French government.[43]

It was a courageous act — the greatest act of John Adams's career. George Logan saw that, and responded with deep thankfulness and rejoicing. He was a forgiving man. He could forget that it had been Adams who had initiated the public ordeal through which he had just passed. He heard the news with quiet satisfaction, with a feeling that he himself had been vindicated, but, more than that, with a sense of relief that the cloud of war had passed.[44]

After a long trial of mockings and scourgings, George Logan and his party stood justified. Just over the horizon lay not only peace but political triumph, for the frustrated followers of Alexander Hamilton, disappointed of their French war, were sharpening their knives for John Adams — and the Republicans could scarcely fail to profit from this internecine strife. Logan's own election to the Assembly had been a portent. His enemies had hoped, by discrediting his French mission, to ring down the curtain not only on his own public career but on his party's as well. Now it seemed as if the curtain were rising on a new drama, to be enacted on a national stage. In that drama Logan would have an important part to play.

*

XI. DAYS of WRATH

ON THE DAY George Logan took his seat in the Assembly, there
was a crowd in the State House yard. When the doors were
opened, they surged up the stairs and crammed the gallery — city
workingmen mostly, with a fair sprinkling of farmers from the
county. They knew that, only a few days before, the Federalist
majority had pushed through the legislature a special address to
President Adams, deploring Logan's 'usurpation of powers,' his
'obscure interference in our external concerns.' [1] The Federalists,
the 'aristocracy,' had spoken in that address. But the democracy
had answered them, the next day, by electing Doctor Logan to
the very chamber that had denounced him. It was the most effective answer the people could have given, and they were waiting in
the gallery now to enjoy his triumph and their own. Someone had
arranged for a new carpet to be unrolled in honor of 'the envoy of
the people.' When Logan made his triumphal appearance, a tumult of huzzas burst out, and Speaker Cadwalader Evans was
able to restore order only by threatening to clear the gallery.[2]

The man who walked down the aisle to affirm his support of
the Commonwealth was hardly a striking or dramatic figure. Still,
there was something about his appearance that commanded attention. Of less than average height, he was clothed from head
to foot in plain homespun. His step no longer had the springy
vigor of youth, for he was beginning to be plagued by recurrent
illness. Nevertheless, though frail in health and approaching middle age, he wore on his handsome face a youthful, ingenuous ex-

pression, a look 'of thought, benignity, and of open, unsuspecting honesty.' About his mouth there was just a suggestion of primness — 'consciousness of rectitude,' Logan himself would have called it. And there was undeniably a determined set to his chin. This was a man of firm will, a stubborn man. 'His person,' wrote Deborah, carefully, with precision tempered by love, 'was formed with exact symmetry . . . He was about the middle size, erect and graceful in his demeanor . . .'[3]

Upon people less sympathetic than Debby or the crowd in the State House gallery, he might make a less favorable impression. Jonathan Roberts, for example, his colleague in the Assembly and a table-mate at his boarding house, regarded Logan with the deference due an older man, but he was not flattering. Roberts set him down in his diary as 'but a little finished character.' The Doctor's educational opportunities had been enviable, he wrote, but they had 'failed to make him more than nature fitted him to be — not great in anything.' He was 'unsteady and eccentric,' but, withal, he was 'a good man.'[4]

It was as 'a good man' that everyone knew Logan. John Dickinson spoke of his 'candor of spirit and boundless benevolence,' and a fellow politician remarked that the Doctor was too honest to be in public life.[5] Even his enemies acknowledged these qualities of character. President Adams, harsh judge of men though he was, spoke of Logan's 'candor and sincerity,' and a sophisticated British Minister, who tried hard to dismiss him as a silly sentimentalist, had to acknowledge in the end that he was 'a very worthy man.'[6]

Men found Logan reserved, gentle, shy in manner. He rarely spoke in public, even as a legislator, and when he did, he was not fluent. He worked hard on committees, he wrote long, carefully pondered letters and memoranda, but he never sought to shine. His nature was normally serene and equable. But sometimes there were sharp eruptions of temper. Charles Jared Ingersoll, a young schoolmate of Albanus, who admired Logan deeply, nevertheless discovered that he was not always 'amiable in his domesticity.' And Deborah herself knew her husband's 'quickness of temper.'[7]

It was a human frailty, this temper, and his political enemies were not slow to make capital of it. They found other facets of his character to mock or to attack. His habitual reserve they 'tortured into haughtiness.' His personal temperance, his disapproval of tavern debauchery, they construed as priggishness. His persistence in wearing homespun they called an affectation, an eccentricity.[8] His liberality in religion could even be twisted into approval of licentiousness and immorality. A Federalist newspaper accused him of proposing Tom Paine's *Age of Reason* as a school textbook, of recommending an avowed infidel as a teacher. With inspired irrelevancy the writer of the squib went on to ask whether the people of Philadelphia County were prepared to surrender their wives and daughters 'to satisfy the lewd cravings of inordinate passion in the most worthless of mankind and the most abandoned of their species.'[9]

But these were not the only calumnies he had to suffer. Intensely devoted to the French Revolution, considering it simply an extension of the American, he had seen his disinterested idealism written down as disloyalty and want of patriotism. To some, his firm, seasoned convictions about democracy were mere airy metaphysics, if not downright sedition. His peace mission to France had been measurably successful — even John Adams could say so — but most Federalists set him down in their books as a silly Quixote, a mischievous busybody.

'Aristocrats' and Federalists could call him fool or knave. But the plain people, the artisans and the yeomen farmers, respected him as a man and were thrilled by his unabashed devotion to equality, freedom, and peace. They showed their feelings unmistakably by crowding into the gallery of the Assembly Chamber at the year's end to do him honor.

The legislative session of 1798–9 was the last to be held in the old State House. Everyone knew the Assembly would soon yield to the persistent demands from the west that the state capital be moved out to Lancaster. It was a stormy session — a local skirmish, preliminary to the greater political struggles that impended in state and nation. Republican chieftains were already laying plans to sweep the fall elections in Pennsylvania, and George Logan, an eligible candidate for the governorship, was assigned an important part in their strategy.[10] Unexpectedly, the Adams administration furnished them an issue.

It was the issue of the window tax. During the previous summer — the war scare at its height and George Logan on the high seas for France — Congress had passed a tax to raise revenue for military purposes. Because of the clamor that Logan and other Republicans had made against indirect taxes, the Federalists had shrewdly planned to catch the opposition in a trap of its own setting by levying a *direct* tax, a tax on lands and houses. But their mistake had been to provide for the counting and measuring of windows as one basis for assessment. It was an old English practice, adopted without sinister intent, but it stirred memories among the Pennsylvania Germans of the oppressive hearth taxes in the old country, from which their fathers and grandfathers had fled.

Liberty poles began appearing in the strongly German counties north of Philadelphia, and taverns rang with cries of 'Damm de President! damm de Congresz! damm de Arischdocratz!' A leather-lunged Bucks County auctioneer named John Fries stuck a feather in his cap, strapped his horse pistol to his side, put himself at the head of a band of fifty or sixty enraged farmers, and began harrying assessors from township to township. (One of the 'insurgents' later admitted to carrying a musket, but added that it was 'goot fer nossing, she would not go loose.' Why had he carried it? 'Oh, I dunnow — I dought mebby I might schkeer some potty.' [11]) White-capped *hausfrauen* defended their homes from the assessors by dousing them with hot water from upper-story windows.

Judge Richard Peters — the same man who had worked with Logan to popularize land plaster — issued warrants for the arrest of the rioters. Eighteen men were taken up in Northampton County and held under guard in the Sun Tavern in Bethlehem. To their rescue marched Fries and his little army. Flaunting their red-white-and-blue cockades, the 'insurgents' milled about the courtyard, drank up the landlord's liquor, and, without firing a shot, terrified the United States Marshal into releasing his prisoners.

By the time news of the incident reached Philadelphia, the tavern brawl had been magnified into a formidable insurrection against the Federal government. President Adams called on Governor Mifflin to send the militia into the disaffected counties. Mifflin in turn handed over the responsibility to the Assembly, which solemnly deplored all 'unlawful and treasonable combinations,' but saw in the present instance no occasion for interference.

Just at this juncture, George Logan arose in the State House and proposed a resolution, requesting the Governor to look into the riots, and report upon 'any circumstances which may be alleged or discovered, tending to show the origin of the same in the agency of foreign incendiaries or the seditious views of domestic traitors.' [12] This maneuver was shrewdly conceived. For years, the party in power had been accusing the Republicans of sedition and treason: here was a chance to turn the tables. It was well known that the disaffected counties were Federalist strongholds; indeed Fries himself was a confirmed Federalist. Should the majority vote down the resolution, it would lay itself open to the charge that it feared an investigation.

The measure was defeated by a party vote, but Republicans were gleeful over the awkward situation into which they had maneuvered their opponents.[13] Meanwhile the Germans, believing themselves the intended victims of oppression by the party in power, went over in droves to the Jeffersonian side. Fries's Rebellion, wrote the perceptive Alexander Graydon, 'was the fatal blow to Federalism in Pennsylvania.' [14]

It seemed almost as if the Federalists were bent upon destroying their party by inviting first ridicule, then hatred. John Adams, impatient with Mifflin's shuffling, now ordered the Governor to raise the militia throughout southeastern Pennsylvania, and send it into the rebellious counties. To make sure that the militiamen did their duty, he detached five hundred regulars from the 'army of the black cockade' — the force originally recruited to fight the French — and sent them in under General Macpherson to face the barrage of hot-water buckets.

The 'Federal Army' — a formidable force — marched bravely up the Ridge Road from Philadelphia, then struck across country into Bucks County, the very center of disaffection. They found Fries at his regular occupation, crying a vendue, at a place called, appropriately, Bunker Hill. At the sight of the troops, he quickly knocked down the article he was selling, jumped off his barrel head, and made for a near-by swamp, the Federal cavalry in hot pursuit. Betrayed by the barking of his little black dog 'Whisky,' he was discovered, made prisoner, and carried off to Philadelphia in irons to stand trial for treason.[15]

Up to this point the incident had been pure comedy, and the more absurd the administration appeared, the more pleased were Logan and his party. Events now took an uglier turn, nearly ending in tragedy for poor Fries — but the Republicans continued to reap political advantage from the insensate folly of the Federalists. The army had used unnecessary brutality in suppressing the 'insurrection.' Back in Philadelphia, the wearers of the black cockade, having no urgent business and little discipline, were swaggering about in uniform, insulting and bullying the citizenry. They broke into the print shop of William Duane, editor of the *Aurora,* beat him savagely, and all but killed him. The public reacted, John Adams later recalled, as if the army had been 'a ferocious wild beast let loose upon the nation to devour it.' [16]

Adams knew that things had gone too far when a Federal court pronounced the Bethlehem riot treason against the United States and sentenced John Fries to death. With the same courage that had dictated his decision to renew negotiations with France, the President pardoned Fries. It was an intelligent and magnanimous act, an act that would console him, he later wrote, to his dying hour.[17] But it came too late to undo the damage his party had done to itself.

Sympathy with John Fries, resentment at the administration's crude attempt to dragoon a free people, and the normal desire for a change after a dozen years of Federalist rule, all had their effect in Pennsylvania politics. The Republicans triumphed in the autumn elections of 1799. As their candidate for Governor the party leaders had chosen Thomas McKean, the former Chief

Justice, a man of changeable political colors, but with an unassailable record as a patriot in 1776. (Logan's lack of a revolutionary record was a serious liability; it finally ruled him out as a candidate for Governor, but he was consoled with the prospect of a seat in the Senate, for which no popular vote was necessary.) McKean was elected, and the Federalist majority in the Assembly evaporated, never to materialize again. In Philadelphia County Dr. Logan's seat was never in doubt.

In December he said good-by to Debby and set out for Lancaster, the new state capital. The seventy-mile journey through the rolling country west of Philadelphia was easier than it once had been, for one could now travel over the hard-surfaced Lancaster turnpike. The man who had led the fight against the turnpike company a few years before now paid his toll cheerfully. He was not a man to nurse old grudges; when experience showed him that he had been wrong, he was never slow to admit it.

In the bustling red-brick and stone market town of Lancaster Logan found lodgings with some other Assemblymen at George Nauman's boarding house on East Orange Street.[18] His closest friend in town, outside the legislature, was the Reverend Henry Ernest Muhlenberg, a robust, warm-hearted man only two months younger than himself. Muhlenberg was Lancaster's leading citizen — a beloved pastor, Principal of Franklin College, an indefatigable botanist, already becoming known to European scientists. The two men shared a common zeal for English agriculture, and though they were surrounded in Lancaster County by the finest farmers in America, they planned to cross-fertilize the traditional German husbandry with the new methods of Coke and Bakewell. Together they founded the Lancaster County Society for the Promotion of Agriculture, Manufactures, and the Useful Arts.[19]

At their first meeting — Logan's influence was unmistakable here — the thrifty German farmers unanimously agreed to use only domestic manufactures.[20] Logan and Muhlenberg promptly published the society's constitution, and Logan wrote an introductory letter, recommending it as a model for other counties to imitate. Once more he exhorted American farmers to fabricate as many of the necessities of life as possible on their own farms and, for the rest, to patronize only American mechanics and manufacturers: 'Let Pennsylvania not only exhibit flourishing enclosures and harvests, but the comfortable houses of industrious artisans and manufacturers. . . Proud of the advantages which our own country will afford, and which our own labor will procure, let us disdain to be the servile imitators of other nations, or to adopt foreign manners inconsistent with our republican form of government.' [21]

In the Assembly, which met in the Court House, Dr. Logan took up the old Quaker fight against slavery. Negro bondage still lingered in Pennsylvania. Laws had drastically restricted the institution and put it in the course of ultimate extinction, but tenderness for property rights had caused the legislators to stop short of abrogating existing titles to slaves. Quakers and other humanitarians had taken the issue to the courts without success. They now started a barrage of petitions to the legislature, praying the total abolition of slavery. On 15 January 1800, George Logan presented a petition from a number of inhabitants of Lancaster County. As the fight got under way, he was in the front ranks of the abolitionists. Their proposal for wholesale manumission met stubborn resistance, but they finally carried a bill to free all Negroes over twenty-eight years of age. The upper house failed to take effective action, however, and the last remnants of slavery were left to die a natural death in Pennsylvania without legislative intervention.[22]

Party feeling was at its peak during this session of the Assembly, the Republicans exultant over their recent victory and looking forward to further triumphs, the Federalists sullen in defeat. All the animosities of that winter came to a head in February in an undignified scuffle on the floor of the House, a scuffle in which Dr. Logan — shy, gentle, aristocratic Dr. Logan — was one of the principals.

The House was debating a new election law. Among its provisions was a section designed temporarily to disfranchise members of the Federal Army and to prevent concentrations of troops near polling places, where they might be used to intimidate voters. Logan had always been suspicious of standing armies, and he was doubly, triply, suspicious of this one, raised to fight Hamilton's war with the French, or — who could doubt it, in the light of recent events? — to put down domestic opposition just as it was about to win at the polls. Moreover, he knew that the revision of the election laws could have crucial national importance: it could determine Pennsylvania's vote in the electoral college, and thus conceivably determine whether Jefferson or Adams should be the next President.

The Assembly canvassed the question of the soldiers' vote on 20 February. The debate was long and acrimonious. The House sat well past the usual hour for adjournment, the members shivering in the drafty Court House. Candles were brought in to shed a flickering light upon an unruly and disorganized House.

Samuel W. Fisher, Philadelphia Federalist, had the floor. He had come in late with a companion, both the worse for liquor. They nevertheless insisted upon delivering long-winded, incoherent speeches. The nation was at war with France in all but the formal sense, they proclaimed drunkenly. In war, soldiers must be treated well. The members stirred restlessly. Repeatedly, during Fisher's maudlin harangue, they called for adjournment. Finally a motion was heard and unceremoniously carried, before the speaker had finished.

On the way out, Fisher taunted a Republican member with being afraid to stay and hear argument. 'You are mistaken,' was the reply, 'we will meet you in argument any time.' Logan, standing near by, could no longer restrain his irritation: 'It is not because we fear argument,' he broke in, 'but because we will not listen to your nonsense, that we will adjourn.' (Testifying later, Fisher was not sure of Logan's precise language. Perhaps he had said 'damned nonsense.')

Aroused, Fisher turned to Logan and demanded, was that remark intended for him? It was, Logan responded. 'Then you are a puppy!' Fisher snapped out. 'You are a damned rascal,' Logan rejoined. And Fisher landed a blow fair in the Doctor's eye.

Logan defended himself with spirit. Quickly, members closed

in and bore Fisher toward the door, but not before he had 'received three blows in the face from Doctor Logan's hands.'

Now George Logan stood only five feet, eight inches, and,
however active he may have been in youth, he was not, at fifty, a
formidable fighter with his fists. Fisher, 'a stouter and younger
man, a practiced pugilist from childhood,' had the better of the
exchange. His one blow, bystanders observed, had more effect
than all three of Logan's. The Doctor went home in mortification.[23]

Next morning from his boarding house, nursing a painfully discolored eye, Logan sent the Speaker a formal complaint: 'Samuel
Fisher, a representative of the city of Philadelphia,' he recited,
'struck me a violent blow on my face, in breach of the privilege
of the House.' Fisher promptly lodged a counter-complaint. Legislative bodies have no humor, and no defense against misconduct.
The Speaker gravely appointed a committee, and the committee
solemnly held hearings. Dr. Logan 'uniformly declined considering himself as a party'; insisting that the whole affair was between
Fisher and the House, he only consented to give testimony when
expressly called by Fisher. When all the evidence had been heard,
the committee found Fisher 'guilty of flagrant acts of disorderly
behavior derogatory to the dignity and privilege of the Assembly.' [24] Logan bore no grudge against his assailant; later, in Philadelphia, he treated him with respect, even friendship.

Republicans could afford to be forgiving this year. Everything
pointed to a complete victory for their party in the election of
1800. For George Logan, however, a family tragedy robbed the
campaign of all the exhilarating expectancy, the sense of triumph
it should have had for him. Suddenly, in August, little Gustavus
sickened and died. He was only thirteen years old, a sturdy, generous, affectionate lad, the image of his father.[25] Deborah was in-
consolable, and Dr. Logan himself had no heart for politics.

Fortunately, little effort was needed. The October election in
Pennsylvania resulted in a smashing victory for the Republicans.
Within three weeks, Logan was off to Lancaster again, ready to
make that victory count in the coming Presidential election. Gov-

ernor McKean had called the new Assembly into special session to settle upon a method of choosing Pennsylvania's electors. The previous legislature had been hopelessly deadlocked over this issue, and time was running out. If no decision could be reached on the procedural question, then Pennsylvania could cast no votes, and would be voiceless in the selection of the next President.

It was already too late to hold a general election. Electors would have to be chosen by the Assembly. Should it be by concurrent vote of the two houses? If so, disagreement was inevitable, for the Senate was still in Federalist hands. Or should it be by joint vote? This would enable the Republicans, through their majority in the lower house, to choose most of the electors. As the Assemblymen wrangled, petitions for a joint vote flowed in, signed with thousands of names, proof that party workers were busy, but also that the people were aroused. The debate lasted nearly a month.

The only solution appeared to be a compromise by which each house should make eight nominations for the state's fifteen places in the Electoral College. This would result in the choice of eight Republican and seven Federalist electors; in effect, it would mean one lone Republican vote from Pennsylvania. But returns from other states showed that the Presidential race between Jefferson and Adams would be close. Better one vote for Jefferson, thought Logan and the other party leaders, than none at all. So the compromise measure was accepted, and an express galloped off to Washington, bearing Pennsylvania's decision.

Undoubtedly, Jefferson was disappointed. Nevertheless, he was able in a few days to write to Dr. Benjamin Rush that 'notwithstanding the annihilation of the Pennsylvania vote, the Republicans seem to have obtained a majority of eight in the late election.' 'If so,' he added, 'the vessel of the Union will be put on her republican tack and show us how she works on that.' [26] Jefferson was right: the Republicans had a margin of eight votes. But it had been a near thing, and the end was not yet. For Jefferson and Aaron Burr, both Republicans, had the same number of electoral votes, and Congress would have to decide between them.

While the nation waited, the Assembly remained in session at

Lancaster, and Logan turned to popular education and internal improvements — two favorite causes of Jeffersonian Republicans everywhere. The Pennsylvania Constitution of 1790 had directed the legislature to establish, 'as soon as conveniently may be,' a system of free schools. But except for a stillborn attempt in 1794, the Federalist Assemblies had made no move. Logan now introduced a bill to spread a network of free public schools over the state. The effort failed, owing largely to the opposition of the Germans. These pious, parochial folk could be goaded into voting Republican, but they could not be converted overnight to the Jeffersonian gospel of universal secular education. In their obstinate way they saw only one outcome — education taken away from their churches, English substituted for German in the schools, their cultural autonomy undermined. And the Germans composed a quarter of the commonwealth's population. They could defeat any proposal for free schools — could, and did, throughout George Logan's lifetime.[27]

With internal improvements Logan had more success. He had grown tired of seeing his horses sink to their knees in mud on the Germantown Road in springtime. And the Philadelphia County farmers, his constituents, were demanding the same ease of access to the Philadelphia market that the Lancaster County farmers, with their fine new turnpike, enjoyed. Even before Governor McKean mentioned internal improvements in his message to the Assembly, Dr. Logan moved that a company be formed for the purpose of turnpiking the Germantown Road as far as the tenth milestone on Chestnut Hill. The bill was quickly passed, and within a few years an 'artificial,' or macadamized road — the third turnpike in Pennsylvania — ran past the Stenton gates.[28]

Soon Logan came up with another project, this time a canal. He dreamed Benjamin Franklin's old dream of linking the rich Susquehanna valley with Philadelphia, in order to prevent its produce from finding its way down to the rival port of Baltimore. The scheme of cutting a canal across from the Chesapeake to the Delaware Bay had been proposed before the Revolution, but had been dropped for want of funds. Lands to the westward were filling up now, and the rising city of Baltimore was reaping the increase. The broad Susquehanna was a natural waterway. Lancaster flour could float cheaply, conveniently, down to the Maryland merchants — in spite of every effort to prevent it. Stubbornly, Pennsylvanians had refused to dredge out the river's channel, to clear away rocks and sand bars. They would not make it any easier for the Baltimoreans to capture the back-country trade. With a canal Pennsylvania could even recover a part of that trade — could counteract Baltimore's natural advantage. Anyone who looked at the map and saw the narrow isthmus separating the two great bays realized that.

Logan took the lead in the Assembly. He introduced a bill reviving the old Chesapeake-Delaware canal project, and fought it through to victory. The House appointed him one of the commissioners to negotiate with the state of Delaware, across whose lands the canal would pass. All winter he conferred, planned, negotiated. Presently a company was incorporated in three states — for even Maryland came in. Books were opened, $400,000 of stock subscribed, surveys were made, and digging commenced. But barely had work started before it came to a halt for the old reason — funds had run out.[29] Dr. Logan's hopes of linking east and west, of solving the inland transportation problem — it was not only Pennsylvania's but all America's problem — had to be deferred.

But meanwhile good news had finally come from Washington. February 1801 had been an anxious month in Lancaster. Governor McKean kept the Assembly in session as Congress took ballot after ballot without reaching a decision between Jefferson and Burr. The Republicans had clearly intended Jefferson for the Presidency, but the Federalists, out of spite, were scheming to elect Burr. It was even darkly hinted that they planned to usurp the Presidency by declaring no election and turning the office over to John Marshall, already both Secretary of State and Chief Justice.[30]

A chain of expresses between Washington and Lancaster brought no news but of continued deadlock. Fearful of the worst, Governor McKean took counsel with Logan and a few other faithful Republicans, and resolved upon extraordinary measures. He drew up a proclamation, calling upon all Pennsylvanians to give their allegiance to Jefferson as President. He secured arms for twenty thousand men, caused old brass field pieces, unused since the Revolution, to be trundled out of armories, prepared orders for the militia to be ready for a march on Washington under General Peter Muhlenberg. These precautions taken, the Governor and Assembly waited.[31]

On the twentieth an express from Washington clattered up brick-paved Queen Street to the Court House with the news: Jefferson elected on the thirty-sixth ballot. As victory bells clashed on the icy air, the Assembly adjourned, Governor McKean quietly committed his desperate plans to the flames, and George Logan sat down to offer his congratulations to his old friend, the new President.[32]

Back at Stenton after a week's reflection, he wrote again to Jefferson. 'Your election,' he confessed, 'has relieved my mind from great anxiety respecting my country.' Like many of the new President's well-wishers, he proffered advice. Let the new administration, he urged in a paternalistic spirit, take 'prompt and decided measures to countenance and promote the useful arts and manufactures.' The suggestion had an almost Hamiltonian ring, but Logan's reasons were not Hamilton's: 'As long as we are dependent on Great Britain for our clothing and other necessaries,' he wrote, with no abatement of his old prejudices, 'we must be influenced by her baneful politics.' Not that the United States should abandon overseas commerce. On the contrary, she should seek to keep the channels of trade open by cultivating the northern powers of Europe, especially Denmark and Holland. She should promote, if not actually join, an 'armed neutrality.' This was the only way to counteract the 'domineering power' of England.[33]

As soon as Jefferson could clear away the heap of correspondence that covered his desk like a snowdrift, he replied to his friend in Pennsylvania. He would have no truck with 'entangling alliances'; he had explained why in his Inaugural Address. The United States, safe behind the broad Atlantic, must keep clear of Europe's conflicts, must even reject the temptation of an 'armed neutrality.' The nations of the Old World, Jefferson declared, depend upon American commerce — so much so that 'they will be glad to purchase it, when the only price we ask is to do justice.' Therefore, he concluded, 'we have in our own hands the means of peaceable coercion . . . the moment they see our government so united as that we can make use of it, they will for their own interest be disposed to do us justice.' [34]

Logan, reading this, could only shake his head. Close as he felt to Jefferson in his attitude toward government, his philosophy of society, his personal tastes and habits, he could never agree with this view of America's foreign relations. Both men abhorred war as the greatest of evils, both coveted perpetual peace for the United States — peace and commerce with all nations. For Logan the way to peace lay in negotiation, understanding, in agreements among governments. Peacemaking was the business of the diplomat, especially the American diplomat. For Jefferson, however, the only real guaranty of peace was the threat of withholding the fruits of peace, the benefits of American neutrality, from warring nations. Not mutual understanding, not the possibility of agreement, but coercion — economic coercion — was America's ultimate resource, her destined strategy. All Republicans, it was plain, did not think alike as they sought to put the Union 'on its republican tack.'

As a prominent Republican, Logan was continually beset with office-seekers, soliciting his influence with the President. Mostly he rebuffed them. To one hopeful, who asked him to sign a petition on his behalf, he responded: 'Sir, I have not the pleasure of knowing you, and therefore cannot sign your recommendation.' 'Oh, sir,' came the answer, 'that is of no consequence. You know the gentlemen who have already signed.' 'True, sir, but I do not know you, and therefore you must excuse me.' [35]

For Dr. Logan himself a higher office was in store. His elevation was delayed by a split in the party ranks — the first of many inevitable schisms in the headless, shapeless mass that was Pennsylvania's new democracy. Just before adjourning, the Assembly had met in joint session to elect a United States Senator to the seat formerly so amply filled by the portly Philadelphia grandee William Bingham. The two leading candidates were General Peter Muhlenberg and George Logan.

Muhlenberg, tall, handsome, courtly in manner, an imposing man, was a veteran of the Brandywine, Germantown, Monmouth, and Yorktown, a veteran too of six years of party battles in the national House of Representatives. He was a devout Lutheran, a member of the most distinguished German family in Pennsylvania, and his voice carried great weight among the people. He had used his influence in the late campaign for Thomas McKean, and it was to him that McKean had looked to lead the state militia on Washington in case of a 'usurpation.' Of General Muhlenberg's Republicanism there was no question. And he was 'safe,' no visionary, no enthusiast; his aristocratic bias, his military experience, his profound belief in Original Sin, all guaranteed that.

Dr. Logan, on the other hand, was not 'safe.' For all his mildness of manner, his natural shyness, his aristocratic heritage, he was a man of stubborn independence, of unlimited optimism, of democratic enthusiasm, and (though not a warm man himself) of warm human sympathies. He was not 'safe'; he was not even, in ordinary political terms, calculable. But though he was less experienced in national affairs than the General, he had a broader vision of America's democratic potentialities and a surer grasp of the means to their fulfillment.

Perhaps that was why the Federalists in a block gave their votes to Muhlenberg. Other reasons — reasons rooted in the contradictions of Pennsylvania politics — explained why fifteen rebellious Republicans joined them to give the General a margin of one vote and send him to Washington. The rebels were either men from the West, who distrusted Logan as an Easterner, or delegates from Berks County, where the German opposition to his public-school bill had centered. Behind these sectional antagonisms was a reluctance to come under the thumb of William Duane, the ambitious, intriguing newspaper editor, who was emerging as the dominant power in state politics.[36]

But the party leaders were not to be thwarted, and Logan did not have to wait long for his place in the Senate. Muhlenberg took his seat during the two-day special session on 4 and 5 March. A month later, he resigned to become Supervisor of Revenue for the Philadelphia District. The Assembly was in recess; Governor McKean appointed Logan to the vacant seat. And when the legislature returned in December, it confirmed him by a big majority.[37]

Stenton, Philadelphia, and Lancaster had prepared George Logan for Washington and a place in the new Republican constellation. He now went to claim that place.

✳

XII. SENATOR LOGAN

STENTON was a different place now, a lonelier place. All winter long, Dr. Logan must be away in Washington City. Deborah must stay behind, to manage the farm, to lie alone at night, listening to the wind sigh through the hemlocks. Deborah never quite reconciled herself to her husband's absence, never grew accustomed to the emptiness of the great house when he was away. And now Stenton would be emptier than ever with Gustavus gone, little Algernon Sydney away at Nazareth Hall, the Moravian school near Easton, and Albanus leaving with his father to enter college. Sadly, Deborah saw the two travelers off to Washington, and turned back to the cares of the farm, to the great empty mansion.

It was early in December 1801 when Dr. Logan and Albanus set out for the Federal City. The journey took two days over frozen, deeply rutted roads. The first day's ride took them over familiar ground — through Darby and Chester, past the mills on Brandywine Creek, on to Wilmington, where cousin John Dickinson lived, and finally, by dusk, into Maryland. An uncomfortable night in a dirty, noisy inn at the Head of Elk, and they pushed on toward Baltimore and Washington, the roads growing steadily worse, the fords and floating bridges more treacherous, the countryside less cultivated. In place of Pennsylvania's neat stone farmhouses, they began to see crude log houses in raw clearings, surrounded by snake fences, with gaunt hogs rooting among the stumps.

This landscape prepared them for their first sight of the new capital. Washington City was little more than a collection of dingy shops and boarding houses clustered around an unfinished Capitol building. Across a broad swamp, standing in bleak and lonely grandeur, was the President's Mansion. A muddy causeway called Pennsylvania Avenue spanned the marsh. At a distance flowed the lordly Potomac. Nearer at hand was a meandering creek called, magniloquently, the Tiber — a stream, observed one resident, 'which feeds without draining the swamps.' [1] It was an unsightly, straggling little village — 'the best city in the world to live in,' remarked a cynical New Yorker, ' — in the future.' [2]

To George Logan it was a good place now, in the present. What if its streets were unlighted, ankle-deep with yellow mud, obstructed with rotting tree-stumps? What if its public buildings were bare, comfortless, unfinished? The very newness symbolized something — a fresh start in government, a break with the rule of the Federalists who had governed America from the elegant parlors of Chestnut Street in Philadelphia. New men, men of firm republican fiber, gentleman farmers and democrats such as Logan himself, walked the muddy streets, inhabited the dingy boarding houses, labored in the unfinished office buildings. Their task was to carry out the unmistakable mandates of 1800 — a simple, frugal government, peace abroad, freedom at home, majority rule, encouragement to agriculture, the spreading of information and education throughout the electorate. These were the very articles of Logan's political faith.

Dr. Logan engaged a room at Mrs. Wilson's boarding house, a few hundred yards north of the Capitol. Mrs. Wilson's was a nest of Republicans. Nathaniel Macon of North Carolina lived there. Speaker of the House now, he was the very embodiment of republicanism with his plain blue coat, his old-fashioned linen, his broad-brimmed Quaker-style hat. John Randolph lived there too, a fantastic figure, with his spidery arms and legs, his boyish countenance — prematurely aged when seen at close quarters — his shrill voice, his burning eyes, his manifest genius. This strange, brilliant, perverse creature was the leader of the Republican forces in the House. Roistering, high-living, keen-minded William Branch Giles of Virginia and quiet, conscientious, scholarly Abraham Baldwin of Georgia, both respected party veterans, also lodged with Mrs. Wilson.[3] Around her dinner table, when Logan arrived, the Republican chieftains were already busy charting their legislative strategy, planning to carry into effect the people's mandate, to consummate what President Jefferson liked to call the 'revolution' of 1800.

Dr. Logan lost no time in going with Albanus to pay his respects to the President. They picked their way through the mud puddles of Pennsylvania Avenue, passed the post-and-rail fence newly put up around the Executive Mansion, and walked up a flight of crude wooden steps into a sparsely-furnished room. There they found Thomas Jefferson — the same tall, raw-boned, informal man they had known at Stenton. Cordially, Jefferson greeted his old friend, inquired for Deborah, expressed regret that she had not come to Washington.

Dr. Logan asked the President's advice regarding Albanus' education. He had intended, he said, to enroll the boy in the near-by college at Georgetown. It was a Roman Catholic school, but Logan cared little about religious differences. Jefferson, however, advised against Georgetown. He suggested his own college — William and Mary. He offered to recommend Albanus to Bishop Madison, its president; indeed, he would ask him to take the lad into his own house, to supervise his education personally.[4] Father and son left the Executive Mansion with a warm feeling that the President was still their good friend.

Bishop Madison, it turned out, was not able to take Albanus into his own family at the moment, but agreed to 'superintend his education with zeal.'[5] Dr. Logan saw his son off to Williamsburg, then turned to the round of visits, receptions, and state dinners which, even in a democratic capital, accompanied the opening of Congress. At these functions he saw more old friends.

He renewed his acquaintance with James Madison, the new Secretary of State. Madison was an inconspicuous man. Some described him as 'shriveled'; he was no taller than Logan himself. He always dressed in black, always appeared preoccupied and solemn when engaged in the public business. Still, he could be bright and cordial, even 'sportive' in company. And his pretty wife was invariably sprightly. Logan had known Dolly Todd as the widow of a young Philadelphia Quaker lawyer who had died of the yellow fever in 1793. He found her now at the very center of Washington's social life, a gay, sparkling hostess, brimming with laughter and vitality. 'Dolly looks extreme well,' he wrote home to Deborah.[6]

He saw Albert Gallatin, the new Secretary of the Treasury, the man who had stood up for him so nobly in the debate on the 'Logan Act.' Gallatin always reeked of cigar smoke, his glasses never fitted him, he still spoke in a pronounced French accent that made it difficult to understand him. But Logan respected him deeply. He knew that this man brought both financial genius and democratic feeling to the post that Alexander Hamilton had once occupied.

Other men he met, men whom he would be seeing daily in the Senate Chamber — lanky John Breckinridge from Kentucky, tall, burly Stevens T. Mason of Virginia, Jefferson's close friend Wilson Cary Nicholas, also of Virginia, Stephen R. Bradley, a Republican from Vermont who told broad stories in a Yankee twang. Some of these men had known the frustration of long service in Congress, always outvoted, always in the minority. Now, by the people's decision, they were the rulers of America.

The Federalists were still there — no longer formidable in numbers but still antagonists to be reckoned with. Foremost in ability among them was the witty, worldly Gouverneur Morris, Senator from New York, who stumped about the capital on his wooden leg, pouring aristocratic scorn on every manifestation of the democratic spirit. Morris was late in arriving at Washington as if by his tardiness to express his contempt for the new government. In time, Logan met the other Federalists — James Hillhouse, Uriah Tracy, Roger Griswold, the whole New England phalanx, bitter over their party's defeat, determined to wage stubborn delaying actions in Congress.

At the state dinners Logan met the diplomatic corps. The handsome Marquis de Casa Yrujo, Minister from Madrid, he already knew, for the Marquis had married Governor McKean's beautiful daughter Sally. At the French Legation he saw Louis André

Pichon, the *chargé d'affaires,* who had been Citizen Genêt's secretary back in that unforgotten spring and summer of 1793. Later he came to know General Turreau, Napoleon's flamboyant Minister, whose gorgeous uniforms cascaded with gold lace and whose domestic life was a well-known scandal. He even came to feel at home at the British Legation, where the supercilious Anthony Merry and his fastidious secretary Augustus John Foster were making a determined effort to offset the town's republican plainness by entertaining in lavish style.

There was no lack of fascinating people in Washington. It was always amusing to take dinner with Dr. Thornton, the designer of the Capitol. Born of a Quaker family in the Virgin Islands, Thornton had been a medical student at Edinburgh only a few years after Logan. Like Logan, he rarely practiced now. But he was interested in everything — steamboats, racehorses, scientific farming, philology, architecture, abolishing slavery, teaching the deaf and dumb to talk, establishing a national university. He even found time to write poetry and novels. Most of Thornton's interests were Logan's too. But it was pleasant to hear him talk on any topic. He spoke slowly, with an unfortunate stammer, but his words were worth waiting for. His company, people said, was a complete antidote to dullness.[7]

Outwardly, the Federal City might be crude, unfinished, lacking in nearly every grace, every comfort, but Logan found it full of congenial men, able men, dedicated men. To his eyes the straggling little capital was a scene of promise as green as the forests that grew in its streets and swamps.

At noon on 7 December 1801, Dr. Logan went to the Senate Chamber in the basement of the Capitol. He found less than a score of Senators there, a bare quorum, a little knot of men in the semicircle around the empty President's chair. His colleague James Ross, a Federalist from Pittsburgh, had not arrived. Aaron Burr, President of the Senate, had not yet left New York.

The hall itself was large and impressive. Full-length portraits of Louis XVI and Marie Antoinette on either side of the President's chair shed an ambiguous splendor : they spoke of monarchy, tyranny, all the evils of the Old Regime, but they reminded Republicans of America's debt to France for indispensable aid in the Revolution. Sixteen Ionic columns supported the Chamber's lofty ceiling — as many columns as states in the Union, almost as many columns as Senators present.[8]

Nearly half of the Senators attending were newcomers, as was Logan. They handed their credentials to Samuel Otis, the Secretary, and took seats in the semicircle, seats brilliantly covered with scarlet morocco leather. The eighteen men organized themselves into the Senate of the United States. They chose Abraham Baldwin President *pro tempore*. The scholarly, soft-spoken Georgian, Logan's table-mate at Mrs. Wilson's, was a veteran of every Congress since the commencement of the national government. The Doctor remembered him kindly for his part in the 'Logan Act' debates, when he had roundly declared that peacemakers deserved public monuments, not fines, imprisonment, and obloquy.

To each of the new Senators in turn Baldwin administered the constitutional oath — to Bradley, to Breckinridge, to Christopher Ellery of Rhode Island, to James Jackson of Georgia. When he came to Logan, the Doctor, remembering his Quaker training, declined to swear, insisting upon a simple affirmation.[9] Senators sat up, looked at each other, then more closely at the new initiate. Had any one ever claimed this privilege before in Congress? This must be a man of scruple, an independent man. Conscientious in small matters, perhaps he would be so in large ones also.

Next day Logan listened to the President's Message. It was read unceremoniously by the Clerk, for Jefferson insisted on cutting loose from the formalities his predecessors had hoped to make into traditions. No more Presidential Messages delivered in person, no more formal Replies by the legislature. All that was a relic of monarchy, of the 'address from the throne,' a typical bit of Federalist flummery, and a waste of the legislators' time. A democratic government should be simple, informal, efficient.

With all this Logan heartily agreed. He approved, too, of the substance of Jefferson's message. Peace was returning to Europe, the President hopefully declared, and with it the prospect that the United States could continue 'to cultivate the earth' in tranquillity, 'to practice and improve those arts which tend to increase our comforts.' This, Logan reflected, was America's calling, her destiny. He had always maintained it; now it was official doctrine. So abundant was the government's income, Jefferson went on, that 'we may now safely dispense with all the internal taxes.' Again Logan inwardly applauded. Indirect taxes had never ceased to excite his distrust, his suspicion.

The judiciary system, 'and especially that portion of it recently erected,' would, of course, 'present itself to the contemplation of Congress.' Here Jefferson touched on a sore point, a special party grievance. The expiring Federalist administration, by the Judiciary Act of 1801, had increased the number of circuit courts and filled them with Federalist judges. There were already enough Federalist judges, the Jeffersonians felt, delivering partisan harangues from the bench. Unquestionably, a struggle impended on this issue.

'That all should be satisfied with any one order of things,' the President concluded, 'is not to be expected; but I indulge the pleasing persuasion that the great body of our citizens will cordially concur in honest and disinterested efforts, which have for their object to preserve the General and State governments in their Constitutional form and equilibrium; to maintain peace abroad, and order and obedience to the laws at home; to establish principles and practices of administration favorable to the security of liberty and property, and to reduce expenses to what is necessary for the useful purposes of Government.' [10] It was a discreet, a disarming message, hardly revolutionary. But it laid down the outlines of a legislative program to which Logan could give himself with zest.

Gradually, Senators trickled into Washington, and the chamber filled to a point where it could transact business. Three days after the President's Message, Logan was appointed to his first Senate committee. There was poetic justice in the appointment. The Convention of 1800, which put a final period to Franco-American hostilities, had been ratified by the previous Senate — but with reservations, concerning claims for French spoliations. Bonaparte, now First Consul of France, had accepted it — with a proviso, rejecting the claims. The French ratification not being 'pure and simple,' Jefferson was now obliged to submit the Convention a second time to the Senate. As presiding officer, Abraham Baldwin named Logan chairman of a committee, with Jackson of Georgia and Tracy of Connecticut, to consider the modified treaty. It was a graceful gesture, the party's way of recognizing the Doctor's role in bringing peace. The committee recommended accepting Napoleon's proviso, and the Senate quickly ratified the treaty.[11] To the unofficial peacemaker of 1798 it was given to put the final touches on the definitive treaty of peace.

The first significant division in the new Senate, the first revelation of Republican party strength, came on 5 January 1802. The question was whether to admit a stenographer to the floor, to make the debates public. Federalists opposed the innovation. Why should the people know what their Senators were saying? they asked. Jeffersonians favored full publicity. What right, they countered, had the people's representatives to debate in secret? Dr. Logan joined the Republicans in a strict party vote, as Gouverneur Morris muttered privately, 'This is the beginning of mischief.' [12]

The 'mischief' commenced the very next day. Breckinridge, the lean, bronzed Kentuckian who had stood sponsor to Jefferson's 'Kentucky Resolutions' in 1798, started it. He moved to repeal the Judiciary Act of 1801, to abolish the sixteen newly created circuit courts. This was the signal that the skirmishing was over, the battle joined.

Dr. Logan sat silent, but approving, as Breckinridge opened for the administration with a cool, logical case against the Act of 1801: it had been both unnecessary and improper; the new courts could and ought to be abolished. He listened with ill-concealed disgust to Gouverneur Morris's mighty rhetorical counterblast. 'Why are we here?' Morris asked his colleagues. 'To save the people from their most dangerous enemy: to save them from themselves.' Government was in the hands of demagogues, he shouted. The Constitution was in danger. 'Can you violate it? If you can, you may throw the Constitution into the flames — it is gone — it is dead.' Mason of Virginia, a huge man of majestic mien, disposed easily of Morris's imaginary fears. Sarcastically,

he dismissed the New Yorker as 'the Ajax Telemon of his party
. . . the hero with his seven-fold shield — not of bull's hide but
of brass.' [13]

In the midst of the great debate, Aaron Burr appeared and
took the chair. Handsome of figure and agile of mind, coarse and
rowdy in his private life, aflame with ambition, but devoid of
principle, the Vice-President was not a man to win Logan's respect. Hardly had he arrived at Washington before he was intriguing with Federalists to defeat the repeal of the Judiciary
Act.[14] A few days later, James Ross, the senior Senator from
Pennsylvania, arrived. A bellicose westerner and a Federalist,
Ross was a man with whom Logan could find little common
ground. For his part Ross had little enough use for Logan: a
man of little talent, he considered the Doctor, one who could only
'babble and disorganize.' [15]

On 20 January 1802 there was no quorum; the Senate met only
to adjourn. Dr. Logan was ill in his boarding-house room. Writing to Deborah, he made light of his indisposition. He was merely
'fatigued,' he said, 'overcome with a sickness of my stomach and
a faintishness.' Others, more concerned, spoke of his having
suffered 'a kind of convulsive fit.' He had known these seizures
before at Stenton. His friends suspected 'some tenderness or defect in his constitution, which requires the utmost attention.' Dr.
Logan declined to take the incident seriously and was back at his
desk in the Senate Chamber the next day, pale, but determined to
take his part in the legislative struggle.[16]

A week later, he helped his party meet and pass its first major
test — the repeal of the Judiciary Act of 1801.[17] Later, he consulted Dr. Joseph Priestley about it. The exiled English scientist
and radical now lived in Northumberland, Pennsylvania. Fearful
Federalists believed that he intended 'to decompose both church
and state' with chemical formulae. But to Republicans he was
a hero, a martyr, and an oracle. Logan had first encountered
Priestley's scientific writings as a medical student at Edinburgh;
he had read the Englishman's political works when he was working out his own philosophy. The old man wrote that he gave little
thought to politics now. Still, it was obvious to him that the new

courts had been created to make 'a permanent provision for the friends of Mr. Adams,' and he implied that Dr. Logan had done well to vote them out of existence.[18]

The democratic forces had taken and destroyed a strategic Federalist redoubt. Now it was time to carry the battle into the enemy's country. But Logan was not fit. He needed rest, a chance to recover from his illness. He obtained leave of absence from the Senate, and spent a few weeks at Stenton under Deborah's tender care. The party leaders, taking advantage of his temporary absence, made an effort to repeal the 'Logan Act,' to clear the statute book of another piece of partisan legislation left over from the last months of Federalist rule. The bill to repeal reached a second reading, but failed to pass, though Senator Mason gave it his powerful backing.[19]

Dr. Logan learned of all this when he returned to Washington, strengthened and refreshed after his holiday. Naturally, he was disappointed. The repeal of the 'Logan Act' would have been a public vindication. But he wasted no tears. More important business was coming before the Senate.

In March, the House passed a bill to repeal all the internal taxes, all those indirect levies — on sugar, stills, spirits, pleasure carriages, stamped paper, auction sales — that had proliferated under Federalist rule. For ten years Logan had chafed, complained, protested, inveighed against these taxes as dishonest, devious, and unfair. Now at last they were to be wiped away. The bill came quickly to a vote, on the last day of March. In unbroken rank the Republicans went for repeal. To a man the Federalists voted 'Nay.' Repeal carried; another Federalist position destroyed.[20]

The Jeffersonian machine was functioning smoothly now. The opposition was listless. The public debt was next on the agenda. No one thought of repudiating any part of it now, as Logan had once counseled. Still, ten years had not brought Republicans around to Hamilton's view that a public debt was a public blessing. Secretary Gallatin had devised a plan to pay it off promptly. A committee was named to consider it: Logan, Baldwin, Breckinridge, Nicholas, all stanch Republicans, with one lone Federalist,

Uriah Tracy of Connecticut.[21] They reported on Gallatin's plan favorably. The bill betrayed the Secretary's unfamiliarity with English and his peculiarly intricate mental processes. With some reason, Gouverneur Morris announced that he could make out its meaning only by resorting to algebra. The sarcastic New Yorker weakened his case, however, by his gratuitous reference to the 'foreigner' who had drawn up the bill. Republicans needed no help from Morris. Their bill passed by a party vote, and another Federalist bastion — Hamilton's favorite policy of a perpetual debt — was seriously undermined.[22]

There was little more to be done in this session. Congress had carried out the President's program to the letter. The more vulnerable parts of the Federalist structure had been leveled. The legislative triumph had been surprisingly easy, the resistance unexpectedly feeble. As a newcomer to the Senate, Dr. Logan had had a minor but still gratifying part to play.

One particular assignment had given him special pleasure. Early in the session Congress had taken measures by a series of joint resolutions, originally prepared by John Randolph, to organize a library for the use of its members. The few books already in hand — about two hundred titles — were installed in the Capitol, in a room just vacated by the House of Representatives, and Logan had been appointed to a committee — the other members were Baldwin and DeWitt Clinton from the Senate, Joseph H. Nicholson, James A. Bayard, and Randolph from the House — to purchase new books.

Always a conscientious committeeman, Logan had written straightway to Debby's cousin, John Dickinson, for advice. The old statesman was in poor health but he had drawn up a list of nearly a hundred titles, chiefly works in history, philosophy, politics, travel, and agriculture, and sent it to Washington City. Meanwhile, Baldwin had besought President Jefferson for a similar list. The committee had pooled its lists of desiderata and begun acquiring books for its working library, the Library of Congress. For the grandson of James Logan, who had built up a great library and given it to the public, it had been a natural, a congenial task.[23]

Dr. Logan returned to Stenton for the spring planting, full of satisfaction at his winter's work, full of hopes for constructive, fruitful sessions to come.

Back in his own state, Logan found a situation that was disturbing, ominous. As a Senator, he was deeply, inextricably involved in state politics. And Republican party politics were nowhere so turbulent, nowhere so vexed by cross-currents, as in the Quaker state. During the long years of opposition, the party had developed an internal harmony, a discipline; but when victory came, when McKean won the Governorship and Jefferson the Presidency, animosities and grudges, long suppressed, burst out in the open, and the party, swollen with spoils, began to fly apart.

The man who aspired to dominate was William Duane. He was Bache's successor as editor of the *Aurora,* and even more fiercely democratic than Bache. Brilliant, fearless, savage as a journalist, he was ambitious, scheming, and unscrupulous as a politician. Faithful service as a writer had won him a place in Jefferson's confidence, though the President was fully aware of Duane's unlovely personality, his driving ambition, his intolerance of other men's opinions. Duane's closest ally was the dapper, perfumed, powdered Dr. Michael Leib, who was as radical in politics as Duane himself. Already Leib had made himself 'Dictator' of Philadelphia County — the district that Logan had always regarded as his own. Hitherto the Doctor had worked harmoniously with Duane and Leib, had been able to conceal his disdain for their devious tactics. But now, as he saw them reaching out, extending their control of the party, consolidating their power, taking up more and more radical schemes, pocketing more and more spoils, he rebelled. He refused to serve with Leib on the state committee of correspondence. Encouraged by his old friend Governor McKean, he spent the summer riding about the County, talking with farmers and mechanics, working day and night to defeat Leib in the fall elections. Often he drove to Philadelphia, to Dunwoody's Tavern on Market Street, to consult with discontented city Republicans.

In the middle of September, he called a meeting at Martin

Ludie's Rising Sun Tavern at the fork of the Germantown and York roads, just a few rods south of Stenton. Thirty anti-Leib Republicans appeared and approved an address that referred pointedly to 'the improper character nominated to represent this county in the congress of the United States.' They voted to hold a general county meeting six days later. Through the *Aurora* Duane promptly scotched the rebellion. He extolled Leib's character, praised his record, and managed to pack the second rally at the 'Rising Sun' with loyal supporters who undid the work of the previous meeting.[24]

Temporarily, Logan's revolt had miscarried. Election day came in October, and Leib was chosen for Congress. Dr. Logan at Stenton scanned the returns and feared for his party's future. Gentlemen of education and principle, he reflected, no longer controlled the Republican party in Pennsylvania; demagogues, hungry for spoils and careless of honor, were in the saddle. Leib's election under these circumstances was a disquieting portent.

To William Duane, sitting at his desk in the *Aurora* office, the post-election scene had another aspect. He surveyed it with satisfaction. To Jefferson he reported that for the moment, at least, all misunderstandings had been checked, all threats to party harmony removed, 'though at the expense of a good man's feelings.' The 'good man,' of course, was Dr. Logan. 'No man esteems him more than I do,' wrote Duane hypocritically; yet he singled out Logan as the chief instigator of party strife, a strife which 'may yet come to an unpleasant issue.' He named the leading Pennsylvania Republicans: Logan, Alexander James Dallas, Peter Muhlenberg, Tench Coxe, Dr. Leib — these were the men who held 'the principal weight' in the party, who led divided councils, who wove their intricate pattern of jealousies and animosities. Logan, he complained, was at odds with everyone except Coxe — and Coxe, as everyone knew, was no true democrat at all, but an old associate of Alexander Hamilton.[25]

These signs of party disharmony, these premonitions of strife to come, were disquieting — to Logan at Stenton, to Jefferson at Washington, to Duane in the *Aurora* office. But two days after the Pennsylvania elections, something happened a thousand miles away, at the mouth of the Mississippi River, to divert everyone's attention from the political broils of the Quaker state. Without warning, on 16 October 1802, the Spanish Intendant at New Orleans closed the Mississippi to Americans, in violation of the Treaty of 1795. When Dr. Logan reached Washington in December, the news was in everyone's mouth. Presently there came further, even more alarming news; Spain was about to cede Louisiana to France, to Napoleon. Americans heard this news with dismay and anxiety. Ever since the Peace of Amiens in the spring they had looked forward to a long period of tranquillity, free from military threats. But already the European powers were indulging in provocative acts, and now the shadow of Bonaparte was falling on the American continent.

President Jefferson was a man of peace. He was deeply concerned at the menacing turn of events, but he was willing to try negotiation. Perhaps Bonaparte, busy in Europe, would sell the mouth of the Mississippi. Soon after the Senate organized, he asked it to confirm Robert R. Livingston and James Monroe as Ministers Plenipotentiary, with authority to purchase the city and island of New Orleans from France.

Dr. Logan was a man of peace too; he could not but wish the negotiators well. He knew from experience, however, that aroused feelings at home could make their path difficult, could even wreck their enterprise before it was well started. Already, word was reaching Washington that parts of the West were up in arms, that hotheads in Kentucky, Tennessee, and Ohio were ready to fight unless free navigation could be restored immediately. This was to be expected. Logan felt sure that Jefferson could restrain his partisans in the West from overhasty action. But he was suspicious when James Ross, his Federalist colleague, arose in the Senate on 13 February 1803 to echo the war whoop of the frontier.

Ross was a Westerner, to be sure; he came from Pittsburgh, 'from a part of the country,' he said, 'where the late events upon the Mississippi had excited great alarm and solicitude.' But there was mischief, irresponsible partisan mischief, in the speech Ross went on to make. A calamity threatened the western country, he announced. Negotiation was useless, dishonorable, a sign of weakness. Let not the Senate trifle, he warned, with 'the feelings, the hopes, and the fears of such a body of men who inhabit the western waters.' These men have arms in their hands; they are bold, daring, aggressive. Only give them a leader, he pleaded, and they will march on New Orleans in force.[26]

Republicans, caught off guard by this inflammatory appeal, forced an adjournment. Obviously this was a Federalist trick to exploit western feeling, to drive a wedge between Jefferson's government and its supporters west of the Appalachians. Never before had a Federalist displayed such solicitude, such respect, for the rough frontiersmen of the western waters.

Two days later, Ross took the floor again. He wished, he said, to propose resolutions. The United States, the resolutions declared, have an indisputable right to free navigation on the Mississippi. The late infraction of this right was an intolerable aggression. The President should forthwith call out the Army, the Navy, and 50,000 western militiamen to seize places of deposit at New Orleans by force of arms. 'War,' cried Ross, 'may be said to be already begun' — by act of Spain.[27]

The Republicans were ready this time. Breckinridge of Kentucky, Joseph Anderson and William Cocke of Tennessee, men from the region directly affected by the closure of the river, deprecated Ross's warlike talk, scouted his pretensions to speak for the West, expressed complete confidence in the President's plan to acquire New Orleans peacefully. Logan kept silent. Better that westerners should carry the brunt of debate, that he should give his colleague from Pennsylvania no opening to impute to him the sectional bias of an easterner. But he rejoiced to see Ross's mischievous resolutions beaten down and the President's policy of negotiation upheld. A unanimous house finally approved a substitute resolution, from which all belligerence, all provocation, had disappeared.[28]

Except for the debate on the Mississippi question, it was not a momentous session of Congress. It seemed as if the revolutionary impulse of 1800 had spent itself in the measures of the previous winter. Most of his time Dr. Logan spent at legislative journeywork. He presented petitions from constituents, served faithfully on routine committees.[29] These were, for the most part, unexciting assignments, but one of his committees — on 'extending the external commerce of the United States' — prepared a bill whose vast consequences neither Logan nor his colleagues, Nicholas of Virginia and Jackson of Georgia, could foresee. The President had recommended sending 'an intelligent officer, with ten or twelve chosen men' to explore the upper reaches of the Missouri and the country beyond, 'even to the Western ocean.' To be sure, the region belonged to France — Livingston had barely opened negotiations for New Orleans in Paris, and in any case, nothing had been said about buying the upper Missouri. Actually the whole territory was still in Spanish hands. Nevertheless, Logan, Nicholas, and Jackson saw no impropriety in the President's suggestion. They recommended an appropriation of $2500 for 'extending the external commerce of the United States.' [30] Within a few months, Meriwether Lewis and William Clark were on the way to the mouth of the Columbia River.

Outside of Congress, there were congenial activities. On 22 February, when the excitement over the Mississippi question was at its height, a group of Senators and Representatives met in the Capitol to realize one of Logan's old dreams — an agricultural organization, national in scope, to link up the local societies of which he had long been so zealous a promoter. James Madison took the chair. Dr. Logan and Dr. Samuel Latham Mitchill, Representative from New York, were elected Vice-Presidents. A Committee of Correspondence was named — a roster, it turned out to be, of the country gentlemen who were ruling America from the halls of Congress — Baldwin, Breckinridge, Nicholas, Randolph of Roanoke, DeWitt Clinton. President Jefferson took a benevolent interest in the undertaking. The Board of Agriculture in England, of which Sir John Sinclair was President and Arthur Young Secretary, provided the model. The new organization even called itself the American Board of Agriculture.

In spite of its impressive sponsorship, its quasi-official character, its elaborate structure, its notable precedent, the enterprise came to nothing.[31] To Dr. Logan, who had seen many agricultural societies rise and fall, it was one more disappointment in a series of disappointments: the auspices so favorable, the results so meager. American farmers could join forces to elect a government. They had proved that in 1800. When would they learn to co-operate to that other great end, that more immediate end — the improvement of their own farms? The problem, he sometimes thought, was not that the farmers lacked information. They had had plenty of opportunities to learn the newer, better methods. 'The fault is with them' — this was a painful conclusion for Logan — 'that they do not act up to their knowledge.' [32]

As Dr. Logan drove back to Stenton early in March, the newspapers were full of new rumors: the men of the western waters were up in arms, buckskin-clad Kentuckians by the hundreds, poised to descend on New Orleans. The story was no sooner scotched for the Federalist canard it was than another tale reached the seaboard from Kentucky. This one was authentic enough, but it was followed by a fantastic sequel, a sequel that put Logan's name once more into everyone's mouth.

An obscure writer in a Frankfort paper, the *Guardian of Freedom,* had proposed that, since eastern politicians had shown themselves indifferent to westerners' rights, Kentucky should forthwith secede from the Union, attach itself to Napoleon's empire. Responsible opinion in the West promptly condemned and disavowed the proposal. It had no support in popular sentiment. The author, Francis Flournoy, was simply rising to the bait cast out by Senator Ross and his party. But even a Federalist could see that Flournoy had gone too far, that his ill-considered screed approached the borders of treason. Moreover, no Federalist could fail to see and shudder at its pro-French implications.

The United States Attorney in Kentucky was a Federalist, Joseph Hamilton Daveiss, an appointee of John Adams, a brother-in-law of John Marshall. By no feat of legal reasoning could Flournoy's letter be tortured into technical grounds for a charge of treason. But there, ready to hand, never yet used, was the law of 1799 which made it a crime to commence or carry on 'verbal or written correspondence with a foreign government

. . . in relation to any disputes or controversies of the United States' — the 'Logan Act.' The resourceful Attorney quickly persuaded a Grand Jury to find an indictment against Flournoy for 'unlawfully commencing a written correspondence indirectly with the government of the French nation . . . with intent to influence the measures and conduct of the said government . . . by means of a certain unlawful writing . . . addressed to the editor of the *Guardian of Freedom.'* [33]

Senator Logan sat in the shade of his noble trees at Stenton and followed the absurd affair in the newspapers. The whole proceeding was too patently preposterous; Flournoy was never brought to trial. But to Logan — and to Debby — it brought back memories of the winter of 1798–9, of the insensate fury with which, on grounds hardly more substantial than poor Flournoy's letter, the Federalists had rushed the 'Logan Act' through Congress.

Early in July, the papers were full of another story — of the gigantic windfall, the sudden stroke of luck, which brought the whole of Louisiana, an imperial domain a million square miles in extent, into the laps of Livingston and Monroe, the American Ministers at Paris. Overnight, the country was nearly doubled in size. What a triumph for Jefferson's peaceful diplomacy!

The President called Congress into session two months early. Dr. Logan barely had time to oversee the harvest at Stenton before he was on his way to Washington. There was important business waiting — the business of taking title to Louisiana. Calmly, modestly, speaking through the Senate Clerk's monotone, Jefferson announced the fabulous bargain, the sudden, tremendous expansion of the nation's territory. 'The fertility of the country,' he said, 'its climate and extent, promise, in due season, important aids to our Treasury, an ample provision for our posterity, and a wide spread for the blessings of freedom and equal laws.'

An ominous note followed. 'The flames of war' had 'lighted up again in Europe.' Wisely, the last Congress had kept the nation clear of the 'sanguinary contest.' As always, the course of neutrality would be difficult. Logan nodded in agreement as the President went on: 'We should be most unwise, indeed, if we were to cast away the singular blessings of the position in which nature has placed us, the opportunity she has endowed us with, of pursuing, at a distance from foreign contentions, the paths of industry, peace, and happiness; of cultivating general friendship, and of bringing collisions of interest to the umpire of reason rather than of force.' [34]

Logan looked about him. Some familiar faces were missing. The two most potent orators on the Federalist side, Morris and Ross, were gone, victims of the ineluctable ebbing of their party's strength in the Middle States. The Republicans had lost their great champion too. Stevens T. Mason, the majestic Virginian, had died a few weeks after the last adjournment. The Senators wore crape for a month in his memory.

No one among the newcomers could compare with those giants for prowess in debate. But there were able men in the new Senate, congenial men, men whose friendship Logan quickly sought. To fill Mason's seat, Virginia had sent John Taylor of Caroline, a tall, slender, red-haired farmer, who had been busy fashioning an agrarian philosophy at his plantation on the Rappahannock when Logan had been composing his pamphlets at Stenton. In Ross's place, the Pennsylvania Assembly had elected Samuel Maclay. A younger brother of old William Maclay, the dyspeptic antique republican of the First Congress, Samuel was every bit as crusty, as honest, and as democratic as his brother.

Massachusetts sent two men who scarcely spoke to each other — John Quincy Adams and Timothy Pickering. Adams was a short, stocky, baldish man, whose precise Yankee speech bespoke an acute mind and an astringent nature. By family tradition he was opposed to Jefferson and all his works. As Minister to Berlin in his father's Presidency, young Adams had delivered some caustic remarks about Logan and his peace mission to Paris. Still, he was no blind Federalist, no party slave; and the Doctor learned to respect his independence of mind. But even a forgiving man like Dr. Logan found it hard to admire Adams's colleague, Timothy Pickering, and found it hard to forget how Pickering had treated him at Trenton in 1798. Nor was Pickering's behavior in this session of Congress calculated to increase one's respect for his patriotism. Already, with other New England Federalists, he was deep in a scheme to separate his section from the Union in protest against Jeffersonian 'tyranny.' The Federalists, their strength on the wane, were growing desperate. They made only a bare handful in Congress now, but they could be fertile in mischief, ingenious in obstruction. As the Mississippi question had been their opportunity in the last session, so the Louisiana treaty gave them their opening in this.

By a party vote the Senate quickly authorized the President to take possession of Louisiana. The struggle came over a bill to create a 'stock' of $11,250,000 to pay for it. The debate turned into a dispute on the very nature of the American government. Oddly, the two parties changed places. It was a strange reversal of roles. The Federalists, so clamorous in the last session for seizing New Orleans by force, now discovered scruples about accepting Louisiana by peaceful purchase. There were defects in the title-deed, said Pickering: Louisiana was not rightfully Napoleon's to sell. The Spanish were not happy about the sale, declared White of Delaware. And anyway, asked Pickering, where in the Constitution was Congress given power to acquire territory? Or to incorporate it into the Union? demanded Uriah Tracy of Connecticut.

It was John Taylor of Caroline, the apostle of strict construction, of states' rights, of limitations on Federal power, who arose to confute the Federalists. It was absurd, he said, to maintain that the Federal government could not acquire and incorporate territory; this was one of the indefeasible attributes of sovereignty. It was John Breckinridge, proposer of the 'Kentucky Resolutions,' who closed for the administration, ridiculing the opposition for its inconsistencies, boldly asserting the government's power, hailing the Louisiana Purchase as a masterpiece of statesmanship, 'one of the most splendid which the annals of any nation can produce.' [35]

Dr. Logan took no active part in the debate. He had genuine scruples about the extent of Federal power. But, like Taylor and Breckinridge, like Jefferson himself, he could not let them stand in the way of such an opportunity. Believing in America's limitless future as an agricultural nation, believing too in the process of peaceful negotiation, how could he help agreeing with the Senator from Kentucky?

To acquire an empire of perhaps half the extent of the one we possessed, from the most powerful and warlike nation on earth, without bloodshed, without the oppression of a single individual, without in the least embarrassing the ordinary operations of your finances, and all this through the peaceful forms of negotiation, and in despite too of the opposition of a considerable portion of the community, is an achievement of which the archives of the predecessors at least, of those now in office, cannot furnish a parallel.[36]

This urgent affair dispatched, the Senate settled down to its routine business. It was a miserable winter in Washington City, a season of pelting rains and heavy snows. Every street became a bottomless morass; Senators often were confined for days to their close, stuffy rooms in the Congressional boarding houses.[37] Nevertheless, committees met, bills were drafted and debated, votes were taken, laws were passed.

Just before Christmas the 'Logan Act' cropped up again. The Marquis Yrujo, Minister from Madrid, had asked a panel of prominent American lawyers — four of them Philadelphians whom Logan knew well — for an opinion on certain old American claims against Spain. The claims arose from French action in 1798 in seizing American ships and having them condemned in Spanish ports. The Marquis had put his question in abstract form, had discreetly referred to the parties as A, B, and C. The lawyers had been just as circumspect. But their opinion was unfavorable to the American claims. Secretary Madison was annoyed; he demanded action against them — for violating the 'Logan Act,' for entering into correspondence with a foreign government on matters pending between the two countries.

Senator Bradley, an administration stalwart, moved that the question be referred to a committee. Francis Rawle, one of the Philadelphia lawyers, he said, had drawn the 'Logan Act' in the first instance; it was fitting that he should be the first to suffer under it. Bradley's remark reached the ears of Roger Griswold, Representative from Connecticut. Indignantly, Griswold denied the story, proudly claiming authorship for himself. The matter never came back to the Senate; as in the Flournoy case, the charge was too patently absurd, the law itself too loose to sustain an indictment.[38] But Logan could not help asking himself : was this why the act — so execrated by his friends in 1798 — had been kept on the statute books — so that a Republican administration could use it for its own purposes ?

Two weeks later, Dr. Logan made one of his rare speeches. The Senate was debating a bill to punish crimes on the high seas — especially the crime of sinking ships for the sake of the insurance. The bill demanded death as the penalty. Dr. Logan moved to substitute banishment or perpetual imprisonment. The principles of humanity, he said, were endangered by the harsh penalty prescribed in the bill. But only six Senators shared his Quaker scruple against taking life, and he was overborne.[39]

Thwarted in one humanitarian effort, he turned to another. The Senate spent much of January and February on a bill to provide a temporary government for the Louisiana Territory. Into this debate, on 23 January 1804, Dr. Logan injected a momentous issue, an issue that stirred bitter feelings in his own party and revealed a deep fissure in its hitherto monolithic unity. He stood up at his desk and read a simple petition, asking that importation of slaves into the new Territory be prohibited by law. The petition came from the American Convention for Promoting the Abolition of Slavery, a group of philanthropists, mostly Quakers, who had just closed their annual session at Philadelphia. Wisdom, virtue, sound policy, ran their plea, all demanded the exclusion of slavery. A beneficent Providence had dowered America with material abundance and tranquillity for enjoying it. 'Does it not become the duty of a nation so crowned with the blessings of peace and plenty and happiness to manifest its gratitude to the whole world by acts of justice and virtue ?' [40]

The Senate took up the question the very next day in the form of an amendment to the territorial-government bill. Temporarily, party lines were obliterated. James Jackson of Georgia, a Republican, opened the debate. Slaves, he said, 'must be admitted into that territory; it cannot be cultivated without them.' Breckinridge of Kentucky and Franklin of North Carolina followed, both Republicans, both Southerners — but both unalterably opposed to slavery. Dayton of New Jersey, a Federalist, spoke next. He came from a state where slavery was virtually dead. Nevertheless, he agreed with Jackson: white people cannot cultivate that country, 'your men cannot bear the burning sun and the damp dews.' John Smith of Ohio, where the Northwest Ordinance prohibited slavery, contradicted Dayton: 'I know that country,' he said, 'I have spent considerable time there — white men *can* cultivate it.' 'I thank God,' he concluded, 'we have no slaves in Ohio!' [41]

The debate raged for more than a week. Southern Senators grew warm, flung out bitter words, even covert threats of secession. The majority of men from above Mason and Dixon's line — and some from below it — stood with Logan. 'I did not expect so soon,' observed a Yankee Federalist, 'to hear on this floor the distinction of eastern and northern and southern men. Has it indeed come to this,' he asked, ominously, 'are we to be designated by a geographical line?' [42]

Finally, on 30 January, the question came to a division. The vote was 21 to 7 to prohibit importation of slaves into Louisiana.[43] In triumph Logan sent news of the result to his father's old friend James Pemberton, now in his eighties, a lifelong opponent of slavery. By this action, he told the aged Quaker, Congress showed that it meant to 'rescue the national character from its greatest degradation.' [44]

Encouraged by this success, heartened still more by an approving letter from old John Dickinson,[45] Dr. Logan was soon on his feet again, to strike a second blow against slavery. It was still possible to import slaves into the states. The Constitution forbade interference with that trade before 1808. But Congress could impose a duty on imported Negroes. By this means, Logan hoped, it might be possible to curtail, perhaps even to stop the traffic altogether. It was an oblique, a devious measure. Still, the Constitution left him no other means of striking at the evil.

Even this avenue, he soon realized, was closed. The same Constitution which protected the slave trade denied the Senate the right of initiating revenue bills. Uriah Tracy, a Federalist from Connecticut, lost no time in reminding him of this. Desperately, Dr. Logan maintained that his was not, in intention, a bill for revenue. But Tracy's challenge showed him the futility of proceeding with his measure. The use of the money power to achieve other ends was too dangerous; it would have antagonized the whole South. John Quincy Adams was right when he prophesied privately that Logan's bill would come before the Senate on the Greek Kalends.[46] But Logan only bided his time. He would never relax his efforts to weaken and destroy the institution of slavery.

The Senate did not adjourn until the end of March. It had been a long session, more than five cold, wearisome months. But as Logan traveled back to Stenton, he could reflect with satisfaction that Federalism was decaying everywhere. In desperation, some New Englanders such as Timothy Pickering were even plotting of disunion, planning a Northern Confederacy, with Aaron Burr — whom Dr. Logan had last seen presiding grandly over the Senate — at its head. The proud party of Alexander Hamilton, the imperious party that Logan had fought for ten long years, had fallen on evil days, had become a scheming cabal in the hands of ignoble men. In the middle of July Dr. Logan heard, with mixed emotions, that Hamilton himself was dead, killed by Aaron Burr's bullet on the dueling ground at Weehawken. Federalism, its pride of place gone, had lost its greatest leader. It was left without strength, almost without honor.

Nowhere was the decay of Federalism more evident than in Logan's own state. But politics there were taking an ominous turn. Thomas Jefferson himself had foreseen it. 'We shall divide among ourselves,' he had written, 'whenever Federalism is completely eradicated.' [47] By the summer of 1804 the President's gloomy prophecy was dismal fact. His supporters in Philadelphia had got themselves 'into such a jumble of subdivision' that Jefferson despaired of ever untangling them.[48] And Senator Logan was deeply involved in the tangle.

County Republican leaders had been meeting for months at the Rising Sun Tavern, laying plans to defeat Michael Leib in the autumn of 1804. Dr. Logan's friend Tench Coxe was at the heart of this junto, its active, directing spirit. The Doctor threw himself energetically into the campaign. General Peter Muhlenberg, disgusted with Leib and Duane, forgot his former coolness toward Logan and Coxe, and joined the 'Rising Sun faction' in the fight.

The need for concerted opposition was greater than ever. Victory in 1802 had set the radicals on a course of reckless, demagogic reforms at Lancaster. The state courts and the Governor's appointive power were their special targets. Governor McKean was frankly alarmed at their excesses, their Jacobinical fury. At his wits' end, he had written to Logan: 'We are here full of chimerical experiments; and my knowledge, acquired with great labor, study, and reflection, and the advantage of a long and public life, cannot at all times stop or check the giddy innovations attempted in our legislature.' [49]

Two things favored the moderates. They had a newspaper of their own now, the *Freeman's Journal*, with an able editor, William McCorkle. And the Federalists chose to enter no candidates in the coming Congressional contest. But Duane's *Aurora* was still a mighty weapon in the hands of the radicals, and even the votes of former Federalists could not quite give victory to the moderates. The County returned Leib to Congress by a bare majority in October.

Duane gave Logan's group a name. 'Tertium Quids,' he dubbed them — neither Republicans nor Federalists, but a third something, a political neuter. Ironically, Tench Coxe had been the first to apply this label to the 'Rising Sun faction,' before his own conversion to it. 'What a hermaphrodite thing,' he had written, 'partaking of two characters, and yet having neither! A *tertium quid* from the combination of good and evil, of the *mule kind,* incapable of propagating itself!' [50] Shortened to 'Quids,' the name stuck.

The breach in Pennsylvania's Democracy was wider, deeper than ever. And the President's worst fears were being borne out: the moderates were joining forces with the Federalists to fight Duane and the radicals. Jefferson's own personal popularity was undiminished in Pennsylvania. The state voted nearly unanimously for his re-election to the Presidency in November. But that sweeping party triumph did little to heal the internal rift.

Dr. Logan tarried at Stenton long enough to cast his vote for the Jefferson ticket, then drove off for Washington. On 8 November he was in the Senate Chamber listening to the President's Message. Happily, the European war had not become general, Jefferson told the legislators. Interference with neutral commerce had been relatively slight. Congress, however, should take notice of the unneutral conduct of certain American citizens. The French Minister had complained that armed merchantmen from American ports were seeking to 'force a commerce' into the insurgent French colony of Santo Domingo. These individuals were, in effect, waging 'private war, independently of the authority of the country.' Congress would, no doubt, take steps to restrain them.[51]

Dr. Logan took note of the suggestion. After all, Congress had censured him in 1798 for waging peace privately. Could nothing be done to stop men from carrying on private warfare?

The Negro population of Santo Domingo had been in rebellion for ten years, first under Toussaint, later under Dessalines. In the eyes of the French government, of the American government, indeed of every government in the world, the island was a French colony in revolt; no nation had recognized the blacks as an independent people. By trading with the island, American ships were inviting action by French corsairs; in arming against attack, they were committing aggression against France. The commerce was illicit, and the arming violated the law of nations. So, at least, argued Jefferson, and his cabinet upheld him. Privately, the President had concluded that trade with Santo Domingo must be completely suspended, that the United States must offer no provocation to Napoleon which might draw her into Europe's wars.[52]

Congress was not prepared to go so far. The House passed a bill merely regulating the clearance of armed vessels, requiring owners to give bond that the armament would be used only for defense. The bill came to the Senate just after Christmas. To Dr. Logan it seemed weak, shuffling, inadequate. He sent a letter off to Wilmington, to Deborah's cousin. What did John Dickinson think of the measure? The old statesman wrote back in vehement terms. The Clearance Bill was 'disgraceful,' 'a real sanction of the trade in its worst aspects.' Congress must put a stop to the illegal traffic, must respect the French blockade. The law of nations required it.[53]

Dr. Logan carried Dickinson's letter with him to the Senate Chamber and showed it to his colleagues.[54] He took the floor and announced his stand: no half-measures would satisfy him; if the present bill were not strengthened, he would move to forbid trade with Santo Domingo. A steady stream of letters arrived from Wilmington to bolster his resolve. Dickinson could find only one explanation for Congress's behavior: it was 'dictated by the eagerness of a commercial spirit, degenerating into an all-confounding rapacity.' 'If our councils are to be warped from a strait course by the violence of peculation,' he concluded, 'we are a lost people.' From Thomas McKean came a letter in the same vein. Peace and tranquillity, the Governor said, must not be set at hazard 'to gratify a few merchants in their cupidity of gain.' [55]

Debate on the Clearance Bill came to an end on 22 February. Reluctantly, Logan voted for it, with his party. But the very next day, he was on his feet, carrying out his promise to introduce legislation prohibiting all clearances to Santo Domingo. The Senate voted on his request for leave to bring in such a bill. A tie vote, half a dozen Republicans going with the Federalists. The President of the Senate gave the casting vote. Party renegade to the last, Aaron Burr pronounced against the permission.[56] Within a few days Burr was making his farewell address to the Senate and leaving the Capitol to pursue his grandiose schemes for an empire in the Southwest.

The final days of the Eighth Congress saw a dramatic scene enacted in the Senate Chamber. The trial of Justice Samuel Chase, which had lasted all through the winter, came to a close. Chase was the Federalist judge who had condemned poor John Fries for treason in 1800. His arbitrary and overbearing courtroom behavior, his political harangues from the bench, had outraged decent people everywhere, though honest men could still differ as to whether he had ever committed an impeachable offense. With the vituperative John Randolph as chief prosecutor and the melodramatic Aaron Burr as stage-manager, the trial had been a brilliant show, enlivening a dull winter. All the ladies of Washington had flocked to it, dressed in their best clothes.

It was obviously a partisan trial, a political purge. Nevertheless, all of John Randolph's corrosive eloquence could not secure a conviction. At the final verdict, when the Senators pronounced their judgment on the eight charges against Chase, Logan found himself taking a moderate position: guilty on four counts, not guilty on the rest. On no single article was there a two-thirds majority for conviction.[57] To John Randolph this was a sore vexation, a bitter disappointment. To him the vote was a test of party regularity, of true Republicanism. His brilliant, tormented, vindictive mind began turning to thoughts of revolt, of insurgency, a break with the apostates.

It had been, Dr. Logan recalled, an acrimonious, a discordant session all along. The Federalists were too few to cause serious trouble, but cracks in Republican solidarity were more and more evident. He could not forget that day in January, in the midst of the Chase trial and the Santo Domingo debate, when, by merely asking leave to read a Quaker memorial, he had laid bare once more the party's disunity on the slavery question.

The document, he had said, was couched in decent, respectful language. It merely expressed the Quakers' conviction that slavery was an evil, and prayed that Congress would exclude it from all Territories, an action perfectly within the constitutional limits of legislative power. Immediately, Southern Senators — Jackson of Georgia, Cocke of Tennessee, Wright and Smith of Maryland — had been on their feet. Fiercely, excitedly they had opposed the reading of the memorial. The Quakers had no slaves, they had shouted; therefore, they had no right to petition on the subject. Every word against slavery uttered in Congress depreciated the value of slave property in the South, made the Negroes 'uneasy, useless, and rebellious.' These petitions were mischievous, meddling, dangerous — they would produce the scenes of Santo Domingo, the bloody horror of a slave revolt in the United States.

Vigorously, John Quincy Adams had defended the right of petitioners to be heard. James A. Bayard of Delaware, just come into the Senate from the House, had ventured the prophecy that 'all the plagues of Egypt united were not equal to the plague that slavery will eventually prove to the southern states.' Brave, conscientious Jesse Franklin of North Carolina had been for hearing the petition. The debate had lasted three hours. Finally, a vote had been taken, and Logan allowed to read the mildly phrased Quaker memorial. No one could overlook the sectional character of the vote. 'This very subject of Negro slavery,' prophesied Senator Plumer of New Hampshire, 'will . . . eventually produce a division of the United States.' [58]

Rumors of war in Europe, the specter of sectional divisions at home, the facts of incipient party discord at Washington, of schisms well advanced in Pennsylvania — all this lay heavy on Logan's spirit as he listened to Jefferson's second Inaugural Address, which followed the adjournment of Congress. Modestly, the President summarized four years of Republican rule. In foreign affairs, he said, 'we have endeavored to cultivate the friendship of all nations . . . convinced . . . that with nations, as with individuals, our interests, soundly calculated, will ever be found inseparable from our moral duties.' At home, internal taxes had been abolished. 'What farmer, what mechanic, what laborer,' Americans could now ask, 'ever sees a tax-gatherer in the United States?' The public debt had been reduced; it was on its way to extinction. The nation's territory had been notably enlarged. Obstructive opposition had dwindled to almost nothing.[59]

Dr. Logan could take deep satisfaction in all these achievements. But when Jefferson spoke of 'the union of sentiment now manifested so generally,' when he listed the auguries of 'harmony and happiness to our future course,' the troubled Senator could not share his President's bland confidence. He made his way back to Stenton, full of anxiety, of misgivings and fears.

＊

XIII. *TERTIUM QUID*

LOGAN was at Stenton in time for the spring planting. After a winter in Washington, it was always a relief to come back to the farm, to exchange the stuffy, hectic, unnatural atmosphere of boarding house and committee room for the simple comfort, the serene, unhurried, healthful outdoor life of a country gentleman. Stenton — with Debby there to hover about him lovingly — was all the tonic, all the restorative Logan needed.

There was no vacation from politics, even at Stenton. For always there were Duane, Leib, the whole 'Jacobin' crew — the epithet came easily to Logan's lips now, though not so long ago, people had been flinging it at him. They had become bolder, more outrageous in their challenge to order and decency. No longer satisfied merely to assail the Governor and the judiciary, they were planning an attack on the very foundations of liberty and property — the common law. They were hatching a convention to revise the state Constitution, to purge it, they said, of 'what yet remains of the dregs of British laws and lawyers.' This was carrying patriotism and the rejection of things English too far; it was turning the spirit of the Revolution against the very principles for which the Revolution had been fought.

So, at least, thought many substantial Republicans. Able, vigorous leaders such as Alexander J. Dallas, who had hitherto been loyal party regulars, were at last beginning to take alarm and make common cause with the Quids, with Logan's Rising Sun faction. The day before Logan left Washington, a group of 'Democratic Constitutional Republicans' had held a dinner at the White Horse Tavern in Philadelphia to celebrate Jefferson's second inauguration. It had been a Quid caucus, and out of it had come formal proposals for a 'Society of Constitutional Republicans,' a new party organization, pro-Jefferson in national politics, anti-Duane in Pennsylvania. Its general headquarters would be in Philadelphia, and there would be branches in each county.[1]

This was what Logan had been hopefully looking for. He was in the thick of the organizing campaign as soon as he was back at Stenton, working harmoniously with Dallas and Muhlenberg. The organization meeting was held at the White Horse on 21 March.[2] General Muhlenberg was chosen president; when he declined because of ill health, Logan was elected in his place. Israel Israel, a Philadelphia businessman, an old friend from the days of the Democratic Society, was vice-president. The Quids now had strong, united leadership. They had the beginnings of a state-wide organization. With aid from the Federalists, they could at last challenge Duane's control of the party. To George Logan all this was immensely encouraging.

To Thomas Jefferson in Washington, however, it was profoundly disquieting. He had barely commenced his second term as President. To protect and extend the achievements of his first administration, he must hold the party together. Democracy must be permanent, always expanding, improving. He wished to hand the succession on to James Madison and with it a strong, united party. But the party was already flying to pieces before his eyes. Within the past few months, he had witnessed the tragic defection of Aaron Burr in New York. He could sense the dissatisfaction, the coming insurgency of the wayward John Randolph in Virginia. Now came this 'bloody schism' in Pennsylvania. He knew well how it would end. The minority faction, whichever it might be, would inevitably coalesce with the Federalists. The Federalists would not 'sell their aid for nothing' — and the principles of 1800 would be fatally compromised. In the end, Republicanism would lose and 'royalism' gain 'some portion of that ground we thought we had rescued to good government.'

Sadly Jefferson wrote to Logan of the 'infinite pain' with which he saw the Pennsylvania Republicans divide. Undoubtedly both factions meant well, but their good intentions, he was convinced, would 'produce great public evil.' As the head of the party and of the nation, the President could not favor one faction over the other. 'The duty of an upright administration is to pursue its course steadily, to know nothing of these family dissensions, and to cherish the good principles of both parties.'

As much as anyone, Jefferson realized that the exhausting battles of the previous decade had left a political malaise: 'The war *ad internecionem* which we have waged against Federalism has filled our latter times with strife and unhappiness. We have met it with pain indeed, but with firmness, because we believed it the last convulsive effort of that Hydra which in earlier times we had conquered in the field . . .' But now if malaise should sink into lethargy and corruption of the mind — 'if any degeneracy of principle should ever render it necessary to give ascendency to one of the rising sections over the other, I thank my God it will fall to some other to perform that operation.' It was a tired, disenchanted man who wrote these lines. He ended wistfully: 'The only cordial I wish to carry into my retirement is the undivided good will of all those with whom I have acted.'[3]

Logan pondered the President's letter long before replying. After all, he too was by nature a man of peace — and a dedicated Republican. It was no slight thing to disrupt the party's unity. But then, he could reflect, it was the others, it was Duane and his crew, who were the wreckers. It was only a handful of scheming, factious, ambitious men, he finally wrote to Jefferson, who were causing trouble in Pennsylvania. These men had initiated 'visionary and mad projects'; they had launched indecent attacks on the republican institutions of the state. It was necessary for good men to unite against them. Soon, he told Jefferson, the Society of Constitutional Republicans would issue an address to the people, and the machinations of the demagogues would stand exposed.[4]

The address was released that very day. It bore Logan's signature as president of the Society, though Dallas had been its principal author. It was a long, closely reasoned, vehemently worded lawyer's brief. It threw back Duane's charge of factionalism,

blamed the disruption of the party on a handful of malcontents —
'men deranged by Utopian theories or corrupted by foreign arts;
men formed turbulent by nature, or become so from necessity;
men who delight in confusion, and subsist upon defamation; idlers
without social attachments; and politicians by trade.' 'Gathering
their scanty numbers into a malignant circle,' these men were busy
scattering 'envy and malice, fear and suspicion throughout the
land . . . indulging a more than Gothic fury for the demolition
of our public institutions,' and incidentally preventing 'the venerable McKean' from closing his patriotic life in peace. In this
strategy there was, of course, nothing new, since 'to the elevation
of bad men, the prostration of good men has always been found
a necessary prelude. The Gironde of Brissot formed a base for the
mountain of Robespierre.'

Vigorously the address defended the common law. Pennsylvania law was simply 'the common law of England as stripped of
its feudal trappings . . . modified by acts of the General Assembly, and . . . purified by the principles of the constitution.' As
such, it was 'the admiration of the world.' Any attack on it was
an attack on the farmer's title to his house and farm, his personal
freedom, his right to a trial by jury. The address ended with a
spirited plea: 'Re-elect our venerable Governor. Exclude from
the legislature all who have avowed a disposition hostile to the
constitution . . . Rescue your country from the impending evil,
and deserve to be happy.' [5] The Quids printed five thousand copies
and scattered them over the state.

As election time drew nearer, Logan spent more and more time
away from Stenton, concerting plans with Dallas, Muhlenberg,
Israel, and Coxe, electioneering through Bucks and Philadelphia
counties for McKean and the Quid ticket, appealing to wealthy
Federalists and thrifty German Democrats alike by dwelling on
the sinister designs of the 'Jacobins,' their disrespect for the Constitution and the rights of property.

Debby deplored this constant activity, this ceaseless coming and
going. It was so undignified for a Senator of the United States, so
exhausting for a man of her husband's frail health, so distracting
for a man whose mind was made for study and contemplation.

Besides, it kept him away from Stenton so much. As if it were not deprivation enough for her to have him in Washington each winter, he must spend the summer in this eternal electioneering. But grave matters were at stake in Pennsylvania, he always told her, and he could not rest at Stenton.

The second Tuesday in October came. McKean was re-elected by a small margin of votes — Federalist votes. The Quids had captured the election but not the party; they had succeeded only by allying with the Federalists. Still, they had elected their man. Logan was relieved at the outcome of the voting, but apprehensive lest the radicals now turn to violence. He confessed his fears to John Dickinson: 'Threats have been made by the Jacobins that they will accomplish their views by force, to which I have no doubt they will resort should they have a prospect of success.' Many Quids believed, he said, that Duane, frustrated and beaten, might now recommend 'an appeal to arms.' [6]

Early in December, the Doctor left Stenton for Washington. He anticipated a strenuous session. He was now one of the President's chief legislative lieutenants; it would be his duty and privilege to help round out the humane, peaceful program of the first Jefferson administration. A new idea had taken root and was flowering in Logan's mind. In his second inaugural address, Jefferson had suggested that, with the national debt almost liquidated, it was time to begin spending public moneys on 'rivers, canals, roads, arts, manufactures, education, and other great objects.' [7] The work of his first four years, Jefferson implied, had been, save for the purchase of Louisiana, essentially negative — a sweeping away of obstacles that the Federalists had placed in the road toward equality and democracy. The task of the next four years would be positive, creative — the improvement of the whole country, physically, intellectually, spiritually, for the benefit of the whole people.

Logan welcomed this new phase. He had steadfastly opposed the use of national power for private ends, as tending to create an aristocracy of privilege. But the government was in the hands of the people now; Jefferson's second, overwhelming victory left no doubt of that. If a democratic government possessed power to buy Louisiana, surely it could encourage internal improvements, promote education, wipe out such obvious crimes against humanity as Negro slavery. It was a challenging prospect.

But the President's Message to Congress, which Logan heard on 3 December, promised ill for these hopes of peaceful progress. It revealed Thomas Jefferson in a new, an unbecoming light. Ominously, he spoke of the renewed war in Europe, how privateers and naval vessels, British and French, were bringing it close to the American shore. He spoke of 'new principles . . . interpolated into the law of nations' by the British, under which American ships trading to the West Indies would henceforth be subject to capture.

Then Jefferson turned to the Spanish. He breathed indignation against them for their refusal to pay the old spoliation claims, their failure to settle the boundaries of Louisiana, their recent aggressions in the Gulf region. To Logan's ears the President sounded for all the world like James Ross, his own bellicose former colleague, whom the Pennsylvania voters had wisely retired to private life. Further efforts at negotiation, Jefferson implied, were useless. Some injuries to the national honor could 'be met by force only.' American troops would repel any future attack. Belligerently, the President called on Congress to increase the nation's land and naval forces, to call up the militia, to authorize the building of seventy-four-gun ships of war.[8]

Logan was aghast. Why this saber-rattling, this warlike talk, this despair of negotiation? Three days later, he knew the answer. In a secret message to Congress, the President revealed a devious scheme. For years, even before the purchase of Louisiana, he had coveted West Florida, a strip of hot, sandy, feverish coast along the Gulf of Mexico. It belonged to Spain, but Spain was embroiled in war now, an unhappy ally of Bonaparte's France. This was the opportune moment, so Jefferson reasoned, to capture the prize.

It was Talleyrand, Logan's old acquaintance of the Rue du Bac, who had suggested the strategy: threaten military action with one hand, he advised, and offer money with the other. The American Minister in Paris, John Armstrong, had sent the suggestion along to Washington, and James Monroe, passing through the French capital, had concurred. The threat of force could be directed at Texas, a vast area adjacent to the Louisiana Purchase, to which a claim might easily be trumped up. The money, if Spain chose to accept it, would go directly to France in payment of subsidies overdue from Madrid; in the end, Jefferson realized, it would further Napoleon's war against Great Britain.

This cynical strategy was laid bare when Jefferson sent in his secret message. All the bluster of his first message was gone. Possibly 'force should be interposed to a certain degree,' he said, but 'formal war is not necessary.' A few days later, he requested two million dollars to buy West Florida. He had once said that, much as he wanted that strip of coast, he would never stoop to a 'French job' to get it. But what else was this? [9]

For John Randolph, already restive and rebellious, it was the signal for open revolt. The whole scheme, he ranted to Jefferson and later to Congress, was dishonorable, cowardly, unworthy. Let the United States make good its threats, move its troops into Texas if the Dons did not truckle — but let the government stoop to no pawnbroker's tricks.

The duplicity of the scheme was just as distasteful to Logan — but his peacemaking instincts carried him in the opposite direction. To his ears the President's first bellicose message had not sounded like mere bluff. Jefferson was telling his friends these days that something must be done to correct a false impression current in some European countries, the impression 'that our government is entirely in Quaker principles, and will turn the left cheek when the right has been smitten.' If Europe was drawing this conclusion from his well-known 'love of peace,' he was saying, then Europe must be set right; there was need for a strong statement that would echo in the chancelleries of Europe like the report of a cannon.[10] To Logan this kind of bluster, this menacing language, was out of character — for Jefferson and for his country. The Doctor was alarmed lest it lead to a break in negotiation, to a needless war with Spain — and that at a time when the unneutral trade with Santo Domingo might any day provoke the French to hostilities.

John Dickinson shared his alarm. The more the old statesman

in Wilmington thought about the President's first message, the less he liked it. War with Spain was unthinkable. There seemed only one possible explanation for the threatening tone: 'that our government has committed momentous errors in the negotiations with Spain, which cannot well be retracted, and now endeavor to cover them by an excitement of national passion.' The United States, he wrote to Logan, had no immediate need of Spain's lands, either east of the Mississippi or west of it. Sooner or later, Texas and Florida would become American anyway; it was fore-ordained by nature. Meanwhile, 'to rush into war . . . for wildernesses beyond the River Mexicano, or on the remote waters of the Missouri would be . . . madness.' [11]

Three days after the secret message, which produced such violent and antithetic reactions among his followers, Jefferson invited the leaders of Congress to dinner at the Executive Mansion. Logan found several Senate friends there — John Quincy Adams, Dr. Mitchill of New York, Samuel Smith, the President *pro tempore* of the upper house. There were a number of Representatives there too — the elegant 'Beau' Dawson of Virginia, Joseph Nicholson of Maryland, two of the President's sons-in-law, John Wayles Eppes and Thomas Mann Randolph — and John Randolph of Roanoke. The only ladies present were Martha Jefferson Randolph and her daughter Anne, eldest of the President's grandchildren.

The guest of honor — the envoy from Tunis — was half an hour late. Meanwhile John Randolph's brown eyes blazed implacable hostility toward his host. Jefferson, gracious as always, might pretend not to notice, but Thomas Mann Randolph could scarcely conceal the contempt he felt for his brilliant, willful, turncoat cousin; within a few months the two men would be sending seconds to arrange a duel. Adams was always stiff and formal in the presence of his father's old enemy. And Logan, deeply troubled by the President's new belligerency, was more than usually reserved and distant. It was not a comfortable half-hour.

Presently, however, the guest of honor arrived to relieve the tension. Sidi Soliman Mellimelni, Ambassador from the Bey of

Tunis, was a celebrity and something of a curiosity. He had only recently arrived on an American man-of-war to negotiate damages for three Tunisian ships seized by the United States Navy in the Mediterranean. His demands, everyone felt, were outrageous — and his conduct was worse. He was being lavishly entertained at the expense of the American government, but already, so gossip had it, he was hinting that he was inconvenienced by the want of his seraglio, that 'a few female domestics would be agreeable.' Nevertheless, Jefferson was anxious — too anxious, Randolph thought — to treat him well, and to pay him the honors he felt were due him.

In deference to the Ambassador's religion — it was the month of Ramadan, when faithful Moslems must fast from sunrise to sunset — the President had ordered dinner served precisely at sundown. The Ambassador made no apologies for his lateness; indeed, no sooner had he arrived than he asked leave to withdraw and smoke his hookah. Jefferson, always fascinated by strange customs, invited him to smoke it in full view of the whole company. Mellimelni agreed, lighted his long sinuous pipe, and puffed contentedly away — while the dinner grew cold. He made an exotic figure with his long beard and his loose flowing garments of silk, velvet, and cashmere, laden with gold and pearls. Every now and then he paused in his smoking to take a copious pinch of snuff, heavily scented with attar of roses.

Finally, long after sunset, the company sat down to dinner. The Ambassador, Adams noted, 'partook freely of the dishes on the table without enquiring into the cookery.' After dinner, when Mrs. Randolph and her daughter retired to the drawing room, the Ambassador insisted on going with them to smoke his pipe once more. His two bearded secretaries, who had piously abstained from wine while their master was present, now hastily gulped down a glass apiece, and followed him out of the room. Without lingering long over their wineglasses, the gentlemen rejoined the Ambassador and the frightened ladies. The evening ended in desultory conversation, laboriously transmitted through an interpreter.[12]

Business presently got under way in the Senate, and Logan immediately found himself in an unhappy position. The administration was now prepared to throw all its weight behind his Santo Domingo bill — the bill he had not even been able to introduce at the last session, to cut off all trade with Dessalines' black republic. Logan had no illusions about the motives for this support; it was a sop to Napoleon, a scheme to curry favor with the French Emperor, to enlist his aid in wrenching the Floridas away from Spain. Logan had no sympathy with this sort of international bribery. But he was still convinced the Santo Domingo trade was illegal, a dangerous threat to peace; and he was committed to putting a stop to it.

On 20 December he rose in his place, requesting permission to bring in his bill. He reminded the Senate of the President's remarks on the subject at the opening of the previous session: the armed trade with Santo Domingo was a species of 'private war,' something which could not 'be permitted in a well ordered society.' He quoted letters from the British Minister and the French *chargé d'affaires,* both complaining that this trade violated the law of nations. The 'Clearance Act' passed by the previous Congress 'had operated as a deception,' he said; it allowed the illicit trade to be carried on more flagrantly than ever. He concluded his brief speech by affirming that he was not 'influenced by views of friendship towards England or France, but to preserve the immediate honor and future peace of the United States.' [13]

The revival of this issue touched off a heated debate. Logan found himself with some strange allies, and opposed by some of his best friends in the Senate. John Quincy Adams was first to speak. He had heard no new reasons advanced, he said, to warrant reopening the question. He scoffed at the danger of war with France. James Jackson of Georgia, on the other hand, seconded Logan's motion. He made it perfectly clear why *he* supported the bill; he feared a slave revolt in the South if the Santo Domingan blacks were encouraged. What new reasons, he asked, were ever given for the proposals to end the slave trade that 'had been rung in our ears by Quakers and others, ever since the Constitution had been in operation?' Two of Logan's closest friends, Dr. Mitchill of New York and Samuel Smith of Maryland, spoke against the principle of the bill; its effect, they said, would only be to abandon a lucrative trade to Great Britain without securing any real advantage to France.[14] Sorrowfully, Logan reflected that the two Senators came from New York and Baltimore — ports actively engaged in fitting out ships for the Santo Domingo trade.

Finally, Logan was given permission to introduce his bill. It surprised almost everyone by its mildness. It declared commerce with ports in the revolted sections of Santo Domingo illegal. By way of enforcement it merely proposed that ships under orders for those ports should be denied clearance. So phrased, the measure struck at least two Federalist Senators as a dead letter, since no penalties were attached, and since vessels for the West Indies seldom cleared out for particular ports anyway, but usually for the islands generally.[15] Logan's chief adviser, John Dickinson, felt the same objection: he wanted heavy penalties imposed; otherwise, he feared the bill would not accomplish its ends.[16] Called upon to defend his bill in private, Logan confessed 'that his only object was to have it in our power to tell the French government that we have prohibited the trade, and that if the merchants would carry it on, they must do it at their own peril, as it would be out of our protection.' [17]

This shuffling, this equivocating, was foreign to Logan's candid nature; to be driven to it was profoundly distasteful. Suddenly, he knew he was no longer independent; he had become a party leader, and he was learning what it meant to lead a heterogeneous, divided party. His Santo Domingo bill had originally had one clear purpose — to safeguard peace in a world at war by avoiding needless provocation. But the administration, having appropriated his measure, was using it for its own ends, as a lever to pry the Floridas loose from Spain. Now, Logan found, he must bow to the administration's strategy. The bill must be all things to all men — at least to all Republicans. For the Southerners who feared a slave revolt, its anti-Negro implications must be brought out. To satisfy the expansionists, it must be, or seem to be, favorable to Napoleon, who could deliver the Floridas to the United States. To satisfy peace-lovers such as Logan and most American farmers, it must discourage an unneutral and provocative armed trade. But to satisfy the commercial interests of New York and Baltimore, who above all wanted profits, it must be mild, unenforcible, nothing more than a nominal prohibition of the lucrative trade. To Logan all this was deeply disillusioning.

Nevertheless, Logan persisted. His main support came from Wilmington, from his aged cousin. John Dickinson in his latter days had adopted the testimonies of the Society of Friends, in which he had been raised, but which he had never actually joined. His letters, written in the Quaker 'plain language,' constantly dwelt on the theme of peace. 'There plays sometimes before my mind,' he wrote, early in 1806, 'an image of policy so pure, so wise, so benignant, that I am charmed by its beauties.' Strict neutrality, patient, undaunted good will toward all nations, readiness to submit every dispute to negotiation — these were the elements of sound policy. Once it had been in Britain's power to pursue such a course, but foolishly she had 'spurned the heavenly present from her.' Now the United States was in a position 'to practice this glorious policy, and to become blessings to mankind.' Dickinson acknowledged that he had nearly lost hope. But to encourage Logan he added, 'perhaps there are more than I know of that possess thy uprightness.' [18]

As winter deepened, the outlook for peace grew darker. John Randolph's implacable grudge against Jefferson and Madison kept the Spanish crisis alive, exacerbated it, made it more serious with the passing weeks. Like a wildcat Randolph fought against the two-million-dollar appropriation for the Floridas; national honor, he cried, required the 'chastisement' of the Spaniards. Meanwhile, Jefferson himself became more provocative, more short-tempered. The Spanish Minister, the Marquis de Casa Yrujo, ventured to criticize the high tone of his message to Congress, and Jefferson peremptorily demanded his recall. While Congress debated the Santo Domingo bill, the armed trade with the island went on, and General Turreau, the French Minister, complained that his master, Napoleon, was growing impatient. As if it were not enough to court war with Spain and France, the administration was bent on measures against England that could only lead — so it seemed to Logan — to a suicidal naval war or, what was still more indefensible in Logan's eyes, a commercial war directed at civilian populations.

A British prize court had lately handed down a momentous decision in the case of the ship *Essex*. The decision struck directly at American commerce with the French West Indies. It held, in effect, that all ships engaging in this trade were violating the 'rule of 1756' — that neutrals might not carry on in wartime a trade that was closed to them in peace — and that violation of this British-made 'rule' was violation of international law. Immediately, an outcry had gone up from the American seaports. The President in his annual message had spoken sharply of 'new principles . . . interpolated into the law of nations.' The national honor was at stake.

To Logan the cry of national honor sounded like the demand of the merchants for more profits. He had always held a low view of the mercantile classes; their insatiable desire for gain, he believed, was incompatible with republican virtue. Moreover, foreign commerce was unnecessary to a nation of farmers. National honor, he said again and again, was not a matter of manifests and bills of lading; it was not to be reckoned in dollars and cents, pounds and shillings. Its true basis was magnanimity, benevolence, generosity — the opposite of the selfish mercantile spirit.

On 14 January 1806, Logan moved for a committee to consider that part of the President's message which dealt with the *Essex* decision and its effects on American commerce. John Quincy Adams was quick to scent a partisan purpose — a desire to have the matter discussed by a committee packed with Republicans.[19] But Logan's motive was only partly political. He knew this was an explosive issue — potentially more explosive than Florida or Santo Domingo. He wanted to have it discussed in a calm, reasonable spirit, to have a voice in the discussion himself, to plead for negotiation.

Calm reason, willingness to negotiate — these seemed more urgently needed than ever, only two days later, when the President sent to Congress a letter from James Monroe, his Minister at

London. Monroe held out little hope for a peaceful solution, advised his government to 'act with energy and decision.' 'Energy and decision' — Logan knew what this language meant. Monroe, he thought, must be out of his mind to contemplate pitting America's puny naval strength against the Mistress of the Seas. It was imprudent of Jefferson even to show the letter to Congress. He vented his feelings in a brief, passionate speech. The letter could only work mischief, he said; it contained 'sentiments unfriendly to peace,' it breathed 'a spirit of war and blood.' 'This Senate,' he stoutly proclaimed, 'is for peace.' [20]

The committee on the President's Message commenced its meetings toward the end of January. Logan's friend, General Smith of Maryland, was chairman. In addition to Logan, the other Republican members were Mitchill of New York, Baldwin of Georgia, and Anderson of Tennessee. There were two Federalists — Uriah Tracy and John Quincy Adams. Sharp differences showed themselves from the very beginning. Smith, the chairman, introduced two resolutions, one an abstract declaration denying the validity of the 'rule of 1756,' the other proposing a non-importation act in retaliation.

John Quincy Adams promptly produced an alternative set of resolutions. He would go far beyond Smith's timid, generalized protest. He would label the recent British captures 'an unprovoked aggression . . . a wanton violation of . . . neutral rights . . . a direct encroachment upon . . . national independence.' He would have the President 'demand and insist upon' restoration of captured property. As for the non-importation act, Adams considered it innocuous; still, knowing it to be a favorite project of the President, he was willing to accept it as a gesture toward 'the conciliation of parties,' the price of a bipartisan foreign policy.[21]

There was little agreement and much wrangling in the committee. Tracy was lukewarm toward any policy that placed national honor above commercial profits, that might interfere with the hazardous but lucrative neutral trade. Logan had no stomach for this mercenary attitude, reckoning treasure before human life. But he could not accept Adams's resolutions. They were too militant, too much of a piece with the administration's provocative language toward Spain. In the confusing cross-currents of foreign relations, Adams the Federalist was rapidly becoming an administration Senator, while Logan, the early, the consistent, the faithful Republican was slowly drifting into opposition.

It would be, he knew, a lonely opposition. Obviously, no man of peace could find common ground with the reckless, truculent, unstable Randolph in *his* revolt against the administration.[22] Just as obviously, despite his temporary alliance with the Federalists in Pennsylvania, a man of Logan's principles could not traffic with Tracy and the New England Federalists, who even now were plotting with Burr and the British to disrupt the Union. He was not prepared, as John Dickinson was, to acquiesce without a murmur in the new British policy.[23] He could only take his stand on his own ground, set his course by the star of his own hope for peace.

He was in favor, he told the committee, of making a solemn, dignified protest against the British policy. He fixed his hopes for redress, however, on an 'armed neutrality' of the northern European powers. A general protest, he thought, was more likely to induce their co-operation than a bill of particulars. The other committee members, except Baldwin, did not share his hopes. Reluctantly, Logan acquiesced in Adams's strong resolution of protest in order to concentrate his opposition on the demand for immediate satisfaction and on Smith's proposal for non-importation.

Peremptory demands, threats of retaliation, he argued, would never create a climate of peace. Let the President send an envoy extraordinary to London. 'Perhaps,' he suggested, 'Mr. Monroe had irritated the British government and aggravated their offenses.' Monroe, as everyone knew, was a tactless, impulsive man, and an inveterate Anglophobe. Why not 'try the effect' of another Minister in London, as Jefferson had done when he sent Monroe himself to Paris for the Louisiana negotiations? Logan quoted the unofficial advice of Anthony Merry, the British Minister, to Secretary Madison: that before the United States risked war, it should 'be very sure that no other measures of a conciliatory nature remained.' [24]

Smith's proposal to retaliate against Great Britain by cutting off all imports Logan rejected outright. Commercial warfare was still warfare. A republican nation, a nation devoted to peace and progress, must rise above it, must put its faith in reason, moderation, indefeasible good will. 'With respect to the injurious commercial acts of Great Britain and France towards the United States,' he wrote on a scrap of paper, 'let her desist from fighting them with such weapons. Let her oppose lenity and moderation to their aggressions, good faith to their treachery, to their violence the mildness of a republican government.' [25] But the committee overrode his objection.

Senator Smith reported the three resolutions to the Senate on 5 February 1806. With a unanimous house Logan voted for Adams's firm declaration of neutral rights — after it had been pruned of its harsher adjectives. The second resolution placed him in a dilemma. It contained two somewhat incongruous clauses. First, it directed the President in emphatic terms to 'demand and insist upon' satisfaction; then, in softer language, language for which he himself was responsible, it called for 'amiable negotiation' to achieve this end. Logan sought to have the first clause deleted entirely, leaving only the provision for negotiation. His effort failed, but he nevertheless voted for the resolution. Privately, to Senator Plumer, he explained why : 'I have no confidence in the President,' he fumed. 'He will not negotiate unless we resolve it is necessary. He has shamefully neglected the interest of this country by not making a treaty with Great Britain years ago. He has sacrificed our interests by sending such a feeble and improper man as Monroe to the Court of London.' [26]

Debate on the third resolution — the call for a non-importation act — was postponed. Logan looked forward to the revival of that issue with a sinking heart. He knew that Jefferson and Madison would make it a question of party regularity, and he dreaded the day when he must go into outright revolt against the party that had so long been the vehicle of his hopes for a peaceful, democratic future.

Yet signs were multiplying that Jefferson was leading the party and the nation into the morass of war — the same morass that the

Federalists had approached less than ten years before, from which only the statesmanship of John Adams, yes, and the private efforts of a few concerned men like himself, had rescued them. Did Jefferson possess John Adams's wise statesmanship? The evidence, unfortunately, all seemed to the contrary.

The warlike atmosphere of this winter of 1805–6 also sent John Dickinson back in memory to the troublous days of 1797 and 1798. He called Logan's attention to passages in his *Letters of Fabius,* written in 1797 to check the 'blind rage for war.' 'A child,' he had warned then, 'may set fire to a house, but a whole city may not be able to prevent the conflagration from leveling the buildings in every street to the ground.' Was not Jefferson, with his blustering to Spain, his scheme for retaliating against England, playing the mischievous child? As in 1797, so in 1806, Dickinson believed, the times called for the conciliatory spirit of a Robert Walpole, ever ready to negotiate, always anxious to avoid war.[27]

Jefferson, Logan reflected sadly, was showing little of Walpole's pacific temper, more of the elder Pitt's imperial ardor, even — though the part fitted him ill — of Bonaparte's cynical, ruthless adventurism. He was continuing to brandish as a club his demand for lower Texas, while he forced a reluctant Congress to pass his 'two-million-dollar bill' to buy the Floridas. At the last moment, Logan tried to block the scheme, offering a substitute resolution directing the President 'to renew our negotiations with the Spanish government, in such a manner as may bring every subject in controversy between the two countries to a speedy termination, equally advantageous to both.' The maneuver failed, and Logan joined two other prominent Republicans, Bradley and Mitchill, in a conspicuous departure from the Senate Chamber.[28] He could not bring himself yet to vote against the President — but neither would he give his support to a shameful 'French job,' for a policy so reckless, so fraught with risk.

Two weeks later, Logan's Santo Domingo bill came to a vote. From the beginning he had been sure of the outcome. Indeed, he had accurately — if somewhat indiscreetly — predicted the final vote one evening over General Turreau's fruit and wine at the French Legation.[29] But already, as he saw how the embargo fitted into Jefferson's plan, Logan began to lose interest in it. He still felt that the United States should avoid unnecessary provocation in a warring world. But he was not prepared, as Jefferson seemingly was, to lend encouragement, however indirectly, to the military designs of Bonaparte. ('Every advantage we bestow on France,' his wise counselor in Wilmington reminded him, 'is a weakening of Britain, already tottering under the mighty contest . . . Will it be wise in us to increase her burthens and accelerate her fall?' [30])

The Santo Domingo bill passed the Senate by a strict party vote on 20 February 1806.[31] From friends of peace everywhere came letters of congratulation. One of the letters was from Nantucket, from Gideon Gardner, master of the ship that had brought Logan back from France in 1798. The Nantucketer added a touching note about his children: 'The two little Republicans, Jefferson and Logan, grow finely.' [32]

For Logan himself, however, there was little satisfaction, little cause for congratulation, in this triumph. He knew well enough why his embargo had been supported — by the Southern Senators because of its pro-slavery ring, by the representatives of the great seaports because it was unenforcible, by the President because it played into his devious plan to acquire Florida.

A few days after the final vote, the Doctor was picking his way among the puddles that transformed Washington's streets into quagmires in February. He met General Turreau, Napoleon's flamboyant Minister. The General thanked him for his exertions, pressed him to take a seat in his carriage. Mortified, the Doctor declined. 'I believe, sir,' protested the Minister, 'you are ashamed to be seen with Mr. Turreau.' Logan did not answer.[33]

Republican leaders, misled by visions of empire, might stray from the paths of peace; they might even lure George Logan into dubious and compromising bypaths. In domestic matters, however, Logan could still work contentedly in the administration harness; indeed, he could lead his party into new, untried roads, roads that led toward a new conception of the democratic state as a positive instrument in the people's hands.

He did not forget the Chesapeake and Delaware Canal Company, for which he had stood sponsor five years before in the Pennsylvania Assembly. He had seen the enterprise launched with enthusiasm; Philadelphians, sensing an opportunity to thwart Baltimore's commercial hopes, had subscribed nearly $75,000 in stock, and digging had commenced in the spring of 1804. On his way to and from Washington he could stop to inspect the ditch as it began to make its way across the narrow isthmus that separated Chesapeake from Delaware Bay. But the work had gone slowly; the shareholders had become discouraged and had fallen behind in their payments. By the end of 1805, construction was at a standstill for want of funds. Hat in hand, the directors were now approaching Congress with a request for a subsidy.

On 28 January 1806 Logan presented their petition. The undertaking, they argued, was one of national importance; it was not merely a local concern. It could be a link in what might eventually become a continuous inland waterway reaching from the Georgia inlets to Boston Bay.[34] The matter was referred to a committee, and Logan was named chairman. The other members — Bayard of Delaware and Bradley of Vermont — were as favorable to the project as he.

In due course, Logan reported the committee's recommendations. As his report moved from the immediate issue to its broader implications, the twenty-one miles of the Chesapeake and Delaware Canal took their place in a grandiose pattern — 'a vast scheme of interior navigation, connecting the waters of the lakes with those of the most Southern States.' Confidently, Logan proclaimed it 'a plan certainly within the compass of industry and art.' If it was beyond present means, it was 'unquestionably within the growing resources of the country.' As a beginning, as the first step toward realizing this grand continental scheme of internal waterways, the committee recommended that the national government should make a grant of land to the Chesapeake and Delaware Canal Company, either as an outright gift or as an investment in the company's stock.[35]

It was a novel idea, this proposal to bestow part of the public domain on a private company to promote 'internal improvements.'

The vastness of the prospect it opened up took the Senators' breath away. The proposal would have to be pondered, digested, seen in perspective. The Senate voted to delay action until the next session.[36]

Another idea, meanwhile, had taken command of Logan's imagination — the idea of a national university. The conception was not new. President Washington had dreamed of founding 'a seminary of learning upon an extensive scale in the Federal City,' where 'the arts, sciences, and belles lettres could be taught in their fullest extent.' Such an institution, he had argued, would make it unnecessary to send American youth to be trained abroad, where they might contract 'principles unfriendly to republican government.' Washington had left fifty shares of stock in the Potomac Company as a nucleus for the university's endowment.[37]

Two of the capital's most picturesque citizens took up the project. One was Logan's friend Dr. Thornton, who was interested in everything. The other was a colorful, pushing, eccentric character with a 'comical look' named Samuel Blodget. He was an architect like Thornton, also an economist, a tireless compiler of statistics, a projector of grandiose schemes for the city's development — and a heavy speculator in real estate. For years the two men had been soliciting funds for the university; Blodget even carried on his financial campaign from the little jail on C Street where he languished for a time as a bankrupt.[38]

Before Congress convened, a third zealous promoter of the scheme arrived in Washington — Logan's friend Joel Barlow, whom he had first met, half a dozen years before, in Paris. Back in his native country after seventeen years abroad, Barlow was bubbling over with ideas — ambitious, far-reaching ideas. The United States, he told everyone, must have a great foundation to advance and diffuse learning in all fields, an institution equal if not superior to the academies and universities of the Old World. In January 1806, Barlow published his *Prospectus for a National Institution.*

Logan read his friend's work with deep interest. He told him everything he knew of Washington's bequest and its sequel — how Blodget, 'the most persevering man in the world,' had kept it alive, how Congress had five thousand city lots at its disposal, which it could devote to the endowment, how Washington had even chosen a site for the university, overlooking the Potomac, opposite Mason's Island. He urged Barlow to draw up his proposals into a bill, and promised to present it in the Senate.[39]

Logan introduced Barlow's bill on 4 March. He bestowed more than his usual care on the speech that he made on its behalf. 'Is it not time,' he asked, 'that Congress should promote and countenance the cultivation of the sciences which enlighten and embellish the human mind, and which are essentially necessary to promote the peace, happiness, and prosperity of our country?' Peace, happiness, prosperity — these were the only proper objects for a republican government to pursue — but from these objects the Senate had allowed itself to be distracted. 'Must we suffer the whole attention of Congress' — Logan spoke slowly, earnestly — 'to be absorbed in contests with foreign nations for the sordid accumulation of money, whilst every study that is calculated for the ornament of the human mind and the improvement of its faculties are [sic] neglected?'

There was no question of Congress's authority to legislate in this sphere. 'Those enlightened citizens who composed the [Constitutional] Convention' had been 'sensible of the cultivation of literature'; they had known how important sound learning was to the maintenance of peace and the preservation of liberty. They had wisely laid upon Congress 'the duty of promoting science and the useful arts.' President Washington, 'whose patriotic and active mind was always alive to the best interests of his country,' had impressed upon the First Congress that nothing deserved its patronage more than 'the promotion of science and literature.'

These were weighty precedents, formidable authorities. No matter that they fell strangely from the lips of a man who had once declaimed against Washington and the makers of the Constitution. He was older now, more experienced in the problems of governing, more respectful of the earlier generation. He passed quickly to an exposition of Barlow's plan for a national academy, reviewed the advantages it would bring to the nation. In his peroration, after quoting Algernon Sidney, one of the fathers of republicanism, he posed the essential problem of republican government: 'Where the rulers are chosen by the people, how necessary is it that the republic should not vegetate in the barbarity of ignorance! What kind of representatives will they choose? What will be their laws?' [40]

The bill was referred to a committee composed of Logan, Mitchill, and Adams. They promptly reported it back without amendment. In a few weeks it reached a third reading, but the Senate was listless. It was referred again to committee and died there, a victim, as Logan had feared, of the government's growing preoccupation with the war and America's relation to it. [41]

War was unquestionably coming closer, and Thomas Jefferson, by his intransigent attitude toward Spain — so Logan felt — was doing nothing to avert it; he was, in fact, doing everything he could to bring it closer. Only Gallatin among the President's advisers counseled caution, and Jefferson no longer listened to Gallatin or consulted him. Indeed John Randolph was charging that Jefferson, these days, consulted nobody. 'There is no longer any cabinet,' he had shrilled one day in the House of Representatives. [42]

At the end of February, the President finally sent to the Senate his nomination of a Commissioner Plenipotentiary to settle the disputes with Spain. [43] But his choice horrified Logan and bore out his worst fears. It was John Armstrong — the man who had first planted in the President's mind the notion of seizing Texas. Logan could scarcely think of a man less suitable for delicate negotiations — if peace were really the aim. Did the President really mean, then, to persist in his mad course of bluster, threats, and bribery?

Logan could no longer suppress his indignation, could no longer contain his anxiety. Abraham Baldwin, who felt the same concern, urged him to carry it straight to the Executive Mansion, to talk it out face to face with Thomas Jefferson. On 12 March, after a sleepless night, Dr. Logan finally dashed off a letter to his old friend at the other end of Pennsylvania Avenue. His language — blunt, forthright, unsparing — revealed the agitation of his mind.

'Your errors in conducting the exterior relations of our country,' he wrote, 'oppress the minds of your best friends with the most anxious solicitude.' Logan paused, drew a dash, then went on: 'You may yet retrieve your character and preserve the confidence of your fellow citizens.' He remembered Gallatin's plaint. 'Call together your too long neglected council,' he pleaded, 'take the state of the Union into consideration, submit every subject with frankness to discussion; and, united with them, determine on such measures as may preserve the peace and honor of our country.'

The President would know what was on Logan's mind, but it would do no harm to be specific. 'Your own reputation,' he continued, 'imperiously demands that you should recede from pretensions and projects which are demonstrably groundless and unjust.' He reminded Jefferson of their old ideals, the noble principles of statecraft they had once discussed beneath the trees at Stenton. Perhaps without realizing it, he echoed the words which President Washington had used in his first Inaugural Address. 'No truth,' Logan wrote, 'is more thoroughly established than that there exists in the affairs of nations an indissoluble union between the generous maxims of an honest and magnanimous policy and the solid rewards of public prosperity and felicity.' [44]

To Jefferson the letter came as a rude shock. He was already wincing under the insensate railings of John Randolph, the defection of a large number of southern Republicans. Now it was Logan, a trusted lieutenant, a leader in the northern wing of the party, who was growing restive. The President could not afford another revolt. He phrased an amiable reply and sent it off at once:

March 12th 1806

Dear Sir, I received your letter as a proof of your friendship. I have been for some time suspicious there was something on your mind unknown to me, and of which I thought I had a right to expect an explanation. We may differ in our opinion of measures: but on matters of fact we cannot differ on due explanation. My present malady keeps me through the whole day incapable of business or conversation, and obliges me therefore to ask an interview any evening that suits you on the subject of your letter.

Accept affectionate salutations,

Th: Jefferson [45]

The very next evening, Logan was facing the President in his spacious study surrounded by books, charts, and scientific instruments, pouring out his misgivings, pleading for moderation, for a reasonable attitude toward Spain, the abandonment of the outrageous claims to Texas. The President was moved by his old friend's earnestness, his obvious concern. He called a meeting of his cabinet the next day, and decided to give up the untenable claim to all of Texas, to say no more of the Rio Grande or the Colorado as a boundary, to be satisfied with the Sabine, several hundred miles to the east.[46]

Logan had made his point — or part of it. Jefferson had yielded ground to conciliate his old friend. But the two men were still far from perfect agreement. Only a few days after the interview, Logan voted against Armstrong's confirmation as Commissioner. A few weeks later, Logan showed the President his most recent letter from John Dickinson. The old gentleman was still convinced that the dispute with Spain had 'proceeded from our mistakes and imperiousness,' he still believed that 'we might almost as reasonably quarrel with her for lands in the moon as for the wildernesses beyond the Mississippi.' The President could only counter lamely that the question of acquiring territory at Spain's expense would have never arisen but for Spain's refusal to pay the spoliation claims.[47]

In the last days of the session, the non-importation bill finally came to a vote. It was a critical moment. William Pitt, Britain's stubborn leader, was dead. Charles James Fox, a liberal and an old friend of America, was the new Foreign Minister. Britain's allies had just suffered a disastrous defeat at Austerlitz. The time was propitious, Logan felt, for 'a reasonable arrangement of all affairs of difference' between the two nations. A declaration of economic war now would only ruin the chance of accommodation. Logan made a last effort to prevent passage of the non-importation bill; he moved to postpone it till the fall, to try once more the effect of negotiation. But the administration, determined on its policy, beat down his motion for postponement easily, and enacted the bill. Every voice in its favor was Republican. Every voice against it — except Logan's — was Federalist.[48]

The irony was not lost on Logan's Senate colleagues: George Logan, the early, faithful, consistent anti-Federalist, the bitter opponent of Hamilton in the 1790's, the loyal supporter of Jefferson and Jeffersonian principles through long years of opposition, now allied with the party of Alexander Hamilton in state, national, and international politics. Ironically, Jefferson, with his shrewd political intuition, had predicted it; Jefferson, with his shrewd sense of political realities, had helped bring it to pass. In Pennsylvania, where Duane's lust for power and spoils had led him into demagoguery, the President, by prudently declining to intervene, had left only one course open to Logan and his friends. In national affairs, Jefferson, the erstwhile apostle of the diminished state, had first extended the national authority by buying Louisiana and then encouraged Logan to join national-minded men such as Adams in working for roads, canals, universities at the Federal government's expense. In foreign relations, Jefferson's unfortunate experiments in the Machiavellian politics of bluster, bribery, and retaliation, his opportunistic appeasement of Bonaparte, his betrayal of the Republican policy of peace, reason, and negotiation, had driven the Doctor into the camp of the Federalists. These ironies weighed heavily upon Logan's spirit as he took his way back over muddy roads to Stenton.

Logan had little relish for active political campaigning in the summer of 1806. The Society of Constitutional Republicans had formally dissolved after re-electing McKean to the Governorship. But old animosities and old suspicions remained, intensified and complicated by new differences on foreign policy. For Duane, Leib, and the 'Jacobins' chose, at the expense of party loyalty, to follow the erratic lead of John Randolph on the Spanish question. Most of the Quids upheld Jefferson in his stand against the British — at the cost of Federalist support. Logan, who desired peace and only peace with all the world, could find common ground with neither group.

Fortunately, he had no strong desire to succeed himself in the Senate. When the Quids — with vague promises of the Governorship in 1808 — politely set him aside for Andrew Gregg, he uttered no protest, even though Gregg had led the movement for non-importation in the House of Representatives. At least, Logan could reflect, Gregg was an honest man, devoted to the farmers' interest, free from 'Jacobinism.' He could be counted on to defeat Michael Leib, who coveted Logan's seat in the Senate.[49]

A disagreeable experience that summer increased Logan's distaste for politics. Just before the autumn election, copies of a scurrilous pamphlet called *The Quid Mirror* began to appear mysteriously, thrown in people's doorways or sent through the mail. Soon everyone was reading it, chortling over its malicious pen-portraits of leading Constitutionalists, or growing indignant over its misrepresentations. The pamphlet produced more than one challenge, and at least one assault and battery, before its echoes died away.[50]

The author — some said it was the radical Lancaster editor William Dickson — characterized the Quids as 'office-seekers and dictators.' Scarcely one prominent figure in the movement did he spare. Governor McKean he described as 'one of Fortune's frolics,' an egotist and a nepotist who bestowed political offices on 'every whelp and every cub of his own.' Dallas was a 'sycophant,' a hypocrite, a coward, a traitor. Israel Israel was the object of an especially vicious attack: this generous, open-hearted Episcopalian, of mixed Dutch and Scotch-Irish ancestry, was set down as 'truly a Jew,' his 'physiognomy . . . indicative of the character of Shylock' and 'money . . . the god of his idolatry.'

Logan came off no better than his friends. He owed his standing in society solely to his large fortune. His learning was contemptible; the 'utmost of [his] genius goes not beyond catching grasshoppers or raising colts.' He had been a Tory in the Revolution, a belated convert to the rights of man in the 'nineties, a craven in the Whisky Insurrection. 'Meanness, cowardice, and malignity are the predominant features of his character.' His mission to Paris in 1798 had been an act of 'lunacy'; 'the reveries of Don Quixote or his knight Sancho Pancha [sic] had not more of the absurd and ridiculous in them.' And this despicable creature, this 'Hottentot,' this 'dirty fellow,' aspired to be Governor of Pennsylvania. The author of the vitriolic pasquinade gave his sarcasm at the end a literary twist: 'Jupiter in his wrath gave the frogs a stork to govern them,' he wrote, 'but really we should suppose him to be in a fantastic mood indeed if he should ordain *an ape* to govern us — a creature whose brain "is as dry as the remainder biscuit after a voyage," and who

> hath strange places crammed
> With observations, the which he vents
> In mangled forms.' [51]

The campaign of vilification was not without its effect. Gregg, who had been spared from attack, won the Senate seat, but the Quids lost ground to the Duane Democrats in the lower house and the state Assembly. The 'Jacobins' redoubled their fury in Lancaster. Soon the embattled McKean was writing to Logan that he might yet be driven to strong tactics of 'opposition and hostility' if the 'Catilinian faction' persisted in its 'seditious measures.' 'It appears to me,' wrote the distraught Governor, 'that the faction would set a church on fire, were it only to roast eggs at it.' [52]

After the crises and conflicts of the previous winter, after the disagreeable affair of the *Quid Mirror,* the Congressional session of 1806–7, Logan's last in the Senate, was unexpectedly harmonious and amicable. For this the President was partly responsible. His messages to Congress breathed a spirit of calm reasonableness, of conciliation, of concern for peaceful progress. Logan could hope, as he listened, that Jefferson had repented of his aberrations, had come back to the true republican course.

William Pinkney, a Baltimore Federalist, had gone to London, the President reported, to join Monroe in ironing out the differences with Great Britain. Meanwhile, Jefferson asked Congress to suspend the Non-Importation Act 'as a mark of candid disposition on our part.' The disputes with Spain were also under negotiation. Turning to domestic affairs, the President was able to report the success of Lewis and Clark in their expedition to explore the Missouri and the Columbia. He called attention to the approach of the year 1808 — the year in which, under the Constitution, Congress could take action to end the foreign slave trade. The national debt was being liquidated as rapidly as the law allowed, and the Treasury would soon be overflowing. What better use for the redundant revenues, he asked, than the construction of 'roads, rivers, canals' to cement the Union with 'new and indissoluble ties'? The President went out of his way to recommend Logan's favorite project of a national university.[53]

All this was hopeful. Logan entered upon his last session as a Senator with a new zest. Enthusiastically he supported Stephen Bradley's bill to end the foreign slave trade forever; triumphantly he saw it pass. Vigorously he continued to press the case of the Chesapeake and Delaware Canal Company. The matter was postponed again and again, and no final action was taken. But Logan could feel that he had helped to plant a momentous new idea. Toward the end of the session, John Quincy Adams proposed referring this and other requests of the same sort to the Secretary of the Treasury, instructing him to draw up a comprehensive plan of national roads and canals. Adams's proposal, in which Logan united wholeheartedly, was eventually carried by a nearly unanimous Senate.[54] Only the plan for a national university, among Logan's favorite projects, failed to have a hearing in this session.

The domestic scene appeared peaceful and propitious, as in the earlier days of the Republican administration. But Logan could not look abroad without anxiety, without a sense that black thunderclouds might blow up at any moment to end the interval of calm. Napoleon, astride the continent of Europe, and Britain, in unchallenged command of the seas, had intensified their deadly war of decrees and orders-in-council, of blockade and counter-blockade. The waves set up by their titanic struggle, Logan knew, would sooner or later wash up on the American shore and affect the peace of the United States. Yet he continued to hope against hope that somehow Monroe and Pinkney might reach an agreement with Britain, an agreement that would save the United States from being drawn into the conflict on the side of Bonaparte.

The negotiations in London were arduous and lengthy. They nearly came to grief over the old question of impressment. Great Britain was fighting with her back to the wall. Survival might depend on keeping the manpower of her Royal Navy and her merchant marine from melting away by deserting to American ships. Lord Holland and Lord Auckland, the British commissioners, would not, could not, give way on the principle. Nevertheless, they made a practical concession; they would agree to a solemn undertaking, in a note to accompany the treaty, that henceforth every precaution would be taken to prevent injury to American citizens. Monroe and Pinkney accepted this assurance, and proceeded without difficulty to negotiate a treaty providing for the settlement of virtually every outstanding difference.

Logan knew nothing of what was going on in London. But when word came, toward the end of the Senate session, that a treaty had been signed, he forgot his earlier distrust of Monroe and rejoiced in the news. He looked forward to ending his Senate service by ratifying a treaty of peace with Great Britain.

But he was to be disappointed. He was never to have a chance even to consider the treaty. The first copy of the document arrived at the British Legation on 3 March 1807. The Ninth Congress would expire that very day. The treaty was promptly carried to the Executive Mansion, where the President lay ill. An expectant Senate remained in session until midnight awaiting a communication from the White House. Ten o'clock came, and no word from the President. A joint committee of the two houses was named — Adams and Mitchill for the Senate — to wait upon the President, remind him of the impending recess.

The five committeemen jolted along Pennsylvania Avenue to the President's House and were ushered into his sickroom. They presented some bills for his signature, spoke of the imminent adjournment. Would the Senate be called back soon to consider the treaty? Senator Mitchill inquired anxiously. 'Certainly not!' exclaimed the President, his voice showing strain and irritation. The treaty was wholly unacceptable, he said. There was not a word in it about impressment. He could not understand what had possessed the two Ministers to sign such a document. No, he had no intention of troubling the Senate with it.[55]

The five Congressmen rode back through the darkness to the Capitol. Mitchill and Adams came into a hushed Senate Chamber, where flickering candles threw long, uncertain shadows on columned walls. The President, they reported, 'had no further communications to make.' There was nothing to do but adjourn.

It was a disappointing end to Logan's Senate career. Sorrowfully, he left the Capitol and hastened to his lodgings. His friend Abraham Baldwin lay gravely ill. He had asked Dr. Logan to attend him as a physician. The patient, he found, was sinking fast. Toward morning he died. Logan tarried in Washington with many of his colleagues for the funeral. As the procession moved from the Capitol to Rock Creek Church — five miles over rutted streets made almost impassable by a recent storm — Logan's mind dwelt mournfully on Baldwin's last words of advice on public affairs. 'Take care,' the dying man had said; 'hold the wagon back; there is more danger of its running too fast than of its going too slow.' [56]

The words lingered in Logan's mind as he started back over the treacherous roads — they were 'never in a more dangerous condition,' he wrote Debby — to Stenton. And the national wagon, he could not but fear, was lurching and careening over a rocky road toward war. Jefferson and Madison, in the drivers' seats, were doing little to check its mad course. Baldwin, Logan's friend and the friend of peace, was gone. Logan himself was no longer in the Senate. Who would hold the wagon back now? Who would keep it from disaster?

XIV. MISSION TO LONDON

ONCE MORE, George Logan was simply a farmer, his responsibilities bounded by the four corners of Stenton. Once more, after years of ceaseless political activity, he could settle into the placid routine of country life, free from the burdens of office, remote from the clamor of place-seekers, the strife of political factions. Once more he could bask in the warm sunshine of Deborah's love and tender care. Once more, life was restored to ideal simplicity — the natural round of plowing, planting, and harvesting, the raising of sheep, steers, and hogs, the elemental, immemorial, rewarding tasks of threshing rye, spreading manure, hauling firewood, sorting potatoes, pressing cider, breaking flax.[1]

A new enthusiasm — a craze for Merino sheep — was beginning to sweep over the farming regions. Two of Logan's friends — Victor Du Pont, the great Physiocrat's son, and Robert R. Livingston, the man who had bought Louisiana — introduced it to the Middle States by importing some Merino rams and ewes from Spain. For years, Logan had been preaching the need to improve the quality of American livestock. For years, he had been trying by precept and example to teach farmers something that George Washington had once impressed on him — that it was possible to double the yield of wool from a flock simply by giving it personal care and attention.[2] For the most part, the Pennsylvania farmers had paid no heed.

Logan welcomed the new breed with its fine, heavy fleece. Perhaps its novelty would do what nothing else had done, would

281

finally persuade the American farmer that it was both sound economy and sound patriotism to raise his own wool and give it to his wife to spin into yarn. With this hope — and an indefeasible faith in the efficacy of farmers' societies — Dr. Logan helped to organize a Merino Society of the Middle States of North America, served faithfully on its Committee of Correspondence, wrote and circulated accounts of the astonishing production of wool from the Spanish sheep.[3]

He had another agricultural project to occupy his mind in these days. Across the Delaware, in Morris County, New Jersey, a day's drive from Stenton, he owned a tract of unimproved land that he had inherited from his father. The place was called Logansville. It lay along a little stream known as Primrose Creek, a tributary of the Passaic River, in a pleasant rolling countryside. For years, Dr. Logan had intended to develop this farm, but he had never had the leisure. Now he turned to it with energy and zest. He drained its low-lying swamps, put its fields into cultivation, settled a steady Quaker farmer on the place.[4] It made a delightful retreat whenever he and Debby grew tired of the noisy traffic that lumbered and rumbled in ever-increasing volume along the Germantown Pike past Stenton's gates.

In the spring of 1808, George and Deborah drove down to Wilmington for Albanus' marriage to John Dickinson's daughter Maria. The couple had been engaged for five years, but they had postponed their wedding until Albanus finished his medical studies. The bride's father had recently died, at the age of seventy-five. He left the young couple a two-hundred-acre estate called Somerville on the Germantown Road. It was only a mile below Stenton, adjacent to Fairhill, where Uncle Isaac Norris's lovely mansion had stood before it was burned in the Revolution. Albanus presently built a fine house at Somerville, and, like his father before him, soon turned his thoughts from medicine to farming.[5]

Living the sequestered life of a farmer at Stenton, Dr. Logan could have felt isolated, cut off from the turbid currents of politics, domestic and international, that swirled and eddied through the last years of Thomas Jefferson's presidency. But he could not be unconcerned about the prospects for peace. In the months that followed his retirement from the Senate, those prospects looked grimmer than ever. Every week, almost every day, came news of American merchant ships stopped and searched on the high seas by British or French warships.

In June 1807 had come the most alarming news: the *Leopard*, a British man-of-war, had actually fired on the *Chesapeake,* an American naval vessel, off Hampton Roads; British guns had killed and wounded American seamen; a British naval captain had unlawfully, brazenly, impressed American citizens from the *Chesapeake*'s blood-spattered decks. In Philadelphia everyone had demanded prompt, condign retaliation. In Washington, Jefferson had exploded to General Turreau: 'If the English do not give us the satisfaction we demand, we will take Canada . . .' In Wilmington even peace-loving old John Dickinson had called the incident a 'horrible outrage . . . against humanity and our country.' [6]

Logan had watched with apprehension to see what his former colleagues in Congress would do when they reassembled in the fall. Obviously, the nation was not prepared for war. Jefferson did not propose it. He was still eager to try the effects of economic strangulation. Congress proved willing to co-operate. The Non-Importation Act, suspended during the Monroe-Pinkney negotiations, went into force early in December. An Embargo Act, forbidding American vessels to clear for any foreign port, passed both houses later in the month. Now the President had a chance to try his favorite weapon of peaceful coercion.

In so far as the Embargo was intended to protect American ships and sailors from danger — its ostensible purpose — Logan approved of it. But that, as everyone knew, was not its real purpose. Designed to bear chiefly upon the British civilian population by cutting off its food supply, it was a device to extort concessions by the grim leverage of starvation. George Logan abhorred war at least as much as Thomas Jefferson did. Yet by no rationalization could he bring himself to consider starvation more humane than shooting, especially when its victims were defenseless, unoffending women and children.

Jefferson's mercantile warfare, he felt, was dishonorable, barbarous, unworthy of an enlightened people. In place of 'the generous disinterested patriotism of the soldier to defend his country,' Jefferson was substituting 'a cowardly sneaking attack on the domestic comforts of the poor.' By imposing the Embargo the United States was 'throwing off the principles of humanity and adopting a measure during the sacred period of negotiations that we fondly contemplate will destroy by famine the wretched inhabitants — men, women and children' — of the manufacturing towns of England. Logan could scarcely conceive of a policy 'more barbarous or more dishonorable to our nation.' [7]

With dismay he saw his old friends among the Quids rallying behind the President's policy — and what was worse, making common cause with Leib and Duane, burying differences of principle to support the Embargo and elect James Madison President.[8] The Embargo was the main issue in the Pennsylvania elections of 1808. Logan's attitude on it was well known. Consequently, nothing more was heard in Republican circles of his succeeding McKean as Governor. He felt as thoroughly alienated now from the Pennsylvania Democracy as from the national leadership.

In the last months of Jefferson's administration, Logan wrote a letter to the President. The reply showed his old friend in utter perplexity and despair, clinging hopelessly to the Embargo in spite of its failure to bring results, half convinced that war was inevitable, yet loath to take any decisive step that would commit his successor. 'As the moment of my retirement approaches,' he wrote poignantly, 'I become more anxious for its arrival, and to begin at length to pass what yet remains to me of life and health in the bosom of my family and neighbors, and in communication with my friends, undisturbed by political concerns or passions.' [9]

Logan could sympathize. He too had longed for release from the burdens of office. But he knew from experience that retirement brought no surcease from political concerns, from anxiety over the country's fate. From New England he heard disturbing reports of growing hardship, of restlessness and disaffection among the workingmen, of Federalism reviving as the Embargo gradually paralyzed trade and produced stagnation in the seaports.[10] More than ever he was convinced that the decision to wage commercial warfare had been a disastrous mistake. More than ever he was persuaded that 'the best mode of securing peace to the United States, and maintaining our respect abroad was by conciliation and unanimity at home.' [11]

Month by month, his anxiety deepened. The Embargo was repealed but in its place was substituted a Non-intercourse Act specifically directed at France and Great Britain. With growing concern, Logan watched James Madison, the new President, persisting in Jefferson's risky policies, making empty but provocative threats of military action, drifting ineluctably toward war. For a moment, in the spring of 1809, it looked as though there might be a basis for peace. A new British Minister, David Erskine, agreed to a settlement of the *Chesapeake* affair and relaxation of the Orders-in-Council. But Erskine, it turned out, had exceeded his instructions; his government repudiated his agreement and called him home. The hopeless drift continued.

When Erskine's successor, Francis J. Jackson, arrived in Washington, matters took a sudden, sharp turn for the worse. Jackson was a short-tempered, truculent, overbearing blusterer. Everyone knew how he had browbeaten the Prince Royal of Denmark before the British Navy had bombarded the Danish capital. 'Copenhagen' Jackson, everyone called him. His insulting language, his blunt charges of American duplicity, precipitated a new crisis. The administration quickly handed the offensive Minister his passport. Congress denounced his behavior as 'highly indecorous and insolent,' charged him with 'outrageous and premeditated insults.' Bills were introduced to build new frigates, to reorganize the militia and put it on a war footing, to raise an army of volunteers.

In December 1810 Logan could restrain himself no longer. He went to Washington, talked with Madison, to Robert Smith, his Secretary of State, implored them not to give up hope of a peaceful settlement. Blandly, Madison turned him off with the assurance that he was always 'willing to renew negotiations.' Logan returned to Stenton unsatisfied. Madison and Smith, he told a New England friend, were 'so strongly influenced by mistaken popular feelings' that he saw little chance of their adopting a genuinely conciliatory attitude. The only hope, he had concluded, lay in the 'dignity, justice, and sound policy' of the British government.[12]

Dimly, tentatively, a project was taking form in Logan's mind, becoming more definite, more urgent, more insistent as the weeks passed. Once before, when peace had been in jeopardy, when only his own government's intransigence had blocked the road to agreement with a foreign power, he had acted on impulse, on a powerful 'concern,' and had gone abroad to try to prevent war. He believed that his intervention then had been useful to the country. Matters now stood in as desperate a state as ever they had in 1798. The new crisis demanded a new venture of faith.

He gave no intimation of his plan in the letter he sent to President Madison on 10 January 1810. But the tone of the letter betrayed the agitation of his spirit, and its contents indicated the trend of his mind. He recalled to the President the state of affairs that had existed just twelve years before, 'during the Federal administration of Mr. Adams.' Then, as Madison well knew, 'a desperate faction' had been 'anxious to involve our country in a war with France.' Providentially, their designs had been thwarted. Now once more the clamor of war hawks, of 'unprincipled demagogues,' was being heard in the land. But now it came from within the Republican party itself, from 'young men in Congress' — men from the South and West — who were casting greedy eyes on Canada and the Floridas.

'My heart mourns,' wrote Logan, 'on account of the political insanity of my country!' There was a desperate accent in his letter, the same urgent, imploring tone he had used in his passionate note to Jefferson in the Florida crisis. 'Make use of your power and your influence as Chief Magistrate of the United States,' he entreated, 'to arrest the progress of the destruction of your country.' He reminded the President of plain facts which he, as an experienced diplomat and politician, should know well enough: 'A war with Britain at once unites us as an ally to Bonaparte, and will dissolve the Union.' He ended with his old plea for a conciliatory spirit and a resumption of negotiations. Send commissioners 'of the most respectable character' to London, he implored Madison. Let them conclude a treaty of friendship and commerce at once. 'You have a precedent in the mission of Mr. Jay by General Washington and a still stronger one in the last mission to France of Mr. Adams, an act of magnanimity which obliterates many of his political blunders.' [13]

Madison wrote a long reply. He honored Logan's well-known desire for peace, he said. Still, 'manifestations of patience under injuries and indignities' could be carried too far; in the end they might leave the United States with 'no choice between absolute disgrace and resistance by force.' He justified his administration's course toward Great Britain and stated his conditions for a renewal of negotiations: full reparation for the *Chesapeake* outrage, unqualified repeal of the Orders-in-Council.[14]

Before he had posted his letter, Madison received a second note from Logan. The Doctor announced his intention to take ship within a week for England, offered to be the bearer of any dispatches the President might have for his Minister in London. Madison accepted the offer, entrusted to him dispatches for Minister Pinkney directing him to resume negotiations upon receiving a promise of satisfaction for the *Chesapeake* attack.[15] As for Logan's precise purpose in going abroad, the President was in the dark. But he knew of the Doctor's 'anxiety . . . for the preservation of peace with England'; he was aware of his 'known benevolence and zeal on the subject.' He could only suppose, he wrote to Pinkney, 'that his views relate, in some form or other, to a mitigation of the hostile tendencies which distress him.' [16]

Obviously, Logan was proposing to violate a Federal statute. No one should know better than he that it was a misdemeanor for a private citizen without authorization to 'carry on any verbal or written correspondence or intercourse' with a foreign government 'in relation to any disputes or controversies with the United States.' But Madison, having no real policy, not knowing which way to turn, could afford to be indulgent. There was no danger that Logan would be prosecuted under the act that, in popular parlance, bore his name.

His departure was delayed for a month. In the interim he went to Washington again and visited Jackson, the disgraced but impenitent British Minister, hoping for introductions to George Canning, the former Foreign Minister, and to Marquis Wellesley, who had just replaced him. 'Copenhagen' Jackson lived up to his reputation. Forewarned by the British Consul in Philadelphia that the Doctor was about to take up 'his old trade of diplomatic adventuring,' he treated Logan as a 'political quack' and curtly refused to give him any letters. He did, however, tell Logan — and Logan promptly relayed the word to the President — that, deeply as he resented the demand for his recall, he did not believe it would cause a complete diplomatic rupture.[17]

A few days after this brusque and inauspicious interview, Dr. Logan sailed from New York in a British packet.[18] His objects, in so far as they were specific, were to take the pulse of popular opinion in England, and, if possible, to persuade British leaders to revoke the obnoxious Orders-in-Council before it was too late.

He was in London by the end of March. He took lodgings in St. James's Place in the West End, near the government offices. He promptly called at the American Legation, delivered the pouch of dispatches to Minister Pinkney, and encouraged him to seek a quick resumption of negotiations. Pinkney was polite, treated him with respect, entertained him at dinner. He grew noticeably cooler, however, when he saw how readily Logan was accepted and listened to by the 'first people in rank and character' in London, people whom Pinkney, the duly accredited Minister, could not always see.

Logan's *entrée* to the 'first people in rank and character' came through Robert Barclay, nephew of the man who had been his adviser and friend when he had been a young medical student, thirty-five years before. A good Quaker, Barclay was naturally eager to help Logan spread his 'pacific creed of peace.' Having lived in America, he was anxious to see friendly relations restored. And being a wealthy and prominent businessman — the owner of a great brewery — he was able to give Logan introductions to many men in high places.[19]

So introduced, Logan lost little time in waiting upon Marquis

Wellesley, Foreign Minister in the Cabinet of Spencer Perceval. Wellesley had been in office only a few months. The oldest brother of Viscount Wellington, commander of the British Army in Spain, he himself had just returned from India and a distinguished viceregal career. He still bore himself with more than a trace of the pomp and formality appropriate for dealing with sultans and rajahs. He was genuinely anxious for peace with the United States, however, and annoyed that he could not carry Perceval and the Cabinet with him.

Logan opened the conversation. Since landing in England, he said, he had heard many people insinuate that President Madison was attached to the French cause, a willing abettor of Bonaparte. This was a mischievous rumor — and perfectly false. The Doctor had known Madison for fifteen years; he could assure Wellesley that the charge was untrue. He then voiced his own deep concern that in view of Napoleon's tremendous power, 'his activity and future prospects of domination,' the two English-speaking nations must forget their jealousies, must cease their 'petty acts of irritation,' and must substitute for them a spirit of 'confidence, justice, and forbearance.' [20]

Wellesley was cordial, sympathetic, friendly. He revealed to Logan an astonishing fact — that the French had boldly proposed to His Majesty's Government not long before that the two nations, though locked in deadly struggle in Europe, should jointly fall upon the United States and divide it between them.[21] More than ever Logan was convinced that the real enemy, the real menace to his country, was not England but Napoleon's France.

A few days later, Logan went to the War Office and had an interview with Lord Liverpool. But he did not confine himself to members of the Government. He sought out as many public figures as he could, especially those he knew to be opposed to the Orders-in-Council. He saw the young Marquis of Lansdowne, a disciple of Charles James Fox and a friend of America. He saw Lord Sidmouth, the former Prime Minister; Sidmouth was a Tory, but he was growing weary of commercial warfare. He saw Henry Brougham, the brilliant young barrister who had pleaded eloquently for the repeal of the Orders at the bar of the House of Commons. At the home of Edward Thornton, a diplomat whom he had known in Washington, he met and talked with Members of Parliament.[22]

Persistently, indefatigably, he sought out prominent men — philanthropists, scientists, religious leaders, literary men — and urged them to exert all their influence on popular opinion, on Parliament, and the Government, for peace. He breakfasted with William Wilberforce, dined with Thomas Clarkson. With these men he stood on common ground, for he had labored as long and vigorously as they for the abolition of the slave trade. He tried vainly to arrange an interview with Sir Samuel Romilly, the law reformer. Romilly was too busy to see him, but Logan wrote out an account of the 'Pennsylvania system' of prison administration for him — the system, incidentally, whose beginnings Logan himself had fought so bitterly twenty-five years before. He saw all the leading Quakers, attended the sessions of London Yearly Meeting, and wrote dutifully to Debby that he had gone to meeting with Friends at Gracechurch Street and Bishopsgate.

He went to Soho Square, to a *conversazione* at the home of Sir Joseph Banks, President of the Royal Society; there he met 'a large company of literary characters.' He went to Slough, near Windsor, to visit William Herschel, the famous astronomer. The kindly old man took him into his garden, proudly showed him the great forty-foot telescope with which, at seventy-two, he was still diligently mapping the heavens. Granville Penn, the grandson of Pennsylvania's founder, entertained him at Stoke Poges, where Thomas Gray had written his famous elegy.

He went to the Board of Agriculture to hear Arthur Young lecture on manures. With another great farmer, Sir John Sinclair, the President of the Board, he commenced a friendship that would last to the end of his life. It began with Sinclair's inquiring about the progress of steam navigation in the United States. Logan told him what he knew of the pioneer experiments of John Fitch and James Rumsey, of the more successful steamboat, 'propelled by two water wheels,' which his friend Robert Fulton had recently sent creaking and fuming up the Hudson River. Such a boat, he added, had recently been navigated on the Delaware, not far from his own farm.[23]

Everywhere he went, Logan inquired of people their views on America, their attitude toward the Orders-in-Council and the possibility of war. Everywhere, he wrote President Madison, he found 'a general anxiety . . . to preserve peace with the United States.' [24] The country people — always wiser than their governments, he thought — were especially eager for peace. Logan spent several weeks in the rural districts talking with farmers, great and small, about Bedford hogs, Merino sheep, the raising of flax, the rotation of crops — and Britain's transatlantic relations. The prosperous state of English agriculture sent him into 'raptures,' and it was heartening to find the country people everywhere friendly to America.

In June he attended the annual meeting of the Agricultural Society of Surrey. 'Above eighty gentlemen of the first characters in the county were present at dinner,' he reported with evident satisfaction to Madison. The two Members of Parliament for the county presided, and the toast of the evening was: 'Dr. Logan, and may harmony be restored between Great Britain and the United States equally honorable and beneficial to both.' A few days later, he was at Woburn for the Duke of Bedford's annual sheep-shearing. 'Many of the first nobility and gentry in the kingdom' were there, and 'a universal desire was expressed to preserve peace with the United States.' [25]

The climactic experience, however, was the great sheep-shearing at Holkham, Thomas William Coke's magnificent estate in Norfolk. Coke was Britain's greatest farmer, a man of boundless benevolence and open-handed hospitality, passionately devoted to country life and the progress of agriculture. He had created at Holkham an immense, inspiring model farm, had created it by a miracle — the miracle of scientific farming — from a sandy waste where once, as he liked to tell his guests, there had been only one blade of grass, and two rabbits fighting over that.

Every year for a third of a century, he had held a great festival at sheep-shearing time, early in July. Hundreds of people gathered at Holkham — members of the nobility, distinguished foreigners, diplomats, scientists, and the humble tenants and farmers of Norfolk. For three crowded days Coke's guests inspected prize cattle, rams, and boars, watched the sheep-shearing in the barn, cheered the contestants in the plowing matches, drove through vast fields of grain, witnessed the awarding of prizes to shepherds, plowmen, and farmers, pausing only to consume enormous quantities of food and drink at Coke's table. No country fair that any American had ever seen could match the sheep-shearing at Holkham for excitement, for crowds of people, for conviviality, for the demonstration of sound farming methods.

For years Logan had admired the 'Norfolk system' of agriculture from afar. It was the system — with modifications to suit American conditions — which he practiced at Stenton. Now at last he could study it at its fountainhead; he could actually discuss the relative virtues of marl and gypsum, of horses and oxen, of turnips and mangel wurzel with the great farmers of England, with Sir John Sinclair, the Duke of Bedford, the great Coke himself. It was exceedingly pleasant to discover that these men accepted him as a peer, recognized him as a scientific farmer in his own right, were eager to question him on his own farming practices. But it was even more gratifying to find that he was welcomed as a peacemaker, a minister of reconciliation between England and the United States. The farmer's calling transcended national frontiers; properly understood, it made nonsense of national rivalries.

The festivities at Holkham culminated on the evening of the third day, after the last sheep had been sheared and the last prize awarded. Late in the afternoon, all the guests — more than three hundred of them — gathered in the lofty Statue Gallery and in adjoining rooms for seven hours of feasting, toasts, and speechmaking. The dinner was a baronial repast. Finally, the platters were removed, the wineglasses refilled, and Coke arose, tall, genial, expansive, his bald head gleaming in the light of hundreds of candles. He bade his guests welcome to Holkham, then proposed the first toast, his favorite motto — 'Live and let live!' To Logan, who knew his host's aversion to war, his affection for America, the toast seemed to have a special meaning. Other traditional toasts followed — 'A fine fleece and a fat carcass!' 'The plough, and a good use of it!' Then a tribute to Coke's efforts to enclose all waste lands — a toast that the farmers always rendered hilariously as 'The enclosing of all *waists!*'

There was a standing rule at Holkham that political topics were never mentioned at a sheep-shearing. On this occasion, however, Coke broke his own rule, and proposed 'Doctor Logan and prosperity to America!' Three hundred and twenty guests lifted their glasses, applauded the Doctor, and echoed the toast. Logan, almost overwhelmed, got to his feet and responded by assuring the company that the prevailing sentiment among all classes in the United States was favorable to peace.[26]

Logan stayed in England till mid-September, hoping vainly for a conversation with Spencer Perceval, the Prime Minister. Finally, despairing of an interview, he wrote him a letter. Perceval, he knew, was a stubborn man, not overly friendly to the United States, grimly determined that the commercial system should stand. Logan expressed himself plainly to this blunt man, as plainly as he was accustomed to address Presidents of the United States. 'The bickering and semi state of warfare, which have existed for several years between our nations,' he wrote, 'have been viewed with deep affliction by the best men in both countries.' Since his arrival in England, he had talked with many 'eminent characters,' with 'respectable men of every situation in life.' Not one person had he met who did not wish a reconciliation with the United States. His own people, he was certain, felt the same way. As a gesture of good will, Congress had just passed a bill sponsored by his friend Nathaniel Macon, revoking the Non-intercourse Act. 'Let Great Britain with the same laudable intent,' he exhorted Perceval, 'remove her Orders-in-Council. Let her declare herself the advocate of neutral rights such as she claimed for herself and conceded to others before she adopted the execrable commercial warfare of the tyrant of Europe.'

Logan begged the Prime Minister to reflect on the consequences of his policy. 'My dear sir, for heaven's sake, pause, and from the elevated and honorable situation in which your sovereign has placed you, contemplate agonizing nations at the feet of a military despot; and say if it is not necessary that Great Britain and the United States at this momentous crisis of the world should lay aside unfounded jealousies and mutual bickerings not only to protect their own existence as independent nations, but to preserve the civil and political liberties of mankind.'

Logan closed his letter with the same words he had often used to Thomas Jefferson and James Madison, words adapted from George Washington's first Inaugural Address: 'I may appeal to your own superior information and understanding if you are acquainted with any truth more thoroughly established than that there exists in the affairs of nations an indissoluble union between the generous maxims of an honest and magnanimous policy and the solid rewards of public prosperity and happiness.' [27]

But Perceval declined to see him, did not even acknowledge his letter. Sorrowfully, Logan embarked for home on the *Golconda*,[28] convinced, as he wrote to Coke just before sailing, that 'the most enlightened and best men' in England, indeed 'the nation in general,' were sincerely anxious for peace. He still believed that the difference between the two countries could be reconciled through negotiation by 'two or three honorable and honest men.' [29] But privately he was not hopeful. 'I am sorry to observe,' he wrote on a scrap of paper which he showed to no one, 'how few, even among public characters in England I find impressed with a due sense of the importance of a sincere reconciliation with the United States. Whilst they abound in professions of friendship, their contracted souls are incapable of looking into futurity.' [30]

If Logan had found 'contracted souls' in power in England, he found equally 'contracted and prejudiced minds' in Washington.[31] The very day he landed in New York, early in November, President Madison, hoodwinked by Napoleon into believing the Berlin and Milan Decrees revoked, revived non-intercourse with England, under the terms of Macon's Act. As returns from the Congressional elections came in, later in the month, it was apparent that a new political generation had arrived — a noisy, aggressive troop of Southerners and Westerners, flaunting grandiose schemes of expansion, infatuated with the old dream of seizing the Floridas from Spain, dazzled with a new vision of conquering Canada from the British. These men, it was clear, would not hesitate to plunge their country into war to achieve their ends.

John Randolph deprecated this frenzy as much as Logan did. He wrote to the Doctor early in December to ask if he did not find the state of the public mind improved since he had left the country, nine months earlier, 'the alarming symptoms of febrile excitement and irregular action happily assuaged.' [32] Logan could not agree. On the contrary, he found the symptoms exacerbated, the disease further advanced, the war fever running higher than ever. In this state of things, he told his old friend Judge Peters, he had little hope that any good would come of his report to the President. For James Madison himself, he feared, was in the grip of the fever, his administration was dominated by the 'war hawks' from the West and South. [33]

Newspaper writers, caught up in the prevalent hysteria, promptly seized on Logan's English trip, accused him of lacking patriotism, of harboring pro-British sympathies. Such charges did not disturb him. He had been through all this a dozen years before — except that then he had been taxed with excessive zeal for France. He gave a dignified statement to the press, then paid no more attention to his critics. [34] In his own heart he knew that he was not for Britain or for France; he was for peace.

In spite of the discouraging face of things, peace was still possible — and while peace was possible, Logan could not be idle. From time to time, as the months went by, he made flying trips to Washington. Mildly, Deborah remonstrated with him. Why could he not relax, seek an inner peace, leave public affairs to those whose duty it was to manage them? The Doctor's reply was always: 'if it was a common time,' he would. But it was not a common time. The emergency was great; the public good was at stake. It was with him a matter of conscience, he said, to do what he could to save his country from the bottomless abyss of war. [35]

Momentarily, in the spring of 1811, his hopes were raised by James Monroe's appointment as Secretary of State. Logan had not always approved of Monroe's diplomacy, but at least he had shown in 1806 that it was possible to negotiate a reasonable settlement with England. Logan immediately wrote to the new Secretary, voicing his conviction that the President was too attentive to the advocates for war in his cabinet, and expressing again the hope that commissioners would be sent to London to renew negotiations.[36] But Monroe made no move.

Again in July, Logan's hopes were revived temporarily. A new British Minister arrived in Washington to succeed the churlish Jackson. It was Augustus John Foster, an affable young man whom Logan had known earlier as Secretary of the British Legation. Foster brought instructions to settle the long-festering *Chesapeake* affair. Logan called upon him at the Legation to express once more his faith in the possibility of agreement.[37]

But it was too late. Events had overtaken the young Minister. While he was still on the high seas, an American ship, the *President,* had fired on the British corvette *Little Belt.* Now American guns had killed and wounded British seamen, thirty-two of them, a heavier toll than the *Leopard* had levied on the *Chesapeake.* Instead of giving redress for an old outrage, Foster found himself obliged to demand it for a new one. In November, there was a new occasion for excitement. Governor William Henry Harrison fought a battle against the Indians at Tippecanoe in Indiana Territory. The guns that the Indians left behind in their retreat, were made — so the frontiersmen firmly believed — in England.

The Congress which assembled in that month was in the hands of the 'war hawks' — men, as Logan observed to Monroe, who met 'not calmly to discuss the most important national subjects . . . but merely to act according to what they call the public opinion of the district they represent.' The conquest of Canada was dancing like a mirage before the eyes of the Westerners. The appetite of the South, long whetted for Florida, was not to be restrained. The clamor for war, blowing like a gale from these two quarters, dismayed Logan, terrified him, drove him to an avowal that came strangely from one who had always preached the doctrine of a government responsive to the popular will: 'A wise and vigorous administration,' he told Monroe, 'does not follow but leads public opinion; and it almost always happens that the governed find in the end that the opinion of the administration is far better than the innumerable clashing opinions which demagogues call the general opinion.' For an example of wise administration he went back to 1793, when Washington had accepted John Jay's unpalatable treaty with England.[38] Monroe may have savored the irony of this illustration, coming from a man who had once shared his own feelings about Jay's treaty. But it is unlikely — for Monroe had gone over to the war party, had become indeed its leader.

In the spring of 1812 new rumors were afloat: there was to be a last-minute effort to avert war, commissioners would be sent to London to demand repeal of the Orders-in-Council, Logan had been called to Washington by the administration for consultations.[39] There was no truth in the rumors. Doctor Logan no longer had the President's ear. Doggedly, desperately, but vainly, he addressed one more plea to him, conjuring him as a friend not to permit an invasion of Canada — 'a subject every rational citizen regards with horror' — urging him to take advantage of the timely accession of George IV, 'a decided Whig,' who would be surrounded by 'friends of the United States.' [40]

Madison showed no sign of listening. The nation was clearly drifting closer and closer to the brink of war. Logan busied himself driving about Philadelphia County among his old constituents, securing signatures to petitions 'deprecating the horrors of war and praying the united efforts of Congress and the President . . . for the continuation of the blessings of peace.' These petitions he sent to Andrew Gregg, his successor in the Senate.[41] Meanwhile, he wrote to his other friends in Congress, imploring them to resist the current that was sweeping the country into hostilities.[42]

Meanwhile, an interesting sequence of events was taking place in England. In the House of Lords the Marquis of Lansdowne moved for a committee to consider repealing the Orders-in-Council. In the Commons, Henry Brougham repeated the motion and argued forcefully for revoking the Orders. These men had powerful supporters — Lord Liverpool, William Wilberforce, Marquis Wellesley, who had finally left the Cabinet in disgust,

Lord Sidmouth, who had just joined the Government, though without commitment on the commercial system. On 11 May, Spencer Perceval was shot by a madman as he entered the House of Commons. Lord Liverpool presently formed a Government. On 16 June Brougham moved the outright repeal of the Orders. At the conclusion of his speech, the Government announced its intention to suspend them promptly. One week later, they were repealed.[43]

Logan, of course, knew nothing of what these men — to whom he had talked face to face only two years before — were doing, nor did Congress or the President. On 18 June — two days after the announcement that the Orders would be suspended, but several weeks before the news could reach America — Congress declared war. George Logan's long struggle for peace had ended — in failure.

Even now, however, he did not give up. He looked hopefully, wistfully toward northern and eastern Europe, remembering the armed neutrality of Revolutionary days, counting on the benevolence of Russia and the Scandinavian kingdoms. He urged the peacemaker's role upon Count Daschkoff, the Russian Minister, and was gratified, some months later, when Daschkoff proffered the good offices of his sovereign, Alexander I, as mediator. But his hopes crashed quickly to earth when he learned that the British refused to accept Russian mediation.[44]

Still, he importuned President Madison to initiate direct negotiations.[45] When his hopes from that quarter died, he appealed from the White House to Monticello. He reminded Jefferson of the humane measures upon which they had once co-operated. He dwelt on the fatal tendency of war to destroy the moral character of a people, to break down 'the fortress of republicanism.' He referred modestly to his own efforts in 1798 and again in 1810 to prevent war. Finally, he begged Jefferson to use his influence with his successor to persuade him to throw off the influence of his bellicose advisers and to return to the true republican path of peace.[46]

Jefferson's reply was friendly but scarcely reassuring. Graciously he acknowledged that Logan's efforts in 1798 'did much towards preventing declared war with France.' But the case was different now. The nation was actually at war. He expressed unreserved support of the administration's policies. If Dr. Logan could suggest any honorable terms for accommodation, terms that had not already been offered and rejected, he would gladly communicate them to the 'proper functionaries' in Washington. Speaking for himself, however, Jefferson saw no hope of peace until the British abandoned impressment, granted heavy indemnities, and established 'such a western frontier [for] Canada as may put it out of their power hereafter to employ the tomahawk and scalping knife of the Indians on our women and children; or what would be nearly equivalent, the exclusive right to the lakes.' [47]

Weary, discouraged, disillusioned, Logan wrote back to Monticello. He was still convinced that 'the weight of public opinion' in England was friendly to the United States, that by a 'candid and magnanimous conduct' his government could negotiate a peace that would be 'honorable and beneficial to all parties.' But he no longer hoped. He had labored long and strenuously for peace, had tried desperately to curb his country's 'rashness,' to point out its 'errors and follies,' to prevent this 'unnecessary,' this 'miserable war.' [48]

Rumors persistently continued to circulate that Logan was about to embark for England on a pacific mission. There was no basis for these reports. Logan knew there was nothing more he could do.[49]

Near the end of 1814 Deborah Logan set down in her diary the latest news from the South. It was Christmas Day, but Christmas was not celebrated in Quaker households. There was, in any event, little reason for celebration. The United States was invaded. British troops were marching on Washington. The news grew steadily more alarming. The Capitol, the President's House, the Treasury, the War Department, the Navy Yard — all had been put to the torch. 'The whole of that part of the country,' she wrote, 'is in the utmost consternation.' Philadelphia itself was 'in great agitation, the militia organizing and troops marching to their rendezvouses.' Everywhere, it was reported, the President was 'spoken of without respect . . . as the author of these needless calamities.' [50]

Sick at heart, George Logan watched while the cruel logic of war worked itself out as he had foretold. The capital city in ruins, republican government in disgrace, a foreign army on American soil, his country virtually allied with the 'tyrant of Europe' — it was almost too bitter to be borne.

*

---

xv. DAYS of PEACE

THE STENTON HOUSEHOLD heard the news of peace on 12 February 1815. An express from New York dashed down the Old York Road, carrying word to Philadelphia of a treaty signed at Ghent on the day before Christmas. The Logans received the tidings with relief, thankfulness, and quiet jubilation. Debby was 'teased' by Mary and Amy, the two maids, to be allowed to go into Philadelphia to see the illuminations on the night of the 15th. Her Quaker conscience disapproved of such celebrations, but she could not resist the girls' pleadings, and finally she sent them off to the city in the gig. They were back by nine o'clock, the dazzling lights still sparkling before their eyes. Awestruck, they described the spectacle — the high shot-tower on Arch Street crowned with a hundred and sixty lamps; the bridges like flaming arches thrown across the Schuylkill; Peale's Museum, the newspaper offices, the fine houses along Chestnut Street blazing with myriads of candles; the great transparency at Eighth and Market, showing an Arcadian shepherdess and a flock of Merino sheep; another, even more beautiful, at Eighth and Sansom, representing Peace, with the motto 'Peace is the Nurse of the Arts.' [1]

Two weeks later, Dr. Logan held his celebration. He took dinner with a party of gentlemen at Miers Fisher's country estate of Ury in the little village of Fox Chase, northeast of Stenton. Fisher was an old friend. As boys, he and Logan had been schoolmates in Robert Proud's classroom at Fourth and Chestnut Streets. After a successful career at the bar, Fisher had retired to Ury, where he lived comfortably in the midst of his books, his fruit trees, his lovely formal gardens. He and Logan had wagered a dinner on the signing of the treaty, Deborah noted in her diary with a faint trace of Quaker disapproval, 'and Dr. Logan won it by a day.' [2]

The treaty was quickly ratified by the Senate. As Logan read its terms, one fact stood out with painful clarity: it contained no word on impressment, no word on the rights of neutrals, nothing on the very issues over which, ostensibly, the war had been fought. Sadly he reflected on the fulfilment of his prophecy, that war had indeed been as futile as it had been unnecessary. But could not something be done even now, through negotiation, to settle these problems, to prevent future irritations that might lead to further wars?

Logan took up his pen, wrote to James Monroe. He congratulated the Secretary on the return of peace, expressed a fervent hope that somehow the rights of seamen would be adjusted satisfactorily. He was writing forthwith, he said, to his friends in England — to Lord Sidmouth, to Wilberforce, to Sir John Sinclair. He would urge them to use their influence for justice and magnanimity, for these were still the only bases of lasting peace.

Another concern weighed heavily on his mind. He was worried, he told Monroe, about a new spirit he saw rising in the country, nurtured at the very heart of the Republican government in Washington. It was not really new. He and Monroe had seen it, had fought it before. It was nothing more, nothing less than a revival of the old grasping, corrupting, mercenary spirit of Federalism, newly clothed in Republican garments, but speaking the old language of tariffs, subsidies, excises, banks, and a national debt. He had seen the effects of that spirit, rampant and unchecked, in England. He had seen 'the vice, wretchedness and dirt in the manufacturing towns,' had compared them with 'the neat habitations, the domestic comforts, the morality of the laborers in the agricultural districts.' What he had seen had convinced him all over again 'how little the most prosperous manufactures contribute to individual comfort or national prosperity.'

Logan and Monroe had once united in opposition to this baneful spirit. In 1800 they and their party had conquered it, laid it to rest, once and for all — or so they had thought. But now unmistakably it was rising again, rising out of the policies of their own party — the mistaken policies of embargo and war. Logan saw it clearly, close at hand, could not avoid seeing it. For Philadelphia was expanding, growing like a cancer, becoming an ugly, tumescent mart of trade, an enormous factory, its smoking mills and filthy, crowded workingmen's hovels almost within sight of Stenton's gates. If this malignancy were not arrested, it would be the end of the old Pennsylvania and the old America he loved.

Peace and prosperity, Logan was convinced, turned on the same peg. They both required that the Republican party return to its pristine faith, cease its whoring after the strange gods of privilege and pelf, and become once more the party of the people, the plain people, the honest yeomanry of the uncorrupted countryside. Almost certainly James Monroe would be the next President of the United States. Before his old friend, Logan laid his fervent hope that 'the great agricultural and permanent interest of both nations' — of England and America — 'will not be sacrificed to the sordid views of manufacturers and merchants.' [3]

Peace, it turned out, was not yet secure. It was only a few days before Deborah was reading in the *Pennsylvania Gazette* the most alarming news: Napoleon had escaped from Elba; he had landed at Fréjus, and was marching toward Paris. 'Now farewell repose to Europe,' she sighed. Dr. Logan returned to Stenton the next day from a trip to Chester. He had heard the same report — direct from Victor Du Pont's enterprising brother, Irenée, who operated a powder mill on Brandywine Creek. 'If it proves true,' Du Pont had said, 'my country is ruined.' [4] By midsummer, however, word of Waterloo arrived. At last Logan could breathe easily, knowing that peace had finally come to the world after nearly a quarter of a century of war.

With the coming of peace old friendships could be restored — friendships that had foundered at one point or another over the long years when the United States had been picking its way through treacherous shoals of international politics, now veering to England's side, now to France's. Logan had always steered by a fixed star — his desire for peace. Now peace had come. There was no longer any reason to harbor distrust of Thomas Jefferson or John Randolph or even Timothy Pickering. Logan was anxious to forget old differences, to end his life at peace with all men.

It was with Pickering, the man who had repulsed him so curtly at Trenton in 1798, on his return from France, that he first became reconciled. The war itself provided the occasion. Both men opposed it, though for different reasons — Pickering because he was still an 'Angloman' at heart, still hostile to Republicans and all their works, Logan because the war seemed unnecessary, futile, and wicked. Judge Peters brought them together — witty, fun-loving Judge Peters, who had known them both since the early days of the Philadelphia Agricultural Society. He persuaded Pickering to forget the Trenton affair; Logan, he said, was 'not now a Frenchman,' and he was a keen and entertaining man.[5]

Pickering often visited Stenton during the war and after. Wherever he was — in Congress at Washington, on his Massachusetts farm — he kept up a running correspondence with Logan. The two men touched on a variety of topics — the errors of the Madison administration, the madness of the land-hungry, bloodthirsty Congressmen from the West and South, the wisdom of the Hartford Convention, the wickedness of the conscription law. But invariably they came back to the character of Thomas Jefferson. Pickering was an unrepentant idolater of Alexander Hamilton. His detestation for Jefferson grew more rancorous, more malignant, with the passing years. No crime was too black, no knavery too foul, to lay at his door. Since Logan had once been close to Jefferson, Pickering besieged him with requests for evidence to build up his case.[6]

Disillusioned by the war, disappointed by Jefferson's unqualified support of it, Logan at first felt some sympathy with Pickering's animus. Half-heartedly he complied with his friend's requests, related some of his less happy memories of Jefferson as President. But soon Pickering's monomania was too obvious. Logan began to protest; Jefferson, he stoutly insisted, had never been as actively anti-British, as hopelessly subservient to Napoleon, as Pickering wanted to believe. Casting about for a way to refute this charge publicly, he decided to give to the newspapers an excerpt from a letter he had recently had from Jefferson — an excerpt containing this categorical statement: 'No man on earth has a stronger detestation than myself of the unprincipled tyrant who is deluging the continent of Europe with blood.' The publication of this excerpt without Jefferson's knowledge was doubly unfortunate: it merely confirmed Pickering in his rooted conviction that the ex-President was an incurable hypocrite, and it displeased Jefferson himself. Not, he later told Logan, that he was unwilling to stand by his harsh words on Napoleon; they spoke his feelings exactly. But their publication out of context, he complained, had 'called for more explanations' than any previous transaction in his life. Some of his friends, to his embarrassment, had drawn the unwarranted inference that he approved unreservedly of England's course.[7]

Temporary vexations, however, could not stand permanently between two men such as Jefferson and Logan, who had once been cordial friends and who still in their hearts cherished the same dream for their country. With the ending of the war, they buried most of their differences over foreign policy, and turned to matters on which they had a common mind. Letters began passing regularly back and forth between Stenton and Monticello, letters which reflected Jefferson's luminous wisdom on one side and Logan's still-eager questing spirit on the other.

They discussed Alexander I of Russia, the baffling ruler whose figure loomed large in Europe behind the pious façade of the Holy Alliance. To Logan, he was a man of sincere good will who could and doubtless would wield immense power for peace in Europe. His offer to mediate between the United States and Britain during the war had been proof of that. Logan now saw nothing but beneficent influences radiating from the land of the Tsars. 'Russia,' he wrote, 'is yet in embryo. The astonishing success which some of her sovereigns have had in civilizing her immense population gives reason to expect that under the paternal care of Alexander, she will become the arbiter of Europe.' The Tsar's old tutor, Laharpe, reported that Alexander was a republican at heart. There was every reason to believe that he was well disposed toward the United States. Thomas Clarkson, the abolition-ist, had had an interview with him at Paris; the Tsar had shown keen interest in the religious principles of the Society of Friends, its humanitarian objection to the slave trade. All these hopeful bits of evidence Logan forwarded to Monticello.

Jefferson was willing to grant that the Tsar had been a force for good in Europe. Only Alexander's magnanimity, he believed, had saved France from being partitioned in 1815. But Jefferson was a little more cautious, a little more skeptical and worldly-wise than Logan. He preferred to reserve final judgment until he knew Alexander's part in the division of spoils behind closed doors at the Congress of Vienna. Jefferson was less disposed than Logan to believe that any permanent good could arise from the broils of Europe. 'Let us turn with abhorrence from their sceptered *scélérats,'* he wrote with an emphasis born of bitter experience, 'and, disregarding our own petty differences of opinion about men and measures, let us cling in mass to our country and to one an-other, and bid defiance, as we can if united, to the plundering combinations of the old world.' [8]

Differ as these old friends still might, in friendly fashion, over America's relation to the world, there was one topic on which per-fect harmony subsisted between them. Their friendship, after all, had commenced over a plow, and now that the storms of politics had subsided and they were both back on their farms, they could once more indulge happily in the interchange of information on country matters. If Logan received from Sir John Sinclair a sample of dried flax or an account of the 'astonishing production of mangel wurzel' on an English farm, he promptly relayed it to Jefferson. Back from Monticello would come a report on the con-tinuing vogue for Merino sheep or some remarks on the growing attention to cotton culture in Virginia.[9] The agrarian faith still burned strong; the vision of America as an agricultural Eden, peopled by a happy, independent, prosperous yeomanry, was scarcely dimmed.

When they turned to religion, they still spoke a common lan-guage. Logan learned one day from a mutual friend — the elderly Charles Thomson, once Secretary of the Continental Congress —

that Jefferson had compiled a little book which he called 'The Philosophy of Jesus,' a collection of moral aphorisms drawn from the New Testament. Why, he asked, did Jefferson not publish it? 'It will remove slanders respecting your unbelief in the Christian religion, and will promote virtue and morality in the rising generation.' He added his own personal confession of faith: 'The more I read of history, the more I contemplate the character of man, the more I am convinced of the necessity of introducing these spiritual doctrines of Christ into government.'

Heartily Jefferson endorsed Logan's views on the moral obligations of government. Nevertheless, he said, he would not publish anything on religion, would not be drawn into any theological controversy. Christianity was hopelessly split into warring sects. 'Into which of the chambers of this Bedlam,' he asked, 'would a man wish to thrust himself?' If one accepted and practiced the sublime ethics of Jesus, surely that was enough. Logan could only agree. He had it much at heart in these days, Deborah later recalled, that men should lay aside sectarian prejudices, forget the interests of particular religious societies, and 'unite to promote the great designs of Christianity.' [10]

Surprisingly enough, it was even possible in these days to discuss 'the great designs of Christianity' with John Randolph of Roanoke. At Mrs. Wilson's dinner table in Washington, Logan had often been shocked by Randolph's blasphemies. The wayward Virginian had never professed to believe in the Christian religion — or pretended to practice the Christian virtues of forgiveness and love. Logan, to be sure, had never felt the sting of Randolph's corrosive scorn as had Jefferson, but he had often been provoked by his vindictive, irresponsible, irrational behavior. In the affair of West Florida, though both men had differed with Jefferson, they had diverged in opposite directions, and their friendship had been temporarily clouded.

It seemed a new, a changed Randolph who came to Stenton for a visit early in 1815 — 'very tall and thin in his person, looking characteristically like a Virginian,' Debby noted, but unexpectedly 'mild and sweet in his demeanor.' Temporarily out of Congress, he spoke of the men in power in Washington, not bitterly, Debby thought, but with 'temperate disdain, as if they were below the standard of hatred.' There was little rancor in his conversation. Even the shrillness had gone from his voice. In rich, flutelike tones, he spoke sadly, elegiacally, of his own Virginia — 'retrograde in all improvements,' the older parts declining into wasteland, the fine brick mansions abandoned and decaying. The old 'habits of regularity productive of civilization and refinement in society' were gone; but this was nothing new, he said mournfully — the decline had commenced as far back as the latter days of George II.

It was wonderful, this change that had come over John Randolph. He told Debby he had lately read Robert Barclay's *Apology for the True Christian Divinity,* the great work of Quaker theology. To her delight he pronounced it infinitely superior to Calvin's *Institutes,* which he considered a blasphemy against the goodness and moral government of God. Later, Debby heard an edifying story about Randolph from Jesse Kersey, a Quaker minister of Chester County. Kersey had paid him a visit, had heard from his own lips how he had 'received the divine illumination of Christianity,' and had been converted from Deism and infidelity. At parting, Randolph had embraced the simple Quaker preacher. All this was heart-warming and interesting. Still, in spite of Randolph's changed manner, Logan detected no signs of forgiveness or Christian love toward Thomas Jefferson.[11]

Many other visitors came and went. In summer they sat under the lofty trees that shaded the lawns, or strolled along Wingohocking Creek to the millpond; in winter they gathered before the tiled fireplace in the parlor or among the books in the great library upstairs. Foreign diplomats often drove out to visit the Doctor and his lady — François Daniel Changuion, the Dutch Minister, Daschkoff, the Russian Minister, the aristocratic Don Luis de Onís, the Spanish envoy. One day Robert Walsh, a young Philadelphia journalist, brought the Abbé Correa de Serra, Minister from Portugal, to Stenton. The Abbé was a noted savant as well as an accomplished diplomatist, and his conversation was rich and curious.

Stenton's gates were wide and hospitable, and sometimes they admitted some surprising visitors. Who should appear, one day, but Joseph Bonaparte, the elder brother of Napoleon. He looked exactly like the pictures of the exiled Emperor, even to the way he dressed his hair. The former King of Spain, now known as the Comte de Survilliers, had bought an estate at Point Breeze, near Bordentown, New Jersey, and was planning to settle down there for the rest of his life. As a country gentleman, Logan could give him useful advice. On political topics there was little they could say to each other.

It was almost as difficult to carry on conversation with General James Wilkinson, another visitor who came now and then to Stenton. A short, stout, pompous man, who looked dashing on horseback but a trifle ridiculous on foot, Wilkinson was living near by, writing his memoirs. He was full of bitterness and self-justification. He accused James Madison of every crime, while he sought to gloss over or explain away his own incredible intrigues with the Spanish, his part in the inglorious conspiracy of Aaron Burr. But the Doctor and his wife were gracious; they listened politely, sometimes demurred gently, but always invited the visitor back.[12]

As in Logan's youth, traveling Quaker ministers — simple, plain-spoken, reverend men such as Nathan Hunt of North Carolina or Jesse Kersey of near-by Chester County — often stopped at the great house. The Doctor welcomed them warmly. If Debby arranged 'a little sitting' in the parlor, he joined the circle in silent worship, listened attentively to the visitors' religious messages, talked earnestly with them afterward about slavery, peace, the other 'great designs of Christianity.' He did not ask to be re-admitted to the Society of Friends, but he usually went with Debby to midweek or First-Day meeting at Germantown or Abington, and often drove into Philadelphia to hear a visiting 'public Friend.'[13]

Many an evening the Logans spent with the venerable Charles Thomson at Harriton, his ancient, high-peaked Welsh-style house on the Gulph Road. Now more than eighty-five years old, Thomson was full of memories. The firebrand and organizer of the patriot party in Philadelphia, later the hard-working Secretary of the Continental Congress, he had been at the very heart of the Revolution. There had been no place for him in the Federal government after 1788, however, and he had retired to his farm at Harriton. There he devoted his leisure and his learning to the translation of the Scriptures.

The old man loved to reminisce with his friends about the great figures of the Revolution. Already, they were becoming demigods — the Adamses, Lees, and Morrises, Patrick Henry and John Hancock, Gates and Conway and Greene — but as he spoke of them, they sometimes seemed all too human. Why did he not write the intimate political history of the Revolution? the Logans asked him. No one could be better qualified. Thomson always gave the same answer. Many a national hero, he would say, 'will go down with *éclat* to posterity, whose laurels would be tarnished if I were to write.' He would pause, as if recalling those distant, tumultuous days. Then, shaking his head, 'No! I have destroyed many an evidence of weakness and folly.' [14]

To Debby — who remembered, as a girl of fourteen, hearing the Declaration of Independence read in the State House yard — the old man's stories were endlessly fascinating. She had more of a taste for history than did her husband. And at Stenton she found a remarkable opportunity to indulge it. In the garret of the great house, stowed away amidst broken furniture and boxes of old clothes, she had found bundles of ancient, tattered, worm-eaten letters, which two generations of Logans had thoughtlessly treated as rubbish. To her, they were not rubbish. For she recognized at once the bold scrawl of William Penn, the more precise, schoolmasterly hand of his secretary, James Logan. Here, she realized, was a priceless historical correspondence, a unique record of Pennsylvania's early days, left behind by its two greatest men. And it was slowly moldering away there in the dark garret. She determined that it should not be lost. Rising before dawn in winter, at daybreak in summer, she laboriously deciphered the letters, one by one, and copied them out in her clear, feminine hand.[15]

The project occupied her for weeks and months. She grew

to have a new respect, a new affection, for James Logan, the strong, masterful, erudite, irascible man who had built Stenton nearly a hundred years before. In the spring of 1815 she expressed her feelings in a sonnet to Stenton:

> My peaceful home! amidst whose dark-green shades
> And sylvan scenes my waning life is spent,
> Nor without blessings and desired content. —
> Again the Spring illumines the verdant glades
> And new-waked Flora calls the Aonian maids
> To grace with song her revels, and prevent
> By charmed spells the nipping blasts, which, bent
> From Eurus or the stormy north, pervades
> Her treasures. — Still 'tis mine among thy groves
> Musing to rove, enamored of the fame
> Of him who reared these walls, whose classic love
> For Science brightest blazed, and left his name
> Indelible — by honour too approved
> And Virtue, cherish'd by the Muses' flame.[16]

After her daily stint of copying, Debby usually devoted the rest of the morning to household tasks. 'I hope I do not overvalue myself,' she wrote in her diary, 'but I am glad I am not of that order of beings who can sit down contentedly in the dirt.' [17] The Doctor, meanwhile, went into the fields to oversee the hired hands, or stayed in the library, reading and writing.

After lunch and a siesta, if the weather was mild, they sat together out under the spruces and oaks in the 'butterfly pasture.' There they read aloud to each other — perhaps from the life of Dr. Beattie, which contained some amusing letters of Mrs. Montagu, the famous bluestocking, or from the *Travels* of Brissot de Warville, which Joel Barlow had translated. Presently, Amy would bring tea, after which the Doctor sometimes got out his flute and played a few airs remembered from his student days at Edinburgh. Debby had little ear for music — it had had no place in her Quaker education — but at times she could confess 'the air he played was in unison with my mind, and the transitory state of our being was brought strongly before me.' As the shadows lengthened, the two usually took a short walk about the farm before going in to a simple supper and the day's newspapers, which came late in the afternoon.[18]

It was a placid life, serene and unperturbed, 'not without blessings and desired content.' Dr. Logan had been separated too often from his wife during the past hectic quarter of a century. He was glad now to spend his days in Debby's company. 'The more I see of life,' he mused, 'the more I become convinced that all the gayest pageantries of life fade before the higher comforts of a domestic life cheered by a mutual desire to please.' [19]

Often, on pleasant days, they drove in the gig to Somerville to see their grandchildren and drink a dish of tea with Albanus and Maria. Every summer they spent several weeks at Logansville. Debby especially loved the little rustic cottage there in its romantic setting — her chamber window darkly shaded by weeping willows through which the light played 'like gleams of silver,' the eastern window with 'the diagonal drapery of a fashionable curtain formed by the ascending branches of a thick Lombardy poplar.' While they were at Logansville, they could go on First Day to the little Friends meeting at near-by Basking Ridge, or take a trip to the seashore, where Dr. Logan sometimes 'went into the sea' before sunrise, and Deborah, following his advice, drank sea water for her weak stomach — even though it made her 'very sickish.' [20]

The bustle, the clamor, the restless stir of postwar America seemed blissfully remote at Logansville. It was becoming all too evident at Stenton. The ever-increasing volume of traffic on the Germantown and York roads told of factory wheels incessantly whirring up and down the Delaware valley. The face of the country was ineluctably changing. With dismay and a growing sense of alienation, Logan saw the Republican leaders at Washington reenact every one of Hamilton's favorite measures — the protective tariff, the excise, the Bank of the United States. The dream of a nation of independent yeomen was fading. The Doctor sadly regretted its passing, deeply deplored the new spirit — the rapacious, mercenary spirit of the manufacturer, the merchant, the banker, which was capturing his party, remaking the face of his country.

In this frame of mind he had little taste for politics. In the summer of 1815, some of his old Quid friends waited upon him at Stenton, asked him to stand for Congress. He replied that he had no wish 'to enter into the public service at this time.' He would only consent to stand, he said, if there were no other means of 'excluding a more exceptionable character proposed on the other side.'[21] Still the conservative Democrats considered Logan a name to conjure with in Pennsylvania, for two years later, despite his poor health and his disinclination to campaign, he was actively considered as a candidate for Governor by a caucus at Carlisle.[22]

In 1817, James Monroe ascended to the Presidency, in succession to Madison. The new President's inauguration caused no great rejoicing in the Logan household. Deborah found the Inaugural Address 'heavy and prolix, and without anything luminous or pleasing — though sufficiently seasoned with flattery to the *dear people.*' There was gentle sarcasm behind that last phrase, for Debby had always listened to political speeches with some degree of skepticism. But she spoke for her husband when she added: 'If he can be kept from doing harm it will be well . . . I am one of those who do not augur much good from his administration.'[23]

In June, three months after the inauguration, President Monroe came to Philadelphia. He was rowed in state up the Schuylkill to Gray's Ferry in a naval barge gaily decorated with bits of bunting; the volunteer cavalry and a company of prominent citizens on horseback escorted him through the streets. Dr. Logan went to town and waited upon the new President. He found Monroe looking much the same as ever, still plainly dressed in short old-fashioned pantaloons and white-topped boots, his blue-gray eyes looking benignly out from his bland, open face.

Together the two men paid a visit to old Governor McKean, now on his deathbed. Never backward about giving advice to Presidents, Logan handed Monroe a letter at parting. It dealt with the old question of the Louisiana boundaries. The Doctor had been assured by the Marquis de Onís that Spain was prepared to give up both East and West Florida peacefully, in return for a generous settlement of the still-disputed western line. With all his old earnestness, Logan urged the President to negotiate while the offer was still open, to prevent another needless and unjustifiable war. Monroe agreed to read the letter with care.[24]

Still the peacemaker, still the volunteer adviser to Presidents, Logan showed himself, a few months later, still the consistent agrarian, the celebrator of rural life, the champion of a yeoman democracy. Recently, after long inactivity, the old Philadelphia Society for Promoting Agriculture had come to life again, with new members and new zeal. As one of its founders Logan was glad to see it revive. He had long outlived the personal and political animosities that had caused him to break with it a quarter of a century before. Still, he could not resist recurring to the theme of his last paper, the paper that had precipitated the break back in 1790. In his first communication to the revived society, after describing a new machine for sowing clover, he casually observed that 'the cultivation of clover is considered the basis of a rotation of crops on which is founded the improved system of agriculture in the United States.' [25] No one murmured. It was a statement of fact now, not a subject for controversy.

In January 1818 Dr. Logan was elected vice-president of the Philadelphia Society. To the younger men he was a venerable pioneer, one of the few Americans who had 'contributed to the advancement of agriculture by their writings.' [26] When they heard him deliver his vice-presidential address on 'The Errors of Husbandry in the United States,' it seemed as though they were listening to a veritable Cato the Elder.

American agriculture, Logan lamented, was still — in spite of the praiseworthy efforts of farmers' societies — too generally in the hands of the poor and ignorant. This was a calamity — not only for the farmers themselves, but for agriculture as a science. For agriculture, he still believed, *was* a science, and, like every other science, 'reducible to fixed, unalterable principles' — principles that could be found out only through constant, patient, enlightened experimentation. But it was useless to expect a poor, ignorant yeomanry to carry on scientific experimentation.

And why, he asked, were the farmers poor? His answer was

his old answer, but the Tariff of 1816, the revival of the Bank of
the United States, gave it new emphasis: the poverty of the American farmer was 'attributable to banking and manufacturing establishments, under the protection of government, absorbing a
portion of capital that might be employed to greater advantage
in agricultural improvements.' Before him — for the Philadelphia Society was still composed mostly of businessmen, not farmers — sat the city's leading bankers and manufacturers, beneficiaries of government protection. He did not spare them. 'Extensive
manufacturing establishments, supported by machinery and the
labor of children,' he warned, 'have been found too frequently
injurious to the morals of the people, wherever introduced.'

He quoted Jefferson, the Jefferson of forty years before. The
famous passage in the *Notes on Virginia* had almost the sound of
an incantation as Logan intoned it once again: 'While we have
land to labor, then, let us never wish to see our citizens occupied
at a work-bench or twirling a distaff . . . The mobs of great
cities add just so much to the support of pure government as sores
do to the strength of the human body.'

Not that Logan was unfriendly to all manufacturing. He still
looked on the small independent artisan as a useful and necessary
citizen — the urban counterpart of the independent yeoman
farmer. 'A flourishing agriculture,' he said, 'inevitably occasions
the possession of such manufactures and commerce as are equal
to the support of numerous and flourishing towns, and to whatever is necessary to form a great and potent society.' But let the
government beware of singling out a special class of men, of
moneyed men, for patronage, for privilege. 'Let government,' he
said in measured words, 'secure to agriculture, manufactures, and
commerce *equal rights,* in exclusion of every idea of monopoly.'

And how could farmers and artisans best advance their status
and their art, best make their contribution to 'a great and potent
society'? Logan still believed in voluntary organizations, in societies for the encouragement of agriculture and domestic manufacturing. But long experience had taught him that societies, with
their premiums and learned treatises on husbandry, were not
enough. Even political organization, in which he had once put his

trust, was not enough. To counteract the ever-present forces of greed and hatred, something more was needed. He ended his address on a note of calm religious faith — a faith compounded of his old philosophy of benevolence and his still older but newly recovered Quaker faith in the Inner Light.

'The catholic charitable disposition which at present prevails amongst the various sects of Christians,' he said, hopefully, gives the ministers of religion an opportunity to 'secure the essentials of Christianity — mildness, gentleness, forbearance, and universal love towards all men.' He praised the peaceful community of Moravians at Bethlehem, 'the private families of Friends and other denominations of Christians, seated on their farms in various parts of our happy country.' In all these groups, though they differed in details of belief, one observed the same 'blessed effects of religion.' For after all — he came back at last to the Quaker doctrine — God has given to all men 'a monitor in their own breasts.' [27] Thus George Logan closed his last public utterance.

His last public act was likewise the act of a Quaker, a humane, conscientious citizen. Ominously, frighteningly — 'like a firebell in the night,' Jefferson said — the slavery question burst into the calm political atmosphere of 1819. The occasion was the debate in Congress over Missouri's admission to the Union. George Logan was sixty-six — a tired, frail, sick man. Nevertheless, on such a portentous issue as this he had to take a stand. To have kept silent would have been to stifle all his warmest human impulses, to betray his Quaker heritage, to turn his back on a lifetime of opposition to human bondage.

The Philadelphia abolitionists held a protest meeting in the State House in November. They passed resolutions deprecating the further extension of slavery, authorizing a memorial to Congress, setting up a Committee of Correspondence to keep the agitation alive. For the most part it was a new generation that led the movement — Horace Binney, Robert Walsh, Peter DuPonceau, Roberts Vaux — but the younger men were eager for Logan's support. He gladly lent them his name and agreed to serve on the Committee of Correspondence, thankful that the heart of Philadelphia was still warm, its conscience still tender.[28]

Logan's heart was still as warm, his conscience still as sensitive as ever, but his mind was troubled and the flesh was growing weak. Deborah noted in her diary in January 1820 that her husband was in a state of unusual depression. The news from Washington — news that told of angry, snarling debates on the Missouri question — did nothing to raise his spirits. Now and again a visitor such as Jesse Kersey, the Quaker minister, would be able to rouse him from his despondency, and for a time he would converse 'very cheerfully.' But always afterward the black pall of melancholy would descend.[29]

His health, never robust, was failing. He was an invalid throughout much of 1820, suffering in his legs the agonies of gout or rheumatism. Debby watched him grow steadily weaker until one day, near the end of the year, she found him 'in a strong convulsed fit, stretched out upon the bed, stiff and speechless.' The end, she knew then, was not far away.[30]

He lingered on through an unusually cold winter, his mind generally clear, but oppressed with an insuperable melancholy. Desperately, Debby sought to cheer him — and herself — by reminiscing in verse over his past triumphs. 'Cheer thee, my love!' she wrote, 'and let the Past/ Gleam brightly o'er the present hour.' She reminded him of the summer of 1798,

> . . . when the patriot dared the wave
> To arrest the dread array of war;
> Steadfast of heart, in counsel wise,
> His virtue over art prevailed,
> And gained of Peace the glorious prize!
> Whilst Calumny and Faction fail'd
> To injure, where they most assail'd.

No peacemaker, she told him, ever lived in vain.

> . . . thy country knows
> The brave resolve, the pure design,
> The counsel and the deed — were *thine*.[31]

The Doctor appreciated — as he had always appreciated — her loving ministrations to his sick mind and body. 'Never shall I forget,' she wrote later, 'the kind and grateful manner in which he received our attentions and the expressions of his affectionate attachment to myself.' [32] On 22 March, when the bluebirds and larks had begun their music in the great trees outside, he signed his will with a tremulous hand. Less than a month later, on 9 April 1821, his heart stopped beating. His body was laid in the family burying ground to the eastward of the mansion, on a hillside overlooking Wingohocking Creek. [33]

The passing of a Logan could not go unnoticed in Philadelphia. Philadelphia had not always understood George Logan, had not always loved him. But Philadelphia knew that he had been a good man, a humane man, a man of learning and public spirit — in short, a Logan. An orator before the American Philosophical Society paused in the midst of an historical discourse on the city to pronounce a florid eulogy:

And art thou gone, Logan? friend of man! friend of peace! friend of science! Thou whose persuasive accents could still the angry passions of the rulers of men and dispose their minds to listen to the voice of reason and justice! Thou whose life was devoted to the cause of humanity and to the promotion of harmony and concord between nations! What though party spirit has in vain endeavored to obscure thy virtues, they will live in the faithful page of history, and thy name will be handed down with honor to posterity! [34]

Under the great trees at Stenton — trees that had outlived three generations of Logans — Deborah was alone. When the first throes of grief were past, she found her own words to limn her husband's character. For nearly forty years she had lived with him in 'the most affectionate love and entire confidence.' No one had known his 'domestic worth' as she had known it. 'He was constant in his attachments,' she wrote, 'a most tender husband, a kind father, a just and good landlord and master, and a steady and efficient friend.'

Of his public life, his contribution to American politics, his place in history, it was not for her to speak. But of one thing she was certain — and historians would have to come back to it, after rendering all their verdicts on his political judgment and wisdom: 'A more kind and humane heart or more upright and just intentions I am sure no man could possess. . . The Roman who wished he had a window in his breast that all men might see his intentions could not have been conscious of greater rectitude of heart. . . He was a most true republican, contemning luxury and despising false glory . . . having in his own mind realized that happy state in which he could call every country his country, and every man his brother.' 35

✳

NOTES

IT will be apparent to anyone who take pains to consult the notes which follow that this book rests primarily on original sources. These sources fall mainly into five categories: (1) George Logan's own letters, journals, etc. among the Logan Papers at the Historical Society of Pennsylvania and elsewhere; (2) the papers of his friends and correspondents — Benjamin Franklin, Thomas Jefferson, Thomas McKean, and others; (3) the proceedings of public and private bodies to which Logan belonged — the Pennsylvania Assembly, the Congress of the United States, the Royal Medical Society of Edinburgh, the Philadelphia Society for Promoting Agriculture, etc.; (4) contemporary newspapers and magazines; and (5) Deborah Norris Logan's *Memoir* of her husband. This last I have felt justified in treating as an original source, fully realizing that it must be used with caution. It was, after all, written a quarter of a century after the major events which it records, and Deborah was, understandably, not always accurate in details. On the other hand, she had the instincts of a historian, and she unquestionably knew more about her husband's public and private life than anyone else.

A few words about my quotations. In matters of spelling, punctuation, and capitalization I have followed modern usage, feeling that no important purpose is served—and that many readers are only irritated — by a pedantic faithfulness to usages which are archaic or, sometimes, merely inadvertent. Wherever it has been possible to refer the reader to a printed version of a letter or other document, I have done so, after comparing its text with the original MS. At several points in the narrative readers will notice bits of conversation or dialogue. In no case have I manufactured these speeches. In every instance the words are taken directly from the sources.

INTRODUCTION

1. John Bach McMaster, *A History of the People of the United States* (New York, 1886–1913), II, 415–16; Henry Cabot Lodge, *George Washington* (Boston and New York, 1889), II, 258; Samuel Flagg Bemis, *A Diplomatic History of the United States* (New York, 1936), 121.
2. William Plumer, *Memorandum of Proceedings in the United States Senate, 1803–1807,* ed. Everett S. Brown (New York, 1923), 595.
3. *Memoirs of John Quincy Adams,* ed. Charles Francis Adams (Philadelphia, 1874–7), I, 404.

CHAPTER I

1. William Logan to ——, 10 May 1753, Maria Dickinson Logan Family Papers (hereafter cited as MDLFP), Historical Society of Pennsylvania.
2. *Memoirs of the Life of Catherine Phillips* (Philadelphia, 1798), 139.
3. William Logan to Susanna Fothergill, 10 June 1755, *Memoirs of the Life and Gospel Labours of Samuel Fothergill* (Liverpool, 1843), 188–9.
4. William Logan to Jared Eliot, 14 October 1755, Jared Eliot, *Essays upon Field Husbandry in New England,* ed. Harry J. Carman and Rexford G. Tugwell (New York, 1934), 230–33.
5. William Logan's journal of this trip is in the *Pennsylvania Magazine of History and Biography* (hereafter cited as *PMHB*), XXXVI (1912), 1–16, 162–86. James Pemberton's diary of the same trip is in the Library of Congress.
6. John F. Watson, *Annals of Philadelphia* (Philadelphia, 1845), II, 31–2.
7. Ibid. II, 168.
8. William Logan's 'Memoranda' are in the Library of the United States Department of Agriculture, Washington, D.C.
9. 'Memoranda in Husbandry.'
10. William Logan to Jared Eliot, 25 July 1754, in Eliot, *Essays,* ed. Carman and Tugwell, 229.
11. Letter signed 'Atticus,' *Pennsylvania Chronicle,* 9 March 1767; cf. F. B. Tolles, 'A Literary Quaker: John Smith of Burlington and Philadelphia,' *PMHB,* LXV (1941), especially 300–310.
12. *Catalogus discipulorum Roberti Proudi,* Proud Papers, Historical Society of Pennsylvania.
13. Minutes of the Overseers of Friends Public School, quoted in James Mulhern, *History of Secondary Education in Pennsylvania* (Philadelphia, 1933), 52–4.
14. Ibid. 52–3.

15. William Logan to Dr. John Fothergill, 11 May 1768, Emmett Collection, New York Public Library; William Logan to David Barclay, quoted by William Logan Fisher in an untitled account of the family of Thomas Fisher (n.p. *c.* 1839), 21. Fisher reads the date of this letter as 1760, but it is clear from other evidence that it should be 1768.

16. Dr. John Fothergill to William Logan, 8 May 1769, Gilbert Collection, II, 141–2, College of Physicians Library, Philadelphia.

17. 23 July 1768, MDLFP.

18. Ibid.

19. Deborah Norris Logan, *Memoir of Dr. George Logan of Stenton* (hereafter cited as *Memoir*), ed. Frances A. Logan (Philadelphia, 1899), 32n. Deborah Logan says he was ten years old at this time, but her memory was frequently at fault in such details, especially when she was dealing with her husband's childhood.

20. 8 May 1769, Gilbert Collection, II, 141–2.

21. Whitfield J. Bell, Jr., 'Thomas Parke's Student Life in England and Scotland, 1771–1773,' *PMHB,* LXXV (1951), 237–59.

22. William Logan, Jr. to his parents, 14 Nov. 1767, Friends' Historical Society, *Journal,* IX (1912), 90–93.

23. William Logan to Dr. John Fothergill, 11 May 1768, Emmett Collection.

24. Quoted by William Logan Fisher, op. cit.

25. Friends' Historical Society, *Journal,* IX (1912), 123–4.

26. *A Collection of Memorials Concerning Divers Deceased Ministers and Others of the People Called Quakers in Pennsylvania, New-Jersey, and Parts Adjacent* (Philadelphia, 1787), 423–5; *The Journal and Essays of John Woolman,* ed. A. M. Gummere (New York, 1922), Appendix, 513.

27. John Reynell's advice to an earlier apprentice, quoted in Frederick B. Tolles, *Meeting House and Counting House: The Quaker Merchants of Colonial Philadelphia* (Chapel Hill, 1948), 60.

28. *Catalogue of the Books Belonging to the Loganian Library: To Which Is Prefixed a Short Account of the Institution* (Philadelphia, 1837), vi; *Memoir,* 33.

29. The books from Dr. Logan's bequest are marked with an *L* in the *Catalogue* of the Loganian Library. See pp. 140–76, for the medical books.

30. *Memoir,* 33.

31. *Journal and Essays of John Woolman,* 291, 560–61.

CHAPTER II

1. All quotations in this chapter, unless otherwise noted, are from Logan's manuscript journal, written in the form of monthly letters to his brother Charles. These are now in the Historical Society of Pennsylvania.

2. Dr. John Fothergill to William Logan, 16 June 1775, typescript copy at the Library of the Society of Friends, Friends House, London.
3. Fothergill to William Logan (quoting a letter of Dr. Sims), 4 Oct. 1775, typescript copy at the Library of the Society of Friends, Friends House, London.
4. —to George Logan, 30 Nov. 1775, extract in Correspondence of Secretaries of State for the Colonies and the Postmaster-General, C.O.5, cxxxiv, 132, Public Record Office, London.
5. *The Autobiography of Benjamin Rush,* ed. G. W. Corner (Princeton, 1948), 44.
6. *List of the Graduates in Medicine in the University of Edinburgh* (Edinburgh, 1867), 13–16.
7. Whitfield J. Bell, Jr., 'Philadelphia Medical Students in Europe, 1750–1800,' *PMHB,* LXVII (1943), 1–29.
8. My descriptions of the style of the introductory lectures are based on the comments of Thomas Parke in 1771. Bell, 'Thomas Parke's Student Life,' *PMHB,* LXXV (1951), 249.
9. Logan's courses are listed in the MS. Matriculation Record, 1762–1785, University of Edinburgh Library.
10. Edward Topham, *Letters from Edinburgh, Written in the Years 1774 and 1775* (Dublin, n.d.), II, 20.
11. John Bell, *Letters on the Education of a Surgeon,* quoted in John D. Comrie, *History of Scottish Medicine* (London, 1932), I, 324.
12. *The Diary of Sylas Neville,* ed. Basil Cozens-Hardy (Oxford, 1950), 147–8.
13. Logan says merely 'Dr. Hunter.' There were two Hunters, both famous anatomists, in London. But only William was called 'Dr. Hunter'; his brother John was always known as 'Mr. Hunter.' Jane M. Oppenheimer, *New Aspects of John and William Hunter* (New York, 1946), 174.
14. Fielding H. Garrison, *An Introduction to the History of Medicine* (Philadelphia, 1929), 339–40.
15. William Hunter, *Two Introductory Lectures,* quoted in Stewart Craig Thomson, 'The Great Windmill Street School,' *Bulletin of the History of Medicine,* XII (1942), 382.
16. Quoted in Betsy Copping Corner, *William Shippen, Jr.* (Philadelphia, 1951), 70.
17. *Two Introductory Lectures,* quoted in Thomson, op. cit. 383.
18. Comrie, *History of Scottish Medicine,* II, 303–4, 453–5, 475–6.
19. *A List of the Members of the Royal Medical Society of Edinburgh* (Edinburgh, 1784).
20. *Diary,* 147–8.
21. MS. Dissertations of the Royal Medical Society, XI (1778), 42–6 (photostat at the Library of the American Philosophical Society).

22. Quoted in Charles P. Keith, *The Provincial Councillors of Pennsylvania* (Philadelphia, 1883), 2.
23. *A Genealogical Account of the Barclays of Urie* (London, 1812), 96–7n.
24. John Robison, Preface to Joseph Black, *Lectures on the Elements of Chemistry* (Edinburgh, 1803), lxii; Topham, *Letters,* II, 19.
25. Wallace Notestein, *The Scot in History* (New Haven, 1947), 221.
26. Bell, 'Philadelphia Medical Students,' *PMHB,* LXVII (1943), 13, 14.
27. Alexander Bower, *The History of the University of Edinburgh* (Edinburgh, 1817), II, 390–91.
28. William Cullen, *First Lines of the Practice of Physic* (Edinburgh, 1784), I, xxxiii–iv, xlvi–xlvii; Richard H. Shryock, *The Development of Modern Medicine* (New York, 1947), 26.
29. MS. Minutes of the Royal Medical Society of Edinburgh, 1778–1784, Library of the Royal Medical Society, Edinburgh. Since the earlier minutes are lost, it is impossible to be certain that no Americans had preceded Logan in this office. In his time, there were four Presidents each year. At an earlier period, the custom had been for each member to serve, in rotation, as presiding officer. Under this system, at least two Americans, John Morgan and Samuel Bard, had presided at meetings of the society.
30. MS. Dissertations of the Royal Medical Society, XI (1778), 173–8.
31. See University of Edinburgh, *Charters, Statutes, and Acts of the Town Council and Senatus, 1583–1858,* ed. Alexander Morgan and Robert K. Hannay (Edinburgh, 1937), 247–50, 252–6.
32. *Tentamen medicum inaugurale de venenis* (Edinburgh, 1779).
33. *Memoir,* 36. Logan's regular letters to his brother come to an end in June 1779. For knowledge of his European travels we are dependent on a single sentence in the *Memoir.*
34. Carl Van Doren, *Benjamin Franklin* (New York, 1938), 654.
35. Franklin to Lord Kames, 3 Jan. 1760, *The Writings of Benjamin Franklin,* ed. A. H. Smyth (New York, 1907), IV, 6.
36. Logan to Franklin, 15 July 1781, Franklin Papers, Bache Collection, American Philosophical Society.
37. *Memoir,* 37–8.
38. Logan to John Adams, 16 April 1780, Adams Papers, Adams Manuscript Trust. Mr. Henry Adams graciously supplied me with a copy of this letter.
39. Logan to Franklin, 15 April 1780, Franklin Papers, XVIII, 24, American Philosophical Society.

CHAPTER III

1. *Memoir,* 45n; William S. Baker, *Itinerary of General Washington* (Philadelphia, 1892), 85; Charles F. Jenkins, *Washington in Germantown* (Philadelphia, 1905), 2–3.

2. Alfred C. Lambdin, 'Battle of Germantown,' *PMHB,* I (1877), 373; Watson, *Annals,* II, 38.

3. Deborah Logan to Alexander Garden, 26 Sept. 1822, Hist. Soc. of Pa., *Collections,* I (1853), 119; *Memoir,* 40; Watson, II, 39.

4. Will of William Logan, LP; *Pennsylvania Archives,* 3rd Ser., XVI, 124; *Memoir,* 41; Accounts of Thomas Fisher, Executor, Logan Papers (hereafter cited as LP), Historical Society of Pennsylvania.

5. Logan to Franklin, 15 July 1781, Franklin Papers, Bache Collection.

6. Hist. Soc. of Pa., *Collections,* I (1853), 131–3.

7. *Memoir,* 42; Harriott H. Ravenel, *Eliza Pinckney* (New York, 1896), 291, 298; 'Josiah Smith's Diary, 1780–1781,' *South Carolina Historical and Genealogical Magazine,* XXXIV (1933), 81–2.

8. Logan to Franklin, 15 July 1781, Franklin Papers, Bache Collection.

9. Sally Fisher, Philadelphia, to Sally Fisher, Duck Creek, Delaware, n.d., Corbit MSS., Historical Society of Delaware.

10. Diary of Anna Rawle (28 Feb. 1781), quoted in *Sally Wister's Journal,* ed. Albert Cook Myers (Philadelphia, 1902), 114–16n.

11. *Our Revolutionary Forefathers: The Letters of François, Marquis de Barbé-Marbois,* ed. Eugene P. Chase (New York, 1929), 153–4.

12. *Hannah Logan's Courtship,* ed. Albert Cook Myers (Philadelphia, 1904), 49–51.

13. Sally Fisher, Philadelphia, to Sally Fisher, Duck Creek, Del., n.d., Corbit MSS. Since this letter is undated, it is impossible to tell whether it refers to the couple's actual wedding or to their 'passing meeting,' which would have occurred a few months earlier. I have felt justified, however, in using it to describe Debby's appearance and manner at the wedding.

14. Marriage certificate of George Logan and Debby Norris, Philadelphia Monthly Meeting, Marriage Certificates, II (1759–1814), 291, Department of Records, Philadelphia Yearly Meeting.

15. Sally Fisher to Sally Fisher, n.d., Corbit MSS.

16. Logan to James Phillips, 17 Jan. 1783, Gibson MSS., IV, 119, Library of the Society of Friends, London.

17. Sally Fisher to Sally Fisher, n.d. (*c.* Jan. 1782), Corbit MSS.

18. *Memoir,* 43.

19. Susanna Dillwyn to William Dillwyn, 2 June 1790, Dillwyn MSS., Library Company of Philadelphia.

20. Keith, *Provincial Councillors of Pennsylvania,* 21; Samuel Hotchkin, *Ancient and Modern Germantown* (Philadelphia, 1889), 29.

21. Deborah Logan to Sally—, 21 Sept. 1791, MDLFP.

22. *American Museum,* x (1791), 18.
23. *Memoir,* 44.
24. Susanna Dillwyn to William Dillwyn, 2 June 1790, Dillwyn MSS.
25. *Memoir,* 99.
26. *The Constitution of the Germantown Society for Promoting Domestic Manufactures* (Philadelphia, 1790), 5–6.
27. William Logan to Jared Eliot, 25 July 1754, Jared Eliot, *Essays,* ed. Carman and Tugwell, 228; William Logan, 'Memoranda in Husbandry.'
28. *American Husbandry* (London, 1775), I, 145.
29. Ibid. I, 180–81.
30. *A Summary View of the Courses of Crops, in the Husbandry of England and Maryland* (Philadelphia, 1784).
31. Olive M. Gambrill, 'John Beale Bordley and the Early Years of the Philadelphia Agricultural Society,' *PMHB,* LXVI (1942), 416.
32. MS. Minutes of the Philadelphia Society for Promoting Agriculture, I, C. J. Marshall Memorial Library, University of Pennsylvania.
33. Ibid. 3.
34. Ibid. II, 18.
35. Deborah Logan to Isaac Norris, 28 Aug. 1785, MDLFP.
36. MS. journal, Misc. MSS., LP.

CHAPTER IV

1. Franklin to John Bard and Mrs. Bard, 14 Nov. 1785, *Writings of Franklin,* IX, 476.
2. *Pennsylvania Journal,* 2 Nov. 1785; *Pennsylvania Gazette,* 2 Nov. 1785; Harold D. Eberlein and Cortlandt V. Hubbard, *Diary of Independence Hall* (Philadelphia, 1948), 213–14, 300–302.
3. *Minutes of the First Session of the Tenth General Assembly* (Philadelphia, 1785), 5; Robert L. Brunhouse, *The Counter-Revolution in Pennsylvania* (Harrisburg, 1942), 178. Much of the background of Pennsylvania politics in this chapter is based on Brunhouse's excellent study.
4. Janet Wilson, 'The Bank of North America and Pennsylvania Politics, 1781–1787,' *PMHB,* LXVI (1942), 3–13; Brunhouse, 173–5.
5. Charles J. Stillé, *Major-General Anthony Wayne* (Philadelphia, 1893), 71.
6. Samuel Bryan to George Bryan, 3 Nov. 1785, *PMHB,* XLII (1918), 287–8.
7. Alfred O. Aldridge, 'Why Did Thomas Paine Write on the Bank?' American Philosophical Society, *Proceedings,* XCIII (1949), 309–15.
8. *Debates and Proceedings of the General Assembly of Pennsylvania on the Memorial Praying a Suspension or Repeal of the Law Annulling the Charter of the Bank,* ed. Mathew Carey (Philadelphia, 1786), 112;

Lawrence Lewis, Jr., *A History of the Bank of North America* (Philadelphia, 1882), 143.

9. *Pennsylvania Gazette,* 5 April 1786.
10. Quoted in Wilson, 17.
11. *Debates and Proceedings,* 75.
12. Ibid. 109, 117, 131, 113.
13. Ibid. 112–13. See also, for a further expression of Logan's views on the Bank, *Minutes,* 10th Assembly, 2nd sess., 265–6.
14. *Minutes,* 11th Assembly, 2nd sess., 159.
15. *Proceedings and Debates of the General Assembly of Pennsylvania* (Philadelphia, 1787–8), I, 50.
16. Journal of Manasseh Cutler (13 July 1787), William P. Cutler and Julia P. Cutler, *Life, Journals and Correspondence of Rev. Manasseh Cutler* (Cincinnati, 1888), I, 267.
17. *Memoir,* 38, 46–7. There are elaborate examinations into the authenticity of this story in Lewis J. Carey, *Franklin's Economic Views* (Garden City, 1928), 106–33; and Thomas D. Eliot, 'The Relations between Adam Smith and Benjamin Franklin before 1776,' *Political Science Quarterly,* XXXIX (1924), 67–96.
18. R. J. Houston, 'The Gap Copper Mines,' Lancaster County Historical Society, *Papers,* I (1897), 292.
19. Franklin to Mrs. Mary Hewson, 6 May 1786, *Writings of Franklin,* IX, 511.
20. *Memoir,* 38.
21. *Proceedings and Debates,* I, 54. A variant version of Franklin's words appeared in the *Pennsylvania Herald,* 20 Sept. 1797.
22. *Proceedings and Debates,* I, 99, 135.
23. 'A Hudibrastic,' *Pittsburgh Gazette,* 3 Nov. 1787, reprinted in *Pennsylvania Gazette,* 21 Nov. 1787.
24. *Proceedings and Debates,* I, 139.
25. Ibid. I, 140.
26. Ibid. II, 140. According to Rush's biographer, the presentation of this memorial marked the *début* of the temperance question as a political issue in the United States. Nathan G. Goodman, *Benjamin Rush: Physician and Citizen* (Philadelphia, 1934), 276.
27. These recommendations looked toward the creation of what would later become famous as the 'Pennsylvania System' of prison administration. Harry Elmer Barnes, *The Evolution of Penology in Pennsylvania* (Indianapolis, 1927), 85–7, 106–7.
28. Logan set out his views at length in the *Pennsylvania Mercury,* 1 April, 6 Sept. 1788.
29. *Proceedings and Debates,* III, 5.
30. *Penna. Mercury,* 6 Sept. 1788.
31. *Proceedings and Debates,* III, 153.

32. *Penna. Mercury,* 22 March 1788.
33. There are clippings of this and several of the later 'Cato' pieces among the Misc. MSS., LP. They bear the notation 'By Dr. Logan' in Deborah's hand.
34. *Penna. Mercury,* 18 March 1788. The italics are in the original.
35. Ibid. 22 March 1788.
36. Ibid. 1 April 1788.
37. *Proceedings and Debates,* III, 201, 203; J. L. Bishop, *A History of American Manufactures* (Philadelphia, 1866), I, 404–9.
38. *Proceedings and Debates,* III, 202–3 (I have altered the punctuation slightly to make sense out of the stenographer's report).
39. *Penna. Mercury,* 12 April, 24 April 1788.
40. Ibid. 3 June, 22 July 1788.
41. In his eighth and last Cato letter (*Penna. Mercury,* 6 Sept. 1788) Logan returned to the theme of the penal laws, still defending death and banishment as the only penalties suitable in a republican government.
42. Anne Bezanson et al., *Prices and Inflation during the American Revolution: Pennsylvania, 1770–1790* (Philadelphia, 1951), 104, 341.
43. *Proceedings and Debates,* IV, 123–6.
44. Benjamin Rush to Jeremy Belknap, 7 Oct. 1788, Massachusetts Historical Society, *Collections,* 6th series, IV, 419; cf. Brunhouse, 216.
45. *Proceedings and Debates,* IV, 216.
46. *The Journal of William Maclay* (New York, 1927), 276, 346.
47. *Minutes,* 13th Assembly, 2nd sess., 89, 107, 110–11; Brunhouse, 219.
48. *Minutes,* 13th Assembly, 2nd sess., 115, 119, 177; 3rd sess., 254, 257.
49. See Chapter V.
50. *Memoir,* 39; Van Doren, *Franklin,* 779–80.

CHAPTER V

1. *Memoir,* 43.
2. The original MS. of this paper is among the archives of the Philadelphia Society for Promoting Agriculture. See also *Minutes of the Philadelphia Society for the Promotion of Agriculture* (Philadelphia, 1854), 32.
3. The paper was duly printed in the *American Museum,* II (1787), 295–7, and in the *Pennsylvania Mercury,* 7 Sept. 1787.
4. The constitution is printed in *American Museum,* V (1789), 161–3.
5. The subscription list is printed at the beginning of III (1788).
6. *Journal of William Maclay,* 346.
7. *American Museum,* VI (1789), 101–2.
8. Ibid.
9. Ibid. VI (1789), 102–3.
10. Ibid. IX (1791), 111; Stevenson W. Fletcher, *Pennsylvania Agriculture and Country Life* (Harrisburg, 1950), 191–3.
11. 'The General Introduction of Working-Oxen on Our Farms, instead of

Horses, a Most Desirable Event,' Misc. MSS., LP. Apparently this essay was never published.

12. *American Museum,* IX (1792), 172.
13. Ibid. XII (1792), 22–3.
14. *Independent Gazetteer,* 5 March 1791.
15. See William Logan to Jared Eliot, 14 Oct. 1755, Eliot, *Essays,* 233.
16. Logan's certificate of membership in the Bucks County Society for the Promotion of Agriculture, Domestic Manufacturing and Economy, dated 11 May 1789, is in LP, v, 5.
17. *American Museum,* VI (1789), 206.
18. Fletcher, 137.
19. William Logan to Jared Eliot, 12 Nov. 1755, Eliot, *Essays,* 234; William Logan, 'Memoranda in Husbandry.'
20. Fletcher, 140.
21. *Independent Gazetteer,* 23 Jan. 1790.
22. Richard Peters, 'On Gypsum,' Phila. Soc. for Promoting Agric., *Memoirs,* I (1808), 158–61.
23. Van Doren, *Franklin,* 736–7, citing J.A.C. Chaptal, *Chymistry Applied to Agriculture* (Boston, 1836), 73.
24. This incident was reported at second or third hand many years later, by Augustus John Foster, a British diplomat, in his 'Notes on the United States of America,' MS. in the Huntington Library; see *PMHB,* LXXV (1951), 389.
25. *Memoir,* 44–5; William S. Baker, *Washington after the Revolution* (Philadelphia, 1898), 83; Richard Peters, *Agricultural Enquiries on Plaister of Paris* (Philadelphia, 1797), 68.
26. *American Museum,* VI (1789), 399–401, 461–3.
27. Watson, *Annals,* II, 486; Fletcher, 131–2.
28. Thomas Jefferson to Thomas Mann Randolph, 28 July 1793, *Thomas Jefferson's Garden Book,* ed. Edwin M. Betts (Philadelphia, 1944), 199.
29. He later wrote a special paper to promote the culture of flax in Pennsylvania. *American Museum,* XII (1792), 271–2.
30. Elizabeth G. Gibson, *Biographical Sketches of the Bordley Family* (Philadelphia, 1865), 123.
31. MS. Minutes of the Philadelphia Society for Promoting Agriculture, 123–7.
32. *Independent Gazetteer,* 26 February, 5 March 1791. The report was published separately six years later as *Fourteen Agricultural Experiments, to Ascertain the Best Rotation of Crops* (Philadelphia, 1797).

CHAPTER VI

1. Unsigned MS., dated 29 March 1798, in the Madeira-Vaughan Colleclection, American Philosophical Society. This account was set down in

1798, just as Dr. Logan was reaching the depths of his unpopularity with the Federalists; it is likely, therefore, that the writer's recollections were colored by partisan feeling. Nevertheless the precision, the details of the account persuade us that some such incident took place. Cf. *Heads of Families at the First Census of the United States* (Washington, 1907–8), VIII, 194.

2. *Independent Gazetteer,* 20 Feb. 1790.
3. MS. Minutes of Philadelphia Monthly Meeting, XI, 52, 58–9, 98, 114, Department of Records, Philadelphia Yearly Meeting.
4. *Pennsylvania Archives,* 6th Series, IV, 430. *The Quid Mirror* (Philadelphia, 1806), 13, refers to Logan as a 'captain of dragoons.'
5. Charles J. Ingersoll, *Recollections* (Philadelphia, 1861), 230, apparently quoting a passage later deleted from Deborah Logan's *Memoir.*
6. Maclay, *Journal,* 199.
7. Ibid. 346.
8. *Independent Gazetteer,* 20 Feb. 1790.
9. Maclay, *Journal,* 229.
10. For Logan's authorship of these and later anonymous or pseudonymous works see Frederick B. Tolles, 'George Logan, Agrarian Democrat: A Survey of His Writings,' *PMHB,* LXXV (1951), 260–78.
11. *Letters* (1791), 3–4, 6.
12. Ibid. 7, 15.
13. Ibid. 9.
14. Ibid. 13–14.
15. Ibid. 18, 20–22, 25–6.
16. Ibid. 23–4.
17. Ibid. 32.
18. Ibid. 33, 34.
19. Ibid. 47; cf. James R. Jacobs, *The Beginning of the U.S. Army* (Princeton, 1947), 50–51.
20. *Letters* (1791), 39, 42–5.
21. Ibid. 35–6.
22. Ibid. 47.
23. *National Gazette,* 20 Feb. 1792.
24. Jefferson to Washington, 9 Sept. 1792, *Writings of Jefferson,* ed. P.L. Ford (New York, 1892–9), VI, 106; to Thomas Mann Randolph, 16 Nov. 1792, ibid. VI, 134; Lewis Leary, *That Rascal Freneau* (New Brunswick, N.J., 1941), 196–7, 346, 403–4.
25. *National Gazette,* 27 Feb., 15 March, 3 May, 1 Aug. 1792.
26. *The Works of Alexander Hamilton,* ed. H. C. Lodge (New York and London, 1904), IV, 70–86.
27. Ibid. IV, 182.
28. See Joseph S. Davis, *Essays in the Earlier History of American Corporations* (Cambridge, 1917), I, 378–87.

29. *National Gazette,* 22 Aug. 1792.
30. *Five Letters,* 3.
31. Ibid. 10–11.
32. Ibid. 11–12.
33. Ibid. 19.
34. Ibid. 22.
35. Ibid. 28.
36. Ibid. 20.
37. *American Museum,* 12 (1792), Appendix II, *22–*23; *National Gazette,* 25 Aug. 1792; *Gazette of the United States,* 29 Aug. 1792.
38. *National Gazette,* 29 Aug., 5 Sept., 19 Sept., 1792; *American Museum,* XII (1792), 159–67, 213–17.
39. L'Enfant to Hamilton, 17 Sept. 1792, Hamilton Papers, Library of Congress.
40. Joseph S. Davis summarizes and evaluates some of this literature in *Essays in the Earlier History of American Corporations,* I, 443–53.
41. Ibid. I, 451–2.
42. Louis Hartz, *Economic Policy and Democratic Thought: Pennsylvania, 1776–1860* (Cambridge, 1948), 69.
43. This tradition is recorded by Paul Leicester Ford in his edition of Jefferson's *Writings,* VI, 116n.
44. *Memoir,* 50.
45. Jefferson to Madison, 28 April 1793, *Thomas Jefferson's Garden Book,* 187, 188; Madison to Jefferson, 30 July 1793, William C. Rives, *History of the Life and Times of James Madison* (Boston, 1878), III, 360–61n; Charles F. Jenkins, *Jefferson's Germantown Letters* (Philadelphia, 1906), 163; Jefferson to Thomas Mann Randolph, *Jefferson's Garden Book,* 199.
46. 'The Anas,' *Writings of Jefferson,* ed. Ford, I, 215.
47. *Letters* (1793), 1.
48. Ibid. 5.
49. Ibid. 8–9.
50. Ibid. 20–22.
51. Ibid. 24.

CHAPTER VII

1. *Dunlap's American Daily Advertiser,* 25 May 1783.
2. *National Gazette,* 29 Sept. 1792.
3. *Independent Gazetteer,* 25 Sept. 1790.
4. J. Thomas Scharf and Thompson Westcott, *History of Philadelphia* (Philadelphia, 1884), I, 467.
5. A copy of the broadside is in Misc. MSS., LP. For its date see my 'George Logan, Agrarian Democrat,' *PMHB,* LXXV (1951), 273n.

6. William Miller, 'The Democratic Societies and the Whiskey Insurrection,' *PMHB,* LXII (1938), 324–49.

7. J. Lee Hartman, 'Pennsylvania's Grand Plan of Post-Revolutionary Internal Improvement,' *PMHB,* LXV (1941), 439–57.

8. Edward Burd to Edward Shippen, 14 June 1792, quoted in Charles I. Landis, 'History of the Philadelphia and Lancaster Turnpike,' *PMHB,* XLII (1918), 133. See also Wilbur C. Plummer, *The Road Policy of Pennsylvania* (Philadelphia, 1925), 46–8; James W. Livingood, *The Philadelphia-Baltimore Trade Rivalry, 1780–1860* (Harrisburg, 1947), 40–44.

9. Henry Simpson, *The Lives of Eminent Philadelphians* (Philadelphia, 1859), 522–4.

10. *Dunlap's American Daily Advertiser,* 24 May 1793; *Independent Gazetteer,* 25 May 1793; *National Gazette,* 25 May 1793.

11. *Dunlap's American Daily Advertiser,* 25 May 1793.

12. Ibid. 30 May, 3 June, 4 June, 7 June, 18 June, 1793.

13. *National Gazette,* 12 June, 15 June 1793.

14. Deborah Logan to Mary Norris, 1 April 1793, MDLFP.

15. Jefferson to James Monroe, 5 May 1793, *Writings of Jefferson,* ed. Ford, VI, 238.

16. *Memoir,* 97.

17. MS. Minutes, 20, 21, 52–3, Historical Society of Pennsylvania.

18. Ibid. 22; Frances S. Childs, *French Refugee Life in the United States, 1790–1800* (Baltimore, 1940), 166; Genêt to Logan, 6 July 1793, LP, V, 11.

19. *Memoir,* 53n.

20. 'The Anas,' *Writings of Jefferson,* ed. Ford, I, 246 (my italics).

21. *Memoir,* 53–4.

22. Jefferson to Madison, 3 Aug. 1793, *Writings of Jefferson,* ed. Ford, VI, 361.

23. John Adams to Thomas Jefferson, 30 June 1813, *The Works of John Adams* (Boston, 1856), X, 47.

24. See J. H. Powell's vivid narrative of the yellow fever, *Bring Out Your Dead* (Philadelphia, 1949).

25. Deborah Logan to Mary Norris, 27 Sept. 1793; Deborah Logan to Mary Norris, 4 Oct. 1793, MDLFP.

26. *General Advertiser,* 18 Sept. 1793; also printed in *National Gazette* and *Federal Gazette.*

27. Rush to Mrs. Rush, 24 Sept. 1793, *Letters of Benjamin Rush,* ed. L. H. Butterfield (Princeton, 1951) II, 678.

28. *Federal Gazette,* 26 Sept. 1793; Powell, 163.

29. *Federal Gazette,* 2 Oct. 1793.

30. *Memoir,* 47–9.

31. MS. Minutes of the Democratic Society of Pennsylvania, 39, 41, Historical Society of Pennsylvania.
32. William Miller, 'First Fruits of Republican Organization,' *PMHB,* LXIII (1939), 123.
33. *New York Daily Advertiser,* quoted by Miller, ibid. 140.
34. MS. Minutes, 43; Eugene P. Link, *Democratic-Republican Societies* (New York, 1942), 60.
35. MS. Minutes, 143–5; Miller, 'Democratic Societies and the Whiskey Insurrection,' 331–2.
36. Monroe to Logan, 24 June 1795 (wrongly dated 1796), *The Writings of James Monroe,* ed. S. M. Hamilton (New York, 1900), III, 6–7.
37. Monroe to Jefferson, 23 June 1795, *Writings of Monroe,* II, 292–304; Beverley W. Bond, Jr., *The Monroe Mission to France, 1794–1796* (Baltimore, 1907), 15–20, 46–7.
38. Monroe to Logan, 24 June 1795, *Writings of Monroe,* III, 6–7.
39. Timothy Pickering, Oliver Wolcott, and James McHenry to Washington, 2 July 1796, *The Writings of George Washington,* ed. W. C. Ford (New York and London, 1889–93) XIII, 216–17n.
40. 'Franklin,' *The Democratic Press,* 31 July 1810, quoted in Harry M. Tinkcom, *The Republicans and Federalists in Pennsylvania, 1790–1801* (Harrisburg, 1950), 144.
41. Fisher Ames to Christopher Gore, 3 Dec. 1796, *The Works of Fisher Ames,* ed. Seth Ames (Boston, 1854), I, 206.
42. Deborah Logan to Mary Norris, 25 Dec. 1796, MDLFP.
43. *American State Papers: Foreign Relations,* I, 577.
44. Samuel Flagg Bemis, 'Washington's Farewell Address: A Foreign Policy of Independence,' *American Historical Review,* XXXIX (1933–4), 263–5.
45. *Penna. Archives,* 4th Ser., IV, 373–4.
46. *Journal of the Pennsylvania House of Representatives,* VII (Philadelphia, 1797), 54; Tinkcom, 203.
47. *House Journal,* VII, 127, 202, 203.
48. Adams to J. Q. Adams, 31 March 1797, *Works of Adams,* VIII, 537.
49. J. D. Richardson, ed. *A Compilation of the Messages and Papers of the Presidents* (Washington, 1899), I, 235.
50. MS. diary of Deborah Logan, LP, II, 169; Albert Gallatin to Hannah Gallatin, 30 June 1797; Henry Adams, *The Life of Albert Gallatin* (Philadelphia, 1879), 187; Bond, 80.
51. Deborah Logan to Mary Norris, 29 May 1796, MDLFP.
52. Napper Tandy to George Logan, 6 May 1797, LP, V, 12.
53. *Gazette of the United States,* 6 Nov. 1798.
54. Obadiah Rich, *Supplement to the Bibliotheca Americana* (London, 1841), 496.

55. *Memoir,* 83.
56. See John C. Miller, *Crisis in Freedom: The Alien and Sedition Acts* (Boston, 1951).
57. *Memoir,* 54, 59n.
58. Scharf and Westcott, *History of Philadelphia,* I, 493.
59. Francis Von A. Cabeen, 'The Society of the Sons of Saint Tammany of Philadelphia,' *PMHB,* xxv (1901), 442–51; xxvi (1902), 346–7; xxvii (1903), 29–48.
60. *An Address on the Natural and Social Order of the World* (Philadelphia, 1798), 6–7, 8, 12.
61. Scharf and Westcott, I, 493.

CHAPTER VIII

1. Memorial signed by James Pemberton, Amos Yarnall, John Elliot, and Owen Biddle, 23 March 1798, LP, v, 14.
2. John Dickinson to Thomas McKean, 3 May 1798, McKean Papers, III, 19, Historical Society of Pennsylvania.
3. Benjamin Rush to George Logan, 24 May 1798, LP, v, 15.
4. *American State Papers: Foreign Relations,* II, 185–6. On war preparations see Gardner W. Allen, *Our Naval War with France* (Boston and New York, 1909), Chaps. IV–V.
5. *Memoir,* 54; cf. Frederick B. Tolles, 'Friends and the Rulers of the People,' *Friends Intelligencer,* cv (1948), 391–3.
6. Jefferson to Elbridge Gerry, 26 Jan. 1799, *The Writings of Thomas Jefferson,* ed. Bergh (Washington, 1903–4), x, 75–6; Jefferson to Edmund Pendleton, 29 Jan. 1799, ibid. x, 89.
7. *Memoir,* 56. The original is in LP, v, 16.
8. *Memoir,* 55–6, 57; McKean to John Dickinson, 24 June 1798, McKean Papers, III, 23. The original certificate in McKean's hand is in LP, v, 17.
9. *Porcupine's Gazette,* 18 June 1798.
10. Quoted in *Memoir,* 59–60n.
11. *Annals of Congress,* 5th Congress, 2nd session, 1972–3.
12. *Memoir,* 59n.
13. *Annals,* 5th Cong., 2nd sess., 2006.
14. Ibid. 1992, 2165–6.
15. *Memoir,* 61; Logan's journal of his trip to Europe (Misc. MSS., LP) 1–14.
16. Logan to Deborah Logan, 28 July 1798, LP, vi, 35–6.
17. Ibid.
18. Murray to Timothy Pickering, 29 July 1798, Pickering MSS., xxii, 326–7, Massachusetts Historical Society; Murray to J. Q. Adams, 2

Aug. 1798, 'Letters of William Vans Murray,' ed. W. C. Ford, American Historical Association, *Annual Report* (1912), 444.

19. Murray to Rufus King, 6 Aug. 1798, Rufus King Papers, Huntington Library; Murray to J. Q. Adams, 6 Aug., 28 Aug. 1798, 'Letters of William Vans Murray,' 449, 460.

20. Murray to Pickering, 6 Aug. 1798, Pickering MSS., XXIII, 10–11; Murray to J. Q. Adams, 6 Aug. 1798, 'Letters of William Vans Murray,' 448–9; Murray to King, 10 Aug. 1798, Rufus King Papers.

21. Murray to J. Q. Adams, 10 Aug. 1798, 'Letters of William Vans Murray,' 452; cf. Murray's Commonplace Book, 1797–9, Murray Papers, Library of Congress; Alexander De Conde, 'The Role of William Vans Murray in the Peace Negotiations between France and the United States, 1800,' *Huntington Library Quarterly,* xv (1952), 187–9.

22. Murray to Pickering, 13 Aug. 1798, 'Letters of William Vans Murray,' 455; Murray to J. Q. Adams, 14 Aug. 1798, ibid. 456; Murray to King, 14 Aug. 1798, Rufus King Papers; J. Q. Adams to Murray, 4 Sept. 1798, *The Writings of John Quincy Adams,* ed. W. C. Ford (New York, 1913), II, 360.

23. MS. journal, 14–17.

24. *Memoir,* 65n; Miecislaus Haiman, *Kosciuszko: Leader and Exile* (New York, 1946), 73–4.

25. Codman to Harrison Gray Otis, 26 Aug. 1798, Samuel E. Morison, *The Life and Letters of Harrison Gray Otis* (Boston and New York, 1913), I, 170. On the authorship of this memorial see Frederick B. Tolles, 'Unofficial Ambassador: George Logan's Mission to France, 1798,' *William and Mary Quarterly,* 3rd Ser., VII (1950), 13–14.

26. *Memoir,* 64; Talleyrand to the Minister of the Interior, 14 Aug. 1798, LP, 18; Talleyrand to Pichon, 16 Aug. 1798, *Archives des affaires étrangères: Correspondance politique, Etats-Unis* (photofilm at Library of Congress), L, 169.

27. *Memoir,* 64.

28. Logan, MS. journal, 28–9; Murray to J. Q. Adams, 11 Sept. 1798, 'Letters of William Vans Murray,' 470.

29. Charles F. Jenkins Autograph Collection, Friends Historical Library of Swarthmore College.

30. See *Memoir,* 130. Logan believed that Temple Franklin suppressed passages that tended to substantiate this view when he later published his grandfather's *Autobiography.*

31. MS. journal, 19–27. After leaving Paris, Logan sent Merlin an *aide-mémoire* repeating the same arguments in substantially the same words, *Memoir,* 129–31. A letter from Nathaniel Cutting to Jefferson, dated 27 August 1798 in the Jefferson Papers, corroborates Logan's account of his interview.

32. Logan, 'To the Citizens of the United States,' *Aurora*, 3 Jan. 1799.

33. *Memoir*, 66.

34. *Le Bien Informé*, 7 *fructidor An* VI (24 Aug. 1798); *Le Journal de Paris*, 9 *fructidor An* VI (26 Aug. 1798).

35. Similar stories appeared in the *Journal des francs, L'Indépendent, Les Annales de la République française, L'Ami des lois, Le Publiciste*, and other papers.

36. Samuel E. Morison, 'Du Pont, Talleyrand, and the French Spoliations,' Mass. Hist. Soc., *Proceedings*, XLIX (1916), 63–79; E. Wilson Lyon, 'The Directory and the United States,' *American Historical Review*, XLIII (1937–8), 524–32; Arthur B. Darling, *Our Rising Empire* (New Haven, 1940), 296–300; Tolles, 'Unofficial Ambassador,' *William and Mary Quarterly*, 3rd Ser., VII (1950), 17–18.

37. *Gazette of the United States*, 26 Oct. 1798. The Mingo chief, according to one theory, had been named after George Logan's grandfather.

38. See Edith Philips, *The Good Quaker in French Legend* (Philadelphia, 1932).

39. Du Pont de Nemours to Jefferson, 27 Aug. 1798, *The Correspondence of Jefferson and Du Pont de Nemours*, ed. Gilbert Chinard (Baltimore, 1931), 6; Du Pont to Jefferson, 13 April 1802, ibid. 43.

40. Logan to Fulwar Skipwith, 11 Sept. 1798, Norris of Fairhill Family Letters, II, 41, Historical Society of Pennsylvania.

41. MS. notes on France, Misc. MSS., LP. Recent scholarship tends to confirm Logan's favorable estimate of political conditions under the Directory. See Crane Brinton, *A Decade of Revolution, 1789–1799* (New York, 1934), 212–21.

42. MS. journal, 29–30; MS. notes on France.

43. Logan's notes on viniculture in the Bordeaux region are among the Misc. MSS., LP. They were published in the *Aurora*, 26 Feb. 1799.

44. *Memoir*, 69–70.

45. Logan to Merlin, 9 Sept. 1798, *Memoir*, 129–31; to Schimmelpenninck, 9 Sept. 1798, ibid. 132–3; to La Revellière-Lépeaux, 10 Sept. 1798, ibid. 133–4; Fulwar Skipwith to Logan, 30 Aug. 1798, LP, V, 23; Logan to Skipwith, 11 Sept. 1798, Norris of Fairhill Family Letters, II, 41; Logan to Deborah Logan, 9 Sept. 1798, *Memoir*, 79–80.

46. *Memoir*, 72–3, 76–7, 78.

47. Ibid. 80; Alexander Graydon, *Memoirs of a Life Chiefly Passed in Pennsylvania* (Harrisburg, 1811), 355.

48. *Memoir*, 72, 74.

49. Ibid. 75–6; Deborah Logan, 'Transactions on the Farm and Memoranda of Various Matters Commencing June 12th, 1798, the day on which my most tenderly beloved husband embarked for Europe,' typescript copy in Misc. MSS., LP.

50. *Porcupine's Gazette*, 21 July 1798.

51. *Memoir,* 83–4.
52. *Porcupine's Gazette,* 10 Nov. 1798.

CHAPTER IX

1. So Jefferson reported to Deborah Logan. 'Transactions . . . and Memoranda'; cf. also Jefferson to Madison, 21 June 1798, *Writings of Jefferson,* ed. Bergh, x, 50.
2. *Memoir,* 84–5; [New York] *Commercial Advertiser,* 15 Nov. 1798; James McHenry to George Washington, 9 Nov. 1798, Bernard C. Steiner, *The Life and Correspondence of James McHenry* (Cleveland, 1907), 351.
3. Pickering's account of this interview is to be found in *American State Papers: Foreign Relations,* II, 236; Logan's is in *Memoir,* 86n (see also 92). The exchange concerning the militia is recorded by Jefferson in his 'Anas,' *Writings,* ed. Ford, I, 281, and by Thomas Paine in a newspaper article, *Complete Writings,* ed. Philip S. Foner (New York, 1945), II, 954.
4. Baker, *Washington after the Revolution,* III, 372.
5. 'Queries propounded to Major Generals Hamilton and Pinckney, 10 Nov. 1798 (actually transmitted on 12 Nov.), *The Writings of George Washington,* ed. J. C. Fitzpatrick (Washington, 1931–44), XXXVII, 14–17.
6. Washington's detailed memorandum of this interview from which all quotations are taken, is in *Writings of Washington,* XXXVII, 18–20. See *Memoir,* 86–7, for Deborah Logan's note on it; also *Gazette of the United States,* 15 Nov. 1798.
7. *American State Papers: Foreign Relations,* II, 199.
8. Darling, *Our Rising Empire,* 333–41.
9. Adams's account of this interview, written from notes made in 1801, was published in 1809. 'Correspondence originally published in the Boston *Patriot,' Works of John Adams,* IX, 243–4. See also *Aurora,* 27 Nov. 1798.
10. *Memoir,* 85. William Branch Giles of Virginia, like Madison, was a veteran Jeffersonian.
11. *Memoir,* 87; Dickinson to Thomas McKean, 29 Nov. 1798, McKean Papers, III, 26.
12. Col. Allen MacLane to Pickering, 6 Dec. 1798, Pickering MSS., XXIII, 353; see also unsigned letter (probably by MacLane) in *Gazette of the United States,* 11 Dec. 1798; ibid. 28 Dec. 1798.
13. Deborah Logan to Mary Norris, 31 Dec. 1798, Norris of Fairhill Family Letters, II, 37; address dated 20 Dec. 1798, LP, v, 29.
14. [New York] *Daily Advertiser,* 18 Dec. 1798; *Gazette of the United States,* 8 Jan. 1798.

15. *Gazette of the United States,* 12 Nov., 15 Nov., 5 Dec. 1798.
16. *Aurora,* 20 Nov. 1798.
17. Ibid. 29 Dec. 1798.
18. *Writings of Monroe,* III, 155n. The memorandum is undated but from internal evidence it is clear that it was written in November 1798.
19. *Works of Adams,* IX, 130–31; George Gibbs, *Memoirs of the Administrations of Washington and Adams, edited from the papers of Oliver Wolcott* (New York, 1846), II, 72.
20. *Messages and Papers of the Presidents,* I, 276.
21. Ibid. I, 277.
22. 24 Dec. 1798.

CHAPTER X

1. *Annals of Congress,* 5th Congress, 3rd session, 2488–9.
2. Ibid. 2493–4.
3. Ibid. 2494.
4. Ibid. 2495.
5. Ibid. 2495–6.
6. Ibid. 2496–9.
7. *Aurora,* 29 Dec. 1798.
8. *Annals,* 5th Cong., 3rd sess., 2502–12.
9. Ibid. 2512–15.
10. Ibid. 2515–19.
11. Ibid. 2522.
12. Ibid. 2523–8.
13. Ibid. 2528–35.
14. Ibid. 2535–41.
15. Ibid. 2542–3.
16. Ibid. 2545.
17. David Redick to William Irvine, 11 Feb. 1799, quoted by Tinkcom, 184.
18. Dram-drinking.
19. *The Political Green-House for the Year 1798* (Hartford, 1799), 8.
20. *Annals,* 5th Cong., 3rd sess., 2602, 2616.
21. Diary of Dr. Nathaniel Ames, 21 Dec. 1798, 1 Jan. 1799, Charles Warren, *Jacobin and Junto* (Cambridge, 1931), 121; Fisher Ames to Christopher Gore, 11 Jan. 1799, ibid. 121–2.
22. Ibid. 2583–4.
23. Ibid. 2600–2603.
24. Ibid. 2603–5.
25. Ibid. 2605–7.
26. Ibid. 2608–13.
27. 12 March 1799, 'Letters of William Vans Murray,' 525–6.

28. *Annals,* 5th Cong., 3rd sess., 2617–26.
29. Ibid. 2637–45.
30. *Aurora,* 12 Jan. 1799; reproduced from Logan's MS. copy in *Memoir,* 89–93.
31. *Aurora,* 16 Jan. 1799.
32. *Annals,* 5th Cong., 3rd sess., 2686–92.
33. Ibid. 2692–6.
34. Ibid. 2696–2702.
35. Ibid. 2705–9.
36. Ibid. 2709–17.
37. Ibid. 2721.
38. Ibid. 2203, 2206.
39. Samuel E. Morison and Henry S. Commager, *The Growth of the American Republic* (New York: Oxford Univerity Press, 1937), I, 273.
40. Charles Warren, *Memorandum on the History and Scope of the Laws Prohibiting Correspondence with a Foreign Government* . . . (Washington, 1917); Lindell T. Bates, *Unauthorized Diplomatic Intercourse by American Citizens with Foreign Powers* (n.p., 1915).
41. Jefferson to Madison, 16 Jan. 1799, *Writings of Jefferson,* ed. Bergh, X, 69.
42. Monroe to Jefferson, 26 Jan. 1799, *Writings of Monroe,* III, 155–6.
43. *American State Papers: Foreign Relations,* II, 239–40.
44. Notes on France, Misc. MSS., LP.

CHAPTER XI

1. *House Journal* (1798–9), 58.
2. *Aurora,* 27 December 1798.
3. *Memoir,* 121–2.
4. 'Memoirs of a Senator from Pennsylvania: Jonathan Roberts, 1771–1854,' ed. P. S. Klein, *PMHB,* LXII (1938), 87, 89.
5. Dickinson to Aaron Burr, 23 Jan. 1802, 'Some Papers of Aaron Burr,' ed. W. C. Ford, American Antiquarian Society, *Proceedings, N.S.,* XXIX (1919), 109; *Memoir,* 159n.
6. Adams, *Works,* IX, 244; Augustus J. Foster, MS. 'Notes on the United States of America'; *PMHB,* LXXV (1951), 390.
7. Ingersoll, *Recollections,* 173, 446; *Memoir,* 122.
8. Letter signed 'Senex,' *Aurora,* 6 April 1801.
9. *Gazette of the United States,* 3 Jan. 1799.
10. Tinkcom, *Republicans and Federalists,* 220.
11. W. W. H. Davis, *The Fries Rebellion* (Doylestown, Pennsylvania, 1899), 106.
12. *House Journal* (1798–9), 344.

13. Tinkcom, 215–17.
14. Graydon, *Memoirs,* 358.
15. Davis, 93–7.
16. *Works,* x, 118; cf. Claude Bowers, *Jefferson and Hamilton* (Boston and New York, 1925), 419–23.
17. *Works,* ix, 270.
18. Lancaster Historical Society, *Papers,* xxviii (1924), 6.
19. *Memoir,* 98.
20. William F. Worner, 'The Lancaster County Society for Promoting Agriculture, Manufactures, and the Useful Arts,' Lancaster Hist. Soc., *Papers,* xxxiii (1929), 145–6.
21. *A Letter to the Citizens of Pennsylvania, on the Necessity of Promoting Agriculture, Manufactures, and the Useful Arts* (Philadelphia, 1800), 12, 14. An earlier edition was published in the same year at Lancaster.
22. *House Journal* (1799–1800), 123, 375–6; Edward R. Turner, *The Negro in Pennsylvania* (Washington, 1911), 82–5.
23. This account is pieced together from the *House Journal* (1799–1800), 274, 276, 278–9, 290; *Report of the Committee Appointed to Enquire Concerning the Complaint of George Logan against Samuel W. Fisher on a Breach of Privilege* (Lancaster [1800]); 'Memoirs of a Senator from Pennsylvania: Jonathan Roberts,' *PMHB,* lxii (1938), 91; LP, vi, 5.
24. *House Journal* (1799–1800), 274, 409–10; *Memoir,* 98.
25. *Memoir,* 100.
26. 14 Dec. 1800, Jefferson Papers, American Philosophical Society, quoted by Tinkcom, 254. I have drawn heavily upon Tinkcom's account of the legislative struggle, 245–52.
27. James O. Knauss, *Social Conditions among the Pennsylvania Germans in the Eighteenth Century* (Lancaster, 1922), 79; Andreas Dorpalen, 'The German Element in Early Pennsylvania Politics, 1790–1800,' *Pennsylvania History,* ix (1942), 176–90; *Aurora,* 6 April 1801.
28. *House Journal* (1800–1801), 22, 80; Joseph A. Durrenberger, *Turnpikes* (Valdosta, Georgia, 1931), 53.
29. *House Journal* (1800–1801), 34–5, 310–11; Livingood, *Philadelphia-Baltimore Trade Rivalry,* Chap. iv.
30. Albert J. Beveridge, *The Life of John Marshall* (Boston and New York, 1919), ii, 541–4.
31. Tinkcom, 254–6; Paul A. W. Wallace, *The Muhlenbergs of Pennsylvania* (Philadelphia, 1950), 297–8.
32. Logan to Jefferson, 20 Feb. 1801, Jefferson Papers.
33. Logan to Jefferson, 27 Feb. 1801, ibid.
34. Jefferson to Logan, 21 March 1801, ibid.
35. *Memoir,* 105.
36. 'Extract of a letter from a member of assembly, dated March 14th, to

his friend in Lancaster,' *Lancaster Journal,* 21 March 1801 ; and answer, signed 'Senex,' *Aurora,* 6 April 1801.

37. *House Journal* (1800–1801), 387, 391 ; ibid. (1801–2), 63.

CHAPTER XII

1. Albert Gallatin to his wife, 15 Jan. 1801, Adams, *Life of Albert Gallatin,* 252–3.
2. *The Diary and Letters of Gouverneur Morris,* ed. Anne Carey Morris (New York, 1888), II, 394–5.
3. *List of Members of the Senate and House of Representatives, with Places of Their Abode* (Washington [?], 1801 [?]), 2.
4. Logan to Deborah Logan, 7 Dec. 1801, LP, VI, 44 ; Jefferson to Bishop Madison, 8 Dec. 1801, Jefferson Papers.
5. Bishop Madison to Jefferson, 16 Dec. 1801, *William and Mary Quarterly,* 2nd. Ser., V (1925), 150.
6. 5 Jan. 1802, LP, VII, 45 ; Margaret Bayard Smith, *Forty Years of Washington Society,* ed. Gaillard Hunt (London, 1906), 51.
7. Logan to Deborah Logan, 5 Jan. 1802, LP, VII, 45 ; Allen C. Clark, 'Doctor and Mrs. William Thornton,' Columbia Historical Society, *Records,* XVIII (1915), 144–208 ; William Dunlap, *A History of the Rise and Progress of the Arts of Design in the United States* (Boston, 1918), II, 8.
8. *Annals of Congress,* 7th Cong., 1st sess., 9 ; Glenn Brown, *History of the United States Capitol* (Washington, D.C., 1900), 26–7.
9. *Annals,* 7th Cong., 1st sess., 9.
10. Ibid. 11–16.
11. *Journal of the Executive Proceedings of the Senate* (Washington, 1828), I, 397–8.
12. *Annals,* 7th Cong., 1st sess., 22 ; *Diary and Letters of Gouverneur Morris,* II, 417.
13. *Annals,* 7th Cong., 1st sess., 23–30, 36–41, 59–69.
14. *Diary and Letters of Gouverneur Morris,* II, 417 ; Claude Bowers, *Jefferson in Power* (Boston, 1936), 123–5.
15. Ross to George Stevenson, 14 Dec. 1798, quoted in Tinkcom, 184.
16. Logan to Deborah Logan, 21 Jan. 1802, MDLFP ; *Diary and Letters of Gouverneur Morris,* II, 417 ; John Dickinson to Aaron Burr, 23 Jan. 1802, American Antiquarian Society, *Proceedings,* New Ser., XXIX (1919), 109.
17. *Annals,* 7th Cong., 1st sess., 183.
18. Priestley to Logan, 15 June 1802, LP, V, 36.
19. *Annals,* 7th Cong., 1st sess., 185, 186, 187, 189.
20. Ibid. 250.
21. Ibid. 263.

22. Ibid. 275–9, 290–91.
23. Ibid. 198, 1301–2; Dickinson to Logan, 20 April 1802, Jefferson Papers, Library of Congress; William D. Johnston, *History of the Library of Congress* (Washington, 1904), I, 23–38; *Catalogue of the Books, Maps, and Charts Belonging to the Library of the Two Houses of Congress* (Washington, 1802).
24. Scharf and Westcott, *History of Philadelphia,* I, 513n; Sanford W. Higginbotham, *The Keystone in the Democratic Arch: Pennsylvania Politics, 1800–1816* (Harrisburg, 1952), 43–5.
25. Duane to Jefferson, 18 Oct. 1802, Mass. Hist. Soc., *Proceedings,* 2nd Ser., xx (1906–7), 277.
26. *Annals,* 7th Cong., 2nd sess., 83–8.
27. Ibid. 91–6.
28. Ibid. 255–6.
29. Ibid. 19, 51, 97–9, 263, 265.
30. Ibid. 25, 27, 104.
31. *National Intelligencer,* 25 Feb. 1803; Jefferson to Sir John Sinclair, 30 June 1803, *The Correspondence of the Right Honorable Sir John Sinclair* (London, 1831), II, 42–3.
32. Logan to John Vaughan, 16 July 1802, Misc. Communications: Trade, Navigation, etc., American Philosophical Society, 33.
33. This was the first—and only—indictment ever found under the 'Logan Act.' The full text, with an account of the circumstances, is found in Charles Warren, *Odd Byways in American History* (Cambridge, 1942), 168–75.
34. *Annals,* 8th Cong., 1st sess., 11–15.
35. Ibid. 60.
36. Ibid.
37. *Memoirs of John Quincy Adams,* ed. Charles F. Adams (Philadelphia, 1874–7), I, 271, 281, 285, 291, 297.
38. *Journal of Executive Proceedings,* I, 463, 468–70; *American State Papers: Foreign Relations,* II, 596–606; *William Plumer's Memorandum of Proceedings in the United States Senate, 1803–1807,* ed. Everett S. Brown (New York, 1923), 94–7.
39. Plumer, 105.
40. The presentation of this memorial has been called 'the first step in the Free-Soil movement.' Mary S. Locke, *Anti-Slavery in America from the Introduction of African Slaves to the Prohibition of the Slave Trade* (Boston, 1901), 106; *Annals,* 8th Cong., 1st sess., 238; 2nd sess., Appendix, 1596–7; *Minutes of the Proceedings of the Ninth Annual American Convention for Promoting the Abolition of Slavery and Improving the Condition of the African Race* (Philadelphia, 1804), 40–42.
41. Plumer, 111–12.
42. James Hillhouse of Connecticut, ibid. 118.

43. *Annals,* 8th Cong., 1st sess., 242.
44. Logan to Pemberton, 30 Jan. 1804, Etting Collection: Scientists, 53, Historical Society of Pennsylvania.
45. Dickinson to Logan, 30 Jan. 1804, Charles J. Stillé, *The Life and Times of John Dickinson* (Philadelphia, 1891), 324–5.
46. *Annals,* 8th Cong., 1st sess., 256, 257; *Memoirs of J. Q. Adams,* I, 295–6.
47. Jefferson to Joseph Scott, 9 March 1804, *Writings of Jefferson,* ed. Ford, VIII, 305n.
48. Jefferson to Thomas Leiper, 11 June 1804, ibid. 304–5.
49. McKean to Logan, 19 Feb. 1803, LP, v, 45; James H. Peeling, 'Governor McKean and the Pennsylvania Jacobins (1799–1808),' *PMHB,* LIV (1930), 330–34.
50. Scharf and Westcott, 117–18; *Aurora,* 22 June 1803.
51. *Annals,* 8th Cong., 2nd sess., 11.
52. *Memoirs of J. Q. Adams,* I, 314; Gallatin to Samuel L. Mitchill, 3 Jan. 1805, *The Writings of Albert Gallatin,* ed. Henry Adams (Philadelphia, 1879), I, 219–26.
53. Dickinson to Logan, 23 Jan. 1805, *Memoir,* 149–50.
54. *Memoirs of J. Q. Adams,* I, 346.
55. Dickinson to Logan, 7 Feb., 11 Feb., 18 Feb., 1805, *Memoir,* 150–52; McKean to Logan 15 Feb. 1805, LP, v, 61.
56. *Annals,* 8th Cong., 2nd sess., 64, 65; Henry Adams, *History of the United States* (New York, 1891), III, 88.
57. *Annals,* 8th Cong., 2nd sess., 665–9.
58. Ibid. 39, 996; Plumer, 251–2; *Memoirs of J. Q. Adams,* I, 336.
59. *Annals,* 8th Cong., 2nd sess., 77–80.

CHAPTER XIII

1. Higginbotham, 82–3; Raymond Walters, Jr., *Alexander James Dallas* (Philadelphia, 1943), Chaps., XII–XIII; Peeling, 'Governor McKean and the Pennsylvania Jacobins,' *PMHB,* LIV (1930), 320–54; William M. Meigs, 'Pennsylvania Politics Early in This Century,' ibid. XVII (1893), 462–90; Elizabeth K. Henderson, 'The Attack on the Judiciary in Pennsylvania, 1800–1810,' ibid. LXI (1937), 113–36.
2. *PMHB,* xxv (1901), 586–7.
3. Jefferson to Logan, 11 May 1805, LP, v, 65 (printed in part in *Writings of Jefferson,* ed. Bergh, XI, 71–2).
4. Logan to Jefferson, 10 June 1805, Jefferson Papers.
5. The full text of the address is in George M. Dallas, *The Life and Writings of A. J. Dallas* (Philadelphia, 1871), 211–33.
6. Logan to John Dickinson, 11 Nov. 1805, LP, v, 68.
7. Richardson, ed., *Messages and Papers,* I, 379.

8. *Annals of Congress,* 9th Cong., 1st sess., 11–16.
9. Ibid. 18–19; Adams, *History,* III, 75–7; Isaac J. Cox, *The West Florida Controversy, 1798–1813* (Baltimore, 1918), 231–6.
10. Jefferson to Thomas Cooper, 18 Feb. 1806, Jefferson Papers.
11. Dickinson to Logan, 19 Dec. 1805, *Memoir,* 152–4.
12. *Memoirs of J. Q. Adams,* I, 378; Charles W. Janson, *The Stranger in America,* ed. Carl S. Driver (New York, 1935), 225–30; Margaret Bayard Smith, *Forty Years of Washington Society,* 400; Ray W. Irwin, *The Diplomatic Relations of the United States with the Barbary Powers* (Chapel Hill, 1931), 161–6.
13. *Annals,* 9th Cong., 1st sess., 26–9.
14. Ibid. 29–41.
15. *Memoirs of J. Q. Adams,* I, 383; Plumer, *Memorandum,* 387.
16. Dickinson to Logan, 11 Feb. 1805, *c.* 2 Feb. 1806, *Memoir,* 151, 156.
17. *Memoirs of J. Q. Adams,* I, 383; cf. Plumer, *Memorandum,* 387.
18. Dickinson to Logan, *c.* 2 Feb. 1806, *Memoir,* 156–7.
19. *Annals,* 9th Cong., 1st sess., 50, 51–2; *Memoirs of J. Q. Adams,* I, 383–6.
20. Plumer, *Memorandum,* 380, 389; for Monroe's letter, see *American State Papers: Foreign Relations,* II, 734–7.
21. *Memoirs of J. Q. Adams,* I, 391–400; Samuel Flagg Bemis, *John Quincy Adams and the Foundations of American Foreign Policy* (New York, 1949), 136–7.
22. Randolph's followers in national and Virginia politics were called *Tertium Quids,* as was Logan's group in Pennsylvania. There was no connection, however, between the two movements.
23. Dickinson to Logan, 6 Feb. 1806, *Memoir,* 157.
24. *Memoirs of J. Q. Adams,* I, 391–3, 395–7, 400.
25. Misc. MSS., LP.
26. *Annals,* 9th Cong., 1st sess., 91, 104–12; Plumer, *Memorandum,* 428–9.
27. Dickinson to Logan, 19 Dec. 1805, *Memoir,* 154; cf. Dickinson, *Letters of Fabius* (Wilmington, 1797), 170–78.
28. *Annals,* 9th Cong., 1st sess., 87; *Memoirs of J. Q. Adams,* I, 403; Plumer, *Memorandum,* 425.
29. Plumer, *Memorandum,* 390.
30. Dickinson to Logan, 6 Feb. 1806, *Memoir,* 157.
31. *Annals,* 9th Cong., 1st sess., 138.
32. Joseph Bringhurst to Logan, 22 Jan. 1806, MDLFP; Gideon Gardner to Logan, 3 March 1806, Library Company of Philadelphia.
33. *Memoir,* 111.
34. *Annals,* 9th Cong., 1st sess., 74, 192–7; Livingood, *Philadelphia-Baltimore Trade Rivalry,* 86–7; Joshua Gilpin, *A Memoir on the Rise,*

Progress, and Present State of the Chesapeake and Delaware Canal (Wilmington, 1821), 33–4.

35. *Annals,* 9th Cong., 1st sess., 192–4.
36. Ibid. 235. In its essentials, of course, this proposal foreshadowed the later Congressional practice of granting lands to railroad companies, which was to be the means of building thousands of miles of railroad across the country. There were partial precedents, but to my knowledge this is the earliest proposal by a committee of Congress to grant public lands to a private corporation for the purpose of improving means of transportation.
37. Washington to Edmund Randolph, 15 Dec. 1794, Columbia Historical Society, *Records,* XVII (1914), 111; same to the Commissioners of the Federal City, 28 Jan. 1795, ibid. 114–16.
38. Wilhelmus B. Bryan, *A History of the National Capital* (New York, 1914), I, 251–3, 553–4.
39. A copy of Logan's memorandum on this subject—written for Barlow's benefit—is among the Misc. MSS., LP.
40. *Annals,* 9th Cong., 1st sess., 161. The heads of Logan's speech and several fragments from it in his handwriting are among the Misc. MSS., LP.
41. *Annals,* 9th Cong., 1st sess., 163, 183, 198. 'Had Barlow's scheme been put into effect,' says a modern scholar, 'the university ideal later exemplified by the Johns Hopkins University would have been realized in the United States seventy years sooner, technical education would have been advanced by a generation, and America would have led the world in systematized advanced studies.' Leon Howard, *The Connecticut Wits* (Chicago, 1943), 329.
42. Henry Adams, *Life of Albert Gallatin,* 339–40.
43. *Journal of the Executive Proceedings of the Senate,* II, 25.
44. Logan to Jefferson, 12 March 1806, Jefferson Papers.
45. Jefferson to Logan, 12 March 1806, ibid.; also in *Memoir,* 110.
46. 'The Anas,' *Writings of Jefferson,* ed. Ford, I, 309–10; *Memoir,* 110–11n.
47. *Jour. of Exec. Proc.,* II, 29; Dickinson to Logan, 31 March 1806, *Memoir,* 159–61; Jefferson to Logan, 7 April 1806, LP, v, 76.
48. *Annals,* 9th Cong., 1st sess., 240. Fox, incidentally, would later confess to James Monroe that the Non-Importation Act, with its 'air of menace,' had been a serious obstacle to his efforts for conciliation. Monroe to Madison, 9 June 1806, *Writings of Monroe,* IV, 447.
49. Higginbotham, Chap. v.
50. Benjamin Rush to John Adams, 24 Oct. 1806, *Letters of Rush,* II, 934.
51. *The Quid Mirror* (Philadelphia, 1806), (2), (3), 4–10, 13–17. The first edition was published in New York; it was republished in Philadelphia after the election.

52. McKean to Logan, 20 Dec. 1806, LP, v, 78.

53. *Annals,* 9th Cong., 2nd sess., 11–16.

54. Ibid. 31, 60, 77, 88–9, 95–7. This was, of course, the origin of Gallatin's great report on roads, harbors, canals, and rivers, presented to Congress at its next session.

55. *Memoirs of J. Q. Adams,* i, 465–6.

56. Logan to Debby Logan, 4 March 1807, LP, vii, 53; Charles B. Todd, *Life and Letters of Joel Barlow* (New York, 1886), 211–12; *Georgia Historical Quarterly,* iii (1919), 172–3.

CHAPTER XIV

1. The Stenton farm diary from 1 Jan. 1810 to 27 April 1812 is extant among the Logan Papers.

2. Logan to John Vaughan, 16 July 1802, MS. Communications: Trade, Navigation, etc., American Philosophical Society, 33.

3. *Constitution of the Merino Society of the Middle States of North America* (Philadelphia, 1811).

4. Logan to William H. Wells, 16 Nov. 1809, Library Company of Philadelphia.

5. Townsend Ward, 'The Germantown Road and Its Associations,' *PMHB,* v (1881), 15–16; Williamina Ridgely to Ann Ridgely, 27 April 1803, *A Calendar of Ridgely Family Letters,* ed. Leon de Valinger and Virginia E. Shaw (Dover, Delaware, 1948), i, 231.

6. Turreau to Talleyrand, 18 July 1807 (wrongly dated 1808), quoted in Adams, *History,* iv, 36; Dickinson to Logan, 7 July 1807, *Memoir,* 163.

7. Undated memorandum in Misc. MSS., LP. For a later expression of the same view see Logan's letter to Madison, 24 Jan. 1810, *Memoir,* 170.

8. Higginbotham, 167–76; Michael Leib, *Long-Talk, Delivered before the Tammany Society, or Columbian Order, on Their Anniversary* (Philadelphia, 1808).

9. Jefferson to Logan, 27 Dec. 1808, *Writings of Jefferson,* ed. Bergh, xii, 219–20.

10. William Rotch to Logan, 9 Jan. 1809, LP, v, 84.

11. Misc. MSS., LP.

12. Logan to William Rotch, 27 Dec. 1809, LP, v, 86; Logan to Madison, 10 Jan. 1810, *Memoir,* 165–7.

13. Logan to Madison, 10 Jan. 1810, *Memoir,* 165–7.

14. Madison to Logan, 17 Jan. 1810, ibid. 167–9.

15. Logan to Madison, 14 Jan. 1810, Madison Papers, Library of Congress; Madison to Logan, 17 Jan. 1810, *Memoir,* 170; Robert Smith to William Pinkney, 20 Jan. 1810, *American State Papers: Foreign Relations,* iii, 349, 356; Logan to Madison, 24 Jan. 1810, *Memoir,* 170–71.

16. Madison to Pinkney, 20 Jan. 1810, *Letters and Other Writings of James Madison* (Philadelphia, 1867), II, 468–70.

17. Phineas Bond to Jackson, 8 Feb. 1810, C. O. Paullin and F. L. Paxson, *Guide to the Materials in London Archives for the History of the United States since 1783* (Washington, 1914), 210; Jackson to R. Söderström, 23 Feb. 1810, copy in Pickering MSS., XLIII, 274; Jackson to Söderström, 27 Jan. 1810, ibid. XLIII, 281; Logan to Madison, 19 Feb. 1810, LP, v, 97.

18. Unidentified clipping, 19 Feb. 1810, Misc. MSS., LP.

19. Logan to Sir John Sinclair, 20 April 1810, *Correspondence of Sinclair,* II, 63; Robert Barclay to Logan, 30 Aug. 1810, LP, v, 120; *Memoir,* 116.

20. Logan to Wellesley, 21 April 1810, *Memoir,* 179–80.

21. Richard Peters to Timothy Pickering, 4 Dec. 1810, Pickering MSS., XXIX, 344–5.

22. Lord Grimston to Logan, 7 May 1810, LP, v, 101; Lansdowne to Logan, 19 June 1810, LP, v, 107; Logan to Deborah Logan, 29 May 1810, *Memoir,* 173; Brougham to Logan, n.d., LP, v, 122.

23. Logan to Deborah Logan, 29 May 1810, *Memoir,* 173; Romilly to Logan, 10 June 1810, LP, v, 104; Logan to Romilly, n.d., LP, v, 123; fragment of diary, 8 Aug.–11 Aug. 1810, Misc. MSS., LP; Logan to Sinclair, 20 April 1810, *Correspondence of Sinclair,* II, 63–4; Logan to Sinclair, 14 May 1810, *Memoir,* 178; Sinclair to Logan, 16 June 1810, LP, v, 106.

24. Logan to Madison, 6 May 1810, Madison Papers.

25. Richard Peters to Timothy Pickering, 4 Dec. 1810, Pickering MSS., XXIX, 344–5; Logan to Madison, [17] July 1810, *Memoir,* 181–2.

26. Norfolk *Chronicle,* 7 July 1810. For a description of the Holkham sheep-shearings see A. M. W. Stirling, *Coke of Norfolk and His Friends* (London, 1908), II, 246–65.

27. Logan to Perceval, 3 Aug. 1810, *Memoir,* 175–7; cf. Logan to Thomas William Coke, 10 Sept. 1810, ibid. 177.

28. Poulson's *American Daily Advertiser,* 5 Nov. 1810.

29. Logan to Coke, 10 Sept. 1810, *Memoir,* 177.

30. Misc. MSS., LP.

31. Logan to Monroe, 10 Nov. 1811, *Memoir,* 185.

32. Randolph to Logan, 4 Dec. 1810, ibid. 180–81.

33. Richard Peters to Timothy Pickering, 4 Dec. 1810, Pickering MSS., XXIX, 344–5.

34. Susanna Dillwyn to William Dillwyn, 3 May 1811, 14 May 1811, Dillwyn MSS.

35. Deborah Logan to Maria Dickinson Logan, 20 Jan. 1811, LP, VI, 60.

36. Logan to Monroe, 14 May 1811, Gratz Collection: U.S. Senators, Historical Society of Pennsylvania.

37. MS. journal, 1811–12, entry for 28 Sept. 1811, Misc. MSS., LP.

38. Logan to Monroe, 10 Nov. 1811, *Memoir,* 185–6.
39. Augustus J. Foster to Marquis Wellesley, 12 March 1812, quoted in E. A. Cruikshank, *The Political Adventures of John Henry* (Toronto, 1936), 129.
40. Logan to Madison, 31 March 1812, *Memoir,* 186–7.
41. Benjamin Rush to John Adams, 2 June 1812, *Letters of Rush,* II, 1137. Senator Gregg presented the petitions on 18 May. *Annals of Congress,* 12th Cong., 1st sess., 242. Logan may have had something to do with the publication at this time in *Poulson's American Daily Advertiser* of 'The Plea of Reason, Religion, and Humanity against War,' a powerful piece of anti-war writing translated by Vicesimus Knox from Erasmus' *Adagia.* Clippings of these essays are among the Misc. MSS., LP. In 'George Logan, Agrarian Democrat' (*PMHB,* LXXV [1951], 276), I mistakenly attributed these essays to Logan.
42. Logan to Nicholas Gilman, 11 June 1812, Gratz Collection: U.S. Senators.
43. Adams, *History,* VI, Chap. VIII.
44. Timothy Pickering to Logan, 26 May 1813, *Memoir,* 189–90; Logan to Pickering, 18 Jan. 1814, Pickering MSS., XXX, 196; cf. Mathew Carey, *The Olive Branch* (Philadelphia, 1815), 59.
45. Logan to Madison, 18 Jan. 1813, *Memoir,* 187–8; Logan to Madison, 4 July 1813, ibid. 171–3.
46. Logan to Jefferson, 18 Sept. 1813, LP, VII, 48.
47. Jefferson to Logan, 3 Oct. 1813, *Memoir,* 135–7.
48. Logan to Jefferson, 9 Dec. 1813, ibid. 137–44.
49. Susanna Dillwyn to William Dillwyn, 22 Dec. 1813, Dillwyn MSS.
50. Deborah Logan's MS. diary, quoted in Stillé, *Dickinson,* 421–2.

CHAPTER XV

1. Deborah Logan, MS. diary, I, 19–21, LP. The part of this diary now extant among the Logan Papers commences on 1 January 1815; cf. Scharf and Westcott, I, 578–9, for a description of the illuminations.
2. MS. diary, I, 31.
3. Logan to Monroe, 22 March 1815, Monroe Papers, Library of Congress; Logan to Sinclair, 20 March 1815, *Correspondence of Sinclair,* II, 65; Miers Fisher, MS. diary, XI, 178, Friends Historical Library of Swarthmore College; undated fragment in Misc. MSS., LP.
4. Deborah Logan, MS. diary, I, 66–8.
5. Peters to Pickering, 4 Dec. 1810, Pickering MSS., XXIX, 344–5; Peters to Pickering, 19 Dec. 1810, ibid. 350.
6. The voluminous Logan-Pickering correspondence can be found in the Logan Papers and the Pickering MSS. (see the useful index to the latter

in Mass. Hist. Soc. *Collections,* 6th Ser., VIII [1896]). Three of Pickering's letters are reprinted in *Memoir,* 189–202.

7. Jefferson to Logan, 19 May 1816, LP, VII, 76; Logan to Jefferson, 5
June 1816, ibid. VII, 77.

8. Jefferson to Logan, 15 Oct. 1815, *Writings of Jefferson,* ed. Bergh,
XIV, 354–5; Logan to Jefferson, 20 Oct. 1815, LP, VII, 66; Jefferson to
Logan, 23 July 1816, *Writings,* ed. cit., XV, 47–9.

9. Logan to Jefferson, 1 Nov. 1816, Jefferson Papers; Jefferson to Logan,
24 Nov. 1816, ibid.

10. Logan to Jefferson, 27 April 1816, 16 Oct. 1816, Jefferson Papers; Jefferson to Logan, 12 Nov. 1816, ibid.; *Memoir,* 122.

11. Deborah Logan, MS. diary, I, 3–5, 53–5. On Randolph's 'conversion' see
Henry Adams, *John Randolph* (Boston and New York, 1899), 264–5.

12. Deborah recorded these and other visits in her diary, vols. I–III.

13. Ibid. I, 48, 106, 109; *A Narrative of the Early Life, Travels and Gospel Ministry of Jesse Kersey* (Philadelphia, 1851), 82.

14. Ibid. I, 253.

15. *Correspondence between William Penn and James Logan,* Historical
Society of Pennsylvania, *Memoirs,* IX (1870), vii–viii, xlviii.

16. *Memoir,* opp. p. 114.

17. MS. diary, I, 188.

18. Deborah Logan, MS. diary, I, 16, 143; II, 120; Deborah Logan to —,
10 Aug. —, MDLFP.

19. Misc. MSS., LP.

20. Deborah Logan, MS. diary, I, 152–3, 160, 179–80; III, 47.

21. Miers Fisher, MS. diary, XI, 178.

22. Deborah Logan, MS. diary, II, 129; cf. Miers Fisher, MS. diary, XIII,
193.

23. MS. diary, II, 127.

24. Ibid. II, 168; Logan to Monroe, 5 June 1817, LP, VII, 85; Scharf and
Westcott, I, 590; cf. Onís to Logan, 7 Jan. 1817, LP, VII, 82.

25. Philadelphia Society for Promoting Agriculture, *Memoirs,* IV (1818),
44–7.

26. Samuel Miller, *A Brief Retrospect of the Eighteenth Century* (New
York, 1803), I, 389.

27. *An Address on the Errors of Husbandry in the United States* (Philadelphia, 1818), 4–6, 9–10.

28. Circular dated 26 Nov. 1819, Misc. MSS., LP; *Aurora,* 23 Nov. 1819,
25 Nov. 1819; Scharf and Westcott, I, 598–9.

29. MS. diary, IV, 9–10; Logan to Harrison Gray Otis, 5 April 1820, Otis
MSS., Massachusetts Historical Society.

30. Deborah Logan, MS. diary, IV, 15–16, 43.

31. 'Recollections Written in 1820 and Inscribed to My Husband,' *Memoir,*
123–6.

32. MS. diary, iv, 46.
33. Ibid. iv, 64; Last Will and Testament of George Logan, Register of Wills, Philadelphia.
34. Peter S. DuPonceau, *A Discourse on the Early History of Philadelphia* (Philadelphia, 1821), 35.
35. *Memoir,* 120–22.

INDEX